FRENCH
ATLANTIC COAST

S. Sauvignier/MICHELIN

Editorial Director   Cynthia Clayton Ochterbeck

THE GREEN GUIDE FRENCH ATLANTIC COAST

Editor   Jonathan P. Gilbert
Principal Writer   Gordon Lethridge
Production Coordinator   Natasha G. George
Cartography   Alain Baldet, Michèle Cana, Peter Wrenn
Photo Editor   Lydia Strong
Proofreader   Gwen Cannon
Layout & Design   Alison Rayner and Nicole D. Jordan
Cover Design   Laurent Muller and Frank Ladd

Contact Us: The Green Guide
                             Michelin Maps and Guides
                             One Parkway South
                             Greenville, SC 29615
                             USA
                             www.michelintravel.com
                             michelin.guides@us.michelin.com

                             Michelin Maps and Guides
                             Hannay House
                             39 Clarendon Road
                             Watford, Herts WD17 1JA
                             UK
                             ☎ (01923) 205 240
                             www.ViaMichelin.com
                             travelpubsales@uk.michelin.com

Special Sales: For information regarding bulk sales,
                             customized editions and premium sales,
                             please contact our Customer Service
                             Departments:
                             USA   1-800-432-6277
                             UK   (01923) 205 240
                             Canada 1-800-361-8236

One Team …
A Commitment to Quality

There's just one reason our team is dedicated to producing quality travel publications—you, our reader.

Throughout our guides we offer **practical information**, **touring tips** and **suggestions** for finding the best places for a break.

Michelin driving tours help you hit the highlights and quickly absorb the best of the region. Our descriptive **walking tours** make you your own guide, armed with directions, maps and expert information.

We scout out the attractions, classify them with **star ratings**, and describe in detail what you will find when you visit them.

Michelin maps featured throughout the guide offer vibrant, detailed and easy-to-follow outlines of everything from close-up museum plans to international maps.

Places to stay and eat are always a big part of travel, so we research **hotels and restaurants** that we think convey the essence of the destination, and arrange them by geographic area and price. We walk you through the best shopping districts and point you towards the host of entertainment and recreation possibilities on offer.

We **test, retest, check and recheck** to make sure that our guidebooks are truly just that: a personalized guide to help you make the most of your visit. And if you still want a speaking guide, we list local tour guides who will lead you on all the boat, bus, guided, historical, culinary, and other tours you shouldn't miss.

In short, we remove the guesswork involved with travel. After all, we want you to enjoy traveling with Michelin as much as we do.

The Michelin Green Guide Team

PLANNING YOUR TRIP

INTRODUCTION TO THE FRENCH ATLANTIC COAST

B. Kaufmann/MICHELIN

SYMBOLS

🛈	**Tourist Information**
🕐	**Hours of Operation**
🕐	**Periods of Closure**
🙂	**A Bit of Advice**
😊	**Details to Consider**
👓	**Entry Fees**
Kids	**Especially for Children**
👣	**Tours**
♿	**Wheelchair Accessible**

CONTENTS

DISCOVERING THE FRENCH ATLANTIC COAST

HOW TO USE THIS GUIDE

Orientation

To help you grasp the "lay of the land" quickly and easily, so you'll feel confident and comfortable finding your way around the region, we offer the following tools in this guide:

- Detailed table of contents for an overview of what you'll find in the guide, and how the guide is organized.
- Map of the French Atlantic Coast with the Principal Sights highlighted for easy reference.
- Detailed maps for major cities and villages, including driving tour maps and larger-scale maps for walking tours.
- Map of French Atlantic Coast Regional Driving Tours, each one numbered and color coded.
- Principal Sights organized alphabetically for quick reference.

Practicalities

At the front of the guide, you'll see a section called "Planning Your Trip" that contains information about planning your trip, the best time to go, different ways of getting to the region and getting around, and basic facts and tips for making the most of your visit. You'll find driving and themed tours, and suggestions for outdoor fun. There's also a calendar of popular annual events. Information on shopping, sight-seeing, kids' activities and sports and recreational opportunities is included as well.

LODGINGS

We've made a selection of hotels and arranged them within the cities by price category to fit all budgets (*see the Legend on the cover flap for an explanation of the price categories*). For the most part, we've selected accommodations based on their unique regional quality, their French Atlantic Coast feel, as it were. So, unless the individual hotel embodies local ambience, it's rare that we include chain properties, which typically have their own imprint. If you want a more comprehensive selection of accommodations, see the red-cover **Michelin Guide France**.

RESTAURANTS

We thought you'd like to know the popular eating spots in France. So we selected restaurants that capture the French Atlantic Coast experience—those that have a unique regional flavor and local atmosphere. We're not rating the quality of the food per se. As we did with the hotels, we selected restaurants for many towns and villages, categorized by price to appeal to all wallets (*see the Legend on the cover flap for an explanation of the price categories*). If you want a more comprehensive selection of dining recommendations, see the red-cover **Michelin Guide France**.

Attractions

Principal Sights are arranged alphabetically. Within each Principal Sight, attractions for each town, village, or geographical area are divided into local Sights or Walking Tours, nearby Excursions to sights outside the town, or detailed Driving Tours—suggested itineraries for seeing several attractions around a major town. Contact information, admission charges and hours of operation are given for the majority of attractions. Unless otherwise noted, admission prices shown are for a single adult only. Discounts for children, seniors, students, teachers, etc. may be available; be sure to ask. If no admission charge is shown, entrance to the attraction is free.

If you're pressed for time, we recommend you visit the three- and two-star sights first: the stars are your guide.

STAR RATINGS

Michelin has used stars as a rating tool for more than 100 years:

★★★	Highly recommended
★★	Recommended
★	Interesting

SYMBOLS IN THE TEXT

Besides the stars, other symbols in the text indicate sights that are closed to the public ⌖; on-site eating facilities ✕; also see ⚭; breakfast included in the nightly rate ☕; on-site parking ℙ; spa facilities Spa; camping facilities △; swimming pool ⤓; and beaches ⌕.

See the box appearing on the Contents page and the Legend on the cover flap for other symbols used in the text.

See the Maps explanation below for symbols appearing on the maps.

Throughout the guide you will find peach-coloured text boxes or sidebars containing anecdotal or background information. Green-coloured boxes contain information to help you save time or money.

Maps

All maps in this guide are oriented north, unless otherwise indicated by a directional arrow. The term "Local Map" refers to a map within the chapter or Tourism Region. See the map Legend at the back of the guide for an explanation of other map symbols. A complete list of the maps found in the guide appears at the back of this book.

Addresses, phone numbers, opening hours and prices published in this guide are accurate at press time. We welcome corrections and suggestions that may assist us in preparing the next edition. Please send your comments to:

Michelin Maps and Guides
Hannay House
39 Clarendon Road
Watford, Herts WD17 1JA
UK
travelpubsales@uk.michelin.com
www.michelin.co.uk

Michelin Maps and Guides
Editorial Department
P.O. Box 19001
Greenville, SC 29602-9001
USA
michelin.guides@us.michelin.com
www.michelintravel.com

Festivities in Coulon on the Sèvre
D. Mar/MICHELIN

PLANNING YOUR TRIP

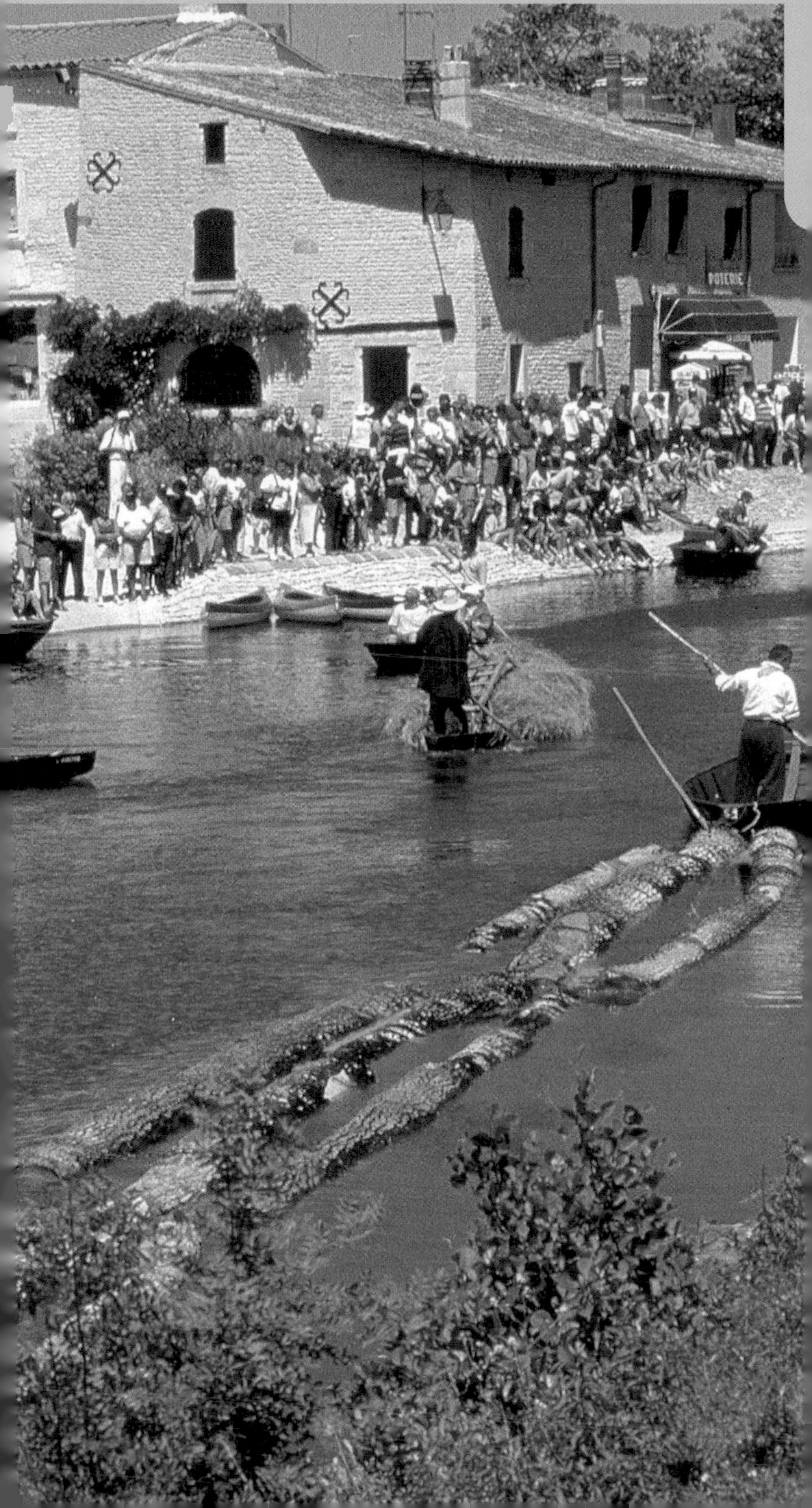

MICHELIN DRIVING TOURS

Read on to explore the areas and driving tours highlighted on the map on the cover flap.

1 PATOU: NORTH-EAST OF POITIERS

230km/143mi starting from Poitiers

The tour begins with a visit to Futuroscope, which has become the symbol of the whole region. East of Poitiers, Chauvigny's ruined castles form the impressive setting of fascinating falconry shows. As a contrast, St-Savin offers the sheer beauty of its 11C biblical frescoes. Head to the spa town of La Roche-Posay via the picturesque village of Angles-sur-l'Anglin. Next, as you walk through the centre of Châtellerault in the footsteps of Descartes, take time to admire the Église St-Jacques, once the rendezvous of pilgrims on their way to Santiago de Compostela, and to enjoy the Auto-Moto-Vélo Museum housed in La Manu. Head north to Loudun, birthplace of the first printed newspaper in France, stopping on the way to look at the Romanesque church in Lencloître and the Château de Coussay, which once belonged to Richelieu. Head back to Poitiers via Moncontour.

Talmont-sur-Gironde

M.Thiery/MICHELIN

2 THE SAINTONGE REGION

210km/130mi starting from Saintes

On your way to Rochefort, with its rich maritime past, stop at the fairy-tale castle of La Roche-Courbon. Southeast of Rochefort, the ramparts of Brouage rise proudly above the surrounding marshland. From Marennes and its famous oysters, make a detour to the picturesque island of Oléron, then follow the coastline south through the Forêt de la Coubre, stopping at La Palmyre - reputedly one of the finest zoos in France. Further south, you will find a succession of seaside resorts, such as St-Palais-sur-Mer, Royan, St-Georges-de-Didonne, Meschers-sur-Gironde and finally, at the end of a peninsula, Talmont-sur-Gironde with its fishermen's huts standing on piles jutting out from the cliffs.

3 THE VENDÉE REGION

225km/140mi starting from Fontenay-le-Comte

The Renaissance town of Fontenay-le-Comte lies between the Marais Poitevin and the Forêt de Mervent-Vouvant, ideal for hiking, riding, biking and climbing. Don't miss the picturesque villages nestling in the heart of the forest. Head north to Le Puy-du-Fou through the rolling hills of Vendée, via Mouilleron-en-Pareds and Pouzauges. Let the spectacular night show at Le Puy-du-Fou take you on an exciting journey back in time before continuing through windmill country to Luçon, Cardinal Richelieu's town. Further south is the dry marsh, an area of the Marais Poitevin where wide open spaces are crisscrossed by canals and dikes. Return to Fontenay-le-Comte after visiting the imposing ruins of the Abbaye de Maillezais and the village of Nieul-sur-l'Autise.

4 SOUTH OF THE LOIRE ESTUARY

255km/158mi starting from St-Gilles-Croix-de-Vie

Drive north-west out of the fishing port of St-Gilles to the seaside resort of St-Jean-de-Monts and its vast sandy beaches ideal for a family holiday. Tear yourself away from the beach and continue north-west to Noirmoutier; enjoy the island's old-world charm, indulge in bird watching and observe the last salt-marsh workers. Follow the coast round the Baie de Bourgneuf to Pornic, a popular seaside resort. Drive on to the rocky Pointe de St-Gildas, then turn back and continue inland to St-Philbert-de-Grand-Lieu and its lake, via the safari park of La Planète Sauvage. Turn south towards Challans, famous for its ducks, and make a detour to Apremont and its castle before returning to St-Gilles.

5 BORDEAUX VINEYARDS

305km/190mi starting from Bordeaux

Châteaux, vineyards and wine cellars dominate this region traditionally dedicated to wine. Drive south-east to Cadillac, a 13C *bastide* (fortified town), then on to the vineyards of Ste-Croix-du-Mont and Sauternes (in particular the exclusive Château Yquem and Château de Malle). Veering north-east, continue to the picturesque village of Sauveterre-de-Guyenne, the ruins of Blasimon Abbey and on to St-Émilion, a jewel of a town set among hilly vineyards. Nearby are the Roman-esque church of Petit-Palais and the Écomusée du Libournais in Montagne. To the north-east, on the River Dordogne, the town of Libourne is the starting point of the journey of Bordeaux wine to every part of the world. Having reached the Gironde estuary, you enter Haut Médoc, an area dotted with famous châteaux, such as Château Margaux and Château Maucaillou, where vineyards and fine architecture blend to offer you an inspiring visit. Fort Médoc is a reminder that the region was, for a long time, torn between English and French domination…no wonder when you see what was at stake laid out before your eyes: elegant rows of vines producing world renown wines whose names are music to the ear of wine lovers: Château Mouton-Rothschild, Château Lafitte-Rochschild and more.

6 THE CÔTE D'ARGENT SOUTH OF ARCACHON

375km/233mi

This is a region of retrieved marshland, lakes, sandy beaches and pine forests. Climb to the top of Dune du Pilat for a splendid panorama of the sea and pine forest. Further south, you can take full advantage of the wealth of sporting facilities on offer at the Lac de Biscarosse, Lac de Parentis and Mimizan-Plage. Boat trips along Courant de Contis enable visitors to savour landscapes of marshes, pine forests and dunes. Inland, Sabres is the starting point of a tourist train leading to Marquèze and the Écomusée de la Grande Lande; part of the museum is in Luxey to the north-east. Continue your journey to the Château de Cazeneuve then to the old town of Bazas nestling round its cathedral and the Château de Roquetaillade. Change direction and drive south-east to Pissos, renowned for its handicraft activities. Drive north to Belhade, Hostens and Belin-Béliet through ideal hiking country then west to Sanguinet and its lake, where water-based activities abound, before returning to Arcachon.

7 THE BASQUE COAST

280km/174mi starting from Biarritz

Follow the coast south to Bidart and Guéthary (why not take a dip in the ocean on the way!) then on to St-Jean-de-Luz and its old town still vibrant with memories of Louis XIV's wedding to the Infanta of Spain. After a short incursion into Spain to visit San Sebastián, return to France and drive inland to La Rhune where a small rack railway

Basque landscape

Crevasses d'Holçarté (narrow gorges) and the grandiose Gorges de Kakuetta. Continue north to see the Gotein Calvary, visit Mauléon-Licharre, a former stronghold, and watch a game of pelota in St-Palais. Drive on to the Isturitz and Oxocelhaya caves and veer southwards to St-Étienne-de-Baïgorry, a typical Basque village. Further south is the Vallée des Aldudes with its characteristic small black pigs, then Spain and Roncevaux, once a traditional stopover for pilgrims on their way to Santiago de Compostela.

9 BÉARN

370km/230mi starting from Pau

Meadows and cultivated areas alternate with slopes covered with vines and pointed Pyrenean summits. The region may sometimes look austere but it is always welcoming. Having strolled through the old town and visited the castle, leave Pau southwards to Nay, where there is an interesting museum devoted to *bérets,* then drive through the mountains via Col de l'Aubisque, one of the passes on the Tour de France route offering superb views. Beyond are the ski resort of Gourette and the small spa of Eaux-Bonnes. A detour to Pic de la Sagette will enable you to hop on a tourist train leading to Lac d'Artouste. Turn back and continue to the cliffs of Aste-Béon inhabited by vultures. Further on is Lescun surrounded by limestone peaks; drive through Issaux forest to the ski resort of Arette-Pierre-St-Martin. Turn north to Oloron-Ste-Marie, then Sauveterre-de-Béarn and Salies-de-Béarn, another spa. The last part of your journey can take in the old town of Orthez, a former capital of Béarn, the Château de Morlanne, Lescar's cathedral and the Église Ste-Foy in Morlaàs.

offers splendid views of the surrounding countryside. Further east you will encounter the picturesque villages of Sare, Ainhoa and Espelette before driving north to Bayonne along the Route Impériale des Cimes. Beyond Bayonne, you will drive through typical Landes landscapes, making a pause for a relaxing boat trip along Courant d'Huchet. Back to the coast and its picturesque resorts of Vieux-Boucau-les-Bains, Hossegor and Capbreton; continue south along the coast road to return to Biarritz, whose striking Rocher de la Vierge can be seen from afar.

8 THE BASQUE MOUNTAINS

285km/177mi starting from St-Jean-Pied-de-Port

This mountainous region dotted with small villages and historic places has a lot to offer. Start your trip from the capital of Basse-Navarre, the medieval town of St-Jean-Pied-de-Port. From there it's a steady climb through the mountains to the convivial winter sports resort of Iraty, then down into the

WHEN AND WHERE TO GO

When to Go

SEASONS

In the **summer** months, the Atlantic shore is very popular with French and foreign holiday-makers, who come to enjoy the bracing atmosphere of the ocean spiced with the balsam scent of pines, a tonic for the body and the spirit. Sea breezes cool the heat of the sun and the light is extraordinary: brilliant and bright at its purest, in the summertime a barely perceptible mist softens the outlines of the landscape. Across the pale blue sky trail wisps of cloud like silk scarves in the wind.

In the **autumn** the crowds and heat subside. When waves batter the coast and rain pounds the shore, the fine weather moves inland. This is the perfect time to visit the vineyards of Bordeaux, busy with the grape harvest. The light falls obliquely from the heavens, saturating the colours of the deepening season: red vine creeping over an old stone wall, purple grapes heavy and ripe, the brown gloss of chestnuts inside their prickly husks, tender mushrooms below the forest bracken.

Winter is a splendid time of year to discover the rugged isolation of the Pyrenées. Whether glimpsed at high speed as your skis cut through fresh powder snow, or contemplated more sedately as you glide across the valley on a cross-country trail, the landscape is memorable.

Spring is a cool season, heralded by a profusion of flowers and flowering trees. As the equinox approaches, storms whip up cold rains which flood the river valleys. Between the dark masses of mountainous clouds, a piercing yellow light highlights the natural and architectural beauty of the land.

CLIMATE

The Atlantic Coast is exceptionally sunny, with over 2 000 hours of sunshine annually. The brightest days are between May and September; over that period the water warms up to an average 20°C/70°F as it hits the beach. Snow is rare and spring comes early. The central part of the coastal area covered in this book is subject to 20 to 30 spectacular thunder storms a year, blown in by prevailing winds from the west. Around Biarritz, on the Basque Coast, the mountains create a different climate with considerably more rainfall. In the winter months, frequent warm spells (up to 20°C/70°F) give the Basque "micro-climate" an exotic feel.

In the high mountains, snow may continue to fall well into spring. Climbers and campers will find late July and early September the most clement for enjoying nature in the part of the Pyrenees covered in this guide (August is often stormy). Skiers seeking fresh *néou* (as snow is called by some locals), will find slopes open from December to April.

WEATHER FORECAST

National forecast: ☎*08 36 68 00 00.*

🛈Weather information is also available on-line at *www.meteo.fr.*

A. Thuillier/MICHELIN

Themed Tours

Travel itineraries with specific themes have been mapped out to help you discover the regional heritage. You will find brochures in tourist offices, and the routes are generally well-marked and easy to follow.

For further information, log on to www.routes-historiques.com or contact:

La Demeure Historique,
Hôtel de Nesmond, 57 quai de la Tournelle, 75005 Paris, ☎01 55 42 60 00; www.demeure-historique.com.

HISTORY

Route des Abbayes et Monuments du Haut-Poitou

Roman vestiges and Romanesque churches, Gothic architecture in the Plantagenet or angevin style, châteaux and feudal fortresses vie for the visitor's attention over this rich historical itinerary.
Information on this route is also available at Ligugé town hall, ☎06 63 06 98 20.

Route des Plantagenets

Eleven itineraries in the western part of France trace this great dynasty. The brochure includes a suggested tour passing through La Sauve-Majeur, Blaye, St-Emillion, Bazas, Dax and Bayonne.

Route des Trésors de Saintonge

A tour around the region of Saintes reveals a wealth of Romanesque churches in the Saintonge style, set like jewels in the beautiful green countryside.
For further information, contact M. Hedelin at the Château de Dampierre, ☎01 46 51 87 15.

Route Historique des Châteaux et Cités au Cœur d'Aquitaine

This tour includes the châteaux of Le Bouilh, Mongenan, Malle, Vayres, Roquetaillade and Cazeneuve as well as the medieval towns of La Réole, St-Macaire and Bazas.
Information on this route is also available at the Château de Mongenan, 33640 Portets, ☎05 56 25 48 16.

Route Historique sur les Pas des Seigneurs du Béarn et du Pays Basque

This tour visits some of the most picturesque manors, châteaux and towns of Béarn and the Basque Country, steeped in the history of Aquitaine, from the 12C to the 18C. The itinerary includes the Château d'Urtubie, Sauveterre, Navarrenx, Oloron-Ste-Marie, Orthez and St-Jean-de-Luz.
For further information, contact the Château d'Urtubie, 64122 Urrugne, ☎05 59 54 31 15; www.chateauxcountry.com.

GASTRONOMY

Route du fromage Ossau-Iraty

Traditional Pyrenean sheep's cheese is produced in the heart of the Béarn and Basque Country. From St-Jean-de-Luz to the Col d'Aubisque (182km/109mi), some 50 stops will give you ample occasion to sample and savour this regional speciality.
For detailed information, contact the Syndicat de défense de l'AOC Ossau-Iraty, Maison Baratchartenea, 64120 Ostabat Asne, ☎05 59 37 86 61.

VINEYARDS

The Atlantic Coast region has a wealth of *caves* (wine cellars) offering *dégustations* (tastings) and visits. Specific addresses for the famous Bordeaux wines are listed under Vignoble de Bordeaux in the *Discovering the French Atlantic Coast* section. While some may prefer to contact their travel agent and set off on a coach tour with an expert, others may prefer to travel the by-ways, stopping at a local wine-grower's *chais* to pick up a bottle to accompany a picnic lunch. A visit to a small proprietor producing local wine, often a family affair generations old, can be as memorable as a tour of one of the great châteaux or distilleries.

Vins de Bordeaux
⚜ **Maison du vin de Bordeaux** – *3, cours du XXX-Juillet, 33075 Bordeaux Cedex, ☎05 56 00 22 88;*

www.vins-bordeaux.fr. ○*Open Jun-mid-Oct Mon-Fri, 8:30am-6:30pm, Sat 9:00am-4:00pm. Mid-Oct-May Mon-Fri 8:30am-6:00pm (Fri 6:30pm).*

☙ **Maison du tourisme et du vin du Médoc** – *La Verrerie, 33250 Pauillac,* ☎*05 56 59 03 08; www.pauillac-medoc.com.*

☙ **Maison des vins de Graves** – *61, cours du Maréchal-Foch, BP 51, 33720 Podensac,* ☎*05 56 27 09 25.*

☙ **Maison du vin des Premières Côtes de Blaye** – *11, cours Vauban, BP 122, 33390 Blaye,* ☎*05 57 42 91 19; www.aoc-blaye.com.*

☙ **Maison du vin des Côtes de Bourg** – *1, place de l'Éperon, 33710 Bourg,* ☎*05 57 94 80 20; www.cotes-de-bourg.com.* ○*Open 15 Jun-15 Sep daily 10am-1pm & 2pm-7pm. Rest of the year hours vary.*

☙ **Maison du vin de Ste-Foy-Bordeaux** – *93, Route de Bergerac, 33220 Pineuilh,* ☎*05 57 46 31 71; www.saintefoy-bordeaux.com.*

☙ **Maison du vin de St-Émilion** – *Place Pierre-Meyrat, 33330 St-Émilion,* ☎*05 57 55 50 55, www.vins-saint-emilion.com.* ○*Open Mar-Nov 9:30am-12:30pm & 2pm-6pm (Aug 9am-7pm). Dec-Feb 10am-12noon & 2pm-6pm.*

☙ **Maison des vins des Premières Côtes de Bordeaux et Cadillac** – *La Closerie, D10, route de Langon, 33410 Cadillac,* ☎*05 57 98 19 20.*

☙ **Maison du vin de Barsac** – *Place de l'Église, 33720 Barsac,* ☎*05 56 27 15 44, www.maisondebarsac.fr.*

Vins Basques

☙ **Cave coopérative des vins d'Irouleguy et du Pays basque** – *64430 St-Étienne-de-Baïgorry,* ☎*05 59 37 41 33.* ●*Guided tours by prior arrangement. 3€.* ○*Open daily May-Sep.*

Vins Béarnais

☙ **Cave des producteurs de Jurançon** – *53, avenue Henri-IV, 64290 Gan,* ☎*05 59 21 57 03; www.cavedejurancon.com.*

Entre-Deux-Mers wine

S. Sauvignier/MICHELIN

☙ **Cave coopérative Béarn-Bellocq** – *64270 Bellocq,* ☎*05 59 65 10 71; www.cavedejurancon.com.*

Vins landais

☙ **Les Vignerons Landais Tursan-Chalosse** – *Place de l'Hôtel de Ville, 40320 Geaune,* ☎*05 58 44 51 25; www.vlandais.com Guided tours every Tues Apr-Sep.*

ℹ The **Guide de Vins du Sud-Ouest** is available from the Comité Interprofessionnel des Vins du Sud-Ouest, ☎*05 61 73 87 06; www.vins-du-sud-ouest.com*

Vins du Lots-et-Garonne

Union interprofessionnelle des vins des Côtes de Duras – *Maison du vin, D 668, 47120 Duras,* ☎*05 53 20 20 70, www.cotesdeduras.com.*

☙ **Les Vignerons de Buzet** – *47160 Buzet-sur-Baïse,* ☎*05 53 84 74 30; www.vignerons-buzet.fr.*

☙ **Cave de Goulens en Brulhois** – *47390 Layrac,* ☎ *05 53 87 01 65.*

☺ A Bit of Advice ☺

While many of the wines in the region covered in this guide are celebrated around the world, some lesser-known vintages are worth tasting, too.

Vins de Mareuil *(Vendée)*

- **Maison Mourat** – *Route de la Roche, ferme des Ardillers, 85320 Mareuil-sur-Lay,* ☎02 51 97 20 10.
- **Domaine des Dames** – *Daniel Gentreau, Follet, 85320 Rosnay,* ☎02 51 30 55 39.

Muscadet de Sèvre et Maine, Gros Plant, Muscadet
(Loire-Atlantique)

- **Domaine La Roche Renard** – *I. et P. Denis, Les Laures, 44330 Vallet,* ☎02 40 36 63 65.
- **Maison des Vins de Nantes** – *Bellevue, 44690 La Haye-Fouassière,* ☎02 40 36 90 10.
- **Domaine des Herbauges** – *44830 Bouaye,* ☎02 40 65 44 92.

APERITIF AND AFTER-DINNER DRINKS

Armagnac

- **Bureau national interprofessionnel de l'armagnac AOC** – *11, place de la Liberté, BP 3, 32800 Eauze,* ☎05 62 08 11 00, www.armagnac.fr.
- **Maison du Floc de Gascogne** – *Rue des Vignerons, 32800 Eauze,* ☎05 62 09 85 41; www.floc-du-gascogne.fr.

Cognac *(Charente)*

The main producers of brandy (Camus, Hennessy, Martell, Otard, Rémy Martin, Hubert de Polignac) are open for tours and sales (*see Cognac Address Book in the Discovering the French Atlantic Coast section).*
For a wealth of information on this famous brandy, log on to www.cognacweb.com or www.le.cognac.com.

Bise dur, La Chouanette, Rosée des Charentes, Kamok, Liqueur des Vendéens *(Vendée)*
Société H. Vrignaud, 1, Place Richelieu, 85400 Luçon, ☎02 51 56 11 48.

Pineau des Charentes

This fortified wine is omnipresent; reds, rosés and golden white varieties are widely available throughout the region.

Trouspinette *(Vendée)*

- **Maison Mourat,** *La Ferme des Ardillers, 85320 Mareuil-sur-Lay,* ☎02 51 97 20 10.

Trinquet Vendéen *(Vendée)*

- **C. et I. Cochain,** *La Rivière, 85160 St-Jean-de-Monts,* ☎02 51 58 82 40.

Fine Bretagne *(Loire-Atlantique)*

- **Distillerie Seguin,** *10, Boulevard St-Rémy, 44270 Machecoul,* ☎02 40 31 40 50.

WINE TOURS

- **Les Routes du vin** – *Maison du vin de Bordeaux, 1 cours du XXX-Juillet,* ☎05 56 00 22 88; www.vins-bordeaux.fr.
- **Route des Vins du Jurançon** – *La Commanderie du Jurançon, 64360 Lacommande,* ☎05 59 82 70 30; www.vins-jurancon.fr.
- **Route des Vins et des Appellations en Entre-deux-Mers** – *Office du tourisme de l'Entre-deux-Mers, Monségur,* ☎05 56 61 82 73.
- **Route du Vignoble en Val de Loire** – *Bureau des vins de la Touraine,* ☎02 47 60 55 00.
- **Les Étapes du Cognac** – Four marked routes with over 200 addresses, including wine producers, monuments, hotels and restaurants, provide an excellent introduction to the Cognac region.
  For further information, call ☎05 45 36 47 35 or log onto www.cognacetapes.com.

OENOLOGICAL COURSES

The **Office du tourisme de Bordeaux** (*12 cours du XXX-Juillet, 33080 Bordeaux,* ☎05 56 00 66 00; www.bordeaux-tourisme.com) offers an introduction to oenology, with a wine-tasting programme every Thursday at 4.30pm (also Saturdays at 4.30pm mid-July to mid-August). Join in the initiation to wine-tasting at the **Maison du Vin de St-Émilion** daily from 11am to noon, mid July to mid-September, and at the **Maison du tourisme et du vin de Pauillac** on Wednesdays at 11am, early July to mid-September. The **Vinoscope du Médoc** (*Château Maucaillou, 33480 Moulis-en-Médoc, ☎05 56 58 01 23*) teaches tasting techniques in a 2-day course. The château also conducts Médoc vineyard discovery tours and weekends combining châteaux, wine and golf.

EQUESTRIAN TOURS

Savour the countryside at a gentle pace aboard a **horse-drawn caravan**. Obtain a brochure from the **Maison Poitou-Charentes** (*68-70, rue du Cherche-Midi, 75006 Paris ☎01 42 22 83 74*) for information on hiring a caravan with bunk beds and kitchen facilities for 2-7 days. The **Comité Nationale au Tourisme Équestre** (*9, boulevard Macdonald, 75019 Paris, ☎01 53 26 15 50; cnte@ffe.com*) will supply general information as well as addresses of local organisations. It is also possible to contact regional associations directly, by writing to any of the following:

- **Comité Départemental de Tourisme Équestre de Gironde**, *153, rue David-Johnston 33000 Bordeaux ☎ 05 56 00 99 28.*
- **Association Régionale du Tourisme Équestre de Poitou-Charentes**, *J-G Mercier, 2, rue du Puits 17330 Villeneuve-la-Comtesse ☎05 46 24 05 94.*
- **Comité Départemental de Tourisme Équestre de Charente**, *Boulevard de Bury 16000 Angoulême ☎05 45 38 94 48*
- **Comité Départemental de Tourisme Équestre de Charente Maritime**, *37, rue Chef de Ville 17000 La Rochelle ☎05 46 41 82 18; www.equitation-17.com.*
- **Comité Départemental de Tourisme Équestre des Deux Sèvres**, *J-G Mercier, 2, rue du Puits 17330 Villeneuve-la-Comtesse ☎05 46 24 05 94.*
- **Comité Départemental de Tourisme Équestre des Landes**, *Chambre d'agriculture, SUA Tourisme, Cité Galianne, 40005 Mont-de-Marsan ☎05 58 85 44 43.*

KNOW BEFORE YOU GO

Useful Websites

www.ambafrance-us.org
The **French Embassy** in the USA has a Web site providing basic information (geography, demographics, history), a news digest and business-related information. It offers special pages for children, and pages devoted to culture, language study and travel, and you can reach other selected French sites (regions, cities, ministries) with a hypertext link.

www.franceguide.com
The **French Government Tourist Office / Maison de la France** site is packed with practical information and tips for those travelling to France. The home page has a number of links to more specific guidance, for American or Canadian travellers for example, or to the FGTO's London pages.

www.FranceKeys.com
This sight has plenty of practical information for visiting France. It covers all the regions, with links to tourist offices and related sites. Very useful for planning the details of your tour in France!

Tourist Offices

FRENCH TOURIST OFFICES ABROAD

For information, brochures, maps and assistance in planning a trip to France travellers should apply to the official French Tourist Office or Maison de France in their own country:

Australia – New Zealand

Sydney – Level 13, 25 Bligh St, Sydney,
New South Wales 2000,
☎(02) 9231 5244;
Fax (02) 9221 8682;
info.au@franceguide.com.

Canada

Montreal – 1981 Avenue McGill
College, Suite 490, Montreal PQ
H3A 2W9, ☎(514) 288 2026;
Fax (514) 845 4868;
canada@franceguide.com.

Ireland

Dublin – 10 Suffolk Street, Dublin 2,
☎(01) 679 0813 or 1560 235 235
(0.95€/minute); Fax: (01) 679 0814;
info.ie@franceguide.com.

South Africa

P.O. Box 41022, Craig Hall 2024,
☎(011) 880 8062;
mdfsa@frenchdoor.ca.za.

United Kingdom

London Maison de France –
178 Piccadilly, London WIJ 9AL
☎(09068) 244 123 (60p/minute);
Fax 020 793 6594;
info.uk@franceguide.com.

United States

New York – 444 Madison Avenue,
16th Floor, NY 10022-6903,
☎(514) 288-1904; Fax (212) 838-
7855; info.us@franceguide.com.

Los Angeles – 9454 Wilshire
Boulevard, Suite 715, Beverly Hills,
CA 90212-2967.
☎(514) 288-1904;
Fax (310) 276-2835;
info.losangeles@franceguide.com.

Chicago - 205 N. Michigan Avenue,
Suite 3770, Chicago, IL 60601,
☎(514) 288-2904
info.chicago@franceguide.com.

🛈 Information can also be requested
from: **France on Call,** ☎(202) 659-7779.

LOCAL TOURIST OFFICES

Visitors may also contact local tourist
offices for more precise information
and to receive brochures and maps.

In the *Discovering the French Atlanti*c
Coast section of this guide, the
addresses and telephone numbers of
tourist offices, indicated by the
🛈 symbol, are listed after the
introduction to the Principal Sight or in
the Address Books.
Following are the addresses of local
tourist offices of the *départements* and
régions covered in this guide.

Three regional tourist offices are
concerned with the area covered by
this guide; address inquiries to the
Comité Régional de Tourisme (C.R.T.):

Aquitaine: Bureaux de la Cité mondiale,
23 parvis des Chartrons, 33074
Bordeaux Cedex, ☎05 56 01 70 00,
Fax 05 56 01 70 07; www.tourisme-
aquitaine.info.

Poitou-Charentes: BP 56, 86002
Poitiers Cedex, ☎05 49 50 10 50,
Fax 05 49 41 37 28; www.poitou-
charentes-vacances.com.

Pays de la Loire (for the Loire-
Atlantique and Vendée *départements*): 2, rue de la Loire, BP 20411,
44204 Nantes Cedex 2, ☎02 40 48
24 20; www.enpaysdelaloire.com.

For each *département* within the
region, address inquiries to the Comité
Départemental de Tourisme (C.D.T.),
unless otherwise stated:

Landes – 4 av. Aristide-Briand, BP 407,
40012 Mont-de-Marsan Cedex,
☎05 58 06 89 89;
www.tourismelandes.com.

Charente – 27 place Bouillaud, 16021
Angoulême, ☎05 45 69 79 09;
www.lacharente.com.

Charente Maritime – Maison de la
Charente-Maritime, 85, boulevard
de la République, 17076 La Rochelle
Cedex 9, ☎05 46 31 71 71;
www.en-charente-maritime.com.

Deux-Sèvres – 15 rue Thiers, 79025
Niort Cedex 9, ☎05 49 77 87 79;
www.tourisme-deux-sevres.com.

Maison du tourisme de la Gironde –
21, cours de l'Intendance, 33000
Bordeaux, ☎05 56 52 61 40;
www.tourisme-gironde.cg33.fr.

Loire-Atlantique – 11 rue du Château
du l'Eraudière CS 40698, 44306
Nantes Cedex, ☎02 51 72 95 40;

www.loire-atlantique-tourisme.com

Lot-et-Garonne – 271, rue de Péchabout, BP 30158, 47000 Agen, ☏05 53 66 14 14; www.lot-et-garonne.fr

Pyrénées-Atlantiques – BP 811, 4 allée des Platanes, 64108 Bayonne Cedex, ☏05 59 46 52 52; www.tourisme64.com

Agence touristique du Béarn – 22 ter rue J-J-de-Monaix, 64000 Pau, ☏05 59 30 01 30; www.tourisme64.com

Vendée – 8, place Napoléon, BP 233, 85006 La Roche sur Yon Cedex, ☏02 51 47 88 22; www.vendee-tourisme.com.

Vienne – 33, place Charles-de-Gaulle, BP 287, 86007 Poitiers Cedex, ☏05 49 37 48 48. www.tourisme-vienne.com

In France, 136 towns and areas have been labelled **Villes et Pays d'Art et d'Histoire** by the Ministry of Culture. They are particularly active in promoting their architectural and cultural heritage and offer guided tours by highly qualified guides as well as activities for 6 to 12-year-olds.

▣ More information is available from local tourist offices and from *www.vpah.culture.fr.*

International Visitors

DOCUMENTS

Passport
Nationals of countries within the European Union entering France need only a national identity card. Nationals of other countries must be in possession of a valid national passport. In case of loss or theft, report to your embassy or consulate and the local police.

Visa
No **entry visa** is required for Canadian, US or Australian citizens travelling as tourists and staying less than 90 days, except for students planning to study in France. If you think you may need a visa, apply to your local French Consulate.

US citizens should obtain the booklet *Safe Trip Abroad (US $1)*, which provides useful information on visa requirements, customs regulations, medical care etc for international travellers. Published by the **Government Printing Office**, it can be ordered by phone – ☏*(202) 512-1800* – or consulted on-line *(www.access.gpo.gov)*. General passport information is available by phone toll-free from the Federal Information Center (item 5 on the automated menu), ☏*800-688-9889*. **US passport application forms** can be downloaded from *http://travel.state.gov*.

CUSTOMS REGULATIONS

Apply to the Customs Office (UK) for a leaflet on customs regulations and the full range of duty-free allowances; available from **HM Customs and Excise**, Thomas Paine House, Angel Square, Torrens Street, London EC1V 1TA, ☏08450 109 000. The **US Customs Service** offers a publication *Know Before You Go* for US citizens: for the office nearest you, consult the phone book, Federal Government, US Treasury *(www.customs.ustreas.gov)*.

There are no customs formalities for holidaymakers bringing their caravans into France for a stay of less than six months. No customs document is necessary for pleasure boats and outboard motors for a stay of less than six months but the registration certificate should be kept on board.

Duty-Free Allowances	
Spirits (whisky, gin, vodka etc)	10 litres
Fortified wines (vermouth, port etc)	20 litres
Wine (not more than 60 sparkling)	90 litres
Beer	110 litres
Cigarettes	800
Cigarillos	400
Cigars	200
Smoking tobacco	1 kg

Embassies and Consulates in France		
Australia	Embassy	4 rue Jean-Rey, 75015 Paris ☎ 01 40 59 33 00 Fax: 01 40 59 33 10 www.austgov.fr
Canada	Embassy	35 avenue Montaigne, 75008 Paris ☎ 01 44 43 29 00 Fax: 01 44 43 29 99 paris@international.gc.ca
Eire	Embassy	4 rue Rude, 75016 Paris ☎ 01 44 17 67 00 Fax: 01 44 17 67 60 paris@dfa.ie
New Zealand	Embassy	7 ter rue Léonard-de-Vinci, 75016 Paris ☎ 01 45 01 43 43 Fax: 01 45 01 43 44 nzembassy.paris@fr.oleane.com
South Africa	Embassy	59 quai d'Orsay, 75007 Paris ☎ 01 53 59 23 23 Fax: 01 53 59 23 68 info@afriquesud.net
UK	Embassy	35 rue du Faubourg St-Honoré, 75008 Paris ☎ 01 44 51 31 00 Fax: 01 44 51 31 27 www.britishembassy.gov.uk
	Consulate	16 rue d'Anjou, 75008 Paris ☎ 01 44 51 31 02 (visas)
	Consulate	353 boulevard du Président Wilson, 33073 Bordeaux ☎ 05 57 22 21 10 Fax: 05 56 08 33 12
USA	Embassy	2 avenue Gabriel, 75008 Paris ☎ 01 43 12 22 22 Fax: 01 42 66 97 83 www.amb-usa.fr
	Consulate	2 rue St-Florentin, 75001 Paris ☎ 01 42 96 14 88

Americans can take home, tax-free, up to US$ 400 worth of goods (limited quantities of alcohol and tobacco products); Canadians up to CND$ 300; Australians up to AUS$ 400 and New Zealanders up to NZ$ 700. Residents from a member state of the European Union are not restricted with regard to purchasing goods for private use, but the recommended allowances for alcoholic beverages and tobacco are as shown in the chart.

HEALTH

First aid, medical advice and chemists' night service rotas are available from chemists drugstores *(pharmacie)* identified by the green cross sign. All prescription drugs should be clearly labelled; it is recommended that you carry a copy of the prescription.
It is advisable to take out comprehensive insurance cover as the recipient of medical treatment in French hospitals or clinics must pay the bill. **Nationals of non-EU countries** should check with their insurance companies about policy limitations. Reimbursement can then be negotiated with the insurance company according to the policy held.

British and Irish citizens should apply to the Department of Health and Social Security **before travelling** for Form E 111, which entitles the holder to urgent treatment for accident or unexpected illness in EU countries. A refund of part of the costs of treatment can be obtained on application in person or by post to the local Social Security Offices *(Caisse Primaire d'Assurance Maladie)*.
Americans concerned about travel and health can contact the International Association for Medical Assistance to Travelers, which can also provide details of English-speaking doctors in different parts of France: ☎*(716) 754 4883; www.iamat.org.*

✚ **The American Hospital of Paris** is open 24hrs for emergencies as well as consultations, with English-speaking staff, at 63 boulevard Victor-Hugo, 92200 Neuilly-sur-Seine, ☎01 46 41 25 25; www.american-hospital.org. Accredited by major insurance companies.

✚ **The British Hospital** is just outside Paris in Levallois-Perret, 3 rue Barbès, ☎01 46 39 22 22; www.british-hospital.org.

Accessibility

The sights described in this guide which are easily accessible to people of reduced mobility are indicated in the admission times and charges information by the ♿ symbol (♿ *see individual sights in the Discovering section*).
On TGV and Corail trains operated by the national railway (SNCF), there are special wheelchair slots in 1st class carriages available to holders of 2nd-class tickets. On Eurostar and Thalys, special rates are available for accompanying adults. All airports are equipped to receive physically disabled passengers.
🔲 Find information for slow walkers, mature travellers and others with special needs at *www.access-able.com*.
🔲 For information on museum access for the disabled contact **La Direction, Les Musées de France**, Service Accueil des Publics Spécifiques, 6 rue des Pyramides, 75041 Paris Cedex 1, ☎ 01 40 15 80 72.
The Michelin Guide France and the **Michelin Camping France** guide indicate hotels and camp sites with facilities suitable for people with physical handicaps.

GETTING THERE AND GETTING AROUND

By Plane

It is very easy to arrange air travel to one of Paris' two airports (Roissy/Charles-de-Gaulle to the north, and Orly to the south). Contact airline companies and travel agents for details of package tour flights with a rail or coach link-up as well as Fly-Drive schemes. For example, some packages include a direct link from Roissy airport to the high-speed TGV train which serves the region, stopping in Poitiers, La Rochelle, Bordeaux and as far south as Biarritz, Hendaye and Tarbes. Alternatively, there are several daily connecting flights from Paris to the regional capital Bordeaux, direct regular flights from London and seasonal flights from a number of destinations outside France, including Montreal, Toronto and Shannon. Information is available from the French Tourist Office in your country (♿ *see WHEN AND WHERE TO GO*) as well as from travel agents and airline companies.
The following **airlines** operate flights from the UK to the Atlantic Coast region:

- ✈ **Ryanair** – *www.ryanair.com* (flights to Poitiers, Pau, Nantes, Biarritz and La Rochelle);
- ✈ **Bmibaby** – *www.bmibaby.com* (flights to Bordeaux);
- ✈ **British Airways** – *www.ba.com* (flights to Bordeaux);
- ✈ **Air France** – *www.airfrance.com* (flights to Bordeaux).
- ✈ **Flybe** – *www.flybe.com* (flights to Bordeaux, La Rochelle);

Visitors arriving in **Paris** who wish to reach the city centre or a train station may use public transportation or reserve space on the **Airport Shuttle** *(for Roissy-Charles-de-Gaulle ☎ 01 45 38 55 72, for Orly ☎ 01 43 21 06 78).*
Air France operates a coach service into town with frequent departures *(☎ 01 41 56 89 00).* The cost and duration of a taxi ride from the airport to the center of town varies with traffic conditions. From Charles-de-Gaulle: about 1hr, 40€; from Orly about 30min, 30€. There is an extra charge (posted in the cab) for baggage; the extra charge for airport pick-up is on the meter; drivers are usually given a tip of 10-15% of the fare.

🔲 For further information on getting to and from Paris airports, log on to *www.aeroportsdeparis.fr*.

The main regional airports are:

🛬 **Aéroport international Nantes-Atlantique** – *(SW of Nantes)* CCI, 44346 Bouguenais Cedex, ☎02 40 84 80 00, www.nantes.aeroport.fr

🛬 **Aéroport de Poitiers-Biard** – *(5km/3mi W of Poitiers)* 86580 Biard, ☎05 49 30 04 40

🛬 **Aéroport d'Angoulême Brie-Champniers** – *(10km/6mi N of Angoulême city centre)* 16430 Champniers, ☎05 45 69 88 09

🛬 **Aéroport La Rochelle-Laleu** – *(N of La Rochelle)* rue du Jura, 17000 La Rochelle, ☎05 46 42 30 26

🛬 **Aéroport d'Agen** – La Garenne, 47520 Le Passage, ☎05 53 77 00 88, www.aeroport-agen.com

🛬 **Aéroport Biarritz-Anglet-Bayonne** – esplanade de l'Europe, 64600 Anglet, ☎05 59 43 83 83

🛬 **Aéroport de Bordeaux-Mérignac** – Cedex 40, 33700 Mérignac, ☎ 05 56 34 50 50

🛬 **Aéroport Pau-Pyrénées** – Lescar, ☎05 59 33 33 00, www.pau.aeroport.fr

LD Lines	In the UK: ☎ 08704 528 4335.
	In France: ☎ 0825 304 304
	www.ldlines.com
Norfolkline	In the UK: ☎ 0870 870 1020
	In France: ☎ 03 28 59 01 01
	www.norfolkline-ferries.co.uk
Brittany Ferries	In the UK: ☎ 0870 907 6103
	In France: ☎0825 828 828
	In Ireland: ☎ 021 427 7801
	www.brittany-ferries.com
Irish Ferries	In the UK: ☎ 08705 17 17 17
	In Ireland: ☎ 0818 300 400
	In France: ☎ 01 43 94 46 94
	In the US: ☎ (772) 563 2856
	www.irishferries.com
Seafrance	In the UK: ☎ 08712 222 500
	In France: ☎ 0825 082 505
	www.seafrance.com

By Ship

There are numerous **cross-Channel services** from the United Kingdom and Ireland. To choose the most suitable route between your port of arrival and your destination use the **Michelin Tourist and Motoring Atlas France**, **Michelin map 726** (which gives travel times and mileages) or **Michelin Local maps** from the 1:200,000 series.

By Train

Le Shuttle-Eurotunnel run a service through the Channel Tunnel for cars from **Ashford** (Kent) to **Calais**, (🔲bookings and information ☎08705 35 35 35; www.eurotunnel.com). **Eurostar** runs via the Channel Tunnel between **London** (Waterloo) and **Paris** (Gare du Nord) in 3hrs (🔲bookings and information ☎08705 186 186 in the UK; ☎1-888-EUROSTAR in the US; |www.eurostar.com). In Paris it links to the high-speed rail network (TGV). TGV departures for the Atlantic coast are from the Gare Montparnasse.

Eurailpass, Flexipass, Eurailpass Youth, EurailDrive Pass and **Saverpass** are three of the travel passes that may be purchased by residents of countries outside the European Union. In the US, contact your travel agent or Rail Europe *(2100 Central Ave. Boulder, CO, 80301 ☎1-800-4-EURAIL)*. If you are a European resident, you can buy a country pass, if you are not a resident of the country where you plan to use it. In the UK, call Rail Europe at ☎08708 371 371. 🔲Information on schedules can be obtained on websites for these agencies and the SNCF, respectively: *www.raileurop.com.us, www.eurail.on.ca, www.raileurope.co.uk, www.sncf.fr.* At the SNCF site, you can book ahead, pay with a credit card, and receive your ticket in the mail at home. There are numerous **discounts** available when you purchase your tickets in France, from 25-50% below the regular rate. These include discounts for using senior cards and youth cards (the nominative cards with a photograph must be purchased – 44€ and 41€, respectively), and lower rates for 2-9 people travelling together (no card required, advance purchase necessary). There are a limited number of discount seats available during peak travel times, and the best discounts are available for travel during off-peak periods.

Tickets must be validated (composter) by using the orange automatic date-stamping machines at the platform entrance (failure to do so may result in a fine).

The French railway company SNCF operates a telephone information, reservation and prepayment service in English from 7am to 10pm (French time). In France call ☎08 36 35 35 39 (when calling from outside France, drop the initial 0).

By Coach/Bus

Eurolines (London), 4 Cardiff Road, Luton, Bedfordshire, LU1 1PP, ☎08705 143219, Fax 01582 400694.
Eurolines (Paris), 22 rue Malmaison, 93177 Bagnolet, ☎01 49 72 57 80 or 08 92 89 90 91, Fax 01 49 72 57 99.
www.eurolines.com
The international website with information about travelling all over Europe by coach (bus).

By Car

PLANNING YOUR ROUTE

The area covered in this guide is easily reached by main motorways and national routes. **Michelin map 726** indicates the main itineraries as well as alternate routes for avoiding heavy traffic during busy holiday periods, and gives estimated travel times. **Michelin map 723** is a detailed atlas of French motorways, indicating tolls, rest areas and services along the route; it includes a table for calculating distances and times. The latest Michelin

route-planning service is available on the Internet at **www.ViaMichelin.com**. Travellers can calculate a precise route using such options as shortest route, route avoiding toll roads, Michelin-recommended route and gain access to tourist information (hotels, restaurants, attractions). The service is available on a pay-per-route basis or by subscription. The roads are very busy during the holiday period (particularly weekends in July and August) and, to avoid traffic congestion it is advisable to follow the recommended secondary routes (signposted as *Bison Futé – itinéraires bis*). The motorway network includes rest areas *(aires)* and petrol stations, usually with restaurant and shopping complexes attached, about every 40km/25mi, so that long-distance drivers have no excuse not to stop for a rest every now and then.

DOCUMENTS

Driving licence
Travellers from other European Union countries and North America can drive in France with a valid national or home-state **driving licence**. An **international driving licence** is useful because the information on it appears in nine langu-ages (keep in mind that traffic officers are empowered to fine motorists). A permit is available (US $10) from the **National Automobile Club**, 1151 East Hillsdale Blvd., Foster City, CA 94404 ☎650-294-7000, www.nationalauto-club.com; or contact your local branch of the **American Automobile Association.**

Registration papers
For the vehicle, it is necessary to have the registration papers (logbook) and a nationality plate of the approved size.

INSURANCE

Certain motoring organisations (AAA, AA, RAC) offer accident insurance and breakdown service schemes for members. Check with your current insurance company in regard to coverage while abroad. If you plan to hire a car using your credit card, check with the company, which may provide liability insurance automatically (and thus save you having to pay the cost for optimum coverage).

ROAD REGULATIONS

The minimum driving age is 18. Traffic drives on the right. All passengers must wear **seat belts**. Children under the age of 10 must ride in the back seat. Headlights must be switched on in poor visibility and at night; use side-lights only when the vehicle is stationary. In the case of a **breakdown**, a red warning triangle or hazard warning lights are obligatory. In the absence of stop signs at intersections, cars must **yield to the right**. Traffic on main roads outside built-up areas (priority indicated by a yellow diamond sign) and on round-abouts has right of way. Vehicles must stop when the lights turn red at road junctions and may filter to the right only when indicated by an amber arrow. The regulations on **drinking and driving** (limited to 0.50g/l) and **speeding** are strictly enforced – usually by an on-the-spot fine and/or confiscation of the vehicle.

Speed limits
Although liable to modification, these are as follows:
- Toll motorways (autoroutes) 130kph/80mph (110kph/68mph when raining);
- Dual carriageways and motorways without tolls 110kph/68mph (100kph/62mph when raining);
- Other roads 90kph/56mph (80kph/50mph when raining) and in towns 50kph/31mph;
- Outside lane on motorways during daylight, on level ground and with good visibility – minimum speed limit of 80kph/50mph.

Parking Regulations
In town there are zones where parking is either restricted or subject to a fee; tickets should be obtained from the ticket machines (horodateurs – small change necessary) and displayed inside the windscreen on the driver's side; failure to display may result in a fine, or towing and impoundment. Other parking areas in town may require you to take a ticket when passing through a barrier. To exit, you must pay the parking fee (usually there is a machine located by the exit – sortie) and insert the paid-up card in another machine which will lift the exit gate.

Tolls
In France, most motorway sections are subject to a toll (péage). You can pay in cash or with a credit card (Visa, Mastercard).

CAR RENTAL

There are car rental agencies at airports, railway stations and in all large towns throughout France. European cars have manual transmission; automatic cars are available in larger cities only if an advance reservation is made. Drivers must be over 21; between ages 21-25, drivers are required to pay an extra daily fee; some companies allow drivers under 23 only if the reservation has been made through a travel agent. It is relatively expensive to hire a car in France; Americans in particular will notice the difference and should make arrangements before leaving; take advantage of **fly-drive offers** when you buy your ticket, or seek advice from a travel agent, specifying requirements. There are many on-line services that will look for the best prices on car rental around the globe. **Nova** can be contacted at *www.rentacar-worldwide.com* or ☎*0800 018 6682 (freephone UK)* or ☎*+44 28 4272 8189 (calling from*

Rental Cars – Central Reservation in France	
Avis:	☎ 08 20 05 05 05 www.avis.com
Europcar:	☎ 08 25 358 358 www.europcar.com
Budget France:	www.budget.com
Hertz France:	☎ 01 47 03 49 12 www.hertz.com
SIXT-Eurorent:	☎ 08 20 00 74 98 www.e-sixt.com
National-CITER	☎ 01 45 22 77 91 www.nationalciter.fr

outside the UK). All of the firms listed below have Internet sites for reservations and information. In France, you can call the following numbers:
A Baron's Limousine ☎*01 45 30 21 21* provides cars and drivers (English-speaking drivers available).

MOTORHOME RENTAL

🚐 **Worldwide Motorhome Rentals**
   Offers fully equipped camper vans for rent. You can view them on the company's web page.
   ☎ 888- 519-8969 *US toll-free*
   ☎ 530-389-8316 *outside the US*
   Fax 530-389-8316, www.mhrww.com

PETROL/GASOLINE

French service stations dispense:
🚗 *sans plomb 98* (super unleaded 98)
🚗 *sans plomb 95* (super unleaded 95)
🚗 *diesel/gazole* (diesel)
🚗 *GPL* (LPG).

Gasoline, is considerably more expensive in France than in the USA. Prices are listed on signboards on the motorways; it is usually cheaper to fill up after leaving the motorway; check the large hyper-markets on the outskirts of town.

WHERE TO STAY AND EAT

👌 *For specific Hotel and Restaurant listings, see the Address Books within the Principal Sights in the Discovering section.*

Where to Stay

Hotels and restaurants for the region are described in the Address Books in the *Discovering the French Atlantic Coast section)*. The Legend on the cover flap explains the symbols and abbrevia tions used in the Address Books. Prices *(based on double occupancy)* and conditions were accurate at press time, but changes in management and other factors may mean that you will find some discrepancies. Please feel free to keep us informed of any major differences you encounter.
Use the **map of Places to stay** on the following pages to identify recommend-ed places for overnight stops. For an even greater selection, use the red-cover **Michelin Guide France**, with its famously reliable star-rating system and descrip-tions of hundreds of establishments all over France. The **Michelin Charming Places to Stay** guide contains a selection of 1 000 hotels and guesthouses at reasonable prices.

Book ahead to ensure that you get the accommodation you want, not only in tourist season, but year round, as many towns fill up during trade fairs, arts festivals, etc. Some places require an advance deposit or a reconfirmation. Reconfirming is especially important if you plan to arrive after 6pm.
For further assistance, **Loisirs Accueil** is a booking service that has offices in some French *départements* – contact the tourist offices listed above for further information or log onto *www.loisirsaccueilfrance.com*.
A guide to good-value, family-run hotels, **Logis et Auberges de France**,

Château de St-Loup

S. Sauvignier/MICHELIN

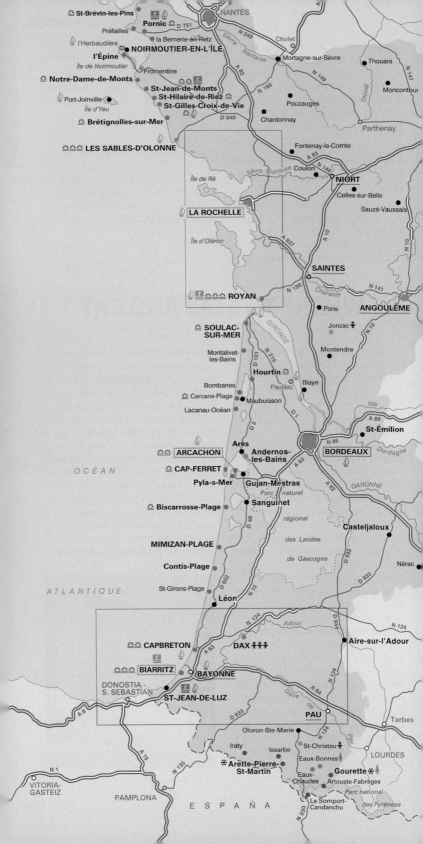

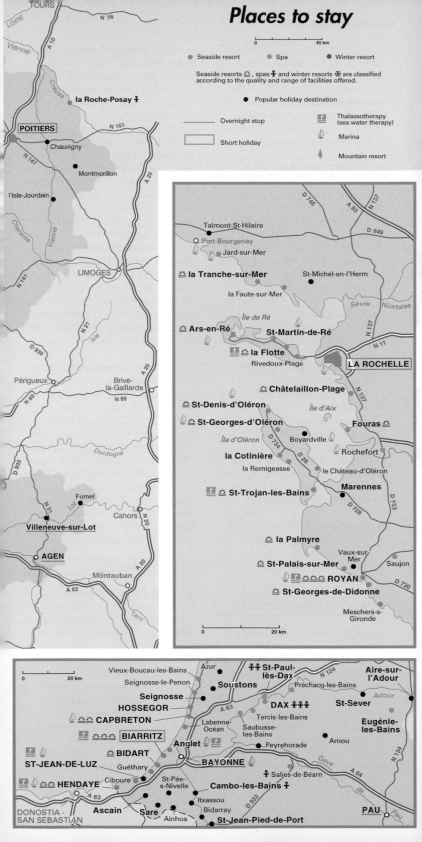

Places to stay

0   40 km

● Seaside resort   ● Spa   ● Winter resort

Seaside resorts ♨, spas ♨ and winter resorts ❄ are classified according to the quality and range of facilities offered.

● Popular holiday destination

— Overnight stop

▭ Short holiday

▣ Thalassotherapy (sea water therapy)

⚓ Marina

▲ Mountain resort

is available from the French Tourist Office, as are lists of other kinds of accommodation such as hotel-châteaux, bed-and-breakfasts etc.

Relais et châteaux provides information on booking in luxury hotels with character: *15 rue Galvani, 75017 Paris, ☎01 45 72 96 69; www.relaischateaux.com*.

ECONOMY CHAIN HOTELS

If you need a place to stop en route, these can be useful, as they are inexpensive (30-45€ for a double room) and generally located near the main road. While breakfast is available, there may not be a restaurant; rooms are small, with a television and bathroom. Central reservation numbers:

- **Akena** ☎01 69 84 85 17; www.hotels-akena.com
- **B&B** ☎08 92 78 29 29 (11am-5pm); www.hotel-bb.com
- **Etap Hôtel** ☎08 92 68 89 00; www.etaphotel.com
- **Mister Bed** ☎01 46 14 38 00; www.misterbed.fr
- **Villages Hôtel** ☎03 80 60 92 70; www.villages-hotel.com

The hotels listed below are slightly more expensive (from 45€), and offer a few more amenities and services. Central reservation numbers:

- **Campanile, Kyriad** ☎0825 003 003; www.campanile.com or www.kyriad.com
- **Ibis** ☎0 803 88 22 22; www.ibishotel.com.

RURAL ACCOMMODATION

The **Maison des Gîtes de France** is an information service on self-catering accommodation in France. Gîtes usually take the form of a cottage or apartment decorated in the local style where visitors can make themselves at home, or bed and breakfast accommodation *(chambres d'hôtes)* which consists of a room and breakfast at a reasonable price. Contact the **Gîtes de France** office (at *59 rue St-Lazare, 75439 Paris Cedex 09, ☎01 49 70 75 75)*, or their representative

in the UK, **Brittany Ferries** (*Millbay Docks; Plymouth, Devon. PL1 3EW, ☎08705 561 600, www.brittany-ferries. com*). The Internet site, *www.gites-de-france.fr*, has a good English version. From the site, you can order catalogues for different regions illustrated with photographs of the properties, as well as specialised catalogues (bed and breakfasts, chalets in ski areas, farm stays etc). You can also contact the local tourist offices, which may have lists of available properties and local bed and breakfast establishments.

The **Fédération Française des Stations Vertes de Vacances**, (6 rue Ranfer-de-Bretenières, BP 71698, 21016 Dijon Cedex, ☎03 80 54 10 50, www.stationsvertes.com), is able to provide details of accommodation, leisure facilities and natural attractions in rural locations selected for their tranquillity.

The **Centre permanent d'initiation à l'environnement** (CPIE, Environment awareness centre, *35 rue Hersent-Luzarche, 36290 Azay-le-Ferron, ☎02 54 39 23 43, Fax 02 54 39 25 12)*, has been entirely renovated and now offers 76 beds (including 6 for disabled travellers) to those who wish to explore the Parc naturel regional de la Brenne. Entertainment for adults and children is organised at weekends. Equipment used for observation is available on location. There are various activities centred on nature and astronomy.

FARM HOLIDAYS

The guide *Bienvenue à la ferme* is published by and available from the **Assemblée Permanente des Chambres d'Agriculture**, (Service "Agriculture et Tourisme", *9 avenue Georges-V, 75008 Paris, ☎01 53 57 11 44, www.bienvenue-a-la-ferme.com)*. It includes the addresses of farmers providing guest facilities who have signed a charter drawn up by the Chambers of Agriculture. *Bienvenue à la ferme* farms, vetted for quality and meeting official standards, can be identified by the yellow flower which serves as their logo.

HIKERS

Hikers can consult the guide entitled *Gîtes d'étapes, refuges* by **A and S Mouraret** *(Rando-Éditions, La Cadole, 74, rue A. Perdreaux, 78140 Vélizy ☎01 34 65 11 89) and www.gites-refuges. com*. The guide and the Web site are intended mainly for those who enjoy hiking, cycling, climbing, skiing and canoeing-kayaking holidays.

HOSTELS, CAMPING

To obtain an **International Youth Hostel Federation card** (there is no age requirement, and there is a senior card available too), you should contact the IYHF in your own country for inform-ation and membership applications *(US ☎202 783 6161; UK ☎01727 855215; Canada ☎613-273 7884; Australia ☎61-2-9565-1669)*. There is a new booking service on the Internet *(iyhf.org)*, which you may use to reserve rooms as far as six months in advance.
The main youth hostel association *(Auberges de Jeunesse)* in France is the **Ligue Française pour les Auberges de la Jeunesse** *(67 rue Vergniaud, 75013 Paris, ☎01 44 16 78 78; www.auberges-de-jeunesse.com)*. Annual membership costs 15.25€ (10.70€ for under-26-year-olds). There are numerous officially graded **camp sites** with varying standards of facilities along the Atlantic Coast and inland, especially round the lakes in the Landes Forest. The **Michelin Camping France** guide lists a selection of camp sites. The area is very popular with campers in the summer months, so it is wise to book in advance.

Where to Eat

Included in this guide are descriptions of selected hotels and restaurants for the region *(see Address Books in the Discovering section)*. The Legend on the cover flap

explains the symbols and abbrevia-tions used in these Address Books.

Coin symbols correspond to the average cost of a meal and are given as guidelines only.
Use the **Michelin Guide France**, with its famously reliable star-rating system and hundreds of establishments all over France, for an even greater choice. If you would like to experience a meal in a highly rated restaurant from the Michelin Guide, be sure to book ahead. In the countryside, restaurants usually serve lunch between noon and 2pm and the evening meal between 7.30-10pm. It is not always easy to find something in-between those two meal times, as the "non-stop" restaurant is still a rarity in small towns in the provinces. However, a hungry traveller can usually get a sandwich in a café, and ordinary hot dishes may be available in a brasserie.
Another guide series to help you with your culinary quest is Michelin's **Les Guides Gourmands** for the various regions of France.
Typical places to enjoy local specialities are the **Bars à Vin** (Wine Bars) of the Bordeaux region and the **Cabanes à Huîtres** (oyster huts) around Arcachon. Near the Spanish border, many bars offer **tapas** to eat with a glass of wine. In the Gers and Lot-et-Garonne depart-ments, foies gras and confits are on almost every restaurant *menu* (fixed price meal) or *carte* (as in *à la carte*). In French restaurants and cafés, a service charge is included. Tipping is not necessary, but French people often leave the small change from their bill on their table, or about 5% for the waiter in a good restaurant.

Sites Remarquables du Gout

French authorities have created a quality label for "remarkable gastronomic sites", places where the unique quality of local produce deserves special mention. In Poitou-Vendée-Charentes these places include: the poultry market in Challans, the town of Cognac, the salt marshes of Ile de Ré, the Marennes-Oléron basin, Noirmoutier Island for its salt and new potatoes, St-Gilles-Croix de-Vie. In Aquitaine and the Basque country: St-Émilion for its wines, Arcachon for oysters and eels,

MENU READER

agneau	lamb	**loukinos**	garlic sausage
alose	shad	**magret**	duck fillet
anguilles	eels	**marrons**	chestnuts
boudin blanc	chicken sausage	**mojettes**	white beans
boudin noir	blood sausage	**moules**	mussels
brioche	sweet egg-and-butter bread	**mouton**	mutton
canard	duck	**noix**	walnuts
cèpes	wild mushrooms	**oie**	goose
chapon	capon	**palombe**	wood pigeon
charcuterie	pork meats	**pastis**	flaky rum-flavoured pastry
chèvre	goat		
chipirones/seiches	squid	**pêche**	peach
choux	cabbage	**pibales**	young eels
confits (canard)	(duck) cooked and preserved in fat	**piperade**	spicy tomato omlette
crevettes	shrimp / prawns	**poule/poulet**	chicken
crudités	raw vegetable salad	**poule au pot**	chicken stew with vegetables
éclade	mussels cooked over pine needles	**prune**	plum
escargots	snails	**pruneau**	prune
esturgeon	sturgeon	**ravigote**	seasoned white sauce
fèves	broad beans		
foie	liver	**salmis**	stew of roast fowl and game
fromage de brebis	sheep's milk cheese		
fruits de mer	seafood	**tournedos**	fillet steak
garbure	hearty vegetable and meat soup	**tourteau fromager**	sweet cake made with cheese
haricots	beans		
homard	lobster	**tourtière**	flaky pastry with prune filling
huître	oyster		
jambon	ham	**tripotcha**	mutton sausage
lamproie	lamprey	**ttoro**	basque fish stew
langouste/langoustines	spiny lobster	well-done, medium, rare, raw =	
lapin	rabbit	*bien cuit, à point, saignant, cru*	

Labastide d'Armagnac for the eponymous spirits and the aperitif wine floc de Gascogne, the prune fair in St-Aubin, Bellocq Abbey and Ossau-Iraty for cheese made from ewe's milk and the mountain village of Espelette for its red hot peppers.

▯ You can find out more on the internet at: *www.sitesremarquablesdugout.com (French version only)*.

WHAT TO SEE AND DO

Outdoor Fun

MOUNTAIN SPORTS

Safety first is the rule for beginners and old hands when it comes to exploring the mountains as a climber, skier or hiker. The risk associated with avalanches, mud slides, falling rocks, bad weather, fog, icy waters from glaciers, the dangers of becoming lost or miscalculating distances, should never be underestimated.

Avalanches occur naturally when the upper layer of snow is unstable, in particular after heavy snowfalls, and may be set off by the passage of numerous skiers or hikers over a precise spot. A scale of risk, from 1 to 5, has been developed and is posted daily at resorts and the base of hiking trails. It is important to consult this *Bulletin Neige et Avalanche* (BNA) before setting off on any expeditions cross-country or *hors-piste*. You can also call Meteo France for a recorded update on ☎ 32504 *(in French)* or log onto www.meteo.fr

Lightning storms are often preceded by sudden gusts of wind, and put climbers and hikers in danger. In the event of lightning, avoid high ground, and do not move along a ridge top; do not seek shelter under overhanging rocks, isolated trees in otherwise open areas, at the entrance to caves or other openings in the rocks, or in the proximity of metal fences or gates. A car is a good refuge.

Skiing

In the western Pyrenees, there are valley resorts, with high curving slopes and plateaux and contemporary, purpose-built mountain top resorts such as Arette-Pierre-St-Martin and Gourette.
Cross-country skiing is especially good in Iraty, Issarbe and Somport-Candanchu.

Log on to *www.lespyrenees.net* (English version available) or *www.pyrenees-online.fr* for information on conditions and accommodation in the main ski resorts.

Hiking

The **Fédération Française de la Randonnée Pédestre** publishes *"topo-guides"* available from its information centre, 64, rue du Dessous des Berges, 75013 Paris, ☎*01 44 89 93 93; www.ffrandonnee.fr*. Some English-language editions are available. The regional guides describe long-distance trails (GR, for *Grande Randonnée* and GRP for *Grande Randonnée de Pays*) and shorter ones (PR – *petite randonnée*) in detail, distances and approximate times.

Rules of the Route

Choosing the right equipment for a hiking expedition is essential, especially in the mountains. Hiking shoes should be flexible, waterproof and have non-slip soles. Always bring a rain jacket or poncho and an extra sweater. Other indispensable items: sun protection (hat, glasses, lotion), drinking water (1-2L per person), something to nibble on between meals (chocolate, cereal bars or bananas), a bag for rubbish and a first aid kit. Of course, you'll need a good map (and a compass if you plan to leave the main trails). Plan your itinerary well, keeping in mind that while the average walking speed for an adult is 4kph/2mph an hour, you will need time to eat and rest, and children will not keep up the same pace. Leave your itinerary with someone before setting out (innkeeper or fellow camper).

Respect for nature is a cardinal rule and includes the following precautions: don't smoke or light fires in forests, which are particularly vulnerable during the dry summer months; always carry your rubbish out; leave wildflowers as they are (certainly don't dig up the roots) and likewise, walk around, not through, farmers' fields. Close gates behind you.

Cycling

Whereas the mountains draw climbers and hikers, the forests, plains, islands, river banks and moors of south-west France are favoured by cyclists. It is not unusual to see coastal travellers pedalling along with camping gear strapped on back; the relatively flat landscape makes for pleasant cycling. The **Île de Ré** is perfect for a one-day tour.

In the **Haut-Saintonge** area around Saintes, 32 mixed-use trails and 18 mountain-bike tours are marked out. Maps are available in tourist offices. On Sunday mornings in **Bordeaux** you can rent a bike for the day and pedal around the city with a guide (details at the tourist office).

The **Marais Poitevin** is a great place for cycling, offering cool shaded lanes, shimmering canals and glimpses of Gothic and Romanesque architecture in the calm, sunny countryside. Other areas particularly suitable for cycling along marked-out tracks include the **Landes, Entre-Deux-Mers** and **Médoc** regions. Information and maps available from the **Comité départemental du tourisme de Gironde** (see WHEN AND WHERE TO GO) and from the **Maison du tourisme et du vin de Pauillac**, ☎05 56 59 03 08.

Organising Your Trip

Some **SNCF** train stations (Châtellerault, Niort, La Rochelle, Royan, Les Sables-d'Olonne, Valence-d'Agen, Verdon) also rent touring and mountain bikes (in French, "VTT" for *vélo tout terrain*). Tourist offices will provide a list of private rental agencies – in summer it is a good idea to reserve.

For more general information concerning cycling in France, contact:

Fédération Française de Cyclotourisme
12, rue Louis-Bertrand,
94200 Ivry-sur-Seine,
☎01 56 20 88 87,
www.ffct.org.

Mountain-bike enthusiasts, contact the following organisation and request the *Guide des centres VTT:*

Fédération Française de Cyclisme
5, rue de Rome,
93561 Rosny-sous-Bois Cedex,
☎01 49 35 69 00,
www.ffc.fr

There are many travel agencies offering **package biking tours**: look for advertisements in travel magazines, search the Internet or contact your travel agent to find the offer that best suits you.

WATER SPORTS

Swimming

Along the Atlantic ocean, it is best to swim from one of the many supervised beaches, where flags *(red = beach closed, orange = some danger, green = safe to swim)* advise bathers. Along the open coast, where the surf is often high, life guards are mobile and attentive, moving the flags marking out the area under their surveillance as rising and falling tides change the danger zones created by depressions in the sea bed and strong undertow. Sheltered beaches (Bassin d'Arcachon, Les Sables-d'Olonne, Capbreton) are more appropriate for small children, who will also enjoy the calm, relatively shallow waters of the inland lakes such as the Lac de Lacanau or the Étang de Léon.

Surfing and Windsurfing

One swimmer's breaker is another surfer's swell. The same deep underwater chasm *(le Gouf)* which makes Capbreton one of the safest swimming beaches on the coast makes **Hossegor** the uncontested capital of surf in France. International competitions are held in **Hossegor**, **Biarritz** and **Lacanau** every August. Novice windsurfers may want to test the waters inland on the calmer waters of a lake before hitting the ocean beach. These sports are restricted to certain areas and subject to regulations for the protection of swimmers.

Surfing the Sands

Sand-yachting and its variant, **speed sailing**, are ideally suited to the vast beaches of the Vendée coast and Côte d'Argent, where large flat areas of sand are left uncovered at low tide. You will find centres in Notre-Dame-de-Monts, Chéray (Oléron), La Faute-sur-Mer, St-Jean-de-Monts, St-Georges-de-Didonne, St-Gilles-Croix-de-Vie, Archachon, La Teste-de-Buch and Hendaye, among others.

🖺 General information from:
Fédération française de Surf, *BP 28, 30, impasse de la Dighe-Nord, 40150 Hossegor,* ☎*+33 (0)5 58 43 55 88,* *www.surfingfrance.com*
Fédération française de Voile, *17 rue Henri Bocquillon, 75015 Paris,* ☎*+33 (0)1 40 60 37 00,* *www.ffvoile.org*
Fédération française de Char à Voile, *17 rue Henri Bocquillon, 75015 Paris,* ☎*+33 (0)1 45 58 75 75,* *www.ffcv.org.*

Canoeing – Kayaking – Rafting

The region's numerous rivers, canals and lakes offer ample opportunities to enjoy these sports.
Sea-kayaks are popular at the Bassin d'Arcachon as well as Fouras *(🕲 see Places to Stay map, south of La Rochelle).* The **Courant d'Huchet** and the **Courant de Contis** are beautiful sights for an introduction to the activity.
In the mountains, rapid water sports are practised on the rivers Garonne, Eyre and Adour. Local tourist offices can provide details.
Canyoning is a technique for body-surfing down narrow gorges and over waterfalls, as though on a giant water slide, whereas **hydrospeed** involves swimming down rapids with a kickboard and flippers; wear a wet suit and a helmet.

🖺 For further information on white-water sports in general, contact:
Féderation française de Canoë-Kayak, *87 quai de la Marne, BP 58, 94344 Joinville-le-Pont,* ☎*01 45 11 08 50,* *www. ffcanoe.asso.fr.*

Funboard

Other Water Sports

For **water-skiing** and **motor boating**, enquire at the tourist offices of the larger seaside resorts. The use of jet-skis is restricted in France.
Diving clubs *(clubs de plongée)* are active in St-Gilles-Croix-de-Vie, St-Hilaire-de-Riez, Royan and Les Sables-d'Olonne.

Fishing

Freshwater fishing enthusiasts will revel in the abundance of rivers, streams, marshland canals and lakes.
Fishing regulations are enforced and anglers must be affiliated with an association, thus obtaining a *carte de pêche* (permit). Apply to the **Conseil Supérieur de la Pêche** (*Le Péricentre, 16 av. Louison-Bobet, 94132 Fontenay-sous-Bois Cedex,* ☎ *01 45 14 36 00*) which also supplies a map, *Pêche en France* (Fishing in France). Permits are easily obtained locally, often sold in cafés where you are likely to pick up a few tips from the regulars.
The extensive coastline, the bays, straits and the wide **ocean** itself offer almost limitless fishing options, the only restrictions being to adhere to local and national regulations and not to interfere with the business of professional fishermen. For fishing trips out to sea on fully equipped boats, ask at tourist offices, or have a walk around the marina and strike up a conversation. You can reserve a spot on a fishing boat (equipment provided).

For general information, apply to:

**Fédération française
des pêcheurs en mer**,
*Résidence Alliance,
Centre Jorlis, 64600 Anglet,*
☎*05 59 31 00 73,
www.ffpm-national.com.*

Pêche à Pied

On the beaches at low tide, the bucket-and-spade brigades are engaging in the popular French pastime known as pêche à pied, digging for shellfish or scooping up shrimp. There are no administrative formalities for this activity, although quantities per fisherman may be limited, and some beaches may be posted off limits. Underwater fishing is subject to strict regulation.
The *Gîtes de France* (◐ *see WHERE TO STAY AND EAT*) have created a special category, *Gîtes de Pêche*, which identifies accommodation most suitable for anglers who are really hooked.

Golf

South-west France has many 9 and 18-hole golf courses, mentioned on a map entitled *Golf, les parcours français*, based on the Michelin map of France 989.

For general information, contact:

Fédération française de Golf
*68, rue Anatole-France,
92309 Levallois-Perret Cedex,*
☎*01 41 49 77 00,
www.ffgolf.org.*

SPECTATOR SPORTS

Certain sports are part of the traditional lifestyle in south-west France, and their heroes are local legends. In addition to major national and international events, there are many local games going on, which will give you a feel for the people and their ways.
Rugby is big in the south-west. An early form of the game was practised in France and Great Britain in the Middle Ages, and rugby as we know it has been played since 1900. Rugby has its own periodical *(Midi Olympique)*; bookstores in the region can track

down over 100 titles; there is a shrine known as Notre-Dame-du-Rugby in Larrivières. There is an ongoing debate between those who favour rugby union (15-a-side) and those who prefer rugby league (13-a-side, as in Carcassonne, Lézignan, Limoux). Women's teams mostly play touch rugby, without tackling each other to the ground (Les Lionnes in Auch).

More information is available from:

Fédération française de rugby,
9, rue de Liège, 75009 Paris,
☎*01 53 21 15 39,www.ffr.fr.*

Local Sports

An unusual event known as **courses landaises** calls on courageous combatants to step into the arena with very large black cows with very long horns. More acrobatic than a Spanish-style bullfight, these events are also more humane, as the animals are not killed. Evolved from the old practices of running the bulls through the streets, the event became especially popular around 1850 with the introduction of the *écarteur*, the equivalent of a toreador.
Pelote Basque (called *jai alai* in Mexico, Havana and Miami, where it is also very popular) is a must-see for visitors to the Basque Country. The most appreciated form is the **grand chistera**, the name of the distinctive curved basket players wear on one hand. Two teams of three players hurl the *pelote* (ball) against the *fronton* (wall). There are many variations on this game, and an unexpected pleasure is listening to the *chacharia* (announcer) sing out the score.
The standard rules are similar to handball rules, except the court is much larger: 53.7m/176ft long. The *pelote*, a hard, wound rubber ball covered by linen thread and two layers of goatskin, is 5cm/2in in diameter and can travel at 240kph/150mph.

Spas

Hot springs, mineral waters, mud and algae packs have been used to treat afflictions and relieve stress since

Roman times. The various therapeutic properties of the different spas are used in the treatment of respiratory ailments, rheumatism, and dermatoses. *Thermalisme* usually refers to medically prescribed, 21-day cures, while *thalassothérapie* sea water facilities serve a more general public for leisure and fitness purposes. In addition to the medical care provided to the numerous *curistes*, many establishments offer short-term packages aimed at improving the general well-being of guests. You can even sign up for a special stay to give up smoking, lose weight, or increase your stamina. Most spa towns have good sports facilities, such as tennis courts and golf courses, and many have their own casinos. Do check the details ahead of time, as some spas require a medical check-up before you can have treatments, and accommodation may be scarce at certain times of year. **The Michelin Guide France** gives the official opening and closing dates of spas.

Time to relax

For general information, write to:
Union Nationale des établisse-ments thermaux,
1, rue Cels, 75014 Paris,
☎+33 (0)1 53 91 05 75,
www.france-thermale.org
Fédération Mer et Santé,
8, rue de l'Isly, 75008 Paris
☎+33 (0)1 44 70 07 57,
www.thalassofederation.com
Chaîne Thermale du Soleil/Maison du Thermalisme,
32, avenue de l'Opéra, 75002 Paris,
☎+33 (0)1 44 71 37 00,
www.sante-eau.com

Here is a description of just three of the many spas in the region:
Dax is France's leading thermal resort, and one of the largest, specialising in the treatment of rheumatism and arthritis of all types. Therapy is based on the application of warm mud packs. To obtain brochures on special 6, 9 and 12-day packages offered by the many different establishments in town, as well as information on sports and entertainment in this busy resort, contact the *Syndicat d'Initiative, place Thiers, BP 177 40100 Dax, ☎+33 (0)5 58 56 86 86, www.ville-de-dax.fr.*

La Roche Posay is hidden deep in quiet countryside, surrounded by gentle valleys and pretty rivers and streams, far from the madding crowd. The spa treats all types of skin problems, using relaxing mineral baths, jet sprays and high-pressure showers. The Mélusine centre (open May to mid-October) offers short cures for relaxation and skin care. The town provides a service for organising business seminars. *Write to the local tourist office (postal code 86270), or Société Hydrominérale de la Roche-Posay, 3 rue Henri-Michaux, 75013 Paris, ☎+33 (0)1 43 13 10 50, Fax +33 (0)1 43 13 10 51.*

In Hendaye, the **Complexe de Thalassothérapie Serge Blanco** *(boulevard de la Mer, 64700 Hendaye, ☎+33 (0)5 59 51 35 35, Fax +33 (0)5 59 51 36 00)* is well-known to sports enthusiasts who appreciate the whirlpools, massages and algae packs, as well as the giant jacuzzi, sauna, weight machines and squash courts. The chic establishment, open year-round in a beautiful setting, offers personalised programmes designed to help you slim down and improve your sports performance.

🛈Information can also be obtained directly from the tourist offices of the spa towns indicated on the map.

Activities for Children 🄺🄸🄳🄨

South-west France has a lot to offer children from swimming and playing in the sand along the sunny Côte d'Argent, backed by a string of peaceful lakes, to cycling through the Landes Forest, having fun in amusement parks, or visiting zoos, safari parks, aquariums and museums of special interest. In this guide, sights of particular interest to children are indicated with a KIDS symbol (🄺🄸🄳🄨). Some attractions may offer discount fees for children.

Calendar of Events

Many Regional Tourist Offices publish brochures listing local *fêtes*, fairs and festivals. Most places hold festivities for France's National Day (14 July) and many organise events on 15 August, also a public holiday.

Fairs and Historical Pageants

1 MAY

Mimizan-Plage – "Fête de la mer" (sea festival), ☎06 32 54 85 41.

JUNE-SEPTEMBER

Le Puy du Fou – Cinéscénie (historical pageant, sound and light show Fri and Sat 10pm, mid-June to July, 10.30pm Aug to early Sept) ☎02 51 64 11 11.
Bougon – "Pierres de Lune", Musée des Tumulus (Aug) ☎05 49 05 12 13; www.deux-sevres.com/musee-bougon.
St-Jean-de-Luz – "Fête de la Saint-Jean" midsummer festival: high mass, concerts, *chistera*, traditional

games, bonfires, ball, *toro de fuego* etc. ☎05 59 26 03 16.

SUNDAY AROUND 14 JULY

St-Étienne-de-Baïgorry – "Force basque" traditional games championship. ☎05 59 37 47 28.

EARLY AUGUST

Clisson – Night-time pageant at the château. ☎ 02 40 54 02 95.
Saint-Sever – Historical pageant: "Life in Town, from the Middle Ages to Today" and sound and light show. ☎05 58 76 34 64.

1ST SUNDAY IN AUGUST

Moncrabeau – This international lying contest coronates the "King of Liars," in a Gascon tradition perpetuated by the Academy of Liars (founded 18C). ☎05 53 65 46 91.
Hagetmau – "Les 5 jours d'Hagetmau:" bullfights, "courses landaises", fireworks, music. ☎05 58 79 38 26.

1ST WEEK IN AUGUST

Bayonne – "Courses de vaches landaises," bullfights, water games, parades with floats, concerts, balls, *toro de fuego*. ☎05 59 46 01 46.

15 AUGUST

Arcachon – "Fêtes de la mer" (sea festival). ☎05 57 22 37 00.
Biarritz – "Nuit féerique": fireworks. ☎05 59 22 37 10.

MID-AUGUST

Dax – "Feria": bullfights, "concours landais", folk dancing and music, balls, fireworks. ☎05 58 90 99 09.

Festivals

JANUARY

Angoulême – International Comic Strip show (at the end of the

month) ☎05 45 97 86 50.
www.bdangouleme.com

MARCH-APRIL

Cognac – International Detective Film
Festival (at the end of the month)
☎05 49 41 80 00;
www.festival.cognac.fr.

APRIL

Bayonne – Foire au Jambon
(ham festival). ☎05 59 46 01 46.

MAY-JUNE

Angoulême – Festival Musiques
métisses (World Music Festival)
www.musiques-metisses-com.
Melle – St-Savinien Classical music
festival (2nd half of May, early June)
☎05 49 29 08 23.
St-Gilles-Croix-de-Vie – International
Jazz Festival (Fri to Whitsunday)
☎02 51 55 03 66;
www.saint-jazz-sur-vie.com

JUNE

Itxassou – Cherry festival.

JUNE-JULY

La Rochelle – International Film
Festival. ☎05 46 51 54 02/03.
Pau – "Festival de Pau" (theatre, music,
dance). ☎05 59 27 27 08.

1ST HALF OF JULY

Parthenay – International Festival
of Games. ☎05 49 94 24 20.
Saintes – "Les Académies musicales de
l'abbaye aux Dames". ☎05 46 97
48 48; www.festival-saintes.org.
Parthenay and area – "De bouche
à oreille" music festival (3rd week
of the month). ☎05 49 94 90 70;
www.deboucheaoreille.org.

2ND HALF OF JULY

Mont-de-Marsan – Flamenco Festival.
☎05 58 06 89 89.

Saintes – International folklore festival.
☎05 46 74 04 35.
Andernos-les-Bains – Jazz Festival.
☎05 56 82 02 95.
La Rochelle – "Les Francofolies",
French song festival (around
14 July). ☎05 46 28 28 28;
www.francofolies.com.

EARLY AUGUST

Oloron-Ste-Marie – "Festival
international des Pyrénées":
folklore, traditional art and
popular traditions. ☎05 59 39 98 98;
www.danseaveclemonde.com.
Cognac – "Blues Passions" Festival.
☎05 45 36 11 81.

2ND WEEK IN AUGUST

Confolens – International folk festival.
☎05 45 84 00 77;
www.festivaldeconfolens.com.
Marciac – Jazz in Marciac.
☎05 62 09 33 33.

3RD WEEK IN AUGUST

Uzeste – "Hestejada de las arts
d'Uzeste": pop music, theatre,
poetry, art exhibits, dance, cinema
etc. ☎05 56 25 38 46.

1ST SUNDAY AFTER 15 AUGUST

St-Palais – "Force basque" traditional
games. ☎05 59 65 71 15.

1ST HALF OF SEPTEMBER

**Anglet, Ascain, Bayonne, Biarritz,
Ciboure, St-Jean-de-Luz** – Classical
music festival. ☎05 59 51 19 95.

OCTOBER-NOVEMBER
Angoulême – "Piano en Valois" |
(mid-October). ☎06 76 41 40 00.

Sports Events

WEEKEND OF WHITSUNDAY

Pau – Grand Prix automobile,
Formula 3000. ☎05 59 27 31 89.

MAY-JUNE

Arcachon – Jumping International d'Arcachon. ☎05 56 83 21 79.
La Rochelle – International Sailing Week (during the Ascension and Whitsunday holidays). ☎05 46 44 62 44.
Beauvoir-sur-Mer – "Les Foulées du Gois", running race against the tide. ☎02 51 68 71 13.

JULY

Arcachon – "18 heures Arcachon Sud-Ouest": sailing race. ☎05 57 52 97 97.
Biarritz – Biarritz Golf Cup. ☎05 59 03 71 80; www.biarritz-cup.com.

AUGUST

Biarritz – Cesta Punta Golden Gloves championships. ☎05 59 22 37 00.
St-Jean-de-Luz – World Championship Cesta Punta tournament. ☎05 59 26 03 16; www.cestapunta.com.
Soustons – "Pelote basque grand chistera" and Landais folk festival. ☎05 58 41 52 62.
Noirmoutier – Historical ships regatta. ☎02 51 39 80 71.
Ascain – "Course à la Rhune" foot race up and down the mountain.
Lacanau – Lacanau Pro: surfboard competition; www.surflacanau.com.

SEPTEMBER

Angoulême – Vintage car rally around the ramparts (2nd week in Sep). ☎ 05 45 94 95 67.
La Rochelle – "Le Grand Pavois" boat show. ☎ 05 46 44 46 39; www.grand-pavois.com.
Val de Garonne – Radofolies; descent of the River Garonne by raft, between Marmande and La Réole.

NOVEMBER

Les Sables-d'Olonne – "Vendée Globe" (departure of the solo sailing race, held every four years since 1988). ☎ 02 51 96 85 85; www.vendeeglobe.fr.

Shopping

OPENING HOURS

Most of the larger shops are open Mondays to Saturdays from 9am to 7 or 7.30pm.
Smaller, individual shops may close during the lunch hour. Food shops – grocers, wine merchants and bakeries – are generally open from 7am to 7 or 7.30pm; some open on Sunday mornings.
Many food shops close between noon and 2pm and on Mondays. Bakery and pastry shops sometimes close on Wednesdays. Hypermarkets usually stay open non-stop from 9am until 9pm or later.
People travelling to the USA cannot import plant products or fresh food, including fruit, cheeses and nuts. It is acceptable to carry tinned products or preserves.

MARKETS

Marchés au Gras

Traditional markets known as *marchés au gras* were previously held in winter months only for the sale of ducks and geese and prepared and raw livers. The most picturesque of these markets are held in the following towns:

Agen (Lot-et-Garonne) – Wed, Sat and Sun mornings, Nov–Mar.
Aire-sur-l'Adour (Landes) – Tue, Nov–Feb.
Dax (Landes) – Sat 7am–noon, in the market hall.
Langoiran (Gironde) – First Sun in Dec.
Montségur (Gironde) – Second Sun in Dec and Feb.
Orthez (Pyrénées-Atlantiques) – Tue 7.30–10am, Nov–Mar.
Villeneuve-de-Marsan (Landes) – Wed morning, Oct–Apr.
Villeneuve-sur-Lot (Lot-et-Garonne) – Tue and Sat, Nov–Mar, in the market hall.

VALUE ADDED TAX

Value Added Tax in France *(TVA)* is 19.6% on almost every purchase (some foods and books are subject to a lower rate). However, non-European visitors who spend more than 183€ (figure subject to change) in any one participating store can get the Value Added Tax amount refunded. Usually, you fill out a form at the store, showing your passport. Upon leaving the country, you submit all forms to customs for approval (they may want to see the goods, so if possible don't pack them in checked luggage). The refund is usually paid directly into your bank or credit card account, or it can be sent by mail. Big department stores that cater to tourists provide special services to help you; be sure to mention that you plan to seek a refund before you pay for goods (no refund is possible for tax on services). If you are visiting two or more countries within the European Union, you submit the forms only on departure from the last EU country. The refund is worth while for those visitors who would like to buy fashion articles, furniture or other fairly expensive items, but remember, the minimum amount must be spent in a single shop (though not necessarily on the same day).

Sightseeing

RIVER CRUISING

Rivers, estuaries, canals and channels offer numerous opportunities to enjoy pleasant **boat trips** (sometimes aboard crafts of a bygone age), thus slowing down the pace and alleviating the stress of a busy touring holiday.

⚓ **Bâteau-promenade L'Escapade**, Boat trips along the canal des Deux-Mers. Canal en Gironde, 6 allée des Ormeaux, 33210 Langon, ☎ 05 56 63 06 45. .

⚓ **Union des Bateliers arcachon-nais,** Boat trips on the Arcachon lagoon. &See Bassin d'ARCACHON

⚓ **Bâteau-Croisière Aliénor**, Boat trips along the Gironde Estuary. &See BORDEAUX

Alternatively, **house-boats**, which can be hired for a day, a weekend or a week,

offer a peaceful glide along rivers (Charente, Sèvre Niortaise, Lot, Baïse) and canals (Canal latéral à la Garonne).

⚓ **Crown Blue Line,** The Port House, Port Solent, Portsmouth PO6 4TH; ☎ +44 (0)870 160 5634; www.crownblueline.com.

⚓ **Aquitaine Navigation,** Port de Buzet, Val d'Albret, 47160 Buzet-sur-Baïse; ☎ +33 (0)5 53 84 72 50; quai de la Baïse 47600 Nérac; ☎ +33 (0)5 53 65 66 66; www.aquitaine-navigation.com.

⚓ **Locaboat Plaisance,** Port au bois, 89303 JOIGNY CEDEX; ☎ 05 53 66 00 74; Central booking: ☎ +33 (0)3 86 91 72 72; www.locaboat.com

TOURIST TRAINS

Several picturesque railways welcome tourists aboard for pleasant rides through fields, woods and marshlands, including a few pulled by steam locomotives. For detailed information, see the following:

⚲ Bassin d'ARCACHON: Cap Ferret (Tourist train to Plage de l'Océan)
⚲ Les HERBIERS (Chemin de fer de la Vendée)
⚲ Île d'OLÉRON: St Trojan-les-Bains (Pointe de Gatseau tourist train)
⚲ Parc naturel régional des LANDES DE GASCOGNE: Marquèze (Train de l'Écomusée de la Grande Lande)
⚲ MARAIS POITEVIN: Coulon (Le Pibalou)
⚲ Haut-OSSAU (Scenic train from La Sagette to Lac d'Artouste)
⚲ ROYAN: Saujon (Chemin de fer touristique de la Seudre)
⚲ SAINT-ÉMILION (Train des Grands Vignobles)
⚲ SAINT-JEAN-DE-LUZ: Le Labourd (Chemin de fer de la Rhune)
⚲ SOULAC-SUR-MER (Pointe de Grave scenic railway)

RAIL-BIKING

Sightseeing with a difference! How would you enjoy pedalling along a disused railway line? It is possible to go for a 10km/6mi ride around St-Gilles-

Croix-de-Vie and along the coast. Each small truck can take up to 5 persons. Call ☎02 51 54 79 99 for information.

BIRDWATCHING

There are guided tours around the **Réserve naturelle des Marais de Müllembourg**, Fort-Larron, Normoutier-en-l'Île, ☎*02 51 35 81 16*.

NATURE AND THE ENVIRONMENT

Parc interrégional du Marais poitevin: Information centre at the Maison des marais mouillés, 79510 Coulon, ☎05 49 35 86 77.

Centres permanents d'initiatives pour l'environnement: these centres organise weekends and longer stays (known as *Sépia*) to encourage people to become aware of nature and the environment.

🖺Information is available from the **Union nationale des centres permanents d'initiatives pour l'environnement**, *2, rue de Washington, 75008 Paris*.

Books

ELEANOR OF AQUITAINE

Eleanor of Aquitaine, Queen of France and England, a 12C divorcee, patroness of poets, source of inspiration for chivalry and Courtly Love, ruler of a kingdom that spanned from Scotland to the Pyrenees, mother of 10 children (including Richard the Lion Heart), lived her 82 years as few women in history before or since. The story of her life is a good introduction to regional history, and a fascinating tale:

Eleanor of Aquitaine: A Life, Alison Weir, Ballantine Books, 2000.

Eleanor of Aquitaine, Marion Meade, Penguin Paperbacks, 1992.

Eleanor of Aquitaine: The Mother Queen, Desmond Seward, Dorset Press, 1986.

Eleanor of Aquitaine and the Four Kings, Amy Kelly, Harvard University Press, Paperback edition 1974.

Beloved Enemy: the Passions of Eleanor of Aquitaine: a Novel, Ellen Jones, Simon and Schuster, 1994.

For Young Readers

A Proud Taste for Scarlet and Miniver, EL Konigsburg, Atheneum, 1974 (illustrated).

Queen Eleanor: Independent Spirit of the Medieval World, Polly S Brooks, Lippincott, 1983 (illustrated).

BOOKS ON WINE

French Wines: The Essential Guide to the Wines and Wine Growing Regions of France, Robert Joseph, DK Publishing, 1999.
This is a very useful book, in a travel-friendly paperback format, for anyone wanting to buy or taste all sorts of wine, whether during a trip to France (includes maps) or to the corner wine shop.

Grands Vins: The Finest Châteaux of Bordeaux and Their Wines, Clives Coates, University of California Press, 1995.
Coates is one of Britain's best-known wine critics, and he has written an extensive survey on the history, geography, grape varieties, and other wine-making idiosyncrasies of the region which produces what many believe to be the world's greatest wines.

The Winemaker's Year: Four Seasons in Bordeaux, Michael Buller, photographs by Michel Guillard, preface by Paul Bocuse, Thames and Hudson, 1991.
Lush photographs and a preface by one of France's most celebrated chefs add to the delicious savour of this tome.

Enjoying Wine, Don Hewitson, Elm Tree Books, 1985.
Friendly, no-nonsense approach to one of life's great pleasures, with useful explanations and illustrations.

The Winemasters, Nicholas Faith, Hamish and Hamilton, 1978.
History and people – two centuries of winemaking in Bordeaux.

The Wines of France, Alexis Lichine, Knopf, 1963.

A classic that ages well.

The Wine Regions of France, Michelin Travel Publications, 2005.
A comprehensive guide to the different wine-producing regions in France.

FICTION

The Three Musketeers, Alexandre Dumas, Grosset and Dunlap Junior Library edition 1953, illustrated.
A perfect choice that is sure to fire the imaginations of young readers. Several film versions are available on video, including Hanna-Barbera's animated feature.

By the River Piedra I Sat Down and Wept, Paulo Coelho, Harper Collins, 1996.
A romantic adventure and search for spiritual sustenance on a journey through the French Pyrenees.

HISTORY AND PERSONAL EXPERIENCE

The Basque History of the World, Mark Kurlansky, Penguin (USA) Paperbacks, 2001.
This rare book in English on the political, economic, social, and even culinary history of the Basque people is an excellent introduction to this rather mysterious culture. Take a look beyond the popular media focus on separatist terrorists and ponder the saying in the Euskara language: *Garean gareana legez* – Let us be what we are.

The Land of My Fathers: A Son's Return to the Basque Country, Robert Laxalt, Joyce Laxalt (Photographer), University of Nevada Press, 1999.
The author, who has written several novels set in the Basque country, here gives a record of the years he spent with his family in the 1960s in a village in the French Basque country. His descriptions of the isolated, beautiful mountain world where the Basques have lived for uncounted centuries complement his wife's photographs and show us Basque market days and festivals, reveal local humour and history, the deep sense of community and pride in the Basque culture and homeland.

The Fronde: A French Revolution, Orest A Ranum, Norton, 1993.
Unrest and turbulence in 1648 ended up in a showdown between the monarchy and insurgents in Bordeaux.

The Lost Uplands: Stories of Southwest France, WS Merwin, Knopf, 1992.
Three narrative portraits of small-town life in the region, from the pen of an award-winning poet.

A House in the Sunflowers: Summer in Aquitaine, Ruth Silvestre, Allison and Busby, 1990.
A British family's search for and discovery of the perfect French holiday home.

Jasmin's Witch, Emmanuel Ladurie, George Braziller, 1987.
Popular tradition and legend, magic, witchcraft and sorcery in the Agen region; the story of a beautiful dancing girl and the poet who recounted her downfall.

Films

FILMS SET IN THE FRENCH ATLANTIC COAST REGION

La Foire aux Femmes (1956). Set in the Vendée this film is the story of an orphan girl who falls in love with Jean-Pierre but is closely guarded by her jealous employer. However tradition has it that at the Fair of Women the young men choose the girl they fancy: Jean-Pierre picks out the orphan girl. The film is set in La Rochelle and Le Vanneau

La Ferme du Pendu (1945). The tragic story of siblings who promise their dying father they will not marry so that his farm will not be split up. Inevitably there ar tragic consequences. Filmed and set in Pouzages and the Marais Poitevin.

Les Demoiselles de Rochefort (1967). The story of tangled relationships of twin sisters and their café owning mother. The former are seeking love and life outside Rochefort but things are not always as simple as we would like them to be. The result is a entertaining musical comedy. As the title suggests the film is set in Rochefort.

César et Rosalie (1972). The film, starring Yves Montard, tells the story of a happy divorcee detoted to her young daughter and her lover César. All is well until an old flame turns up and battle commences between the two men to claim the woman they both love. Meanwhile Rosalie cannot decide who she loves. Set and filmed on the Île de Noirmoutier.

La Revolte des Enfants (1991). Set in 1847 during the Industrial Revolution the film tells the story of rebellion against their cruel and repressive gaoler by the child inmates of a prison for young offenders. Filmed on the Île d'Yeu.

THE FRENCH ATLANTIC COAST CONNECTION

These films have connections with the French Atlantic Coast even though much of the action is set elsewhere. some scenes were shot in the area covered by this guide.

The Three Musketeers (1922, 1948, 1973, 1993). Alexander Dumas' novel has probably spawned more films that any other book. The three musketeers and D'Artagnan all come from Gascony but seek adventure in Paris serving the King. Later versions have scenes set in the Gascogne countryside.

Cinq Tulipes Rouge (1948). A mystery thriller in which a journalist and a police inspector race against time to find the killer of five riders in the Tour de France. Each rider is wearing the yellow jersey and the killer leaves a red tulip near his victims. Set and filmed, among other location, in Bordeaux and Biarritz.

Le Promeneur du Champs de Mars (2005). A story about a young journalist helping the French President, François Mitterand, to compile his memoirs.

ON LOCATION IN THE FRENCH ATLANTIC COAST REGION

The Sun Also Rises – Hemmingway's story of expatriates in Europe between the wars. Locations in Bayonne.

The Sign of Zorro – Parts of the the earlier version were shot in Biarritz and St-Jean-de-Luz.

The Longest Day – This epic about the Normandy D-Day landings uses locations in and around La Rochelle for Normandy.

Tomorrow Never Dies – Part of the Arms Bazaar Sequence was shot in Bayonne.

USEFUL WORDS AND PHRASES

SIGHTS

abbaye...abbey
beffroi..belfry
chapelle ....chapel
château .... castle
cimetière.. cemetery
cloître...cloisters
cour..courtyard
couvent ....convent
écluse ....lock (canal)
église .... church
fontaine ....fountain
halle ....covered market
jardin ....garden
mairie...town hall
maison..house
marché..market
monastère..monastery
moulin...windmill
musée...museum
parc ....park
place ....square
pont ....bridge
port ....port/harbour
porte ....gate/gateway
quai...quay
remparts...ramparts
rue ....street
statue..statue
tour...tower

NATURAL SITES

abîme..chasm
aven ....swallow-hole
barrage..dam
belvédère ....viewpoint
cascade...waterfall
col...pass
corniche..ledge
côte...coast, hillside
forêt..forest
grotte..cave
lac...lake
plage...beach
rivière..river
ruisseau..stream
signal ....beacon
source ....spring
vallée ....valley

ON THE ROAD

car park ....parking
driving licence.........permis de conduire
east...Est
garage (for repairs) .... garage
left ....gauche
motorway/highway...............autoroute
north...Nord
parking meter ....horodateur
petrol/gas...essence
petrol/gas station..........station essence
right ....droite
south...Sud
toll ....péage
traffic lights........................ feu tricolore
tyre...pneu
west ....Ouest
wheel clamp ....sabot
zebra crossing................passage clouté

TIME

today.................................. aujourd'hui
tomorrow ....demain
yesterday ....hier
winter...hiver
spring..printemps
summer...été
autumn/fall..automne
week ....semaine
Monday...lundi
Tuesday .... mardi
Wednesday .... mercredi
Thursday...jeudi
Friday ....vendredi
Saturday..samedi
Sunday ....dimanche

NUMBERS

0 ....zéro
1 .... un
2 ....deux
3 ....trois
4 ....quatre
5 .... cinq
6 .... six
7 ....sept
8 ....huit
9 ....neuf
10..dix

11	onze
12	douze
13	treize
14	quatorze
15	quinze
16	seize
17	dix-sept
18	dix-huit
19	dix-neuf
20	vingt
30	trente
40	quarante
50	cinquante
60	soixante
70	soixante-dix
80	quatre-vingt
90	quatre-vingt-dix
100	cent
1000	mille

SHOPPING

bank	banque
baker's	boulangerie
big	grand
butcher's	boucherie
chemist's	pharmacie
closed	fermé
cough mixture	sirop pour la toux
cough sweets	cachets pour la gorge
entrance	entrée
exit	sortie
fishmonger's	poissonnerie
grocer's	épicerie
newsagent, bookshop	librairie
open	ouvert
post office	poste
push	pousser
pull	tirer
shop	magasin
small	petit
stamps	timbres

FOOD AND DRINK

beef	bœuf
beer	bière
butter	beurre
bread	pain
breakfast	petit-déjeuner
cheese	fromage
chicken	poulet
dessert	dessert
dinner	dîner
fish	poisson
fork	fourchette
fruit	fruits
glass	verre
ice cream	glace
ice cubes	glaçons
ham	jambon
knife	couteau
lamb	agneau
lunch	déjeuner
lettuce salad	salade
meat	viande
mineral water	eau minérale
mixed salad	salade composée
orange juice	jus d'orange
plate	assiette
pork	porc
restaurant	restaurant
red wine	vin rouge
salt	sel
spoon	cuillère
sugar	sucre
vegetables	légumes
water	de l'eau
white wine	vin blanc
yoghurt	yaourt

TRAVEL

airport	aéroport
credit card	carte de crédit
customs	douane
passport	passeport
platform	voie
railway station	gare
shuttle	navette
suitcase	valise
train	billet de train
plane ticket	billet d'avion
wallet	portefeuille

CLOTHING

coat	manteau
jumper	pull
raincoat	imperméable
shirt	chemise
shoes	chaussures
socks	chaussettes
stockings	bas
suit	costume
tights	collant
trousers	pantalon

USEFUL PHRASES

goodbye	au revoir
hello/good morning	bonjour

how .... comment	When is breakfast served?.......................
excuse me .... excusez-moi	À quelle heure sert-on le petit-déjeuner?
thank you ....merci	What does it cost?....................................
yes/no................................... oui/non	..................................Combien cela coûte?
I am sorry....................................pardon	Where can I buy
why.......................................pourquoi	a newspaper in English?.........................
when.......................................quand	....Où puis-je acheter
please ....s'il vous plaît	un journal en anglais?
Do you speak English?	Where is the nearest
.... Parlez-vous anglais?	petrol/gas station?..................................
I don't understand	..............................Où se trouve la station
...............................Je ne comprends pas	essence la plus proche?
Talk slowly .... Parlez lentement	Where can I change
Where's...? .... Où est...?	traveller's cheques? ....
When does the... leave?...........................	..............................Où puis-je échanger
...............................À quelle heure part...?	des traveller's cheques?
When does the... arrive?	Where are the toilets?.............................
...........................À quelle heure arrive...?	...............................Où sont les toilettes?
When does the museum open?	Do you accept credit cards?....................
..............À quelle heure ouvre le musée?	.... Acceptez-vous les cartes de crédit?
When is the show?	
....À quelle heure est la représentation?	

BASIC INFORMATION

Discounts

Significant discounts are available for senior citizens, students, youth under age 25, teachers, and groups for public transportation, museums and monuments and for some leisure activities such as movies (at certain times of day). Bring student or senior cards with you, and bring along some extra passport-size photos for discount travel cards. The **International Student Travel Conference** (www.istc.org), global administrator of the International Student and Teacher Identity Cards, is an association of student travel organizations around the world. ISTC members collectively negotiate benefits with airlines, governments, and providers of other goods and services for the student and teacher community, both in their own country and around the world. The non-profit association sells international ID cards for students, youth under age 25 and teachers (who may get discounts on museum entrances, for example). The ISTC is also active in a network of international education and work exchange programmes. The coorporate headquarters address is:

> Herengracht 479,
> 1017 BS Amsterdam,
> The Netherlands,
> ☎ +31 20 421 28 00;
> Fax +31 20 421 28 10.

See GETTING THERE: BY RAIL for other discounts on transportation.

Electricity

The electric current is 220 volts. Circular two-pin plugs are the rule. Adapters and converters (for hairdryers, for example) should be bought before you leave home; they are on sale in most airports. If you have a rechargeable device (video camera, portable computer, battery recharger), read the instructions carefully or contact the manufacturer or shop. Sometimes these items only require a plug adapter, in other cases you must use a voltage converter as well or risk ruining your appliance.

Emergencies

Emergency numbers	
Police:	17
SAMU (Paramedics):	15
Fire (Pompiers):	18

Public Holidays

Public services, museums and other monuments may be closed or may vary their hours of admission on the following public holidays:
National museums and art galleries are closed on Tuesdays; municipal museums are generally closed on Mondays. In addition to the usual school holidays at Christmas and in the spring and summer, there are long mid-term breaks (10 days to two weeks) in February and early November.

1 January	New Year's Day (Jour de l'An)
	Easter Day and Easter Monday (Pâques)
1 May	May Day (Fête du Travail)
8 May	VE Day (Fête de la Libération)
Thurs 40 days after Easter	Ascension Day (Ascension)
7th Sun-Mon after Easter	Whit Sunday and Monday (Pentecôte)
14 July	France's National Day (Fête de la Bastille)
15 August	Assumption (Assomption)
1 November	All Saint's Day (Toussaint)
11 November	Armistice Day (Fête de la Victoire)
25 December	Christmas Day (Noël)

Mail/Post

Main post offices open Monday to Friday 8am to 7pm, Saturday 8am to noon. Smaller branch post offices generally close at lunchtime between noon and 2pm and at 4pm.
Postage via air mail:
✉UK: letter (20g) 0.50€
✉North America: letter (20g) 0.90€
✉Australia and NZ: letter (20g) 0.90€

Stamps are also available from newsagents and *bureaux de tabac*. Stamp collectors should ask for *timbres de collection* in any post office.

Money

CURRENCY

There are no restrictions on the amount of currency visitors can take into France. Visitors carrying a lot of cash are advised to complete a currency declaration form on arrival, because there are restrictions on currency export.

Notes and coins
The European currency unit, the **euro**, went into circulation as of 1 January 2002, and since 17 February 2002, euros have been the only currency accepted as a means of payment in France. Notes in francs will be accepted by the Banque de France until 2012; coins in francs were accepted until 2005. (⬛ *For more information, go to www.banque-france.fr.*)

BANKS

Although business hours vary from branch to branch, banks are usually open from 9am to noon and 2pm to 5pm and are closed either on Mondays or Saturdays. Banks close early on the day before a bank holiday. A passport is necessary as identification when cashing travellers cheques in banks. Commission charges vary and hotels usually charge more than banks for cashing cheques.

American Express ☎ 01 47 77 72 00
Visa ☎ 0 800 901 179
MasterCard/Eurocard ☎ 0 800 901 387
Diners Club ☎ 0 800 314 519

One of the most economical ways to use your money in France is by using **ATM machines** to get cash directly from your bank account (with a debit card) or to use your credit card to get a cash advance. Be sure to remember your PIN number, you will need it to use cash dispensers and to pay with your card in shops, restaurants etc. Code pads are numeric; use a telephone pad to translate a letter code into numbers. Pin numbers have 4 digits in France; inquire with the issuing company or bank if the code you usually use is longer. Visa is the most widely accepted credit card, followed by Mastercard; other cards, credit and debit (Diners Club, Plus, Cirrus etc) are also accepted in some cash machines. American Express is more often accepted in premium establishments. Most places post signs indicating which card they accept; if you don't see such a sign and want to pay with a card, ask before ordering or making a selection. Cards are widely accepted in shops, hypermarkets, hotels and restaurants, at tollbooths and in petrol stations. **Before you leave home,** check with the bank that issued your card for emergency replacement procedures. Carry your card number and emergency phone numbers separate from your wallet and handbag; leave a copy of this information with someone you can easily reach. If your card is lost or stolen while you are in France, call one of the 24-hour hotlines above: These numbers are subject to change, but you can also check at ATM machines, where they are usually listed. You must **report any loss or theft** of credit cards or travellers cheques to the local police who will issue you with a certificate (useful proof to show the issuing company).

Telephones

Most public phones in France use pre-paid phone cards *(télécartes)*, rather than coins. Some telephone booths accept credit cards (Visa, Mastercard/Eurocard). *Télécartes* (50 or 120 units) can be bought in post offices, branches

To use your personal calling card	
AT&T	☎ 0-800 99 00 11
Sprint	☎ 0-800 99 00 87
MCI	☎ 0-800 99 00 19
Canada Direct	☎ 0-800 99 00 16

of France Télécom, *bureaux de tabac* (cafés that sell cigarettes) and newsagents and can be used to make calls in France and abroad. Calls can be received at phone boxes where the blue bell sign is shown; the phone will not ring, so keep your eye on the small digital screen.

NATIONAL CALLS

French telephone numbers have 10 digits. Paris and Paris region numbers begin with 01; 02 in north-west France; 03 in north-east France; 04 in south-east France and Corsica; 05 in south-west France.

INTERNATIONAL CALLS

To call France from abroad, dial the country code (33) + 9-digit number (omit the initial 0). When calling abroad from France dial 00, then dial the country code followed by the area code and number of your correspondent.
International information,
US/Canada: 00 33 12 11
International operator:
00 33 12 + country code
Local directory assistance: 12

International Dialling Codes (00 + code)			
Australia	☎ 61	New Zealand	☎ 64
Canada	☎ 1	United Kingdom	☎ 44
Eire	☎ 353	United States	☎ 1

MOBILE PHONES

In France these have numbers that begin with 06. Two-watt (lighter, shorter reach) and eight-watt models are on the market, using the Orange (France Télécom) or

SFR networks. *Mobicartes* are prepaid phone cards that fit into mobile units. Mobile phone rentals (delivery or airport pickup provided):

- **A.L.T. Rent A Phone –** ☎01 48 00 06 06; altloc@jve.fr.
- **Rent a Cell Express –** ☎01 53 93 78 00, Fax 01 53 93 78 09.
- **Ellinas Phone Rental –** ☎01 47 20 70 00.

Time

France is 1hr ahead of Greenwich Mean Time (GMT). France goes on Daylight-Saving Time from the last Sunday in March to the last Sunday in October.

When it is **noon in France**, it is	
3am	in Los Angeles
6am	in New York
11am	in Dublin
11am	in London
7pm	in Perth
9pm	in Sydney
11pm	in Auckland

In France "am" and "pm" are not used but the 24-hour clock is widely applied.

Prices and Tips

Since a service charge is automatically included in the prices of meals and accommodation in France, it is not necessary to tip in restaurants and hotels. However, if the service in a restaurant is especially good or if you have enjoyed a fine meal, an extra tip (this is the *pourboire*, rather than the *service*) will be appreciated. Usually 1.5 to 3.5 euros is enough, but if the bill is big (a large party or a luxury restaurant), it is not uncommon to leave 7 to 8 euros or more.

As a rule, the cost of staying in a hotel and eating in restaurants is significantly higher in Paris than in the French regions. However, by reserving a hotel room well in advance and taking advantage of the wide choice of restaurants, you can enjoy your trip without breaking the bank.

Restaurants usually charge for meals in two ways: *a menu*, that is a fixed price menu with 2 or 3 courses, sometimes a small pitcher of wine, all for a stated price, or *à la carte*, the more expensive way, with each course ordered separately. **Cafés** have very different prices, depending on where they are located. The price of a drink or a coffee is cheaper if you stand at the counter (*comptoir*) than if you sit down (*salle*) and sometimes it is even more expensive if you sit outdoors (*terrasse*).

CONVERSION TABLES

Weights and Measures

1 kilogram (kg) 6.35 kilograms 0.45 kilograms **1 metric ton (tn)**	**2.2 pounds (lb)** 14 pounds 16 ounces (oz) **1.1 tons**	**2.2 pounds** 1 stone (st) 16 ounces **1.1 tons**	*To convert kilograms to pounds, multiply by 2.2*
1 litre (l) 3.79 litres 4.55 litres	**2.11 pints (pt)** 1 gallon (gal) 1.20 gallon	**1.76 pints** 0.83 gallon 1 gallon	*To convert litres to gallons, multiply by 0.26 (US) or 0.22 (UK)*
1 hectare (ha) **1 sq. kilometre (km²)**	**2.47 acres** 0.38 sq. miles (sq.mi.)	**2.47 acres** 0.38 sq. miles	*To convert hectares to acres, multiply by 2.4*
1 centimetre (cm) **1 metre (m)**	**0.39 inches (in)** 3.28 feet (ft) or 39.37 inches or 1.09 yards (yd)	**0.39 inches**	*To convert metres to feet, multiply by 3.28; for kilometres to miles, multiply by 0.6*
1 kilometre (km)	**0.62 miles (mi)**	**0.62 miles**	

Clothing

Women	🇪🇺	🇺🇸	🇬🇧
Shoes	35	4	2½
	36	5	3½
	37	6	4½
	38	7	5½
	39	8	6½
	40	9	7½
	41	10	8½
Dresses & suits	36	6	8
	38	8	10
	40	10	12
	42	12	14
	44	14	16
	46	16	18
Blouses & sweaters	36	06	30
	38	08	32
	40	10	34
	42	12	36
	44	14	38
	46	16	40

Men	🇪🇺	🇺🇸	🇬🇧
Shoes	40	7½	7
	41	8½	8
	42	9½	9
	43	10½	10
	44	11½	11
	45	12½	12
	46	13½	13
Suits	46	36	36
	48	38	38
	50	40	40
	52	42	42
	54	44	44
	56	46	48
Shirts	37	14½	14½
	38	15	15
	39	15½	15½
	40	15¾	15¾
	41	16	16
	42	16½	16½

Sizes often vary depending on the designer. These equivalents are given for guidance only.

Speed

KPH	10	30	50	70	80	90	100	110	120	130
MPH	6	19	31	43	50	56	62	68	75	81

Temperature

Celsius (°C)	0°	5°	10°	15°	20°	25°	30°	40°	60°	80°	100°
Fahrenheit (°F)	32°	41°	50°	59°	68°	77°	86°	104°	140°	176°	212°

To convert Celsius into Fahrenheit, multiply °C by 9, divide by 5, and add 32.
To convert Fahrenheit into Celsius, subtract 32 from °F, multiply by 5, and divide by 9.
NB: Conversion factors on this page are approximate.

Kakuetta Waterfall
B. Kaufmann/MICHELIN

NATURE

The Atlantic coastline from the Loire in the north to the vast barrier of the Pyrénées in the south, travels past the great plain of Poitou; the lush meadows of Le Bocage; the great wine-growing landscapes of Charentes and Bordelais; the lagoons and dunes of Landes; the valleys of Agenais; and the hills of Gascony.

Landscapes

POITOU

This large and ancient province centred on the town of Poitiers incorporates the Pays de Retz, Vendée and the Marais Poitevin (the Poitou marshlands).

The plain

The limestone plateau between the ancient massifs of the **Vendée** (which are the southern extremity of the Armorican peninsula on which Brittany sits) and Limousin (the region east of Angoulême) comprises a crescent stretching from Loudun to Luçon. Almost denuded of trees and cut through with deep valleys, the plain seems to roll away to infinity, its succession of fields, meadows and moors scarcely interrupted by the occasional village.

Certain subtle differences are discernible: in the north the plain is actually part of **Touraine** (the region around Tours); from Thouars to Châtellerault there are outcrops of local chalk, carpeted with thin patches of cultivation and moor-

land cropped by sheep. Here and there deposits of sand occur, and fields of asparagus can be seen in the middle of pinewoods. On the exposed hillsides bordering the River Thouet and River Vienne, the scattered wine-growers' houses are built of tufa (a hard crystal-line chalk with a high mica content). The areas around Chauvigny and Montmorillon (on the Poitou borders), composed of sands and clay, were once a region of infertile heaths or **brandes.** In certain areas this heathland still subsists, supporting flocks of sheep and goats (the goat's cheese of Chauvigny is well known). In other places, where the heath has been cleared, Charollais or Limousin bullocks are raised. Flocks of *pirons* (a variety of goose raised for its skin and *duvet* or down) wander near the farms. West of Clain, continuing as far as Melle and St-Maixent, the Jurassic limestone, lacerated by valleys, has decomposed on the surface into what is locally called **terre de groie** (a compound soil part clay, part gravel, part lime, of proverbial fertility – especially for cereals and fodder plants such as clover and alfalfa).

Le Marais Poitevin

Le Bocage

The Vendée and the **Gâtine de Parthenay,** south and west of the River Thouet, have many features in common. This is the region known as *le bocage* – an area of lush meadows bordered by hedge-rows of hawthorn or broom, with sunken lanes leading to smallholdings and farms half-hidden in leafy copses. The speck-led brown Parthenay bullocks, bred and fattened for beef, are often seen grazing in this patchwork of small fields. The

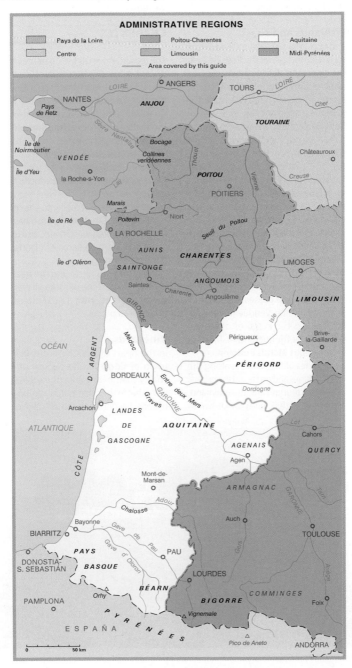

ADMINISTRATIVE REGIONS

Pays de la Loire   Poitou-Charentes   Aquitaine

Centre   Limousin   Midi-Pyrénées

Area covered by this guide

area is dotted with apple orchards and the occasional field of fodder plants grown to feed the cattle. A chain of low, rounded hills forms the backbone of this productive agricultural area, and these are known as **Les Collines Vendéennes** (the Hills of the Vendée).

Marshlands and coast

The marsh (Marais) area extends from the schist landscapes of the **Pays de Retz** to the limestone cliffs of the **Aunis** – an ancient region centered on La Rochelle. Between these cliffs, which mark the limit of the prehistoric Bay of Biscay (or Golfe de Gascogne as it is known in France), and the sea, salt-marshes transformed into oyster farms glitter in the sun and sheep and cattle graze in the water-meadows. Early fruit and vegetables ripen on the alluvial soil and wild duck paddle the canals beneath over-hanging hedgerows alive with smaller birds. The marshland, formed from debris accumulated by rivers and ancient ocean currents, lies sheltered behind the coastal dunes; rocky islets from the ancient coastline define the area's inner limit. From north to south the route passes successively through the Breton-Vendée marshland, which includes the marshes of Monts, the marshes of Olonne and of Talmont and the famous **Marais Poitevin**.

Huge beaches of fine sand lie along the foot of the dunes and on the offshore bars; between Noirmoutier and the mainland, on either side of the causeway known as the Passage du Gois, enormous stretches of mudflat are exposed at low tide. Noirmoutier itself and the more southerly Île d'Yeu (Isle of Yeu) provide yet more contrast: the one flat, peaceful and gentle, the other rocky and savage on its western coast.

CHARENTES

The region known as the Charentes comprises the two *départements* of Charente and Charente-Maritime, separated by the green and placid valley of the River Charente, which themselves embrace the ancient provinces of **Angoumois** (the Angoulême region), **Aunis** and **Saintonge** (the region around Saintes).

Charente itself, abutting the foothills of the Massif Central, divides into four natural geographic areas: to the west the wine country of Cognac, at the centre the cereal-growing Angoumois, in the northeast the Confolentais with its plateaux, and to the south the Montmorélien, a hilly landscape of mixed farming.

Charente-Maritime, facing the Atlantic, presents a coastline of rocks, dunes and sandy beaches, with a rural interior of forests and plains.

Vineyards

In the heart of the Charentes lies the town of **Cognac**, the capital of that chalky champagne area (the soil is similar to that in the Champagne region, east of Paris) bordering the south bank of the

Vineyards of the Cognac region

river that nourishes the grapes from which the world-famous brandy bearing the name of the town is distilled.

The Plain

The limestone plateau which extends from Angoulême to La Rochelle provides a slightly monotonous landscape, only rarely cut by valleys (such as that of the Boutonne), dotted with small towns and an occasional whitewashed hamlet. As in Poitou, the Jurassic bedrock is cloaked with a reddish *terre de groie* or a fertile alluvium on which cornfields take second place to crops of clover and alfalfa or fields of sugar-beet grown as fodder.

Coast

The Charentais coast is unusual because, especially towards its centre, alluvial deposits from the River Charente and River Seudre have combined with marine currents to form an area of marshland not unlike that in Poitou. Most of this swampy land has been either reclaimed as **polders** (low-lying lands protected by dykes) on which crops are grown, or transformed – especially near Marennes – into shallow basins in which mussels and oysters are farmed. The distance the tide goes out varies from 2km/1mi to 5km/3mi.

Not far offshore, the low-lying and sandy islands of Oléron and Ré, scattered with pretty white houses, define the outer limit of an inner sea – the **Mer de Pertuis,** so-called because the only way its waters can reach the open sea is via one or other of the straits (pertuis) dividing these isles from the mainland.

BORDELAIS

The region known as Le Bordelais, at the heart of the ancient province of **Guyenne** (Aquitaine), centres on the confluence of the River Garonne and River Dordogne. This transitional area between the limestone plains of Charentes to the north and the vast sandy expanse of the Landes to the south is drained by the Garonne and its tributaries towards the zone of subsidence around the estuary.

Agriculture here is dominated by the cultivation of vines.

Gironde Estuary

The Gironde is the name given to the great estuary which lies between the Garonne-Dordogne convergence and the sea. It is a modest reminder of the marine reaches which covered the Aquitaine basin long ago in the Tertiary era.

The northern bank of the estuary is bordered by limestone hills known as the **Côtes de Bourg** and **Côtes de Blaye**. On the south bank, where the land on the whole is lower, similar limestone formations have been eroded and then covered by gravels, producing the topsoil in which the famous vines of the Médoc flourish. Covering the limestone bedrock of the Gironde are deposits washed down by the two great rivers; these deposits, stirred by the action of the tides, have determined the formation of marshes, which are separated from the running water by an alluvial belt, the **palus.**

Some of the marshland has been transformed, in the Dutch manner, into polders where meadows now lie; the rest remains the province of hunters and waterfowl. Artichokes are grown on the *palus,* and certain vines which produce a palus wine.

Over the centuries the movement of the water has created a number of elongated islands as well as sandbanks which are revealed at low tide.

Médoc

This world-famous wine-producing area is divided into three separate zones: the region of viticulture proper, a zone of coastal forest, and the *palus* which punctuates the limestone bluffs of St-Estèphe and Pauillac. Fine red wines come from the first zone: north of St-Seurin-de-Cadourne these are produced mainly by local cooperatives and sold under the simple overall description of Médoc; to the south, from St-Seurin to Blanquefort, lies the district meriting the more distinguished Haut-Médoc appellation.

LANDES

The word *landes* (moors) still conjures up a vision of the more desolate aspect of this part of the coast which existed prior to the 19C, when a remarkable

The Bassin d'Arcachon and the Dune du Pilat

project of reforestation transformed the area into a huge pine forest.

Coast and Dunes

The Landes sit on an enormous plain, roughly triangular in shape, covering an area of 14 000km²/5 400sq mi. The side of the triangle runs down the 230km/143mi of coast from the Gironde estuary to the mouth of the Adour, and turns eastwards from the two points to meet at the triangle's apex 100km/62mi inland. This ruler-straight shoreline, known as the **Côte d'Argent** (Silver Coast), is essentially one vast beach on which the sea deposits sand at an annual rate of 15 to 18m³ per metre/20 to 24cu yd per yard of coast. The sand – especially in those reaches of the strand only reached by the highest equinoctial tides – is then dried and blown inland by the west wind, where it accumulates in dunes. Until the last century these dunes then moved away from the sea at a speed varying between 10m/32ft and 27m/88ft per year. Today, fixed in position by the plantation of shrubs, grasses and forest trees, the dunes form a continuous but static coastal belt 5km/3mi wide. The strip is the longest – and highest – series of dunes in Europe.

Lakes, Lagoons and the Plain

Most of the watercourses in the region find themselves blocked by the dune barrier, the one exception being the Leyre (known also as the Eyre in its lower reaches) which finds its way directly to the sea via the Bassin d'Arcachon. Elsewhere the streams have formed lakes, the surfaces of which are 15m/50ft to 18m/60ft above sea level. Most of these lakes intercommunicate; their waters force a passage through to the ocean with difficulty, via turbulent currents popular with water-sports enthusiasts; the Huchet and Contis currents are typical examples.

The lakes and currents are well stocked with fish (such as trout, tench, carp and eel) but the huge areas of water involved make these coastal lakes and lagoons particularly suitable for the use of large-scale boating equipment.

Sands distributed over the inner areas of the Landes originally formed part of material gouged from the Pyrenees by Quaternary Era glaciers; they exist now as a layer of brown sandstone, no more than 50cm/20in thick, known as the **alios**. This bed inhibits the percolation of water and blocks the extension of roots, and this, combined with the poor drainage of the plains because of their negligible slopes, adds to the dampness of the region and the sterility of its soils. Until the middle of the 19C this inner zone was no more than an unhealthy stretch of moorland, transformed into a swamp when the rains came, and supporting only a scanty shepherd population which went about on stilts. Even the sheep were raised more for their manure than for their meat or wool.

Wayward River

Over the centuries the course of the **River Adour** and its outlet to the sea has been altered by the region's shifting sands. Documents reveal that in AD 907 the

A. Thuillier/MICHELIN

river left Capbreton to carve a route to the sea via Vieux-Boucau-Port-d'Albret; in 1164 it again channelled a new path, this time near Bayonne, but later returned to Capbreton. A terrible storm in the 14C blocked the river's way and so it once again flowed to Port-d'Albret. Meanwhile, the port at Bayonne was being engulfed by sand. In 1569 Charles IX insisted that the river should be given a fixed estuary, which saved the harbour at Bayonne; nine years later a channel leading through 2km/1mi of dunes beyond Bayonne was opened, and the port at Boucau-Neuf was created.

Consolidation of the Dunes

As early as the Middle Ages it was known that mobile sand dunes could be fixed by the use of maritime pines or plants with spreading roots. A number of experiments were made in the Landes but it was **Nicolas Brémontier** (1738-1809), an engineer from the Roads and Bridges Department, who perfected the process and started the gigantic task here in 1788. First he constructed a dyke designed to check the movement of the sand at its starting point, then, about 70m/230ft from the high-water mark, he planted a palisade of stakes against which the sand could pile up. Adding to the height of the palisade as the accumulated sand rose higher, he progressively formed an artificial coastal dune 10m/33ft to 12m/39ft high, which acted as a barrier. He fixed the surface sand by sowing **marram grass,** a variety of grass with a thick network of rapidly spreading roots. He then turned his attention to the problem of the inland dunes.

Brémontier mixed the seeds of maritime pines with gorse and broom seeds, sowing them beneath brushwood which temporarily held back the sand. After four years the broom had grown into bushes nearly 2.5m/7ft high. These sheltered the slower-growing pines, which eventually outgrew the bushes, and, as they died and rotted, provided fertiliser for the young trees. By 1867 the work was almost complete: 3 000ha/7 500 acres of coastal dunes were carpeted with marram grass and 80 000ha/198 000 acres of inland dunes were planted with pine trees.

Cleaning up the Interior

At the beginning of the 19C the inner part of the Landes area was still a fever-swamp unfit for cultivation; it was badly drained and resisted all attempts to establish an agricultural presence. Under the Second Empire, however, an engineer named **Chambrelent** found the answer: he systematically broke up the unfertile layer of *alios* and then drew up a scheme of drainage, clearance and reforestation. The results justified the large-scale planting of maritime pines, cork-oaks and ilex trees: the Landes *département* soon became one of the richest in France as the many products made from pine trees brought large returns.

The Forest Under Threat

For maritime pines the greatest danger, which in a dry climate can never be entirely eliminated, is fire, especially when allied with wind. Today the pine forest covers nearly 1 000 000ha/2 350 000 acres in the Landes, and to preserve it a special corps of forest firefighters has been created. Numerous observation posts linked by telephone and radio ensure the rapid detection of an outbreak of fire. Air assistance can be called up. Everything possible has been done to facilitate the firefighters' access in all weathers and with the least delay. Commercial developments, access for traffic and especially camping are strictly controlled.

AGENAIS

The Agenais is a transitional region lying between the southern section of the Périgord, Bas-Quercy (Lower Quercy, to the east) and the Landes. This fertile area is lent a certain unity by the valley of the River Garonne.

In the damp northern sector herds of dairy cows graze in the pastures covering the clays; further east, pinewoods and plantations of oak and chestnut appear. In the area around Fumel, on the River Lot, a number of small metallurgical works exploit the local sands rich in iron ore.

Pays des Serres

This area stretches as far as the southern part of the Lot *département*. Unlike nearby Quercy which has retained a variety of crops, this region of long, narrow hills tends to specialise. On the muddier plateaux of Tournon-d'Agenais wheat is the most important crop; the hillsides are used for the cultivation of vines.

Lot Valley

The Lot Valley is one immense orchard punctuated by nurseries and fields of tobacco. Fresh peas, green beans and the melons of Villeneuve-sur-Lot are among the renowned local products.

Valley of the Garonne

The alluvial soils and mild climate here allow more delicate crops, most of them grown on terraces, to flourish; each town and village has its speciality. Agen, for example, is famous for its onions and its prunes: hand-picked, specially graded fresh plums, grown on grafted trees, are subsequently dried either naturally or in a slow oven to produce the **pruneaux d'Agen.** The use of grafted plum trees here dates back to the Crusades. In the 16C the monks of Clairac, near Tonneins, were the first to foresee the commercial possibilities of the plum, and 200 years later the market had grown to such an extent that it had to be government-controlled. The plum variety used almost universally in the region today is the *Robe-Sergent* (Red Victoria plum). Marmande is famous for its tomatoes and pumpkins; Ste-Marie produces peaches and cherries. Since the 18C even poplar trees have been pressed into service: plantations on land subject to flooding provide wood used in carpentry and the manufacture of paper.

GASCOGNE

The Aquitaine basin is part of a series of French sedimentary beds which resulted from the silting up of an ancient ocean depth; what distinguishes Gascogne (Gascony), the region lying between the Pyrenees and the River Garonne, is the upper covering provided by enormous masses of debris washed down by the rivers after the erosion of the mountains during the Tertiary Era.

The most common formation in Gascony is known as the **molasse** – layers of sand frequently cemented into a soft yellow sandstone penetrated by discontinuous marl and limestone beds. This geological structure has resulted in a hilly landscape of mixed topography.

From an agricultural point of view the soils here vary between **terreforts,** which are clayey and heavy to work, and **boule-bènes** – lighter and slightly muddy, but less fertile and more suitable for grazing and cattle-breeding.

The Hills of Gascony

The rivers, all tributaries of the Garonne, fan out northwards from the foothills of the mountains and cut through the hills of Armagnac in thin swathes. Those emerging from the major Pyrenean valleys – the Neste d'Aure and the Gave de Pau (Aure and Pau torrents) for instance – are already discharging the deposits they carry, and this material, mixed with the detritus from ancient glacial moraines, has produced a soil that is relatively poor. As a result there is a succession of moors between the high **Plateau de Lannemezan** and Pont-Long, north of Pau, via the Ger Plateau on the western side of Tarbes.

In the hills themselves, careful watering has led to the establishment of market gardens specialising in produce such as strawberries and melons.

Vines in this region form only a part of the traditional polyculture; production of *appellation contrôlée* wines, such as the Jurançon and Madiran whites and reds, and VDQS *(vins délimités de qualité supérieure)* from Béarn and Tursan, remains limited.

Pays d'Adour

The great curving sweep of the River Adour – northwards from its source, then west and finally back towards the south – creates a major demarcation line on the hydrographic chart of the region; the convergence towards Bayonne of all the rivers within this arc is evidence of a continuous sinking of the earth's crust beneath the ocean, which has persisted since the end of the Secondary Era.

Within the area encompassed by the Adour is a hilly landscape cut through by the tributaries of the river. The lower slopes of the valleys are terraced as they drop towards the cultivated alluvial strips flanking these streams.

LES PYRÉNÉES

The customary division of this mountain range into three large natural areas succeeding one another from west to east is justified by major differences in structure, climate and vegetation. The distinction is underlined by the traditions and language of the inhabitants (the Central Pyrenees and the Mediterranean section of the chain are described in the *Michelin Green Guide Languedoc – Roussillon – Tarn Gorges*).

Formation of the Chain

The remarkable view from the town of Pau of the Pyrenean mountains rising above the hills of the Béarn district presents a seemingly endless series of finely serrated crests – a mountain barrier revealing at that distance neither individual peaks, with the exception of Pic du Midi d'Ossau, nor saddles.

The barrier itself, stretching 400km/248mi from the Atlantic to the Mediterranean, is relatively narrow (30km/19mi to 40km/25mi on the French side of the frontier) yet also massive and continuous: the average height of the Pyrenees is 1 008m/just over 3 300ft.

History of the Range

Approximately 250 million years ago a Hercynian (Paleozoic) mountain mass similar to the Massif Central or the Ardennes stood on the site occupied by the Pyrenees today; however, whereas the central and northern heights experienced a relatively tranquil existence, this chain between the Atlantic and the Mediterranean was sited in a particularly unstable zone. Already vigorously folded, and then partially levelled by erosion, the Hercynian block was submerged about 200 million years ago beneath a continental sea and covered by Secondary Era sedimentary deposits, before being totally resurrected – and literally shaken from top to bottom – by the Alpine folding, the earliest spasms of which occurred here.

Under the enormous pressure of this mountain-building movement the most recent beds, still comparatively pliant, folded without breaking but the rigid ancient platform cracked, broke up and became dislocated. Hot springs burst through near the fractures; mineral deposits formed and metal-bearing ores appeared. During the geological eons that passed while this was occurring, the mountain mass, now tortured and misshapen, was ceaselessly worn down by erosion, and the material torn from it washed out by rivers across the plains below.

Central Pyrenees

The overall structure of the Pyrenean region is characterised by the juxtaposition of large geological masses arranged longitudinally. Starting from the Upper Garonne, the relief encompasses:

♦   The rises known as the Petites Pyrénées, of only medium height but remark-

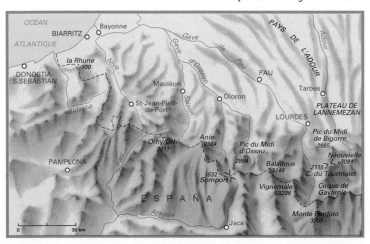

A. Thuillier/MICHELIN

Le Pic du Midi d'Ossau

able for the alignment of limestone crests pleated in a fashion typical of the Jurassic period;

♦ The real foothills, formations of the Secondary Era (either Cretaceous or Jurassic), with folded beds more violently distorted;

♦ The **Axial Zone,** the true spine of the Pyrenees along which granitic extrusions, recognizable by sharply defined peaks chiselled by glacial erosion, thrust through the Primary sediments: the Balaïtous, the Néouvielle and Maladetta massifs, the Luchon Pyrenees. The summits however are not made up entirely of granite, since patches of extremely hard schist and limestone exist which are even more resistant to erosion;

♦ The southern Secondary Era sediments, under-thrust to a height of more than 3 000m/9 840ft at Monte Perdido, which are to be found largely on the Spanish side of the frontier. Two masterpieces of mountain scenery stand out among this limestone relief: in Spain the canyon of the **Ordesa Valley** (a National Park); in France the lower part of the **Gavarnie** amphitheatre, with its gigantic platforms of horizontal strata piled one upon the other.

Valleys

The inner part of the chain lacks a channel, parallel to the backbone of the range, which could link up the many transversal valleys. This makes internal communications difficult, a problem exacerbated in the Central Pyrenees by the fact that most passes are impracticable in winter. Each of these valleys was therefore isolated for much of the time, and this led to a survival of socially autonomous lifestyles of the kind still to be found in such *petit pays* districts as the **Couserans**, the **Quatre Vallées** (Four Valleys) region, and the **Pays Toy.** The valleys are nevertheless far from being inhospitable; despite being hemmed in, they seem no more than a hilly extension of the plains of Lower Aquitaine – with the additional advantage of a sheltered climate.

Glaciers

A hundred centuries ago the ancient glaciers thrust their abrasive tongues across the mountain landscape, gouging out the terrain as far as the present sites of Lourdes and Montréjeau. Since then these giant ice rivers have shrunk to negligible proportions (less than 10km²/4sq mi for the Pyrenees, compared with 400km²/155sq mi in just the French part of the Alps). There is only one whole glacier, complete with tongue and terminal moraine, in the entire range: **the Ossoue**, on the eastern slopes of the Vignemale.

Many of the most dramatic and appealing features to be found at the heart of the Pyrenees were formed by the old glaciers: hanging valleys, amphitheatres, canyons transformed into pastoral sweeps, jagged crests and scatters of huge boulders, lakes (over 500 in the French Pyrenees), cascades, bluffs, sudden morainic platforms and powerful waterfalls, some of which are harnessed for the production of hydroelectric power.

Summits

The frontier between France and Spain is marked by the peaks of Balaïtous (3 146m/ 10 321ft) and Vignemale (3 298m/ 10 820ft), though the greatest heights of the Pyrenees are located on the Spanish side of the border: the impressive massifs of the Maladetta (3 404m/11 168ft) and Posets (3 371m/11 059ft). The French side nevertheless boasts **Pic du Midi d'Ossau** (2 884m/ 9 462ft), which owes its majestic silhouette to the extrusion of volcanic rocks, and **Pic du Midi de Bigorre** (2 865m/ 9 400ft), notable also for the way it towers over the plain below. The **Massif de Néouvielle** (3 192m/10 472ft at Pic Long) includes an extraordinary water tower, the contents of which are now almost totally reserved for the hydroelectric installations in the valleys of the Pau and Upper Neste torrents.

Picturesque Pyrenees

The **Cauterets Valley** perfectly illustrates those traditional and well-loved aspects of the Pyrenees which have inspired so many artists: steep-sided, narrow valleys opening up in the higher reaches of their rivers into huge upland pastures, gently sculptured, jewelled with lakes and webbed with torrents both turbulent and limpid. Such attractions, added to the benefits of the hot springs, the individuality of local customs and the proximity of Spain, appeal to romantic natures. Despite the progressive abandonment of temporary dwellings (such as mountain refuges and summer sheepfolds), of upland tracks and some of the highest pastoral slopes, the Central Pyrenees retain – at least in the Axial Zone – that friendly and characteristic image of mountains that have been in some way humanised.

Atlantic Pyrenees

This part of the range is characterised geographically by the disappearance of the Axial Zone, which has led to a confusion of the general relief, there being no longer a continuous spine or backbone to act as a "natural" frontier.

It is among the calcareous beds covering the eastern extremity of the Axial Zone that the most noticeable examples of geomorphological disturbance occur. These are the twisted contortions of the 2 504m/8 213ft **Pic d'Anie** and the savage gashes of the **Kakuetta** and **Holcarte** gorges. The subterranean levels of these fissured limestones riddled with potholes have provided an immense area of exploration and study for speleologists.

The slopes of these Lower Pyrenees are abundantly wooded and relatively difficult to cross (the Forest of Iraty for example). Nearer the ocean a more placid topography characterises the Basque Country, typified by **La Rhune**, **Mont Ursava** (at Cambo-les-Bains) and the mountains surrounding St-Jean-Pied-de-Port. The landscape between the Adour estuary and Spain mainly comprises hills sculpted from a heterogeneous mass of marine sediments.

Basque Pyrenees

The charm and cohesion of this region derives mainly from its oceanic climate, and the colourful language and culture of the Basque people, so closely interwoven with those in the neighbouring Spanish provinces of Guipuzcoa and Navarra. Trans-Pyrenean traffic is largely concentrated on the coastal route but the inland passages remain very popular with tourists and locals who have used them ever since the era of the great pilgrimages to Santiago de Compostela in Spain.

Coast

The dunes and pinewoods of the Landes region stretch beyond the mouth of the River Adour, as far as Pointe de St-Martin near Biarritz.

Farther south however the coastline bites into the Pyrenean folds, and the rocks – sedimentary beds violently arched over, foliated into thin laminated layers – form the low, slanting cliffs responsible for the picturesque appearance of the Basque Corniche.

Flora

There are three main types of vegetation in the Pyrenees, associated with the different geographic zones. To the west, the climate is affected by the Atlantic; the central Pyrenees is a continental-mountain zone; on the far eastern end of the range, the Mediterranean climate prevails. The diversity of species also depends on altitude, as in other mountainous areas. Below 800m/2 625ft, in the foothills, the forest is mostly common oak, typical of Atlantic regions. As the hills rise to 1 700m/5 580ft, the mountain sides are covered with beech on the lower slopes, and pine higher up, where the undergrowth is thick. From this level up to 2 400m/7 874ft, a robust species of hard pine (*pinus uncinata* – it proliferates in the rocky soil around the Cirque de Gavarnie) joins birch and *serbus domestica*, a fruit-bearing tree resembling mountain ash. At this limit, the forest grows sparse, rhododendrons and alpine meadows strewn with wild flowers predominate. From here up to 2 800m/9 186ft, few trees subsist, apart from the dwarf willow; other multicoloured vegetation hugs the ground. Beyond this altitude, the wintry landscape is one of rocks covered with the barest layer of moss and lichen, growth which resists the long months spent under snow.

There is an extraordinary wealth of native species of plants, flowers which are found nowhere else on earth. Some of them, such as *ramondia*, a small plant with deep violet blossoms and fuzzy leaves, can be traced back to the Tertiary Era, when the climate was subtropical. Countless species flourish in the mountainous, sub-alpine and alpine zones. Among the loveliest and best known are the lily of the Pyrenees, long-leafed saxifrage, blue Pyrenees thistle, campion, sisymbrium, Welsh poppies (blown in, no doubt, by the western wind), and wild iris (especially around the Cirque de Gavarnie). These delightful and rare plants flower in June and July, as well as in August at high altitudes.

Fauna

A range of mountain species can be found in the different altitude zones. Among the protected species, the brown bear, now unfortunately a rare sight, lives in the mountainous zone. In the beech and pine woods, the last of the lynx roam (it is uncertain how many of them survive in the wild). The isards (a local name for the indigenous chamois) prefer the grassy meadows and rocky outcroppings of the alpine altitudes. Beyond 1 500m/4 921ft, the river banks provide shelter for musk-rat; the local species is known as *desman*, and these rodents grow to about 25cm/10in. The lakes and streams of the Pyrenees had been fished out, but recent efforts to reintroduce species have been successful, and trout and salmon again swim the waters. An amphibian of the *uridela* order, resembling a newt with a yellow underside and flattened tail, known as the Pyrenean euprocte, likes to hide under flat stones in rivers and ponds (10-20cm/3-8in). The area is also home to many birds of prey, including the royal eagle, the griffon vulture, and the rare bearded vulture (*Gypaetus barbatus*), the largest bird of prey in Europe, also known as a lammergeier. The wood grouse is found in the underbrush, where it feeds on grains, berries and pine buds. During mating season, its courtship routine is a particularly noisy affair. Marmots come out in the early morning to start their daily routine of eating, napping, playing and keeping watch for predators.

Observing Mountain Animals

It is unusual to encounter wild animals casually, because they prefer to keep well away from the human species. However, you can increase your chances by using a few simple techniques. Firstly, walk as quietly as possible, avoid snapping branches, keep your voice low. In relative silence, animals are less likely to run away, and you may be able to hear tell-tale sounds such as rustling in the underbrush, or even an animal's cry. Through careful observation, you may discover tracks in the snow or on the ground, remains of a meal (nut shells, pine cones or berries which have been nibbled), or droppings, which tell naturalists a good deal about an animal's habits. Certain times of day or periods of the year are more propitious: many animals are more easily spotted at dusk or dawn, while spring mating season encourages males to wander farther afield, and even close up to paths used by people. In the winter, most mountain animals hibernate, and reappear with the vernal melt.

HISTORY

Prehistory

The Quaternary Era began about 2 million years ago. It was during this period that glaciers developed (the Günz, Mindel, Riss and Würm glacial stages), spreading over the highest mountains. However, the most significative event of the period was the appearance of the first humans in Europe, and more particularly in the Pyrenees.

Archaeology and scientific methods of dating have made it possible to classify various phases of evolution – Palaeolithic (Old Stone Age), Mesolithic (Middle Stone Age), Neolithic (New Stone Age) – which can themselves be subdivided into different periods.

THE STONE AGE					
PERIOD	HOMINID EVOLUTION	STAGE OF CIVILISATION	SITES	FAUNA	CLIMATE
MEGALITH AGE — 1 500		Dolmens and tumulus			
NEOLITHIC		Points and arrows / Polished stone choppers			Warm
— 7 500					
MESOLITHIC / AZILIAN — 10 000		Painted stones / Carved Venus figures / Needles / Burins		Reindeer	
MAGDALENIAN / SOLUTREAN	Cro-Magnon		Lespugue / Brassempouy / Gargas / Aurignac	Mammoths, Bears, Cave Hyena, Woolly Rhinoceros, Hippopotamus	Würm Glacial Period
UPPER PALEOLITHIC		Harpoons / Convex side scrapers / Spears			
AURIGNACIAN		Bone tools			
PERIGORDIAN	Homo sapiens	Cave paintings and engravings			
— 35 000					
MOUSTERIAN		Oval flints			
MIDDLE PALEOLITHIC		Blades, Disks, Arrows, Scrapers, Biface flint tools			Warm
LEVALOISIAN — 150 000				Mammoth Elephant	
TAYACIAN	Neanderthal Man			Appearance of Mammoth Ox, Lion	
ACHEULIAN		Handaxes in flint or quartzite / Awls / Scrapers / Saws			Riss Glacial Period
LOWER PALEOLITHIC				Aurochs/Bison, Rhinoceros, Tiger	Warm
CLACTONIAN	Montmaurin Man	Handaxes, shaped on both sides ("bifaces")	Montmaurin	Hippopotamus, Rhinoceros, Big Bear	Mindel Glacial Period
ABBEVILLIAN					Warm
	Java Man / Pithecanthropus erectus				Günz Glacial Period
— 2 million					
	Lucy (Ethiopia) / Australopithecus afarensis				
	Homo erectus				
3 million years ago					

R. Corbel/MICHELIN

LOWER PALAEOLITHIC

The Lower Palaeolithic period is represented in the Pyrenees by Tautavel man, who came to light when the remains of a human skull were discovered in a layer of ancient sediment in the **Caune de l'Arago** in 1971 and 1979.

Tautavel man belongs to the *Homo erectus* genus, which inhabited Roussillon 450 000 years ago. He was between 20 and 25 years old and was able to stand upright, about 1.65m/5ft 6in tall. He had a flat, receding forehead, prominent cheekbones, and rectangular eye sockets beneath a thick projecting brow. Since no trace of any hearth has been found, it is assumed that this intrepid hunter, who had not mastered the use of fire, ate his meat raw.

The first hunters who came to live in the Caune d'Arago used it for several purposes: as a look-out to keep track of the movements of animals which had come to drink from the Verdouble, as a temporary place to set up camp and dismember their prey, and as a workshop for manufacturing tools.

Palynology (the analysis of fossilised pollen grains) has helped to determine the specific characteristics of flora and fauna from different prehistoric periods. Although the alternation of climates produced changes (from grassy steppes to deciduous forests), Mediterranean plant species (such as pines, oaks, walnut trees, plane trees and wild vines) have always been present. There was much game in the area: large herbivores included various types of deer and mountain goats, prairie rhinoceros, bison, musk ox and an ancient species of wild sheep. Carnivores (bears, wolves, dogs, polar foxes, cave lions, wild cats) were hunted for their fur. Small game comprised rodents (hares, voles, beavers, field mice) and birds still to be found today (golden eagles, lammergeier vultures, pigeons, rock partridges, red-billed choughs).

The tools found are in general quite small (scrapers, notched tools). The largest tools found are pebbles, measuring on average 6-10cm/2-4in, made into choppers, or flat two or poly-sided implements of varying degrees of sharpness. These early humans used material they found nearby such as quartz or schist, and more rarely limestone, flint and jasper.

MIDDLE PALAEOLITHIC

The presence of numerous Mousterian deposits is evidence that Neanderthal man was present in the Pyrenees. Taller than *homo erectus*, he had a well-developed skull (1 700cm^3/103cu in). He was forced to adapt to the climatic conditions of the Würm glacial period.

Neanderthal man produced more sophisticated, specialised tools. He fashioned numerous double-sided implements, stone knives with curved edges, chisels, scrapers, pointed tools and all kinds of notched implements. His evolution is also evident in the construction of vast dwelling and burial places.

UPPER PALAEOLITHIC

With the advent of *homo sapiens*, there was now a significant human presence in the Pyrenees. During the Aurignacian period, stone implements were supplemented with bone and horn. The appearance of long thin wooden spears with metal tips (assegais), awls and spatulas pointed to a technical evolution which progressed still further during the Solutrean and Magdalenian periods. Towards the end of the last Würm glacial period (Würm IV), a transformation in landscape and fauna occurred, with boar and deer predominating from now on. Humans both hunted and fished. However, the most revolutionary change was the birth of art. Sculpted human figures (the Aurignacian "Venuses") and cave paintings are of exceptional archaeological interest. The animals, painted in red or black, on the walls of **Niaux** cave look strikingly realistic.

MESOLITHIC AGE

At the end of the Ice Age, the historical landscape of the Pyrenees became established. The Mesolithic Age is, in fact, an intermediary phase during which a multitude of civilisations appeared. During the Azilian culture (named after the **Mas d'Azil** cave), which began at the end of the Upper Palaeolithic period, the harpoon became an increasingly important weapon. Art, on the other hand, was restricted to enigmatic pebbles with symbolic markings.

NEOLITHIC AGE

The Neolithic Age is characterised by polished (as opposed to chipped) stone tools and the use of earthenware. This evolution was accompanied by a decisive change in economy and life style. However, in the eastern Pyrenees and the Ariège, evolution appears to have been slower, for it has been recorded that the local post-Palaeolithic population, who were joined by groups from outside the Pyrenees, remained static; they continued to live in caves and earthenware came into use only sometime later.

Further north, valuable ethnological information was discovered in the Font-Juvénal shelter, between the River Aude and the Montagne Noire. As early as the fourth millennium, agriculture and cattle-rearing had become a means of subsistence, with wheat and barley being cultivated. At the same time, dwellings were adapted to meet increasingly elaborate domestic requirements, a fact borne out by the discovery of flat hearths for cooking, air vents to raise the combustion temperature, supporting structures (posts and slabs) and silos for storage. In the Narbonne region, rural communities with specialised activities, using very elaborate implements, started to barter and trade with each other. Megalithic constructions (dolmens and tumili) were introduced to the Pyrenees from the western zone during the third millennium. The middle mountain slopes were the most densely populated. Activities included stock-rearing, and, increasingly, the making of weapons (arrows, axes and knives). Jewellery (necklaces and bracelets) and earthenware (bowls and vases) became more widespread. In the Catalan region, the Megalithic culture lasted until the Bronze Age.

Time Line

THE ROMAN CONQUEST

72 BC	Foundation of Lugdunum Convenarum (St-Bertrand-de-

Comminges), religious capital of the population south of the River Garonne, by Pompey.

56	Aquitaine conquered by Crassus, Caesar's lieutenant.

INVASIONS, THE RISE OF THE CAROLINGIAN EMPIRE AND THE HUNDRED YEARS WAR

2C-4C AD	**Introduction of Christianity** in Gaul. St Hilaire elected Bishop of Poitiers.
276	Germanic invasion.
5C	**Visigoth kingdom** in Aquitaine: continuation of the Latin culture and Roman law.
End 6C	**The Vascons**, Basque mountain people from the south, driven back by the Visigoths, settle in the flat country Gascogne (Gascony).
507	Defeat of **Alaric II**, King of the Visigoths, by Clovis at Vouillé (north of Poitiers).
732	The Arab advance into Europe is halted by Charles Martel at **Moussais-la-Bataille**.
778	**Kingdom of Aquitaine** created by **Charlemagne**.
801	Barcelona taken from the Arabs by Charlemagne and Spanish Marches organised.
820	Start of the Norman incursions. Destruction of Saintes, Angoulême (c 850) and Bordeaux.
c 950	Beginning of pilgrimages to Santiago de Compostela.
1058	**Union of the duchies** of Aquitaine and Gascogne. The southwest under the hegemony of the Comtes (Comtes of Poitiers and Angoulême).
1137	Marriage of Eleanor of Aquitaine to Louis, son of the French king.

ELEANOR OF AQUITAINE (C1122-1204) AND THE PLANTAGENET TERRITORIES

The marriage in 1137 of Eleanor, the only daughter of **William of Aquitaine,** to Louis, the French *dauphin,* brought with it a dowry which included the duchies of Guyenne, Gascogne, Périgord, Limousin, Poitou, Angoumois and Saintonge, plus suzerainty over the Auvergne and the Comté of Toulouse. Her husband was crowned Louis VII the same year. Fifteen years later, in 1152, the marriage ended in divorce; Eleanor retained all the lands of her dowry.

Eleanor's subsequent marriage to **Henry Plantagenet** in 1154 was a political disaster for the Capetian dynasty: the combined possessions of the bride and groom, extending from the English Channel to the Pyrenees, were as vast as those of the French crown. Henry's crowning as Henry II of England finally upset the fragile international equilibrium; the resulting Anglo-French struggle lasted on and off for 300 years.

Later, separating from her second husband, Eleanor left London for Poitiers where she held a brilliant court. From 1173 her various intrigues – she supported her son Richard the Lionheart in the fight against his father, Henry, for example – resulted in her being imprisoned in London by her husband, and she was only released on his death 15 years later in 1189. She took up her plotting again, this time against her youngest son, John (Lackland), and Philippe Auguste, King of France.

Eleanor spent her later life peacefully at her castle on the Isle of Oléron and finished her days at Fontevraud Abbey, where she is buried, together with her husband Henry Plantagenet *(for further details of her life, ↻ see Eleanor of Aquitaine).*

1224	Poitou attached to the French crown.
1345	Start of the **Hundred Years War** in Aquitaine.
1356	The French King, **Jean le Bon**, captured by the English at the Battle of Poitiers and taken prisoner by the **Black Prince**.
1360	**Treaty of Brétigny**: the duchies of Aquitaine, Aunis, Saintonge and Angoulême become possessions of the English crown.
1369	**Jean de Berry** installed as Governor of Poitou.
1380	Restriction of the English presence in the southwest to Bordeaux and Bayonne, thanks to the formidable Constable Du Guesclin (who had chased the *grandes compagnies* – bands of terrorising mercenaries and brigands – into Spain).
1422	**Charles VII** proclaimed King in Poitiers.
1450-1500	Dismantling of English Gascony; re-attachment of the Comtés of Armagnac and Comminges to the French crown.
1453	Final battle of the **Hundred Years War**, won by the Bureau

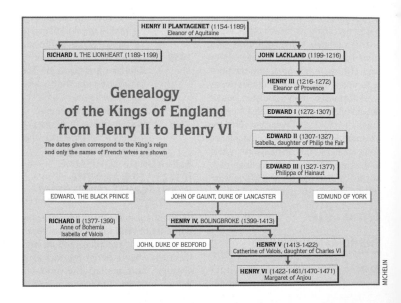

Genealogy of the Kings of England from Henry II to Henry VI

The dates given correspond to the King's reign and only the names of French wives are shown

HENRY II PLANTAGENET (1154-1189)
Eleanor of Aquitaine

RICHARD I, THE LIONHEART (1189-1199)

JOHN LACKLAND (1199-1216)

HENRY III (1216-1272)
Eleanor of Provence

EDWARD I (1272-1307)

EDWARD II (1307-1327)
Isabella, daughter of Philip the Fair

EDWARD III (1327-1377)
Philippa of Hainaut

EDWARD, THE BLACK PRINCE

JOHN OF GAUNT, DUKE OF LANCASTER

EDMUND OF YORK

RICHARD II (1377-1399)
Anne of Bohemia
Isabella of Valois

HENRY IV, BOLINGBROKE (1399-1413)

JOHN, DUKE OF BEDFORD

HENRY V (1413-1422)
Catherine of Valois, daughter of Charles VI

HENRY VI (1422-1461/1470-1471)
Margaret of Anjou

MICHELIN

brothers at Castillon-la-Bataille. Progressive abandonment of France by the English.

FROM THE RENAISSANCE TO THE REVOLUTION: WARS OF RELIGION

1484 **The Albrets** – Kings of Navarre – become all-powerful in the Gascon Pyrenees.

1494 Birth of **François I** in Cognac.

1515 Accession of François I. Battle of Marignano: victory for François over the Swiss and the Italians; northern Italy becomes French.

1533-34 The doctrine of the Reformation preached by **Calvin** in Saintonge, Angoumois and Poitiers (in 1558, from Basle in Switzerland, Calvin tells his fellow Protestants of the Confession of La Rochelle, a sign of the town's early conversion to Reformation principles).

1539 The administration of justice reshaped by the Edict of Villiers-Cotteret, which imposed French as the official language of the judiciary, instead of Latin or the Langue d'Oc.

1555 **Jeanne d'Albret** crowned Queen of Navarre (until 1572).

1562 Beginning of the **Wars of Religion**.

1569 Victory for the **Duc d'Anjou** over the Protestants in the battles of **Jarnac** and **Moncontour**. Poitiers under siege from Protestants.

1570-71 Imposition of the **Protestant faith** on Béarn by Jeanne d'Albret. Bloody rivalry between her lieutenant, Montgomery, and his Catholic adversary, Blaise de Monluc.

1579 An attempt made, with les grands jours de Poitiers, to end religious discord in the region.

1589 Accession of **Henri IV**, the son of Jeanne d'Albret.

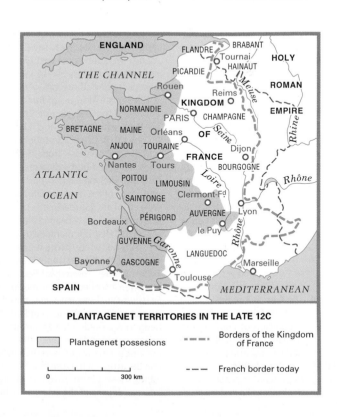

PLANTAGENET TERRITORIES IN THE LATE 12C

Plantagenet possesions

- - - - Borders of the Kingdom of France

- - - French border today

0   300 km

Richelieu during the Siege of La Rochelle (H. Motte)

1598	End of the Wars of Religion. Protestants granted freedom of worship, and 100 safe places (among them La Rochelle) in which to practise their religion, through Henri IV's promulgation of the **Edict of Nantes**.
1608	The future **Cardinal Richelieu** created Bishop of Luçon.
1627-28	Siege of La Rochelle and eventual submission to Richelieu.
1659-60	Treaty of the Pyrenees. Marriage of Louis XIV and the Infanta Maria Teresa at St-Jean-de-Luz.
1685	Revocation of the Edict of Nantes by Louis XIV. Persecution of Protestants in Béarn by the King's Dragoons *(Dragonades)*. Evacuation of many Huguenots from the country.
18C	A decisive impetus to the country's economic development brought during the era of the Intendants (stewards or governors): the Comte de Blossac in Poitiers, Reverseaux in Saintes, Tourny in Bordeaux.
1789-99	The **French Revolution** and the end of the Ancien Régime (execution of Louis XVI in January 1793); establishment of the Convention.
1793-95	The **Vendée War**.
1794	Deportation of priests aboard the hulks of Rochefort.

THE VENDÉE WAR (1793-95)

By early 1793 a combination of the execution of Louis XVI, years of resentment over the religious issue capped by the rounding up and persecution of priests, the imposition of arbitrary taxes and the Convention's decision to conscript 300 000 men triggered an insurrection and a wave of riots in the west of France.

In Maine, Normandy and Brittany where the rebels were known as the *chouans* and were fairly loosely dispersed, operating in a guerrilla fashion, the authorities did regain control; in the territories south of the River Loire, however, where fewer troops were available and communications were more difficult, the government collapsed. In this area, collectively known as the **Vendée Militaire,** the rebels were able to form the Catholic and Royal Army. Their strongholds were in the Gâtine, the *bocage* and the marshes – difficult country to penetrate, crisscrossed with hedgerows and perfect for ambushes, and in the Retz district, around the Lac de Grand-Lieu. Led at first by royalists of peasant stock such as **Cathelineau,** a pedlar, and the game-keeper **Stofflet,** the peasants themselves soon called on their gentlemen (local nobles, estate stewards, priests) for help: these included **Gigost d'Elbée,** the Marquis of Bonchamps, Sapinaud, the Chevalier de **Charette, La Rochejaquelein** and **Lescure,** among others. They also sought help – with limited success – from the British. These so-called brigands, armed at first only with pitchforks and scythes and later with guns taken from the Republicans, worked in cells grouped parish by parish, each wearing a cloak bearing the insignia of a Sacred Heart surmounted by a Cross; their flag was white (hence the royalists' nickname, the **Whites;** republicans were known as **Blues**), covered with fleurs-de-lis, and often inscribed with the motto *Long live Louis XVI.* Their tactics were based on surprise: skilled marksmen, hidden in the hedgerows, would silently surround an enemy patrol and open fire, after which the ambushers would hurl themselves into the attack. If the resistance was too robust, the whole troop would melt away into the depths of the *bocage* – which

B. Kaufmann/MICHELIN

was bitterly referred to by the Republican general, **Kléber**, as "the labyrinth." From the spring of 1793 superior Republican troops led by generals Westermann, Kléber and Marceau were deployed in the area. Battles were won by both sides until the winter of 1794 when the Republicans got the upper hand; thousands of Whites were shot or guillotined, while the Blue **"Infernal Columns"** devastated the entire province. Following more battles and treaties the tired rebels eventually submitted to the Revolution through the diplomacy of the astute Republican General Lazare **Hoche.** Stofflet and Charette were finally captured and subsequently shot, the latter with the cry "Long live the King!" on his lips.

FROM THE FIRST TO THE SECOND EMPIRE

1804 Consecration of **Napoleon I** as Emperor of the French, and founding of the town of Napoleon-Vendée (today, La Roche-sur-Yon).

1806 The continental blockade, designed to ruin England by denying the country its economic outlets on mainland Europe, also severely reduced activity in the ports along the Atlantic Coast of France.

1815 Embarkation of the deposed Napoléon for the Isle of Aix.

1822 Plot by the **Four Sergeants of La Rochelle** to overthrow the Restoration government.

1832 Attempts by the Duchesse de Berry to provoke another Vendée uprising, this time against Louis-Philippe.

1845 Birth of the town of Arcachon.

1852-70 The **Second Empire** – a period of splendour for the Basque coast and country and the spas in the region.

1855 Opening of the Poitiers-La Rochelle railway link.

1860 Opening of the Eaux-Bonnes to Bagnères-de-Bigorre Thermal Cure route.

1867 The topography of the Landes revolutionised by the extensive planting of pines.

1868 Appearance of the Portuguese oyster in the Gironde.

FROM THE THIRD REPUBLIC TO THE PRESENT DAY

1870 Installation in Tours and then in Bordeaux of a delegation from the National Defence government, headed by Gambetta.

1876 **Phylloxera crisis** in the vineyards.

1905 A law separating the Church from the State pushed through by Émile Combes, Mayor of Pons, and Georges Clemenceau, a Deputy in the National Assembly.

1914 President Poincaré, the government and both chambers of the Assembly moved temporarily to Bordeaux before the first German offensive in the First World War.

1929 Death of Clemenceau at St-Vincent-sur-Jard.

1939 End of the Spanish Civil War. Seizure of the Spanish gold reserves (lodged in Mont-de-Marsan) by the Fascist victors; 500 000 refugees flood into the southwest of France.

1940 Refuge again taken in Bordeaux by the authorities of the Third Republic after the German advance southward following the breakthrough at Sedan during **WWII**.

1945 German forces still entrenched in the Atlantic pockets (among them Royan) besieged by Free French soldiers and members of the Resistance.

1951 Death of Marshal Pétain on the Isle of Yeu.

1954 Inauguration of the oil wells of Parentis.

1966 Oléron becomes the first French island to be linked to the mainland via a bridge.

1988 Completion of the bridge leading to the Isle of Ré.

1990 Opening of the new high-speed Paris-Bordeaux rail link, with the **TGV**-Atlantique (*train à* *grande vitesse*) making the journey in less than 3hrs.

1996 President **Mitterrand** is buried in his native village of Jarnac.

1997 The Cirque de Gavarnie is added to UNESCO's World Heritage list.

1998 The mint in Pessac begins production of **Euro** coins.

1999 December – a terrible storm uproots trees and damages buildings across the southwest.

1999 Oil spill from the Crude oil carrier *Erika* pollutes beaches in the Vendee and the Charentes

2000 Construction begins on the A89 motorway linking Bordeaux to Clermont-Ferrand.

2001 Ellen MacArthur sails into Les Sables-d'Olonne as runner-up in the 2001 Vendée Globe around-the-world yacht race.

2008 Scheduled completion date of A89 motorway between Bordeaux and Clermont-Ferrand.

Pilgrim Routes

History and legend

St James the Great, beheaded in Jerusalem in the year AD 91, was the first Apostle

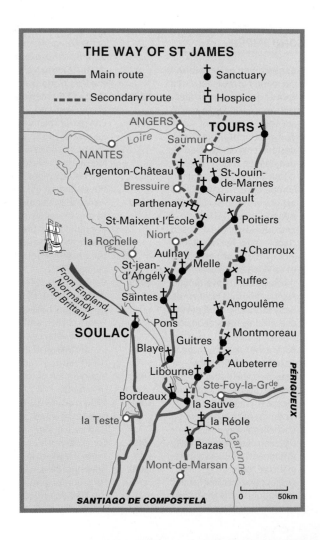

martyred for his beliefs; according to legend, his body and head were transported to northwestern Spain in a stone boat and buried on the coast of Galicia. On the site of his tomb, miraculously rediscovered in the early 9C, a church was built, and around it grew the town of Compostela. When the Moors were driven from Spain, St James (Santiago in Spanish) became the patron saint of Christians: in the year 844, it is said, at the height of a decisive battle at Clavijo in Rioja, he appeared on a white charger and vanquished the enemy – a manifestation which earned him the nickname of *Matamore* (Moor-slayer).

The Pilgrimage

Soon after the building of the church to St James, the faithful from far and wide began flocking to the site to venerate the relics. They travelled from hostel to hostel visiting churches, abbeys and holy places along a number of well-defined routes. Throughout the Middle Ages the number of pilgrims grew to such an extent that the church of **Santiago in Compostela** became a shrine equal in importance to Jerusalem or Rome.

The first French pilgrimage was led by the bishop of Le Puy in the year 951. Subsequently millions of **Jacquets,** Jacquots or Jacobites (*Jacques* in French means James) set out from Paris, Tours, Le Puy, Vézelay and Arles, which developed into assembly points for pilgrims from all over Europe.

Pilgrims to Santiago wore a uniform of a heavy cape, an 8ft stave with a gourd attached to carry water, stout sandals and a broad-brimmed felt hat, turned up at the front and marked with three or four **scallop shells,** the badge of the saint, which identified the pilgrim's destination. The shells, found in great banks along the Galician coast and still called *coquilles St-Jacques* (St James' shells) in France today, were also used as a receptacle to collect alms. A scrip or pouch, a bowl and a small metal box for papers and passes completed the equipment. The network of hostels and hospices where pilgrims could find food and shelter for a night, or receive attention if they were unwell, was organised by the Benedictine monks of Cluny, the Premonstratensians and other orders. The Knights Templars and the Hospitallers of St John with their commanderies policed the routes, marked with carved mileposts or cairns; everything was done to provide for the pilgrims' spiritual and physical welfare.

There was even a *Pilgrims' Guide,* the first tourist guide ever written, which was produced in Latin in c 1135, probably by Aymeri Picaud, a monk from Parthenay-le-Vieux. This outlined local customs, gave advice on the climate and weather conditions to be expected, spiced the more mundane information with comments on the morals, customs, and mentality of the inhabitants of each region, and listed the most interesting routes, towns, and the sights on the way – the pilgrim in those days was in no hurry and frequently made detours that took weeks or months to complete, to visit a sanctuary or shrine.

The main routes all converged in the Basse-Navarre district before crossing the Pyrenees. The most important junction was at Ostabat; St-Jean-Pied-de-Port was the last halt before the climb towards the frontier. The pilgrims reached Roncesvalles by a mountain route which was once part of the Roman road linking Bordeaux with Astorga via the Valcarlos gap. The bell of the monastery at Ibañeta pass would toll when it was foggy – or sometimes for much of the night – to signal the right direction to those pilgrims who might have got lost or lagged behind.

With the passage of time, however, the faith that fired people to set out on pilgrimages began to wane; false pilgrims seeking gain by trickery and robbery, and known as *coquillards,* increased; the Wars of Religion, when Christians fought among themselves, reduced the faithful even more. In the late 16C, when Francis Drake attacked Corunna, the relics were removed from the cathedral to a place of safety, after which the pilgrimage was virtually abandoned. By the 18C anyone wishing to make the journey to Santiago de Compostela was obliged to provide the authorities, when requested, with a letter of introduction from their parish priest and other documents certified to be true by a police official or signed by the pilgrim's local bishop.

ART AND CULTURE

ABC of Architecture

Religious architecture

CHAUVIGNY - Ground plan of St-Pierre (11C-12C)

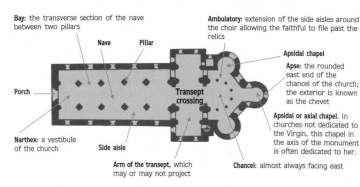

Bay: the transverse section of the nave between two pillars

Nave

Pillar

Ambulatory: extension of the side aisles around the choir allowing the faithful to file past the relics

Apsidal chapel

Apse: the rounded east end of the chancel of the church; the exterior is known as the chevet

Porch

Transept crossing

Apsidal or axial chapel. In churches not dedicated to the Virgin, this chapel in the axis of the monument is often dedicated to her.

Narthex: a vestibule of the church

Side aisle

Arm of the transept, which may or may not project

Chancel: almost always facing east

ANGOULÊME - Cross-section of the transept of the Cathédrale St-Pierre (12C)

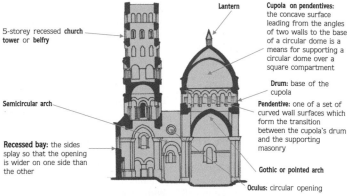

Lantern

5-storey recessed church tower or **belfry**

Semicircular arch

Recessed bay: the sides splay so that the opening is wider on one side than the other

Cupola on pendentives: the concave surface leading from the angles of two walls to the base of a circular dome is a means for supporting a circular dome over a square compartment

Drum: base of the cupola

Pendentive: one of a set of curved wall surfaces which form the transition between the cupola's drum and the supporting masonry

Gothic or pointed arch

Oculus: circular opening

AULNAY - South portal of St-Pierre (12C)

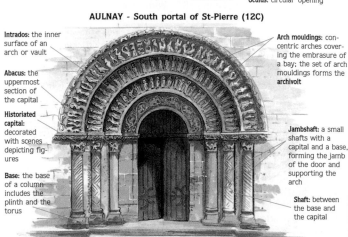

Intrados: the inner surface of an arch or vault

Abacus: the uppermost section of the capital

Historiated capital: decorated with scenes depicting figures

Base: the base of a column includes the plinth and the torus

Arch mouldings: concentric arches covering the embrasure of a bay; the set of arch mouldings forms the **archivolt**

Jambshaft: a small shafts with a capital and a base, forming the jamb of the door and supporting the arch

Shaft: between the base and the capital

R. Corbel/MICHELIN

74

PETIT-PALAIS - The Église St-Pierre (end 12C)

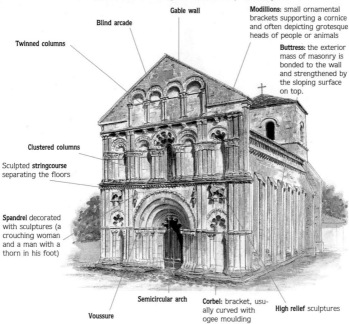

Gable wall

Blind arcade

Twinned columns

Modillions: small ornamental brackets supporting a cornice and often depicting grotesque heads of people or animals

Buttress: the exterior mass of masonry is bonded to the wall and strengthened by the sloping surface on top.

Clustered columns

Sculpted **stringcourse** separating the floors

Spandrel decorated with sculptures (a crouching woman and a man with a thorn in his foot)

Semicircular arch

Corbel: bracket, usually curved with ogee moulding

High relief sculptures

Voussure

POITIERS - Façade of Notre-Dame-la-Grande (12C)

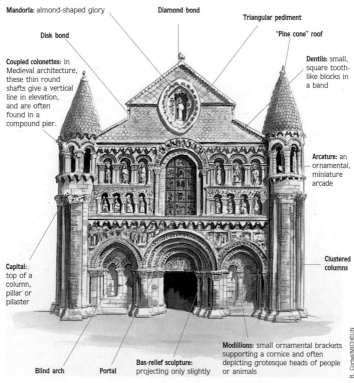

Mandorla: almond-shaped glory

Diamond bond

Triangular pediment

Disk bond

"Pine cone" roof

Coupled colonettes: in Medieval architecture, these thin round shafts give a vertical line in elevation, and are often found in a compound pier.

Dentils: small, square tooth-like blocks in a band

Arcature: an ornamental, miniature arcade

Capital: top of a column, pillar or pilaster

Clustered columns

Modillions: small ornamental brackets supporting a cornice and often depicting grotesque heads of people or animals

Blind arch

Portal

Bas-relief sculpture: projecting only slightly

SAINTES - Belfry of the Église de l'Abbaye aux Dames (12C)

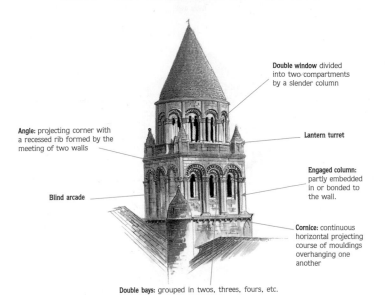

Double window divided into two compartments by a slender column

Angle: projecting corner with a recessed rib formed by the meeting of two walls

Lantern turret

Engaged column: partly embedded in or bonded to the wall.

Blind arcade

Cornice: continuous horizontal projecting course of mouldings overhanging one another

Double bays: grouped in twos, threes, fours, etc.

Military architecture

ROQUETAILLADE - Château neuf (14C - restored 19C)

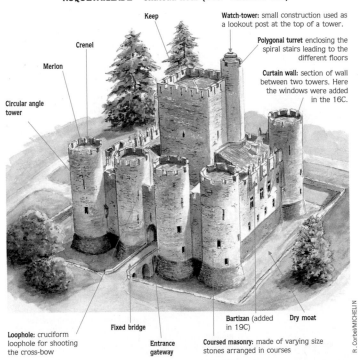

Keep

Watch-tower: small construction used as a lookout post at the top of a tower.

Crenel

Polygonal turret enclosing the spiral stairs leading to the different floors

Merlon

Curtain wall: section of wall between two towers. Here the windows were added in the 16C.

Circular angle tower

Loophole: cruciform loophole for shooting the cross-bow

Fixed bridge

Entrance gateway

Bartizan (added in 19C)

Dry moat

Coursed masonry: made of varying size stones arranged in courses

R. Corbel/MICHELIN

Civil architecture

Château de MALLE (17C)

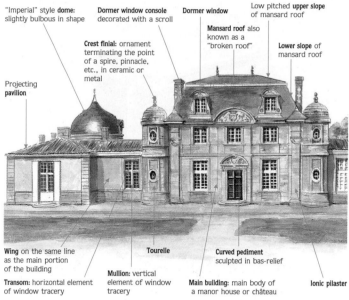

"Imperial" style **dome:** slightly bulbous in shape

Dormer window console decorated with a scroll

Dormer window

Low pitched **upper slope** of mansard roof

Crest finial: ornament terminating the point of a spire, pinnacle, etc., in ceramic or metal

Mansard roof also known as a "broken roof"

Lower slope of mansard roof

Projecting **pavilion**

Wing on the same line as the main portion of the building

Tourelle

Curved pediment sculpted in bas-relief

Transom: horizontal element of window tracery

Mullion: vertical element of window tracery

Main building: main body of a manor house or château

Ionic pilaster

BORDEAUX - Palais de la Bourse (18C)

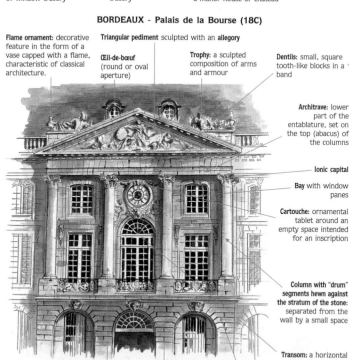

Flame ornament: decorative feature in the form of a vase capped with a flame, characteristic of classical architecture.

Triangular pediment sculpted with an **allegory**

Œil-de-bœuf (round or oval aperture)

Trophy: a sculpted composition of arms and armour

Dentils: small, square tooth-like blocks in a band

Architrave: lower part of the entablature, set on the top (abacus) of the columns

Ionic capital

Bay with window panes

Cartouche: ornamental tablet around an empty space intended for an inscription

Column with "drum" segments hewn against the stratum of the stone: separated from the wall by a small space

Transom: a horizontal member above a window or door

Colossal order: order of columns and pilasters that extend more than one storey

Rusticated course. Rustication is texturing on the facing of cut stone

Groovings: cut into the façade to simulate or accentuate the stone-work pattern

R. Corbel/MICHELIN

BORDEAUX - Staircase of the Grand Théâtre (end 18C)

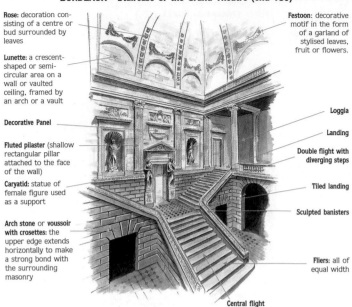

Rose: decoration consisting of a centre or bud surrounded by leaves

Lunette: a crescent-shaped or semi-circular area on a wall or vaulted ceiling, framed by an arch or a vault

Decorative Panel

Fluted pilaster (shallow rectangular pillar attached to the face of the wall)

Caryatid: statue of female figure used as a support

Arch stone or **voussoir with crosettes:** the upper edge extends horizontally to make a strong bond with the surrounding masonry

Festoon: decorative motif in the form of a garland of stylised leaves, fruit or flowers.

Loggia

Landing

Double flight with diverging steps

Tiled landing

Sculpted banisters

Fliers: all of equal width

Central flight

ARCACHON. Winter house - Villa Trocadéro (end 19C)

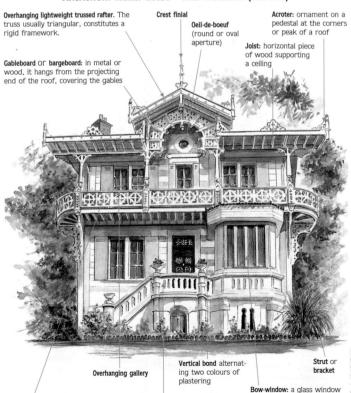

Overhanging lightweight trussed rafter. The truss usually triangular, constitutes a rigid framework.

Gableboard or **bargeboard:** in metal or wood, it hangs from the projecting end of the roof, covering the gables

Crest finial

Oeil-de-boeuf (round or oval aperture)

Acroter: ornament on a pedestal at the corners or peak of a roof

Joist: horizontal piece of wood supporting a ceiling

Balustrade with cross-bars

Overhanging gallery

Stone balcony

Vertical bond alternating two colours of plastering

Bow-window: a glass window in a protruding bay

Strut or **bracket**

R. Corbel/MICHELIN

Architecture

GALLO-ROMAN ERA

Despite the institutionalised vandalism of the 19C, many examples still remain of the arts which flourished in the Roman colony of Aquitaine, the capitals of which were Bordeaux, Poitiers and Saintes. The ruins of amphitheatres, theatres, temples and bathhouses, and votive arches scattered throughout these areas offer a broad view of Gallo-Roman civilization.

ROMANESQUE PERIOD (11C-12C)

After the turbulent period of the early Middle Ages, marked by conflicts between the great feudal houses, the year AD 1000 saw a renewal of faith exemplified in the Crusades and the great pilgrimages. In the southwest of France the most important religious sanctuaries were all built along the routes leading to Santiago de Compostela in Spain (◐ see PILGRIM ROUTES in the History chapter).

Church Design
In Poitou, Romanesque churches generally comprised a high, barrel-vaulted central nave, buttressed by side aisles of almost equal height. Light entered through the window bays of these aisles.
In Angoumois and Saintonge (the regions around Angoulême and Saintes) the wide, single nave was sometimes barrel-vaulted, sometimes topped by a **line of**

domes showing influence from the Périgord region.

West Fronts
The façades were characterised by arcades or tiers of blind arcades. Arcading at the upper level was nevertheless typical more in Angoumois and Saintonge, whereas churches in Poitou were often distinguished by a tripartite division vertically, with large arcades separated by columnar buttresses (Notre-Dame-la-Grande in Poitiers is an exception).
The west front was usually surmounted by a triangular pediment and flanked by columns or groups of columns sometimes crowned by pierced lanterns with conical roofs. These roofs, and often those of the church belfries, would be covered by overlapping tiles. The façade itself was normally decorated with statues and low-relief sculptures, intended to deliver a message. Notre-Dame-la-Grande in Poitiers is one of the most successful examples of these façade-screens; the Biblical stories depicted on the façade are easily identified and understood.
In Angoumois the west fronts are generally more sober, although that of St-Pierre in Angoulême is famous for its depiction, through 70 different characters, of the Last Judgement.

East Ends
Churches with an ambulatory at their east end and radiating chapels buttressed by columns are common in Poitou:

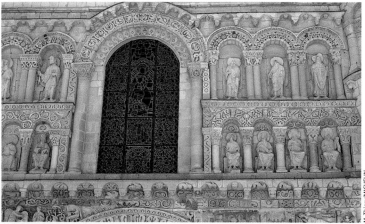

Façade of Notre-Dame-la-Grande, Poitiers

M. Thiery/MICHELIN

St-Hilaire, in Melle, is typical. Certain east ends in Saintonge, on the other hand, were built to a simpler design, like the church at Rioux, with a five-faced apse and columnar buttresses; the bays separating the columns have archivolts at the middle level, decorated with a row of blind arcades and miniature columns above. The whole is topped by an elegant frieze running beneath a cornice with carved, double-scroll brackets.

Sculpture

The use of sculpture – on façades, east ends, corbels, arches, consoles and capitals – was facilitated by the nature of the local limestone, which is relatively easy to work; Romanesque edifices are notable for the abundance, variety and finesse of the religious ornamentation. On these surfaces foliage, acanthus leaves in the antique style and pre-Romanesque plaited stonework rival in complexity images of oriental monsters, biblical illustrations, legends of the saints and scenes of everyday life.

One of the most lavishly decorated west fronts in the Poitou area is that of Notre-Dame-la-Grande in Poitiers; however, it is the Saintonge that is best known for its wealth of sculpted decor. Whilst the richness of the overall decoration can be almost overwhelming, it is also worth looking closely at the wonderful individual details.

Frescoes and Mural Paintings

A fresco (from the Italian word *fresco* meaning fresh) is a wall or ceiling painting executed on a surface of freshly applied, still-damp plaster, into which the design is incorporated before the plaster dries. The number of colours that can be used is limited, since only pigments made from natural earths and iron oxides suit the technique.

The most extraordinary murals of the Poitou School are found in St-Savin, where the compositions are remarkable as much for the beauty of the colours, the harmony of the design and the perfection of the technique as for their lively content.

FROM ROMANESQUE TO GOTHIC: THE PLANTAGENET STYLE

In the west of France the Plantagenet style, also known as **Angevin,** marked the transition between Romanesque and Gothic styles. This architectural style reached its highest point at the beginning of the 13C and had died out by the end of the century.

Angevin Vaulting

In normal Gothic vaulting all the keys are situated at approximately the same height. Plantagenet architecture, however, is characterised by steeply recessed quadripartite vaulting – probably derived from an earlier use of the dome – in which the keystones of the diagonals are higher than the stringer or transverse keys by as much as 3m/10ft.

At the end of the 12C these Angevin vaults became lighter as the number of ribs increased and arched more gracefully, springing from slender circular columns. The early 13C saw the style at its finest,

Château d'Oiron

S. Sauvignier/MICHELIN

the tall, slim pillars supporting an airy tracery of lierne vaulting.

Examples of the style can be seen in Vendée, Poitou (Poitiers Cathedral, Airvault, St-Jouin-de-Marnes southeast of Thouars), Saintonge and as far away as the region around the Upper Garonne.

Gothic Period (12C-15C)

Apart from its appearance in the Plantagenet style, which nevertheless retains many elements of the Romanesque, Gothic art raised scarcely an echo in the west and southwest of France; such examples as there are tend to be Southern Gothic, the style of the Mediterranean, characterised by a single, very wide nave and no transept. Certain English influences are evident in the square, Flamboyant towers of a few 14C and 15C churches in the Saintonge (St-Eutrope in Saintes, Marennes).

RENAISSANCE PERIOD

Renaissance ideas were first introduced to France following the Italian wars at the end of the 15C. Although this new style did not take hold overnight, the arrival of a score of Neapolitan artists brought from Italy by Charles VIII at the end of 1495 brought new life to French architecture.

Civil Architecture

The Renaissance style was brought to the west by members of the court of François I who were natives of the Saintonge or Angoumois regions and had been influenced by the architecture of the Loire Valley. The François I Wing of the Château d'Oiron, for example, displays a characteristic series of basket-handled arches, whereas the Château de la Rochefoucauld, with its celebrated courtyard surrounded by a three-tiered gallery, is reminiscent of an Italian *palazzo*.

Extensive use of decorative arabesques and grotesques, as well as hints of Antiquity, distinguishes the châteaux of Dampierre-sur-Boutonne, Oiron and Usson: the roofs are tall, with all the slopes on each side at the same angle; the inclusion of splendid staircases accounts for the projecting façades of the central blocks.

Similar features can be found in other châteaux of the region – the old royal Castle in Cognac, for instance (guardroom and gallery) – or in such Renaissance mansions as the Hôtel Fumé in Poitiers and the Hôtel Saint-Simon in Angoulême.

CLASSICAL PERIOD

The accession of the Bourbon dynasty in 1589, following the era of stagnation that characterised French art and architecture toward the end of the Renaissance, heralded a radical shift in direction: the period of material prosperity that coincided with the reign of Henri IV fired artists eager for change with new ideas and new interpretations of classical, antique themes. Classical art held sway in France from 1589 to 1789.

Classical Fortifications

From the 16C onwards fortifications were constructed above all to protect frontier towns, and consisted of curtain walls and bastions surmounted by platforms from which cannon could be fired. Overhanging turrets allowed the defenders to survey the surrounding ditches and keep watch over the terrain beyond.

The acknowledged master of fortifications was **Sebastien le Prestre de Vauban** (1633-1707). Developing the ideas of his predecessors – military engineers employed by the king – he evolved a system based on the use of massive bastions complemented by ravelins or demilunes, the whole being protected by very deep defensive ditches. Vauban's designs are notable for the way he made use of natural obstacles, used only local materials, and added aesthetic value to the functional works he produced, incorporating monumental stone entrance gates, often adorned with sculpture. His talent can be admired at Blaye, where the citadel protecting the entrance to the port of Bordeaux is part of a complex defence system; further south, Bayonne and Navarrenx (south of Orthez) are also examples of the genius of this great military architect.

BASQUE RELIGIOUS ARCHITECTURE IN THE 17C

Most of the churches in the Basque country were renovated during the period of the

Council of Trent (1545-63), which generated a movement within the Catholic clergy and laity for widespread religious renewal and reform that yielded substantial results in the 17C, even affecting religious architecture. In this region, the belfry is a particularly distinguishing element. Around La Soule, a distinctive form of **belfry-calvary** is common, such as the one in Gotein. The flattened belfry rises up like a wall, with three pointed gables, each crowned with a cross. The shape symbolises the Holy Trinity, whereas the crosses recall Jesus and the two thieves crucified. In lower Navarre and Labourd, the belfry-wall is rounded, resembling the fronton of a pelota court. Certain churches have massive, tiered **belfry-porches.** Often the porch, whatever its dimensions, is surmounted by a room used to hold town council meetings or catechism classes.

In the northern Basque regions of Labourde and Basse Navarre, the inner layout is characteristic: a wide nave is surrounded by two or three tiers of **galleries,** which are in theory reserved for men. The pulpit is integrated into the lower gallery. The main altar is often monumental **baroque** in style, a profusion of gilding, sculpture, curls and wreaths typical of Catholic baroque churches all over Europe.

In the cemeteries, the oldest and most remarkable tombstones – some dating from before the 16C – are known as **discoidal tombstones:** atop a plinth, a round, flat stone is often carved with a swastika figure, or *cruz gammata,* believed to have been a symbol of solar power and movement, possibly of Hindu origin. The exact source of the design remains a subject of speculation and debate, along with the many other unique aspects of Basque culture.

1830-1930: ARCHITECTURE ON THE ATLANTIC COAST

19C Eclecticism

In the 19C, European architecture was characterised by a penchant for eclecticism, bringing styles from the past (Antique, Romanesque, Gothic, Renaissance and Classical) back into fashion, and borrowing largely from foreign architectural styles, especially those of the Far East. Such buildings are found from the Gironde to the Basque country, along the shore and in spa towns in the Pyrenees. Some of them are highly original, many are luxurious villas, lending their image to the reputation of certain resorts. In the Bordeaux area, neo-Classicism is the dominant architectural style (early 19C), especially in the châteaux of local wine-growers. But some odd mixtures can be found here as well, as at the Château Lanessan where the Spanish Renaissance meets Dutch tradition, or the Cos d'Estourel, rising pagoda-like from the vines.

The popular Bassin d'Arcachon inspired a building boom in the 19C, as holiday homes owned by families from Bordeaux went up in styles ranging from the Algerian villa to the Swiss chalet, the Basque house to the English cottage. These hideaways can still be seen around Cap Ferret and in the Ville d'Hiver section of town, so successfully promoted by the Pereire brothers.

Biarritz became a fashionable seaside resort thanks, in part, to Napoléon III and his neo-Classical Villa Eugénie. Luxury beach houses in a range of different styles were built right up to the 1930s: the Villa de la Roche-Ronde is neo-Medieval (towers and look-outs); the Boulard château (1870-71) neo-Renaissance; and the Françon Villa adopts the Old England look. In Hendaye, the Château d'Abbadia is influenced by Gothic architecture. Its interior is inspired by Moorish architecture, a style also in evidence at the Casino de la Plage.

Art Deco

This 20C style is most evident along the Basque coast: the town casino, the Maritime Museum (1932-35) and the interior decoration of private homes in Biarritz; the Atrium Casino (1928) and the Splendid Hotel (1932) in Dax; the Leïhora Villa (1926-28) in Ciboure. Like the Art Nouveau movement which preceded it, Art Deco draws from classical motifs, but they are reduced to geometric stylizations, and the noodle, whiplash, tapeworm, and cigarette-smoke style curves of Art Nouveau give way to straight and pure lines. Architects used wrought iron, glass (creating luminous

rooms within buildings) and ceramics to express these colourful designs.
During the 1920s and 1930s, villas built in Hossegor, in the Landes region, were inspired by rural houses of the Basque country and a neo-regional style developed, which combined timber-framing, typical brick bond from the Landes, overhanging roofs, projecting load-bearing walls and white roughcast façades with Art Deco ornamentation.

Medieval Town Planning

MILITARY ARCHITECTURE

From the 9C to the 12C the weakness and remoteness of the central power in medieval France contributed to the establishment of powerful dukedoms and counties. When the enforced feudalism began to crumble, one of the results was a generalised increase in the scattering of new strongholds. Fortresses proliferated in the southwest and in particular in the former Aquitaine, which had been disputed for three centuries by two different crowns. Outside the towns where, through the consolidation of existing Gallo-Roman protective enclosures, defence could usually be assured, crude new strongholds spread across the open countryside. Comprising a surrounding ditch, a palisade, and a wooden tower (later built of stone) rising on a hillock, these fortresses provided basic refuge for local inhabitants.

Keeps

Rectangular keeps built of stone made their appearance in the early 11C. They initially had a purely defensive role: the stonework was not particularly thick and there were no loopholes from which to fire at the enemy. The ground-floor level, which was dark, served as a store. The keep could only be entered at first-floor level, via either a ladder or a retractable footbridge. This design (illustrated by the keep at Bassoues), which persisted until the 14C, explains why the spiral stone staircases of so many of these structures only started at the higher level.

Before the Hundred Years War there was a 13C-14C Gascon variant of the keep known as a **salle** – a fortified dwelling flanked by one or two rectangular towers, set along the diagonal. Again, only the upper storeys were inhabited and provided with windows.

Castles of Brick

Certain castles in the Béarn district bear the trademark of **Sicard de Lordat,** a military engineer employed by Gaston Fébus, the 14C overlord of Béarn. For reasons of economy they were built of brick rather than massive stonework. The single square tower astride a polygonal defensive perimeter served both as a keep and as a gateway. The living quarters and the barracks were built against the inside of the curtain wall.

Thuillier/MICHELIN

Château de Montaner

Fortified Churches

Fortress-churches occupy a special place in the history of French military architecture, and are numerous in the southwest. Two types of machicolation were employed in their construction: the classic variety supported by corbels, and another in the form of arches curving between the buttresses (as at Beaumont-de-Lomagne). They appeared for the first time in France in the late 12C, in the Langue d'Oc country. The churches were traditionally places of asylum with their robust architecture and their belfries which could be used as watchtowers; moreover the Truce of God ordered by the Vatican Council in the 10C and 11C stipulated a "zone of inviolability", extending for 30 paces around each church, in which refugees might not be touched. The Council's orders forbade the waging of war on certain days of the week and during Advent, Lent and Easter week. Violation of the Truce was punished with excommunication.

Examples of these fortified churches still exist in the Upper Pyrenees, in the valleys once subject to cross-frontier raids from Aragon; the best-known are Luz Church, enclosed within a crenellated curtain wall, and Sentein Church, which has three towers.

NEW TOWNS OF THE MIDDLE AGES

Medieval urban development in southwestern France has left only three sites still substantial enough today to be called towns: Montauban (southeast of Agen), founded by the Comte de Toulouse in 1144; the lower part of Carcassonne (1247), built on the west bank of the Aude by St Louis to shelter the homeless after the town was sacked; and **Libourne** (east of Bordeaux), named after Sir Roger Leyburn, Seneschal to Edward I of England (1270) (for details of Montauban and Carcassone, & see the *MICHELIN GREEN GUIDE LANGUEDOC - ROUSSILLON - TARN GORGES*). Aquitaine, however, at first strewn with *sauvetés* and *castelnaux* (refuges and fortified towns), was above all characterised by an abundance of new towns known as *bastides* – semi-urban, semi-rural settlements which were characterised by a geometric ground plan. Many of these small country towns and villages ha retained their traditional character an original layout.

Sauvetés and Castelnaux (11C and 12C)

The **Sauveté** (including Sauvetat and Sauveterre) usually arose as the result of an ecclesiastical initiative. Prelates, abbots or dignitaries of a military Order of Chivalry would found the village or hamlet; the inhabitants would clear, prepare and cultivate their lands; a host or overseer, installed perhaps in a small manor house, would supervise the work. These rural townships also provided sanctuary for fugitives.

In a similar fashion, the **castelnau** (including Châteauneuf and Castets) originated with the dependencies built by a seigneur around his château. Auvillar (southwest of Agen), Mugron and Pau were once *castelnaux*. In Gascony the name Castelnau is completed by the name of the local fief; for example, Castelnau-Magnoac, Castelnau-Barbarens.

Bastides (1220-c1350)

The *bastide* was an entirely new concept, a purpose-built and efficiently planned town or village where people could live. By the middle of the 14C something like 300 *bastides* had been created between Périgord and the Pyrenees. In Gascony and Guyenne these new towns were so numerous that it suggests that at one time they were the most important form of collective habitation in the region. Although not all of them were fully developed, and despite their relative lack of importance today – some have disappeared altogether – the *bastides* in their time were a genuine response to demographic, financial and economic needs as well as to military and political imperatives.

The construction of many *bastides* arose from a contract of *paréage*. Such contracts, frequently drawn up between the king and a local seigneur or between an abbot and a lay seigneur, could also permit two neighbouring seigneurs to detail the rights and powers of each over territories they might hold in common; or they could stipulate that a less powerful seigneur would enjoy the protection of his stronger neighbour in return for a fixed proportion of the former's revenues. The contracts also affected the inhabitants of the *bastide*, establishing their status, outlining the allotment of building plots and specifying the taxes to be paid. To encourage people to move into the *bastide*, new arrivals were granted – among other privileges – the right of asylum and exemption from any military service due to the seigneur. The immigrants were free to bequeath property to their inheritors and dispose of their other possessions as they wished. Penalties, on the other hand, could be imposed on those who were slow to build.

Place names of the *bastides* followed three different principles: they could evoke the settlement's status – Villefranche (Free Town); they could carry the name of the founder – Montréjeau (Mount Royal), Beaumarché, Hastingues (Hastings); or they could suggest a symbolic twinning with some famous foreign city such as Valence (after Valencia in Spain), Fleurance (Florence), Cologne or Tournay.

These settlements were fairly rigidly planned, based on the model of a right-angled grid, either square or rectangular (with the exception of Fourcès, a rare circular *bastide*). Variations on this plan were due either to the lay of the land or to considerations of defence. The use of professional surveyors at the planning stage is evident in the rectilinear layout of the streets, always meeting each other at right-angles to form a symmetrical pattern of equal-area lots. Those moving in were allowed so much on which they could build, so much for a garden, and – outside the built-up area but not too far away – an allotment which they could cultivate.

The road system was ahead of its time: the principal streets were usually 8m/26ft wide, a generous size when none of the buildings had more than two floors.

In the centre of the grid was the main (and only) square, normally closed to traffic and reserved for markets; many of the central, covered market places still stand today. The square was effectively an open lot islanded among the regular ranks of buildings; the four streets framing it passed from the open air to the *couverts,* and then out again on the far side, retaining their continuity and frequently their street names. The **couverts,** most of them unfortunately now truncated or lost altogether, were covered passages surrounding the square running beneath either stone-built arcades or projecting upper storeys supported by wooden pillars.

Bastide Churches

The proliferation of *bastides* from the 13C onwards led to the construction of many new churches. They were built either close to the market square or out on the periphery of the grid, on the specified lot assigned for church and cemetery; here, therefore, the Languedoc single-nave-no-transept style was particularly suitable. Churches in Gascony share a family likeness, with their belfry-porches (Mirande, Marciac) and their wide, dark naves lit mainly through the clerestory windows of a cramped apse.

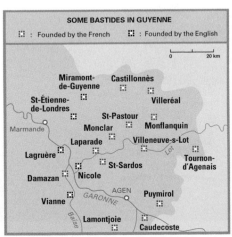

SOME BASTIDES IN GUYENNE

▯ : Founded by the French ▯ : Founded by the English

0   20 km

Miramont-de-Guyenne   Castillonnès

St-Étienne-de-Londres   Villeréal

Marmande

St-Pastour

Monclar   Monflanquin

Laparade   Villeneuve-s-Lot

Lagruère   Lot

St-Sardos   Tournon-d'Agenais

Damazan   Nicole

AGEN

Vianne   GARONNE   Puymirol

Baïse

Lamontjoie

Caudecoste

THE REGION TODAY

Economy

FISHING AND THE FRUITS OF THE SEA

Since the western part of the region enjoys a favoured situation beside the sea, fishing is naturally one of its principal commercial assets.

Deep-Sea Fishing

Modern trawlers are ideally suited to fishing on the high seas – a branch of the industry which supplies most of Europe's fresh fish and which concentrates its activities at the limit of the continental shelf, where the depth is often 500m/ 1 640ft or more. Sole, bream and hake landed by these trawlers play an important part in the economy of La Rochelle, Les Sables d'Olonne, the Île d'Yeu, St-Gilles and other ports in the northern coastal section.

Fishing for the huge **tuna fish** takes place from June to October, from boats equipped with dragnets and live bait (sardines, anchovies etc). The great white Atlantic tuna, known locally as *germon,* is fished at the beginning of the season between Portugal and the Azores, and the fleets then follow its migration north from the Bay of Biscay as far as the southwest of Ireland. Tuna is the main catch brought back to St-Jean-de-Luz.

Coastal Fishing

Though coastal fishing is more limited in its scope than deep-sea fishing, it nevertheless supplies a particular demand – for varieties of fish and seafood which are especially prized when they are absolutely fresh. Small trawlers, motor-boats and local fishing smacks bring in sole, whiting, mullet, mackerel, skate etc, according to the season and the locality. To fish **sardines,** fishermen use "turning" nets – seines from 200m/656ft to 300m/984ft long. The catch is landed daily and sold immediately at quayside auctions. The increasing rarity of sardine banks off the Vendée coast has, however, driven the fleets further towards the coast of Morocco, where ships with deep-freeze compartments have to be used.

Recreational fishing uses lines, cords, fixed nets, seine nets from the beach, or regionally typical **carrelets** (suspended nets manoeuvred via pulleys from a landing stage). Carrelets remain popular, particularly in the Gironde estuary, although a certain picturesque quality may weigh more in their favour than any particular effectiveness. In the spring, when fish swarm upriver to spawn, the catches of shad and lamprey in the Gironde are at

Fishing along the coast

M. Thiery/MICHELIN

their most plentiful. The eels return at the same time; their tiny **pibales** (elvers) are fished from the shore, thousands at a time, with fine-meshed shrimping nets.

Crustaceans
Lobsters, crabs and crayfish are caught – in wicker pots or hoop nets – mainly in the cold waters off the rocky coasts of the Vendée and the Île d'Yeu. Langoustines (crayfish) are fished further out by the trawlers. Fishermen from Royan and La Cotinière seek out shrimps and prawns on the banks off the Gironde estuary.

Salt marshes
From the 11C to the 18C the marshes, bordering almost the entire Poitou coast, were one of the principal economic assets of that area, especially in the Aunis and Saintonge regions. The salt trade played an important part in both sea and river traffic. Merchants sailing to northern Europe carried salt as far as the Hanseatic ports, where it was used to preserve fish. Then the receding sea withdrew further still; the marshes silted up and transformed themselves into *gâts* (fever swamps). Today the only salt pans still worked are on the Île de Noirmoutier and the Île de Ré, with a few more among the Breton-Vendée marshes. The rest have been turned into pastureland, market gardens, nature reserves or *claires* (basins) for fattening oysters.

The working of salt flats is a delicate operation. The marsh is divided into a grid, squared off with small *bossis* (banks) of earth bearing a large proportion of clay. Sea water, brought by the rising tide, is carried into the grid via narrow canals or *étiers*, allowed to settle, and then concentrated in a series of reservoirs that become shallower and shallower. The water in the final pans, known as *œillets*, is no more than 5cm/2in deep. It is here, once the liquid evaporates, that the salt crystallises.

From May to September the *paludier* (salt-worker) "draws" with the help of a large rake (known as a *las* or *rabale*) the grey salt deposit from the bottom of the pan after skimming the white salt off the surface with a flat shovel. The harvest is then assembled in *mulons* (small heaps) at the side of the pan – today often protected against bad weather by plastic sheeting – to be stocked later in the local *salorges* (special salt stores, usually built of wood).

OYSTERS

The Marennes-Oléron basin, which extends from the River Charente to the mouth of the Gironde, is among the most important oyster-farming regions in France: the Charente-Maritime *département* alone supplies almost half the national market in these epicurean delicacies. Brittany is the country's other major oyster-producing area.

History and biology
The two main varieties, the flat oyster *(plates)* and the concave or deep-shelled oyster *(creuses)*, live in their natural state, respectively, on sandbanks or in beds attached to undersea rocks. The **flat oyster** is hermaphrodite and viviparous (the young are produced live and do not have to be hatched). This variety has been found in the region since Gallo-Roman times, and has been gathered or dredged since then; it was a delicacy on the table of Louis XIV, who was a great oyster-lover. In 1920, however, the species was almost entirely destroyed by a disease, and flat oysters can only be found now – in very small quantities – in the region of Marennes.

The fleshier, richer **deep-shelled oyster,** with a taste that is less delicate and very different, is unisexual and oviparous (the young are hatched from eggs) as well as being less sensitive to changes in the weather. The variety was introduced into the area accidentally in 1868: a ship sheltering from a storm stayed too long in the Gironde on its way from Portugal to England with a cargo of these oysters; the cargo was in danger of going bad and the oysters had to be thrown into the sea. The surviving oysters then imposed themselves on the majority of local farms.

When disease struck again in 1971, these *portugaises* were in turn supplanted by *japonaises (Crassostrea Gigas)* – oysters bred in the Pacific and imported from Japan or Canada (British Columbia).

Sea snail

Scallop

Periwinkle

Treasures from
the sea

Starfish

Donacidae

Clam

Razor shell clam

Limpet

*Knotted
wrack*

Cockle

Mussels

R. Corbel/ MICHELIN

Exploitation

Ostreiculture (oyster breeding) in France remains very much a cottage industry – frequently a family affair – and still a fairly uncertain business: apart from the risk of disease, oyster farms can be destroyed by pollution, silting up, excess salinity, storms, an unusually cold spell or degeneration of the oysters – which can also be attacked by crabs, starfish or even winkles.

The **nassain** (young seed oysters or spats), drifting this way and that with the currents, become attached in summer to **collectors** – lime-washed tiles, slates, wooden stakes or stones according to the region; these are then transported to the first oyster park. After a year or two the oysters are prised off the collectors – a technique known as **détroquage** – and placed in a second park. They remain a further year or two here, usually in special *pochons* (containers) placed on tables. In the Marennes-Oléron basin the oysters receive a final treatment to mature and refine them, giving them their characteristic pale greenish-blue hue, in fattening pools known as **claires** full of microscopic blue algae.

Oysters sold as **spéciales** have spent longer in the *claires,* and are less densely distributed in them, than the ordinary **fines de claires.**

MUSSELS

The mussel is a bivalve with a blue-black shell, and in the wild lives in colonies on rocks pounded by the sea. It has been farmed since the 13C and is reared commercially along the coast of the province of Aunis – separated (except in the Baie de l'Aiguillon) from the oysters, since the two shellfish are biologically incompatible. The centres of mussel production today are the coast near Brouage, the Île d'Oléron (Baie de Boyardville) and the Anse de Fouras to the south of the province; the Baie de l'Aiguillon to the north of it.

Mytiliculture

This is the French term for mussel breeding, including their fattening and beautifying for the market. The mussels attach themselves to **bouchots** (stakes) driven into the mud or silt in long lines or arranged in

Gathering mussels

grids, where they fatten and increase in size. The arrangement of the *bouchots* varies from district to district and is subject to strict control. In the Breton Straits the *bouchots à nassain,* for the very young mussels, are well off-shore, and those where the shellfish grow to commercial size much nearer the coast. The *boucholeurs* visit their mussel beds in small, flat-bottomed boats or, if the tide is low, on their *accons* – flat wooden crates which they slide across the mud with a hefty kick from their boot.

Mussels serve as the base for the preparation of a regional delicacy known as *mouclade.*

AGRICULTURE

Poitou, the Charentes and the region around Bordeaux all rely heavily on agriculture, with crops on the limestone plains and vines on valley slopes. In the Landes, the forest overshadows everything.

Mixed Farming

Mixed agriculture is still the norm in these areas; tenant farming (with a generous percentage of the crop being given to the landlord), although rapidly disappearing, still exists and the average property rarely exceeds 50ha/125 acres.

Cereals (wheat, maize, oats) in the small farms grow side by side with meadows of clover, alfalfa and other **fodder plants.** A number of slightly less common crops are also grown: in the coastal regions, for example, with their humid atmosphere warmed by the ocean, **early fruit and vegetables** flourish; on the islands (with the exception of the Île d'Yeu) and in the rich alluvial soil of the marshlands, it is easy to grow new potatoes, artichokes, carrots and peas. The melons known as Charentais also grow in this same area and in recent years these have been so successful that they have spread as far as the Rhône Valley, where they have threatened to supplant the Cantaloupe melon.

Market gardens abound in the lower parts of the Vienne, Thouet and Garonne valleys and those of their tributaries. The Garonne basin, in addition, specialises in tomatoes, various fruits and even tobacco.

Tobacco, largely a family business, is grown in small fields in the region around Bazas and on the alluvial soil flooring the valleys of the Dordogne, the Lot and the Garonne, where the principal centres are Marmande and Tonneins.

The Pines of the Landes

The huge forest covering the Landes consists mainly of maritime pines, although parasol varieties occur here and there. The maritime pine, with its tall bole ringed by tufts of needles, is not a beautiful tree though it does have a certain elegance – and it grows quickly; it has also brought prosperity to what was once a poor and desolate region.

Since ancient times it has also been the base of the traditional activity of **gemmage** (resin harvesting). Formerly, the *gemmeur* (gum collector) periodically tapped the tree with the aid of a tool known as a *hapchot*. From the wound made, resin would then bleed into small earthenware cups (called *cramponnés* because they were clamped to the trees). Every few weeks the resin was collected, packed into barrels and sent to distilling plants. Today this practice has largely been superseded by the use of sulphuric acid, which activates the process and has the advantage that it does far less damage to the tree. Today the region serves as a processing centre for turpentine, pitch, transparent wrapping material and other solids.

Even when they are very old, the pines remain useful; after they have been "bled dry" of their resin, they are felled and sent to factories which transform them into parquet flooring, crates and wood-fibre boards (especially compressed woodchip sheeting). Large factories producing paper, wood pulp and pine cellulose exist across the region, in particular at Facturen, which is responsible for half of the country's cellulose production.

LIVESTOCK

Cattle

Cattle are reared throughout the region, both for their meat and milk. Fattening, particularly of the distinctive white Charolais breed, takes place in the fields of the Pays de Retz, the Gâtine de Parthenay, the *bocages* of the Vendée, and on the polders of marshland. Bressuire and Parthenay, important cattle markets, handle thousands of tawny Parthenay cattle and an increasing number of Charolais. To the east, towards the Massif Central, the Charolais and the chestnut-coated Limousin breeds predominate. French breeds (Black-and-Whites and Normans) are bred between Poitiers and La Rochelle and between the Vendée and the Charentes, providing milk to numerous cooperatives. These areas produce cheese, long-life milk and the famous *beurre des Charentes,* a rich, creamy butter.

Resin harvesting in the Landes forest

A. Thuillier/MICHELIN

Ducks from the Gers

Sheep, Goats and Horses

Sheep, which originally appeared indigenously on the heaths and pastureland of the region, are increasingly important in these otherwise poor farming areas, in particular the eastern reaches of the Poitou, in the Berry, and in the Gâtine de Parthenay (renowned for its tender Charmoise lamb).

Goat-rearing has considerably increased in the southern parts of the Deux-Sèvres and Vienne, based around dairy cooperatives that produce 50% of the country's goat-milk products. **Chabichou,** the celebrated goat's cheese, is a traditional speciality of the region.

Horse-rearing has been in steady decline for decades; breeding racehorses, however, remains a thriving business, especially in the Vendée. The Poitou **baudet** (donkey) and the Mellois mule, on the other hand, have become rare to the point where measures have been taken to preserve them from extinction.

Poultry

Poultry is of great economic importance from Clisson to Mont-de-Marsan, with the emphasis on Poitou geese, Bressuire and Barbezieux hens, and white ducks from Challans. Specialised poultry production is particularly important in the north of the Deux-Sèvres and in the Vendée.

In the east and south of the Landes forests, crops (mainly maize) and poultry farming (yellow, corn-fed chickens; geese, ducks, turkeys) are the mainstays of local agriculture alongside a flourishing *foie gras* industry.

WINES AND SPIRITS

The areas to the north and the south of the Gironde are known throughout the world for their fine wines, fortified wines, cognacs and armagnacs, which have long been exported and play a major role in the local economy.

Wines of Bordeaux

The world-famous Bordeaux vineyards, 105km/65mi from north to south and 130km/81mi from west to east, cover an area of approximately 105 000ha/ 405sq mi. The region, widely considered the best in the world for fine wines, contains over 8 000 wine-producing *châteaux* (which can mean an estate or simply a property, and not necessarily something resembling a castle) which between them produce wines within 53 different controlled *appellations* under six main "family" headings. Added to these are the *Crémant de Bordeaux,* a sparkling wine, and the local **digestif** spirit called *Fine de Bordeaux.* Red wine accounts for approximately 75% of production and white wine for 25%, with an output of around 600 million bottles per year; 40% of wine is exported to the United Kingdom, Belgium, Germany and the Netherlands.

Red Wines

According to a local saying, "all the edges are rounded off in the bottle" – and red wines do indeed have a remarkable ability to improve with age. The wines of the region include the elegant wines of the Médoc, the delicate, slightly spicy and vigorous Graves to which they have a family resemblance, and the wines of St-Émilion, with their strength of character.

The Pomerol district is renowned its warm, deep red wines, while the lesser-known Fronsacs – coarse when first bottled but refining with age – are characterised by their full favour and body. Farther downstream, the vineyards of Bourg and Blaye are known for their *grands ordinaires* – admirable wines both white and red. Production is similarly diversified in the Premières Côtes de Bordeaux region on the east bank of the Garonne.

White Wines

The range of white wine available is equally impressive. Pride of place must go to the great wines of Sauternes and of neighbouring Barsac, which produce the best sweet white wines in the world, pressed from grapes benefiting from the effects of the famous noble rot. Less well-known but also of note are the whites of Ste-Croix-du-Mont and Loupiac, on the other side of the Garonne.

The dry white Graves are wines of distinction which, for many, typify the whites of Bordeaux: fresh on the palate, slightly fruity and vigorous.

The finely fragranced Cérons wines, ranging from quite dry to liquoreux, are a cross between the best wines of the Graves district and the great Sauternes.

The town of Cadillac, in the *Premières Côtes de Bordeaux* appellation, produces mellow,

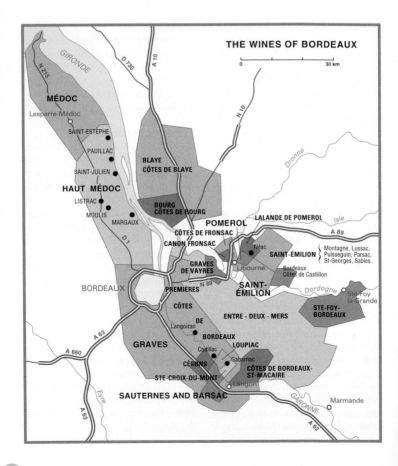

THE WINES OF BORDEAUX

velvety white wines that are agreeably light, while the huge area known as Entre-Deux-Mers (between two seas: the Atlantic and the Mediterranean), with its network of cooperatives, is a very important supplier of dry white wines and reds which are marketed as *grands ordinaires.*

Appellations

The term **"appellation d'origine contrôlée" (AOC)** on a wine label is an assurance of a wine's origins, carrying with it an implication – though not necessarily a guarantee – of quality.

The Médoc, thanks to the variety of its *terroirs* (soils), is classified into eight *appellation contrôlée* zones: Médoc and Haut-Médoc, and more specifically St-Estèphe, Pauillac, St-Julien, Moulis, Listrac and Margaux.

Serving Bordeaux Wines

The red wines of Bordeaux should not be drunk too young; the whites, on the other hand – especially the dry whites – are at their best relatively soon after bottling.

Wines of Gascogne

The region, situated northeast of the Landes and extending south to the Gers and the Pyrenees, produces palatable red wines such as the spicy Madiran and dry or sweet white wines such as the Pacherenc.

Wines of Agenais

Buzet is a light red wine which becomes full-bodied with age. The Côtes de Duras wines, produced in the north of the Lot-et-Garonne *département,* include light, fruity reds and refreshing whites. North of Marmande, the Côtes du Marmandais region is known mainly for its full-bodied fruity red wines.

Wines of Béarn

The Béarn region (& *see BÉARN*) produces several wines of note including the famous Jurançon, a heady wine grown on the left bank of the Gave de Pau, and the Rosé du Béarn, once exported to northern Europe, as far as Hamburg.

Wines of the Basque Country

The best known Basque Country wines are the Irouléguy *appellation* red wines.

The region also produces a yellow or green liqueur distilled from mountain plants, known as Izzara.

Muscadet

This well-known dry white wine which forms, with the Gros Plant and Côteaux d'Ancenis, part of the **Vins de Nantes** group, was accorded *appellation d'origine contrôlée* status in 1936. The vineyards producing the wines of this group extend south of the Loire.

Muscadet is made from the Melon grape, which came originally from Burgundy. The vines were imported and planted in the Nantes area after the terrible winter of 1709 because of their resistance to frost. There are three *appellations,* corresponding to three different regions: the Muscadet de Sèvre-et-Maine, which accounts for the major part of the production, the Muscadet des Côteaux de la Loire (which comes from around Ancenis) and plain Muscadet (from the neighbourhood of St-Philbert-de-Grand-Lieu). All of them yield wines that are light and dry, with an alcoholic content limited to 12%. Served cold, Muscadet is the perfect accompaniment to fish and seafood.

The **Gros Plant du Pays Nantais** has been classed as a VDQS *(vin délimité de qualité supérieure* – a superior wine) since 1954. It is made from the Folle-Blanche grapes grown in the Charentes since the 16C. This light wine (11%) complements seafood in general and shellfish in particular.

Cognac

Cognac, famous for centuries throughout the world, is a distillation of white wines produced in the region of the Cognac *appellation* (essentially the Charentes

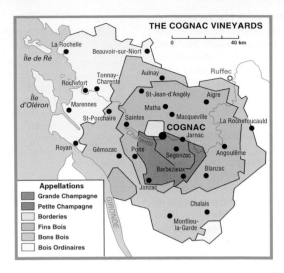

THE COGNAC VINEYARDS

Appellations
- Grande Champagne
- Petite Champagne
- Borderies
- Fins Bois
- Bons Bois
- Bois Ordinaires

département). A good cognac should taste like the very essence of fresh grapes, strong and heady. More than 80% of the production is exported; Britain and the United States alone account for 40% of those sales.

History

The distillation of wine to make spirits, practised in the region since the 16C, became generalised in the early 17C. The local vintners at first distilled just the wines that did not travel well but later realised that the process could help turn-over, reduce excise duties and facilitate storage (between seven and ten barrels of wine are used to make one barrel of cognac). The taste for the resulting *eau-de-vie* (spirit) spread and it began to be exported, like the wines before it, to the countries in the north of Europe as an adjunct to the salt trade.

Much of the wine trade at that time was in the hands of the Dutch – who, learning that the people of Charentes burned their wine, dubbed the result *brandewijn* (burnt wine). From this the English coined the word brandy, which has been used in the Anglo-Saxon world ever since. In France the spirit took the name of the town where it was first commercialised, Cognac.

From Cognac the barges and tenders laden with barrels sailed down the River Charente to Tonnay-Charente and La Rochelle, where the cargo was trans-ferred to full-rigged merchantmen bound either for northern Europe or for the colonies. In the late 17C and early 18C, brandy became increasingly popular in London society and as the Dutch lost commercial supremacy of the Cognac market, English merchants and traders began to play a stronger role in the pro-motion of the drink; the names of several famous Cognac brands still have an Anglo-Saxon ring about them.

Ruined by the devastating outbreak of phylloxera (American aphids) in the 19C, the Cognac vineyards were replanted by the burghers of Cognac, who had them-selves escaped ruin because of the huge stocks they held in store ageing.

The vineyards

Almost 90 000ha/222 400 acres are planted with vines, most of which are the Ugni Blanc variety (incorrectly termed St-Émilion des Charentes in the region). The vineyards are planted in an area of temperate climate – wet in winter, sunny in summer – and chalky soil similar to that found in the Champagne region, east of Paris. The finest Cognac, known as Grande Champagne, is produced from vines planted in the centre of this region, where the chalkiest soil is found; the other five classified *crus* or growths – producing more full-bodied and highly flavoured brandies – radiate outwards from this area.

Development of Cognac

Distilling is simply a means of concentrating the strength and flavour of any alcoholic drink by removing most of the water content. The technique stems from the fact that alcohol in chemical terms is more volatile than water: it boils at a lower temperature. All the alcohol and most of the aromatic elements in a heated wine will therefore evaporate long before the water boils. If this vapour is collected and condensed, the resulting liquid will contain virtually all the alcohol, certain other volatile elements – known as the congenerics – and very little water.

The system of distilling first came west with the Arabs in the 14C (the Arabic term al embic is the root of the French *alambic* – a still – and *al kohol* is the root of alcohol). The cognac distillation process consists of two stages. During the first distillation, which lasts for about 8hr, the wine is heated in a copper Charentais still to produce a liquid containing 25-35% alcohol, known as the **brouillis**. This liquid is then passed back into the still for a period of about 12hrs to produce a clear liquid, which has a maximum alcohol content of 72%. During the distillation process vapours compressed in the still head pass through the swan's neck into a condensing coil, which cools the vapours to produce the liquid.

The brandy, fiery but colourless when it leaves the still, is only faintly flavoured; all its character is derived from the maturing process, which takes place in barrels left in the darkness of the producer's well-aired *chais* (stores). Here the pale oak of these barrels, brought from the hills of the Limousin, stimulates the oxidization of the spirit, adds tannin and the characteristic amber colour of the brandy. The incredible amount of evaporation from the barrels is equivalent to the loss of 12 million bottles of spirit every year, referred to as the "angels' share". Finally, the spirit is diluted with distilled water to the accepted legal strength for the market. It is cut and blended with brandies of different ages, from different crus, and sugar and caramel are added to obtain the required colour, until a consistent quality is arrived at with characteristics recognizable as typical of a particular brand.

There are several different categories of cognac, classified according to the length of time they have spent maturing in the oak casks.

The three-star label signifies a brandy of normal quality, between five and nine years of age. The acronyms VO (Very Old) and VSOP (Very Special Old Pale) apply to cognacs aged on average between 12 and 20 years. The terms Vieille Réserve, Grande Réserve, Royal, Vieux, XO, Napoleon, Extra etc are used to distinguish cognacs that are 20 to 40 years old or even older. The words Fine Champagne on the label identify a cognac that is a blend of the Grande and Petite Champagne growths.

Armagnac

Armagnac is very different from cognac both in style and in the technique used to make it. This spirit should be velvety

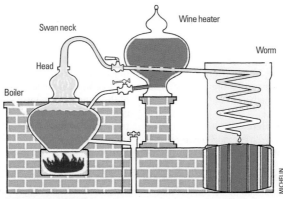

A Charentais Pot Still

smooth, dry and with a pungent smell; it is considered to have less finesse than cognac.

The region legally permitted to sell its products under the name "Armagnac" extends over an area of 35 000ha/ 35sq mi, which is roughly triangular in shape. This area is divided into three sections: **Haut-Armagnac** (Upper Armagnac, the hilly region of Auch) in the east; **Ténarèze** (around Condom) in the centre; and **Bas-Armagnac** (Lower Armagnac, the Eauze region) in the west. Armagnac from Ténarèze is full and rich in flavour, whereas the brandy made in Bas-Armagnac has a more fruity character. Only white wines made from 10 approved varieties of vine may be distilled to make Armagnac, and their common characteristic is a strong, fixed level of acidity. The most popular of these grapes are the Ugni Blanc and the Folle-Blanche varieties (known as Gros Plant in the Nantes area).

Armagnac is distilled in a sort of double boiler, at a much lower temperature than cognac. This results in a stronger flavour and aroma which, combined with the effect of the sappy black oak casks in which it is stored, adds character; it also matures faster than cognac.

Like cognac, each brand of Armagnac has its expert *maître de chai,* the Master Blender who creates the finished product with its particular identity.

Fortified Wines and Aperitifs

Floc

Floc is the old Gascon word for flower. Floc de Gascogne – a fortified wine between 16° and 18°, about the strength of port or sherry – is either red or white and is drunk chilled as an aperitif. It is made from selected wines grown in the region of the Armagnac *appellation* and is a blend of the must from these wines with Armagnac of more than 52°. The aperitif is aged in oak barrels.

Pousse-rapière

Also drunk as an aperitif, Pousse-rapière was invented in the 16C at Château Monluc, near the town of Condom, by Marshal Blaise de Monluc, an army commander and man of letters. It is made from Armagnac mixed with fruit. Add it to dry sparkling wine for an excellent cocktail!

Pineau des Charentes

This is a fortified aperitif wine, classified *appellation d'origine contrôlée* and produced in the same area as Cognac; it is made in both red and rosé forms, and it should be served chilled.

The aperitif was created by accident in the 16C, when a wine grower accidently poured grape juice into a barrel which still had some cognac left in the bottom. He was agreeably surprised, some years later, to discover in the barrel a strong wine that was smooth, heady and deliciously fruity.

Pineau is produced from the same growths as Cognac. The grape juices utilised before the *mutage* (the addition of Cognac) should have an alcoholic content of 10%. After the *mutage* the strength of the drink should be at least 16.5%. The blend is then transferred to oak casks and kept for several months in dark stores.

When it has sufficiently matured, it is submitted to an official Commission of Tasters who will decide whether or not it merits the *appellation* Pineau des Charentes.

Pineau sells very well in France and is exported to Belgium, Canada, Germany, Britain, Luxembourg and the United States.

The Basque Country

TOPOGRAPHY

The landscape of the Basque Country (Pays Basque) presents a dramatic contrast with that of Bordeaux and the moors to the north. Suddenly, there are mountains all around and the cliffs and rugged rocks along the coast are a complete contrast to the long, level beaches of the Landes. The Basque hinterland consists of green valleys dotted with traditional white houses. The Basque Country is one of the most distinctive regions in France.

The geology of the Basque region seems somewhat chaotic, marked by the last collapse of the folds of the Pyrenees. The valleys are full of winding roads making

Spanish or French name and its Basque equivalent

Bayonne/Baiona
Biarritz/Miarritze
Bilbao/Bilbo
Hasparren/Hazparne
Mauléon/Maule
Pamplona/Iruña
St-Jean-de-Luz/Donibane-Lohizun

St-Étienne-de-Baïgorry/Baigorri
St-Jean-Pied-de-Port/Donibane-Garazi
St-Palais/Donapaleu
San Sebastián-Donostia
Tardets-Sorholus/Atharratze-Sorholüze
Ustaritz/Uztaritze

communications between them difficult. One 17C chronicler described it as "very bumpy country". This partly explains the former division of the country into small states, each with its separate identity. The seven Basque provinces nevertheless share a unique linguistic and cultural heritage, on both the French and Spanish sides of the Pyrenees. Their common motto, in the Basque language, is *Zaspiak-bat* – Seven-in-One.

This guide describes the three provinces on the northern side of the border, those in the French sector of the Basque Country: **Le Labourd, La Basse Navarre** (Lower Navarre) and **La Soule.**

MYSTERIOUS ORIGINS

The origins of the Basque people and their common tongue has always been an enigma. All that is known for certain is that they were driven out of the Ebro Valley in Spain by the Visigoths and founded the kingdom of Vasconia in the western Pyrenees. The Vascons of the plain then intermarried with the local peoples of Aquitaine and became Gascons. Those who remained in the mountains fiercely safeguarded their own traditions and their language, **Euskara,** which binds the race together.

BASQUE AUTONOMY AND NATIONALISM

In the 9C, Iñigo Arista founded the Basque dynasty and became king of Pamplona. Two centuries later, Sancha the Great ascended to the throne of Pamplona and reunited the Basques on either side of the Pyrenees. This is where the history of the Basque Country begins, intimately linked to that of both Spain and France. Before the French Revolution, the French Basque provinces held on to their political autonomy. Leaders from each village met to discuss territorial matters, after which each province would hold an assembly. Royal emissaries regularly consulted these assemblies before making political decisions.

The French Revolution in 1789 brought an end to these special rights and the three French Basque provinces joined Béarn to form the Basses-Pyrénées *département*.

At the end of the 19C, the Spanish Basques were quick to join the great nationalist movement which was spreading throughout Europe. In 1895, **Sabino Arana Goiri** (1865-1903) founded the **Partido Nacionalista Vasco** (Basque Nationalist Party) in Bilbao. His aim was to reunite the seven Basque provinces in France and Spain and form one confederate state

The Basques Go to the Americas

Unable to partake in their father's estate, younger children often left to seek their fortune elsewhere, emigrating in particular to Latin America (Argentina, Uruguay, Paraguay, then Chile, Colombia and Mexico). During the 19C, 90 000 French Basques travelled across the Atlantic where they raised animals, exported wool, cut wood and traded in timber, just as they had done in their homeland. Having made their fortune, the **Americanuaks** returned to their native country or encouraged their descendants to join them.

From the turn of the century until 1960, the Basques emigrated to the United States, and more especially, California. Most of them were shepherds from Basse Navarre. With the help of an immigration agency, they went to tend sheep in the Rocky Mountains, where they had to endure far harsher weather conditions than they had known in the Basque Country. Some remained, totalling 43 140 in 1980. Although they are now a part of American society, they have been careful to keep up their old traditions.

which he first called Euskeria, changing it in 1896 to **Euskadi,** the name still used today by the Basque Separatist Movement. In 1894, Arana designed the **Ikurrina** – a red flag with two green and white crosses. Autonomy was granted to the three Spanish Basque provinces on 11 October 1936, in exchange for Republican support against Franco's followers during the Spanish Civil War. In 1937, however, the new Basque government was suppressed in Guernica, and Franco's regime set out to repress and persecute Basque culture. This was the beginning of the ETA *(Euskadi Ta Askatasuna* meaning Basque country and liberty), the underground armed separatist movement. After Franco's death, the Spanish Basque Country gained greater autonomy and in 1978 became Euskadi.

BASQUE HOUSES

The traditional houses in Labourd, perhaps the most attractive in the Basque Country, have inspired the design of many suburban villas and holiday homes. The exposed wooden framework, usually painted a reddish-brown, contrasts with the original walls of cob (compressed loam, clay or chalk reinforced with straw) coated with whitewashed rough cast. Houses are east-facing and are sheltered from rain, brought by the westerly winds from the Atlantic, by a huge overhanging tiled roof.

The houses in Basse (Lower) Navarre have a stone framework and semicircular balconies. The darker, slate roofs found in La Soule are an indication of the region's proximity to the Béarn region. Basque houses all share the characteristic white finish, and many proudly carry over their front doors the date of their construction or their owner's name. Nowhere else is the family so closely connected with the home.

Before the French Revolution, furniture, the right to use common land, church rights (the place occupied in church determined one's social status) and burial rights were attached to the house, which was a veritable economic and social entity passed down from generation to generation. The master of the household, the **etcheko jaun,** had ultimate authority and his main concern was to safeguard the family inheritance. The house was left to the son or daughter designated by the father as the eldest child.

A BASQUE TRILOGY: TOWN HALL/CHURCH/PELOTA COURT

The town hall, the church and the *pelote* court are the three focal points of Basque community life. They are all centred around the main square at the heart of village life. The **Basque church** plays a fundamental role, and the village is symbolically constructed around it. Many worshippers attend daily church services, usually celebrated in the Basque language.

The traditional game of *pelote basque*, played against a high, orange-coloured wall or **fronton,** is very popular among the men and boys all over the region. One version, known as *le grand chistera* (the name of the long wicker scoop strapped to one arm), is the most frequently played in official competitions and tourist exhibitions. The ball is flung against the fronton wall and caught up immediately or after a single rebound, and flung back. In professional games, it is not uncommon for the hard ball, covered with goatskin, to travel at speeds of 240kph/150mph!

A more recent variation, *la cesta punta,* has gained fans. This is the jai alai *(jai alai* comes from the Basque for merry festival) played in Latin America, against three walls (front, left and back). Points are marked by hitting the ball between vertical lines marked on the left wall. Spectators sit on the open side, with the front wall to their right, the left wall in front of them, and the back wall on their left.

There are also older, subtler variations, which some traditionalists prefer, including *yokogarbi* (with a small glove) and barehanded pelota. Different games are played by teams of three or two, or one-on-one. In the *pasaka* game, players face each other across a net, as in tennis, and wear gloves. And in all the small villages in the Basque Country, wherever you see a fronton, there will always be boys with their *palas* (wooden rackets) practising the sport.

LA FORCE BASQUE

If you attend a local fair, you may witness competitions between the men of neighbouring villages. There are eight established tests of strength, performed by teams of 12; each team member has his own special prowess. The feats they perform include spinning a 350kg/770lb wagon around with one hand, chopping or sawing tree trunks at top speed, running a race with a sack weighing 80kg/176lb slung across the shoulders – all concluding with a great game of tug-of-war between the teams.

FOLKLORE

The Basque people have a rich tradition of dancing, singing and communal activities. The young men – most of the

Basque tombstone

traditional dances do not include female partners – travel from village to village for local festivities.

The dances are numerous and complex. They are generally accompanied by a tchirulä (three-holed ocarina or flute) and a *ttun-ttun* (small drum) or a stringed tambourine, though an accordion, cornet or clarinet are sometimes used. The famous Basque leaps (danced by men only) have many different steps. The striking contrast between the stillness of the torso accompanied by an expressionless face, and the incredibly agile leg movements, is common to all of them.

The **Fandango,** a dance described as "both chaste and passionate", refers to man's eternal pursuit of his female ideal. The movements of the woman's arms and the upper part of her body harmonise with alternating rhythms representing invitation and flight.

For the celebrated "Wineglass Dance", the fleet-footed men from La Soule wear dazzling costumes. The *zamalzain* (a dancer who appears, in a wicker frame, as both a horse and its rider) and the other dancers perform complicated steps around a glass of wine placed on the ground. Each of the dancers stand on the glass for a fraction of a second, without breaking it or spilling a drop of its contents.

Basque songs are haunting melodies with lyrics inspired by everyday life (in much the same way as the American Blues). French Basques sometimes sing *Guernikako Arbola* (The Tree of Guernica), the sacred song of the Spanish Basques which has practically become their national anthem. In it, the Oak of Guernica – the Basque village devastated by Fascist air raids during the Spanish Civil War and immortalised by Picasso – symbolises *fueros*, or local freedom.

Food and Drink

Visitors to the Atlantic Coast region of France have a rich variety of choice local products to enjoy.

All along the coast itself good, fresh seafood is available whereas inland, in Poitou and the Charentes, the "simple, honest and direct, even rustic" cuisine – according to the great chef Curnonsky (1872-1956) – is based on fine, fresh ingredients and careful preparation. In the Bordeaux region the accent is naturally on wines and wine sauces.

HORS-D'ŒUVRES

For lovers of seafood the obvious starter must be oysters from Arcachon or Marennes, or perhaps mussels from Aiguillon; *pibales* (elvers) from the Gironde, either grilled or *à la ravigote* (with a highly seasoned white sauce) are a delicious alternative.

Those who prefer *charcuterie* might like to try the famous Bayonne ham or the ham from Poitou, or such Basque specialities as **loukinkos** (miniature garlic sausages) and **tripotcha,** a mutton boudin or blood sausage not unlike a small black pudding. Gourmets will also delight in the rich *foies gras* (prepared goose and duck livers) of Gers and the Landes.

A glass of chilled Pineau des Charentes may be taken as an aperitif or savoured with *foie gras,* whereas a chilled white wine such as a Graves or an Entre-Deux-Mers served at 8° to 10°C is a delightful accompaniment to oysters, fish, crustaceans and other shellfish.

FISH DISHES

This area favoured with an abundance of water – both fresh and salt – offers the choice of sole or turbot from the *pertuis* (straits), fresh sardines from Royan or Les Sables d'Olonne, stuffed carp in the Poitou fashion or **chipirones** – tiny cuttlefish, stuffed or cooked in a casserole.

Near Bordeaux a wide range of fish is caught in the Gironde estuary, including shad, smelt, salmon, sturgeon, eels and lamprey.

Seafood platter

D. Mar/MICHELIN

B. Kaufmann/MICHELIN

Espelette peppers and Basque charcuterie

MEAT, POULTRY AND VEGETABLES

The quality of meat in the region, whether it be a *chevreau* (young goat), Charmoise mutton or lamb from Pauillac, is invariably excellent. Many dishes around Bordeaux are served with a wine sauce; tender steaks accompanied by this sauce will be described on the menu as *à la Bordelaise*.

The superb quality of vegetables grown in Charentes help form the base for the delicious *pot-au-feu* (beef stew) known locally as **le farci;** the local broad beans, haricots, peas and Chinese cabbage can equally well be cooked *à la crème* (with cream) or with *beurre de Surgères* (a butter sauce).

Poultry specialities include *poule-au-pot* (chicken stew), Poitou goose with chestnuts, Challans duck and green peas, Barbezieux capon or chicken, and wood-pigeon *salmi* (casserole or ragout). Duck, if it is not conserved in its own fat (the delicious *confit de canard*), may be roasted or served as a *magret* (slices of breast).

Red wines from Médoc or Graves, served cool (cellar temperature) are an ideal complement to poultry, white meat and light dishes, while those from St-Émilion, Pomerol or Fronsac, served at room tempera-ture, are wonderful accompaniments to game, red meat, mushrooms and cheese.

CHEESE

In the Poitou, Vendée and Charentes regions it is normal to start off the dessert course with cheeses, for the local varieties are essentially unsalted cottage cheeses made from curdled milk or cream which can be taken with sugar if desired. These include **Caillebote d'Aunis,** a crustless sheep's cheese (sometimes made with goats' or cows' milk), and **Jonchée niortaise,** a goats' cheese served on a rush platter. Equally delicious is the Poitou **Chabichou,** another strongly-flavoured goats' cheese. The sheep's cheeses of the Basque Country and Béarn remain characteristic local products. A traditional way to finish a meal in the Basque Country is with a slice of cheese topped with cherry preserves from Itxassou.

FRUIT AND DESSERT

Delicious Charentais melon is served in the summer months as a dessert, as are peaches and plums from the valley of the Garonne, or succulent prunes steeped in Armagnac. Baked desserts include Poitou cheesecake *(tourteau fromager)*, macaroons from St-Émilion, Charentais gâteau, and *clafoutis* (dark cherries baked in a sweet batter). Sweetmeats include Poitiers *nougâtines,* chocolate *marguerites* and *duchesses* from Angoulême, and angelica-based sweets from Niort.

The exquisite dessert wines of Sauternes, Barsac, Ste-Croix-du-Mont and Loupiac, served very cold (5°C), are the perfect accompaniment to sweet dishes; a fine cognac makes an excellent digestive.

A TASTE OF THE REGION

A Rare Treat

Authorities on Bordelais cooking agree that a genuine **entrecôte bordelaise** is hard to find. First of all, it must be grilled over two different sorts of dried clippings *(sarments)* from the Bordeaux vineyards.

- Begin with Cabernet Sauvignon branches, which burn at a high temperature, for searing the meat.

- Grill the steak on both sides until the juice begins to appear on the surface.

- As the juice rises, toss on a bunch of twigs from Merlot vines, which add a subtle smoky flavour.

- Top off the steak with fresh chopped shallots.

The ideal side dish is a generous helping of the wild mushrooms known as *cèpes*, sprinkled with finely chopped garlic and parsley. The traditional preparation *Boletus edulis* mushroom is an exact science. Lightly grill the mushrooms to remove excess moisture, separate the cap from the stem, make a small cut in each cap with the point of a knife, then poach the caps in peanut oil (this releases the tannin).

Nowadays, the steak is usually served with a wine-based sauce, although this was most likely the invention of 19C Parisian chefs. Culinary historians tell us that the *entrcôte* steak was introduced to France by the English in the late 18C. Previous to that, the vintners and winegrowers of Bordeaux made their special dish with the meat of vineyard rodents who had grown plump and tasty amid the rows of ripening grapes.

À la Basquaise

Chicken and tuna dishes are frequently listed on menus as "in the Basque style." The term does not appear in French cookbooks before the early 20C, but seems to refer to chicken or fish cooked in a thick, orange-red sauce consisting mainly of tomatoes and red peppers. Another regional tomato-based sauce is **piperade,** which makes excellent use of the moderately hot, thin red peppers that festoon villages around Espelette (dried ground peppers can be purchased in the region and substituted for fresh ones, or use any fresh chili peppers).

- Skin four large sweet red, yellow and green peppers; remove the cores and cut the peppers into strips.

- Heat 60ml/¼ cup of olive oil in a heavy pan; sauté a sliced onion until it is tender.

- Add the pepper strips, four large peeled tomatoes (cut into chunks), chopped garlic to taste, one half of a hot pepper, a bay leaf and a sprig of thyme.

- Cook this aromatic mixture over a low flame for at least 30 minutes, or until it reaches the desired thickness, stirring regularly.

- Salt to taste.

- *Piperade* is especially good added to an omelette as it begins to set. Mix it in gently with the eggs, the fold the omelette over while it is still a bit runny.

For the best little places, follow the leader.

Looking for the latest news on today's best hotels and restaurants? Pick up the Michelin Guide and look for the Bib Gourmand and Bib Hotel symbols. With 45,000 addresses in Europe, in every category and price range, the perfect place to dine or stay is never far away.

Point du Devin, Île de Noirmoutierx

B. Kaufmann/MICHELIN

AGEN★
POPULATION 69 488
MICHELIN MAP 336: F-4

Agen sprawls across the fertile plain between the River Garonne and the Ermitage Hills. This modern, well-planned town has wide avenues and the impressive green expanse of Esplanade du Gravier. Midway between Bordeaux and Toulouse, Agen is an economic centre for the Middle Garonne region. Its practical location has made it an important market for fruit and vegetables, especially peaches, Chasselas (white) grapes and plums. **Pruneaux d'Agen,** the best-known prunes in France, are dried from local plums. They are often steeped in brandy.

- ℹ **Information:** 107 bd Carnot, 47000 AGEN. ☎05 53 47 36 09; www.ot-agen.org.
- ▶ **Orient Yourself**: Either the A 62 or the N 113 (Bordeaux-Toulouse) is the most direct route into the town. If you have time, follow the D roads through the attractive countryside surrounding Agen. The canal latéral à la Garonne runs to the north of the town and the River Garonne to the west. The busy town centre is formed by the intersection of Boulevard de la République with Boulevard Carnot, and the small streets in the surrounding area.
- 🅿 **Parking**: There are several car parks on the outskirts of the town centre *(see map).*
- 🚫 **Don't Miss**: The Musée des Beaux-Arts; rue Beauville; Pierre-Boisson confectionery for an introduction to the famous Agen prunes, including a tasting.
- 🕐 **Organising Your Time**: Allow half a day to explore the old town and visit the Musée des Beaux-Arts *(open all day; closed Tue).* Good choice of boat trips in summer.
- 📷 **Especially for Kids**: Culture and fun at the Musée des Beaux-Arts; the Walibi Aquitaine amusement park; pony riding in Les Vallons des Marennes (👶 *see Address Book).*
- 👶 **Also See**: NÉRAC, VILLENEUVE-SUR-LOT.

A Bit of History

Artists and Scholars
Leading lights of the Renaissance were particularly prominent in Agen. **Matteo Bandello** (1485-1561), monk, diplomat and courtier, banished from Milan by papal decree after the publication of his scandalous stories in the style of Boccaccio, found peace and tranquillity as an exile on the banks of the Garonne. He later became Bishop of Agen.

Julius Caesar Scaligero (1484-1558), born in Padua but settled in Agen, brought fame to his adopted home with his sparkling personality, extensive learning and influence on many literary figures. His tenth son, Joseph Justus Scaligero (1540-1609), born in Agen, was an eminent philologist, humanist and Protestant philosopher.

Old-fashioned prune box

A. Thuillier/MICHELIN

Walking Tours

Old Town

2hrs. Start from place Dr-Pierre-Esquirol.

Place Docteur-Pierre-Esquirol
The square, named after a former Mayor of Agen, is surrounded by the town hall (the office of the provincial governor in the 17C), Ducourneau Theatre, built at

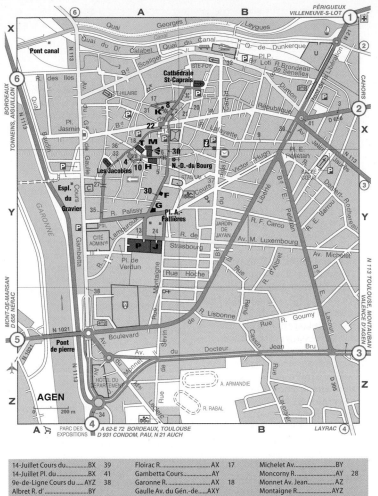

AGEN

Address Book

PRACTICAL INFORMATION

GUIDED TOURS

☞ *Contact the tourist office for times of guided tours of the town.*

WHERE TO STAY

☝ *For coin ranges, see the Legend on the cover flap*

⊜**Régina Hôtel** – *139 bd Carnot* – ☎*05 53 47 07 97* – *reginagen@wanadoo.fr* – 🅿 *– 24 rooms*. This central hotel has modern comfortable facilities. Pretty colours provide each room with a personal touch; many of them are spacious and all have double-glazed windows. There is a Breton fresco adorning the hall.

⊜⊜**Atlantic Hôtel** – *133 av. Jean-Jaurès – E of Agen via the N 113* – ☎*05 53 96 16 56* – *atlantic.hotel@wanadoo.fr* – *closed 23 Dec-3 Jan* – 🅿 *– 44 rooms*. This hotel built in the 1970s behind a petrol station is a short distance from centre city. Don't let the surroundings daunt you – the rooms are pleasant and the more recent ones are modern and sizable. Breakfast is by the pool.

⊜⊜**Chambre d'hôte Domaine de Bernou** – *47340 La Croix-Blanche – 14km/ 9mi N of Agen along the Villeneuve-sur-Lot road* – ☎*05 53 68 88 37 or 06 17 36 50 32* – *www.domainedebernou.com* – 🖨 *– reserv. recommended out of season – 3 rooms – meal* ⊜⊜. Built in 1780, in the middle of a large estate (25 ha/62 acres), this attractive mansion now houses a bed and breakfast, a riding school and a stud. The spacious guest rooms here are quiet and peaceful. Warm welcome and good food.

BARS AND CAFES

Place Jasmin – *Pl. Jasmin*. Noisy with conversation and the clinking of glasses and cutlery, this square houses a multitude of bars and brasseries whose terraces attract crowds of locals in the summer months. Don't miss the Bodega and its Thursday evening Latino music concerts.
Colonial Café – *10 av. du Gén.-de-Gaulle* – ☎*05 53 48 28 10* – *Mon-Tue 8am-3pm, Wed 8am-7pm – Thu-Sat 8am-2am – closed Sun and public holidays*. A former Agen rugby player, Gérald Mayout, runs this

friendly bar. Modern and bright, it attracts a clientele of all ages.

WHERE TO EAT

⊜**Fleurs des T** – *13 r. des Héros-de-la-Résistance* – ☎*05 53 47 32 83* – *closed for a week in Mar, a week in Aug, Sun except Nov-Dec*. This attractive tea room is the ideal place for a quick snack at lunchtime, an evening meal in summer, or tea, coffee and hot chocolate during the day. The tea room is on the first floor and a small shop on the ground floor sells gifts such as tea-pots and mugs.

⊜**Restaurant Oasis** – *46 r. Molinier* – ☎*05 53 66 89 33* – *closed evenings, Sun and public hols* – *reserv. recommended*. This little restaurant situated on a shopping street has a choice of two dining rooms, one small and modern and the other decorated in typical southern colours. The menu is deliberately limited – savoury quiches, plats du jour and pastries. Tea salon in the afternoon. Friendly welcome and reasonable prices.

⊜⊜**Margoton** – *52 r. Richard-Cœur-de-Lion* – ☎*05 53 48 11 55* – *closed 21-28 Feb, 15-30 Aug, 22 Dec-3 Jan, Sun evening from 1 Oct-30 Jun, Sat lunchtime, Sun evening and Mon from Jul-Sep*. Decorated with painted furniture and wooden panelling, this family-run restaurant has a warm, friendly atmosphere. Conveniently located near Agen's old town, the Margoton serves traditional, yet creative cuisine.

⊜⊜**L'Atelier** – *14 r. du Jeu-de-Paume* – ☎*05 53 87 89 22* – *restaurant.latelier@wanadoo.fr – closed 9-22 Aug, Sat lunchtime and Sun*. This former joiner's workshop is now a popular restaurant, which is especially busy at lunchtime, full of locals attracted here by the efficient service, good food and reasonable prices . The atmosphere is more relaxed in the evening, when diners take their time to savour the excellent regional cuisine, served and prepared with care.

⊜⊜⊜**Mariottat** – *25 r. L.-Vivent* – ☎*05 53 77 99 77* – *contact@restaurant-mariottat.com – closed Feb school holidays, Sat lunchtime, Sun evening and Mon*. This old 19C mansion, with its sculptured door pediment and slate roof, exudes character. Climb the handsome stone steps to reach the simply furnished dining rooms. Pleasant terrace under the trees. Appetizing cuisine prepared from fresh ingredients.

SPORT AND LEISURE

Méca Plus – Vélo et Oxygen – *18 av. du Général-de-Gaulle* – ☎*05 53 47 76 76* – *http://meca.plus.free.fr* – *open daily except Mon morning and Sun 9.30am-12.30pm and 2-7pm*. This is the only place that rents bicycles in Agen – mountain bikes and childrens' bicycles available.

Canoë-Kayak club de l'Agenais – *2 quai du Canal* – ☎*05 53 66 25 99* – *daily 9am-noon and 2-6pm, Sat-Sun by prior arrangement – closed 2 weeks in Sep, 2 weeks in Dec and public hols*. This club rents kayaks and organises water trips. Open to all, including novices, it also offers beginners' lessons.

Poney-club de Darel en Agenais – *Darel – 7.5 km/4.5 mi NE of Agen via D656 – 47480 Pont-du-Casse* – ☎*05 53 96 90 33 – Mon-Sat 8am-noon and 2-7pm – closed public hols*. Located on the hills outside Agen, this centre organises lessons and horse or pony rides.

Les Vallons de Marennes – *47340 Laroque-Timbaut* – ☎*05 53 95 97 32* – *open 15 Jun-15 Sep 10am-7pm; out of season by prior arrangement*. It's worth taking a whole day to make the most of the various activities available on this farm (22ha/55 acres), with its 800 animals, arboretum and nature trails. A great day

out for children. Picnic area and snack bar on site.

Locaboat Plaisance – *Port de la Gare du Pin* – ☎*05 53 66 00 74* – *www.locaboat. com* – *Mar-Oct Mon-Sat 8am-noon and 1.30pm-7pm; Nov-Feb Mon-Thu 8am-noon and 1.30-4.30pm – closed Dec*. Discover the region's rivers and canals by hiring a boat or a barge at the marina.

SHOPPING

Confiserie P. Boisson – *20 r. Grande-Horloge* – ☎*05 53 66 20 61* – *pierre. boissonsarl@wanadoo.fr* – *Mon-Sat 9am-12.30pm and 2pm-7.30pm, Sun and public hols: groups by prior arrangement*. The Boisson family has been manufacturing delightful confectionery from the prunes for which Agen is famous since 1835. Its success dates from 1876, when a pastry cook's boy was inspired to stuff prunes with filling. A free slide show tells the history of this illustrious lineage. Tastings.

MARKETS

Traditional markets – Open daily at the market hall; Wed, Sun at the Halle du Pin.

Farmers' markets – Sat morning on the Esplanade du Gravier and place des Laitiers; Wed morning and Sun morning at the Halle du Pin.

Organic market – Sat morning at place des Laitiers.

Marché au gras – Duck and goose products – Sat and Sun mornings Nov-Mar.

---

the beginning of the 20C, and the Fine Arts Museum.

Rue Beauville

The street is lined with restored medieval houses. Note, in particular the fine timber-framed building with corbels at no 1.

▶ *Turn right onto rue Richard-Cœur-de-Lion.*

At the intersection with rue Moncorny there is another half-timbered house.

▶ *Rue Garonne leads to place des Laitiers.*

Place des Laitiers

This square, with its arcades and shops, lies at the heart of the oldest part of the town which has been a major trading place since the Middle-Ages. In the square, note the contemporary sculpture of a pilgrim on the Way of St James, recognisable from the scallop shell that he is wearing.

▶ *Cross boulevard de la République and turn left onto rue Puits-du-Saumon.*

Maison du Sénéchal

The upper storey of this 14C steward's house has fine Gothic windows. On the ground floor, various items from the Fine Arts Museum (sarcophagi, 17C busts, the

A dedicated potter

Bernard Palissy (1510-90), born locally, wrote technical and philosophical treatises, though he is better known as a glassblower and potter. He worked with endless determination and at great personal sacrifice (he allegedly burnt his own furniture to fuel his furnaces) and rediscovered the art of enamelling. He created a type of pottery halfway between Italian faience and glazed earthenware. His rustic bowls, decorated with fruit, plants and animals in coloured relief were extremely successful.

bell from the old town hall) are on display behind a glass door.

Rue des Cornières

Half-timbered houses (nos 13, 17 and 19) and stone houses built over arcades make this busy shopping street very picturesque.

▶ *Turn right onto rue Floirac then follow rue des Cornières to place de la cathédrale.*

Cathédrale St-Caprais

This former collegiate church, founded in the 11C, was granted the status of cathedral in 1802. Its most remarkable feature is the 12C east end, which comprises an apse flanked by three radiating chapels each pierced by semicircular arched windows with scrolled corbels in the form of carved human and animal heads. The interior, restored in the 19C, is decorated with frescoes which depict the patron saints of Agen. There is a view of the east end from place Raspail.

▶ *Return to rue des Cornières then take rue Banabéra on the left.*

On the corner of rue Jacquard is a charming timber-framed house.

▶ *Cross boulevard de la République in the direction of the covered market which you then leave on the left before reaching rue Montesquieu.*

Rue Montesquieu

Note the picturesque 13C-14C church, **Notre-Dame-du-Bourg**, with its brick and stone construction and belfry-wall. **Hôtel Escouloubre** is 18C.

Place Armand-Fallières

The préfecture, the 18C former bishop's palace, stands next to the imposing 19C law courts in this shady square planted with magnolias and cedar trees. The 18C Hôtel Lacépède on the north side houses the public library.

▶ *Turn left onto rue Palissy, right onto rue Louis-Vivent then follow rue Richard-Cœur-de-Lion opposite.*

Église des Jacobins

The only remains of a convent founded by the Dominicans in the 13C. The vast, brick Gothic building has two identical naves separated by circular pillars and a flat chevet. Exhibitions are hosted in the church

▶ *Rue Beauville on the right leads back to place Dr-Pierre-Esquirol.*

Along the Garonne

The banks of the River Garonne and of the canal offer relaxing walks.

Esplanade du Gravier

Plane trees and lawns on either side of a circular pond make this the most popular walk along the Garonne. The footbridge provides a good view of the river, town and bridge-canal.

On the right is the **Pont Canal**, a 500m/547yd long bridge with 25 arches, which carries the Canal Latéral across the Garonne.

The **stone bridge** on the left was commissioned by Napoleon when he stayed in Agen.

Sights

Musée des Beaux-Arts★★

Place du Dr-Esquirol. ⊙*Open daily except Tue 10am- 6pm.* ⊙*Closed 1 Jan, 1 May, 1 Nov, 25 Dec.* ⊕*3. 70€. No charge on the*

first Sunday of the month. ☎05 53 69 47 23; www.ville-agen.fr/musee.

The Fine Arts Museum is made up of elegant 16C and 17C mansions – Vaurs, Vergès, Monluc and Estrades – which, though their interiors have been reorganised to make room for the exhibits, have largely retained their original façades.

Medieval archaeology – Romanesque and Gothic capitals carved with leaves and fantastic animals adorn the walls of one of the rooms. The main exhibit is the **tomb of Étienne de Dufort** and his wife. Note also the 16C Brussels tapestry titled The Month of March, and various funerary stones.

Gallo-Roman archaeology – Among the mosaics, amphorae and small bronzes of this section stands the museum's finest exhibit, the **Vénus de Mas**. This 1C BC Greek marble statue, discovered near Mas d'Agenais in the 19C, is noted for its elegant contours, perfect proportions and the graceful flow of its draperies.

War and hunting – In a neighbouring room, which features an impressive Renaissance chimney-piece, are exhibits based on the themes of War and Hunting. Ancient weapons are on display. The 17C tapestry, The Stag Hunt, is after a cartoon by Van Orley, and the 15C marble profile of a woman is attributed to Mino da Fiesole. Nearby stands a large bronze Minotaur by a local artist, François-Xavier Lalanne.

Prehistoric and mineral collections – The cellars of Hôtel de Vaurs, once used as the local prison (note the chains and shackles still fixed to the walls), today house the museum's prehistoric collections, ranging from the most primitive stone implements, to more sophisticated stones from the Neolithic period, as well as a collection of minerals.

Paintings and decorative arts – A fine spiral staircase leads to the upper floors which house a collection of 16C and 17C French and foreign canvases. Most notable among them are The Temptation of St Anthony by Teniers the Elder and Portrait of a Man by Philippe de Champaigne. Also on view are displays of porcelain and 14C-19C **ceramics**, both French and foreign, including dishes by Bernard Palissy. On the same floor is a striking series of **cameos** (porcelain cameos set

in glass), on religious, historical and mythological themes, by Boudon de Saint-Amans (1774-1856). He was a local artist, also responsible for unique examples of earthenware designed to rival products from English porcelain factories.

The 18C paintings feature portraits by Greuze and a fine canvas, The Dying Page by Tiepolo. The highlight of this section, however, is a **series of five works by Goya** which were donated to the museum by a former Spanish ambassador. Note in particular the expressive Self Portrait, showing a keen, lively expression under rather heavy features.

Impressionism – Fine collection displayed on the first and second floors. French painting in the 19C is represented by Corot with his masterpiece, **L'Étang de Ville-d'Avray**, Courbet and Isabey, a collection of pre-Impressionists (numerous views by Boudin) and Impressionists (Lebourg, Caillebotte, Sisley, Guillaumin and Lebasque). Head of a Romanian Peasant Woman was the work of the Romanian artist Grigoresco. The 20C is ushered in by a Picabia, On the Banks of the Loing, unusual for its Impressionist flavour.

Docteur-Esquirol Room – This room houses paintings, furniture and Asiatic figurines. The paintings include two fine portraits by Clouet; and a fine Head of a Child by Greuze.

Excursions

Walibi Aquitaine★

4 km/2.6mi SW on the D 656, route de Neyrac, from the city centre. From the A 62 motorway, take exit 7 to Agen. ⏱Open daily mid-Jun to Aug, Sat-Sun and public hols mid-Apr to mid-Jun and Sep-Oct. ☜25.70€; children 21.70 €. ☎05 53 96 58 32; www.walibi.com.

This amusement park is perfect for a family outing, with a wide range of attractions for young and old. Younger children will enjoy the gentle carousel rides, while teenagers will want to try spinning above the ground on the Fandango chairs or rafting down the turbulent Raja River. Other popular entertainment includes a musical fountain sound and light show and a spectacular sea-lion show. For lunch, choose between a picnic or eating at the restaurant on site. Take the time to observe the two-hundred-year-old cedar trees and the rare birds of prey which can be seen around the castle.

Moirax
9km/5.6mi S.
The **church**★, which belonged to a priory of the Cluniac order founded in the 11C, is a fine example of 12C Romanesque architecture. The long edifice is surmounted by a conical pinnacle and a campanile over the west front. The most interesting decorative motifs are those adorning the east end and the apsidal chapels.

Inside, the forward part of the chancel is no doubt the most original: square at the base, it is octagonal higher up and is topped by a cupola. The capitals are decorated with foliage and figures (note Daniel in the lions' den, near the crossing on the left, and the original sin on the right). The statue of the Virgin Mary in the chancel, the stalls and the walnut panels in the aisles were carved by Jean Tournier (late 17C).

Layrac
The terrace of the place du Royal is surrounded by Notre-Dame church (12C) to the south and Saint-Martin church to the north, but the only vestige left of the Saint-Martin church is its steeple. It is worth stopping for a moment to admire the view of the River Gers running into the Garonne valley. When Notre-Dame church was last restored and the choir regained its original height, a fragment of a Romanesque mosaic was found. It represents Samson fighting the lion.

AINHOA★
8KM/5MI SW OF CAMBO-LES-BAINS
POPULATION 599
MICHELIN MAP 342: C-3

Ainhoa, a typical Basque village, grew up around a walled redoubt founded in the late 12C by monks of the Premonstratensian order as a staging post on the pilgrims' route to Santiago de Compostela. This brotherhood from northern France combined evangelism and work in their parish with a contemplative life. The D 20, which passes through the village, is one of the oldest pilgrimage and trade routes to Spain in the Nive-Nivelle region.

WHERE TO STAY
Hôtel-restaurant Etchartenea – ☎05 59 29 90 26 – *Dancharia – on the Spanish border.* This family-run restaurant has an attractive shady terrace overlooking the river. A short stroll over the bridge takes you across the border into Spain.

SHOPPING
Pierre-Oteiza – *Rue Principale, D 422* – ☎05 59 29 30 43 – *www.pierreoteiza.com – open daily 10am-11pm – closed 25 Dec, Jan and Mon in winter.* This small shop specialises in typical *"pie noir"* hams from the Vallée des Aldudes and other traditional Basque dishes.

Visit

Main street★
The picturesque main street is lined with 17C and 18C houses, their overhanging roofs, often asymmetric, covered with very old tiles.

The sunlit façades are freshly whitewashed each year for the Feast of St John, the shutters and half-timbering painted and the main beams sometimes embellished with inscriptions. The vast porches, known as lorios, decorating the front of houses, have retained the metal rings used to tie mules long ago, when Ainhoa was a stopover for merchants on their way to Spain.

Church

This traditional Basque church is notable for its two-tiered galleries, wooden ceiling and gilded woodwork in its chancel. The war memorial at the entrance to the cemetery bears the characteristic disk motif of Basque headstones.

Notre-Dame-de-l'Aubépine

Take the street to the left of the town hall and follow the red and white markers of the GR footpath – allow 2hrs round trip. Pilgrimage Whit Monday with mass cele- *brated in the Basque language at 10.30am. Mr Audiot.* ☎*05 59 29 90 16.*

This rocky path, which lies along the GR10 footpath, is a Stations of the Cross *(general view from Ainhoa)* leading to Notre-Dame-de-l'Aubépine, a tiny chapel perched on the side of Mont Ereby. The Virgin Mary is said to have appeared there in a hawthorn bush. Basque pilgrims flock here every year on Whit Monday. It offers a beautiful panoramic view of the harbour of St-Jean de-Luz and Socoa and the Spanish villages in the foothills of the lofty Navarrese mountains.

ÎLE D'AIX★
POPULATION 199
MICHELIN MAP 324: C-D 3

Île d'Aix (the final x is not pronounced) is a small island in the Atlantic, only 133ha/329 acres in area. It has a mild climate and clear skies, which combined with its attractive layout and impressive fortifications, make it an interesting place to visit. As the boat approaches Île d'Aix, sandy beaches and magnificent cliffs appear along the coast. Inland, pine trees, ilex and tamarisk, flourishing in the mild climate, give the landscape an almost Mediterranean air.

- 🚗 **Driving:** Motor traffic is restricted to service vehicles, which means that the island can only be explored on foot, by bike or barouche.
- ▶ **Orient Yourself**: The island is accessible by boat, from **Pointe de la Fumée** and, during the high season, from La Rochelle, Île d'Oléron and Île de Ré. The direct route *(30min)* offers interesting views northwards along the coast up to La Rochelle and out towards Île de Ré; westwards to the offshore forts of Enet and Boyard and to Île d'Oléron. Boats land at the jetty at Pointe Ste-Catherine, below Fort de la Rade citadel.

A Bit of History

Memories of Napoleon at the time of his downfall are an important part of this solitary island, still steeped in the past.

It was on Île d'Aix that **Napoleon Bonaparte** last stood on French soil. In July 1815, the frigate, which was supposed to take the exiled Emperor to America, was anchored off Fort Enet. Meanwhile a potentially threatening British naval force was cruising in the Antioche Straits, blocking the frigate's exit to the open sea.

The following day, Napoleon landed on Île d'Aix and visited the fortifications, to wild acclaim from the islanders and the garrison of 1 500 sailors (he had previously inspected the stronghold in 1808, at the height of his power). On his return to the ship, he learnt what options lay open to his guards. If combat with the British could be avoided, they would sail past to the ocean, and if not, they would discuss terms. Negotiations lasted three days, during which time the Emperor's envoys were assured (falsely) that he would be permitted to seek asylum in England. Finally, escape appearing impossible, Napoleon accepted the advice of his officers and decided to surrender himself to his adversaries.

On 12 July, Napoleon had gone ashore, again to stay with the garrison commander, and on 14 July he wrote his now-famous letter (€*see Musée Napoléonien*) to the Prince Regent in London. The next day he

Address Book

ACCESS

Regular service (30min) leaving from Fouras (Pointe de la Fumée). May-Oct 11.20€ (children aged 4-12: 7.70€); Jan-Apr and Nov-Dec 7.20€ (children aged 4-12: 5€). ☏08 20 16 00 17.

LEISURE ACTIVITIES

Bicycle hire – It is easy to find bikes for hire at the port or in the village. Trailers available for small children.

Horse-drawn carriage rides – ☏05 46 84 07 18. Apr-Sep. Look for the carriages on Place d'Austerlitz, where the horses wait patiently in the shade for customers. Tour with commentary lasts for 50min. Maximum 50 passengers per tour.

Swimming – Beaches on the island (most pleasant at high tide) do not have lifeguards. On the western side, there are long sandy beaches (from Anse de la Croix to La Batterie de Jamblet). There is a small beach on the eastern shore (Anse du Saillant), and attractive little coves to the NE (Les Sables Jaunes, Baby Plage), where holm oak trees provide shade.

SPECIALITIES

Oysters – These are sold by the basket (une bourriche d'huitres) from oyster shacks at the NE end of the town and at some fish shops in the centre (in season). **Atelier-Boutique de la Nacre** – Place de l'Eglise – ☏05 46 84 09 40 – Open 9.30am-12.30pm and 2-6pm – Closed Nov-Apr. This boutique sells items and souvenirs made from mother-of-pearl by local craftsmen.

---

donned the green uniform of a colonel in the Imperial Guard – the uniform he had worn at the Battle of Austerlitz – and embarked on a brig which was met by an admiral's barge. The barge then took him to the warship Bellerophon, where he was taken aboard. This was to be his last voyage, carrying him to exile on another small island, St Helena, where he was to end his days.

The Village

Wide streets intersecting at right angles, and a double line of fortifications separated by deep dykes, give the impression of a large town. However, the small church and single-storey whitewashed cottages surrounded by hollyhocks, reveal it as a small village where the sight of a motorised vehicle is still a rarity. From here, visitors

Typical white-washed cottages and hollyhocks

S. Sauvignier/MICHELIN

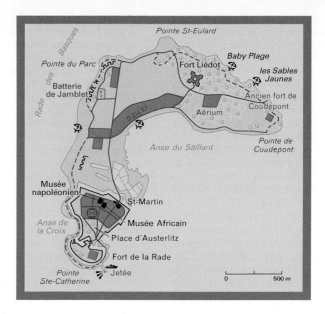

can tour the island on foot (*2hrs 30min*) or enjoy a horse-drawn carriage ride.

Place d'Austerlitz

At the mainland end of Pointe Ste-Catherine, a gate with a drawbridge leads to this pleasant open space, once the parade ground, with its shady walks between rows of fine cypress trees. Just beyond the drawbridge, on the right, stands the arcaded harbour office.

Fort de la Rade

This citadel overlooking the harbour was originally designed in 1699 by Vauban, the brilliant military architect. Work on the five bastions and ring of fortifications was completed in 1702 but 55 years later, most of it was destroyed by the British. The island's strategic importance was again recognised in 1793 by the powerful State Security Committee, although it was not until 1810 that Napoleon gave the order for rebuilding to start. Work was completed in 1837. The fort today is an isle within an island, completely surrounded by a wide, water-filled moat and a circle of anti-siege defences. There are two lighthouses on the fort. The jetty below provides a view of the massive Fort Boyard (3km/1.75mi away), rising straight up out of the sea.

Église St-Martin

This was once the church of a priory occupied by Benedictine monks from Cluny. All that remains today are the transept, apse and apsidal chapel. The 11C crypt has fine columns with foliate capitals.

Fort Liédot

During the 19C, Île d'Aix became a prison, and a variety of lodgers were housed within the walls of Fort Liédot, on the northern coast, including Russian prisoners from the Crimean War and the First World War, Prussian prisoners from the War of 1870 and convicts whose boat had foundered on the rocks on the way to Devil's Island. More recently Ben Bella, one of the leaders of Algeria's outlawed National Liberation Front (FLN), was detained here for seven years, along with his colleagues, during the Algerian War in the late 1950s and early 1960s.

Sights

Musée Napoléonien

⏲*Open Jun-Sep daily except Tue 9.30am-6pm (last admission 30min before closing); Apr-May and Oct daily except Tue 9.30am-*

12.30pm and 2- 6pm; Nov-Mar 9.30am-
12.30pm and 2-5pm. ◐Closed 1 May. ◉3€
(age 18-25: 2.30 €). No charge 1st Sunday
in the month. ☎05 46 84 66 40.

The museum (part of the Gourgaud Foundation) is housed in the building which
was constructed on Napoleon's orders in
1808, and where he took refuge in July
1815. It is one of the few buildings on the
island with an upper storey, surmounted
by the imperial eagle. Two Classical columns frame the entrance. Baron Gourgaud,
great-grandson of the Emperor's aide-de-
camp, bought the building in 1925 and
left it to the nation.

The 10 rooms contain memorabilia of
Bonaparte, his family and his entourage
– weapons, works of art, clothes, furniture,
documents, and portraits by Isabey, Gros,
Appiani and others. In the garden stands
an oak tree which was grafted to an elm
by Napoleon himself in 1808, and a Clas-
sical-style bust of the Emperor which
once served as a ship's figurehead.

Napoleon's room on the first floor is particularly evocative, as nothing in it has been
changed since the days when he stood
outside on the balcony, watching the
manœuvres of the British fleet through
his telescope. It was in this room that he
composed the famous letter to the Prince
Regent in London:

*"Faced with the factions dividing my
country and with the enmity of the
great powers of Europe, I have ended
my political career and I come, like*

*Themistocles, to seat myself at the
table of the British people. I place myself
under the protection of their laws and
the indulgence which I crave from your
Royal Highness as the most powerful,
the most steadfast and the most generous of my enemies."*

General Gourgaud was entrusted with
delivering the letter to London, but he was
refused permission to land at Plymouth.
Napoleon made the General a gift of the
document, and a facsimile of the Emperor's
rough draft of the letter is on view in the
museum.

Musée Africain

◐Open Jun-Sep 9.30am-6pm (last admission 30min before closing); Apr-May and
Oct daily except Tue 9.30am-12.30pm and
2-6pm; Nov-Mar daily except Tue 9.30am-
12.30pm and 2-5pm. ◐Closed 1 May.
◉3€ (age 18-25: 2.30 €). No charge 1st
Sunday in the month. ☎05 46 84 66 40.

This museum (another part of the Gourgaud Foundation) is housed in a former
army barracks. It displays ethnographic
and zoological items collected by Baron
Gourgaud in Africa between 1913 and
1931.

Slides are used to illustrate interesting
examples of African fauna. The white
dromedary ridden by Napoleon during
the Egyptian campaign was later taken
to the Jardin des Plantes in Paris and
stuffed after its death. It was transferred
to Île d'Aix in 1933.

ANGLES-SUR-L'ANGLIN★

POPULATION 365
MICHELIN MAP 322: L-4

The terraced village of Angle is sited above the River Anglin and beneath the
ruins of a castle. Like England, its names derives from Angles, a warlike tribe
from Germania that invaded Britain in the 5C. In the 9C, Charlemagne dispatched
the descendants of these northern peoples southwards, to settle on the banks
of a tributary of the River Gartempe, the Angla, which subsequently became
the Anglin. The inhabitants of Angles are called Anglais, also the French for English.
Les jours d'Angles, a highly prized form of drawn-thread embroidery, is still made
in the village today. Archaeological excavations carried out in neighbouring
rock shelters have unearthed important carvings dating from the Magdalenian
(Late Palaeolithic) Era.

🛈 **Information**: Le Bourg, 86260 ANGLES-SUR-L'ANGLIN. ☎05 49 48 86 87.

Ruins above the village

A Bit of History

A Cardinal Sin

Like the proverbial victim "hoisted on his own petard", **Cardinal Balue**, a native of Angles born in 1421, was condemned by Louis XI to be locked up in a *fillette*, a small, uncomfortable type of iron cage allegedly designed by the cardinal himself.

Balue came from a modest family but rapidly gained wealth and power, rising through the ranks of King's Chaplain, Financial Steward, Secretary of State to become Bishop of Evreux. Subsequently, he became Bishop of Angers, after which he was made Cardinal. Foolishly, Balue betrayed the King's confidence and sold state secrets to the Duke of Burgundy. Once discovered, he was sentenced to prison for treason. Eleven years later he was freed at the request of the Pope, emigrated to Rome, and lived another 11 years, showered with honours.

Sights

Site★

There is a splendid **view**★ of the village from the south-eastern end of the bluff where the castle stands, beside a roadside cross and a small Romanesque chapel. Beyond a breach in the cliff are what remains of the walls and towers of the old castle. To the north, on another promontory, the Romanesque belfry of the upper church rises above the roof tops, and at the foot of the escarpment, the River Anglin, with its reeds and water-lilies, winds peacefully between two rows of poplars. Beyond the turning wheel of an ancient water mill, a stone bridge leads to the Sainte-Croix quarter, where the former abbey church has a fine 13C doorway.

Castle ruins★

🕐*Open Jul-Aug daily except Tue 10.30am-12.30pm and 2.30-6.30pm; Apr-Jun and Sep-Oct, Sat 2.30-6.30pm, Sun and public hols 10.30am-12.30pm and 2.30-6.30pm.* 🎫*1.50€.* ☎*05 49 48 61 20.*

Angles Castle, an important stronghold in the Middle Ages due to its commanding position and the strength of its defences, was abandoned in the 18C. The Revolution (1789) added to its downfall as local builders were allowed to use the uninhabited castle as a stone quarry.

ANGOULÊME★★

POPULATION 43 171
MICHELIN MAP 324: K-6

Like many old towns, Angoulême is best explored on foot, with its labyrinth of narrow streets, attractive old buildings and the fine views from its ramparts.

Every year in January, a festival, created in 1974, crowns Angoulême as the world capital of the comic strip *(bande dessinée)*, a form of graphic art celebrated in the **Centre national de la bande dessinée et de l'image**, which includes a museum and a multimedia library.

▶ **Orient Yourself**: From the N 141, northwest of the town, there is a fine view of Angoulême and its impressive site above the River Charente. The town is divided into an upper town known as Le Plateau, built on a promontory and ringed by ramparts, and a lower town, which includes most of the outlying areas.

🅿 **Parking**: There are car parks dotted around the ramparts and near the town hall and tourist office (*see map*).

☺ **Don't Miss**: The façade of Cathédrale St-Pierre; the attractive narrow streets of the old town.

Kids **Especially for Kids**: Le Centre national de la bande desinée et de l'image; Swimming and watersports at the Base Nautique Eric Tabarly. (*see Address Book*).

👍 **Also See**: COGNAC, LA ROCHEFOUCAULD.

A Bit of History

Marguerite d'Angoulême

Marguerite de Valois, François I's sister, also known as **Marguerite des Marguerites**, was born in the town in 1492 and spent much of her youth here. She was a woman of great culture and learning – her *Heptameron,* a collection of stories in the style of Boccaccio, won her a permanent place in French literature. She was also famous for her fêtes and parties, and was very influential in court life. Her name lives on in two kinds of local confectionery: *marguerites* (a chocolate confection) and *duchesses*.

The two Balzacs

The local *lycée* is named after the author **Guez de Balzac** (1597-1654), who was born in Angoulême. A rigorous stylist, he was dubbed "the man who restored the French language." The other writer, **Honoré de Balzac** (1799-1850), the famous French author of *La Comédie Humaine* (The Human Comedy), was adopted by Angoulême and described the town in his famous work *Les Illusions Perdues* (Lost Illusions).

Upper Town Tour★★

It is possible to walk around the fortifications in an anti-clockwise direction.

▶ *Start this walk from place des Halles and aim for the northern section of the ramparts to admire the view.*

North Ramparts

Here there are impressive views over the river bridge, the suburb of St-Cybard, the valley of the River Charente and the industries dotted along it. In 1806, General Resnier (1728-1811), born in Angoulême, launched himself from the top of the Ladent Tower in a flying machine which he invented himself, and thereby became the first man to achieve a non-powered flight. However, since he broke his leg on landing, the General abandoned plans to exploit his invention which, it is said, was intended for a future airborne invasion of England by the Imperial Army.

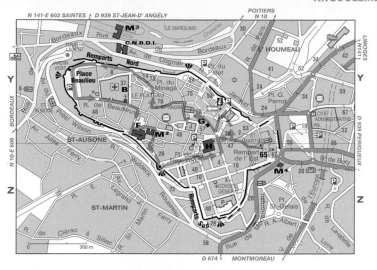

A plaque commemorates General Resnier and his attempt.

▶ *Retrace your steps along rue du Chat and follow rue de Genève on the left.*

Hôtel de ville
See SIGHTS.

▶ *Walk along rue de la Cloche-Verte.*

Note the Hôtel St-Simon at n° 15, with its fine Renaissance courtyard.

Hôtel St-Simon
FRAC Poitou-Charentes – *See SIGHTS.*

▶ *Continue straight on along rue St-André.*

In **square St-André**, note the mural entitled Souvenir of the 20C, after an original drawing by Yslaire. Farther on, the imposing neo-Classical façade of the law courts dominates the tree-lined place du Murier, giving the square a southern French feel.

▶ *Turn right onto rue Taillefer.*

Step inside St-André Church to admire the fine furniture, the carved wooden pulpit and Baroque altarpieces.

▶ *Turn immediately left onto rue du Soleil.*

Note the interesting Louis XVI façade overlooking the courtyard of n° 17.

Address Book

TOURIST INFORMATION

TOURIST OFFICE

7bis r. du Chat – pl. des Halles, 16007 Angoulême, ☎ 05 45 95 16 84; www.ot-angouleme.fr

GUIDED TOURS OF THE TOWN

Rates and schedules vary. For further information, contact the Service Patrimoine, ☎ 05 45 38 70 79 or www.vpah.culture.fr.

WHERE TO STAY

☝ For coin ranges, see the Legend on the cover flap.

La Templerie Bed and Breakfast – Denat – 16430 Champniers – 9.5km/6mi N of Angoulême. Take the N 10 dir. Poitiers then the D 105 to Balzac – ☎ 05 45 68 73 89 – 5 rms. You will be lodged in the old utility rooms of this magnificent vineyard farm. Not to worry – every room is very pleasant and colourful. Two of the ground-floor bedrooms look out on the pool. Self-catering cottage for six.

Vieille Etable – 16440 Roullet-St-Estèphe – ☎ 05 45 66 31 75 – vieille.etable@wanadoo.fr – closed Sun eve Oct-May – 🅿 – 29 rms – meals ⊜⊜. Despite lying close to the N 10 road, this restored farmhouse offers quiet accommodation in small chalets dotted around its peaceful grounds. The open fireplace makes for cosy evenings in winter, while the attractive terrace is perfect in summer.

Hostellerie du Moulin du Maine Brun – 16290 Asnières-sur-Nouère – 10km/6mi NW of Angoulême on the N 141 then the D 120 – ☎ 05 45 90 83 00 – hostellerie-du-maine-brun@wanadoo.fr – closed 26 Oct -24 Jan, Sun evening off-season, Mon except evenings 11 Apr-30 Sep and Tue lunch – 🅿 – 18 rms – restaurant ⊜⊜⊜. If you dream of sleeping in Louis XIII, Louis XV or Empire-style rooms, then this distinctive mill on the banks of a charming Charantaise river is perfect for you. A pretty terrace and pool overlook the peaceful country-side. On site the Cognac distillery and cellars can be visited.

WHERE TO EAT

Preuve par Trois – 5 r. Ludovic-Trarieux – ☎ 05 45 90 07 97 – closed Sun. A boutique for bargain-hunters and gourmands in the heart of the old city. Light, simple cuisine for lunch; scones, homemade pastries and tea at teatime – just what you need before spending some time browsing in the little second-hand shop here. Dinner on Fri only.

Le Palma –4 rampe d'Aguesseau – ☎ 05 45 95 22 89 – lepalma16@aol.com – closed 19 Dec-3 Jan, Sat noon and Sun. Fresh regional cuisine served in a light, spacious dining room. The restaurant also specialises in Spanish dishes.

La Chouc' – 16 pl. du Palet – ☎ 05 45 95 18 13 – lachouc@tiscali.fr – closed Aug, 25 Dec, 1 Jan, public hols, Sat lunch, Sun and Mon. As the name suggests, choucroute (sauerkraut) is the speciality of this small, discrete restaurant, although you'll also find food fresh from the marketplace, simple and well prepared. Service swift but not rushed - a must.

BARS AND CAFES

Le Tire-Bouchon – 18 r. de la Cloche-Verte – ☎ 05 45 95 00 12 – summer Tue-Fri noon-3pm and 5pm-2am, Sat 5pm-2am; rest of the year, Mon eve, Sat eve, Tue-Fri noon-3pm and 5pm-2am. This hospitable wine bar entirely decorated with second-hand finds offers a fine selection of wines to be savoured with fresh cuisine. An excellent place to unwind.

Chez Paul – 8 pl. Francis-Louvel – ☎ 05 45 90 04 61 – www.chez-paul.com – daily 11am-2am. Old flooring, red benches, designer chairs and a pleasant inner courtyard all contribute to the relaxed atmosphere of this large café. In the background, a trompe-l'oeil fresco turns a banal stone wall into a country landscape.

SPORTS AND RECREATION

Base Nautique Éric Tabarly – Plan d'eau de la Grande Prairie – Direct access from the N 10 – 16710 St-Yrieix-sur-Charente – ☎ 05 45 68 42 46 – cvac16002@oreka.com – daily 8am-10pm – closed late Nov to late Mar. This 25ha lake run by the dynamic French Sailing School is the stage for two exceptional yearly events: the magnificent 14 August fireworks display and the 'Active Summer' which lasts two months.

During this period the lake becomes a theatre where a multitude of free concerts and other activities take place. In the meantime, you can enjoy canoeing and sailing while your children safely play in the water and swim under supervision.

Moulin du Got – [Kid] – *16410 Dirac* – ☎ *05 45 61 52 72; 06 82 06 32 84* – *dalsemeponeyclub@voilà.fr* – *Sep-Jun Wed, Sat-Sun 9am-7pm; Jul-Aug Mon-Fri 9am-7pm* – *closed beginning to mid-Aug.* This riding club, established in a superb mill, puts the accent on developing an autonomous and responsible relationship between child and horse. Courses of one day or one week take place in a family atmosphere and include rides in the woods, lunch and snack. The sort of children's holiday life-long memories are made of.

SHOPPING

Markets – Covered market every morning at place des Halles. Market Tue-Fri mornings at place Victor Hugo. Flea market held Oct-May 8am-6pm the third Sun of every month at place Mulac; large market twice a month on place du Champs-de-Mars.

Les Halles – *Open daily 7am-1pm.* This attractive market hall, built in 1888 and restored in 2000, is a replica of the famous *halles* in Paris. Colourful market, popular with locals.

Letuffe – *10 pl. Francis-Louvel* – ☎ *05 45 95 00 54* – *Mon-Sat 9am-noon and 2-7pm* – *closed public hols.* Founded in 1873, this renowned establishment has opened the doors of its confectionery atelier to visitors. Specialities include cognac and pineau-flavoured chocolates as well as the famous *'duchesses of Angoulême'*, nougatines with praline filling.

▶ *Walk along rue Vauban on the right then turn left to reach rue de Turenne.*

N° 15 has a Louis XIII doorway; opposite is the doorway of the former Carmelite convent (1739).

▶ *Continue along the Beaulieu rampart.*

Place Beaulieu

This esplanade is at the end of the promontory, where a school has replaced the old Benedictine abbey. It offers views of the St-Ausone district and the church of the same name, built in the 19C by Paul Abadie (1812-84), one of the architects responsible for the Sacré-Cœur Basilica in Paris. Beyond, the confluence of the River Charente and River Anguienne can be seen. Immediately below is a small park, *"le Jardin Vert"* filled with contemporary sculptures. A large wooden cross is a reminder of the former hermitage of Saint-Cybard, one of the main evangelists in Aquitaine in the 5C.

▶ *Walk along rue de Beaulieu.*

N° 79 boasts an imposing façade flanked with three square turrets and decorated with an Ionic colonnade (1783). On the corner of rue de Beaulieu and rue Guérin stands the Chapelle des Cordeliers.

Ancienne chapelle des Cordeliers

This chapel was once a convent church belonging to the Franciscan friars. In 1556, one of the monks, André Thevet, brought the first samples of tobacco – which he called Angoulême grass – back from Brazil.

Now the hospital chapel, the building has an elegant Gothic belfry with a projecting side supported on two small squinches. The nave contains the tomb of Guez de Balzac (*see A Bit of History*), who was buried here in 1654.

▶ *Continue along rue de Beaulieu then turn right onto rue du Minage leading to the cathedral and town hall district.*

Cathédrale St-Pierre★
See Sights.

Musée municipal des Beaux-Arts
See Sights.

▶ *Walk towards the southern section of the ramparts to admire the view.*

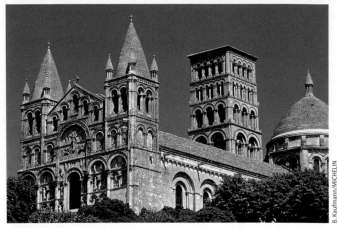

Cathédrale St-Pierre

South Ramparts

From here there is a fine view of the Anguienne Valley with its tree-covered slopes.

▷ *Walk along the tree-lined place de New-York to the town hall and enter the St-Martial shopping district via rue Marengo.*

Sights

Cathédrale St-Pierre★

Built in the 12C, the cathedral was partially destroyed by the Calvinists in 1562, and restored in 1634, followed by a more complete restoration started by Abadie in 1866.

Façade★★ - The impressive façade, decorated in the Poitiers style, is an enormous sculpted tableau in which 70 characters, statues and bas-relief sculptures, portray the Last Judgement. The ensemble is presided over by a glorious Christ in Majesty surrounded by angels, saints set in medallions and symbols of the Evangelists. Both the archivolts and friezes above and around the side doors are decorated with intricately carved foliage, animals and figures. On the lintel of the first blind doorway, on the right, are strange scenes of combat based on episodes from *La Chanson de Roland* (Song of Roland).

The tall tower with six diminishing storeys which rises above the far end of the north transept was partly restored by Abadie.

Interior - The inside has several striking features. Domes resting on pendentives represent an extremely bold concept, and in the north transept, a huge chapel sits beneath the Abadie tower, its supporting columns embellished with remarkable capitals.

Also of note is the Romanesque bas-relief in the nave depicting a Madonna and Child, and the 18C organ loft.

In the chancel, the capitals with floral decoration originate from the 9C cathedral built by Grimoald de Mussidan.

Musée municipal des Beaux-Arts★

⊶ *Closed for renovation. Reopening scheduled in 2008.*

The Fine Arts Museum, housed in the 12C former Bishops' Palace rebuilt in the 15C and 16C, is best known for the quality and wealth of its exhibits from the South Pacific region and Africa (ritual statues from the Congo, masks and Kota reliquaries) and for the famous **Casque d'Agris**★ (Agris' Helmet) on the upper floor, a masterpiece of 4C BC Celtic goldsmith's work. In addition, there are collections of medieval treasures (capitals, crosses, sculptures),

The cathedral façade

B. Kaufmann/MICHELIN

ceramics (mainly regional) and 18C and 19C French paintings (*on the ground floor*), as well as a wide selection of 17C and 18C Italian and Flemish paintings, and French works and sculptures by local artists (*on the upper floor*).

Musée de la Société Archéologique

🕒*Open daily Mon-Fri 2-5pm.* 🕒*Closed between Christmas and New Year's Day and public hols.* ◎*No charge.* ☎*05 45 94 90 75. www.archeologie-charente.com.*
This museum devoted to the work of the local archaeological society displays, indoors and outside in a garden, examples of prehistoric finds in the neighbourhood, along with Gallo-Roman mosaics, lapidary collections from Roman times to the 18C, and various regional antiquities (weapons, pottery, trinkets and enamels from the Limousin area).

Hôtel de Ville

🕒◦◦*Guided tours (1hr) Jul and Aug at 3pm and 4pm (3pm Sun and public hols); Jun and Sep daily at 3pm; Apr, May and Oct Sat-Sun at 3pm.* ◎*4€.* ☎ *05 45 38 70 79.*
Abadie built this Gothic-Renaissance town hall on the site of the old castle which was the seat of the Comtes d'Angoulême. All that remains of the castle today is the polygonal tower – a 13C and 14C keep from which a fine **panorama** can be

enjoyed – and the 15C round tower where Marguerite d'Angoulême was born. The staircase and the Second Empire style sitting rooms can also be visited.

Hôtel St-Simon – FRAC Poitou-Charentes

15 rue de la Cloche-Verte. 🕒 *Open daily except Mon and Sun 10.30am-noon and 2-7pm.* 🕒 *Closed public hols; no exhibition from mid-Dec to mid-Jan.* ◎ *No charge.* ☎ *05 45 92 87 01.*
This is the regional centre of the Poitou-Charentes Contemporary Art Collection, which houses a collection of recent artistic works from around the world.

Le Centre national de la bande dessinée et de l'image★ (CNBDI)

▶ *From the upper town, take a bus or walk down the road from the Tour Ladent. Entrance: rue de Bordeaux. Alternatively, a stairway leads up from avenue de Cognac.*

♿🕒*Jul-Aug Tue- Fri 10am-6pm, Thu 10am-7pm, Sat-Sun 2-7pm; rest of the year hours vary.* 🕒*Closed 1 Jan, 1 May, 25 Dec.* ◎*5€; children no charge.* ☎*05 45 38 65 65. www.cnbdi.fr.*
Kids The Comic Strip Centre, housed in a group of turn-of-the-century industrial buildings which the architect Roland

Castro remodelled with resolutely modernistic elements, is as inventive as the works on display.

Inside, the **Médiathèque** (*1st floor*) houses almost all of French comic strip production since 1946. Since 1982, all comic strips published in France have been legally registered here for reasons of copyright. A very large media bank (video cassettes, comic strip books, magazines etc) can be freely consulted.

In the **museum**, rich collections of original drawings are displayed in rotation. Rooms on the ground floor pay tribute to the great masters of the comic strip (through one or several plates or original illustrations or an illuminated screen with a commentary). Videos retrace significant moments in the history of the comic strip.

Among comic strip pioneers are the Swiss Töpffer (mid-19C), Christophe (*La Famille Fenouillard*, 1889), Pinchon (*Bécassine*, 1905), Forton (*Les Pieds Nickelés*, 1908) and Alain St Ogen (*Zig et Puce*, 1925). Innumerable later talents represented include the Belgians Hergé (*Tintin*, 1929) and Franquin (*Gaston Lagaffe*, 1957); the Americans Raymond (*Flash Gordon*, 1934) and Schulz (*Peanuts*, 1950); and the French artists Goscinny and Uderzo (*Astérix*, 1959). A host of contemporary creators include Gotlib, Claire Bretécher, Reiser, Bourgeon, Wolinski, Loustal, Bilal, Baudoin, Tardi and Teule.

There are activities and workshops for children and an internet area

Musée du Papier "Le Nil"

  Jul-Aug daily except Mon noon-6.30pm; Jan-Jun daily except Sun and Mon 2-6pm. Closed public hols. No charge. 05 45 92 73 43.

The former Bardou-Le-Nil paper mill, which specialised in the production of cigarette papers, operated here on the banks of the River Charente until 1970. The building has since been converted into a museum devoted to the paper industry, which brought wealth and prosperity to the region. Angoulême was particularly suited to this traditional activity as a result of the clean, unpolluted water of its river.

One of the six metal-vaned waterwheels which powered the machinery until the end of the 19C is on view, together with an exhibition detailing the different stages in the industrial production of paper and cardboard. The raw material – first rags, then wood and waste paper – is turned into a paste and subsequently into a continuous sheet by a machine invented by Nicolas Robert in 1799. Once dried, the sheet undergoes numerous other treatments before the final product is obtained.

Two other exhibitions – one devoted to industry in Charente, from the earliest times to the present day, the other following the history of the paper trade worldwide – give a comprehensive survey of papermaking. Rooms on the 3rd floor also have displays of contemporary art.

Excursion

Grottes du Quéroy★ *(16km/10mi E via the D 699 and the D 412)* – Labyrinth of impressive caves.

ARCACHON ♨♨

POPULATION 11 454

MICHELIN MAP 335: D-7

The seaside resort of Arcachon is built on a lagoon and is reputed for its oyster farms. For decades the town's Winter Resort was the favourite haunt of celebrities from Alexandre Dumas to Jean Cocteau and Marilyn Monroe. Today, several festivals bring the town to life; Festival Jeunes Solistes (classical music) in April; the parachuting competition in June; Not'Ambules (street festival) and Les 18 heures d'Arcachon (sailing competition) in July; Fêtes de la Mer (blessing of boats, music in the evening) in August; and September's Festival du cinéma au féminin.

- **Information:** Esplanade G. Pompidou. ☎05 57 52 97 97. www.arcachon.com
- ▶ **Orient Yourself**: The most direct routes to Arcachon from Bordeaux (60km/37mi away) are the N 250 or the A 63. The town sits on the Bassin d'Arcachon and is divided into four separate districts, the most popular of which is the summer resort facing the sea.
- **Parking**: There is a car park near the railway station, as well as near Cours Lamraque de Plaisance in the town centre (*see MAP*).
- **Don't Miss**: The promenade along the sea front; the view from the jetty; the Winter Resort; the Boulevard de la Mer; watching the fishing boats unload their catch.
- **Kids**: The local aquarium and maritime museum; the region's sandy beaches.
- **Also See**: BASSIN D'ARCACHON; BORDEAUX.

A Bit of History

Birth of Arcachon

In 1841, a new branch line extended the railway from Bordeaux to La Teste, a favourite bathing place for holidaymakers from the famous wine capital. In 1845, a deep-water landing-stage was constructed 5km/3mi north of La Teste and the two towns were linked by a road across the salt-marshes. Villas were subsequently built along the road, and Arcachon was born.

In 1852, the **Pereire brothers**, Émile and Isaac, founded a railway company, Compagnie des Chemins de Fer du Midi, and took over the Bordeaux-La Teste line which they extended to Arcachon. At the beginning of the 1860s, they purchased forest land from the State. To make the line and land profitable, they started building facilities to attract clients – a station, a Chinese-style dining room, a luxury hotel, a Moorish casino and several mansions. The plans for the first buildings were mainly the work of Paul Régnault assisted by the young Gustave Eiffel. Already a summer resort popular for sea bathing, the town also became a winter resort in 1866, attracting tuberculosis patients. It was not until after 1935 that Arcachon became a popular seaside and tourist resort as well as a health resort.

Fishing in Arcachon

Arcachon is considered to be a pioneer port in the history of sea fishing. It was here that the *Turbot*, **the first steam-operated trawler in the world** (with a paddle wheel), put to sea in 1837.

Plage Péreire

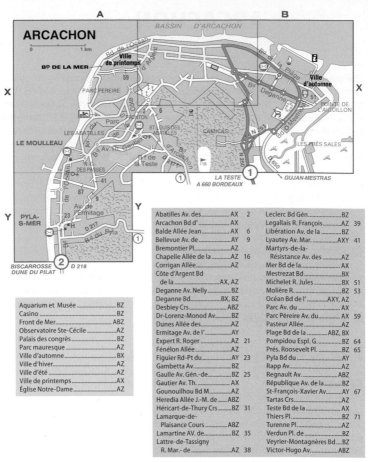

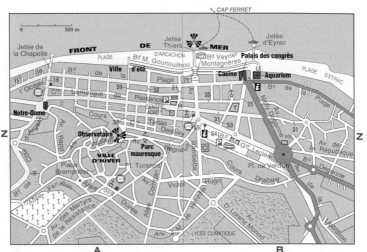

In 1865, Arcachon saw the first French steamers with propellers and iron hulls. At the turn of the last century, it was the second largest fishing port in France after Boulogne-sur-Mer. In the same spirit of innovation, the first motorised trawler in France, the **Victoria**, was commissioned in 1927. Commercial fishing in Arcachon declined in the 1950s, as the trawlers left for the more profitable Breton ports, and fishing in Arcachon returned to traditional methods.

Every year, 2 000t of fine quality fish – sole, bass, hake, mullet, turbot and squid – fetching high market prices, are unloaded onto the Arcachon jetties (do not miss the unloading of the catch which often takes place around 6.45am). The fleet which fishes in the **Bay of Biscay** is made up of traditional fishing smacks and catamarans with nets. In the lagoon itself, apart from holidaymakers and locals who gather clams, cockles and winkles at low tide, traditional methods are still employed. Methods include the use of – the *jagude* – three increasingly smaller-gauged nets one inside the other; the loup – a horn-shaped net for fishing sea bass; the *palet* – similar to the *loup* but with a spiral base; the *balai* – bunches of broom used to trap prawns; *esquirey* – a term in local patois meaning landing net; the *trahine* – a seine-net, one end of which is drawn along the beach and the other out to sea; and the *foëne* – a two-pronged fishing spear for catching eels.

Visit

The **Summer Resort** stretches along the seafront between Jetée de la Chapelle and Jetée d'Eyrac, attracting tourists to its terrace cafés, casino and nautical events (sailing regattas, speedboat races). The **Autumn Resort** is the maritime quarter with its large marina and busy fishing port animated by a regular stream of trawlers. The unloading of fresh fish early in the morning is a sight not to be missed. The **Winter Resort**★, farther inland and more sheltered from the sea breezes, is a quiet, pine-shaded area whose broad avenues are lined with handsome late-19C and early-20C villas. The green expanse of its Moorish park lying above the town

centre makes it Archachon's most peaceful district.

To the west, Pereire Park with its large sports complex (bowling, swimming pool, tennis courts, golf course and riding centre) and avenues lined with wealthy mansions forms the **Spring Resort**. Mineral water from the **Abatilles** spring, which once supplied a local spa, is now bottled for sale. Pereire beach is lined by a shaded pedestrianised alleyway. The southern end, known as Les Arbousiers, is the surfing enthusiasts' favourite spot.

The Sea Front★

The pleasant promenade along the tamarisk-shaded boulevard Gounouilhou and boulevard Veyrier-Montagnères, by Jetée Thiers, overlooks Arcachon's fine, sandy beaches. To the east can be seen the white façade of the **Palatium** conference centre, part of the neo-Renaissance Château Deganne, which also houses the casino. The jetty offers a general **view**★ of the resort and the lagoon.

Église Notre-Dame

This 19C church is located along Jetée de la Chapelle, just beyond the Sailors' Cross. Inside, **Chapelle des Marins**, adorned with numerous thanksgiving offerings, houses the revered statue of Our Lady of Arcachon.

Boulevard de la Mer★

This charming seaside walk, bordered by pine trees growing in the sandy ground, skirts Pereire Park and offers fine views of the Cap Ferret peninsula.

The Winter Resort★

2hrss. From place du 8-Mai, take the lift up to the edge of the grounds of the Moorish Casino which overlooks the Summer Resort below. Guided tours of the Winter Resort (1hr 30min) ⏲Apr-Oct Mon, Wed and Fri 10.30am-noon and Sat 2.30-4pm. ✆6€. ☎ 05 57 52 97 97.

As a result of a real estate project inaugurated by the Pereire brothers in 1860, the Winter Resort is a sort of city park, crisscrossed with winding avenues skirting the dunes that protect it from the

Address Book

For coin ranges, see the Legend on the cover flap.

WHERE TO STAY

Hôtel Orange Marine – *35 bd Chanzy – ☎05 57 52 00 80 – 21 rooms – restaurant*. Here, a stone's throw from the fishing docks, an address where you needn't spend a fortune. The rooms are simple and impeccably maintained. Ask for a seaside room, unless you prefer one overlooking the pretty patio where diners are seated in the summer.

Hôtel Les Mimosas – *77 bis av. de la République – ☎05 56 83 45 86 – contact.hotel@wanadoo.fr – closed 31 Dec-1 Mar – 21 rooms.* From the outside, this villa looks like an old bourgeois residence. Albeit rather modest, the small rooms are cool and clean. Even in the summer, prices are relatively reasonable for this seaside resort town.

Hôtel Le Dauphin – *7 av. Gounod – ☎05 56 83 02 89 – P – 49 rooms.* Housed in an attractive 19C mansion, this hotel enjoys an excellent location 300m/330yd from the sea in one of Arcachon's quiet districts. The hotel has comfortable, air-conditioned rooms and a swimming pool. Friendly staff.

WHERE TO EAT

Le Cosy – *116 cours Desbiey – ☎05 57 52 15 70 – closed Sun, Mon and Tue except public hols.* This wine bar serves a good selection of wines from different regions to accompany their mixed salads and large sandwiches. Relaxed, friendly atmosphere.

Le Pavillon d'Arguin – *63 bd du Général-Leclerc – ☎05 56 83 46 96 – closed 2 weeks in Jan and 2 weeks in Nov.* Young, friendly staff, fresh ingredients and an attractive maritime decor make this restaurant a pleasant place to eat.

Cap Pereire – *1 av. du Parc-Pereire – ☎05 56 83 24 01 – closed Tue.* Far from the crowds, with a view of the sea, this attractive colonial-style restaurant is situated next to the tranquil Parc Pereire. The restaurant specialises in fish and seafood.

SPORTS AND LEISURE

L'Étrier Sportif – *25 av. Pierre-Frondaie – ☎05 56 83 21 79 – winter daily 8am-9pm; rest of the year 7am-10pm.* This riding school organises lessons, courses and outings in the woods or on the beach *(Oct-May)*. It has an indoor school, two outdoor arenas and a club house with terrace.

Le Fronton – *14 av. du Parc, Quartier les Abatilles – ☎05 56 83 17 87 – pierre.cleaz@wanadoo.fr – open daytime every day; wall: 9am-11pm – 6/10€ (per person, according to the game).* This pelota Basque fronton was built in the Parc des Abatilles in 1932. Each Saturday evening in July and August, chistera matches are held here. Note the excellence of the Arcachon players of this discipline – they hold several Champion of France titles in grand chistera (one of the forms of the sport).

Tennis Club d'Arcachon – *Av. du Parc – ☎05 57 72 09 50 – tcarcachon@aol.com – summer: 8am-8.30pm; off-season: daily 9am-noon and 2pm-6.30pm – closed 25 Dec and 1 Jan.* This splendid tennis club boasts twelve clay courts (two are covered) and ten hard courts. Modern club house with bar.

Centre nautique Pierre-Malet – *Quai de Goslar – BP 82 – ☎05 56 22 36 83 – www.port-arcachon.com – open Mon-Sun 9am-noon and 2-6pm except Tue off-season – closed mid-Sep to beg. Apr.* In addition to courses and sailboat rentals, the Centre Pierre-Malet offers various water activities, including sea kayaking, rowing and diving.

Dingo Vélos – *1 r. Grenier – between jetée de Thiers and jetée d'Eyrac – ☎05 56 83 44 09 – dingovelos@wanadoo.fr – open Apr-Jun, Sep: daily 9:30am-6:30pm; Jul-Aug: 9am-midnight; rest of the year: call 06 87 27 39 86.* In addition to traditional bicycles (touring and mountain bikes), this rental shop offers a range of unusual bikes, including tandems and bikes with three or even five seats. Go-karts, family quadri-cycles and electric scooters also available.

Golf course – *35 bd d'Arcachon – 33120 La Teste-de-Buch – ☎05 56 54 44 00 – golfdarcach@aol.com.* This 18-hole course is situated near the lagoon.

Casino de la Plage – *163 bd de la Plage – ☎05 56 83 41 44 – casino-arcachon@g.partouche.fr – daily 10am-4am.* This casino has a traditional games room and 100 slot machines. Also a restaurant, bars and the discotheque

(Le Scotch-Club) with frequent cocktail hours and theme evenings.

CAFES

Au Cornet d'Amour – *Av. N.-D.-des-Passes* – ☎*05 56 54 52 16 – cornedamour@ wanadoo.fr – summer: daily 9am-1am; off-season: 2pm-7:30pm – closed Jan.* The biggest homemade ice cream parlour of the Arcachon Basin has 70 different flavours of ice cream and sorbet and makes its own cones. Have a seat and savour their iced desserts, such as the marmite nougatine with 16 ice creams (for 8), or the pinasse en nougatine, filled with 30 scoops (for 15).
Café de la Plage – *1 bd Veyrier-Montagnères* – ☎*05 56 22 52 94 – daily 8am-2am; mid-Jun to mid-Sep daily 8am-3am.* This century-old bar lies in an ideal location on the Arcachon beach, near the casino and palais des congrès (convention hall). People come here to be seen and to sip whisky on the terrace; there's no better place to do it – their drinks menu features no fewer than 90 different brands. Jazz concerts every fortnight; excellent musical ambience in the evening.

EVENTS

International Piano Competition – *Mar.*
Sailing regatta – *Jul.*
Fêtes de la mer – *14 and 15 Aug* – Blessing of boats, music in the evenings.
Dance festival – *Five days in Sep.*

---

sea winds. This picturesque neighbourhood, planted with pine trees and filled with the fragrance of balsam, considered beneficial for tuberculosis patients, turned Arcachon into a popular resort. In 1863, the Emperor Napoleon III visited the Winter Resort, and for decades, it remained a meeting place for famous politicians, authors and artists of the time. Today, there is a strong movement towards consolidating and renovating this highly original and charmingly outdated architectural heritage, characterised by the sculpted wood of its gables, balconies and external staircases.

☞*Below are some suggestions for places to visit on foot.*

Parc Mauresque

Featuring numerous exotic species, the park offers an excellent **view** of the town and the Arcachon lagoon. Many of the original buildings, including the Moorish Casino, destroyed by fire in 1977, and inspired by the Alhambra in Grenada and the mosque in Cordoba, have now disappeared.

Observatoire Ste-Cécile

This metal-framed observatory by Gustave Eiffel can be reached by a footbridge over Allée Pasteur. The platform affords a **view** of the Winter Resort, Arcachon and the lagoon (☺*to be avoided if you suffer from vertigo*).

Villas

Even though there is a variety of styles (Swiss and Basque chalets, English cottages, Moorish villas, neo-Gothic manors and colonial-style houses), villas usually follow the same basic design. A raised first floor above a semi-basement service floor contains the reception rooms and veranda-lined living room. The bedrooms are on the next floor. The opulent villa roofs emerge from the vegetation, mainly tall Atlantic pines, interspersed with oaks, maples, black locust (robinia), Japanese ornamental cherry trees, nettle trees, plane and lime trees. When in bloom, mimosas, catalpas and magnolias offer a vibrant display of colour amid the dark green foliage of the pines.

Allée Rebsomen

Villa Theresa (*no 4,* now Hôtel Sémiramis).

Allée Corrigan

Villa Walkyrie (*no 12*), **Hôtel de la Forêt**, **Villa Vincenette** (bow window with beautiful leaded glass).

Allée Dr-F.-Lalesque

Villas l'Oasis, Carmen and **Navarra**. On the corner of rue Velpeau and allée Marie-Christine – **Villa Maraquita** (*no 8*).

Allée du Moulin-Rouge

Villa Toledo (*no 7*, carved staircase).

Allée Faust

Villas Athéna, Fragonard, Coulaine, **Graig-crostan** (no 6), Faust and Siebel.

Allée Brémontier

Villas Brémontier (no 1, turret and balcony), Glenstrae (no 4) and Sylvabelle (no 9).

Allée du Dr-Festal

Villas **Trocadéro** (no 6, finely carved balcony – *see illustration in the INTRODUCTION: ARCHITECTURE*) and **Monaco**.

Allée Pasteur

Villas Montesquieu and Myriam.
On the corner of Allée Pasteur and Allée Alexandre-Dumas – Villa A.-Dumas (no 7).

Sights

Aquarium and Museum

2 rue Jolyet Open Jun-Aug 9.45am-12.15pm and 1.45-7pm; Feb school hols, mid-Mar to late May and Sep-Oct 9.45am-12.15pm and 1.45-6.30pm (last admission 30min before closing time). Closed early Jan to mid-Feb. 4.50€ (children 2.80€). 05 56 54 89 28.

In the aquarium on the mezzanine floor, 30 glass tanks display marine life found in the lagoon and the nearer reaches of the ocean beyond.

Upstairs the museum boasts a special section devoted to oyster farming, and collections of birds, fish, reptiles and invertebrates native to the region. Another section displays finds from local archaeological digs.

BASSIN D'ARCACHON ★

MICHELIN MAP 335: D-E 6

The Bassin d'Arcachon (Arcachon lagoon), a vast triangular-shaped inlet, is the only major indentation along the Côte d'Argent (Silver Coast). It is almost cut off from the sea by the narrow promontory of Cap Ferret, which leaves an exit channel barely 3km/1.8mi wide.

The region's prosperity is based on **oyster farming**, pine plantations (sawmills and paper mills), and fishing and tourism; note the many weekend cottages, holiday homes and camp sites. With an annual production of 18 000 tonnes, the Arcachon lagoon is one of the major European centres for oyster production, covering almost 1 800ha/ 4 447 acres of the lagoon's surface. The lagoon is the main regional breeding centre and supplies seed oysters or spats to other oyster beds in Brittany, Normandy, Languedoc and the Netherlands.

- **Don't Miss**: The Dune du Pilat; Parc Ornithologique du Teich; boat trips of the lagoon; tasting the local oysters.
- **Especially for Kids**: Parc de loisirs de la Hume; les jardins du Bassin botanical gardens (*see Address Book*).
- **Also See**: ARCACHON; BORDEAUX.

Geographical Notes

Several small rivers flow into the bay, the most important being the Eyre which irrigates the Parc Régional des Landes de Gascogne. At low tide *crassats* appear (silty sandbanks full of underwater vegetation) surrounded by secondary channels called *esteys*.

The inlet extends over an area of 25 000ha/ almost 100sq mi, four-fifths of which is exposed at low tide. The 9 500ha/23 475 acres which remain above water at high tide contain dykes enclosing the fish reservoirs of Audenge and Le Teich, and include the low, almost treeless relief of **Île aux Oiseaux** (Bird Island). The 80km/50mi of shoreline enclosing the lagoon, flat to the east and south and bordered by wooded dunes on either side of the entrance channel, includes a number of small oyster ports and attractive bathing resorts among the pine trees and mimosa.

Oyster country – The famous oysters from Arcachon lagoon have long been a delicacy. The Roman poets, Ausonius and Apollinaris Sindonius, and later, Rabelais, praised their excellent gastronomic qualities in their writing. Over-exploitation of their natural beds, however, exhausted the supply, until the naturalist Victor Coste stepped in and started developing oyster-farming or ostreiculture in 1859. Until 1920, the flat oyster from Arcachon, or *gravette (ostrea edulis)*, was the most intensely cultivated in the lagoon, followed by the Portuguese deep-shelled oyster *(crassostrea angulata)*. In the same year, a disease struck the flat oyster beds, but left the Portuguese oysters untouched. The latter were then closely observed and became the predominant species until 1970, when disease struck again and they were replaced by a Japanese variety *(crassostrea gigas)*.

The oyster cycle lasts for about four years. It starts in July when the oyster spats are gathered in collectors consisting of sand and lime-washed semicircular tiles which are then put in wooden cages or baskets, and strategically placed along the canal. The following spring, the oysters are prised off the collectors and placed in beds sealed off with wire netting which protects them from their predator, the crab. After 18 months, the oysters are detached from the cultch to be fattened for another year in pools of water rich in plankton. During this period, they are repeatedly turned, to give them a uniform shape. Having reached maturity, the oysters are sorted, and left in degorging tanks to rid them of their impurities. They are washed for a last time and then packed up in small wooden crates and delivered.

The Pinasse, emblem of the lagoon – The brightly coloured streamlined fishing smack called the *pinasse* is the symbol of the Arcachon lagoon. It was originally made of pinewood (hence its name) and pegged together. Nowadays, it is made of iroko (African wood), locust

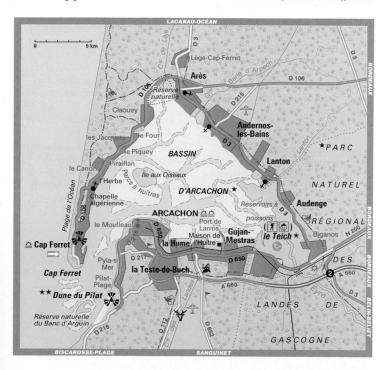

or walnut and assembled with rivets. Formerly used for coastal fishing, the pinasse was adopted by the lagoon's oyster farmers in the 19C. Since it is flat-bottomed, it can be easily pulled aground and pass through even very shallow channels. It is generally motor-driven and 9m-10m/30ft-33ft long; the *pinasotte*, a smaller version, is 6m-7m/20ft-23ft long with either sails or oars.

Few of these fishing smacks are produced nowadays (only two pinassayres, the yards which make these boats, are still in operation in the lagoon). However, because of their similarity to Venetian gondolas and Mediterranean caiques, they are highly prized and looked after with great care. The old smacks are refurbished, cosseted and raced in the lagoon during regattas.

Address Book

For coin ranges, see the Legend on the cover flap.

WHERE TO STAY

Chambre d'hôte Les Tilleuls – *17 bis r. des Écoles – 33380 Mios – ☎05 56 26 67 85 – gitemios@club-internet.fr – closed 1 Nov-30 Apr except Sat-Sun and school hols – ⊘ – 4 rooms.* Quite a pleasing blend of red brick and wood in these entirely renovated barns and stables far from the crowded resorts of the Bassin d'Arcachon. Tastefully decorated rooms with period furniture. Attractive garden with hundred-year-old linden trees.

WHERE TO EAT

Pinasse Café – *2 bis av. de l'Océan – 33970 Cap-Ferret – ☎05 56 03 77 87 – pinassecafe@wanadoo.fr – closed 16 Nov-7 Feb.* An original, laid-back bistro. The wood-panelled walls are decorated with paintings of boats and drawings of fish – not surprising, considering its situation overlooking the Basin and the oyster-breeding pools. Homemade regional cuisine.

L'Escalumade – *8 r. Pierre-Dignac – port de Larros – 33470 Gujan-Mestras – ☎05 56 66 02 30 – closed 2 weeks in Jan, 6-28 Oct, Sun evening and Mon except 1 Jun-31 Aug.* A delicious, unassuming seafood meal. The charm of this cool, tranquil oyster breeders' cabin-cum-restaurant is enhanced by its wood furnishings and bay windows. The oysters come directly from the oyster ponds below the terrace. Shellfish prepared with care.

La Côte du Sud – *4 av. du Figuier – 33115 Pyla-sur-Mer – ☎05 56 83 25 00 – cote.du.sud@wanadoo.fr – closed Dec-Jan.* Fish and seafood enthusiasts, this pleasant restaurant near the ocean is for you. The colourful dining room ends on a terrace with a view of the sea. Comfortable rooms with an exotic touch.

SPORT AND LEISURE

Les jardins du Bassin – *Rte des Lacs – 33470 La Hume – ☎05 56 66 00 71 – open daily except Sat 2am-6am – closed 26 Aug-29 May. 5€.* Adults and children alike will enjoy a visit to these botanical gardens, with their fruit trees, vines, cacti, exotic plants and vegetable plots.

Aéro-club du Bassin d'Arcachon – *Aérodrome de Villemarie – 33260 La Teste-de-Buch – ☎05 56 54 72 88 – www.acba-fr.com – reception: daily 9am-noon and 2-6pm; aero club: summer 8am-10pm – flights over the lagoon from 70€-110€ (30min).* This aero club organises first flights and introductions to air acrobatics as well as piloting lessons. There are also parachuting and hang-gliding clubs at the Aérodrome de Villemarie.

École Pyla parapente – *Maison forestière Gaillouneys – 33115 Pyla-sur-Mer – ☎05 56 22 15 02 –early May to late Sep: opening times available every day upon request.* Located near the 118m-high Dune de Pilat, this school offers para-gliding and hang-gliding flights.

EVENTS

Oyster Festivals – *Mid-Jul in Lanton, Lège-Cap-Ferret and Andernos-les-Bains; mid-Aug in Gujan-Mestras and Arès.* Many of the small ports around the lagoon hold festivals in the summer months, with oyster tastings, music and dances. Look out for the oyster farmers in their traditional costume.

Boat Trips

Tours of the lagoon, or fishing trips and oyster-bed tours are available at several locations.

Île aux Oiseaux

This small flat island covered with dwarf vegetation used to be a birds' paradise until oyster-breeders took possession of the surrounding mud flats. Do not miss the two *cabanes tchanquées* ("tchanque" meaning stilt in the Gascon language). They can be spotted above water at high tide.

The Banc d'Arguin Nature Reserve

Guided tours. SEPANSO, 1 r. Tauzia, 33800 Bordeaux, ☎05 56 91 33 65.
Banc d'Arguin is a small, sandy island at the mouth of the channels, constantly changing shape as the Atlantic changes mood. It was made a nature reserve in 1972 and is visited from March to August by a large colony of Cabot's sterns (4 500 mating couples) and oyster-catchers. In winter, the curlew, bar-tailed godwit, red-backed sandpiper, grey plover, seagull and black-headed gull live here in great numbers.

Driving Tour from Cap Ferret to Dune du Pilat

76km/47mi – allow one day

Although the roads cited in the itinerary below offer few glimpses of the water, you are never far from a stretch of shore or a small jetty giving at least a partial view of the lagoon.

Cap Ferret

The long thin promontory of Cap Ferret runs north-south at the entrance to Arcachon lagoon, sheltering narrow straits leading into the basin. The area has been developed into a seaside resort, with hotels and holiday villas scattered among the pines. It is also an oyster-farming centre, with the most accessible oyster beds in the lagoon.

Lighthouse

Jul and Aug 10am-7.30pm; Apr-Jun and Sep 10am-12.30pm and 2-6.30pm; Oct-Mar daily except Mon and Tue 2-5pm. Closed 1 Jan, 1 May, mid-Nov to mid-Dec and 25 Dec. 4.50€ (children: 3€). ☎05 57 70 33 30 or 56 03 94 49; www.lege-capferret.com
This landmark (rebuilt in 1947) is 52m/171ft high, with a revolving lantern which can be seen 50km/31mi out to sea. An audio-visual show and a screen gallery inform visitors about the peninsula and the lighthouse. From the platform (258 steps) there is a fine **panorama**★ embracing the whole of the peninsula, the lagoon, the straits, the open sea and Pilat Dune.

Plage de l'océan

Departs Bélisaire Jul-Aug: 11.15am, 11.50am, 12.30pm, 2.10-6.10pm (every 20 min); 15 Jun-7 Jul and 29 Aug-18 Sep 11.15am, 2.45-5.45pm (every 30 min); from early Jun to mid-Jun and from mid-Sep to end Sep: 2.45pm, 3.15-5.15pm (every hour); from mid-Jun to end Jun and from mid-Sep to late-Sep, 2.45, 3.15-5.15pm (every 30 min); Apr-May 2.45pm-4.45pm (every 30 min). Departs ocean Jul-Aug 11.30am, 12.05pm, 12.45pm,

Bird Sanctuary

A traditional stopover in the spring and autumn for tens of thousands of migratory birds (such as the spoonbill, greylag goose and black-headed gull), the meadows and dikes along the Eytre and around the old fish tanks also shelter numerous birds in the winter including teal, dunlin and cormorant. There are also nesting species such as a colony of herons consisting of more than 1 000 couples of common heron, little egret and cattle egret. In summer, the rare bluethroat rewards patient visitors with his pure song and vibrant colours.

The rich, varied vegetation will delight botany enthusiasts: wild berries (arbutus, brambles) highly appreciated by the frugivorous species; water irises, rushes and oaks planted to consolidate the dikes, as well as tamarisk and alders used by ducks and moorhens to build their nests.

2.30-6.30pm (every 20 min); 15 Jun-7 Jul and 29 Aug-18 Sep 11.45am, 3-6pm (every 30 min); from early Jun to mid-Jun and mid-Sep to late-Sep 3-5.30pm (every 30 min); Apr-May: 3-5pm (every 30 min). ☞Price list posted at the railway station. ☏05 56 60 60 20.
A narrow-gauge railway service operates between Bélisaire landing-stage (eastern side) and this splendid beach on the ocean side of the promontory.

▶ *Drive out of Cap Ferret along avenue de la Vigne towards Bordeaux.*

The road runs through wooded dunes dotted with villas. The smell of the sea mingles with the scent of pine trees.

Villa Algérienne
4km/2.5mi N.
This site, named after a building in the Moorish style which was demolished in 1965, offers a good view of the lagoon and Bird Island. The oriental influence remains in a chapel, built about 150 years ago, looking out across the sea.

Oyster-breeding villages
Le Canon, Le Four, Les Jacquets, L'Herbe: these picturesque oyster-breeding villages alternate with beaches along the edge of the Bassin d'Arcachon; crates and lime-washed tiles lie in front of their wooden huts (those of L'Herbe, one of the prettiest villages, are always freshly painted).

Chapel entrance, Villa Algérienne

▶ *The D 106 wends its way between the edge of the forest and the shore of the lagoon.*

Arès
Arès was originally an oyster port; it now also harbours pleasure boats and is a sea-side resort. A Romanesque church stands on the town's central square. Inside, the carved capitals of the columns are illuminated by modern stained-glass windows. The round tower (restored) on the waterfront was once part of a windmill.

▶ *From Arès to Biganos, the road passes through a landscape of endless pine forests, linking the towns and villages along the lagoon's eastern shore.*

Andernos-les-Bains
This sheltered site at the far end of the lagoon has been inhabited by man since prehistoric times. Today, the town is one of the major local resorts, very popular in summer, with beaches stretching for over 4km/2mi and a casino.
Opposite the beach and next to the small church of St-Éloi, with its 11C apse, lie traces of a 4C Gallo-Roman basilica. The jetty offers extensive views over the lagoon, the town's oyster port, the beaches and the marina.

Audenge
The town, an oyster-farming centre, is also known for its fish reservoirs (a system of locks which encloses the catch at low tide).

▶ *Beyond Biganos take the D 3E12 to join the D 650. Opposite the junction is the impressive smoking bulk of the Cellulose du Pin paper mill, visible for miles around.*

The route crosses the inner end of the marshy Eyre delta (bridge over the river) and follows the lagoon's southern shore, which remains pleasantly leafy all the way to the outskirts of Le Teich.

Parc Ornithologique du Teich★
&.☼Jul and Aug 10am-8pm; mid-Apr to Jun and early to mid-Sep: 10am-7pm; mid-Sep to mid-Apr: 10am-6pm. ☞6.80€

A. Thuillier/MICHELIN

(children: 4.80€). ☎05 56 22 80 93; www.
parc-ornithologique-du-teich.com

Kids The **nature reserve** covers a surface
area of 120ha/300 acres in the Eyre delta,
including 80ha/200 acres of water used
in the past for fish breeding and now
linked to Arcachon lagoon via a system
of locks. The reserve promotes the preservation of species of wild fowl threatened
with extinction, and encourages the public
to discover European bird species.

The reserve is divided into four parks:
Les Artigues, La Moulette, Causseyre and
Claude Quancard.

The visitor is given a choice of tours
on foot, all well marked and equipped
with look-outs: the short tour (2.4km/1.5mi),
the long tour (3.6km/2mi) and the complete tour (6km/3.6mi). *We recommend
that you rent binoculars.*

Gujan-Mestras

This busy town with its six oyster farms
is the oyster capital of the Arcachon area.
It is extremely picturesque with tile-roofed
cabins, canals crowded with fishing smacks,

Parc ornithologique du Teich – Stork

J. Malbouret/MICHELIN

oyster-purging tanks and waterfront kiosks
where oysters can be sampled, ordered
and dispatched to family or friends.

In the port of Larros, at the **Maison de
l'Huître** (& Open Jun-Aug 10am-
12.30pm and 2.30-6pm, Sep-May daily
except Sun 10am-12.30pm and 2.30-6pm;
closed 25 Dec-8 Jan; 4.50€; ☎05 56
66 23 71; www.maisondelhuitre.com), an
exhibition and film explain the different

Low-Tide Fishing

At low tide, the Archachon lagoon offers the possibility of fishing for shellfish and
other seafood.

Cockles and **clams** can be gathered by just scraping the surface of the sand to a
depth of 4cm/2in. Clams are easier to locate as two small holes in the sand indicate
their presence. They can be found in large numbers near the Arquin sandbank and
on the mudflats uncovered at low tide. It is advisable to leave them to sweat in salt
water for a few hours before eating them.

Winkles can be gathered by hand on the mudflats. In order to eat them as an appetizer
before a meal, it is necessary to plunge them for a few minutes in boiling water.

Wild **mussels**, found near the oyster beds, can be dislodged with a knife.

Green crabs also abound on the beaches at low tide; they can be caught with a net
and cooked in seasoned boiling water.

Fishing for **shrimps** is done with the help of a net.

As for gathering **razor-shells**, it is real fun. They can be detected by the key-shaped
mark they leave on the sand; place two or three grains of coarse salt on this mark to
trick them into coming up to the surface as they believe the high tide is returning.
Razor-shells are not a refined kind of seafood but they make an excellent bait for
line fishing.

Gathering oysters, even wild ones, is strictly forbidden.

Fishing for cockles and clams is on the other hand allowed but restricted to 2kg/4lb
per person at every tide. Shell-gathering is sometimes forbidden for health reasons
(in case of excessive heat for instance). Be careful when walking on mudflats as
there is always a risk of getting bogged down.

Ch. Faurie/MICHELIN

Dune du Pilat

stages of oyster-farming, from preparation of the collectors to consumption.
A *pinasses* yard (local fishing smacks) and oyster-packaging unit are visible.
You can then sample and compare oysters in fishermen's huts in the heart of the port of Larros.

Parc de Loisirs de la Hume
Kids This park, at the intersection of the N 250 and the D 652, offers a range of leisure facilities including a **medieval miniature golf; Aqualand** (*Open Jul-Aug: 10am-7pm, Jun and early Sep 10am-6pm; 23.50€ (children under 12: 17€); 05 56 66 39 39; www.aqualand.fr)*, a water park; and **La Coccinelle** (*End of Jun to end of Aug: 10.30am-7.30pm, end of May to end of Jun: 10am-6.30pm; 8€ (children: 6.50€); 05 56 66 30 41)*, a menagerie for younger visitors, where they can feed lambs, kids and calves themselves.

La Teste-de-Buch
La Teste was once the capital of the former kingdom of the Buch family and is now part of one of the biggest municipalities (18 000ha/44 500 acres) in France. Settled by the Boli or Boians before the Roman colonisation, it was later developed by the English and subsequently became an important oyster port. Today the municipality includes the ancient forest of La Teste, Cazaux and its lake *(south)*,

and the resorts of Pyla-sur-Mer and Pilat-Plage with its famous dune *(south-west)*. Note, near the tourist office in place Jean-Hameau, the façade of the 18C **Maison Lalanne**, adorned with representations of an anchor, rigging and the heads of the owner's children.

Arcachon ♠♠
See ARCACHON.

▶ *The road passes through the neighbouring resort of Moulleau and then Pyla-sur-Mer and Pilat-Plage, where hotels and villas are scattered beneath the pines, before climbing in a series of hairpin bends towards the famous dune.*

Dune du Pilat★★
This colossal sand dune, at 114m/374ft the highest in Europe, is 2.7km/over 1.5mi long and 500m/550yd wide. Created by the combined action of wind, waves and the land itself, the dune is still constantly changing. The west face slopes gently towards the Atlantic rollers, whereas the hollowed landward side to the east drops sharply to the woodland pines below.
To reach the summit, either scale the flank of the dune (a fairly difficult ascent) or climb the 154-step staircase *(in summer only)*. From the top, the **panorama**★★ over the ocean and the forests of the Landes – the finest of all views over the Silver Coast – is breathtaking, especially at sunset.

AUBETERRE-SUR-DRONNE★

POPULATION 365
MICHELIN MAP 324: L-8

Aubeterre is a very old village huddled in a semicircle at the foot of its castle One of the finest villages in France, it has steep, narrow streets, and stands out against the line of white chalk cliffs that give Aubeterre its name (*alba terra* in Latin, meaning white land). The writer Pierre Véry (1900-1960) was born in Bellon, a few miles away from Aubeterre. One of his most famous books was 'Les Disparus de St-Agil'.

▶ **Orient Yourself**: Situated half-way between the Charente and Aquitaine regions, Aubeterre-sur-Dronne sits on the cliffs overlooking the Dronne Valley. The village is centred on place Trarieux, a quiet square containing a bust of Ludovic Trarieux, native of Aubeterre and founder of La Ligue pour la Défense des Droits de l'Homme et du Citoyen (the League for the Defence of Human Rights). From here, visitors can climb up to Église St-Jacques, or walk down to the monolithic church.

🅿 **Parking**: Park the car near the tourist office.

⊘ **Don't Miss**: The rock-hewn monolithic church.

⚲ **Also See**: ANGOULÊME.

Sights

Monolithic Church★★

🕓*Mid-Jun to mid-Sep 9.30am-noon and 2-7pm; mid-Sep to mid-Jun: 9.30am-noon and 2-6pm.* 🕓*Closed 1 Jan, 25 Dec.* ✆*4€.* ☎ *05 45 98 65 06.*

The church, dedicated to St John, is one of a rare type which has been hewn from a single, solid block of rock. Another example of a monolithic church is to be found in St-Émilion near Bordeaux. A passageway lined with funerary recesses leads to a vast rocky cavern, whose crude materials and stark interior make it a captivating and impressive sight. The 5C or 6C baptismal font, carved in the form of a Greek cross, indicates the existence of a previous church, at the time when baptism by immersion was practised. The crypt would have housed worshipers of Mithras, the ancient Persian deity. The main rival of early Christianity, this cult, characterised by the sacrifice of a bull whose blood was used to baptise worshipers, was spread throughout Gaul by the soldiers of the Roman empire.

Monolithic church

Work on the church probably began in the 12C, to house the relics of the Holy Sepulchre from Jerusalem, brought back from the Crusades by Pierre II de Castillon, owner of the nearby castle. Used as a saltpetre works during the Revolution, it was the local cemetery until 1865.

The 12C nave, which runs parallel to the cliff, is 20m/69ft high. A small spring still filters up through the single side-aisle. Its waters were no doubt considered beneficial and venerated by the early pilgrims. The apse houses a solid rock reliquary of monumental size set aside when the church was hewn. It used to enclose the shrine containing the relics of the Holy Sepulchre. At the opposite end of the nave is the original 6C chapel, turned into a necropolis in the 12C when the church was refurbished. A series of tombs have been hollowed out of the rock.

In the upper part of the nave, a gallery with a suspended ambulatory affords an interesting view of this once primitive place of worship. In former times, a castle stood above the church, linked by a hidden staircase still visible today, providing the lords of the castle with easy access to the gallery, from which they could spy on the congregation and attend religious services.

Église St-Jacques

This former Benedictine abbey church has a Romanesque west front enhanced by arcading delicately carved with geometric motifs in Moorish style. Note in particular the interesting frieze on the left of the central doorway, which depicts the various tasks to be performed throughout the year.

Below the church, a machicolated tower guards the residential quarters of the chapter.

ÉGLISE ST-PIERRE D'AULNAY★★

MICHELIN MAP 322: G-3

Église St-Pierre-de-la-Tour, standing on the borders of Poitou and the Saintonge, along the age-old pilgrims' route to Santiago de Compostela, rises in solitary state among the dark cypresses of an ancient cemetery *(on the side of D 950, NW of the village)*.

▶ **Orient Yourself**: The church of St-Pierre-d'Aulnay stands on the D 950 to the NW of Aulnay village, 17km/11mi NE of St-Jean-d'Angely.

Visit

Guided tours from May-Sep. Contact the tourist office for further information. ☎05 46 33 14 44.

The rare harmony of the composition, the abundant and ornate yet restrained decoration, and the warm patina of old stone combine to make this 12C church a masterpiece of regional Romanesque architecture. The best overall view of the church is from the far end of the cemetery, just to the left of the west front.

West front

The west front is crowned with small lanterns. In its centre stands a porch of broken arches flanked by blind arcades forming funerary niches. The Crucifixion of St Peter is carved on the tympanum of the northern arcade. On the southern tympanum, Christ in Majesty is seen with two figures presumably representing St Peter and St Paul.

The receding arches behind the archivolt are carved with graceful sculptures illustrating the favourite themes of the Poitou image makers – 1st arch (*below*), angels worshipping the Lamb of God; 2nd arch, Virtues exterminating Vices; 3rd arch, the Wise (*left*) and Foolish Virgins; on the 4th arch, Signs of the Zodiac and Labours of the Months. The central blind bay on the upper level of the façade once framed a statue of the Emperor Constantine on a horse.

St-Pierre d'Aulnay

Transept

The square belfry-tower, which stands over the transept crossing, served as a landmark for pilgrims and other travellers. The arching over the **south transept doorway** features rows of superbly carved figures and animals. The carvings are as follows.

Outer arch: mythological characters and creatures – the musical ass, a goat, a deer, an owl, and a mermaid.

3rd arch: the Old Men of the Apocalypse – 31 here instead of the usual 24 – each holding a phial of perfume and a musical instrument. The intrados (underside) of the arch is carved with kneeling atlantes (male figures used as pillars).

2nd arch: the Disciples of Christ and the Apostles (seated atlantes adorn the intrados).

Inner arch: animals (centaurs, griffins) and foliage of Eastern inspiration in light relief.

A tall opening above the porch features a central arch with four fine sculptures of the Virtues conquering the Vices.

East end

On each side of the axial window, strange, Eastern-style wreaths of foliage encircle enigmatic figures.

Interior

The nave is roofed with broken-barrel vaulting and buttressed by tall aisles. Note the unusually deep openings, narrower on the north side than on the south, and the massive pillars cut by two layers of capitals.

A handsome dome on pendentives crowns the inside of the transept crossing, its ribs radiating from a circular opening through which bells in the tower above can be rung.

The capitals in the church, especially those in the transept, are exceptionally fine with carvings of tiny eared elephants *(south transept, by the entrance to the aisle)*, Samson, sleeping, being bound by Delilah while a Philistine cuts his hair with enormous scissors *(north-west pillar, transept crossing)* and imps pulling the beard of a poor man *(north transept, entrance to the aisle)*.

Cemetery

The burial ground, strewn with tombstones in the form of sarcophagi, still has its 15C **hosanna cross**, complete with lectern from which the priest read the lessons on Palm Sunday, and the canopied statues of Saints Peter, Paul, James and John.

BAYONNE★★

POPULATION 178 965
MICHELIN MAP 342: D-2

The heart of this lively and interesting town combines good shopping facilities with picturesque old streets, ramparts and quays on the south bank of the Adour. The main ramparts extend from the 16C Château Vieux (Old Castle) to the Spanish Gate. **Parc de Mousserolles,** on the eastern side of the town known as Petit Bayonne, is a pleasant place for a stroll, with children's playgrounds and a small lake. The citadel overlooking the suburb of St-Esprit, on the northern bank of the river, was built by Vauban.

- **Information:** Pl. des Basques, 64108 Bayonne.
  ☎08 20 42 64 64. www.bayonne-tourisme.com.
- ▶ **Orient Yourself:** Bayonne lies near the coast on the boundary between the Landes and the Basque country, where the River Nive joins the Adour.
- **P Parking:** There are several car parks along the river banks, as well as in the centre of town *(see MAP).*
- **Don't Miss:** Cathédrale Ste-Marie; Museé Basque; Musée Bonnat; the Fêtes de Bayonne at the beginning of August.
- **Organising Your Time:** Allow half a day to explore the old town and visit the Cathédrale Ste-Marie.
- **Also See:** BIARRITZ; SAINT-JEAN-DE-LUZ.

A Bit of History

In the 12C, Bayonne was part of the dowry of **Eleanor of Aquitaine**. When Eleanor's second husband, Henry Plantagenet, assumed the crown of England in 1154, Bayonne became English, and remained so for three centuries.

During the Hundred Years War, a naval force from Bayonne served with the English fleet. The port was bursting with merchandise and the town flourished. However, after the city fell to the French in 1451, the integration of Bayonne into the Kingdom of France brought heavy penalties. A war indemnity had to be paid and the English market, which had made the town prosperous, was lost.

The French Kings encroached on local freedom more than their English counterparts, and laws and legal documents which they decreed, from then on, had to be written in French and not in Gascon. This created deep-rooted resentment among the inhabitants of Bayonne. In the 16C, Charles IX decided to re-open the port, which in the meantime had silted up. The direct channel to the sea was completed in 1578 and trading began again.

Zenith

The prosperity of Bayonne reached its peak in the 18C. The Chamber of Commerce was founded in 1726. Trade with Spain, Holland and the West Indies together with cod-fishing off Newfoundland and local shipbuilding, gave the port as much business as it could handle.

Bayonne was declared a free port in 1784, and this trebled its traffic. In the same year, it was included in the famous series by the painter Joseph Vernet, Great Ports of France. The spoils of war on the high seas were considerable, and affluent citizens commissioned many privateers. The Ministers of Louis XIV – Seignelay, the eldest son of Colbert, and Pontchartrain – officially decreed a system of dividing the spoils: one-tenth was to go to the Admiral of France, two-thirds to the ship-owners, and what was left to the crew. A sum was also set aside for widows, orphans and ransoms to release prisoners from the Barbary pirates.

The town's Corporation of Ironworkers and Armourers is well known: their members invented the **bayonet** – named after Bayonne and first used by the French infantry in 1703.

Walking Tour of the Old Town 3 hr

Cathédrale Ste-Marie★

St Mary's Cathedral was built between the 13C and the 16C in the characteristic style of churches built in northern France. Initially, there was only one south tower. The north tower and both steeples were added in the 19C.

A 13C sculpted knocker, known as a sanctuary ring, is fixed to the north door, leading to the transept. Any fugitive criminal who seized the knocker was assured of sanctuary within the church. Inside, the windows in the nave incorporate fine examples of Renaissance stained glass. In the second chapel on the right (dedicated to St Jerome), a splendid window dating from 1531 depicts *The Canaanite's Prayer*. In the sixth chapel, a commemorative plaque (1926) recalls the Miracle of Bayonne (a celestial apparition in 1451), when English Bayonne was under siege. According to legend, a great white cross surmounted by a crown appeared in the sky, and then the crown turned into a fleur-de-lis, the emblem of France. The townsfolk interpreted this as a sign from God that He wished them to be French, and so discarded the banners and pennants bearing the red cross of St George in favour of those bearing the white cross of France. The following day, Bayonne surrendered.

The harmonious lines and beautiful proportions within the cathedral can best be appreciated from the centre of the three-tiered nave, with its ribbed vaulting, triforium and clerestory windows. Proceed to the ambulatory where the architecture is reminiscent of the Champagne region; the ribbed vaulting of the five radiating apsidal chapels was decorated by Steinheil at the end of the 19C.

Cloisters★

Access from place Louis-Pasteur. &. ©*From mid-May to mid-Sep 9am-12.30pm and 2-6pm (early Oct to mid-May 9.30am-12.30pm and 2-5pm).* ©*Closed 1 Jan, 25 Dec.* ©*No charge.* ©*05 59 46 11 43. Entrance from place Louis-Pasteur.*

The three galleries which remain form a fine 14C Gothic ensemble, with attractive twinned bays. A number of ancient funerary stones can be seen.

From the south gallery, there is a fine view of the Cathedral and its windows, celebrated for their vast dimensions and unusual design.

▷ *Leave via the west door, turn right and then left onto rue de la Monnaie; continue as far as rue du Port-Neuf.*

At the junction with rue Orbe, an attractive half-timbered house stands on the left.

Rue du Port-Neuf

This charming pedestrian precinct is lined with low arcades, beneath which famous pastry shops and confectioners tempt passers-by with mouth-watering displays of chocolates. The art of chocolate-making was brought to Bayonne in the 17C by Jews whose ancestors had been banished from Spain and Portugal.

Place de la Liberté

This is a busy square at the western end of Pont Mayou; the bridge crosses the River Nive at the northern end of the old town. The town hall, the local administrative offices and the theatre, all under the same roof, stand at one end of the square. The town's motto *nunquam polluta* (never spoilt) is engraved on the marble paving.

▷ *Walk along quai Dubourdieu then across Pont Marengo.*

Petit Bayonne

This is the town's popular district; the narrow streets covered with graffiti are lined with small bars which come to life in the evening. The Musée Bonnat and Musée Basque are located in this area.

▷ *Cross back via Pont Pannecau.*

Unfaithful or loose women used to be thrown over the bridge in an iron cage! The bridge leads to rue Poissonnerie; note the fine timber-framed house on the left.

▷ *Walk to the end of rue Poissonnerie then turn left onto rue d'Espagne and*

Address Book

⏱ *For coin categories, see the Legend on the cover flap.*

WHERE TO STAY

⊖⊜ **Chambre d'hôte M. et Mme Ladeuix** – *26 av. Salvador-Allende – 40220 Tarnos – 5km/3mi N of Bayonne via the N 10 –* ☎ *05 59 64 13 95 – heleneladeuix@hotmail.com –* ✉ *– 5 rooms.* The perfect spot for those looking for peace and quiet. A park with oaks, chestnuts, mimosas, banana trees, pears, maples...A vast lawn with a pool, a pen where ewes graze near the rabbit hutches and chicken cages...The rooms are simple but comfortable. Self-catering cottage for four.

⊖⊜⊜ **Grand Hôtel** – *21 r. Thiers –* ☎ *05 59 59 62 00 – infos@bw-legrandhotel.com – 54 rooms – restaurant* ⊖⊜. Near the cathedral, this traditional hotel proposes rooms with a slightly passé charm. Ask for one of the quieter rooms overlooking the internal courtyard. Small, luminous dining room under a glass roof.

WHERE TO EAT

⊖ **Le Bayonnais** – *38 quai des Corsaires –* ☎ *05 59 25 61 19 – closed 13-28 Jun, 28 Jul-4 Aug, 7-29 Nov, Sun from Sep to Jun and Mon.* With a name like Le Bayonnais, this restaurant on the docks of the Nive has no choice but to serve native cooking. And the owner does just that, concocting local dishes with great care. Photos and posters tip their beret to Basque sports. Our kind of address.

⊖⊜ **Iltsaski** – *43 quai Jauréguiberry –* ☎ *05 59 46 13 96 – closed Sun evening and Tue except in high season.* This restaurant on the docks of the Nive is often packed. The dining room has a boat-like interior and the seafood-rich cuisine is a hit. The terrace looks out on the Petit Bayonne.

⊖⊜ **El Asador** – *pl. Montaut –* ☎ *05 59 59 08 57 – closed 7 Jun-2 Jul, 20 De-7 Jan, Sun eve and Mon – reserv. required.* The grilled specialities à la plancha of this little restaurant transport one to the Spanish Basque country. The owner, who prepares local dishes with passion and talent, is quite proud of the freshness of her fish and prawns. Images of San Sebastian in the 1930s on the walls.

BARS AND CAFES

Le Petit Bayonne – Right where the Nive River meets l'Adour, le Petit Bayonne is the quarter where the city's young folk gather – the beating heart of local nightlife. As soon as the weather warms up, so does the general party atmosphere, thanks to the bars and restaurants crowding the neighbourhood. Between la rue des Cordeliers, la rue Pannecau and la rue des Tonneliers, there are a good thirty establishments. Among them, you may want to try the Txalupa (26, rue des Cordeliers) and the Killarney Pub (35, rue des Cordeliers).

Chai Ramina – *11 r. Poissonnerie –* ☎ *05 59 59 33 01 – Tue-Thu 9.30am-8pm, Fri-Sat until 2am – closed 1-15 Jan, Sun and Mon.* Ramina, a former rugby champion, found a new calling 25 years ago when he opened this pub, a locals' bar with a lively atmosphere. A good place to sample whisky – there are 300 varieties to choose from!

ENTERTAINMENT

Arènes de Bayonne – *Av. Alfred-Bouland –* ☎ *05 59 46 61 00 or 05 53 25 48 19 – daily 9:30am-12:30pm and 3-6.30pm.* From bull fighting to pop concerts, a large variety of shows are organised in the Bayonne arenas.

La Luna Negra – *R. des Augustins –* ☎ *05 59 25 78 05 – www.lunanegra.free.fr – Wed-Sat 7pm-2am – closed Aug (except fêtes de Bayonne beg. Aug.) – 5-10€.* This dynamic café-theatre offers a different show every evening: plays, songfests, cabarets, one-man shows, jazz, blues or rock concerts, story-telling sessions and readings of great literary works. Painting and photography exhibitions are also organised regularly.

Théâtre de Bayonne – *Pl. de la Liberté –* ☎ *05 59 59 07 27 – snbayonne@wanadoo.fr – information/reservations: Tue-Sat 10am-1pm and 3-6pm – closed mid-Jul. to late Aug, public hols. 4-32€ depending on the show.* This is the national theatre of Bayonne and the Sud Aquitain. All sorts of performances are put on here – plays, dance, opera. They hold a yearly festival called 'Jazz in the Ramparts' in mid-July.

SHOPPING

M. Leoncini – *37 r. Vieille-Boucherie –* ☎ *05 59 59 18 20 – Mon-Fri 4-6.30pm, Sat 10am-noon.* Mr. Leoncini is one of the last craftsmen to continue the makila-making tradition. A *makila* is a Basque cane used for hiking and defence made of medlar wood, sculpted while still green, that contains a long, sharp blade.

Market – *Mon-Fri 7am-1pm.* Located on the banks of the Nive, this traditional fruit and vegetable market delights the senses with its vivid colours and heady aromas.

Maison Montauzer – *17 r. de la Salie –* ☎ *05 59 59 07 68 – charcuterie.montauzer@ wanadoo.fr – open Tue-Sat 7am-12.30pm and 3.30-7.30pm; Mon 7.30am-12.30pm – closed Sun and public hols.* Among this delicatessen's specialities, their Ibaïona ham comes from pigs raised exclusively on Basque country grains. In accordance with tradition, it is dried 15 to 18 months outside, where it soaks up the flavours of the different seasons.

Pierre Ibaïalde – *41 r. des Cordeliers –* ☎ *05 59 25 65 30 – pierre.ibaialde@ wanadoo.fr – open summer Mon-Sat 10am-12.30pm and 2am-7pm; rest of the year Mon-Sat 9am-12.30pm and 2-6pm – closed Sun and public hols.* After having visited this cottage-style canning factory, you'll know Bayonne ham from A to Z. Pierre Ibaïalde will explain each step of the ham-making process and will invite you to taste his products, ham and foie gras.

Chocolat Cazenave – *19 r. du Port-Neuf –* ☎ *05 59 59 03 16 – www.lantegiak.com – open school hols: Mon-Sat 9am-noon and 2-7pm; general hours: Tue-Sat 9am-noon and 2-7pm – closed 3 wks in Oct.* Early in the 17C, Bayonne was the first French city to produce chocolate. Of the numerous chocolatiers who set up shop in the rue du Port-Neuf, only two remain: Cazenave (since 1854) and Daranatz (since 1930).

SPORTS AND LEISURE

Tennis -L'Aviron Bayonnais – *Garage de la Nive –* ☎ *05 59 63 33 13 – www.aviron-bayonnais.asso.fr – open Apr-Aug daily 9am-1pm and 4-8.30pm, Wed and Sat 9am-6pm; Sep-Mar schedule may change daily– closed public hols.* The ancient fortifications of Vauban are the setting for this distinctive tennis club, founded in 1922. Two important tournaments take place at Easter and during the first fortnight of August. 12 courts.

Trinquet Moderne – *60 av. Dubrocq –* ☎ *05 59 59 05 22 – open daily from 9am.* Many barehanded pelota matches take place between the glass walls of this covered *trinquet* (court). The French are among the finest players internationally.

Trinquet St-André – *2 r. du Jeu-de-Paume –* ☎ *05 59 59 18 69 – open Mon-Sat 8.30am-10pm.* This 17C *trinquet* is among the oldest in France. The Basques come here for a game of pala before having a drink at the bar. Bare-handed matches are held from the first Thursday of October to the last Thursday of June. Wooden palettes are let by the hour.

EVENTS

Fêtes de Bayonne – *Early Aug.* The Bayonne summer festival includes bullfights, fairs, dances and concerts of traditional Basque music.

right onto rue Tour-de-Sault skirting the ramparts.

Botanical Gardens

🕐*Open from mid-Apr to mid-Oct daily except Sun and Mon, 9.30am-noon and 2-6pm.* ⊗*No charge.* ☎*05 59 46 60 84.* Overlooking the ramparts is a Japanese-style garden with over 1 000 plant species.

▶ *To return to the cathedral, follow the avenue du 11-Novembre and then turn right into rue de la Monnaie.*

Museums

Musée Bonnat★★★

5 rue Jacques-Laffitte. ♿ 🕐*Open Jul-Aug 10am-6.30pm (Wed 9.30pm); May-Jun and Sep-Oct daily except Tue 10am-6.30pm; Nov-Apr daily except Tue 10am-12.30pm and 2-6pm.* 🕐*Closed public hols, except Jul-Aug.* ⊗*5.50€, no charge 1st Sunday in the month in Jul-Aug.* ☎*05 59 59 08 52.*

A chronological tour of the museum's works of art begins on the second floor, where the Primitive and Old Master paint-

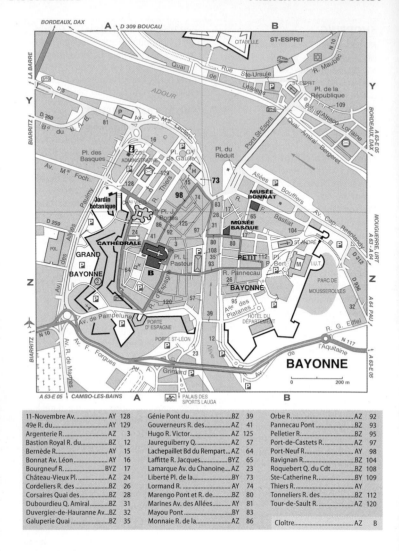

BAYONNE

ings hang. Among those dating from the 14C and 15C, are a *Head of Christ Dead* from the Venetian School and a *Virgin and Child with Pomegranate* attributed to the School of Botticelli.

The Rubens Room contains canvases showing Apollo and Daphne and The Triumph of Venus.

The 17C and 18C artists represented include Vouet *(Roman Charity)* and Tiepolo (study for the royal palace in Madrid). From the Spanish and English schools from the 17C to the early 19C, there are works by Ribera *(Woman Tearing Out Her Hair)*, Murillo *(San Salvador de Horta and*

the Inquisitor of Aragon), Goya *(Portrait of Don Francisco de Borja)*, Constable *(Hampstead Heath)* and Hoppner *(Head of a Woman)*. 19C French painting is represented by The *Oath of the Horati (*School of David*)*, several works by Ingres including *The Bather, Study of a naked young Man* by Flandrin and, on the first floor, paintings by Delacroix, Géricault, Degas, Puvis de Chavannes and Bonnat – the artist who assembled this superb collection during his long lifetime (1833-1922) and left it to his native town. His works are exhibited in a gallery surrounding the ground floor terrace.

The museum's Drawings Department houses a selection by the Grand Masters, French and foreign; there is a permanent collection of drawings by Paul Helleu and an alternating display. Another room has sketches by Rubens and terracottas from the Cailleux collection.

Musée Basque et de l'histoire de Bayonne★★★

Maison Dagourette, 37 quai des Corsaires. ⏰*May-Oct daily except Mon 10am-6.30pm; Nov-Apr daily except Mon 10am-12.30pm and 2-6pm.* ⏰*Closed public holidays.* ✆*5.50€, no charge 1st Sun in the month.* ✆*05 59 46 61 90; www.museebasque.com*

The museum, which was created in 1924, has a vast collection of objects, pictures and books which relate to the history and people of the Basque country and the western region of the Pyrenees. The **Maison Dagourette** houses the permanent collection, whereas the **Château-Neuf** site is used for temporary exhibits. The approach has been to liven up the ethnographic displays with music and images creating a space which is dynamic as well as informative.

The exhibits are centred around the themes of work on the farm (shepherding, traditional crafts and cheese-making); architecture and interior furnishings; boats, shipping and other economic activities; games, sports, arts and music and religious traditions.

Excursions

Croix de Mouguerre★

10km/6mi E. Exit Bayonne via the D 312 – road to Bidache. Turn right and follow the mountain road through Mouguerre, then right again to the Crucifix.

Along the river Nive

B. Kaufmann/MICHELIN

This French national monument commemorates battles fought by the troops of Maréchal Soult against the invading English, Spanish and Portuguese troops, commanded by Wellington in 1813-14. There is a **panoramic view**★ of the Landes region, Bayonne, the Basque coast and the Pyrenees.

Route Impériale des Cimes★ (Napoleon I's Scenic Highway)

From Bayonne to Hasparren, 25km/ 15mi. Leave Bayonne to the SE by the D 936. At the far end of St-Pierre-d'Irube turn right onto the D 22.

Napoleon I had this winding route carved out through the mountains, as part of a strategic link between Bayonne and St-Jean-Pied-de-Port. The **view**★ opens out on the Basque coastline and the summits of the Pyrenees nearest the sea – La Rhune, the jagged crest of Les Trois Couronnes and Le Jaizkibel, which at this distance looks like a steeply contoured island. As the road approaches **Hasparren** the Basque Pyrenees of the upper Nive basin stretch from La Rhune to L'Artzamendi.

BAZAS★

POPULATION 4 379
MICHELIN MAP 335: J-8

Surrounded by ruined Gothic ramparts, Bazas is situated in a region of fertile hills and since the 15C has been the seat of a bishopric (the title of which, since 1937, has belonged to the archbishop of Bordeaux). The 4C Latin poet Ausonius, born in Burdigala (Bordeaux), stayed here several times. Recent excavations have brought to light foundations of the ancient oppidum (settlement), which date back to the 7C BC.

- **Information:** 1 pl. de la Cathédrale, 33430 Bazas. ☎05 56 25 25 84. www.ville-bazas.fr.
- ▶ **Orient Yourself**: Bazas stands on a narrow promotory above the Beuve valley, 60km/37mi SE of Bordeaux and 40km/25mi SW of Marmande.
- **Parking**: Park on place de la Cathédrale in the centre of town.
- **Don't Miss**: Cathédrale Saint-Jean; Château de Roquetaillade *(11km/7mi NW of Bazas)*; Château de Cazeneuve *(10km/6mi SW of Bazas)*.

Visit

Place de la Cathédrale

This lovely square is lined with 16C and 17C houses. No 3 called **maison de l'Astrologue** is decorated with astrological symbols (serious looking faces of the moon and the sun, oriental astrologer wearing a pointed hat).

Cathédrale St-Jean★

Guided tours available. Contact the tourist office for further information. ☎*05 56 25 25 84.*

The cathedral dates from the 13C-14C and was built on the model of the great Gothic sanctuaries of northern France. The blood of John the Baptist was venerated here. The west front is of an attractive and harmonious design, despite the differences in style between the three storeys. The first dates from the 13C, the second from the 16C, and the top storey, from the 18C.

Doorways – Their tympana and coving still have fine 13C sculptures which the locals saved from Protestant vandals by paying the sum of 10 000 *écus*. The central

Place de la Cathédrale

B. Kaufmann/MICHELIN

Address Book

WHERE TO STAY AND TO EAT

⊖**Ferme-auberge Aux Repas Fermiers de Haoun Barrade** – *34430 Cudos – 5km/3mi S of Bazas. Take D 932 towards Mont-de-Marsan – ☎05 56 25 06 69 – open 10 Jul-1 Sep; lunch Sat-Sun and public hols –* 🍽. This plain and simple *auberge* in the countryside serves produce made by farmers belonging to a co-op. Try patés, *rillettes* and meat stews made from duck, kid, chicken, rabbit or young boar, accompanied by good local wines.

⊖⊖⊜**Chambre d'hôte Château d'Arbieu** – *Route de Castel – Bazas exit on the right of route de Casteljaloux via the D 655 – ☎ 05 56 25 11 18 – arbieu@ wanadoo.fr – closed Feb school hols and All Saints'Day – reserv. required – 4 rooms.* A rocky road through the country leads to this 19C château with a vast park. Its spacious, regal rooms are graced with numerous handsome period pieces. Unwind in the reading room, or with a game of billiards or table football.

---

doorway shows the Last Judgement and the story of John the Baptist, and the side doors, the Virgin and St Peter.

Interior – The long, narrow nave, with no transept, gives a striking impression of grandeur.

In the chancel, the Louis XV-style high altar in different coloured marbles is somewhat fussy. The axial chapel contains paintings by François Lemoyne (18C).

Jardin du Chapitre

This garden is a haven of peace located over the ramparts, on the right side of the cathedral. It looks like a mediaeval garden with a few relics (from the iron age to the 15C) There is a fine view of the Beuve Valley.

▶ *Return to the cathedral and turn left (before the town hall) onto rue Théophile-Servière then walk along the Maurice-Lapierre ramp.*

Promenade de la Brèche

Before enjoying the walk under the lime trees, beneath the old ramparts covered with moss and ivy, take some time to visit the rose garden in the **jardin du Sultan**.

Excursions

Collégiale d'Uzeste★

8km/5mi W by the D 110. ⏰*Open weekends and public holidays, 3-6pm.* ☎*05 56 25 87 48.*

The collegiate church in the village of Uzeste is somewhat of a rival to Bazas Cathedral. **Pope Clement V** played a major part in building the church. He raised it to a collegiate church in 1312, and named it in his will as the site for his tomb. Outside, note the arrangement of the east end and the belfry, the latter completed only in the 16C.

Enter the church by the south door, with its tympanum decorated with a fine Coronation of the Virgin. Behind the altar, holding a crucifix, thought to date from the 15C, lies the white marble figure of Clement V which was damaged by the Protestants. In the axial chapel is a 13C figure of the Virgin which was venerated by Pope Clement (born Ber-

Château de Cazeneuve - Henri IV's room

trand de Got, in Villandrault) in his youth and, in the neighbouring chapel, a 14C funerary effigy.

Château de Villandraut

13km/8mi W along the D 110 then the D 3. ⏱*Jul and Aug 10am-7pm; Sep-Oct and Mar-Jun 2-6pm; Nov to mid-Dec and mid-Jan to end Feb 2-6pm; Sat-Sun and public hols 2-6pm.* ✎*3.20€.* ☎*05 56 25 87 57.* This striking example of Gothic castle architecture was built for Pope Clement V, who often stayed here. A fairly large area

was for residential use, which was characteristic of medieval castles in Italy and the Middle East. The south side is more spectacular due to the alignment of its four large towers, the one on the right having been levelled in 1592 on the orders of the Parliament of Bordeaux.

Château de Roquetaillade★★

8km/5mi NW by the D 1 and D 223.

Château de Cazeneuve★

10km/6mi SW by the D 9.

LE BÉARN★★

MICHELIN MAP 342: I-K 3-5

Béarn, the largest of the formerly independent Pyrenees States, is crossed diagonally by Gave de Pau and Gave d'Oléron. Meadows and ploughed fields rise in terraces on either side of these fast-flowing streams, while orchards and vines flourish on the lower slopes of the long ridges above, mainly covered in moors.

In the southern part of the region, the Pyrenees rise to the dramatic heights of Pic du Midi d'Ossau (alt 2 884m/9 462ft) and Pic d'Anie (alt 2 504m/8 215ft). The route to the pass, Col d'Aubisque (alt 1 709m/5 610ft), linking Béarn to the Bigorre region through the mountains, is the most picturesque in the area.

- ▸ **Orient Yourself**: The Béarn region covers about two-thirds of the Pyrénées-Atlantiques *département* and is bordered to the south by Spain.
- **Don't Miss**: The Route de l'Aubisque; the Haut Ossau.
- **Especially for Kids**: The zoo at Asson; Falaise aux Vautours wildlife centre at Aste-Béon.
- **Also See**: PAU.

The Béarnais

The people of Béarn (the Béarnais) are used to an isolated existence. Unlike the Basques, they are very communicative. They often converse in a variant of the old Gascon tongue.

Traditional Béarn can be seen most clearly during the 15 August procession at Laruns, in the Vallée d'Ossau. The men wear red jackets, waistcoats with wide lapels, knee breeches, gaiters and berets. The women are dressed in black or brown wide, pleated skirts, partly covered by a small lace apron. They also wear an embroidered shawl and a silk-lined, scarlet hood which falls to the shoulders. A white traditional *bonnette*

crowns the women's plaited hair. Only heiresses can wear a red skirt and the family gold jewellery.

Young men and women dance the Ossau *Branle* (swing or shake) to the music of the three-hole *fluto* (a flageolet like the Basque *txirulä*) and tambourines – both played by the same musician.

In spite of its name, sauce *béarnaise* is not a local culinary speciality; it was invented in 1830 in the kitchens of the Pavillon Henri IV in St-Germain-en-Laye, near Paris. However there is a connection: good King Henri IV was a native of Béarn!

Address Book

For coin ranges, see the Legend on the cover flap.

WHERE TO STAY

Chambre d'hôte La Ferme aux Sangliers – *Micalet* – *64570 Issor* – *10km/6mi W of St-Christau. Take the D 918 to Asasp, then the N 134 and the D 918 to Arette* – *☎05 59 34 43 96* – *reserv. required* – *5 rooms - meals*. Tastefully restored with the original farm in mind, this isolated house is remarkably situated facing the Pyrenees. Pretty rooms with a blend of stones and exposed beams. Try the home-made products, notably the *civet de sanglier* made from boar raised in the park.

Hôtel Au Bon Coin – *rte des Thermes* – *64660 Lurbe-St-Christau* – *☎05 59 34 40 12* – *closed Sun evening, Mon and Tue noon from 10 Oct-30 Mar* – *restaurant*. This long edifice surrounded by trees faces the countryside. The rooms are modern and comfortable; half of them have a view of the mountains. Meals are served in the rustic dining room or on the veranda. Garden with a pool across the way.

WHERE TO EAT

La Pimparela – *plateau d'Ipère* – *64490 Osse-en-Aspe* – *☎05 59 34 52 23* – *reserv. required off-season*. Perched above the Aspe valley, this authentic mountain stable is set amid fields covered with *pimparelas* (daisies). A delightful array of home-made products to savour on the terrace or in the charming dining room featuring floral bouquets and blue-tinted wood.

SHOPPING

Cave des Vignerons du Jurançon – *53 av. Henri-IV - 64290 Gan* – *☎05 59 83 05 91 or 06 85 20 53 23* – *open 9am-noon and 2-7pm*. This local wine producer makes sweet and dry Jurançon wine which is aged in oak barrels for a period of three years.

Tissage de Coarraze – *R. Louis-Barthou* – *64800 Coarraze* – *☎05 59 61 19 98*. Basque fabrics are renowned for their quality and durability and are ideal for household linen of all types.

Driving Tours

Gave d'Aspe★

1. **From Oloron-Ste-Marie to Col du Somport**
66km/41mi – 3hrs

Today, despite improvements to the roads and the opening in 1928 of a trans-Pyrenean railway (currently not operating south of Bedous), the glaciated valley of the Gave d'Aspe – narrowing into wild gorges, and sometimes opening out into fertile basins – retains all the harshness of its mountain heritage. The villages here make no concession to being picturesque or charming. The occasional bear (these days protected by the National Parks authority) still roams the lonely forests. The population of the long valley now numbers less than 5 000. However, the Somport Tunnel linking Pau and Zaragossa should bring considerable changes and breathe new life into this area.

One of its famous emigrants was Pierre Laclède (1729-78), who was born in Bedous and later founded the city of St Louis, Missouri.

Oloron-Ste-Marie

See OLORON-STE-MARIE.

▶ *Leave Oloron to the SE via rue d'Aspe.*

The road, following the east bank of the Aspe, crosses a rural valley planted with maize and wheat, divided occasionally by windbreaks of poplar trees. Ahead, Pic Mail-Arrouy (alt 1 251m/4 100ft) appears to block any passage south.

St-Christau

The air in this small spa is fresh and cool. The waters are rich in iron and copper and the cure centre, standing in a 60ha/ 148 acre park, specialises in treating ailments of the mucous membranes.

▸ *Continue S to Escot*

Escot

This was the first Aspe village, strikingly perched on a terrace at the mouth of Vallée du Barescou. In accordance with the local formalities, the Viscount of Béarn had to exchange hostages with representatives of the valley before setting foot in Escot. Louis IX, on a pilgrimage to Notre-Dame-de-Sarrance, indicated that he was leaving his own kingdom by ordering his sword-bearer to lower his blade.

Sarrance

Sarrance, a place of local pilgrimage was visited by both Louis XI (1461) and Marguerite d'Angoulême (Queen of Navarre), who wrote part of her book of tales, *Heptameron*, here. The **church**, rebuilt in 1609, has a very Baroque octagonal belfry-porch with concave sides surmounted by a lantern. Inside, are 15C wooden panels with naïve carving. The **cloisters** of the former 17C monastery have a slate roof supported by 14 small transverse gables.

At Bedous, a pronounced humpback rise affords an unexpected view of the valley's central basin and its seven villages. In the background the crests of Arapoup are visible and, to the right in the distance, the first summits of the Lescun cirque (Pic de Burcq).

▸ *The road again enters a narrow gorge. Turn right to Lescun.*

Lescun★

Lescun is a favourite village with mountain lovers, owing to the surrounding cirque with its needle-like limestone peaks.

To admire the full **panorama★★**, park in the car park behind Hôtel du Pic d'Anie and walk to the viewpoint *(30min round trip on foot)*. Follow the GR10 footpath as far as the church.

Beyond a public wash-house with a crucifix, the footpath winds around a hillock. From here, looking back, there is a fine view of Pic d'Anie to the right and, to the left, Le Billare and Dec de Lhurs.

The **Route du Somport★** *(N 134)* continues to climb the valley, which is now an almost continuous succession of gorges and narrow passes. The villages, built in pairs on opposite sides of the valley, seem to be watching over one another (Eygun and Cette, Etsaut and Borce).

Fort du Portalet

This stronghold is perched on a sheer cliff above the river in one of the narrowest, most steep-sided sections of the valley. It was built in the early 19C, and later used for the internment of prominent anti-Nazis during the Occupation (1941-45). From the road, the walled ramps leading to the casemates commanding the road to Urdos can be seen.

Leaving the gorge, the peaks marking the Spanish border appear as a jagged crest cut through by Pas d'Aspe. The scene is dominated by Pico de la Garganta (2 636m/8 660ft), which is usually flecked with snow.

Beyond Urdos, on the left, is Arnousse Viaduct.

Col du Somport★★

At an altitude of 1 632m/5 351ft, this pass (the only one in the Central Pyrenees accessible the whole year round) has been famous since the passage of the Roman legions. Until the 12C, it was used by pilgrims on the way to Santiago de Compostela. An important staging post at the time was St Christine's Hospice (now demolished) on the southern slopes of the range.

The high ground behind the restaurant affords an impressive view of the Aragon Pyrenees on the far side of the border.

Le Haut Ossau★★

See LE HAUT OSSAU.

Frange Des Pyrénées★

2 **Round tour from Pau**
79km/49mi – about 4hrs 30min

▸ *Leave Pau to the SW via the suburb of Jurançon; the N 134 follows the*

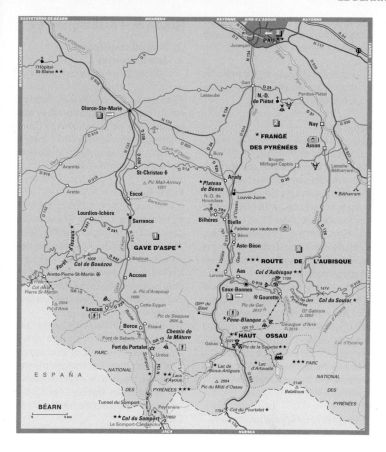

valley of the River Nez. At Gan turn
left onto the D 24.

Notre-Dame-de-Piétat

Opposite the 17C pilgrims' chapel, at the
end of the esplanade, there is a roadside
crucifix. Behind this is a viewing table
providing a **panorama**★ of the Gave de
Pau Valley and its many villages. Pic du
Midi de Bigorre is visible in the distance
(south-east), beyond the line of wooded
foothills.

▸ Continue to D 37 and turn right
along the valley.

Between Pardies-Piétat and Nay the road
passes through several pretty Béarn villages whose splendid houses have gateways decorated with piers surmounted
by stone urns.

Nay

Nay (pronounced nigh) is a *bastide*
typical of the Béarn region.
The **Musée du Béret**, situated at the
entrance of the village, relates the history of the genuine beret from Béarn
and illustrates the various stages of its
manufacture. ◯*Jul-Aug 10am-noon and
2-7pm; Sun 2-7pm; Apr-Jun and Sep-Oct,
daily except Sun and Mon 10am-noon and
2-6pm; Nov-Mar Tue 10am-noon and 2-6pm,
Wed and Sat 2-6pm; school hols daily
except Sun and Mon 2-6pm.* ◯*Closed 1 Jan,
1 May and 25 Dec.* ◈*4€.* ☏*05 59 61 91 70;
www.museeduberet.com*
In the main square, the **Maison Carrée**
(16C), also called Maison de Jeanne
d'Albret, was built in the Renaissance
period. The inner Florentine-style courtyard shows three classical forms of architecture and is a unique example of this

style in south-west France. It houses collections from the Musée béarnais and temporary exhibitions.

▶ *3km/1.8mi W of the village (towards Bruges) a road branches off to the Jardin Exotique.*

Zoo d'Asson

🕐*Apr-Sep 9am-7pm; Oct-Mar 9am-6pm.* ➡*8.50€ (children: 6€).* ☎*05 59 71 03 34.*
The **zoo** 🖼 is planted with about a hundred palm-trees and adorned with a fine Napoleon III style greenhouse. It is home to a raucous and colourful collection of parrots, parakeets, pink Cuban flamingos, emus, panthers, lorikeets, chimpanzees and gibbons,a colony of lemurs from Madagascar, and one of the largest kangaroo parks in Europe.
The road continues through a series of villages with flower-filled gardens. Fields of maize make way for orchards, and these in turn are succeeded by trellised vines. As the road drops down finally to the Lower Ossau Valley, the stone belfry of **Louvie-Juzon church**, with its distinctive outline of an inverted chalice, comes slowly into view.

▶ *Right on N 134 beyond Louvie-Juzon.*

Arudy

Industrially, this is the most developed town in Lower Ossau, due to the surrounding marble quarries and the various factories built on the outskirts.
Maison d'Ossau (🕐*open Jul and Aug daily except Mon, 10am-noon and 3-6pm; Jan-Jun and Sep daily except Mon 2-5pm, Sat, Sun and public hols 3-6pm; Feb and Easter school hols daily except Mon 3-6pm;* 🕐*closed Oct-Dec and 1 Ma;* ➡*2.50€;* ☎*05 59 05 61 71)*, a 17C house near the east end of the church, contains displays on prehistoric life in the Pyrenees in its basement. The former residential rooms on the ground floor include an exhibit on the flora, fauna and geology of Vallée d'Ossau. Displays on the attic floor are devoted to the history of the valley and the life of the local shepherds.

▶ *To return to Pau, follow the D 920 to Buzy then turn right onto the D 34 which leads back to the N 134.*

Route de l'Aubisque★★★

③ **Round tour from Eaux-Bonnes**
107km/66mi – allow one day

🚗*As a rule, Col d'Aubisque (Aubisque Pass) is blocked by snow from November to June. The cliff road beyond Col de l'Aubisque is very narrow which makes it difficult for vehicles to pass. Consequently, traffic alternates every 2hrs.*

Eaux-Bonnes

🅂🄿🄰 This spa, nestling in the wooded Vallée du Valentin, offers thermal cures initially developed by the great doctor from Béarn, Théophile de Bordeu, to treat respiratory disorders. The promenades, laid out in the 19C in the wooded foothills of the Gourzy, are witness to the refined appreciation of nature and the creature comforts of the times.
The esplanade in Darralde Gardens, bordered by mansions typical of Second Empire spas, is the hub of local activity. After skiing, there is nothing better than a shower, a sauna or a bath session at the spa in Eaux-Bonnes. For further information, contact the tourist office in Eaux-Bonnes.

▶ *Turn left to Aas.*

Aas

In this village typical of the Ossau region, with its steep, narrow streets, some of the locals still use the whistling language once used by shepherds to communicate with one another throughout the valley, at distances of up to 2 500m/ 7 000ft. A similar language is also used on Gomera Island in the Canaries, in the Görele Valley in Turkey and by Mexico's Maztec and Zapatec Indians.
The road crosses the River Valentin (🚗 *note the waterfall*) and starts the long haul up the side of the mountain, offering splendid views of the Pic de Ger massif, especially in the early morning and at dusk.

Gourette⁎

🅸*Pl. Sarrière, 64440 Gourette,* ☎*05 59 05 12 17, www.gourette.com.*

A. Thuillier/MICHELIN

Col de l'Aubisque under snow

Gourette is a popular winter sports resort, which owes its existence to Henri Sallanave, a native of Pau, who pioneered downhill skiing in the Pyrenees in 1903. Although international skiing championships had been held here yearly since 1908, the resort was not opened until 1930. Apartment blocks nestle in an cirque scarred by the rugged strata of Pic du Ger (alt 2 613m/7 316ft) and the rocky jagged formation of Pène Médaa, which is an impressive **site**★ in the limestone mountains of the Pyrenees.

Pène Blanque★

1hr 30min round trip using the gondola lift from Gourette.

The upper platform of the **gondola lift** is in the northern cirque of Pène Blanque, at the foot of Pic de Ger and not far from a group of small mountain lakes. From here, there is a fine **view**★ of Gourette and the road to Col d'Aubisque.

A difficult footpath, zigzagging between Pic de Ger and Géougue d'Arre, leads to a pass *(allow an extra 2hr round trip for this excursion)* from which there is an interesting view of the border peaks of the **Balaïtous**. Below is a lake and Vallée d'Artouste. Cows and horses graze freely in the pastures along the roadside. Not far beyond Gourette, from a corner of the Crêtes Blanches (White Crests), a splendid panorama unfolds. In the distance you can see Pic du Midi de Bigorre.

Col d'Aubisque★★

The pass is at an altitude of 1 709m/5 608ft. Sports enthusiasts will recognise it from the annual Tour de France bicycle race. The south knoll *(TV relay – 15min on foot from the car park)* affords a striking view of the whole Gourette cirque, and an immense **panorama**★★ from Pic de Gers to Pic de Montaigu *(due east, in the distance)* with nine major peaks in between. Beyond the pass, the road *(D 918)*, carved into the mountainside, offers views of the Vallée de Ferrières and, in the distance, the Béarn plain. After that, the **Corniche des Pyrénées** skirts Cirque du Litor at a height of almost 300m/1 000ft. This is one of the most impressive sections of the drive, along a road which was one of the boldest feats of 19C engineering.

Col du Soulor★

The pass lies at an altitude of 1 474m/4 740ft. Grass-covered peaks form the foreground to a sweeping mountain vista. Beyond the Vallée d'Azun the summits between Pic du Midi de Bigorre and, farther to the left, Pic de Montaigu, rise into view.

▶ *Turn left onto the D 126.*

Asson

See 2 above.

In the distance, after crossing the bridge to Louvie-Juzon, the great mass of Pic du Midi d'Ossau comes into view.

The Tour de France Bicycle Race

Every year cyclists in the Tour de France take on this awe-inspiring challenge through the passes of the Pyrenees, bringing glory to a few and disappointment to the rest. Aubisque, Tourmalet, Aspin, Soulor are synonymous not only with pulled muscles, violent summer storms, steep inclines and extremely narrow roads, but also with huge crowds from all over France and Spain cheering on the leader in the yellow jersey.

The Pyrenees joined the Tour in 1910, with a segment from Perpignan to Bayonne, and a stopover in Luchon. In 1918, Envalira Pass was included, at an altitude of 2 407m/ 8 063ft. In the 1960s, the Tour went through the newly established winter sports resorts of Superbagnères, La Mongie, Luz-Ardiden, Hautacam and Val-Louron etc. The 1990s, saw the five consecutive victories of the unbeatable Spanish cyclist, Indurain. Most recently, the American Lance Armstrong, now retired, holds the record for consecutive wins: a total of 7.

▷ *Beyond Louvie-Juzon, turn left onto the D 934.*

The road enters the **Vallée du Gave d'Ossau**★★.

Bielle

This former county seat, split in two by a tributary of Gave d'Ossau, retains a certain sleepy dignity. Several 16C town houses can be seen in the south bank district, between the main road and the church. On the north bank stands a castle built by the Marquis de Laborde (1724-94), a banker during the time of Louis XV and the Duc de Choiseul.

▷ *Follow the D 294 to Bilhères.*

Bilhères

▷ *Drive right through the village.*

This is a scattered village containing several houses with 16C and 17C decorative elements – embellished keystones, for example, in the arched doorways.

Plateau de Bénou★

Above Bilhères the view opens out southwards as far as Pic de Ger. The chapel of Notre-Dame-de-Houndaas *(rest stop facilities)*, shaded by two lime trees, appears in a **site**★ which is kept fresh by running water from several main springs. The road then runs into the pastureland of the Bénou basin where large flocks of sheep graze in summer.

▷ *Return to Bielle and drive upriver towards Laruns.*

Aste-Béon

▷ *On the right bank of the Ossau Torrent.*

On the way into Béon village is the **Falaise aux Vautours**, (Vulture's Cliff) an interpretation centre (Kids ◷ *Open Jun to Aug 10.30am-12.30pm and 2-6.30pm - last admission 1hr before closing time; Sep 2-6pm, Apr and school and public hols 2-5pm; ⊚6€ (children: 5€); ☎05 59 82 65 49; www.falaise-aux-vautours.com).*
At the foot of a limestone cliff are nesting grounds for a large colony of tawny vultures. The Ossau Nature Reserve was set up to protect these and other raptor's breeding habitat. These include bearded vultures, Egyptian vultures, black and royal kites, peregrine falcons and kestrels
The exhibit, divided into 12 sections, offers an insight into the lifestyles of these birds of prey. Of particular interest is the three-dimensional model of the cliff with a panoramic screen projecting images of the vultures' seasonal behaviour patterns, from the courting display, nest-building, hatching of the solitary egg, to the feeding and flying away of their young. There are other displays on cattle farming, tales and legends from Vallée d'Ossau and the fauna and flora of the Pyrenees.

▷ *Drive back to Eaux-Bonnes along the D 918.*

SITES DE BÉTHARRAM ★

The Bétharram caves and sanctuary are located near the former bastide of Lestelle-Bétharram, founded in 1335 by Gaston de Foix. Several beautiful Renaissance and 18C houses still line the streets laid out at right angles to each other. The sanctuary, an age-old place of pilgrimage, used to enjoy considerable popularity.

▶ **Orient Yourself**: Lestelle-Bétharram is situated 20km/12mi SE of Pau. To get to the sanctuary, head south along the D 937 from the village; the caves are a further 2.5km/1.5mi from here along the D 526 .

Chapelle-Notre-Dame

The chapel has an austere Classical façade (1661) of grey marble. The interior and furnishings are Baroque in style. On the left as you go in, behind a screen, is a 14C polychrome wood statue of the Madonna Nursing her Child; on the right, an 18C Scourging at the Pillar and, at the high altar, a plaster statue of Notre-Dame-de-Bétharram (1845).

Against the chevet *(access through a door to the left of the chancel)* the chapelle **St-Michel-Garicoïts** (1926) (⏱*open Jul-Aug, 9am-noon and 2-6pm; Apr-Jun and Sep, 9am-noon and 2-5pm; early Oct to Easter, 2-5pm;* ☎*05 59 71 92 30)* contains the shrine of the priest (1797-1863) who restored the sanctuary and calvary and founded the congregation of the Sacred Heart of Jesus.

Overlooking Chapelle de Notre-Dame is a hill with 19C chapels marking the Stations of the Cross. Note the eight bas-relief sculptures by Alexandre Renoir (1845).

Grottes de Bétharram ★

2.5km/1.5mi from the southern exit of Lestelle-Bétharram on the D 152. ☛*Apr-Oct, guided tours (1hr 20min) 9am-noon and 1.30-5.30pm; Feb-Mar daily except Sat-Sun at 2.30pm and 4pm.* ☜*10€ (children: 6€).* ☎ *05 62 41 80 04; www. betharram.com.*

The caves were discovered in 1819 by local shepherds and explored the same year by naturalists from Pau. A more

systematic exploration, begun in 1888 by three speleologists took 10 years and unearthed 5 200m/over 3mi, of underground galleries. In 1898, the caves were brought to the attention of Léon Ross, a painter from St Malo in Brittany, who had settled in Bigorre. It took him four years to prepare the caves for the first regular stream of tourists. In 1919, he finished excavating the exit tunnel. It was opened to the public for the first time in 1903. The first floor is now accessible to handicapped people.

Tour

The underground tour covers 2.8km/ more than 1.5mi, and leads through five tiers of galleries, hollowed out of the limestone mountain by the river (which later flows into Gave de Pau). The upper level is the largest, comprising huge interconnected chambers. Their most interesting feature is their porous roof, which has led to the formation of beautiful stalactites in the *Salle des Lustres* (Chandelier Room), and a stalagmite column. This process is very slow, 1cm/0.4in every century in our temperate climate. The collapsed pot hole into which the subterranean stream finally plunges is 80m/262ft deep and contains scattered boulders and curious Romanesque cloisters. The old river bed is a deep and narrow fissure containing different examples of erosion. The lowest galleries are on the same level as the river which visitors follow by boat over a short distance. A miniature train takes them through a tunnel and back into daylight.

BIARRITZ ☼☼☼

POPULATION 30 055
MICHELIN MAP 342: C-2

Biarritz, on the borders of the Basque Country, is the most fashionable and most frequented seaside resort in south-west France. The setting is magnificent, with Atlantic rollers breaking against rocks and reefs, impressive cliffs, a small port, and superb bathing beaches. The town's international status has been enhanced by nine easily accessible golf courses, two casinos and numerous sports facilities in the town itself.

- **Information:** Square d'Ixelles (Javalquinto), 64200 Biarritz. ☎05 59 22 37 00. www.biarritz.fr.
- **Orient Yourself:** The towns of Biarritz, Bayonne and Anglet form one large populated area along the Atlantic Coast, just north of St-Jean-de-Luz and the Spanish border.
- **Parking:** As parking is difficult in Biarritz, it's best to leave your car on the outskirts (such as near the lighthouse) and explore the town on foot.
- **Don't Miss:** The views from La Perspective, Pointe St-Martin and the lighthouse.
- **Especially for Kids:** Musée de la Mer; Musée du Chocolat; Grande Plage, the town's sandy beach; Plage du Port Vieux, a sheltered family-friendly beach.
- **Also See:** BAYONNE, ST-JEAN-DE-LUZ.

A Bit of History

Empress Eugénie's town

At the beginning of the 19C Biarritz was but a small, whale-fishing harbour. The people of Bayonne, when they started coming here to enjoy the sea, made the 5km/3mi journey on donkeys or mules. Then Spanish nobility from the far side of the border discovered its charms, and from 1838 onwards, the Countess of Montijo and her daughter Eugénie came each year. When Eugénie became Empress of France she persuaded her husband, Napoleon III, to accompany her on her annual visit to the Basque coast and he too became captivated by the area. Their first trip together was in 1854. The following year, he had a house built and named it Villa Eugénie (today Hôtel du Palais). Suddenly, Biarritz was famous.

The charm of the town and its growing reputation for discreet luxury, drew the rich, famous and aristocratic from all over Europe. Villas overlooking the sea testify to the growing attractiveness of this seaside resort, whose illustrious list of visitors is hard to rival. In 1956, while he was filming *The Sun Also Rises*, the

---

VIPs in Biarritz

Since the beginning of the 19C, Biarritz has been a holiday resort for many of the rich and famous, starting, of course, with Napoleon III and Eugénie, who commissioned the neo-Classical Villa Eugénie. Kings, queens and aristocrats from all over the world came to sun themselves in Biarritz, including Edward VII, then Prince of Wales. At the turn of the last century, two casinos were built, providing Sarah Bernhardt and Lucien Guitry with the opportunity to perform for a very fashionable audience. The 1920s saw celebrities such as Rostand, Ravel, Stravinsky, Loti, Cocteau, and Hemingway. After the Second World War, the Marquis of Cuevas gave sumptuous parties, whereas the Duke and Duchess of Windsor came here to rest and relax. It was not unusual to run into some of the great film stars of the 50s and 60s, such as Frank Sinatra, Rita Hayworth and Gary Cooper.

American script-writer Peter Viertel had a go at the Atlantic waves with a surf board he ordered from California. The new sport became a craze overnight!

Beaches

Biarritz owes much of its charm to its hydrangea-lined garden promenades, which follow the contours of the cliffs, over the rocks and along the three main beaches, which have become an international meeting place for surfers and a focal point for local entertainment both day and night.

Grande Plage
Kids Overlooked by the Municipal Casino, the Grande Plage is the largest and most fashionable of Biarritz's beaches. In former times, only the most daring of bathers would swim here, which led to its now-forgotten nickname of *Plage des Fous* (Madman's Beach). To the north, it becomes Plage Miramar.

Plage du Port-Vieux
Kids Sheltered by two overhanging cliffs, it is a small family beach and a local favourite.

Plage de la Côte des Basques
Lying at the foot of a cliff which periodically has to be shored up against landslides, this is the most exposed and best surfing beach in Biarritz, because of its long reach; it owes its name to a traditional trip to the coast held on the first Sunday after the 15 August every year, which brought Basques from the inland provinces to the seaside.

Walking Tour

Rocher de la Vierge★
The Virgin's Rock, crowned with a statue of the Virgin Mary, is Biarritz's main landmark. It is surrounded by reefs and joined to the shore by a footbridge, which impassable in rough weather by the breaking waves. It was Napoleon III who had the idea of hollowing out the rock and linking it to the cliff by a wooden bridge. This has since been replaced by a metal one built by Gustave Eiffel.
A gently sloping footpath shaded by tamarisks leads to Rocher du Basta and Grande Plage. Throughout the year, the shoreline is illuminated from nightfall until 1am in the wintertime and 3am in the summertime.

Plateau de l'Atalaye
This open stretch of ground lies between Basta Rock and the promontory bearing the town's last remaining *atalaye* or watchtower from which smoke signals were sent to fishermen when whales were sighted.

Seafront

B. Kaufmann/MICHELIN

Address Book

For coin ranges, see the Legend on the cover flap.

WHERE TO STAY

Hôtel Gardenia – *19 av. Carnot – ☎05 59 24 10 46 – www.hotel-gardenia.com – closed Dec-Feb. – 19 rooms.* This central hotel with a pink facade has all the charm of a private home. Its quiet, attractive rooms are regularly re-decorated. Prices are reasonable considering the location.

Hôtel Atalaye – *6 r. des Goëlands, Plateau de l'Atalaye – ☎05 59 24 06 76 – contact@hotelatalaye.com – closed 14 Nov-15 Dec – 24 rooms.* This imposing turn-of-the century villa owes its name to the superb Atalaye plateau overlooking the Atlantic ocean. Rooms with a sea view are the especially attractive. Free parking nearby.

Chambre d'hôte Maison Berre-terrenea – *Quartier Arrauntz – 64480 Ustaritz – 11km/6.6mi SE of Biarritz. Take the D 932, Arrauntz exit – ☎05 59 93 05 13 – ⌷ – 4 room.* Facing a cider apple orchard, this 17C Basque house dominates the Valley of the Nive. Now a bed and breakfast, the house has been sympathetically renovated in traditional style, with white-washed stone walls. Simply furnished rooms adorned with beams and old doors.

Hôtel Maïtagaria – *34 av. Carnot – ☎05 59 24 26 65 – closed 1-15 Dec – 17 rooms.* A warm, friendly reception in this little hotel near the garden, just 500m/550yd from the beach. The rooms, of varying sizes, are bright and functional. Small flower-filled garden in the back.

Le Petit Hôtel – *11 r. Gardères – ☎05 59 24 87 00 – www.petithotel-biarritz.com – 12 rooms – restaurant .* This appealing hotel is ideally located for exploring the town or spending time on the beach. Its soundproofed rooms have been renovated in tones of blue or yellow; all have Internet access. The hotel has a seminar room above its restaurant, just 100m/110yd from the hotel.

WHERE TO EAT

La Goélette – *4 r. du Port-Vieux – ☎05 59 24 84 65 – closed 1 Dec-11 Jan.* Take a break from shopping and treat yourself to a meal in this pleasant restaurant. The decor is inspired by the nearby sea, fishing nets, and other nautical objects. Cuisine with an accent on fish and salads.

Tikia – *1 pl. Ste-Eugénie – ☎05 59 24 46 09 .* Tikia means 'small' in Basque. There's not much space in this little restaurant, but its attractive ambience makes it a pleasant place to linger. The decor has a cabin-type feel, with varnished wood panelling on the walls, porthole-shaped mirrors and other marine knick-knacks. Giant kebabs on the menu.

La Pizzeria des Arceaux – *20-24 av. Édouard-VII – ☎05 59 24 11 47 – closed 6-26 May, 14 Nov-6 Dec, Sun eve and Mon.* This lively pizzeria just a stone's throw from the city hall is particularly popular with a young, trendy crowd. Attractive decor with tile frescos and mirrors and an excellent choice of desserts.

Le Clos Basque – *12 rue Louis-Barthou – ☎05 59 24 24 96 – closed 16 Feb-5 Mar, 23 Jun-3 Jul, 19 Oct-6 Nov, Sun eve and Mon except in Jul-Aug.* Excellent local cuisine and a warm, friendly atmosphere mean that there's rarely a spare table in this popular restaurant. Exposed beams and azulejos tiles add an Iberian flavour.

Plaisir des Mets – *5 rue du Centre – ☎05 59 24 34 66 – closed 15-30 Jun, 15-30 Nov, Mon noon and Tue noon in Jul and Aug, Tue eve and Wed from Sep-Jun.* This attractive small restaurant is situated near the market hall, just a few hundred yards from the sea. The modern cuisine highlights seasonal and regional produce. Light, modern decor.

BARS AND CAFES

L'Impérial (Hôtel du Palais) – *1 av. de l'Impératrice – ☎05 59 41 64 00 – www.hotel-du-palais.com – daily 9am-midnight – closed Feb.* "La Villa Eugénie", the scene of Napoleon III's love affair with the Empress Eugénie, became the majestic Hôtel du Palais in 1893. Enjoy a glass of champagne and savour the atmosphere in the hotel's elegant bar, the Impérial, where a pianist makes the ambience complete from 8 to 11 every evening.

Le Caveau – *4 r. Gambetta – ☎05 59 24 16 17 – daily 10.30pm-5am.* One of the trendiest bar-discotheques in the region, Le Caveau is popular with locals and visitors, as well as the inevitable stars on holiday. *The* place to be seen in Biarritz.

La Santa Maria – *Espl. du Port-Vieux –* ☎ *05 59 24 92 25 – Apr-Jun, Oct daily 10am-2am; Jul-Sep daily 9am-3am*. The splendid view of the Rocher de la Vierge and the Port Vieux beach is one of the attractions of this little bar perched on a rock. A terrace, a few stools and a bar counter in a cave make this a pleasant, unpretentious spot where you can sample tapas while listening to the little orchestra.

ENTERTAINMENT

Gare du Midi – *21 bis av. du Mar.-Foch –* ☎*05 59 22 37 10 – tickets available from the tourist office: daily 10am-6pm*. The city's main theatre, with a seating capacity of 1,400, puts on a range of plays, music concerts and ballets. It is also the home of the Biarritz ballet company.

Casino de Biarritz – *1 av. Édouard-VII –* ☎*05 59 22 77 77 – www.lucienbarriere.com – Sun-Thu 10am-3am, Fri-Sat until 4am*. Located on the Grande Plage, this enormous casino has a table games room (roulette, Black Jack) and 180 slot machines as well as Le Café de la Plage brasserie, Le Baccara restaurant, Le Flamingo discotheque, a show room (theatre, dance) and a ballroom.

SHOPPING

Cazaux et fils – *10 r. Broquedis –* ☎*05 59 22 36 03 – Mon-Sat 10am-12.30pm and 3pm-7pm, public hols by appointment*. The Cazaux family has been involved in making ceramic pottery since the 18C. Jean-Marie Cazaux is happy to talk about his profession, describing it as 'austere and solitary'. The boutique also offers personalised creations – each step can be undertaken according to the customer's wishes, from extracting the clay to hand-painting the finishing touches.

Fabrique de chistéras Gonzalez – *6 allée des Liserons – 64600 Anglet –* ☎*05 59 03 85 04 – Mon-Fri 9am-noon and 2-7pm; tours 5pm Mon, Wed and Fri – closed Sat afternoon, Sun and public hols*. Founded in 1887, the Gonzalez company produces hand-made cestas (wicker scoops that extend from the protective pelota glove). In one hour you will learn everything about the history and manufacture of pelotas and cestas.

Chocolats Henriet – *Pl. Clemenceau –* ☎*05 59 24 24 15 – chocolat.henriet@ wanadoo.fr – daily 9am-7pm*. Established after WWII, Henriet is the local guiding light in chocolates and confectionery, featuring *calichous* (Échiré butter and fresh cream caramels), and *rochers de Biarritz* (bitter chocolate, orange rinds and almonds). Serge Couzigou, maître chocolatier responsible for the creation of the Musée du Chocolat (located 4 Ave. de la Marne), has been running the shop for the past twenty years.

Maison Arostéguy – *5 av. Victor-Hugo –* ☎*05 59 24 00 52 – www.maison-arosteguy.com – Mon-Sat 9.30am-1pm and 3-7.30pm – closed 25 Dec*. Founded in 1875, this famous Biarritz grocery store (formerly the 'Epicerie du Progrès') has kept its original walls, shelves and facade. The shop specialises in regional fare and also stocks many products difficult to find elsewhere: rare bottles of Bordeaux, prestigious Armagnacs, Basque products, flavoured teas and spices.

SPORT AND LEISURE

Euskal-Jaï Fernand Pujol – *R. Cino-del-duca –* ☎*05 59 23 91 09 – open match days*. This pelota Basque school organizes cesta punta competitions nearly every Wednesday and Saturday from June to September.

Hippodrome des Fleurs – *Av. du Lac Marion –* ☎*05 59 43 91 56 – open racing days*. Horse races have been held this trotter's hippodrome on July and August evenings for over fifty years.

Piscine municipale – *Bd du Gén.-de-Gaulle –* ☎*05 59 22 52 52 – schedule depends on school calendar*. Located on the shore, this municipal complex features heated seawater pools as well as a jacuzzi, hammam and sauna.

Thermes Marins – *80 r. de Madrid –* ☎*05 59 23 01 22 – Apr-Oct, Mon-Fri 8.30am-12.30pm and 2.30pm-6.30pm, Sat 8.30am-12.30pm, Sun 10am-noon and 4-7pm; Nov-Mar Mon-Fri 9am-noon and 2.30-6.30pm, Sat 8.30am-12.30pm, Sun 10am-noon and 4-7pm – closed one week in Jan*. This spa features a leisure pool and jacuzzi and offers various treatments, such as affusion or underwater showers, seaweed treatment booths, massages, sea-air bath booths.

Paths lead down to **Port des Pêcheurs**, a charming fishing village of white-washed fishermen's cottages, below.

"La Perspective"

This fine promenade overlooking Plage des Basques offers a splendid **view**★★ south towards the last of the Basque summits – La Rhune, Les Trois Couronnes and the Jaizkibel massif.

Pointe St-Martin

⊙*Jul-Aug, 10am-noon and 3-7pm; May, Jun and Sep, Sat, Sun and public hols, 3-7pm.* ∽*1.55€.* ☎*05 59 22 37 00. www.biarritz.fr*
The gardens and, in particular, the **light-house,** towering 73m/240ft above the sea, offer an excellent **view**★ of the town and the Basque Pyrenees. You will not regret having climbed 248 steps!

Villas

☜*A guided tour of the town's villas (Jul-Aug) is organised by the tourist office.*
The small fishing port of Biarritz suddenly became extremely fashionable during the second half of the 19C and many sumptuous villas were built in the eclectic style of the period. Thus, Villa Belza, standing on a rocky spur at the extremity of the Côte des Basques and built in 1880 for Marie-Belza Dubreuil, became a Russian cabaret during the roaring 20s. Villa La Roche Ronde (avenue de l'Impératrice), on the other hand, was built by Alphonse Bertrand in neo-Gothic style, complete with crenellated roof and bartizan. Château Javalquinto is another neo-Gothic building designed by its owner, the Duke of Osuna; it now houses the tourist office. By contrast, Villa Etchepherdia,

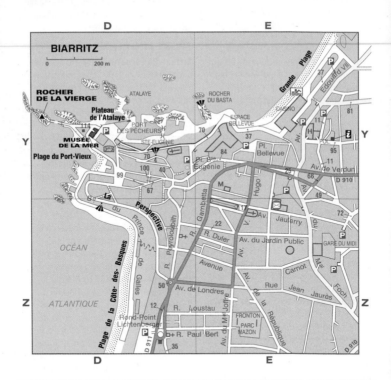

Atalaye Pl.	DY	4	Gaulle Bd du Gén.-de	EY	37	Mazagran R.	EY	84
Barthou Av. Louis	EY	11	Goélands R. des	DY	40	Osuna Av. d'	EY	95
Beaurivage Av.	DZ	12	Helder R. du	EY	49	Port-Vieux Pl. du	DY	99
Champ-Lacombe R.	EZ	22	Hélianthe Rd-Pt.	DZ	50	Port-Vieux R. du	DY	100
Clemenceau Pl.	EY	25	Larralde R.	EY	66	Rocher de la Vierge Espl. du	DY	114
Édouard-VII Av.	EY		Larre R. Gaston	DY	67	Sobradiel Pl.	EZ	117
Espagne R. d'	DZ	35	Leclerc Bd Mar.	DEY	70	Verdun Av. de	EY	
Foch Av. du Mar.	EZ		Libération Pl. de la	EZ	72	Victor-Hugo Av.	EYZ	
Gambetta R.	DEZ		Marne Av. de la	EY	81			

situated near the lighthouse of Pointe St-Martin, is more in line with the local architectural style, since it is modelled on a farm from the Basque country.

Chapelle impériale

Rue Pellot. Empress Eugénie ordered the chapel built in the 19C. Its style is both Romanesque-Byzantine and Hispano-Moorish. *Enquire at the tourist office for touring schedule.*

Russian Orthodox church

8 av. de l'Impératrice. Built in 1892, the year of the alliance between France and Russia, it used to be frequented by many Russians who spent their holidays in Biarritz, many of whom were famous. The inside of this Byzantine church is more interesting than the outside: the icons are from St-Petersburg.

Museums

Musée de la Mer★

Esplanade du Rocher-de-la-Vierge. ₫Jul and Aug, 9.30am-midnight; Easter school hols, Jun and Sep, 9.30am-7pm; Christmas and Feb school hols, Sat, Sun and public hols 9.30am-6pm; Nov-Mar, daily except Mon 9.30am-12.30pm and 2-6pm. Closed second and third week in Jan, 1 Jan (morning), 25 Dec . 7.20€ (children: 4.60€). 05 59 22 75 40. www.museedelamer.com.

This marine museum and scientific research centre stands opposite Rocher de la Vierge, with its back to Atalaye Plateau. It exhibits a wide range of marine life, the human activity connected with it, and a general presentation of the close relationship between Biarritz and the ocean throughout the centuries. In the basement a series of **aquariums** display the remarkable wealth and variety of the ocean fauna in the Bay of Biscay.

On the first level, **Salle de Folin**, named after the pioneer of oceanography in the Bay of Biscay, contains an exhibit on the history of the museum, founded in 1935. Also on this level, in the **cetacean gallery,** a presentation on whaling has animal skeletons and models of animals caught or washed ashore along the coast (finback and killer whales, dolphins etc).

Models of boats and navigational instruments complete the section devoted to fishing methods.

The second level contains further information on the resort, including conservation of the coastline, a study of the ocean around Biarritz, and an underwater display of seals and sharks in their natural habitat. The seals' acrobatics – especially at feeding time *(10.30am and 5pm)* – is wonderful entertainment for young children.

The terrace affords a **panoramic view** of the coast from the Landes to Cape Machichaco in Spain. The ornithological gallery at the end of the tour offers a complete display of all the sedentary and migratory species to be found along the coast and in the Pyrenees. The birdsong of 40 different species resonates in an aviary equipped with an interactive system.

Musée du Chocolat

14 av. Beaurivage. ₫Jul-Aug, guided tour (45 min) 10am-noon and 2-6pm; school hols, 10am-noon and 2-6pm; rest of the year, daily except Sun 10am-noon and 2-6pm. Closed 2nd and 3rd week in Jan. 6€ (children aged 4-12: 3.50€). 05 59 41 54 64; www.lemuseeduchocolat.com.

Let yourself be guided by the delicious aromas from this interesting museum devoted to chocolate making. A display of sculptures , each one in chocolate, is a highlight of the visit.

Excursions

Anglet

The town links Biarritz and Bayonne and its success as a resort and tourist centre followed that of Biarritz during the Second Empire. However, geographically it is closer to the countryside of the Silver Coast north of the Adour estuary with its long straight beaches bordered by dunes, and a flat hinterland planted with pines.

Just off Plage de la Chambre d'Amour (the main beach), steps lead to the cave in which it is said that two lovers, caught unawares by the rising tide, were trapped and died.

Each summer an International Festival of Humorous Drawings is held in Anglet. The festival was founded in 1979 and features amateur as well as professional artists.

Bidart

6km/3.7mi S. The small resort of Bidart, halfway between Biarritz and St-Jean-de-Luz, is built at the highest point on the Basque coastline, on the edge of a cliff. From Chapelle Ste-Madeleine *(accessible from rue de la Madeleine)*, the clifftop **view**★ looks over the Jaizkibel (a promontory closing off the Fontarabia natural harbour), the Trois Couronnes and La Rhune.

The charming **Place centrale** (main square) is framed by the church, the pelota *(jai alai)* fronton and the town hall. Local pelota matches and competitions are always watched by enthusiastic crowds.

The church is typically Basque in style with its belfry-porch, fine wooden ceiling, and enormous, brightly coloured 17C altarpiece. The mezzanine galleries were reserved for the men attending services; women sat below.

Rue de la Grande-Plage and promenade de la Mer lead steeply down to the beach.

Guéthary

8.5km/5.3mi S. Originally a traditional fishing port on a small inlet along the Basque coast, Guéthary is now a seaside resort with well-to-do Labourd-style villas nestled in spacious grounds. The view from the terrace above the beach stretches north-east as far as Biarritz. Beyond N 10, on Elizalda hill, the **church** houses a 17C Crucifixion, a 17C *Pietà* and a statue of Monsignor Mugabure (1850-1910), who was born and bred in the region and became the first archbishop of Tokyo.

BISCAROSSE

POPULATION 9 281

MICHELIN MAP 335: E-8

Once famous for its high-flying aviation pioneers and now the paradise of surfers, Biscarosse is located along the Atlantic coast, just south of the Bassin d'Arcachon. Its name refers to the dunes that abound in the area. 3 000ha/7 413 acres of coastal dunes were covered with marram grass and another 8 000ha/19 768 acres of inland dunes have been planted with maritime pines as part of a vast project to prevent them from shifting.

▶ **Orient Yourself:** The resort of Biscarosse includes three distinct sites: Biscarosse-Plage on the coast, Biscarosse-Bourg inland and Étang de Biscarosse et de Parentis, one of several lakes along this stretch of coastline.

◔ **Also See:** BORDEAUX, DUNE DU PILAT.

Sights

Biscarosse-Plage

Ideal for those who enjoy exciting surfing possibilities. Fishing is a less strenuous alternative.

Étang de Biscarrosse et de Parentis

This magnificent stretch of water, also known as the Southern Lake covers an area of 3 600ha/8 900 acres. There is only one beach with a marina, and Kids games for children.

Étang de Cazaux et de Sanguinet

This body of water, also known as the Northern Lake, is linked with its neighbour by a canal. It offers sailing and various water sports. From Biscarrosse to Navarrosse the road runs through a pine forest, ideal for hiking, cycling and horse riding.

Musée Historique de l'Hydraviation

332 av. Louis-Breguet, in Biscarrosse-Bourg. ♿ ◔*Jul-Aug, 10am-7pm; (last admission*

1hr before closing time); Jan-Jun and Sep-Dec, daily except Tue 2-6pm. *Closed public hols.* *4.20€ (children aged 6-12: 0.90€).* *05 58 78 00 65.*

The Seaplane and Flying Boat Museum is housed in four pavilions which trace the evolution of these aircraft at a time, between the wars, when concrete runways did not exist and landing gear was unable to support the weight of ever-larger aircraft. Numerous documents, models and original parts (engines, propellers etc) tell the story the aircraft, the pioneers who designed them, the inauguration of an airmail service, the Biscarrosse seaplane base, the first long-distance flights, and the evolution of larger and larger civil planes and military craft. Highlights include a reconstruction of a cockpit and an 18min film *(afternoons only, in French)* on the giant flying boats' brief hour of glory.

Opposite the museum, seaplanes and flying boats can be viewed in a huge glass hangar. It is also possible to visit a laboratory in which the remnants of aircraft shot down during the war are protected by electrolysis against corrosion.

Excursions

Sanguinet

13km/8mi NE (E of the Étang de Cazaux).

The interesting **Archaeological Museum** in the village displays finds from local digs and excavations in and around the lake. The dugout canoes from the Iron Age made out of a single piece of pine are well worth seeing. *Jul-Aug, 10am-12.30pm and 2.30-7pm.* *3.50€.* *05 58 78 54 20; www.musee-de-sanguinet.com*

Parentis-en-Born

9km/5.6mi SE (E of the Étang de Biscarosse).

The name of this small town is familiar in France today, thanks to the oil wells which have sprouted up there. It is worth going there to enjoy the activities around the lake.

BLAYE

POPULATION 4 666

MICHELIN MAP 335: H-4

LOCAL MAPS IN INTRODUCTION (WINES OF BORDEAUX) AND VIGNOBLE DE BORDEAUX

Blaye (pronounced Bly) is known mainly for its citadel, its Côtes de Blaye wines and its port. The port includes a deep-water landing-stage and an extended dock basin, at right angles to the Gironde, used by coastal steamers and sailing ships. Fishing boats land lampreys and shad in the spring. The Gironde estuary is also a natural reserve of sturgeon which is now a protected species and the local caviar therefore comes from sturgeon farms.

- **Information:** Allées Marines, 33390 Blaye. 05 57 42 12 09. www.blaye.net.
- **Orient Yourself:** Blaye is situated on the eastern bank of the Gironde, 43km/27mi downstream from Bordeaux.
- **Parking:** There are car parks just outside the citadel and along the banks of the estuary *(see map)*.
- **Don't Miss:** The citadel.
- **Also See:** BORDEAUX, VIGNOBLE DE BORDEAUX, ST-ÉMILION.

Citadel★ *1hr 15min*

Guided tours (1hr) Jul-Aug, Tue, Wed, Thu, Sun and public hols at 3pm, Fri at 8.30pm; mid-Apr to Sep, Sun and public hols at 3pm. Contact the tourist office. *4.60€.* *05 57 42 12 09.*

Access is either on foot via Porte Dauphine to the south, or by car through Porte Royale to the east. Both gateways are decorated with shields carrying fleur-de-lis, both protected by ravelins in the curtain wall.

B. Kaufmann/MICHELIN

The Citadel

The citadel, built by Vauban in 1689 and still partly inhabited, is a real town within a town, very lively in season thanks to the local craftsmen. It becomes all the more animated during music and theatre festivals. The landward side, which is 45m/148ft above the river, is defended by bastions protected by a dyke.

Château des Rudel

This medieval castle is triangular in shape, and has a romantic history. It was the birthplace of the 12C troubadour **Geoffroy** (or **Jaufré**) **Rudel**, who fell poetically in love with "a distant princess", Melisande of Tripoli, without ever seeing her. According to legend, he sailed across the sea to join her, fell ill on the voyage, and died on arrival in the arms of his beloved. Only two towers of the castle still stand. However, the bridge, which led to the entrance, and the foundations of the walls are also visible. In the middle of the courtyard, the coping around the ancient well can be seen, grooved by the constant rubbing of the chain or rope which lowered the bucket. From the top of the tower, Tour des Rondes, there is a good **view** of the town, the Gironde estuary and the surrounding countryside.

Tour de l'Éguillette

From the side of the tower, which rises at the north-western end of the citadel, there is a fine **view**⋆ of the estuary, studded with islets as far as the open sea.

▶ *Take the pathway on the western side of the citadel.*

Place d'Armes

From the esplanade on the edge of the cliff overlooking the Gironde there is another view of the estuary and the islands. Nearby there stands a former monastery belonging to the mendicant order of Minims (17C), complete with its chapel and cloisters. Temporary exhibitions are regularly hosted here.

La Manutention

This square building erected in 1667 to house the jail of both the citadel and the city was then used as a bakery, a warehouse and a storehouse. It houses interesting exhibitions: **Estuaire vivant,** (with model ships and the maritime history of Blaye), the bakery museum (the history of bread explained in front of two antique ovens), and an archaeological museum.

CHÂTEAU DE BONAGUIL★★

MICHELIN MAP 336: I-2

This majestic fortress is one of the most perfect examples of military architecture from the late 15C and 16C. It is unique in that it appears to be a traditional defensive stronghold but its design was also a response to the development of firearms, such as the cannon and the harquebus. Bonaguil, which was built neither as a lookout post nor as a fortress, but as a secure place of refuge, pioneered the use of firearms essentially for defensive purposes (from 1480 to 1520).

▶ **Orient Yourself:** The Château de Bonaguil is situated on the edge of the Périgord Noir and Quercy regions, NE of Villeneuve-sur-Lot and NW of Cahors.

⏱ **Also See:** VILLENEUVE-SUR-LOT, AGEN.

Visit

A Bit of History

🕐 *Open Jun-Aug, 10am-6pm; Apr-May, 10.30am-1pm and 2.30-5.30pm; Sep, 10.30am-1pm and 2.30-5pm; Feb-Mar, 11am-1pm and 2.30-5.30pm; Oct, 11am-1pm and 2.30-5pm; Nov, school hols, Sun and public hols, 11am-1pm and 2.30-5pm; Dec, during school hols 2.30-5pm. 🕐Closed Jan, 25 Dec. ⊗6€ (children aged 7-16: 3.50€). ☎05 53 71 90 33. 1hr 30min. www.boaguil.org*

It was a strange quirk of character that made Bérenger de Roquefeuil proclaim himself the "noble, magnificent and most powerful lord of the baronies of Roquefeuil, Blanquefort, Castelnau, Combret, Roquefère, Count of Naut". He belonged to one of the oldest families of Languedoc and was a brutal and vindictive man who, in his determination to be obeyed, did not hesitate to use force. However, the extortion and other outrages he perpetrated incited revolt. In response, Bérenger transformed Bonaguil Castle, which had been built in the 13C, into an impregnable fortress from which he would be able to observe and quell any signs of uprising without delay. It took him nearly 40 years to build his fortified eagle's eyrie, which seemed an anachronism when compared with the châteaux being erected by his contemporaries for a life of ease at Montal, Assier and along the Loire. However, his castle was never attacked and stayed intact until the eve of the Revolution. Although demolished during the Revolution this colossus (notwithstanding its mutations), still evokes the absolute power it once represented.

This masterpiece of military architecture, while still keeping the traditional defences against attack by escalade or sapping, was also designed to make use of artillery and other new battle equipment.

Tour

After passing through the outer wall, the visitor comes to the barbican. This was an enormous bastion on its own with a separate garrison, powder store, armouries and escape route. The barbican formed part of the 350m/ 380yd-long first line of defence whose embrasures were designed for cross-firing.

The second line of defence consisted of five towers including the **Grosse Tour,** which is among the strongest round towers ever to have been built in France. It is 35m/115ft high and crowned with corbels. The upper storeys served as living quarters, whereas the lower contained weapons, such as muskets, culverins and harquebuses.

WHERE TO EAT

Ferme-auberge Les 4 Saisons – *47500 St-Front-sur-Lémance – 3.5km/ 1.8mi N of Château de Bonaguil towards St-Front – ☎05 53 40 69 88 – closed Sun eve and Tue.* This inn serves home-reared farm poultry, foie gras and pâtés.Children will enjoy the farm animals all gathered in an enclosure.

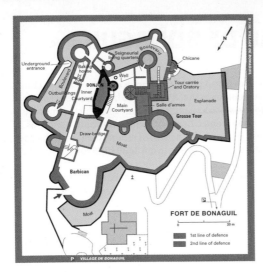

steeply sloping streets, sometimes spanned by covered passages known as pontets, climb up to the attractive place des Arcades covered market, where the four *cornières*, gateways to the bastide's main square, are still in place. The 15C fortified façade of the Southern Gothic style church has been restored.

A street encircling the upper town provides a pleasant walk with panoramic **views**★ of the surrounding countryside and the River Lède, tributary of the Lot. To the north-east, overlooking a crest line, the Château de Biron stands out clearly on the horizon.

Overlooking both lines of defence, the keep **(donjon)** with its cant walls, served not only as a watchtower but also as a command post. It was shaped like a vessel, with its prow – the most vulnerable point – turned towards the north. It was the last bastion of defence. Inside, a room houses arms and objects found during excavation of the moats.

Equipped with a well sunk through the rock, outbuildings (including the **baking house**) in which provisions could be stored, monumental chimneys, drainage systems, dry internal ditches and vaulted tunnels enabling the troops to move about quickly, the castle garrison of about 100 men could easily withstand a siege provided they were not betrayed or starved out.

Excursions

Bonaguil stands at the heart of an area rich in *bastides* and strongholds that bear witness to the troubled history of Aquitaine.

Monflanquin
28km/17mi W via the D 124.
The distinctive tiled roofs of this venerable bastide, founded in the 13C by Alphonse de Poitiers, are clustered together on a hill dominated by the slender silhouette of the church. Narrow,

Villeréal
13km/8mi N of Monflanquin via the D 676.
This *bastide* founded by Alfonse de Poitiers, the brother of St Louis, has kept its original right-angled grid plan, corbelled houses and overhanging roofs. In the centre of the *bastide,* the two-storied 14C markets are supported by oak pillars. Cornières (corner gateways typically found on the central square of a *bastide*) stand on the main square. The fortified 13C **church** dominates the *bastide* with its slender silhouette, combining charm and severity. The high façade is framed by two towers crowned with pinnacle turrets connected by a crenellated watch-path; the left-hand tower is pierced with arrow slits.

A lake with water sports facilities lies at the foot of the village.

Fumel
25km/15mi NE of Villeneuve-sur-Lot via the D 911.
This is both a historical and an industrial city. You might be surprised at first sight, but try to look beyond the grey smoke and you will be charmed by the château overlooking the River Lot and by the surroundings of the city.

BORDEAUX★★★

POPULATION 753 931
MICHELIN MAP 335: H-5

Bordeaux, built 98km/61mi upriver at the first bridging point of the tidal River Garonne, is the regional capital of Aquitaine and one of the most important ports in Europe. The elegant city boasts a wealth of Classical architecture, which contrasts with the small store houses lining the narrow cobbled streets of some districts. As a trade centre, the town is renowned not only for the export of the world-famous **Bordeaux wines** and spirits distilled in the south-west of France but also for its farming, food-processing and timber connections, and for its place in the high-tech world of aeronautics, electronics and chemicals. Bordeaux is also part of a powerful communications network that was further enhanced by the completion of the TGV high-speed rail link with Paris at the end of 1990. The development of international exhibition sites and the construction of such projects as the tramway, the World Trade Centre and the staging of international exhibitions, testify to the spirit of enterprise that has made Bordeaux an important junction between Northern Europe and the Iberian peninsula.

- **Information:** 12 cours du XXX-Juillet, 33000 Bordeau. ☎05 56 00 66 00. www.bordeaux-tourisme.com.
- ▶ **Orient Yourself:** Bordeaux is situated on the banks of the River Garonne, just 48km/30mi from the Atlantic Coast.
- **Parking:** There are a number of car parks alongside the river, easily accessible from the ringroad (see map).
- **Don't Miss:** The Grand Théâtre; Église Notre-Dame; Place de la Bourse; Porte de la Grosse Cloche.
- **Especially for Kids:** Croiseur Colbert.
- **Also See:** VIGNOBLE DE BORDEAUX; ST-ÉMILION; DUNE DU PILAT.

A Bit of History

Dukes of Aquitaine

Bordeaux (or Burdigala before it was colonised and developed under the Romans) was built on a choice site repeatedly attacked by Visigoths, Normans, Saracens and Moors. It was Good King Dagobert who, in the 7C, regained the town and the surrounding territory for the Frankish empire and the Merovingian dynasty, creating a Duchy of Aquitaine with Bordeaux as its capital. One of these dukes of Aquitaine was the legendary **Huon of Bordeaux,** who is said to have killed one of the sons of Charlemagne, without knowing who he was. Exiled by the Emperor, Huon was subsequently involved in a number of adventures before he eventually married the daughter of the Emir of Babylon. A celebrated 13C *chanson de geste* (a long epic poem featuring a single hero) was based on an embroidered version of this amorous exploit. According to the myth, the hero's pardon depended on Huon going to Babylon, cutting off the Emir's beard and bringing it back, together with four of the potentate's molars, to Charlemagne. The task was successfully accomplished with the help of Oberon, that same King of the Fairies used by Shakespeare 300 years later in *A Midsummer Night's Dream.*

Eleanor's Dowry

In 1137, Louis, son of the French king, married **Eleanor of Aquitaine,** the only daughter of another duke of Aquitaine, William. The bride's dowry comprised the Duchy of Guyenne, the regions of Périgord, Poitou, Limousin, Angoumois, Saintonge and Gascony – practically the whole of south-western France – together with the suzerainty of the Auvergne and the Comté de Toulouse. The marriage, solemnised in Bordeaux Cathedral, was not a success. Louis, who

The Claret Connection

It was the Romans who introduced viticulture to the Bordeaux region. The red wine, christened claret by the English occupiers, was much appreciated by the Plantagenets – 1 000 casks were set aside for the coronation celebrations.

The grape at that time was a sacred fruit (the punishment for thieves was the loss of an ear) and the quality of the wines even then was all-important. Six sworn tasters testified to its excellence or otherwise, and no innkeeper dared broach a barrel before it had been submitted for their approval. Merchants who adulterated the wine were severely punished, and so were coopers whose casks proved to be defective.

became King Louis VII, was a religious man and an ascetic, contrary to his queen, who was frivolous and enjoyed the good things in life. After 15 years of unhappy marriage, Louis returned from the Crusades and obtained a divorce (1152) through the Council of Beaugency. The settlement gave Eleanor her freedom, and she retained the whole of her dowry. Two years later, she married **Henry Plantagenet,** Duke of Normandy, Count of Anjou, ruler of Maine and Touraine. Politically, this marriage was a disaster for the Capetians. Henry and Eleanor's combined territories covered an area as vast as that ruled by the King of France. When, barely two months after the marriage, Henry succeeded to the throne of England and became Henry II, the resulting imbalance proved too much for the French. The conflict it provoked lasted, intermittently, for three centuries.

Black Prince's territory (14C)

Bordeaux was known as the capital of **Guyenne** (an old English corruption of the word Aquitaine, which remained in use until the French Revolution). Under English rule the town had the right to choose its own mayor and its councillors or *jurats,* and throughout the Hundred Years War, trade continued to flourish in the port. Wine was still exported to England, and the Bordelais (the people of Bordeaux) cheerfully sold arms to belligerents on both sides. At the same time, nobles and jurats built themselves substantial stone houses, known as *taules* or *hostaux,* and the son of the English king, Edward III, known as the Black Prince, possibly because of his dark armour, established his headquarters and held court here.

The Black Prince was one of the most talented military leaders of his time and

Monument to the Girondins

The Port

Bordeaux stands strategically upriver of the Gironde estuary, just 98km/61mi from the coast, and commands the shortest land link between the Atlantic Ocean and the Mediterranean Sea, via the valley of the River Garonne and the Midi Canal (240km/149mi long) which includes Naurouze Pass. The city's importance as a port dates back to the blossoming of the wine trade during the English domination, when the exportation of claret began. This was markedly increased in the 18C by a heavy traffic in colonial products from the French West Indies.

More recently, the activity of the inner-city docks has declined in favour of the new container terminal downstream at Le Verdon where the Gironde meets the ocean.

The inhabitants of Bordeaux are rediscovering the banks of the river. On the west bank the quays (4.5km/2.7mi long and 80m/0.48mi wide) have been redevloped for us by pedestrians, bikes, trams and cars as well as venues for various events and open air cafés.

one of the most savage plunderers. From his Bordeaux base, he sallied forth for one campaign after another, terrifying in turn the people of the Languedoc, Limousin, Auvergne, Berry and Poitou regions. A victim of dropsy, however, the heir to the English throne died before having reigned anywhere but in Bordeaux.

In 1453, Bordeaux and the whole of Guyenne was retaken by the French Royal Army, and the Hundred Years War was over.

Bordeaux and the Intendants

These high-ranking provincial representatives of the French Crown, or stewards, first appointed by Richelieu during the reign of Louis XIV in the 17C, were made an effective instrument of central government by Jean-Baptiste Colbert (1619-83), the King's Secretary of State, Controller-General of Finances and Superintendent of Buildings. In the 18C the Intendants' broad vision of a spacious, well-planned city to replace the tangle of medieval streets in Bordeaux brought them into conflict with the short-sighted and penny pinching representatives of the local population, but they succeeded in their aims. The work of Claude Boucher, the Marquis of Tourny, Dupré and St Maur turned a maze of narrow, twisted and stinking lanes surrounded by swamps into one of the most beautiful towns in France. Grandiose urban concepts such as

Tourny's avenues, the Bordeaux quays, the Stock Exchange complex and monuments such as the Customs House, the City Hall and the Grand Theatre date from this period. Once the new Bordeaux was established, its position on the Atlantic seaboard was exploited to the full, and it soon became the leading port in France.

Trade boom

The Empire period (early 19C) was a bleak time for the city, as the maritime trade on which it depended was badly affected by the Continental Blockade. The Restoration, however, revived the fortunes of the people of Bordeaux. The great stone bridge and the huge Quinconces Esplanade, dating from this era, were both projects which the Intendants had no time to complete.

Under the Second Empire, the city's role as a trade centre continued to develop, largely because of improved communications and the drainage of the Landes marshes to the south.

In 1870, during the siege of Paris, in 1914 before the German offensive and again in 1940, the French government fled south to take refuge in Bordeaux – dramas which earned the town the nickname of the Tragic Capital. After the Second World War, Bordeaux once again found the dynamic spirit of enterprise that its shipbuilders, financiers and merchants had enjoyed in the 18C.

Address Book

For coin ranges, see the Legend on the cover flap.

WHERE TO STAY

Hôtel Acanthe – *12 r. St-Rémi* – ☎ *05 56 81 66 58* – *www.acanthe-hotel-bordeaux.com* – *closed 23-30 Dec* – *reserv. required* – *20 rooms* – ⌑*6€.* A central location and very reasonable prices are the strong points of this hotel. The bright rooms are well sound-proofed and the reception is welcoming.

Hôtel Opéra – *35 r. de l'Esprit-des-Lois* – ☎*05 56 81 41 27* – *hotel.opera.bx@wanadoo.fr* – *closed 24 Dec to 2 Jan* – *27 rooms* – ⌑*6€.* A modest family hotel near the Grand Théâtre and the Allées de Tourny. The rooms are functional with those on the street well sound-proofed. Good value for money.

Hôtel Notre-Dame – *36 r. Notre-Dame* – ☎*05 56 52 88 24* – *hotelnotredame@free.fr* – *21 rooms* – ⌑*6€.* An unpretentious little family hotel in an 18C house just behind the Quai des Chatrons. Rooms small but well-kept; reasonable prices.

Hôtel Presse – *6 r. de la Porte-Dijeaux* – ☎*05 56 48 53 88* – *www.hoteldelapresse.com* – *closed 25 Dec to 2 Jan* – *27 rooms* – ⌑*8€.* In the pedestrian shopping quarter of the old city, this is a nice little hotel despite the rather difficult access by car. Superb stairway with crimson carpets. Modern, functional, cosy rooms.

Hôtel Continental – *10 r. Montesquieu* – ☎*05 56 52 66 00* – *www.hotel-le-continental.com* – *closed 24 Dec to 3 Jan* – *50 rooms* – ⌑*8.50€.* An 18C mansion in the old city with a fine staircase in the hall. Breakfast room under a glass roof. Modern rooms with waxed wood furnishings.

WHERE TO EAT

La Table du Pain – *6 pl. du Parlement* – ☎ *05 56 81 01 00* – *closed Christmas and New Year's Day.* This very successful restaurant genre originated in Belgium. The dining room is quite inviting. The menu has a wide selection of sandwiches, toasts and salads.

Lou Magret – *62 r. St-Rémi* – ☎*05 56 44 77 94* – *closed 7-21 Jul, Sun and public holidays.* If overwhelmed by the choice of restaurants in this street, try this pleasant establishment whose speciality is canard de Chalosse, duck served grilled or with a delicious sauce. No-frills decor and outdoor terrace.

Bar Cave de la Monnaie – *34 r. Porte-la-Monnaie* – ☎*05 56 31 12 33* – *latupina@latupina.com* – *closed Sun* . This wine bar decorated with photos of old Bordeaux bistros has an original flair. Customers choose their dishes first (omelettes or salads), then they draw their glass of Bordeaux from one of four taps in the wall. Affordable prices.

Chez Mémère – *11 r. de la Devise* – ☎*05 56 81 88 20.* Under the vaulted ceiling of this 16C workshop, experience the flavour and ambience of a fine meal chez mémère (at granny's): garbure landaise (soup), agneau de Pauillac, encornets frais aux piments d'Espelette and, at the end of the week, la sanguette, a sort of black pudding made of poultry blood. Also has a cave dégustation of reional wines.

Le Bistro du Musée – *37 pl. Pey-Berland* – ☎*05 56 52 99 69* – *closed 2 weeks Christmas, 3 weeks in Aug and Sun.* This bistro with a pretty green wood entrance makes a promising impression from the start. Thoughtful decor with exposed stone walls, oak parquet, moleskin seats and wine paraphernalia. Southwest cuisine and a fine Bordeaux wine menu.

Hôtel des 4 Sœurs – *6 bis cours du 30-Juillet* – ☎*05 56 81 19 20* – *4sœurs@mailcity.com.* Close to the Grand Théâtre, this hotel's café is charming with its stucco, mirrors, mosaic and red velvet wall seats. Choose an omelette aux cêpes, a jambon piperade, a morue basquaise or some chipirons frais à l'encre with a glass of wine.

Café Louis – *2 pl. de la Comédie* – ☎*05 56 44 07 00.* Intelligent renovations have given new life to this ex-brasserie of the Grand Théâtre de Bordeaux, built in the 18C. The interior design – gilded pilasters, high ceiling with frescos and crystal chandeliers – is based on its glorious past. Pleasant terrace under the arcades. Traditional menu.

ON THE TOWN

Bodega Bodega – *4 r. des Piliers-de-Tutelle – ☎05 56 01 24 24 – Mon-Sat noon-2:30pm, 7pm-2am, Sun 7pm-2am*. The exuberance of the Spanish music and the range of flavours as you savour a variety of tapas will transport you to Castille, at least for the evening.

Chez Brunet – *9 r. de Condé – ☎05 56 51 35 50 – Tue-Sat 10am-2pm, 5pm-10pm – closed 1st week of Jan and and 3 wks in Aug*. A charming woman runs this little restaurant where you can discover one of the region's specialities – oysters with grilled sausages.

SHOWTIME

L'Onyx – *11 r. Fernand-Philippart – Quartier St-Pierre – ☎05 56 44 26 12 – www.theatre-onyx.com - office: 6pm-8pm performance evenings; Oct-May: Wed: 1-6pm, Thu-Fri:9.30-12pm, 1-6pm – closed Jul-Sep – 12.5€*. The oldest café-theatre of the city, L'Onyx is a requisite stop for discovering local culture.

La Boîte à Jouer – *50 r. Lombard – ☎05 56 50 37 37 (reserv.) – ticket office: Wed-Sat 8pm; performances 8:30pm – closed Jul-Sep*. This theatre has two small rooms (60 and 45 seats) where lesser known regional, national or international troupes specializing in contemporary or musical theatre perform.

Opéra de Bordeaux-Grand théâtre – *Pl. de la Comédie- BP 95 – ☎05 56 00 85 95 – www.opera-bordeaux.com – ticket office: Tue-Sat 11am-6pm; – closed public holidays*. The Grand Théâtre de Bordeaux is one of the most attractive in France – its architectural assets are a showpiece for its impressive cultural wealth. Henri Tomasi's Sampiero Corso (1956), Jean-Michel Damase's Colombe (1961) and the French adaptation of Benjamin Britten's Gloriana (1967) are among the significant performances that premiered here. Symphonies, operas and ballets are performed here under excellent acoustic conditions.

Théâtre du Port-de-la-Lune – *Sq. Jean-Vauthier – BP7 Quartier Ste-Croix – ☎05 56 91 98 00 – ticket office: Tue-Sat 1pm-7pm – closed 25 July to 25 August, Sun, Mon and public holidays*. This theatre's repertoire includes classic and contemporary drama staged by the Centre Dramatique National Bordeaux Aquitaine.

SHOPPING

Baillardran Canelés – *Galerie des Grands-Hommes – ☎05 56 79 05 89 – Mon-Sat 8:30am-7:30pm*. This boutique makes delicious canelés, the small brown Bordelais cakes, irresistibly delicate and caramelised, that take on the shape of the ribbed (canelé) cake tins.

Cadio-Badie – *26 allées de Tourny – ☎05 56 44 24 22 – www.cadiotbadie.com – Mon 9am-noon, 2pm-7pm, Tue-Sat 9am-7pm – closed 2 weeks in Aug, Sun and, public holidays except Christmas and Easter*. A charming old-fashioned style boutique founded in 1826 where incredible chocolates are made and sold. The truffe de Bordeaux and guinette alone are worth a special trip.

Chocolaterie Saunion – *56 cours Georges-Clemenceau – ☎05 56 48 05 75 – Mon 2pm-7:15pm, Tue-Sat 9:30am-12:30pm, 1:30pm-7:15pm – closed 15-22 Aug, Sun and Mon morning, public holidays except Christmas, New Year and Easter*. One of the illustrious chocolatiers of Bordeaux.

Conseil Interprofessionnel des Vins de Bordeaux – *1 cours du XXX-Juillet – ☎05 56 00 22 66 – www.vins-bordeaux.fr – Mon-Fri 9am-5pm – closed Sat-Sun and public holidays*. This is where you'll find information, workshops and tastings on Bordeaux wines and vineyards. Several different wine cellars are to be found nearby, including La Vinothèque Bordeaux (8 cours du XXX-Juillet), L'intendant (2 allées de Tourny) and Bordeaux Magnum (3 rue Gobineau).

Darricau – *7 pl. Gambetta – ☎05 56 44 21 49 – Mon-Fri 10am-7pm, Sat 11am-7pm – closed 1 to 15 Aug and public holidays*. Since the turn of the century, this chocolatier pampers the city with the irresistible pavé Gambetta (praline with raisins soaked in wine), Bordeaux bottle-shaped chocolates *(confits de sauterne or de médoc)* and *niniches* (soft caramel with dark chocolate).

Old Bordeaux★★

Situated between the Chartrons and St-Michel districts, the old town, which includes some 5 000 buildings dating from the 18C, has undergone large-scale restoration in an effort to return the city's ancient stonework to its original splendour.

1 From the Quinconces to the Chartrons

At the centre of this area is the triangle formed by the intersection of cours Clemenceau, cours de l'Intendance and allées de Tourny.

Esplanade des Quinconces

The sheer size (about 126 000m^2/150 700sq yd) of this rectangular esplanade is very impressive. It was laid out during the Restoration (early 19C) on the site of the old Château Trompette.

The **Monument aux Girondins** with its bronze statuary was erected between 1894 and 1902, in honour of the *députés* from Bordeaux who fell under the guillotine in 1792, and of the Republican spirit. The huge work (65m/214ft long, 44m/145ft wide, and 50m/165ft high) is bursting with allegory: *Liberty Breaking Her Chains* atop the central column; various vices (Ignorance, Deceit etc) and virtues (Labour, Public Education, etc) on the Republique **fountain**★ facing the Grand Théâtre; Fraternity, Abundance and Happiness on the Concorde **fountain**★ opposite. The sea-shell shaped Triumphal Chariots are drawn by chimerical beasts with the forequarters of a horse and the tail end of a fish or reptile.

Statues of the writers Montesquieu and Montaigne (1858) preside over the Esplanade. Between the Esplanade and the waterfront stand two rostral columns (ship figureheads), decorated with figures representing Commerce and Navigation.

Grand Théâtre★★

⅏ The recently restored Grand Théâtre, which overlooks the **Place de la Comédie**, is among the most beautiful in France, and is a potent symbol of the richness of both French architecture and French cultural ideas at the time.

The building was designed by the architect Victor Louis (1731-1802) and erected between 1773 and 1780 on the site of a Gallo-Roman temple. From the outside, it is distinguished by its Classically inspired peristyle, surmounted by a balustrade supporting 12 statues representing Graces and Muses. (⅏ *see QUARTIER DES QUINCONCES: GRAND THÉÂTRE*)

▷ *Rue Mautrec, opposite the theatre leads to place du Chapelet; take passage Sarget on the left and turn right onto cours de l'Intendance.*

Cours de l'Intendance

Cours de l'Intendance is the main street for high-fashion and luxury goods stores. From no 57, along rue Vital-Carles, there is a fine view of the towers of Bordeaux Cathedral. No 57 itself, the house where the artist Goya lived and died (1828), is now a Spanish cultural centre.

Place Gambetta

This square was formerly known as place Dauphine. All the houses were built in the Louis XV style (with arcades at street level and mansard roofs), giving a pleasing architectural unity. An attractive English garden has been laid out at the centre of the square which, during the Revolution, was the site of the scaffold.

▷ *Walk along rue du Palais-Gallien, then turn left to join the entrance to rue du Dr A. Barraud.*

Palais Gallien

Rue du Dr-Albert. ⏱*Jun-Sep, 2-7pm.* ⌾*2.50€. Contact the tourist office or log onto www.bordeaux-tourisme.com.*
All that remains of this Roman amphitheatre which could seat 15 000 spectators are a few rows and arcades overgrown with weeds.

▷ *Continue along rue du Dr A. Barraud, cross rue Fondaudège and take rue St-Laurent, just in front of it.*

Petit Hôtel Labottière

Laclotte, an architect at the Musée des Arts Décoratifs, designed this neoclassical private mansion (18C). It has been restored in its original style. The staircase at the right of the vestibule is worth seeing.

Jardin public

This 18C French-style garden was turned into an English-style park during the reign of Napoleon III. Palm trees and magnolias provide shade among colourful flower beds. It houses the **Muséum d'Histoire Naturelle** (Natural History Museum).

The **quartier des Chartrons** gets its name from a former Carthusian monastery which was transformed into a huge wine warehouse in the 18C. The Golden Age of this area was in the 18C, when the high society of Bordeaux, enriched by trade, built fine hotels.

Cours Xavier-Arnozan

Formerly known simply as *le pavé* (the cobbled street), this avenue reflects the wealth of the great merchant and wine-growing families of the 1770s, who had their sumptuous town houses built conveniently close to but sufficiently removed from the noisy bustle of the port. Such private projects nevertheless combined to form an architectural ensemble of remarkable unity. The three-storey Classical façades have arches at ground level. Above, squinches support magnificent **balconies**★ with ornamental wrought-iron railings.

② Round Trip from La Bourse

This stroll leads you through a network of picturesque narrow streets between the St-Pierre and St-Michel districts.

Place de la Bourse★★

Named after the Stock Exchange (La Bourse), this magnificent square was formerly called place Royale and was the work of the father and son architects Jacques Jules (1667-1742) and Jacques-Ange (1698-1782) Gabriel.

On the north side is the Stock Exchange itself. On the southern side is the former Hôtel des Fermes (tax assessors) housing the National Customs Museum. (&see *QUARTIER DE LA BOURSE: MUSÉE DES DOUANES*)Three Graces Fountain stands in the middle of the square.

▶ *Continue, via rue F.-Philippart, to place du Parlement.*

A. Thuillier/MICHELIN

Place de la Bourse

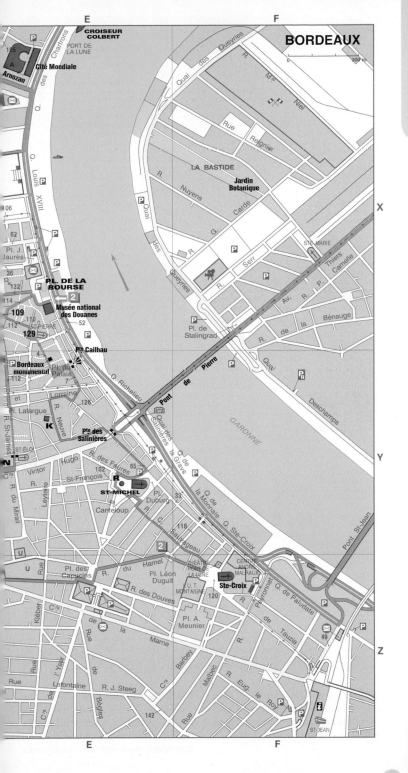

BORDEAUX

- 3-Conils R. des DY
- Abbé-de-l'Épée R. CX
- Albret Crs d' CY
- Allo R. R. CX
- Alsace-et-Lorraine Crs d' DEY
- Argentiers R. des EY 4
- Argonne Crs de l' DZ
- Arnozan Crs Xavier DEX
- Audeguil R. F. CZ
- Ausone R. EY 7
- Aviau R. d' DX
- Barbey Crs EFZ
- Baysselance R. A. DZ
- Bègles R. de EZ
- Belfort R. de CYZ
- Belleville R. CY
- Bénauge R. de la FX
- Bir-Hakeim Pl. de EY
- Bonnac R. G. CXY
- Bonnier R. C. CY
- Bordelaise Galerie DX 21

- 3-Conils R. des DY
- Abbé-de-l'Épée R. CX
- Albret Crs d' CY
- Allo R. R. CX
- Alsace-et-Lorraine Crs d' DEY
- Argentiers R. des EY 4
- Argonne Crs de l' DZ
- Arnozan Crs Xavier DEX
- Audeguil R. F. CZ
- Ausone R. EY 7
- Aviau R. d' DX
- Barbey Crs EFZ
- Baysselance R. A. DZ
- Bègles R. de EZ
- Belfort R. de CYZ
- Belleville R. CY
- Bénauge R. de la FX
- Bir-Hakeim Pl. de EY
- Bonnac R. G. CXY
- Bonnier R. C. CY
- Bordelaise Galerie DX 21

- Bourse Pl. de la EX
- Briand Crs A. DYZ
- Burguet R. J. DY
- Cadroin R. DZ
- Camelle R. P. FX
- Canteloup Pl. EY
- Capdeville R. CX 30
- Capucins Pl. des EZ
- Carde R. G. FX
- Carles R. V. DXY
- Carpenteyre R. EFY 33
- Chapeau-Rouge Crs EX 36
- Chapelet Pl. du DX
- Chartres Allées de DX 37
- Chartrons Quai des EX,BTU
- Château-d'Eau R. du CXY 40
- Clemenceau Crs G. DX
- Comédie Pl. de la DX 43
- Costedoat R. E. DZ
- Course R. de la CDX
- Croix-de-Seguey R. CX 45
- Cursol R. de DY
- Deschamps Quai FX
- Dr-A.-Barraud R. CX
- Dr-Nancel-Pénard R. CX 48
- Domercq R. C. FZ 49
- Douane Quai de la EX 52
- Douves R. des EZ
- Duburg Pl. EY
- Duffour-Dubergier R. DY 57
- Duguit Pl. Léon EFZ
- Duhen R. P. CDZ
- Duplessy R. DX 58
- Esprit-des-Lois R. de l' EX 62
- Faures R. des EY
- Ferme-de-Richemont Pl. de la DY 63
- Ferrère R. DEX
- Foch R. Mar. DX 64
- Fondaudège R. CDX
- Fusterie R. de la EY 65
- Gambetta Pl. DX
- Gaulle Espl. Ch.-de CY
- Grands-Hommes Pl. des DX 75
- Grassi R. de DX
- Grave Q. de la EFY
- Hamel R. du EZ
- Huguerie R. DX
- Intendance Crs de l' DX
- Jean-Jaurès Pl. EX
- Joffre R. du Mar. DY
- Johnston R. D. CX 81
- Judaïque R. CX
- Juin Crs Mar. CY
- Jullian Pl. C. DY
- Kléber R. EZ
- Lachassaigne R. CX
- Lafargue Pl. EY
- Lafontaine R. EZ
- Lamourous R. de CDZ
- Lande R. P.-L. DY
- Leberthon R. DZ
- Leyteire R. EYZ
- Libération Crs de la CDY
- Louis-XVIII Quai EX
- Malbec R. FZ
- Marne Crs de la EZ
- Martyrs-de-la-Résistance Pl. des CX
- Mautrec R. DX 100
- Mazarin R. DZ
- Meunier Pl. A. FZ
- Meynard Pl. EY 102
- Mie R. L. CZ
- Mirail R. du EY
- Monnaie Quai de la FY
- Mouneyra R. CYZ
- Naujac R. CX
- Neuve R. EY
- Niel R. du Mar. FX
- Notre-Dame R. EX 105
- Nuyens R. FX
- Orléans Allées d' EX 106
- Palais Pl. du EY
- Palais Gallien R. du CX
- Paludate Quai de FZ
- Parlement Pl. du EX 109
- Parlement St-Pierre R. du EX 110
- Pas-St-Georges R. du EXY 112
- Pasteur Crs DY
- Paulin R. CX
- Pessac Barrière de CZ
- Pessac R. de CZ
- Peyronnet R. FZ
- Philippart R. F. EX 114
- Pierre Pont de EFY
- Porte de la Monnaie R. FY 118
- Porte Dijeaux R. de la DX
- Pressensé Pl. de DY
- Queyries Quai des EFX
- Quinconces Espl. des DX
- Reignier R. FX
- Remparts R. des DXY
- Renaudel Pl. P. FZ 120
- République Pl. de la DY
- Richelieu Quai EY
- Rioux R. G. DZ
- Rousselle R. de la EY 126
- Roy R. Eug. le FZ
- St-François R. EY
- St-Genès R. de CDZ
- St-James R. EY
- St-Jean Pont FY
- St-Nicolas R. DZ
- St-Pierre Pl. EX 129
- St-Projet Pl. DY 130
- St-Rémi R. EX 132
- Ste-Catherine R. DXY
- Ste-Croix Quai FY
- Salinières Q. des EY
- Sarget Passage DX 133
- Sauvageau R. C. EFY
- Serr R. FX
- Somme Crs de la DZ
- Sourdis R. F. de CYZ
- Stalingrad Pl. de FX
- Steeg R. J. EZ
- Tauzia R. de FZ
- Thiac R. CX
- Thiers Av. FX, BU
- Tondu R. du CZ
- Tourny Allées de DX
- Tourny Pl. de DX
- Treuils R. des CZ
- Turenne R. CDX
- Verdun Crs de DX 139
- Victoire Pl. de la DZ
- Victor-Hugo Crs EY
- Vilaris R. EZ 142
- Villedieu R. DZ
- Yser Crs de l' EZ
- Zola R. Émile CDX

- Basilique St-Michel EY
- Basilique St-Seurin CX
- Bordeaux monumental EY
- Cathédrale St-André DY
- Centre Jean-Moulin DY
- Cité Mondiale EX
- Croiseur Colbert EX
- Grand Théâtre DX
- Hôtel de Région CY
- Hôtel de ville – Palais Rohan DY H
- Jardin Botanique FX
- Jardin Public DX
- Maison de Jeanne de Lartigue EY K
- Monument aux Girondins DX L
- Musée Beaux-Arts CDY M4
- Musée Goupil DY M1
- Musée d'Aquitaine DY M1
- Musée d'Art contemporain DX M2
- Musée des Arts décoratifs DY M3
- Musée national des Douanes EX
- Muséum d'Histoire naturelle DX
- Palais Gallien CX
- Petit Hôtel Labottière CX
- Porte Cailhau EY
- Porte Dijeaux DX
- Porte d'Aquitaine DYZ
- Porte de la Grosse Cloche EY N
- Porte des Salinières EY
- Tour Pey Berland DY Q
- Tour St-Michel EY R
- Église Notre-Dame DX
- Église Ste-Croix FZ

The façades and the variety of their sculpted decoration combine to form one of the best architectural examples of the Louis XV style.

Place du Parlement★

Parliament Square was once a royal market. This pleasant quadrangle of Louis XV buildings is arranged around a central courtyard paved with old cobblestones *(restored)*. A Second Empire fountain is set in the centre of the square. There are many fine houses, some with ground-floor arcades, delicate fanlights and mask decorations. They are surmounted by open-work balustrades.

▶ *Take rue du Parlement-St-Pierre to place St-Pierre.*

Many 18C houses in the St-Pierre district have been restored. The 14C-15C church of St Peter was altered substantially in the 19C. On Thursdays the square is livened up by a market of organic produce where one can enjoy a delicious healthy meal in pleasant surroundings.

▶ *Follow rue des Argentiers.*

The house at no 14, known as **Maison de l'Angelot,** dates from c 1750. The carved ornamentation of the façade includes a haut-relief of a child, and keystones in the Louis XV rough-cast style known as *rocaille*. At number 28 an 18C building houses the **Bordeaux monumental exhibition,** which chronicles the development of Bordeaux from Gallo-Roman town to the modern city of today.

▶ *Continue to place du Palais.*

The square owes its name to the old Palais de l'Ombrière, which was built by the dukes of Guyenne in the 10C, rebuilt in the 13C, used subsequently by the kings of England and finally, under Louis XI, became the seat of the Bordeaux Parliament in 1462. The Palace was demolished in 1800 to make way for the present rue du Palais.

Porte Cailhau
🕐*Jun-Sep, 2-7pm.* ⊗ *2.50€.* ☎*05 56 00 66 00; www.bordeaux-tourisme.com*
This triumphal arch derives its name either from the Cailhau family, who were members of the Bordeaux nobility, or from the *cailloux* (pebbles) washed up around its base by the Garonne and used as ballast by ships. Built on the site of an ancient city gate, east of the old Palais de l'Ombrière, it was completed in 1495, The arch is dedicated to Charles VIII who won the Battle of Fournoe in the same

La Cité Mondiale

Inaugurated in 1992, this complex located in quai des Chartrons, was designed by the local architect Michel Petuaud-Letang. Its harmonious curved structural glass façade includes a round tower. Until 1995, Cité Mondiale was given over to wines and spirits. Nowadays, it has become a business and conference centre with shops and restaurants.

year. This might explain the juxtaposition of the decorative and defensive elements. Inside, on three different levels, an exhibit retraces the history of old Bordeaux, outlines the important stages of urban expansion and reveals plans for the future. The top floor offers an unusual **view** across the quays of the Garonne to the stone bridge.

▶ *Follow rue Ausone, cross cours d'Alsace-et-Lorraine and fork right; turn right onto rue de la Rousselle.*

This street is lined with the shops in which the city's wine merchants, grain and salted meat sellers once plied their trade. The buildings are characterised by tall ground floors surmounted by low-ceilinged mezzanines. No 25 was the town house of the 16C philosopher-essayist Montaigne.

▶ *Turn left onto rue Neuve and continue to the cul-de-sac (right).*

Still preserved is a 14C wall, pierced with two windows surrounded with stone tracery. Through the porch to the right, stands the city's **oldest house**, where Montesquieu's wife, **Jeanne de Lartigue,** lived. On the other side of cours Victor-Hugo there is a view of **Porte des Salinières** (Salt Sellers' Gate), formerly Porte de Bourgogne (Burgundy Gate).

▶ *Take rue de la Fusterie, opposite, to place Duburg and Basilique St-Michel.*

Basilique St-Michel★
🕐 ⌛*Guided tours 1st and 2nd Sun in the month 3-6pm.* ☎*05 56 94 30 50.*

Pont de Pierre

The construction of St Michael's Basilica began in 1350, and lasted for two centuries, during which time the original design was much modified. The side chapels were added after 1475.

The generous dimensions of the restored basilica are impressive. Inside, the two-storey elevation is emphasised by high arcades, topped with tall clerestory windows, and wide side aisles. The lines of the flattened east end are barely affected by the three small chapels.

In the first chapel off the south aisle, stands a statue of St Ursula sheltering 1 000 virgins beneath her cloak. The modern stained-glass windows, behind the high altar, are by Max Ingrand. The moulded coving of the north transept doorway frames a tympanum decorated with an allegorical scene representing Original Sin (left) and Adam and Eve being expelled from the Garden of Eden (right). The organ loft and pulpit date from the 18C. The latter, mahogany with marble panels, is surmounted by a statue of St Michael slaying the dragon.

Tour St-Michel

🕙 *Jun to end of Sep, 2-7pm.* 🎫 *2.50€.* *www.bordeaux-tourisme.com*
The people of Bordeaux are justly proud of this late-15C hexagonal Gothic belfry, which stands apart from the basilica. At 114m/374ft tall, it is the highest tower in all of southern France (the tallest tower in the country belongs to Strasbourg

Cathedral: 142m/468ft). The tower easily dwarfs the cathedral's Pey-Berland Tower, also a separate structure, a mere 50m/164ft high. Beneath the slender spire and superbly decorated facades lies a circular crypt. In the first chapel on the right aisle stands a statue of Saint Ursula sheltering a thousand virgins under her coat.

▶ *Take rue Camille-Sauvageau.*

Église Ste-Croix

🕙 *Aug, Sat 10am-noon and 3.30-6pm; rest of the year, Thu 10am-noon.* 🚫 *Closed Sunday afternoon.*
Built in the 12C and 13C and considerably restored during the 19C, this church has a Romanesque **west front**★ typical of the Saintonge region; The north tower is modern. The arches of the blind windows surrounding the main doorway are decorated with interesting carvings depicting Greed and Lust.

▶ *Walk to place de la Victoire (a favourite haunt of elderly people in the afternoon and of students in the evening) via place Léon-Duguit and place des Capucins.*

Porte d'Aquitaine

This imposing 18C triumphal arch, erected in the centre of place de la Victoire, is surmounted by a triangular pediment bearing the royal arms and those of the city.

▷ *Follow the pedestrianised rue Ste-Catherine and turn right onto cours Victor-Hugo.*

Porte de la Grosse-Cloche★

The 15C arched gateway (Great Bell Gate) with its three round turrets and conical roofs, is another source of local pride. The clocks date from 1592 (inside) and 1772 (outside); the bell was cast in 1775. The gateway stands on the site of an older structure, Porte St Éloi (St Eligius' Gateway), which was one of the entrances to the 13C walled town. When it existed, this belfry was used to ring out the news that the grape harvest was to begin.

▷ *Follow the narrow rue St-James, which passes through the gateway, cross place Lafargue to rue du Pas-St-Georges and continue to place C.-Jullian. Turn left and continue to rue Ste-Catherine.*

Rue Ste-Catherine

Farther along the street a number of houses are built over ground-floor arcades, with wide semicircular bays opening at first-floor level. At the junction with rue de la Porte-Dijeaux note the Galeries Bordelaises *(opposite)*, a covered passageway and shopping arcade built by Gabriel-Joseph Durand in 1833.

▷ *Rue St-Rémi, on the right, leads back to place de la Bourse.*

Quartier des Quinconces

Grand Théâtre★★

☞ *Guided tours (1hr) according to the rehearsal schedule.* ☞5.20€. *Booking essential. Contact the tourist office.*

Inside the theatre, the coffered ceiling of the foyer is supported by 16 columns. Beneath the dome at the far end, a handsome staircase rises in a single flight then divides into two (an arrangement copied by Garnier when he designed the Paris Opera House; ◔ *see INTRODUCTION: ART AND CULTURE).*

The panelled auditorium with its 12 gilded columns, provides a splendid interior with perfect acoustics. From the centre of the ceiling, painted by Roganeau after the primitive frescoes of Claude Robin,

La Grosse-Cloche

A. Thuillier/MICHELIN

hangs a chandelier glittering with 14 000 drops of Bohemian crystal.

Église Notre-Dame★

🕐 *8.30am-12.30pm and 2.30-6.30pm.* ☞ *Guided tours available 2.30-5.30pm; summer: 3-6pm.* ☎05 56 81 44 21.

This church, dedicated to the Virgin, was formerly a Dominican chapel. It was built between 1684 and 1707 by the engineer Michel Duplessy. The **façade,** in typical baroque style.

The stonework in the **interior** is especially impressive, including barrel vaulting, pierced by the lunettes of the clerestory windows for the nave, groin vaulting in the side aisles, and an organ loft extended on each side by gracefully curving balconies. The quality and design of the wrought-iron work – in particular the gates around the chancel – provide a fitting complement to the architecture. **Cloisters** dating from the 17C adjoin the wall on the right side of the church.

Quartier de la Bourse

Musée des Douanes

♿ 🕐 *Daily except Mon 10am-6pm.* 🕐 *Closed 1 Jan and 25 Dec.* ☞3€ ☎05 56 48 82 82.

The Customs Museum is housed in a large hall with fine vaulting *(restored)*. On the right-hand side, the history of the customs administration is followed chronologically with the help of documents, uniforms, an old Customs Director's office, professional equipment, and prints and paintings including a portrait of St Matthew, the patron saint of customs officers.

On the opposite side, different themes are presented including seizure of drugs and the arrest of counterfeiters. The tour ends with a display on the customs officer's latest weapon – the computer.

Quartier Pey-Berland

Cathédrale St-André, with its famous tower, stands in the middle of place Pey-Berland, which is flanked by the city's most important museums. On the first Sunday of every month, the town centre is closed to traffic (bikes can be hired on place des Quinconces) and admission to museums is free.

Cathédrale St-André★

9-11.30am and 2.30-5.30pm, 1st Sun in the month 2.30-5.30pm. closed Mon

This cathedral, dedicated to St Andrew, is the most impressive of all the religious buildings in Bordeaux. The 11C-12C nave was altered in the 13C and again in the 15C. The Gothic chancel and the transept were rebuilt in the 14C and 15C. Later, when the roof of the nave threatened to collapse, the building was strengthened by buttresses and flying buttresses, added at irregular intervals.

▶ Approach the cathedral from the north and circle it to the left (clockwise).

Porte Royale★ – This 13C entrance to the right of the north doorway is renowned for its sculptures, inspired by the outstanding statuary adorning religious buildings in île-de-France (the region surrounding Paris, where Gothic architecture originated). Most remarkable are the Twelve Apostles in the entrance bay and, on the tympanum, the fine Gothic Last Judgement.

North Doorway – The 14C sculptures here are hidden by a wooden porch.

East End – The exterior is distinguished by its fine proportions and by its elevation: the two-tiered flying buttresses soar over the side aisles. Between the supports separating the axial chapel from the one on the left, note the statues of St Thomas, patron saint of architects, holding his square, and Mary Magdalene, in 15C costume, with her jar of sweet-smelling ointment.

South Transept Doorway – This entrance to the cathedral is below a pediment pierced by an oculus and three rose windows. The upper part, embellished with trefoil arcades, also boasts an elegant rose window set within a square. The west front, destroyed in the 18C and then rebuilt, remains unadorned.

Interior – The impressive nave features late-Gothic upper parts, resting on 12C bases. Note the lierne and tierceron vaulting over the first three bays. The pulpit, fashioned from mahogany and coloured marble, is 18C. The different height of the **chancel**★, also Gothic, contrasts with the nave and is accentuated by the slenderness of the tall arches, above which a blind triforium is illuminated by Flamboyant clerestory windows. An ambulatory with side chapels encircles the chancel.

▶ Enter the ambulatory from the southern side.

Against the fourth pillar to the right of the chancel, there is a charming early-16C sculpture group depicting St Anne and the Virgin. The axial chapel closes off the 17C choir stalls. Opposite, a fine 17C door of carved wood separates the chancel from the nave.

On the inner face of the west front is the **Renaissance organ loft.** Below it two bas-relief sculptures trace the development of Renaissance sculpture. The group on the right shows Christ, harried by pagan deities from Hell, descending into Limbo, whereas that on the left shows the Resurrection, with the Saviour mounted upon an eagle, like Jupiter.

Tour Pey-Berland★

Jun-Sep, 10am-6pm; Oct-May, daily except Mon 10am-12.30pm and 2-5.30pm. Only accessible by stairs (231 steps). Closed

1 Jan, 1 May and 25 Dec. 4.60€. 05 56 81 26 25.

The tower was built in the 15C on the orders of Archbishop Pey-Berland. It has always stood separate from the main body of the cathedral, beyond the east end. The steeple, shortened by a hurricane in the 18C, now supports the statue of Notre-Dame d'Aquitaine installed in the 19C and restored in 2002. 229 steps up a narrow spiral staircase *(beware of low door lintels)* take you to the top from where there is a panoramic **view**★★ of the town and its steeples.

It is worth standing back a little (to the south), for an overall view of the twin spires above the north transept of the cathedral and, in the foreground, the massive, square, terraced towers flanking the south transept.

Centre Jean-Moulin

Daily except Mon 11am-6pm, Sat-Sun 2-6pm. *Closed public hols.* *No charge.* 05 56 79 66 00.

This museum, devoted to the Resistance and deportation under the German occupation, presents a panorama of the Second World War. Jean Moulin, the most famous of France's Resistance heroes, became President of the clandestine National Resistance Council after a secret visit to General de Gaulle in Britain. Subsequently betrayed, he was caught by the Gestapo, tortured and murdered in 1943.

On the ground floor, the Centre displays Resistance pamphlets, secret communications, underground newspapers, illegal radio transmitters and other items – particularly relating to Jean Moulin – which developed as a result of the Nazi occupation. The first floor concentrates on the spread of Nazi tyranny and the deportations which followed. The displays on the second floor are devoted to the men of the Free French Forces and their exploits, and include the boat *S'ilste-Mordent* (If They Bite You) which, crammed with volunteers, linked the Brittany fishing port of Carantec with England. There is also a reconstruction of Jean Moulin's secret office.

Hôtel de Ville

Guided tours (1hr) Wed at 2.30pm. 2.50€. *www.bordeaux-tourisme.com.*

The City Hall is installed in the former bishop's palace, built in the 18C for Archbishop Ferdinand Maximilian de Meriadek, Prince of Rohan. The building marks the introduction of neo-Classicism to France. The most notable interior features are the state staircase, the salons with their fine 18C panelling, and a banqueting hall decorated in grisailles by Lacour.

Musée des Beaux-Arts★★

Open daily except Tue 11am-6pm. *Closed public hols.* 4€ (temporary exhibitions: 5.50€), no charge 1st Sun in the month. 05 56 10 25 17.

The Fine Arts Museum bordering the gardens of City Hall displays a fine collection of 15C to 20C paintings in the north and south galleries. The **south wing** houses paintings from the Italian Renaissance (Titian's *Tarquin and Lucretia),* 17C French works, such as Vouet's *David Holding the Head of Goliath* directly inspired by Caravaggio, works from the 17C Dutch School, such as Ter Brugghen's *The Lute Player,* the captivating *Oak Struck by Lightning,* by Van Goyen, and paintings from the 17C Flemish School including the admirable *Wedding Dance,* painted in a popular rustic style by Jan I (Velvet) Brueghel. The 18C and early 19C are represented, among others, by the graceful *Portrait of Princess Louise of Orange-Nassau* by Tischenbein, Chardin's *Still Life* and four paintings by the local artist Pierre Lacour, who was the museum's first curator in 1811.

The **north wing** is given over to modern and contemporary works. The Romantic School is represented by Delacroix' famous *Ruins of Missolonghi,* whereas *The Forest of Fontainebleau* by Diaz de la Peña (born in Bordeaux) is an illustration of work by the Barbizon School, the first school to paint in the open air. Bertrand-Jean, better known as Odilon Redon (1840-1916) was born in Bordeaux. A small room in the Fine Arts Museum pays tribute to him and shows some of his works: *Char d'Apollon* (Apollo's Chariot, 1909), *Chevalier mystique* (mystic Knight, a charcoal and pastel work), *la Prière* (the Prayer), *la Lecture* (the Reading). The second half of the 19C is introduced by the outrageous *Rollas* by Henri Gervex, a nude refused by the 1878 Salon, followed by Henri Martin's *Chacun sa Chimère,* a large canvas inspired by the symbolist movement. From the 20C, there is the impressive *Eglise Notre-Dame à Bordeaux* by the Austrian Expressionist Kokoschka, the sinuous, tormented *Homme Bleu sur la Route* by Soutine and the extremely beautiful *Portrait of Bevilacqua* (1905), outlined in blue, by Matisse. Recent acquisitions include *Entrée du bassin à flot à Bordeaux* (1912) by the local artist, André Lothe, who incorporates Cubist concepts into figurative painting. The last room is dedicated to contemporary works.

The **Galerie des Beaux-Arts** in nearby place du Colonel-Raynal holds temporary art exhibits.

Musée des Arts Décoratifs★

Daily except Tue 2-6pm. *Closed public hols.* 4€ , no charge 1st Sun in the month. 05 56 00 72 53.

The Lalande mansion which houses the Museum of Decorative Arts was designed by Laclotte in 1779. It has tall slate roofs and dormer windows.

A tour of the right wing begins with the Jeanvrot Collection (items relating to the lives of the last kings of France), presented in a setting furnished in 19C fashion, and continues through rooms of elegant woodwork and fine furniture, such as the Compagnie room, containing an 18C terracotta statue symbolising America (on the chimney-piece), and a marble bust of Montesquieu signed by Jean Baptiste Lemoyne. In the dining room is a display of local faience decorated with a pewter glaze, and a collection of fine 18C porcelain. Next door, the Guestier room typifies an elegant bourgeois lifestyle, displaying carved furniture and bronze statues by Barye. The two antechambers with their blue and white panelling are evocative of 18C town life style in Bordeaux. The central staircase, embellished with a fine wrought-iron balustrade, leads to the first floor rooms. The first two of these are dedicated to French and foreign ceramics. The Jonquille lounge is decorated with a magnificent Venetian glass candelabra and splendid 18C decanters and flasks. The second floor houses an exhibit of faience from southwestern France. Ornamental ironwork, enamel inlay and pre-18C collections of the locksmith's craft are displayed on the attic floor.

Musée d'Aquitaine★★

Daily except Mon 11am-6pm. *Closed public hols.* 4€, no charge 1st Sun in the month. 05 56 01 51 00. This regional museum, housed in the former Literature and Science Faculty and laid out on two levels, traces the life of Aquitaine Man from prehistoric times to the present day.

Collections in the **prehistory section** contain precious relics of arts and crafts practised by the hunters of the Stone Age. These include the famous Venus with a Horn (20 000 BC) from the Great Grotto in Laussel, and bison from the Cap Blanc grotto (Middle Magdalenian Age). A display of axes unearthed in the Médoc region illustrates the variety of tools fashioned by the metallurgists of the Bronze Age (4 000-2 700 BC). Iron Age spoils include funerary items (urns, jewellery, weapons) discovered in the Gironde burial grounds or Pyrenees tumuli, and the prestigious **Tayac Treasure** – a quantity of gold artefacts comprising coins, small ingots and a remarkable torque (necklace or collar) which dates from the 2C BC.

In the **Gallo-Roman section,** aspects of day-to-day religious and economic life in the Aquitaine provincial capital are illustrated through ceramics, glassware, mosaics, fragments of cornices and bas-relief sculptures. Of particular note are a grey Pyrenean marble altar, an imperious **statue of Hercules** in bronze, and the **Garonne Treasure** which comprises 4 000 bronze alloy coins bearing the effigies of emperors from Claudius to Antoninus Pius.

Early Christian times and the Middle Ages are illustrated by grey marble and limestone sarcophagi and mosaics, including a 4C representation of *The Holy Sepulchre*. Excavations and public works in the city have uncovered significant pieces, which have been added to the collections – Romanesque capitals from St Andrew's Cathedral and a Flamboyant Gothic rose window from the Carmelite monastery.

Bordeaux's golden age (18C) saw the development of grandiose urban projects and the building of splendid mansions which were luxuriously furnished. Several displays focus on country life and farm-

Meriadeck District

Named in honour of Prince Ferdinand Maximilien de Rohan, Archbishop of Bordeaux in the 18C, this ultra-modern complex is the administrative centre of the Aquitaine region.

The area includes offices, administrative buildings, apartment blocks, a shopping centre, an ice-skating rink and the municipal library. Esplanade Charles-de-Gaulle is an example of the formal gardens and ponds here. Suspended footbridges lead to roads bordering the complex. Some of the cubed and rounded concrete and glass buildings are encased in metal super-structures. The most distinctive are the **Caisse d'Épargne** building with its superposed curved and rectangular forms, the mirror-walled **Bibliothèque** (Library), the **Hôtel de Région** with its harmonious, vertically lined façade made of concrete, and the **Hôtel des Impôts** (Tax Office) which is a gleaming mass of metal.

---

ing in former times. The accent is always placed on the natural resources of Aquitaine, which embraces the rural landscape of Béarn, the Landes (moors) of Gascony, the Gironde and its vineyards, and of course Arcachon and its oyster farming.

Several rooms show regional rural society and traditional activities, **19C Bordeaux** and modern, **20C Aquitaine**.

Quartier des Chartrons

Musée d'Art Contemporain★

Entrance at 7 rue Ferrère. &. ⏰*Daily except Mon 11am-6pm, Wed 11am-8pm.* ⏰*Closed public hols.* ☞*5.50€, no charge 1st Sun in the month.* ☎*05 56 00 81 50.*

The former **Lainé warehouse**★★, built in 1824 for storing goods imported from the French colonies, has been successfully remodelled into a Museum of Contemporary Art. It houses the collections of the Centre d'Arts Plastiques Contemporains de Bordeaux (CAPC), which are particularly strong on works from the 1960s and 1970s.

Inside, a tall, twin-aisled central section runs the length of the building. The huge amount of space available allows even the largest exhibits to be mounted here, accommodating individual works of great dimension. The sober character of the original structure of the building was further accentuated during its conversion by the use of black metal.

The museum also functions as a cultural centre with conferences and debates, guided tours on a particular artist or

aspect of contemporary art, children's workshops and film projections.

Vinorama

12 cours de Médoc. ⏰*Jun-Aug, daily except Mon 10am-noon and 2-6.30pm, Sun and public hols 2-6.30pm (last admission 30min before closing time); Sep-May, daily except Sun, Mon and public hols 10am-noon and 2-6.30pm.* ☞*5.40€.* ☎*05 56 39 39 02.*

Thirteen tableaux with costumed figures recount the history, production and commercialisation of Bordeaux wines from antiquity to the present day. The tour ends with a wine-tasting session including a vintage wine from 1850, a modern wine and wine drunk in Roman times with the addition of honey and spices.

Croiseur Colbert★★

⏰*Jul-Aug, 10am-8pm; Jun, 10am-7pm; Apr-May, Sep, 10am-6pm, Sat, Sun, public and school hols, 10am-7pm; Oct-Mar and zone C school hols, Wed, Sat, Sun and public hols 10am-6pm (last admission 1hr before closing time).* ⏰*Closed 1 Jan, 25 Dec.* ☞*7.80€.* ☎*05 56 44 96 11.*

The tour of the ship consists of three sign-posted circuits. The last two include steep steps and are not recommended for the less agile.

Kids The **Colbert** has been berthed in Port de la Lune near cours de la Martinique since 1993, casting its imposing triangular silhouette onto the waters of the River Garonne. This anti-aircraft warship was launched in 1959 and carried out its first mission in Toulon as the Mediterranean Squadron's flagship. She was then converted into a missile-launcher and served during the 1970s in the Atlantic Squadron in Brest. Although she performed few military operations, she went on some memorable missions, including the rescue of victims of the Agadir earthquake in March 1960, repatriation of Maréchal Liautey's ashes in 1961, General de Gaulle's trips to South America in 1964 and Quebec in 1967 and Operation Salamander (summer 1990 in the Gulf War). The exhibits vary according to the circuit chosen – weapons' room (Masurca and Exocet systems), the engine room, the control rooms, the two officers' quarters, the crew's galley, a medical centre, including an operating room and dentist, post office and many other facilities designed for daily life on board a warship in the second half of the 20C. The cabins belonging to the different members of the crew can also be viewed, including the Admiral's cabin with its chimney piece, where famous guests such as Général de Gaulle were entertained. From the decks, fore and aft, the pad for helicopters and other war machinery can be seen.

Additional Sights

Musée d'Histoire Naturelle
◯ Daily except Tue 11am-6pm, Sat-Sun 2-6pm. ◯ Closed public holidays. ∞ 5.50€, no charge 1st Sun in the month. ☎ 05 56 48 29 86.
The **Natural History Museum** is housed in an 18C building near the public gardens.

Jardin Botanique
◯ Summer 8.30am-5.30pm. ∞ No charge. ☎ 05 56 52 18 77.
This garden, designed by the landscape gardener Catherine Mosbach, is a new kind of botanical garden with the scientific aim of studying and preserving species, but with a thematic presentation. The visitor becomes aware of ecological problems in an "environmental gallery" and to ethnobotanics with "culture fields". Besides an aquatic and an

urban garden, looked after by the inhabitants of the area, a tropical greenhouse completes the whole landscape.

Excursions

Vignoble de Bordeaux★
See Vignoble de BORDEAUX.

Marais de Bruges
280ha/691acre of land is all that is left of the former large marshes of Bruges. This natural reservation is located on one of the major migratory axis in Europe.

Établissement Monétaire de Pessac★
Southern suburbs of Bordeaux. Follow the signs to Parc Industriel de Pessac. At the roundabout turn right on avenue Archimède leading to Voie-Romaine (Roman Way).
This concrete fortress has housed France's Mint since 1973. The hall contains an exhibit of coins and medals. A 350m/400yd-long upper gallery gives a good view of the whole process from delivery, melting and laminating of the metal ingots to cutting, finishing and conditioning of the coins. The 180 000 rough coins, called blanks, produced per hour, are given a preliminary check, then turned into coins at the rate of 250 per minute. The Ministry of Finance thus produces 4 million copper and silver coins a day, not only for France but also for several foreign countries (Israel, Lebanon, Cyprus, French-speaking Africa). The first French Euro was minted here in March 1998.

Floirac
The **observatoire astronomique de Bordeaux-Floirac** (astronomical observatory of Bordeaux-Floirac) is located at the top of the road leading to the church. ◯ Oct-Jun, guided tour from 10am to noon, 1st Sat per month. Write a request two weeks in advance to Mme Élisabeth Speletta, BP 89, 33270 Floirac. ∞ No charge. ☎ 05 57 77 61 00. www.obs.u-bordeaux1.fr.

VIGNOBLE DE BORDEAUX★

MICHELIN MAP 335: F-3 – H-5 AND I-5 – K-8

Bordeaux is synonymous with world-famous wines. The Bordeaux wine-producing region covers 135 000ha/520sq mi in the valleys of the River Garonne and River Dordogne in the département of Gironde; it includes several distinct areas each producing characterictic wines: Côtes-de-Bordeaux, Entre-Deux-Mers, Sauternais, St-Émilion and Médoc.

Côtes-de-Bordeaux

1 Round-trip from Bordeaux

105km/65mi – allow 1 day

▶ *Drive out of town along D 113 and D 10, which follow the River Garonne SE of Bordeaux.*

Château de Langoiran

🕐*9am-12.30pm, 1.30-5.30pm; Sep-Jun: 2-6pm, Sun 10am-12.30pm, 2-6pm.* 🕐*Closed 22 Dec-2 Jan.* ☎*05 56 67 08 55. www.chateaulangoiran.com.*
All that remains of the 13C castle is a ruined outer wall and an imposing circular keep among luxurious vegetation.

Rions

This small fortified town is entered via the 14C Porte du Lhyan, which has kept all its original defensive features – guard-rooms on either side, grooves guiding the portcullis, and an *assommoir* (a platform from which objects could be dropped on attackers) etc. It is very enjoyable to walk around the old houses and to take a look at the 18C covered market. The path on the ramparts is lined with small gardens.

Cadillac

The town, originally a *bastide* founded in 1280, is situated on the north bank of the Garonne, and is known for its sweet white wines. The remains of the 14C town walls are still visible. The austere **château**, built between 1589 and 1620 for the Duc d'Épernon then devastated during the Revolution and later rebuilt, stands inside its own defensive walls with bastions at the corners. Inside, there are enormous rooms with coffered ceilings and monumental, richly carved and decorated marble fireplaces. The 17C tapestries relating the history of Henri III were woven in the huge vaulted basement. 🕐*Jun -Sep: 10am-6pm (last*

Château de Cadillac

A. Thuillier/MICHELIN

Address Book

WHERE TO STAY

◎**Chassagnol Bed and Breakfast** – *33410 Ste-Croix-du-Mont – at Peyrat on D 10 – ☎05 56 62 00 58 – ⌐ – 4 rooms.* A very nice stop for wine enthusiasts is this large 19C house set in the heart of the Ste-Croix-du-Mont vineyards. A few period pieces in the spacious bedrooms. The garden and terrace with a barbecue are quite popular.

◎◎**La Lézardière Bed and Breakfast** – *Boimier-Gabouriaud – 33540 St-Martin-de-Lerm – 8km/4.2mi SE of Sauveterre-de-Guyenne. Take D 670, D 230 and D 129 – ☎05 56 71 30 12 – lalezardiere@free.fr – closed Jan-Feb – ⌐ – 4 rooms, 1 gite – meals 20€.* Colourful rooms have been nicely fitted out on the upper level of this 17C smallholding overlooking the valley of the Dropt. Table d'hôte in the upper barn. Room with documents about wine and the region behind the cribs where the cattle used to eat. Pool.

◎**Château Cap Léon Veyrin Bed and Breakfast** – *33480 Listrac-Médoc – 4km/2.4mi from Listrac via D 5E2 – ☎05 56 58 07 28 – capleonveyrin@aol.com – closed Christmas to New Year's – ⌐ – 5 rooms.* The same family has been running this long residence situated in the heart of a 20ha winery since 1810. The Louis XV-style rooms are endowed with lovely bathrooms. The breakfast room opening onto the chai is superb.

◎◎**Château du Broustaret Bed and Breakfast** – *33410 Rions – 6km/3.6mi N of Cadillac. Take D 11 toward Targon then D 120 – ☎05 56 62 96 97 – www.broustaret.net – closed Nov to Easter school holidays – ⌐ – 5 rooms.* Hospitality is a 25-year-old tradition in this winery amid the Premières Côtes de Bordeaux grape vines. Woods and fields surround this noble house and its simple, comfortable rooms. A tranquil halt, perfect for discovering the vineyards.

◎◎**Domaine de Carrat Bed and Breakfast** – *rte de Ste-Hélène – 33480 Castelnau-de-Médoc – 1km/0.6mi SW of Castelnau-de-Médoc – ☎05 56 58 24 80 – closed Christmas – ⌐ – 4 rooms. ⌐.* Surrounded by a pine and deciduous forest, this majestic, red-shuttered house used to accommodate the stables of the neighbouring château.

Considerate reception and very cosy rooms. You'll enter via the splendid paved porchway that horse-drawn carriages used to pass through.

◎◎**Le Manoir de James Bed and Breakfast** – *rte de Ste-Colombe – 33580 St-Ferme – ☎05 56 61 69 75 – midubois@wanadoo.fr – closed 15 Dec to 15 Jan – ⌐ – 3 rooms.* In the 19C, the addition of handsome towers topped with pointed roofs gave this 17C farm its present noble appearance. A verdant setting, rooms with fireplaces, Gironde tiles in blond shades gracing the front entrance, a warm welcome and the pool combine to ensure a lovely stay.

◎◎◎**Château le Foulon Bed and Breakfast** – *Route de St-Raphael – 33480 Castelnau-de-Médoc – ☎05 56 58 20 18 – closed 15 Dec to 2 Jan – ⌐ – 4 rooms. ⌐.* This château dating from 1840 is the perfect starting point for your discovery tour of the great vintages of the Médoc. The rooms, furnished with antiques, have preserved their spacious feel. All overlook the park and the swans gliding on its waterway.

WHERE TO EAT

◎**Le Lion d'Or** – *pl. de la République – 33460 Arcins – 6km/3.6mi NW of Margaux via D 2 – ☎05 56 58 96 79 – closed Jul, 24 Dec to 1 Jan, Sun-Mon and public holidays – reserv. required.* Bistro ambience in this restaurant, with wall seats and big mirrors reflecting the Châteaux de Bordelais wine racks. Generous and well-prepared fare is quite popular, especially because prices are so reasonable.

◎◎**Auberge de Savoie** – *1 pl. Trémoille – 33460 Margaux – ☎05 57 88 31 76 – closed Feb and Christmas school holidays and Sun evening.* A very friendly reception awaits you in this handsome 19C stone house. Two colourful, pleasant dining rooms and agreeable terrace in the back. Well-prepared cuisine at affordable prices.

◎◎ **Ferme-auberge Château Guittot-Fellonneau** – *33460 Macau – 6km/3.6mi SE of Margaux. Take D 2 and D 211 – ☎05 57 88 47 81 – closed Feb school holidays and 16 Aug to 5 Sep.* In this wine-producing property in Médoc, the alchemy of the grape is combined with the science of good cookery. On a shady terrace overlooking the vineyards, let yourself be tempted by the pleasures of an authentic Southwest repast, featuring rillettes, confits, foie gras prepared by the proprietor herself.

⊜⊜**Le Flore** – *1 Petit-Champ-du-Bourg – 33540 Coirac – 7.5km/4.5mi W of Sauveterre-de-Guyenne. Take D 671 then*

D 228 after St-Brice – ☎*05 56 71 57 47 – closed Wed and Sun evenings and Mon.* Whether you choose the shaded terrace or the big, flower-filled dining room of this little house, prepare yourself for a first-rate meal, prepared by a very creative young chef. Affable and professional, his wife will gladly help you choose from among the subtly flavoured dishes.

---

admission 30 minutes before closing time); Oct to May: daily except Mon 10am-12.30pm, 2-5.30pm. ❊*Closed 1 Jan, 1 May, 25 Dec.* ⊜ *4.60€. (children under 18: no charge), free on the 1st Sun. of the month (Oct-May).* ☎*05 56 62 69 58.*

Ste-Croix-du-Mont★

The village is noted for its strange **caves**★ hollowed out from a thick fossilised oyster bed laid down by the ocean in the Tertiary Era. One of these has been turned into a **cave de dégustation** *(tasting cellar – *❊*Early-Apr to mid-Oct: daily except Wed 2.30-7pm, Sat-Sun and public holidays 10.30am-13pm, 2.30-7.30pm.* ⊜*No charge.* ☎*05 56 62 01 54.)*, where you will be able to appreciate the white wines which made the reputation of Ste-Croix-du-Mont. There are also splendid **views**★ from the Château de Tastes (now the town hall) stretching towards the distant Pyrenees. At the end of the hill, the church, which has undergone many changes throughout the centuries, still has its Romanesque portal.

St-Macaire★

This small, medieval town of dark, narrow streets, perched on a rock above the river, still has the original 12C walls, with their 15C machicolations and three gates. The **Église St-Sauveur** (☛ *Guided tours available by appointment.* ☎*05 56 63 34 52)* is a huge, imposing church with an unusual trefoil-shaped Romanesque apse. Other features include the 13C murals near the chancel, the Gothic nave and polygonal belfry, and the 13C porch crowned by a Flamboyant Gothic rose window. A 13C priory and its cloisters stand nearby.

Verdelais

Basilique Notre-Dame is an important place of pilgrimage. Worshippers come to venerate the 14C wooden statue of the Virgin, said to prevent drowning and heal paralytics.

The painter **Henri de Toulouse-Lautrec** (1864-1901) is buried in the cemetery of this small town.

▶ *Drive along D 117.*

After Verdelais, the road crosses the vine-covered hills of a district known for its sweet white wines affected by the noble rot which concentrates the grape juice by dehydration. Here, the châteaux are hidden among clumps of trees. There are views of Ste-Croix (in the foreground), the valley of the Garonne and the distant forests of the Landes.

Loupiac

Loupiac, famous for its white wines, already existed in Roman times and is said to have been home to the Latin poet Ausonius (4C). The vestiges of a **Gallo-Roman villa** are a witness to this period and remarkable mosaics can still be seen in its thermae.

▶ *Beyond Langoiron, turn right onto D 20 to enter Entre-Deux-Mers country.*

St-Genès-de-Lombaud

The church in this village, halfway up a valley slope, is a place of pilgrimage venerating the Black Virgin. It is built on a site thought to have been occupied by a Roman villa. The west front, with its belfry-gable, is pierced by a Romanesque doorway beneath coving carved with animals and small human figures, most of them comic. There are Romanesque capitals in the nave and, on the north side, carved stonework which was probably once part of a domestic altar.

▶ *To return to Bordeaux, continue along D 20, then turn left onto D 14 which joins D 113.*

Entre-Deux-Mers

② **Round-trip from Bordeaux**

55km/34mi – 4hrs

The gentle slopes of the Entre-Deux-Mers region, carpeted with vineyards, fields of ripening corn, and an occasional copse, undulate between the valleys of the Dordogne and the Garonne.

▶ *Leave Bordeaux to the E via D 936, then turn right on D 115.*

Sadirac

The town is an important pottery centre, where craftsmen mainly work with the local blue clay. The heyday of this traditional activity was in the 18C, and fine examples can be seen in **La Maison de la Poterie – Musée de la Céramique Sadiracaise** *(Daily except Sun and Mon 2-5pm. Closed public holidays. 1€. 05 56 30 60 03)*. This local museum, on the site of a former workshop built in 1830 (the original furnace can be seen at the far end of the gallery), displays examples of local work (ceramics used domestically and in sugar refining) dating from the 14C to the 18C, along with models of furnaces from other periods. Production today, from the three remaining workshops, concentrates on garden pottery, building materials, and the recreation of traditional designs.

The **Ferme-parc Oh! Légumes Oubliés** *(Mid-Apr to early-Nov. 2-6pm. 7.50€ (children: 5.90€). 05 56 30 62 00. www.ohlegumesoublies.com)* is a farm devoted to preserving "forgotten" varieties of vegetables and plants, offering a tour of its orchard and kitchen gardens.

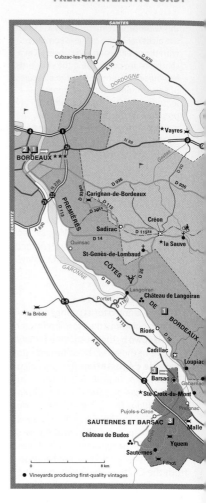

● Vineyards producing first-quality vintages

▶ *D 115E8 and D 671 lead to Créon.*

Créon

Once a bastide (13C arcaded square), the capital of Entre-Deux-Mers is an important agricultural market. The surrounding area has so many valleys that it has been nicknamed Little Switzerland.

La Sauve

There are two interesting churches in this village built on the former site of a large forest cleared by monks. The **old abbey**★ was founded in 1079 by St Gérard and was once very powerful; its dependencies stretched from Spain to England. The Romanesque and Gothic ensemble was, however abandoned in the 16C, though re-inhabited by monks in the

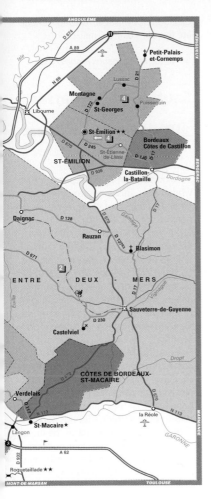

The church is distinguished by a superb **Romanesque doorway**★ in the Saintonge style, with lavishly carved capitals and covings. Scenes illustrated include the labours of the months *(first cove, from the top)*, the combat between the Virtues and the Vices *(second cove)* and human figures linked by a rope, symbolising the community of the faithful *(third cove)*.

The capitals include the Holy Women at the Tomb, and, on the right, the beheading of John the Baptist, on the left, the Seven Deadly Sins *(the first capital on the extreme left represents Lust)*.

Sauveterre-de-Guyenne

This is a typical *bastide*, created by Edward I in 1281. It eventually became French in 1451 after changing sides ten times. It still has four fortified gates and the vast central square is very lively on market days, each Tuesday.

Ancienne Abbaye de Blasimon

&⋅🔊*guided tours by appointment at the town hall.* ☎05 56 71 59 62.

Nestling in the hollow of a valley are the ruins of an old Benedictine abbey which was once encircled by fortified walls (a tower still remains). The 12C-13C church has both Romanesque and Gothic elements (rounded and pointed arches) and a 16C open-work belfry-gable. The coving of the main doorway

17C until the time of the Revolution; the vaulting collapsed in 1809. The 12C-13C abbey church has magnificent **capitals**★ carved with scenes from the Old and the New Testaments, and 13C ruined cloisters.
🕐*Jun to Sep: 10am-6pm; Oct to May: daily except Mon 10.30am-1pm, 2.30-5.30pm.* 🕐*Closed 1 Jan, 1 May, 25 Dec.* 💳 *4.60€.* ☎05 56 23 01 55.

St-Pierre is late 12C. The west front, with its belfry-wall and buttresses, presents an austere grandeur. Between the bays of the flat east end stand 13C statues of St Michael, St James, the Virgin and St Peter.

Église de Castelvieil

🔊*Guided tours by appointment with the mayor.* ☎05 56 61 99 27

Doorway of the Castelvieil church

is carved with fine hunting scenes etc. Only a few arcades (with Romanesque capitals) remain from the **cloisters**, together with a section of the chapter-house.

Rauzan

Château des Duras – ⏰ *Jul-Aug: 10am-noon, 2.30-6.30pm; rest of the year: daily except Mon 10am-noon, 2-5pm.* 🚫 *3€. Contact the Tourist office.* ☎ *05 57 84 03 88.*

Rauzan, one of the market towns of Entre-Deux-Mers, features the romantic ruins of this château, built at the end of the 13C. It is a testimony to the conflict between the French and the English during the Hundred Years War. The castle was protected by fortified walls with merlons, and has a seigniorial dwelling (14-15C) pierced by mullion windows and a majestic circular keep 30m/98ft high. From the top of the keep there is a fine view of the surrounding countryside. The *tour d'honneur* (end of 15C) with its palm-tree shaped vault is also remarkable. On the far side of the valley stands the village **church** with its three splendid 13C doorways, and a belfry-gable in a style more typically found in the Pyrenees.

Grotte Célestine

⏰ *Visit by guided tour (45min) only. Open Jul-Aug daily 10am-noon 2pm-5pm. Sep-Jun daily except Mon 10am-noon, 2pm-4pm. 6.50€. Reservation required.* The galleries of a subterranean river were discovered in the middle of the 19C when a well was dug in the centre of the village. Visits were organised until 1930 whenthe site was closed to the public, in order to preserve the caves. During the Second World War, the caves were used as a hiding place by two members of the French resistance. They have now reopened and you can go down, dressed like a perfect speleologist, see the subterranean river and explore the various concretions.

▷ *Follow D 128 to Daignac.*

Daignac

This is a picturesque village, spanning a ravine carved out by a stream called Le Canedone. Downstream of the old bridge are the ruins of a 13C mill.

▷ *Return to Bordeaux along D 936.*

Sauternes and Barsac

③ **Round-trip from Barsac**

30km/19mi – allow 2hrs

Small in size, but highly reputed for its white wines, this wine-growing area is limited by the lower valley of the Ciron, near its confluence with the Garonne. The *terroir* – the land producing a given *appellation* – covers the five municipalities of Sauternes, Barsac, Preignac, Bommes and Fargues. The vines grow on the valley slopes, in walled vineyards, generally planted in rows at right angles to the river. Only three grape varieties are used – Sauvignon, Muscadelle and Sémillon.

The original feature of this part of the Bordeaux region is the harvesting method used. The grapes, once ripened, are not picked right away. They are left on the branch so that they can be affected by **noble rot** or *botrytis*, a fungus peculiar to the district which increases the sugar content of the fruit. The overripe or candied grapes are then picked, one by one, and transported to the press with infinite care.

Barsac

The **church** (⏰ *Apr-Sep: 9am-6pm;* ☎ *05 56 27 15 39*), a curious building dating from the late 16C and early 17C, has three aisles of equal height, and vaults demonstrating the survival of the Gothic style in the Classical period. The furnishings – gallery, altars, reredos, and confessionals – are in the Louis XV style, and the sacristies are wood-panelled or stuccoed.

Budos

The village of Budos, a little outside the actual Sauternes area, has preserved the **ruins** of an early-14C feudal castle built by a nephew of Pope Clement. The sloping approach to the old esplanade passes through a fortified gateway crowned by a square, crenellated tower. The massive strength of the curtain wall and towers, shored up with timber, is best appreciated from inside the moat protecting the west façade.

Sauternes

This is a typical wine-growers' village. A little way to the south stands the 17C **Château Filhot**.

Château Yquem

The château is the home of the most prestigious Sauternes in the world. Its wines have been famous since the 16C.

Château de Malle

Apr to end of Oct: ✆ Guided tours (30min) *by appointment 10am-noon, 2-6pm (last admission 30 minutes before closing time).* ✆7€. ✆05 56 62 36 86. www.chateau-de-malle.fr.

Château d'Yquem stands unique as the sole *premier grand cru* (or classified first quality) of the Sauternes-Barsac region. Immediately below it, are the fine 11 *premiers crus* and 13 *deuxièmes crus* – the Château de Malle being classed among the latter.

Entrance gates, adorned with superb wrought-iron work, lead into the property. The attractive château and gardens were created at the beginning of the 17C by an ancestor of the present owner. The château itself is charming, with a layout similar to that of some of the isolated manor houses in the Gironde. The outbuildings house the wine-stores or cellars.

The interior of the château, resplendent with fine period furniture, boasts a collection of 17C *trompe-l'œil* silhouettes which is unique in France. They were used in former times as part of the setting of the small rockwork theatre set up in the gardens.

Italian-style terraced gardens are embellished with 17C carvings and statues depicting mythological themes, hunting or grape-harvest scenes.

Beyond the gardens, the vineyard – the only example of its kind in the Gironde – extends over two different terroirs: Sauternes (white wine) and Graves (red wine).

▶ *Return to Barsac via D 8E4 to Preignac, and N 113 leading N.*

Château Yquem

St-Émilion

④ Round-trip from St-Émilion

52km/32mi – 6hrs

It is best to visit the wine country in autumn, when a soft golden light bathes the contours of the landscape and the bronze rows of vines are alive with the fever of the grape harvest, usually the second fortnight in September. The picturesque landscape of neatly planted slopes crowned by the châteaux set in groves of trees, with glimpses, here and there of the valleys of the River Dordogne and River Isle, can nevertheless be appreciated at any time of the year.

St-Émilion★★
👆 *See St-ÉMILION.*

▶ *Leave St-Émilion via D 122 heading N.*

Just before the village of St-Georges, its fine Louis XVI château can be seen on the right, crowned with a balustrade and pots-à-feu (classical urns from which stone flames leap).

Pomerol

In order to discover these vineyards close to those of St-Emilion, contact Château la Fleur de Plince. No magnificent estate, no immense cellars in this 28-hectare/ 0.70-acre property (the smallest in Pomerol which counts 150), but the landlord will be happy to share his passion with you. He will show you around and explain to you how he makes his wine, before inviting you to a wine-tasting session. Moreover, M. Choukroun owns lovely B&Bs in St-Emilion and will be able to advise you.

St-Georges
This small 11C Romanesque church has a square tower wider at the top than at the base, and a curved apse with modillions carved with saucy subjects, treated in an almost Cubist style.

Montagne
The Romanesque church in this small town has three polygonal apses, topped by a square tower containing a strong room. From the terrace, beside the church, there is a view of St-Émilion and the Dordogne Valley.
The **Écomusée du Libournais** nearby, offers visitors a trip into the rural world of the past. ⚷ ⚲ *Early-Apr to mid-Nov 10am-noon, 2-6pm; Apr to mid-Nov: Sat, Sun and public holidays 2-6pm.* ⚲*Closed from mid-Nov to end of March.* ⚲*5.50€ (children: 2.60€).* ⚲*05 57 74 56 89*
There are two museums, presenting the traditional activities and social background of local wine growers in Libourne in the late 19C and the early 20C. Temporary exhibitions explain present-day wine-growing techniques.

▶ *Continue along D 122 – 2km/1mi beyond Lussac turn left into D 21 and continue for 4.5km/3mi.*

Petit-Palais-et-Cornemps
The late-12C church with its delightful Romanesque **façade**★ in the Saintonge style is surrounded by its cemetery. The scale is small, but perfectly proportioned, and the decorations are carved in a profusion of motifs.
The elevation presents three tiers of arches and blind arcades of different designs, some of them multi-lobed in the Arabic style. The archivolt of the central doorway is carved with a series of animals chasing one another and, in the corners, two amusing figures of a woman, and of a man pulling a thorn from his foot. The entrance is flanked by two blind doorways, which give a false impression of the interior which in fact only has a nave and no side aisles. A disparity between the two blind bays at the extremities of the façade's second tier, one multi-lobed, the other plain, is another peculiarity of this fascinating building.

▶ *Return to D 17 and turn S.*

Castillon-la-Bataille
Castillon was the site of the battle, in 1453, that put an end to English domination of Aquitaine. The English troops led by General Talbot were decimated by a French army under the command of the Bureau brothers (14C-15C) who modernised French artillery, which was instrumental in defeating the English here.
The town is built on a hillock overlooking the north bank of the Dordogne. The surrounding slopes produce a wine called Côtes de Castillon, classed as a Bordeaux Supérieur.

▶ *Return to St-Émilion via D 130 to St-étienne-de-Lisse and D 245.*

Haut Médoc★

5 Round-trip from Bordeaux
125km/78mi – allow one day

▶ *Leave Bordeaux to the NW via N 215. In Eysines turn right on D 2 and continue for about 15km/9mi.*

The Upper-Médoc district, with its exceptional natural conditions and fine-wine tradition dating back to the time of Louis XIV, is true château country and the origin of many wines classed as *grands crus*, which are carefully kept in wine stores or **chais**. The Médoc is particularly attractive during the autumn.
A number of different wine stores welcome visitors, the most interesting are described below.

Château Siran
At Labarde. ⚷⚲*Guided tours (30min, last tour leaves 30min before closing time)* ⚲*10.15am-6pm.* ⚲*Closed 1 Jan and 25 Dec.*

No charge. ☎05 57 88 34 04. www.cha-teausiran.com

You will see objects related to coo-perage, a collection of antique bottles, *jacquot* jars and labels of the château, which have been illustrated each year by a different artist since 1980. After visiting the wine store, you will discover a few rooms fitted out in the outbuild-ings of the château. The latter, a manor house (17C-Directoire), surrounded by a wood which is carpeted with cyclamens in the autumn, used to belong to the comtes de Toulouse-Lautrec, the ances-tors of the 19C painter. In the corridors, note the engravings signed by Rubens, Velasquez, Boucher and Daumier. A painting in the style of Caravaggio, *The Young Bacchus*, hangs above the stair-case leading to the first floor. The dining hall – named the Décaris Room, after the artist who depicted wine-related subjects in his paintings – displays inter-esting glazed earthenware decorated with twining vine motifs. On the first floor, in the reception room, do not miss the collection of richly decorated Vieillard dessert plates (hunting and wedding scenes etc). This room also holds inter-esting 19C furniture.

Château Margaux

Guided tours (1hr and 30min) daily except Sat-Sun and public holidays 10am-noon, 2-4pm by appointment two weeks in advance from Château Margaux, bureau des visites, 33460 Margaux. Closed Aug and during the grape harvest. No charge. ☎ 05 57 88 34 04. www.chateau-margaux.com

The wine from this estate is one of the five wines of Bordeaux classed as a premier *grand cru classé*, the aristocrats of the Médoc. The **vineyards** which produce it cover an area of 85ha/210 acres including rows of extremely old and valued vines, which are gnarled and twisted.

Visitors are shown the **wine stores**, various wine-making installations and an inter-esting collection of old wine bottles.

The château itself is a finely proportioned building. It was constructed in 1802 by an architect named Combes and comprises a basement, two storeys and an attic. The informal appearance of the English-style gardens contrast with the formal lines of the building.

▶ *Beyond Margaux, route D 2 follows the contour of the hillside rising above the* **palus** *(the alluvial soil at the foot of the valley).*

▶ *At Arcins turn left to Grand-Poujeaux. From here, turn right on D 5 towards Lamarque.*

Château Maucaillou

May-Sep guided tours (1hr 30min) every hour 10am-5pm, by appoint-ment. Oct to Apr 10am, 11am, 2pm, 3pm, 4pm. Closed 1 Jan. 6.90€ (children under 12: no charge). ☎05 56 58 02 58.

This estate offers a visit to the stores fol-lowed by a tour of the **Musée des Arts et Métiers de la Vigne et du Vin**, a museum

Wine-Growing in Médoc

Although the gravel deposited in the past by the Gironde estuary has not produced very fertile soil, at least it has the advantage of storing heat during the day and releasing it slowly at night, thus minimising spring frosts. Médoc vines are pruned down very close to the ground to take advantage of this. Also, the steep-sided valleys, known as *jailles*, at right angles to the Gironde estuary facilitate the run-off of excess water, offering growers a variety of exposures. The climate also helps – while the water mass in the estuary tends to keep the temperature mild, the pine forest of the Landes acts as a screen, sheltering the Médoc from Atlantic breezes.

The Médoc supplies 8% of the appellation wines of Bordeaux. They are exclusively red and are made principally from the Cabernet grape producing a wine which is light, has a nice bouquet, is elegant, even a little astringent, and a delight to a discern-ing palate. The most highly rated are Château Lafite, Château Margaux, Château Latour and Château Mouton.

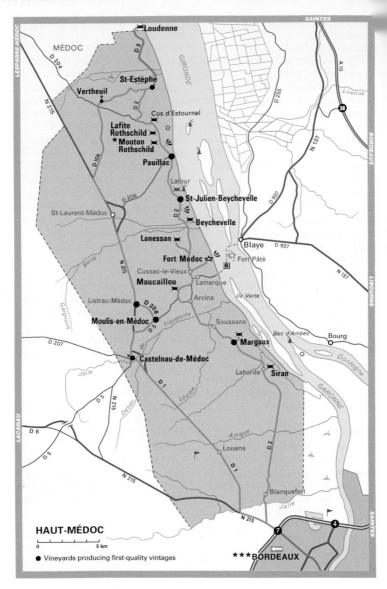

HAUT-MÉDOC

0 ———— 5 km

● Vineyards producing first-quality vintages

★★★BORDEAUX

which illustrates wine-making methods, ancient and modern, on this estate.

▶ *Rejoin D 2 and continue N. At Cussac-le-Vieux turn right.*

Fort Médoc

&. ◐ May-Sep 9am-7pm. Apr and Oct 10am-6.30pm. Nov-Mar 10am-5pm. ◎2.20€ (children under 12: no charge). ☎05 56 58 98 40.

This fort, designed by Vauban in 1689 to prevent the English fleet from penetrating the Gironde and approaching Bordeaux, could pepper the estuary with cannon fire, adding to the defences of Fort Pâté and the citadel of Blaye on the far side. Beyond a gateway, Porte Royale with its pediment carved with a sun (the emblem of Louis XIV, the Sun King), lies the courtyard and the main features of the fort – guard-room, powder magazine, bakery and gun emplacements etc. Beyond the courtyard, a bastion offers interesting views of the Gironde and over to Blaye and beyond, the vine-covered slopes.

▶ *Continuing N along D 2, a lane on the left leads to Château Lanessan.*

Château Lanessan

♿🍷🚌 *Guided tours (1hr and 30min) 9.15am-noon, 2-6pm.* *Closed 1 Jan and 25 Dec.* *7€ (children: no charge).* *05 56 58 94 80. www.lanessan.com*

The château, stands on a ridge in the middle of a 400ha/988-acre estate. It was built in 1878 by Abel Duphot, and displays a strange marriage of styles – a mixture of Spanish Renaissance and what looks like traditional Dutch, with stepped gables and tall, monumental stone chimneys. The outbuildings house the **Musée du Cheval** which includes an interesting collection of horse-drawn vehicles dating from 1900, including a 15-seat stagecoach. A collection of saddles, harnesses, bits and stirrups is on view in the tack room. The feeding troughs in the stables are made of marble. The wine stores, which date from 1887, can also be visited, and the visit ends with a wine-tasting session.

Château Beychevelle

🕐🍷🚌 *Guided tours Jul-Aug (1hr) daily except Sun 10-11.45am, 1.30-5pm; Sep-Jun: daily except Sat-Sun 10-11.45am, 1.30-5pm.* *Closed during Christmas and public holidays.* *No charge.* *05 56 73 20 70. www.beychevelle.com*

This is a delightful white manor house, rebuilt in 1757, extended in the 19C and recently restored. The wine store may be visited upon reservation. The name of Beychevelle (allegedly derived from *baisse-voile* meaning lower sail) is a reminder of a ship's salute; customary in the 17C when vessels passed the property. It belonged then to the Duc d'Éperon, Grand Amiral de France, who exacted a toll from masters navigating the Gironde.

St-Julien-Beychevelle

This is one of the better-known names of the Médoc. The region includes such famous châteaux as Lagrange, Léoville,

Beaucaillou, Talbot – after the English general who lost at Castillon-la-Bataille – and Gruaud-Larose (its proprietor, it is said, used to hoist upon the château tower a different coloured flag to signal the quality – excellent or otherwise – of each year's vintage).

Pauillac

Halfway between Bordeaux and "la pointe de Grave", Pauillac is a riverside town, a port with fine quays equipped to accommodate cruise liners. It is known above all, however, as a major centre of the wine trade, honoured by such famous vineyards as Château Lafite Rothschild, Château Latour and Château Mouton Rothschild. There is also a wine cooperative, La Rose Pauillac, the oldest in the Médoc.

Château Mouton Rothschild★

🕐🍷🚌 *Apr to Oct: guided tours (1hr) daily except Sat-Sun 9.30-11am, 2-4pm (3pm Fri).* *Closed 25 Dec-1 Jan and public holidays.* *5€.* *05 56 73 21 29. www. bpdr.com.*

At the heart of the vineyards above Pauillac rises Château Mouton Rothschild, one of the most exalted names of the Médoc. Its wine was classed *premier cru* in 1973. The **wine stores** are open to the public. The superbly furnished reception hall of the château is embellished with paintings and sculptures on the theme of wine and vineyards. The banqueting hall beyond is hung with a magnificent 16C tapestry illustrating the grape harvest. Also on view is an interesting collection of wine labels commissioned from Braque, Dali, Masson, Carzou, Villon and other modern artists. The tour finishes at the main wine store, where the barrels containing the most recent vintage are stored, and the cellars in which bottles of the precious wine, thousands upon thousands, ageing and aged, are racked.

Another series of very old cellars has been converted into a **museum**★★. It contains an extraordinary selection of paintings, sculptures, tapestries, ceramics and glasswork, celebrating wine and its production. It includes precious stones and a dazzling collection of 16C and 17C gold plate. Among the contemporary pieces, note the fine work by the American sculptor Lippold.

Château Mouton Rothschild storehouse

Château Lafite Rothschild

🍷🍷⏱*Guided tours (45 min) daily except Sat-Sun at 9,10.30am, 2 and 3.30pm.* ⏱*Closed Aug-Oct, public holidays. No charge.* ☎*05 56 73 18 18. www.lafite. com.*

This is perhaps the most famous of the premier *grands crus* of the Médoc. Among the treasured bottles of wine stored in the château's impregnable cellars are some known as *Comète* vintage, commemorating a celestial phenomenon of 1811. The name Lafite corresponds to the Gascon term *la hite* (originally derived from the Latin *petra ficta* meaning carved stone), and was used initially because the château was built on a small rise. The terrace on which it stands is planted with fine cedar trees and bordered by an elegant Louis XIV balustrade. It has belonged to the Rothschild family since the Second Empire (1868).

Beyond Château Lafite Rothschild, on the right-hand side of D 2, the silhouette of **Château Cos d'Estournel** appears, reminiscent of 19C Indian-style pagodas. In fact, the founder of the château exported his wine as far as India and had this exotic mansion constructed as a reminder of his far-off business dealings.

▶ *Turn right (D 2) to St-Estèphe.*

St-Estèphe

This little town, clustered around its church, rises like an island in a sea of vines. From the small port on the Gironde, east of the town, the view includes the slopes around Blaye, formerly the banks of the estuary.

▶ *About 2km/1.2mi before St-Izans-de-Médoc, take a lane on the right.*

Château Loudenne

⏱*May-Oct daily except Sun 9am-noon, 1-6pm.Nov-Apr daily except Sat and Sun by appointment. 5€* ☎*05 56 73 17 80. www.lafragette.com.*

This lovely 17C pink manor house has belonged to two Britons for 125 years until it was purchased back in 2000. The terrace opens onto **English gardens** (including a rose garden), which lead down to the estuary where the small port of the property is located. The Victorian wine stores house a **museum** explaining the history of wine making (with antique tools and objects) and vineyards (interesting fresco representing the four seasons).

Vertheuil

The 11C **Romanesque church**, modified in the 15C, is a former abbey church whose importance can be seen in its two belfries, three aisles, and a chancel with an ambulatory and radiating chapels. On the north wall are the remains of a handsome Romanesque doorway with covings, decorated with figures.

The interior, with its 15C ribbed vaulting and aisles almost as tall as the nave, is reminiscent of the Poitou style. In the chancel, where the vaulting is reinforced by radiating ribs, are stalls carved with scenes from monastic life, and a suspended gallery. The unusual ambulatory is roofed with a series of transverse barrel vaults. In the nave stands a 15C font, carved from a single stone block.

Impressive 18C buildings remain in the grounds of the old abbey, along with traces of its Gothic cloisters. The village is overlooked by the (restored) 12C keep of a ruined castle.

▶ Turn S along D 104.

Moulis-en-Médoc
The **Romanesque church** here was slightly altered during the Gothic period, the south apsidal chapel being replaced by a round turret enclosing a spiral stairway that led to a belfry with a strongroom. Peasants pruning vines are visible on the Romanesque portal. At the angles of the transept crossing, the columns supporting the church tower had to be reinforced at one time, thereby reducing the width of the supporting arches. The remarkable apse has carved modillions and blind arcades on the outside, and blind arcades in the interior, their capitals naively carved with historiated cats and birds. The fourth on the left (Tobias carrying the fish whose venom will cure his father's blindness) is especially noteworthy. The *bénitier* (stoup) outside the church, built into the façade, was reserved – according to local history – for lepers. Notice the frescoes from the 12-15C. Recent archaeological digs have unearthed the foundations of a 4C-5C place of worship and several Merovingian sarcophagi. The Grand-Poujeaux vineyards have made wines from Moulis famous.

Castelnau-de-Médoc
Three features of particular interest distinguish the church in Castelnau – a stained-glass Renaissance window portraying the Crucifixion, a wood carving dating from 1736 representing Pentecost, and a 14C alabaster bas-relief of the Holy Trinity, which hangs above the font.

▶ Return to Bordeaux via D 1.

TUMULUS DE BOUGON★★
MICHELIN MAP 322: F-6

This important Megalithic site, parts of which dates back to c 4700 BC, lies hidden in a wood near Bougon, a village known today for its goat's cheese. The site comprises five tumuli or barrows (ancient burial mounds), predating the Egyptian pyramids by 2 000 years. These barrows, circular or rectangular in shape, built with stones and earth, are one of the oldest examples of funerary architecture in the world, and were the work of Neolithic tribes living in the neighbourhood; of their dwellings, very little remains.

Museum

&.◷Open May-Sep: 10am-6.30pm, Wed, 1-6.30pm. Oct to Dec and Feb-Apr 10am-5.30pm, Wed, Sat-Sun 1-5.30pm. Jan Sun 1-5.30pm. ◷Closed 1 Jan and 25 Dec. ✆3.90€ (6-18: 1.50€) ☎05 49 05 12 13. www.deux-sevres.com/musee-bougon. This elegant, ultra-modern metal and glass structure, built on limestone, encompasses the ruins of a Cistercian priory. Start here for a walk through prehistory, from the creation of the universe to the necropolis of Bougon.

The modern-style exhibition retraces human, technological, geological and climatic evolution from the very beginning of man's existence. Partial, life-size reconstructions give a more true-to-life idea of a primitive world which is still the basis of our society – dwellings from the Çatalhüyük village in Anatolia (one grotto is painted with huge vultures carrying off tiny men), a dwelling made with

Tumulus FO

branches and rushes from Charavines in Isère, a chamber with a megalithic passage grave from Gavrinis (Morbihan) and lastly an exhibition room dedicated to the Tumuli of Bougon where offerings and skulls – one cut into three pieces – lie in a reconstructed funerary chamber. There is a 12C **chapel** on the way from the museum to the Neolithic site.

Neolithic Site

The site is accessed via a footpath lined with interesting reconstructions such as a sun and lunar calendar (based on Stonehenge in England), and the erection of a megalithic flagstone. There is also a botanical garden.

Tumulus A

This circular construction, the first to be discovered in modern times (1840), dates from c 4000 BC. The funerary chamber, one of the largest known (7.8m/27ft long), is roofed with a single stone slab weighing 90t. A smaller slab, standing vertically, divides the chamber in two. As well as the 220 skeletons seen here, the tumulus also yielded a rich collection of funerary objects.

Tumulus B

The shape of this barrow is elongated. The interior revealed two funerary vaults

at the east end and two passage graves at the west. Shards of pottery discovered here have been dated to the middle of the fifth millennium BC, which makes this the oldest monument on the site.

Tumulus C

This circular mound, 5m/17ft high, dates from 3500 BC. It shelters a small passage grave and also has a rectangular platform which may have been used for religious ceremonies. A 35m/115ft long wall runs between Tumulus C and Tumulus E. It appears to have been designed to separate the sanctuary into two separate zones.

Tumulus E

The barrow contains an east-facing passage which leads to two chambers where bones and funerary objects dating from 4000 to 3500 BC were found. These are the oldest-known passage graves in the centre-west of France.

Tumulus F

This, the longest enclosure (80m/262ft), encompasses two more barrows. F2, to the north, dates from 3500 BC and has a passage grave of the type known here as *angoumoisin* (in the Angoulême style). The passageway leads to a rectangular chamber. FO to the south dates from c 4700 BC.

CHÂTEAU DE LA BRÈDE ★

MICHELIN MAP 335: H-6

In the Graves region, bordering the moors of Gironde, the austere lines of the Château de la Brède are reflected in the waters of its wide moat. The fortified castle appears to be an island in a lake. There has been no change to the property since the days when the angular-faced, but kindly figure of **Baron Montesquieu** (1689-1755), the writer and philosopher, could be seen pacing around the outer edge of the moat. Château de La Brède (*brède* in the local dialect means bush or thorn) still belongs to his descendants today.

A Bit of History

Charles de Secondat, future Baron of Labrède and Montesquieu, was born within these castle walls in 1689. As a sign of family humility he was carried to the baptismal font by a beggar.

Montesquieu's kinsmen were Bordeaux magistrates and he himself – mediocre by his own admission in that profession – eventually became President of the Bordeaux Parliament. Like Montaigne, he had a passionate love of the countryside, withdrawing frequently to his castle, which he described as "the most peaceful and beautiful rural retreat that I know". Here, he looked after his business affairs (he exported a lot of wine to England), supervised the cultivation of his vines with his steward – conversing with his staff in the local dialect – and visited his cellars.

Montesquieu, who was by nature easygoing and even-tempered, found relaxation (again like Montaigne) in scholarship and the intellectual life. "Learning, for me," he said, "is the supreme remedy against world-weariness. I never suffered a disappointment that could not be dispelled by an hour's reading." Two of his best-known works, *Thoughts on the Rise and Fall of the Romans* and *The Spirit of the Law* were written at the castle.

Every year, the Baron spent the winter in Paris, where he was welcomed by the intellectual elite of the Académie Française, to which he himself was elected in 1727. It was in the capital that he died, quite suddenly, of an attack of fever, on 10 February 1755.

Visit 45min

Château

♿ 🚌 *Guided tours (45min) Jul to Sep daily except Tue 2-6pm. Apr to Jun Sat-Sun and public holidays 2-6pm. Oct to mid-*

Château de La Brède

A. Cassaigne/MICHELIN

Nov Sat-Sun and public holidays 2-5.30pm.
7€.

A wide avenue, laid out by Montesquieu, skirts the moat and leads, indirectly, to the austere 12C-15C Gothic castle. The original interior courtyard was converted into a terrace during the Renaissance by levelling one section of the outer wall. Small bridges which link two ancient fortifications, their doorways surmounted by Latin inscriptions, cross the moat and lead to the vestibule supported by six spiral columns. From the vestibule, which contains the Baron's travelling chests, visitors pass into the salon adorned with family portraits and a fine 16C cabinet. Montesquieu's own simple **sanctuary** remains exactly as it was when he was alive. A worn mark visible on one side of the chimney-piece was the result of Montesquieu's shoe repeatedly rubbing against it – he used to sit by the fire here and write with his papers in his lap. Notice the **library**, which has panelled barrel-vaulting and used to contain 5 000 books.

Park

Montesquieu took a great interest in the grounds of his castle.

BRESSUIRE

POPULATION 17 799
MICHELIN MAP 322: D-3

Bressuire is the chief town of the Vendée bocage – a patchwork of farmlands criss-crossed with hedges and woods south of the River Loire. It is an important agricultural market, as attested by the huge dimensions of place Notre-Dame, the size of the covered food market, and the cattle market in which large local sales are held every Tuesday. The low houses, roofed with their convex tiles, cling to the hillside on the banks of the River Dolo.

A Bit of History

Ravages of War

The Vendée Wars (1793-96) raged as the result of an anti-revolutionary insurrection involving Royalist-Catholic forces in south-western districts of the Loire. Bressuire, at that time, was under the sovereignty of the Royalist **Marquis de Lescure**, the Saint of Poitou and Lord of Clisson. The town consequently became the headquarters of the Royalist forces.

As a result it was set ablaze and attacked, on 14 March 1794, by the Infernal Columns of General Grignon – a former cattle merchant who kept a scrupulous tally of the number of Royalists killed by his men and who prided himself on the fact that 200 were massacred in a single day on the outskirts of Bressuire.

Sights

Église Notre-Dame

The architecture of this church resembles that of sanctuaries in the Loire Valley. The single, very wide nave with Gothic vaulting but with doorways and capitals still in Romanesque style is characteristic of the 13C Plantagenet (Angevin) style. In addition, the huge quadrangular chancel in Flamboyant Gothic style appears also to show an Angevin influence, despite the fact that it dates from the late 15C. The tower, conceived as a whole in the 16C, achieves a harmonious marriage between Gothic and Renaissance styles.

WHERE TO STAY

Hôtel de la Boule d'Or – *15 pl. Émile-Zola* – *05 49 65 02 18 – closed 6 to 22 Feb, 1 to 22 Aug, Sun evening and Mon lunch –* **P** *– 20 rms –* *6€.* Not far from the train station, this hotel could be a stopover for limited budget travellers. Its outmoded rooms are of varying sizes; some are a bit more comfortable than others. Several fixed-price menus are proposed in the restaurant.

Crowned with a dome and lantern, it rises above the town and surrounding farmlands to a height of 56m/184ft.

Musée Municipal
🕐 *Open Jul-Aug daily except Sun-Mon 2.30-6pm. Rest of the year Sat-Sun 3-6pm.* 🕐 *Closed Jan and public holidays.* 🚗 *No charge.* ☎ *05 49 65 26 79.*
This small museum, devoted to the history and culture of the region, is housed in a former granary. It stands near the town hall in an attractive square. Inside, in a typically regional setting, the displays include collections of local enamelware, and mementoes of the Vendée Wars.

Château
🕐 *Open access to the outside. Temporary exhibitions in the château, schedule information available.* ☎ *05 49 74 46 30.*

On the western side of the town stands the castle, now partly in ruins, which was once the headquarters of the powerful Barony of Beaumont-Bressuire. It comprises two separate walls punctuated by 48 semicircular towers. The outer wall, dating from the 13C, has a circumference of c 700m/770yd. Following it around on the left for just over 92m/100yd, the visitor is rewarded with a romantic view of curtain walls and crumbling towers. The inner wall dates back to the 11C. A postern leads into the main courtyard. The ruined 15C domestic quarters, which were burned down during the Revolution, have since been replaced with a Troubadour-style building.
There is a fine view of the castle and its curtain walls from the bridge across the River Dolo *(on the road to Cholet)*

BROUAGE★
POPULATION 498
MICHELIN MAP 324: D-4

The ramparts and turrets of Brouage, still extremely well-preserved despite constant assault from the sea winds, soar above the desolate marshland around them. Memories of lost love and lost wars haunt the old walled town, now sunk into silence. Brouage still stands today as a stoic memorial to the friendship between France and Quebec, flags flapping in the ocean breeze.

🖪 **Information:** Forges Royale – 2 r. de Québec, 17320 Brouage. ☎ 05 46 85 19 16.

A Bit of History

Grandeur and decadence
In medieval times Brouage played an important commercial role. The town, sheltered by Île d'Oléron at the inner end of "the finest haven in France", was the salt capital of Europe. Some 8 000ha/19 768 acres of salt-marshes provided the precious mineral which was to be refined and sent abroad – particularly to Flanders and Germany.
At some time between 1567 and 1570, **Samuel de Champlain** was born into a Protestant family living in Brouage. The boy became an expert navigator and, on the orders of King Henri IV, sailed away to colonise parts of Canada. In 1608, he left Honfleur in Normandy and discovered Quebec, opening up the fur trade in beaver and mink. A monument marks the place in Brouage where he was born. During the siege of La Rochelle in 1628, Brouage became the arsenal of the royal army, and Cardinal Richelieu instructed the Picardy engineer, Pierre d'Argencourt, to rebuild the fortifications. By the time the work was finished 10 years later, Champlain's birthplace, with a garrison of 6 000 men, was the most impregnable stronghold on the Atlantic coast.
At the end of the 17C, Brouage entered a period of decline. The founding of Rochefort and the re-establishment of La Rochelle as a military base, removed most of the military reasons for its exist-

The fortifications are well preserved

M. Thiery/MICHELIN

ence. Vauban, nevertheless undertook to reinforce the ramparts once more. However, the haven silted up, the salterns degenerated into rot-marshes which bred fever, and the garrison was reduced. **Love affairs and Affairs of State** – In 1659, the 21-year-old Louis XIV was in love with **Marie Mancini**, the raven-haired niece of Richelieu's successor, Cardinal Jules Mazarin. The young couple wanted to marry, but their dreams were thwarted. The Cardinal had decided that, for "reasons of State", the King must marry the Infanta of Spain to guarantee the peace brought by the Treaty of the Pyrenees, recently signed by the two countries. Marie Mancini was sent to La Rochelle, where she heard, with despair, of the forthcoming marriage. From September to December that year, she withdrew to

Brouage, where another of her uncles was Governor, "because solitude is the only solace for my broken dreams". Mazarin subsequently allowed her to return to Paris.

Six months later, after the royal marriage in St-Jean-de-Luz, Louis contrived to absent himself from the official cortège, returning to the capital, and then rode to Brouage, where he occupied the room in which Marie had stayed, pacing the ramparts, as he too sighed for the love he had lost.

Racine was inspired by this melancholy episode to write his tragedy *Bérénice*.

Ramparts★★

Kids ✏ *The Tourist Office organises guided tours of Pierre d'Argencourt's ramparts.* Constructed between 1630 and 1640, the ramparts are a perfect example of the art of fortification before the Vauban era. They describe an exact square measuring four times 400m/440yd, and are protected by seven massive bastions, each equipped with gracefully corbelled turrets. The walls, 13m/43ft high, are topped by a brick parapet pierced with apertures for cannon fire. Two gateways, Porte Royale and Porte de Hiers, allow access to the enclave. The western rampart is additionally protected by a ravelin detached from the curtain wall.

Though most of the houses in Brouage, including the Governor's mansion where Marie Mancini and Louis XIV stayed at different times, have disappeared, the military dependencies have better resisted the erosions of time.

Watch-path

It is possible to walk almost entirely around the town's

circumference along the top of the old ramparts, now carpeted with grass. From here the neat rectilinear layout of the plan is apparent, and there is a good view across the marshes to Île d'Aix and Île d'Oléron.

Porte Royale

Located in the northern **Bastion Royal**, this gateway once opened onto the quays. On the right-hand wall of the vaulted passage, leading out, ancient graffiti showing different types of ships can be seen. The outside of the gateway is surmounted by a pediment with the armorial bearings – partly worn away – of France and Navarre.

Forges Royales

The old blacksmiths' forges back onto Bastion Royal. In the middle of the one occupied today by the tourist office, an imposing furnace chimney can still be seen. Left of the forge, **Escalier Mancini** is the stone stairway that was used by the King's beloved each time she climbed to the ramparts to dream her solitary dreams. Parallel to the steps is a ramp that was used to hoist cannons. To the left are the **hangars de la Porte Royale**, a row of one-time workshops and stalls, today converted into shops. The Governor's mansion was just to the south.

▶ **Église St-Pierre; Halle aux Vivres** – restored food market; **Ancienne Tonnellerie** – old cooper's workshop; **Poudrière de La Brèche** – old powder magazine; **Port Souterrain** – underground harbour.

CAMBO-LES-BAINS✤

POPULATION 4 416
MICHELIN MAP 342: D-4

Haut Cambo, the upper residential district of this small spa, has a number of hotels and villas on the edge of a plateau overlooking the River Nive, whereas Bas Cambo, the lower town, is an old Basque village nestling in a wide curve of the river. At one time Cambo was the navigable limit for barges bringing cargoes inland from Bayonne. Farther upstream, the thermal cure centre is active once again. It was built in 1927 in neo-Classical style with Art deco mosaics and wrought-iron work.

A Bit of History

It is the exceptionally mild climate and a visit by the well-known poet and writer, Edmond Rostand (1868-1918), made Cambo a fashionable health resort at the turn of the last century. Arriving for the first time in the autumn of 1900, Rostand at once fell in love with Cambo and decided to live here permanently. He built a huge villa with beautiful gardens *(now open to the public)* overlooking the Bayonne road. Rostand was inspired by his walks in the Basque countryside around Cambo to write *Chantecler*, the successor to his *Cyrano de Bergerac*.

Arnaga★

The spacious **Villa Arnaga** (Musée Edmond Rostand) *(⏲ ⚒ guided tours (1hr) Jul-Aug 10am-7pm; Apr-Jun and Sep 10am-12.30pm, 2.30-7pm; Mar Sat-Sun and public holidays: 2.30-6pm; Oct 2.30-6.30pm. ⚒5.50€. ☎05 59 29 83 92)*, in the Labourdes Basque style was built under Rostand's supervision between 1903 and 1906. It stands on a promontory which the writer turned into French-style formal gardens.
The spacious house, with its great Basque roof, decorative painting and wooden balconies, contains Rostand memorabilia – furniture, documents, the original costume designs for *Chantecler*, and portraits of Rostand and Rosemonde Gérard by Pascau and Caro.

Address Book

WHERE TO STAY

⊜ **Hôtel Chez Tante Ursule** – *Quartier Bas-Cambo – 2km/1.2mi N of Cambo –* ☏ *05 59 29 78 23 – chez.tante.ursule@ wanadoo.fr – closed 15 Feb to 28 Feb and Tue –* 🅿 *– 17 rooms –* ⊑ *6.50€ – restaurant 15/35€.* A small, discrete hotel across from the fronton, well-placed for watching a game of Basque pelota. Very well-kept, classic rooms – ask for one in the more modern annex. Traditional fare in the dining room under the wooden ceiling.

⊜ **Soubeleta Bed and Breakfast** – *64250 Itxassou –* ☏ *05 59 29 78 64 –* 🍽 *– 5 rooms.* ⊑. Perched above the town, this imposing 17C edifice's tourelle and finely sculpted granite frame are still intact. The spacious rooms are decorated with family furniture; two have marble fireplaces.

⊜⊜ **Domaine Silencenia Bed and Breakfast** – *64250 Louhossoa – 10km/6mi SE of Cambo dir. St-Jean-Pied-de-Port –* ☏ *05 59 93 35 60 – domaine. de.silencenia@wanadoo.fr –* 🍽 *– 5 rooms – meals 25€.* A sweet quietude permeates this fine 18C house where a true art de vivre prevails. Each room echoes one of the owner's passions – rugby, fishing, wine and good food. The kitchen honours local cuisine.

WHERE TO EAT

⊜ **Venta Burkaitz** – *Col des Veaux – 64250 Itxassou – from Itxassou, take Pas de Roland, then Artzmandi –* ☏ *05 59 29 82 55 – closed evenings and Wed –* 🍽. On the Spanish side of the mountain range, a venta with two dining rooms. The more authentic has a traditional counter where you can have a before-dinner drink or buy liquor and conserves; the second offers a pretty view of the valley from the veranda. Plentiful local cuisine.

⊜⊜ **Domaine Xixtaberri** – *4km/2.4mi E of Cambo-les-Bains via D 10 –* ☏ *05 59 29 22 66 – reserv. recommended.* It's a steep drive to this house but you'll be rewarded by a splendid view of the Basque coast and the Pyrenees. Basque specialities to savour under the arbour or in the pleasing dining room with classic art on the walls. Comfortable rooms, decorated with a personal touch.

Driving Tour

Montagnes d'Itxassou★

15km/9mi S via D 918 – 3hrs
The road climbs out of the last farmlands of the Lower Nive.

Itxassou★

The hamlet's cottages are set in clusters among cherry orchards, which supply the main ingredient of the famous local cherry jam. The rustic-looking **church**★, standing alone near the River Nive, has three tiers of galleries adorned with statues and turned balusters, an 18C gilt wood altarpiece and a fine pulpit with decorations picked out in gold.

▶ *N of the village, take the road to the gliding field (terrain de vol à voile).*

Mont Urzumu

From the viewing table, near a statue of the Virgin, there is a remarkable **pano-** rama of the Basque Pyrenees and the coast from Pointe Ste-Barbe to Bayonne.

▶ *The narrow minor road runs along the west bank of the Nive.*

Pas de Roland

Park where the road widens, just beyond the parapet with a roadside crucifix. Beyond the crucifix, there is a view down to Pas de Roland, a rock with a large aperture said to have been formed by a kick from Roland's mount when he was being pursued by the Vascons.

▶ *Turn right at Laxia; the road becomes very narrow, and climbs steeply.*

Artzamendi★

Next to the telecoms station, there is a **panorama**★ extending northward towards the lower valley of the Nive, the Nivelle basin and its up-land pastures, and southward, beyond the border, to the slopes above the Bidassoa Valley.

CELLES-SUR-BELLE

POPULATION 3 480

MICHELIN MAP 322: E-7

The small town of Celles grew up in the shadow of the tall, imposing belfry of an old Augustinian abbey built on a terrace above the valley of the River Belle.

Sights

Église Notre-Dame

This former abbey church is the site of a pilgrimage to the Virgin known as the Septembresche (first Sunday of each September). King Louis XI was a regular worshipper here. The church was destroyed by the Huguenots in 1568, but rebuilt a century later, in 15C style, by the architect **François Leduc**. He was known as François the Tuscan because of his taste for Tuscan architecture.

The Romanesque main **doorway**★ of the original abbey church, is most unusual. Its multi-lobed arching, decorated with grimacing masks, betrays an Eastern influence which can be seen throughout France on the pilgrims' route to Santiago de Compostela.

Inside, the church is striking for the luminosity of the nave and aisles, and for the purity of line seen in the pillars soaring towards the high, curved vaulting.

Abbaye

Guided tours (1hr 15min) from mid-Jun to mid-Sep. 10.30am-12.30pm, 2.30-6.30pm. 3.50€ (children under 14: 1.50€). Closed 13 Jul. 05 49 32 14 99. Access the abbey via the doorway below the church.

Three of the presiding abbots here left their mark on history – Geoffrey d'Estissac, Cardinal de La Rochefoucauld, who was Louis XIII's prime minister, and the famous minister Talleyrand.

The monastic buildings and their dependencies were, like the church, the work of Leduc. The attractive main façade (85m/279ft long) features Ionic columns resting against scrolled buttresses. The right wing of the building was unfortunately never completed. Inside, there is a fine staircase, the old refectory, kitchen and a cloister gallery, all dating from the 17C.

Excursion - Maison du Protestantisme Poitevin

Beaussais

Early. Jul-Aug daily except Mon 10.30am-noon, 2.30-6.30pm. Apr-Jun and Sep-Oct Sat-Sun and public holidays 2.30-6pm (school holidays: daily). 5€. 05 49 32 83 16.

This **temple**, a former 12C Catholic church with a Romanesque oven-vaulted chancel, now houses a small museum. Panels and displays at the entrance relate to the activities of Protestants in the 20C, while those in the nave trace the history of the movement in France, with special emphasis on Poitou. A multimedia show tells the history of Reformation through the story of Jean Migault, a Protestant school teacher who had to go into exile. Major events are highlighted, such as the coming of Calvin to Poitiers, the history of Reformation, wars of religion and the consequences of the revocation of the Edict of Nantes A Huguenot footpath links Beaussais to La Couarde *(4km/2mi, details from the museum).*

▷ *Take D 10 N to La Couarde.*

La Couarde

This section of the **Maison du Protestantisme Poitevin** is housed in a church built in 1904. The showcases and displays concentrate on the period known as the Desert, the period of resistance and repression which followed the revocation of the Edict of Nantes in 1685. Among the exhibits are *méreaux*, tokens used by Huguenots at that time to identify themselves as members of the faithful. There is a reconstruction of a Desert Assembly (a meeting or service held in secret) with a collapsible pulpit which could be quickly dismantled and hidden.

LOGIS DE LA CHABOTTERIE★★

MICHELIN MAP 316: H-6

It is in the woods of La Chabotterie that the Vendée War ended with the capture of the Royalist leader, Charrette (1796).

The Manor

⏱Jul-Aug 10am-7pm. Jun and early Sep. to 11 Nov 9.30am-6pm. Sun and public holidays 10am-7pm. 12 Nov to end of Mar, Sun and public holidays 10am-6pm. ⏱Closed last 3 weeks in Jan and Christmas. ∽6€ (children under 18: no charge). ☎02 51 42 81 00.

A new type of construction appeared in Vendée in 1560 known as the logis clos, so-called because the fortified courtyard enclosed the seignorial manor and its attendant outbuildings. This typical configuration was found in Vendée until the 18C.

The refined atmosphere of the 18C century – a mixture of country ways and gracious living typical of the rural society of the time in Bas-Poitou – has been brought to life again through careful restoration of the manor house to which Charette was brought after his capture, thus putting an end to the Vendée War.

Salles historiques

They feature authentic period pieces in a reconstructed dining room (table laid for a meal, hallmarked chairs, cut-crystal chandelier), bedroom (canopied bed made of fabric from Nantes, 1783), and study (17C and 18C Aubusson tapestries).

Salle des maquettes

It contains scale models of many traditional houses of the Vendée region.

Parcours spectacle

☺Children and particularly sensitive people may find the subject matter here disturbing. In the modern building, visitors walk through rooms illustrating great moments in local history, including the main episodes of the Vendée War.

Walled garden

It is divided into flower beds where roses are tended, and a vegetable plot, where the flowers can also be spectacular.

Croix de Charette

This granite cross can be reached from La Chabotterie (🚶30min on foot there and back). Erected in 1911 in La Chabotterie Woods, the cross marks the place where the Royalist leader was captured.

This canopied bed is known as a lit à la duchesse

M. Thiery/MICHELIN

Excursion

Château du Bois-Chevalier

20km/12mi W. ⏰Open Jul to beginning of Aug 10.30am-4.30pm. 🚶3€.
The central body of this Louis XIV château is crowned by a dome and flanked by six wings with high French roofs; the ensemble is reflected in the waters alongside. Charrette stayed here during the Vendée War.

Driving Tour

Charrette's footsteps

45km/28mi round-trip – allow 3hrs

▶ *From Logis de la Chabotterie, rejoin D 18 and turn right; cross D 763 and continue to La Copechagnière, turn left onto D 86 to Les Brouzils, then right onto D 7 towards Les Essarts.*

Roads D 7 then D 6 (towards Belleville-sur-Vie) run close to the edge of **Grasla Forest** where Charrette and his troops sought refuge on 11 January 1794. A commemorative cross stands at the entrance of an unusual village hidden at the heart of the forest.

Refuge de Grasla

♿⏰*Open early Jun to mid-Sep 11am-6pm; May Sat-Sun and public holidays 2-6pm. Mid-Sep to mid-Oct Sun 2-6pm.🚶5€. (children: 3€). ☎02 51 42 96 20 or 02 51 43 85 90.*
In 1793, many inhabitants of the surrounding parishes, fleeing the Blues (Republican army) sought refuge in Grasla Forest. Some 2 000 of them built a village of wooden huts in order to survive.

▶ *Continue along D 6. In St-Denis-la-Chevasse, turn right onto D 39 to Les Lucs-sur-Boulogne.*

Les Lucs-sur-Boulogne

On 28 February 1794, one of General Cordelier's Infernal Columns slaughtered many of the inhabitants of Grand-Luc, and, on 5 March, parishioners of Petit-Luc who had sought refuge in the church. This, however, was not the only place where the Republican Infernal Columns held sway, and the memorial inaugurated in May 1993 was erected to the memory of all their victims.
The historiated stained-glass windows of **Église St-Pierre**, built in 1902, tell of the 1794 massacres (🎧*a tape recorder can be turned on next to the organ*).

▶ *Drive NE out of Les Lucs along D 18. After crossing the River Boulogne, turn right onto a minor road leading to a vast parking area.*

Le Chemin de la Mémoire des Lucs★

⏰*Open jul-Aug daily 10am-7pm. Sep-Jun 9.30am-6pm. Sun and public holidays 10am-7pm. ⏰Closed last 3 weeks in Jan, 1 Jan, 25 Dec. 🚶No charge. ☎02 51 42 81 00.*
Dedicated to the memory of the martyrs and victims of the Reign of Terror, the memorial in Les Lucs is a contemporary creation, an architectural and landscaped ensemble leading from the banks of the Boulogne to the hilltop chapel.
Many historical landmarks lie along the **Allée de l'Histoire** recalling the major events in the Vendée War from March to December 1793.
In the foreground stands the **Memorial de Vendée**, of intentionally sober architecture. The corridor of memory, divided into four rooms, evokes the end of the insurrection and the destruction of Vendée through reconstructed scenes and symbolic objects (monstrance, Sacred Heart tapestry, a peasant's scythe upturned for use as a weapon). The crypt, its floor covered with dozens of stelae, perpetuates the memory of all the unknown victims.
On the other side of the footbridge over the Boulogne, stands a blackened wall, symbolising the mass burning of villages. A path leads to the **Chapelle Notre-Dame-du-Petit-Luc**, built in 1867 on the remains of the former church which was burned to the ground.

▶ *Rejoin D 18 and turn right towards St-Sulpice-le-Verdon to return to Logis de la Chabotterie.*

CHARROUX ★

POPULATION 1 320
MICHELIN MAP 322: I-8

Charroux, which lies 50km/31mi south of Poitiers in a valley on the east bank of the Charente, grew up around a Benedictine abbey dedicated to the Holy Saviour, on the way to Santiago de Compostela. A 15C wooden market is still standing in the main square.

Informations: 2 r. de Chatain, 86250 Charroux. ☎05 49 87 60 12.

Kids: In the tourist office, you can see a scale model of the abbey as it must have appeared in its former glory. Price 1€.

A Bit of History

Holy Relics, a Source of Wealth

The success of Holy Saviour Abbey was assured from the start because the original monks were under the patronage of Charlemagne himself. Ecclesiastical Councils were held here from time to time, one of which, in 989, laid the foundations for the Truce of God. The abbey church was consecrated by Pope Urban II in 1096.

The abbey, the guardian of priceless relics (flesh and blood of Jesus Christ, parts of the True Cross), attracted impressive numbers of pilgrims; at one time 25 000 of the faithful would visit it each June. Wealthy pilgrims enriched the treasury with gifts of money and magnificent works of art. Eventually the abbey had possessions as far away as England.

Decline

The Wars of Religion in the 16C put an end to this prosperity, and the abbey was sacked. In 1762, its function was suppressed altogether and by the beginning of the 19C, over half of the buildings had been demolished.

The preservation of what remained is the work of Mérimée, Inspector-General of Historic Monuments under the Second Empire. Excavations and restoration work carried out between 1946 and 1953 have exposed the ground plan of the abbey church and revealed the crypt. The cloisters have been restored. Building works in the chapter-house led to the discovery of sarcophagi containing a fine collection of funerary items.

Abbaye St-Sauveur ★

&.☉Jun-Sep 10am-12.30pm, 2-6.30pm. Oct-May 10am-12.30pm, 2-5.30pm. ☉Closed 1 Jan, 1 May, 1 and 11 Nov, 25 Dec. ⊜4.60€ (children under 18 no charge). ☎05 49 87 62 43.

Abbey church

The ground plan here allied the traditional Latin cross outline with the circular design of the Holy Sepulchre Church in Jerusalem. The church comprises a narthex, a nave, a transept with side chapels, and an apse with radiating chapels. In the centre of the transept crossing was a circular sanctuary surrounded by three concentric aisles, positioned above a crypt. It was surmounted by a tall tower (still standing). The building as a whole, which was 126m/413ft long, suggested certain early Middle Eastern churches.

The church was built in the Poitou Romanesque style with the exception of the west front which was Gothic. Several elements from this façade are incorporated in the walls of a nearby house.

The polygonal **tower**★★ dates from the 11C and was in the exact centre of the church. It stands like a gigantic canopy above the rotunda sheltering the high altar, which itself surmounts the crypt in which the sacred relics were displayed. The first two storeys of the tower, now empty, were actually inside the church. The upper part was probably crowned by a spire.

Cloisters

The cloisters – today open to the sky and extensively plundered – were reconstructed in the 15C under the direction of Abbot Chaperon, whose heraldic arms, three hoods, are reproduced on the capitals of the columns in the chapter-house.

Chapter-house

The large, impressive building houses a number of excellent 13C **sculptures**★★ which once adorned the main doorway of the west front. These include Christ in Judgement, originally on the tympanum, and several figures decorating the arches – kings, prophets, former abbots of Charroux, and the delightful statuettes of the Wise and Foolish Virgins so often seen in the Poitou region. These works are attributed to the sculptor who worked on the doorways of Poitiers Cathedral.

Treasury★

The treasury houses a fine collection of Romanesque pastoral staffs and pieces by Gothic goldsmiths and silversmiths, discovered in the abbots' tombs exca-

Polygonal tower

vated beneath the chapter-house. Two magnificently worked silver-gilt reliquaries stand out among the gold and silver plate – one, dating from the 13C, is particularly remarkable: two angels hold a box which contained the relics.

THERMES DE CHASSENON★

MICHELIN MAP 324: O-4

In 1958 a remarkable Gallo-Roman site was discovered in the Charente and Limousin area. It seems that Chassenon was a health resort in Roman times and was eventually abandoned in the 6C.

▶ **Orient Yourself**: The site is situated 5.5km/3.5mi NW of Rochechouart.

A Bit of History

Cassanomagus or Cassinomagus?

The etymological origin of this term remains a debatable point. For some, Cassanomagus is composed of the Celtic words *cassanos* (oak) and *magos* (market). Another interpretation gives Cassinomagus, from Cassinus (a man's name) and magos. Either way, both names are related to the Gauls. Even though its role before the Roman Conquest remains unknown, it is certain that the Romans were familiar with a site located at an important road junction, possibly endowed with thermal springs. For a long time, it was

even thought that a large town was built here and what we see today was a Roman governor's palace.

Chassenon had one or several temples, a theatre, a forum and thermal baths.

The Rise and Fall

The sanctuary reached its peak in the 2C. It is easy to imagine the grandiose style of these richly ornate marble baths, decorated with sumptuous works of art. Its decline began in the late 3C, accelerated by the spread of Christianity. Defaced statues found in the gutter and sewers testify to the exhaustive destruction of all pagan symbols. The barbarian invasions also contributed to the ruin of the building, which was later partly converted into a foundry after making alterations to the ovens. For a while, it was even used to make sarcophagi out of local stone. It would appear, however, that certain medical practices associated with continuing local paganism lasted up until the 6C, when the miraculous healings performed by St Junien made the old Gallo-Roman sanctuary redundant.

The Thermal Baths

Traces of a high curtain wall and a few remnants of the temple and theatre can still be seen but nothing of the forum, which is still buried. Only the thermal baths have survived intact. These baths were unusual, not only because they had two sets of everything, but also because they were used for healing. The people who came here were mainly pilgrims with health problems, who observed a specific religious ritual (the temple was 230m/760ft away). When people came to the thermal baths, they entered through a doorway in the eastern façade (the side opposite the present pathway). They then went into the changing room before going through to another heated room, where they may have paid or been checked – the exact use remains unknown. After that, they went through to the large central room, and into the *tepidarium* (warm room), where the skin was thoroughly scraped with a curved metal instrument called a strigile; the *caldarium* (hot room) contained the steam room and boiling hot baths designed to make the bather sweat profusely, and the *frigidarium* (cold room) was used for taking a cold plunge after leaving the *tepidarium*. The *palestra* next to the southern frigidarium was used for all types of physical activities, including swimming. The baths would almost certainly have had additional rooms adapted to specific therapies.

Visit

⏱ 👣 *Guided tours (1hr, last departure 45min before closing time) from early Jun to mid-Sep, 10am-noon and 2-7pm. Apr-May and mid-Sep to 11 Nov, 2-5.30pm.* 🎫 *4.90€.* ☎ *05 45 89 32 21.*

The building, whose walls are still 5m/16.5ft high, had three floors. The south wing, better preserved, was the mirror image of the north wing. Two aqueducts provided the building with a constant flow of water and a drainage system.

The tour starts with the north wing: follow the cart track (where the fuel was off-loaded) along the foot of the high walls, into the dark, vaulted underground chambers which seem to have been built to carry water. The zigzag passageways connecting the chambers were designed for maximum decantation. Items collected during the excavations are displayed in one of the passageways.

The service or boiler rooms were located on the intermediate level. Note the ingenious underground heating system using a hypocaust, or hollow space under the floor. The coal-fired furnaces could be heated to more than 300°C/570°F. The resulting heat was routed to the hypocaust, a layer of tiles laid in a bed of clay mortar, and radiating flues distributed the heat into the room above. The temperature of about 20°C/68°F to 25°C/77°F was obtained in the rooms above.

The ground floor in the south wing has remained relatively intact, and the visitor can easily imagine what the rooms were like when they were full of bathers. The southern cold room and several other rooms lead into the largest room in the very heart of the baths. Several hypotheses have been put forward concerning the function of this 232m²/763sq ft room, with its six windows and six doors – a place of worship, a waiting hall, a physician's surgery or a room dedicated to the god of healing.

CHÂTELLERAULT

POPULATION 34 126
MICHELIN MAP 322: J-4

Châtellerault is a pleasant town for a stroll, with wide tree-lined avenues and an attractive pedestrianised district. The city lies on the banks of the River Vienne, at the upper limit of its navigable reach, and owes its name to Ayraud, Vicomte de Poitou, who built a château on the site in the 10C.

- **Information:** 2 av. Treuille, 86100 Châtellerault. ☎05 49 21 05 47.
- ▶ **Orient Yourself:** Situated 35km/22mi NE of Poitiers, Châtelleraut town centre is surrounded by wide avenues. The most direct access to the town is via the A 10.
- **P Parking:** There are several car parks in the town centre, including along the boulevard de Blossac, which separates the old town from the more modern suburbs (☝see MAP).
- Ⓒ **Also See:** ANGLES-SUR-L'ANGLIN.

A Bit of History

The growth of the modest local metal-working trade from the 13C onwards led to the establishment of a cutlery industry in the city in the 18C. Later (1820), the metallurgy business expanded into arms manufacture and an arsenal. The former, which operated until 1968, played an important role in the economic success of Châtellerault.

Walking Tour

Allow 2hrs.

▶ *Start from the tourist office on boulevard de Blossac and enter the pedestrianised district. Follow rue Bourbon on the right.*

Maison Descartes

The philosopher Descartes spent several years of his childhood in this 16C family home, currently undergoing restoration.

Église St-Jacques

▶ *Walk along the pedestrianised rue Bourbon to a small square then turn right to reach the church.*

The west front and the two neo-Roman-esque towers of this former priory church dedicated to St James date only from the 19C, but the transept and the east end with its buttress-columns were built in the 12C-13C.

The nave has quadripartite vaulting in the Anjou Gothic style whereas the south side chapel has lierne and tierceron vaulting with historiated keystones.

A 17C statue of St James in polychrome wood stands in the northern arm of the transept. The figure is dressed as a pilgrim on his way to Santiago Compostela, a reminder that Châtellerault was one of the stages on the pilgrims' route (Santiago means St James).

A **carillon** of 52 bells is housed in the north tower.

▶ *Go past the Musée Municipal to the Henri IV Bridge.*

Saint James (Jacques to the French)

S. Sauvignier/MICHELIN

Pont Henri-IV

The bridge (144m/472ft long and 21m/69ft wide) was built between 1575 and 1611 by Charles Androuet du Cerceau, a member of a famous family of architects. Two massive slate-roofed towers, once linked by a central block, protected the entrance to the west end – a wise precaution so soon after the Wars of Religion. In the middle of the bridge, on the upstream side, two anchors hanging from a cross are a reminder of the time when inland river transport was a thriving business.

▶ *Walk across the bridge then upriver along an avenue shaded by plane trees until you reach the Manu.*

La Manu

This former weapons' foundry, set in shady grounds on the left bank of the River Vienne has been restored and now combines culture, teaching and leisure activities.

Musée Auto Moto Vélo

see SIGHTS.

Comme deux tours

In 1994, the artist Jean-Luc Vilmouth added a platform and a spiral staircase to a couple of high factory chimneys so that people could climb up and admire the town and its surroundings.

▶ *From here, it is possible to continue the walk as far as the Envigne Canal.*

Canal de l'Envigne

Situated on the west bank of the River Vienne and framed by the skating rink and a park planted with cedar trees and sequoias, the canal offers water-sport activities.

Museums

Musée Sully

Currently closed ☎05 49 21 01 27. *www. alienor.org.*

The museum stands at the far end of a splendid courtyard, in Hôtel Sully, a man-

sion built in the 17C by Androuet du Cerceau. Collections of weapons, knives, 17C to 19C porcelain and earthenware are on view, together with carved wooden chair backs, sculptures, paintings and other works of art. One room is devoted to Rudolph Salis (1851-97) who was born in Châtellerault and later founded the famous Parisian cabaret, Le Chat Noir. Menus and wine lists from the cabaret are on display with posters and a number of metal shadowgraph silhouettes representing an army on the march. The silhouettes were projected onto a screen, producing an effect rather like a primitive animated cartoon. Salis himself added a spoken commentary, and one of his shadow theatre shows was an entire Napoleonic saga.

Local history from prehistoric times to the present day is traced in another department, including an archaeological display of the Gallo-Roman site of Vieux-Poitiers, prints and engravings of Châtellerault, bills from coaching inns including lodging for the traveller's horse.

Documents, photos and explanatory tableaux in a section on the Acadians follow their odyssey to the New World and back, and examine the economic and cultural role played by Acadia today (New Brunswick and Nova Scotia).

Regional headdresses, bonnets, shawls and christening robes from the 18C to the early 20C can also be seen. The considerable skill of the local linen workers is reflected in the variety of shapes and the richness of the embroidery.

Musée Auto Moto Vélo

Early Jul to 1st week in Sep daily except Tue 10am-noon and 2-6pm. Feb-Jun and mid-Sep to late Dec, daily except Mon and Tue 2-6pm. Closed Jan and 25 Dec. 5€ *(children under 13 no charge).* ☎05 49 21 03 46.

 This interactive museum, covering a surface area of 4 300m^2/46 300sq ft, retraces the very early beginnings of the motor vehicle and its subsequent popularisation through a series of gleaming motor cars. The motorbike collection is remarkable.

CHAUVIGNY★

POPULATION 7 025
MICHELIN MAP 322: J-5

Chauvigny was an important medieval stronghold, which later developed as a trade and industrial centre specialising in the manufacture of porcelain. Traditional quarrying of local freestone – a fine-grained limestone with regular cleavage – has also remained important.

▶ **Orient Yourself**: Chauvigny is situated on the right bank of the River Vienne, 23km/14mi E of Poitiers.

▣ **Parking**: Parking is available In the Upper Town.

⊚ **Don't Miss**: The Upper Town; Église St-Pierre and the capitals in the chancel; Donjon de Gouzon.

▧ **Especially for Kids**: Falconry show at the château.

⌕ **Also See**: POITIERS; ABBAYE DE ST-SAVIN.

Upper Town★

Standing on a spur, the upper town *(ville haute)* is surmounted in turn by the jagged ruins of forts and castles dominated by the elegant belfry of St Peter's.

Château baronnial

This 11C baronial castle, built when the bishops of Poitiers were also the lords of Chauvigny, comprises both an upper section – with an enormous keep – and a lower section surrounded by ramparts, revealing traces of the Château Neuf (New Castle) ruins.

Falconry show

⌕*(for the show).* ◷ *Jul-Aug (45min) 11.15am, 2.30pm, 4pm and 5.30pm. End of Mar to end of Jun and Sep-Oct, 2.30pm, 4pm.* ◷*Nov-Mar and 14 Jul.* ⊚*8.50€ (children 5-12: 5.50€).* ☎ *05 49 46 47 48; www.geantsduciel.com*

▧The castle precinct lends itself perfectly to demonstrations of birds of prey in flight (eagles, falcons, vultures).

Château d'Harcourt

The castle originally belonged to the earls of Châtellerault, who built it between the 13C and 15C, on the crest of the promontory. Massive ramparts with a fortified entrance gate still exist.

Église St-Pierre★

The construction of this former collegiate church, founded by the lords of Chauvigny, started in the 11C with the apse and was completed in the following century by the erection of the nave. The style is Romanesque, and the building material a fine grey stone. There are two different levels of open-work in the square belfry. The east end, richly decorated with sculptures, is notable for the pleasing proportions of the apse and chapels.

The interior of the church has unfortunately suffered from over-enthusiastic 19C repainting.

The capitals of the columns, supporting the broken-barrel vaults in the nave, are decorated with palm leaf designs. The **capitals in the chancel★★** are particularly interesting, embracing a fascinating selection of biblical, evangelical and mythical scenes – the Annunciation, the Adoration of the Magi, the Weighing of the Souls, the Arrival of the Shepherds, the Temptation and other religious subjects alternate with an extraordinary phantasmagoria of winged monsters, sphinxes, sirens and demons subjecting resigned humans to the worst possible torments.

Donjon Gouzon★

Just north of the church. This keep is all that remains of a castle acquired in the late 13C by the Gouzon family and subsequently (around 1335) bought by Bishop Fort of Aux. The square keep was originally supported by rectangular buttresses, which were later surmounted by rounded buttresses.

Capitals in Église St-Pierre

Espace d'Archéologie Industrielle

&🕙*Apr to mid-Jun and Sep-Oct, 2-6pm; Sat 2.30-6.30pm, Sun 11am-6.30pm; Nov-Mar, Sat-Sun and public hols 2-6pm.* 🕙 *Closed 1 Jan and 25 Dec.* ∞*4.60€.(children no charge)* ☎*05 49 46 91 56.*

A local archaeological exhibition was set up in the keep after its restoration in 1988. A glass lift, encased in the spiral staircase of the tower with its transparent dome, leads up to the exhibition rooms (computer and video displays). The terrace at the top of the keep commands a fine view of the surrounding countryside.

Musée de Chauvigny

🕙*Mid-Jun to end of Aug, daily 10am-12.30pm and 2.30-6.30pm, Sat-Sun and public hols 2.30-6.30pm; Apr to mid-Jun, Sep and Oct, daily 2-6pm; Nov-Mar, Sat-Sun and public hols 2-6pm.* 🕙*Closed 1 Jan and 25 Dec.* ∞*1.70€ (children no charge).* ☎ *05 49 46 40 31.*

This typical example of local traditional architecture houses a display on objects relating to life in Chauvigny in bygone days and an archaeology room (1C ceramics).

▶ **Église Notre-Dame** – 14C fresco; **St-Pierre-les-Églises** (2km/1mi south) – pre-Romanesque church with 9C-10C frescoes. 🕙*Jul to end of Aug: 10am-6pm.* ☞*guided tours available with reservation Fri at 10.30am.* ☎*05 49 46 39 01.*

Excursions

Château de Touffou★

6km/3.6mi NW. ☞*Unaccompanied visit (30 min) of the garden. From mid-Jun to mid-Sep, guided tour (1hr) daily except Tue 10am-noon and 2-6.30pm. Early May to mid-Jun, Sat, Sun and public hols 2-6pm; from mid-Sep to end Sep, Sat-Sun 2-6pm (gardens only).* ∞*7€.* ☎*05 49 56 40 08.*

The warm, ochre-coloured stone of this château with its terraces and hanging gardens overlooking the River Vienne helps to form a unified whole, despite the four different architectural styles.

The oldest part of Touffou Castle is the massive keep, which was formed during the Renaissance by joining two older keeps dating from the 11C and 12C. At each of the outer corners the buttresses are crowned by elegant turrets. Four huge round towers were added in the 14C: Tour St-Georges, with finely sculpted openings, Tour St-Jean, Tour de l'Hostellerie, restored in 1938, and Tour de la Chapelle with its prison cells.

The Renaissance wing, linking Tour St-Georges with the keep, was added c 1560. It is adorned with mullioned windows and dormers; the triangular pediments carry a series of 17 different coats of arms, representing the genealogy of the Chasteignier family.

The main features are François I's Chamber (also known as the Four Seasons Room), which is embellished with fine frescoes illustrating work in the fields, the chapel, the guard-room and its cells, the bakery and kitchen.

Archigny
13km/8mi N.
The name of this village is inextricably linked with the story of the Acadians – early-17C emigrants from the Poitou region who settled in the eastern part of French Canada. Acadia, corresponding roughly to the present-day Canadian provinces of Nova Scotia and New Brunswick, was ceded to the British in 1713. After the Treaty of Paris at the end of the Seven Years War (1763), the British government in Canada colonised the area and, in 1773 and 1774, forcibly repatriated the 10 000 French living there to make room for English immigrants. Returning to Poitou, the dispossessed Acadians settled south-east of Châtellerault on fallow land given to them by the Marquis de Pérusse des Cars.

La Ligne Acadienne, the Acadian Line, was the name given to a series of similar farms established on the heath between Archigny and La Puye: 58 clay and brushwood houses on rubble foundations, which the ex-colonists hoped eventually to own. Some, impatient because the charter they awaited was delayed, moved to Nantes and later to French Louisiana. Those that remained received their title deeds only in 1793.

Today, 34 of these houses are still standing. Each year on 15 August, in the hamlet known as **Huit-Maisons** (Eight Houses),

descendants of the Poitou Acadians organise a fête to commemorate this period in their history.

Ferme acadienne des Huit-Maisons
&. ⏲*Apr–end of Oct guided tours (45min) Sat-Sun and public hols 3-7pm (Jul and Aug, daily except Mon).* � *2€ (schools: 1€).* ☎ *05 49 85 57 46.*

An old Acadian farm at Huit-Maisons (6km/ 3mi E of Archigny, signposted) has been converted into a museum. Here, under the same roof, visitors can see living quarters with furniture of the period, a cow shed containing agricultural implements, and the barn, where documents relating to the history of the Acadians and their return to Poitou are on display.

Civaux
15km/9mi S.
The number of rare archaeological treasures found around Civaux confirms the importance of this modest village in relation to the spread of Christianity in the Poitou region.

Nécropole Mérovingienne★
This ancient burial ground dates from Merovingian times (AD c 500-750) when the Frankish dynasty founded by Clovis reigned over Gaul and Germany.

The origin of the burial ground remains a mystery. It is thought that the graves might have been those of warriors who fell in a battle between Clovis and Alaric, the King of the Visigoths, or perhaps they were the tombs of penitents who had

---

Address Book

&*For coin ranges, see the Legend on the cover flap.*

WHERE TO STAY
⊖**Chambre d'hôte La Veaudepierre** – *8 r. du Berry –* ☎*05 49 46 30 81 – http:// perso.club-internet.fr/laveaudepierre –* ⊟ *– 5 rms.* Overlooked by the castle ruins, this beautiful 18C mansion has plenty of charm. The collection of old instruments will appeal to music lovers, while all guests will appreciate the views.

WHERE TO EAT
⊖**Les Choucas** – *21 r. des Puys –* ☎*05 49 46 36 42 – www.leschoucas.net – closed last week in Jan, Tue and Wed.* Across from the donjon, this small restaurant is housed in a medieval building. Choose between the bar-crêperie on the ground floor and the restaurant with mullion windows, fireplace and wooden beams on the first floor. Regional cuisine or medieval menu (must be ordered in advance).

expressed a wish to be buried on the site of their conversion.

A ruined chapel, dedicated to St Catherine, had been remodelled several times since the Romanesque period.

Musee archéologique

30 pl. de Gomelange. ⏰*Mid-Jun to mid-Sep daily except Mon 10.30am-1pm and 3-7pm. Rest of the year hours vary.* ⏰*Closed 20 Dec-3 Feb.* ⬤*3€.* ☎*05 49 48 34 61.*

This small museum not far from the cemetery contains exhibits from Merovingian and Gallo-Roman times (stelae, tombstones, ceramics, funerary items). Of special interest are the reconstructions of various types of grave discovered in the necropolis – both with and without coffins, directly in the earth or surrounded by a drystone frame, in sarcophagi or in simple cairns.

Église St-Gervais et St-Protais

The church was built on the site of a Roman temple, the ruins of which still contain a loggia converted into a baptistery. The apse, which dates from the 4C, has a stone belfry adorned with two tiers of blind arcades. In the barrel-vaulted nave (10C), the cylindrical columns are topped by **historiated capitals** embodying themes which reflect fears of hell and damnation. Sealed into the south wall of the apse is a 4C funerary stone engraved with the Greek letters Alpha and Omega on either side of a *chrisma* (a monogram formed from the first two letters of the Greek word for Christ).

CLISSON★

POPULATION 5 939
MICHELIN MAP 316: I-5

The small town of Clisson is dominated by its imposing medieval fortress, which stands on a spur overlooking the River Sèvre Nantaise. The town is also home to La Garenne-Lemot, a magnificent neo-Classical villa built in the Italian style.

▶ **Orient Yourself**: Clisson stands on a picturesque site at the junction of the River Moine and the Sèvre Nantaise.

🅿 **Parking**: There are several car parks in the town centre.

⊙ **Don't Miss**: Domaine de la Garenne-Lemot.

A Bit of History

In 1794, the Infernal Columns of the Republicans attacked the town and set it ablaze so savagely that, by the end of the Revolution, virtually every inhabitant had fled. In the early years of the 19C, Clisson rose phoenix-like from its ashes, largely owing to the enthusiasm of the Cacault brothers, who were natives of nearby Nantes, and the sculptor, Frédéric Lemot. They had spent some time in Italy, and under their influence the restored town was progressively Italianised. Today, houses in Clisson itself and a number of watermills and small factories in the neighbourhood (recognisable by their brick-dressed, rounded-arch windows) are evidence of that architectural trend, the first examples of which appeared in Garenne-Lemot park (⊙*see BELOW*).

Old Town

Château d'Olivier de Clisson

⏰*Apr-Sep daily except Tue 9.30am-noon and 2-6pm (last admission 20min before closing). Oct-Mar, daily except Mon and Tue 9.30am-noon and 2-6pm.* ⏰*Closed 1 Jan, 1 May and during Christmas school hols.* ⬤*2.20€.* ☎*02 40 54 02 22.*

The ruins rise impressively above the Sèvre Nantaise. The castle, located on the border of the Duchy of Brittany, was designed to repel attacks from both Anjou and Poitou. The first overlords were the Sires of Clisson, among them the famous Constable, Olivier de Clisson

(1336-1407). In 1420 the castle was confiscated by the Duc de Bretagne.
An earlier castle had been built in the 11C and 12C. This was enclosed within a polygonal structure flanked by towers in the 13C. A keep, also polygonal, was added in the 14C (a section of wall topped by machicolations still exists). The kitchens, the chapel and the lords' living quarters also date from the 14C.
The Duc de Bretagne, François II, modernised the fortifications in the 15C with the addition of a second enclave, which included a prison and a huge gateway. This new entrance was protected by a drawbridge, replacing the ancient barbican. Finally, fearing an attack by the Catholic League, the overlords strengthened the defences still further in the 16C by building three new bastions.
In the middle of the central courtyard stands a well into which, in 1794, the Republicans flung 18 citizens of Clisson who had sought refuge in the castle.

Bridges

From the viaduct carrying route N 149 across the Moine, there is an attractive view of the castle, the river with its green banks, and the 15C Pont St-Antoine (St Anthony's Bridge). From the second bridge, spanning the Sèvre, there is an equally picturesque vista of the river with the awe-inspiring castle towering overhead.

Les Halles

The covered market originated in the 15C, though the fine timber framework was fashioned from oak in the 17C and 18C.

Domaine de la Garenne-Lemot★

Access via the N 149

In 1805, Frédéric Lemot purchased Bois de la Garenne, a wood just south-east of Clisson, and employed the architect Mathurin Crucy to carry out a number of projects in the Italian style.

Park

Apr-Sep, 9am-8pm; Oct-Mar, 9.30am-6.30pm. No charge. 02 40 54 75 85; www.culture.cg44.fr
Scattered throughout the park are statues and follies in the style of classical antiquity (a Temple of Vesta imitating the one in Tivoli in Italy, an oratory, a military monument and a tomb), the Grotto of Héloïse, two rocks engraved with poems and, notably, a charming rocky site on the banks of the Sèvre known as the Baths of Diana.

Villa Lemot

Open is dependent on current exhibition Closed 1 Jan, 1 May, 25 Dec. 2.20€ (children under 18: no charge). 4.20€. 02 40 54 75 85.
This villa was built in neo-Classical style and fronted by a semicircular colonnade, recalling the famous Bernini columns in front of St Peter's in Rome. It is used as a venue for art exhibitions. The terrace

Address Book

WHERE TO EAT

La Gétignière – *3 r. de la Navette – 44190 Gétigné – 3km/1.8mi SE of Clisson; take the N 149 towards Cholet – 02 40 36 05 37 – closed 6-27 Aug, 24 Dec-2 Jan, Sun eve, Mon eve, Tue eve, and Wed all day.* In a small street in the heart of the town, this restaurant run by a young couple serves excellent, simple food. Spotless dining room renovated in a contemporary style; plenty of room between the tables and an innovative, modern cuisine. Interesting lunch menu.

La Bonne Auberge – *1 r. O.-de-Clisson – 02 40 54 01 90 – closed 13 Feb-2 Mar, 8-31 Aug, Sun eve, Tue lunch, Wed lunch and Mon all day.*
An attractive restaurant a little off the beaten track, away from the town centre. The dining rooms at La Bonne Auberge are light and pleasant, running one into the other to the back of the building, where a veranda opens onto the garden. Mouth-watering dishes on the menu include lobster millefeuille, baked pikeperch and veal kidneys.

A. Thiery/MICHELIN

Clisson – Villa Lemot

behind the villa offers a **view** over the town, the castle, the River Sèvre and the Temple of Friendship, a columned building in which the remains of Frédéric Lemot lie.

Maison du Jardinier (Gardener's House)

To the right on entering the park. ◔*Jun-Sep 10am-noon and 2-7pm, Mon 2-7pm. Mar-May and Oct daily except Mon 10am-noon and 2-6pm. Nov-Feb daily except Mon 10am-noon and 2-5pm, Sat-Sun and public hols, 2-5pm.* ◔*Closed 1 Jan, 1 May, 25 Dec.* ≈*No charge.* ☎*02 40 54 75 85.*

The building, with its dovecote tower, is an imitation of an Italian country house, and served as a model for a number of others in the area. Inside, there is a scale model of the park, a video display and a permanent exhibition on Italian architecture in Clisson.

Driving Tour

Muscadet and Sèvre-et-Maine

Round-trip of 65km/40mi – 4hrs

Clisson is one of the gateways to the vineyards of the Sèvre-et-Maine region (&*see INTRODUCTION*) which produces the popular Muscadet wine and the lesser-known Gros Plant white wine. The wine-growing estates are built on the slopes on either side of the green and fertile valley of the winding Sèvre Nantaise.

▶ *Leave Clisson by D 763 then N 149 towards Nantes.*

Le Pallet

This is the birthplace of **Pierre Abélard** (1079-1142), a scholastic philosopher, dialectician and theologian, whose genius profoundly influenced the thinking of his time. He is also famous for his tragic love affair with Héloïse, niece of the cruel Fulbert.

Musée du Vignoble Nantais

&◔*Mid-Jun–mid-Sep 11am-6pm Early Mar–mid-Jun and mid-Sep–mid-Dec 2-6pm.* ◔*Closed Mon, 1 Nov and 11 Nov.* ≈*4€ (children under 12 no charge).* ☎*02 40 80 90 13.*

The museum, housed in a large modern-style glass building, is devoted to wine-growing in the Nantes area.

After a presentation on the different areas of production, there is a display of the wine-grower's work: grafting methods, grape-picking, pressing, wine-making and marketing. Tools and machinery used in former times (pruning shears and knives, copper-sulphate sprayers, carts and tractors), include a monumental 18C long barrel **winepress**. The final section is dedicated to cooperage (tools and scales to weigh barrels) as well as local crafts and folk traditions.

▶ *Leave Le Pallet eastwards on the road which runs along the River Sanguèse.*

Mouzillon

The wine festival, *La Nuit du Muscadet*, is celebrated here in early July. South of the church is a **Gallo-Roman bridge** across the River Sanguèse.

▶ *Leave Mouzillon N via the D 763.*

Vallet

This wine-growers' town is considered to be the Muscadet capital.

▶ *Leave Vallet on the D 37 NW*

Château de la Noë de Bel-Air

🕐*Unaccompanied visits of the château grounds 11am-6.30pm.* ⟐*No charge.*

This elegant château, rising above the vineyards, destroyed during the Revolution and rebuilt in 1836, now has an enormous loggia with Tuscan columns facing onto the park. The use of bricks in the orangery and outbuildings is characteristic of the houses in Clisson.

▶ *Continue along the D 37.*

Les Moulins du Pé

From the top of one of these disused mills, there is a captivating view of the vineyards and marshlands of the Goulaine region.

▶ *Return to and continue along the D 37.*

Le Loroux-Bottereau

During the insurrection of 1793, the inhabitants of the town formed an elite corps, incurring the anger of Turreau, who destroyed the town in 1794.

Église St-Jean-Baptiste

The church has two 12C frescoes telling the legend of St Gilles. The vine-covered slopes can be admired from the belfry.

▶ *Leave Le Loroux-Bottereau SE, via the D 7.*

Marais de Goulaine

🕐*Apr-Sep, boat hire.* 🕐*Closed during the hunting season. Keys and oars available at the tourist office.* ⟐ *10€ for a 4-seater boat (half day).* ☎*02 40 03 79 76.*

This green stretch of marshland covering 1 500ha/3 700 acres is crisscrossed with little canals, bordered with reeds. Nature enthusiasts can explore the marshes by **boat** or on foot along the canal paths. By road, Butte de la Roche near the legendary **Pont de l'Ouen** (bridge), offers a fine view.

▶ *Turn right onto the D 74.*

Château de Goulaine

🕐⟐*Mid-Jun–mid-Sep guided tours (1hr 30min) daily except Tue 2-6pm. End of Mar–mid-Jun and mid-Sep–mid-Nov Sat-Sun and public hols 2-6pm.* ⟐*7€ (Children 3.50€.* ☎*02 40 54 91 42.*

The château, surrounded by vineyards, was built between 1480 and 1495 by Christophe de Goulaine, Groom of the Bedchamber to Louis XII and François I. Remains from the military past include a machicolated tower and a small castle in front of a bridge spanning the moat. This handsome residence consists of a 15C Gothic main building made of limestone tufa from the Saumur region, and two wings added in the early 17C.

Interior

A spiral staircase leads to the first floor, which opens into the **grand salon** (monumental Renaissance chimney-piece), the **salon bleu**, the **salon gris** (remarkable panelling and interesting mythological scenes on the piers).

Butterfly aviary

Kids An enormous greenhouse next to the curtain wall of the castle contains exotic butterflies in among tropical flowers and shrubs.

▶ *Return via the D 74. At Haute-Goulaine, follow the D 105 S. On reaching Vertou, turn left and take the D 59 towards Clisson. In 500m/550yd turn left onto the D 359.*

La Haye-Fouassière

The village probably derives its name from a kind of flat cake, *fouace*, which is a local speciality. The **Maison des Vins de Nantes,** (🕐*daily except Sat and Sun 8.30am-12.30pm and 2-5.45pm.* ⟐*No charge.* ☎*02 40 36 90 10 www.muscadet. org*) next to the water tower, is the headquarters of the Nantes wine-growers' association which provides information on local wines and runs wine-tasting sessions.

▷ *Leave La Haye-Fouassière to the S, crossing the River Sèvre Nantaise on the D 74, then turn left onto the D 76 following the river.*

Monnières

The village church dates from the 12C and 15C but the interesting stained-glass windows are modern, with wine and the vine providing the main decorative themes.

▷ *The D 76 leads back to Clisson.*

COGNAC

POPULATION 19 534
MICHELIN MAP 324: I-5

Cognac is a peaceful little town, the birthplace of François I and cradle of the fine brandy that bears its name. The buildings around its famous cellars and stores have been darkened over the years by the microscopic fungi that thrive on the alcohol fumes.

🖪 **Information:** 16 r. du 14-Juillet, 16100 COGNAC.
☎05 45 82 10 71; www.tourism-cognac.com.

▷ **Orient Yourself**: Cognac lies on the N 141 between Saintes and Angoulême, 28km/17mi SE of Saintes. Place François I, a busy square with an ornamental fountain, links the old part of Cognac, huddled on the slope above the River Charente, with the sprawling modern town.

🅿 **Parking**: There are car parks in place Beaulieu and alongside the river near the Musée du Cognac.

🕲 **Don't Miss**: The old town; a visit to one of the Cognac distilleries.

🕲 **Also See**: PONS, ANGOULÊME.

A Bit of History

Royal Childhood

The literary and artistic House of Valois-Angoulême held court in the town from the late 14C until the accession of **François I** in 1515. It was here that François, the son of Charles of Angoulême and Louise of Savoy, was born "about ten hours after midday on the 12th day of September", in 1494. Part of his youth was spent in the Valois château near the River Charente, where he lived a carefree life with his sister Marguerite d'Angoulême and Charles' two illegitimate daughters, Madeleine and Souveraine.

Old Town

Porte St-Jacques and Rue Grande

The restored 15C gateway, flanked by two round towers with machicolations, once commanded a bridge which has since disappeared. However, it still leads to rue Grande, originally the main street in Cognac. On the left, at the foot of the hill, is a Renaissance fountain. The winding street is typically medieval, lined with 15C houses with their projecting, half-timbered upper floors (note in particular the *Maison de la Lieutenance).*

Rue de l'Isle-d'Or

This street is lined with 17C town houses with fine façades *(restored).*

Rue Saulnier

In contrast to rue Grande, rue Saulnier is bordered by aristocratic Renaissance buildings. Its name recalls one of the traditional activities of Cognac – the salt trade. The street, which was very wide for the period, has retained its irregular cobblestone surface and its handsome 16C and 17C houses. At the far end is a Renaissance house with a shop.

Address Book

For coin ranges, see the Legend on the cover flap.

WHERE TO STAY

Hôtel Résidence – *25 av. Victor-Hugo* – ☎*05 45 36 62 40* – *laresidence@free.fr* – *closed 20 Dec-3 Jan* – *18 rms*. The sober façade with its exposed stones is a striking contrast to the hotel's colourful interior. The lounge is decorated in tones of green and dark red, the modern breakfast room in pink and fuchsia and the guest rooms in brightly coloured prints.

L'Échassier – *quartier l'Échassier, 72 r. Bellevue* – ☎*05 45 35 01 09* – *echassier@wanadoo.fr* – *closed 30 Apr-17 May and 24 Oct-3 Nov* – P – *22 rms* – *restaurant*. This hotel comprises two buildings on either side of a garden, one of which is a recent villa featuring cosy modern rooms. The hotel restaurant is housed in the old stables of the Château

de l'Yeuse (19C). Contemporary interior. Terrace beneath the linden trees; traditional yet inventive cuisine.

WHERE TO EAT

Taverne du Coq d'Or – *pl. François-Ier* – ☎*05 45 82 02 56*. Opened in 1908, this is Cognac's oldest restaurant. The restaurant has an attractive 1920s look, with a decor of wood, mirrors, earthenware and molten glass. From noon to midnight, the bistro menu includes oysters, sauerkraut, etc.

Les Pigeons Blancs – *110 r. J.-Brisson* – ☎*05 45 82 16 36* – *pigeonsblancs@wanadoo.fr* – *closed 1-15 Jan, Sun eve and Mon lunch*. This 17C post house was turned into a restaurant in 1973. Located in a garden outside the city, the restaurant is popular with locals who appreciate the friendly service and the good food. Bourgeois-style decor, attractive terrace and a few rooms.

Rue du Palais, rue H.-Germain, rue Magdelaine and **Maison de la Salamandre** are also of interest.

Église St-Léger

Daily except in the afternoon on Sun and public hols.

This 12C church has been extensively remodelled. The most interesting part is the Romanesque west front, pierced in the 15C with a large Flamboyant Gothic rose-window. The archivolt of the doorway below is adorned with carvings representing the Signs of the Zodiac and the Labours of the Months. The vast nave dates from the 12C. In the south transept hangs a fine 17C Assumption of the Virgin.

On the right-hand side of the doorway, 18C cloisters lead to the library.

Couvent des Récollets

This restored convent houses exhibitions and the headquarters of several charities. Note the beautiful hall with its ribbed vaulting and the covered well in the middle of the cloisters.

Parc François-Ier

The park, bordered to the west by the River Charente, was part of the former castle grounds, prolonged by a thicket of tall trees. So dense was the growth that Louise of Savoy used to call it her *dedalus* or maze. It is mainly planted with ordinary oaks and holm oaks.

Wine Cellars and Stores

The cellars and wine stores *(chais)* spread out along the riverside quays, near the port and in the suburbs.

Camus

29 rue Marguerite-de-Navarre. *Guided tours (1hr 15min) Jun-Sep daily 10.30am-12.30pm and 2-6pm.Sun, Mon and public holidays 2-6pm. Rest of the year times vary.* *6€(Jun-Sep) 8€ (Oct-May) (children: no charge).* *05 45 32 28 28. www.camus.fr.*

The tour offered by this cognac trading company, founded in 1863, concentrates on the history of cognac, its distillation, ageing and blending. Visitors are conducted through the cooper's shop and wine stores before watching the bottling process.

Hennessy

&♿○●⌚ *Guided tours (1hr 15min) Jun-Sep 10am-6pm (last departure). Mar-May and Oct-Dec 10am-5pm.* ○ *Closed 1 May, 25 Dec.* ○9€ *(children under 16 no charge).* ☎05 45 35 72 68. www.hennessy. com.

After 12 years' service with Louis XV's Irish Brigade, Captain Richard Hennessy, wearying of army life in 1760, discovered the Charente region and settled in Cognac.

Attracted by the taste of the delicious elixir distilled here, he sent several casks to his relatives in Ireland and, in 1765, founded a trading company which was an immediate success. The Captain's descendants still head the company today.

Quais Hennessy

The stores of this company are located on both banks of the River Charente. A modern white-stone building, standing on the right bank, was designed by Wilmotte, who has used the three symbols of Cognac: copper (for the still), oak (for the casks) and glass (for the bottles). As an introduction to the world of Cognac, visitors are first taken across the river by boat and led into the wine stores where the various stages of brandy making are explained with the help of special effects involving sounds and smells: double distillation, manufacture of oak casks, maturing and blending of the different brandies. After watching a film and being shown round an exhibition, visitors can take part in a tasting session and enjoy Cognac on the rocks.

Martell★

&♿○●⌚ *Guided tours (1hr) Apr-Oct 10am-5pm, Sat-Sun and public hols noon-5pm.* ○ *4€.* ☎ 05 45 36 33 33; www.visitez-martell.com.

The oldest of all the Cognac distilleries owes its name to Jean Martell, native of Jersey, who settled in the town in 1715. The tour includes the semi-automated bottling process, and the stores and cellars where the brandy is left to age for six to eight years in oak barrels – this wood is preferred because of the slight tannin content which gives Cognac its beautiful colour, and the fine grain which limits evaporation of the alcohol. In the blending room which follows, brandies of different origins are mixed to ensure consistently high quality. Access to the tasting room is limited to brandy specialists and creators of blends such as the highly renowned Cordon Bleu. Three rooms have been restored in the house of this famous entrepreneur in order to recreate his life and work in the early 18C.

Before going back to the hall for a tasting session, the visitor is invited to take a look at the most prestigious wine

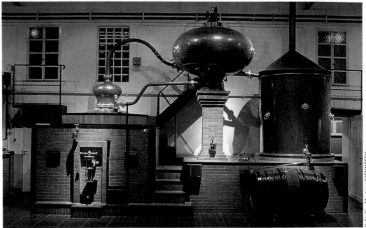

Hennessy distillery

© Atelier Martron/HENNESSY

stores, known as *purgatoire* (purgatory) and *paradis* (heaven) in which some of the brandies have been ageing in demi-johns for over 100 years.

Otard★
🚸 *See ANCIEN CHÂTEAU.*

Prince Hubert de Polignac
4km/2mi SE along the N 141. Drive towards Angoulême and leave by the first exit; pass beneath the main road and follow signs for Z.A.

🚸🕐*Shop open from Mon to Fri all year. For further information, call ☎05 45 82 51 72. www.polignac.fr.*

This cooperative, set up in 1949, brings together a number of local growers. A tour can be made of the different facilities in Pavillon du Laubaret.

Rémy Martin
4km/2mi SW along the D 732. Drive towards Pons then turn left onto D 47 to Merpins.

🕐 *Open Apr-Oct. Reservation recommended.* ◈*Admission charge.* ☎05 45 35 76 66.

This firm, founded in 1724, creates its cognac exclusively from the elite Grande Champagne and Petite Champagne vintages. A **miniature train** takes visitors on a tour of the plant. It goes through the cooper's shop (the largest in Europe), where the coopers can be seen at work on the casks, and then travels through part of the vineyard and various cellars used for stocking and ageing the spirit. Two different commentaries *(in French)*, illustrated with slides, punctuate the journey.

Ancien Château

🕐◈ *Guided tour (1hr, last departure 1hr before closing time). Apr-Oct 11am-noon, 2-6pm. Nov-Dec daily except Sat-Sun and public holidays 11am-noon, 2-6pm.* 🕐*Closed Jan-Mar, 1 May, 25 Dec.* ◈*6€ (aged 12-18 3€).* ☎05 45 36 88 86; www.otard.com.

This 15C and 16C château recalls the memory of the Valois family and François I, who was born here. It became the property of the Comte d'Artois (the future Charles X)

under Louis XVI and was sequestrated by the Republicans during the Revolution. Since 1795 it has been used as a wine store by the firm **Otard**, which was originally founded by an old Scottish family.

The façade overlooking the Charente has a fine balcony, known as the King's Balcony, the supports of which are sculpted with salamanders, the emblem of François I.

Inside the old château, it is possible to visit Helmet Hall, where Richard the Lionheart married his son Philip to Amélie de Cognac. The room contains a magnificent chimney-piece surmounted by a helmet, the work of Jean le Bon. In one corner are traces of the Lusignan family's original 13C feudal castle. The huge rooms, with their ribbed vaulting (including the Guard-room) are extremely elegant. The tour ends with a visit to the wine stores.

Musée d'Art et d'Histoire

🚸🕐*Apr-Oct daily 10am-6pm. Nov-Mar daily except Tue 2-5.30pm.* 🕐*Closed 1 Jan, 1 Nov and 25 Dec.* ◈*4.50€ (children no charge).* ☎05 45 32 07 25.

This municipal museum is housed in Hôtel Dupuy d'Angeac, in the grounds of the town hall.

Ground Floor
(Local arts and crafts)
The displays here cover the history and civilisation of the Cognac area from the earliest times to the present through maps, plans, prints and photographs; headdresses, bonnets and traditional costumes; glasswork from the collection of Claude Bouiher (who invented a bottle-moulding machine in 1897); fine glazed earthenware, and fossils (mainly shellfish) found in the region's Secondary limestone formations. A section devoted to archaeology contains prehistoric stone artefacts such as ceramics and a Neolithic dugout canoe, pottery, statuettes and bracelets from the Gallo-Roman period.

There is also a reconstruction of the interior of a rural house, evoking the life of a local wine-grower c 1875.

Basement
(Cognac Ethnology Gallery)

The first display is a documentary illustration of the history of brandy. In the next six rooms, tools and machines recreate vine-growing and winemaking, distillation, the brandy and Pineau des Charentes trade, related crafts, cooperage and saddlery. Another room is devoted to traditional agriculture.

First Floor (Fine Arts)

This section houses paintings, sculpture, furniture and objets d'art, both French and foreign, from the 15C to the 19C. On the landing, are interesting works in molten glass by Émile Gallé (1846-1904), one of the main pioneers of Art Nouveau. The period paintings originate from countries which were clients of the Cognac brandy trade. Particularly noteworthy are two works from the 16C Antwerp School – *Lot and his Daughters* by Jan Massys, and *Adam and Eve* by Frans Floris. One room on this floor has a display of contemporary paintings.

Excursion

Gensac-la-Pallue

9km/5mi SE via the N 141, then the D 49.
Before arriving at Gensac, route D 49 skirts the *pallue* or marshland from which the small town derives its name. The interesting 12C **church** has a Romanesque west front decorated with haut-relief sculptures of the Virgin (left) and St Martin *(right)*, the patron saint of the church, being carried heavenwards by angels. The Romanesque nave, with its four domes supported by pendentives, leads to a Gothic chancel.

Driving Tours

1 Les Borderies

35km/22mi round tour – about 2hrs.

▶ *Drive W out of Cognac along the road to Saintes. At the roundabout, drive to Javrezac then follow the D 401.*

Richemont

The church and the castle ruins rise, half-hidden, among the trees crowning a spur. The **church** (*Guided tours available Jul-Aug. 05 45 83 25 69 - town hall.*) is built on the site of an ancient stronghold (its loopholes and arrow slits are still visible) and contains a delightful pre-Romanesque crypt (10C).

▶ *Continue N beyond Richemont towards l'Épine. Turn right onto the D 731 then, 1km/0.6mi farther on, turn right again onto the D 85 to Cherves.*

Château-Chesnel

This curious residence was built between 1610 and 1625 by Charles Roch-Chesnel. Architecturally, the château seems to hesitate between the Renaissance style and 17C Classicism while retaining a strong flavour of medieval military architecture (the deep dry moats around it). The central block and the towers at each corner are crowned with a castellated parapet. The complex as a whole forms a huge square, surrounded by large agricultural buildings.

▶ *Continue along the D 85. Shortly after Vignolles, turn left onto the D 120.*

Migron, Écomusée du Cognac

2km/1mi N; follow the signs. May-Sep 10am-12.30pm and 2.30-6.30pm. 4€ (children between 12 and 18 2€) 05 46 94 91 16.
This little craft museum located among vineyards, is dedicated to brandy making. A home distillery has been reconstructed, where the old-fashioned pot still, or *alembic* stands nearby the ever-vigilant moonshiner's bed. As he slept with one eye open, alcohol vapours rose while the fermenting liquid boiled; trapped and recondensed, the powerful distillate could be bottled and sold. Also on view are winepresses, one of which required treading feet, a cooper's workshop, vine-growers' tools and examples of the huge copper stills used in the trade today. This area has been making Pineau des Charentes (a fortified wine made from brandy and grape-must) and Vieux Cognac since 1850.

▷ *Drive S out of Migron along the D 131. In Burie, take the D 731 to return to Cognac.*

② Vignoble des Fins Bois

40km/25mi round tour – about 2hrs

▷ *Drive NE out of Cognac along the D 24. In Ste-Sévère, take the direction of Les Buges and continue along the D 24.*

Macqueville

This peaceful village, in the heart of the Fins Bois vineyards, north-east of Cognac, has modern distilleries devoted exclusively in the production of cognac. The white houses, with their tiled roofs, have Empire-style porches and closed courtyards. A façade with decorated gable and pepper-pot turret is all that remains of the former 11C **Château de Bouchereau**. In the shady square, **Église St-Étienne** (St Stephen's Church) is a charming example of the Romanesque art which flourished in the ancient province of Saintonge during the 12C. The north transept is replaced by a bell-tower with radiating chapels, the east end is flattened, and the north doorway has a carved archivolt. Equally characteristic are the semicircular blind arcades of the walls and the amusing modillions on the cornices. Inside, recessed pillars with elegant capitals support the Gothic vaulting of the wide nave. The ribbed transept crossing is magnificent.

▷ *Leave Macqueville eastwards along the D 227.*

Neuvicq-le-Château

This is another village of picturesque low houses with tiled roofs. The château, which overlooks a small valley and gave the village its name, incorporates a 15C main block with a charming staircase-tower, and a 17C pavilion crowned by a tall, steep, typically French roof. Today, it houses the post office.

▷ *Leave Neuvicq-le-Château southwards along the D 23. In Sigogne, take the D 15 to return to Cognac.*

CONFOLENS

POPULATION 2 855
MICHELIN MAP 324: N-O 3

An attractive medieval town with a pleasant, relaxed atmosphere, Confolens lies at the confluence of the River Vienne and River Goire, hence its name.It was the home of a disciple of Louis Pasteur, **Doctor Émile Roux** (1853-1933), who discovered how to treat diphtheria in 1894. Confolens is also known for its International Folklore Festival, held every August.

- 🖹 **Information:** Pl. des Marronniers, 16500 CONFOLENS. ☎ 05 45 84 22 22.
- ▷ **Orient Yourself**: Confolens lies on the border between the regions of Limousin and Angoumois, 40km/25mi NE of La Rochefoucauld.
- 😊 **Don't Miss**: The Old Town.
- 🚶 **Also See**: LA ROCHEFOUCAULD.

Old Town Walking Tour

1hr 30mins.

▷ *From place de l'Hôtel-de-Ville (parking) follow rue de la Ferrandie to the left.*

Pont-Vieux★

The bridge was probably built in the 12C and modernised in the early 19C. For a long time it looked like a fortress, with its three towers – one in the centre and one on either bank. The tower on the west bank had a drawbridge, making it

The pont Vieux ("old bridge") seen from the pont Neuf ("new bridge")

possible to cut off all access to the town, until it was replaced by an arch in the 18C.

It leads to the Fontorse district (named after an elegant ornamental fountain), the old town's busy suburb.

▶ *Turn right on rue E.-Roux, then, at place de la Liberté, turn left on rue des Buttes. Half way up the street, a passageway leads to a fortified gatehouse.*

Porte de ville

On the other side of the gatehouse, once the obligatory passageway for those seeking to enter the town, is a façade pierced by two Romanesque clerestory windows, no doubt built in the late 11C. The wartime residence of the local overlord, it contained a court-room and prison and was an integral part of the fortifications surrounding the town on the east bank of the River Vienne.

Go back through the gateway and take rue des Buttes to the 11C **keep**, which stands on what used to be the moat. In former times, travellers arriving from the south-east went through a doorway here, traces of which can still be seen at the base of the keep and on the lower tower opposite.

Plan d'Olivet nearby, a public garden, offers an attractive **view** of the rooftops of the town.

▶ *Go back towards the centre via rue du Vieux-Château, then take rue Pinaguet.*

Rue Pinaguet

The street is lined with medieval houses (one of them, very tall, has a tower with a spiral staircase inside).

On the corner of rue Bournadour, another tower juts out, with a square half-timbered upper section.

▶ *Go back as far as the crossroads and turn left on rue Fontaine-de-Pommeau.*

Église St-Maxime

Restored in the 19C, this church has an octagonal Gothic Troubadour tower surmounted by a spire with crockets. At its east end there is an attractive half-timbered house.

▶ *Take rue de la Côte.*

Le Manoir

Rue de la Côte leads to a manor house with high gables and decorative carved finials. It was built in the 16C by the Comte de Confolens.

▶ *From the bridge over the River Goire, take rue du Soleil.*

Rue du Soleil

This was the main street until the 19C. It is lined with tall houses backing onto hanging gardens and grounds which are not visible from the street. On the left, is **rue des Francs-Maçons**, a staircase-street so narrow that the eaves of facing houses nearly cover it. Just beyond is the **Maison du Duc d'Épernon**★, used by the Duke of Épernon as a meeting point for the conspirators who helped Marie de Medicis to escape in 1619. The house dates from the 15C and 16C. It has three half-timbered upper storeys set back from the ground floor and sealed with cob (compressed loam, clay or chalk, reinforced with straw).

▷ *Return to place de l'Hôtel-de-Ville.*

Driving Tour

Vallée De La Vienne

Round trip of 75km/47mi – allow 4hrs

▷ *Leave Confolens by the north along the east bank of the Vienne (D 952).*

St Germain-de-Confolens
St Germain-de-Confolens, once the site of an important feudal castle, is located in a picturesque setting at the junction of the River Vienne and River Issoire. Perched on a mound overlooking the valley of the River Issoire are the ivy covered ruins of the huge towers of Château de St-Germain, at the foot of which is a tiny Romanesque chapel.

▷ *Drive SE out of St-Germain along the D 952 then turn left onto the D 82.*

Lesterps
8.5km/6mi east along the D 30. Pronounced Laytair.
Église St-Pierre – The remains of an abbey founded in the early 11C are preceded by an impressive grey granite **belfry-porch★**. Above the porch with its three bays, decorated with rather coarse capitals, is a massive belfry. Inside, the narrow side aisles contrast with the wide barrel-vaulted nave which houses the remains of the old chancel and 12C capitals.

▷ *D 29 S, then the D 30.*

Brigueuil
This historical burg perched on a hill still has many of its medieval fortifications ramparts with seven towers and two gatehouses. Near the Romanesque church (additions made in the 14C and

15C) are the remains of an old castle (11C truncated keep) and a manor house rebuilt in the 16C. There are also several other historical houses, a graveyard lantern, and in nearby Boulonie, a strange Romanesque mausoleum, said to be the tomb of Saint George.

▷ *Drive W along the D 165; in Saulgond, turn left onto the D 193.*

Château de Rochebrune
◐ Guided tours (45min) Jul–Aug daily except Tue 2–6pm. 5€ (children 2€). ☎05 45 65 26 69.
Built on a basalt rock, on the border of Poitou and Limousin, the castle is flanked with towers reflecting in the still water of the moat. In the 16C, its owner, the governor of Guyenne, Marshall Blaise de Monluc, led a pitiless fight against the Protestant community.
One enters the main courtyard, past the outbuildings covered with curved tiles and across a small stone bridge spanning the moat. The four 11C-13C round towers are linked by three buildings. The arms of Marshall de Monluc are carved above the doors. The apartments are furnished in Renaissance and Empire style and contain numerous mementoes of the Napoleonic period.

▷ *Continue along the D 193, cross the River Vienne; right onto the D 160.*

Thermes de Chassenon
◔ *See THERMES DE CHASSENON.*

▷ *Continue W along the D 29. In Chabanais, take the N 141; then right onto the D 370 2km/1.2mi farther on.*

Exideuil
The 16C Château de la Chétardie overlooks the town and the river. Built as a priory in 1200, **Église St-André** has a flattened chevet and ovolo mouldings over the porch. The broken-barrel-vaulted nave with its recessed pillars is invitingly simple. It houses three stone tombs and a 13C baptismal font in the middle of the baptistery.

▷ *Return to Confolens via the D 370 then the D 16.*

PHARE DE CORDOUAN★★

MICHELIN MAP 324: C-6

Cordouan watches over the approaches to the Gironde estuary, which are frequently rough and at the mercy of dangerous currents. The architecture of this lighthouse is as captivating as its isolated setting; the rocky outcrop on which it stands was once part of Pointe de Grave, but was separated from the mainland and reduced to an islet during the 16C and 17C. Today, the ancient land link is revealed only at exceptionally low tide.

▸ **Orient Yourself**: The lighthouse can be reached from Royan or Pointe de Grave in Verdon-sur-Mer.

A Bit of History

A Feat of Engineering

In the 14C the Black Prince had an octagonal tower built on the promontory, at the top of which a hermit was to keep a fire blazing at all times. A chapel and a few small cottages were added around the base of the tower. At the end of the 16C, however, the main structure was in danger of collapsing so Maréchal de Matignon, governor of Guyenne, called in the architect-engineer **Louis de Foix,** who had just finished diverting the River Adour, a huge undertaking in those times. De Foix arrived with a work force of more than 200 men and built a sort of belvedere surmounted by domes and lanterns and surrounded by a protective platform on the rocky base. In 1788 the engineer Teulère remodelled the upper part of the structure in the Louis XVI style; its sobriety forms a vivid contrast with the richness and flamboyance of the lower levels.

Visit

🕐 *Open daily Apr-Sep. Visits are governed by the tide and weather conditions; wear boots or an old pair of shoes as there is a chance of getting your feet wet. 3-4 hrs round trip. ⊜ 26€ (boat crossing and entrance to the lighthouse, children aged 1-12: 16€). Reservation required. ☎ 05 56 09 62 93 or 06 09 73 30 84.*

The Renaissance architecture of the lower storeys separated from the upper Classical portion by a balustrade, makes the 67.5m/221ft-high lighthouse a bold and majestic presence.

A postern leads into the circular bastion which protects the building from the fury of the seas and contains the lighthouse-keepers' quarters. On the ground floor of the tower itself a monumental doorway provides access to the vestibule from which 311 steps lead up to the modern lantern (with a flashing light). On the first floor, surrounded by an outside gallery, is the King's Apartment. There is a **chapel** on the second floor, also circled by a gallery, and crowned with an elegant dome. The bust above the entrance door is of Louis de Foix.

The **Musée du Phare de Cordouan** is located on Pointe de Grave (🕐 *see SOULAC-SUR-MER).*

DAMPIERRE-SUR-BOUTONNE

POPULATION 297
MICHELIN MAP 324: H-3

Dampierre-sur-Boutonne is known for its Renaissance château, built in an attractive setting on a tiny island in the river. Since 1981, Dampierre has also become famous as a breeding centre for the celebrated *baudets* (donkeys) of Poitou.

▸ **Orient Yourself**: The village is situated in the green valley of the River Boutonne, 8.5km/5mi NW of Aulnay.

🄺🄸🄳🄼 **Especially for Kids**: The Maison du Baudet de Poitou (donkey museum).

🕭 **Also See**: Église St-Pierre at Aulnay.

Sights

Château

🕐 *Jul-Aug, 10.30am-7pm; mid-Jun to end of Jun and early Sep to mid-Sep, 2-6pm; mid-Mar to mid-Jun and mid-Sep to mid-Nov, Sun and public hols 2-6pm. ⊶The château is currently under restoration; only the upper gallery and garden are open to the public.* ⊜ *4.50€.* ☏ *05 46 24 02 24.*

Of the four wings originally framing the inner courtyard, only the living quarters remain. The building is flanked by two massive towers designed to defend the building from attack. From the courtyard itself, the château seems less forbidding. The most impressive feature is a two-tiered Renaissance **gallery**★ of basket-handle arches, with its two levels separated by a frieze of carved foliage. The upper gallery features a coffered ceiling whose 93 sections are carved with crests (a swan pierced by an arrow, the emblem of Claude of France, wife of François I), insignia (Catherine de' Medici and Henri II), and allegorical scenes and symbols (a labyrinth and a cherub astride a chimera etc). These are often bordered by scrolls bearing Latin mottoes. An interpretation and explanation of these decorations was proposed by Fulcanelli in his alchemical work, *Les Demeures Philosophales,* in 1931.

Among the furnishings on view in the apartments are fine Flemish tapestries and a superb Italian ebony cabinet (16C). In the guard-room, above the chimney-piece, reads the inscription: *Estre, se cognestre et non parestre* (To be is to know oneself rather than be known).

There are two exhibitions in the castle reception area – "Art and Alchemy" (which analyses details of the coffered ceiling) and "Dali's Horses" (paintings inspired by the ceiling).

S. Sauvignier/MICHELIN

Poitou donkey

Maison du Baudet de Poitou

At La Tillauderie, 5km/3mi NE on the D 127 towards Chizé. ⏲ *Jun-Sep, 10.30am-noon and 2-6.15pm (5.30pm in Jun and Sep); Apr-May daily except Mon, 10am-noon and 2-5.30pm; Feb-Mar and Oct-Nov, Wed, Sat and Sun, 10.30am-noon and 2-4.30pm.* ☞ *3€ (aged 12-16: 2.20€).* ☎ *05 46 24 68 94.*

Kids The **baudet du Poitou**, an unusually large donkey, reddish-brown in colour with a long, woolly coat, has been bred in this region for centuries. Crossing a mare with the male ass of this breed produces a hybrid, sterile mule known as a *mule Poitevine* which is particularly suited to carrying heavy loads over difficult terrain. Most were bred in St-Martin-les-Melle, near the town of Melle, and were in great demand until the beginning of this century, when they were replaced by more modern methods of transport.

Display panels and video in the small museum illustrate the history of the Baudet and the efforts being made to preserve the breed. Nearby, she-asses from Portugal and local Baudets can be seen grazing peacefully together. The centre's robust, mule-producing stallion may also be seen in the stables.

DAX

POPULATION 19 515

MICHELIN MAP 335: E-12

Spa Dax, the most popular spa in France, is reputed for its hot mud treatments. The maceration of silt from the River Adour in water from the hot springs encourages the development of vegetable and mineral algae. The mud is particularly effective in treating rheumatic complaints. The town, built on the edge of the Landes pine forest, is also an important commercial centre. Riverside walks, colourful public gardens, interesting churches, and even bullfights, combine to make the town an enjoyable place to visit.

- 🅱 **Tourist Office** – 11 cours Foch, 40100 Dax. ☎05 58 56 86 86; www.dax.fr.
- ▶ **Orient Yourself:** Situated between Mont-de-Marsan and Bayonne, Dax lies 35km/22mi NE of Capbreton and 21km/13mi N of Peyrehorade.
- 🅿 **Parking:** There are car parks near the cathedral and along the banks of the Adour. Note that some of the streets in the town centre are pedestrianised.
- 😊 **Don't Miss:** The Fontaine Chaude and the town's parks and gardens; the duck and goose market *(marché au gras),* which is held every Saturday morning in the market hall.
- 🕐 **Organising Your Time:** If you enjoy a festival atmosphere, then August is the best time to visit Dax. This is when the town holds its annual *feria*, a week-long festival of bullfights and other organised events.
- **Kids** **Especially for Kids:** Musée de l'Aviation.
- 👣 **Also See:** HOSSEGOR, PEYREHORADE.

A Bit of History

A lake village, with houses on stilts, once stood on the site where Dax is built today. However, alluvia from the Adour gradually silted up the lake and the village developed on dry land.

After the Romans settled in the region, the hot springs of Aqua Tarbellicae, named after the first tribe to inhabit the area, became famous. When Emperor Augustus brought his daughter Julia here to treat her rheumatism, the town received favours from Rome and consequently prospered. After celebration of the marriage between Louis XIV and Maria Teresa in St-Jean-de-Luz, the King and his bride stopped at Dax on their way home to Paris. The townsfolk set up a triumphal arch at the entrance to the town as a sign of welcome. The painting on the arch of a dolphin emerging from the water, and an inscription in

Dax – Fontaine chaude

Latin, were a pun on the words dolphin and *dauphin* (identical in French) in the hopes that the couple's stay in Dax would bear fruit.

Town Centre

Cathédrale Notre-Dame

The Romanesque cathedral was built in the 11C on the site of a very ancient chapel. It was destroyed in 1295 after the English laid siege to Dax. The Gothic building which replaced it in the 14C collapsed in 1645. The present cathedral was built in the Classical style – a fine 13C Gothic doorway still remains in the north transept. The embrasures of the double doorway are decorated with 12 columns supporting large statues of the Apostles; a statue of Christ adorns the pier.

Fontaine Chaude

The hot spring at the centre of town is the main attraction in Dax. Its waters, of meteoric origin, and tapped since Roman times, gush forth at a temperature of 64°C/147°F into a huge basin surrounded by arcades. Nearby is the statue of **Borda**, an 18C marine engineer born in Dax (*see BOX*).

Banks of the Adour

There are several **riverside walks**. Upstream from the bridge, on the south side, is **Parc Théodore-Denis**, where Gallo-Roman ramparts provide a shady walk under a row of plane trees. In the centre of the park, the arenas are the site of the Feria de Dax, a festival held in August every year. Downstream is **Jardin de la Potinière**, leading down into the heart of the thermal district, whereas just beyond is the *Trou des Pauvres* or paupers' hole, once a public bath. Farther west lies the Bois de Boulogne, a vast open space offering pleasant walks (*6km/3.7mi through the woods*).

A Great Seaman

Jean-Charles de Borda was born in Dax in 1733. He was a marine engineer, mathematician, surveyor and all-round seaman, worthy of being the namesake of ships serving in the Navy school until the beginning of the 20C.

Borda made great progress in nautical calculation and observations. He was part of a mission directed by the Constituent Assembly, which included Méchain and Delambre, charged with establishing the metric system and measuring the meridian arch between Dunkirk and Barcelona. The museum is named after him and his statue stands in place Thiers.

Address Book

For coin ranges, see the Legend on the cover flap.

WHERE TO STAY

Chambre d'hôte Capcazal de Pachiou – *606 rte de Pachiou – 40350 Mimbaste – 12km/7.5mi SE of Dax. Take the D 947 and C 16 –* ☎ *05 58 55 30 54 – – reserv. required – 4 rooms – restaurant*. You won't want to leave this 17C house with its sculpted wooden fireplaces, antique furniture and canopied beds in the bedrooms. The friendly hosts and the real family cooking are an extra bonus.

Hôtel Calicéo – *r. du Centre-Aéré, at the lac de Christus – 40990 St Paul-lès-Dax –* ☎ *05 58 90 66 00 – caliceo@thermesadour.com –* 🅿 *– 50 rooms – restaurant*. Recharge your batteries in this modern hotel facing the Lac de Christus. Aquatic fitness facilities open to the public feature round pools with currents and fountains, a cardiovascular-training room, hammams and saunas. The rooms are furnished in the style of the 1940s, as is the dining room.

Grand Hôtel Mercure Splendid – *cours de Verdun –* ☎ *05 58 56 70 70 – closed Jan and Feb –* 🅿 *– 155 rooms – restaurant*. This resort hotel near the River Adour has a Belle Époque atmosphere. Built in 1930, the spacious rooms have been fitted with comfortable modern facilities while preserving their original character. The huge dining room has been entirely restored in the Art Deco style. Garden with pool under the trees.

WHERE TO EAT

Ferme-auberge de Thoumiou – *chemin de Thoumiou – 40180 St-Pandelon – 4km/2.4mi S of Dax via the D 29 –* ☎ *05 58 98 73 41 – closed Jan-Feb, open Fri eve to Sun lunch from 13 Sep-13 Jun, daily except Sun eve and Wed from 20 Jun-12 Sep – reserv. recommended.* Enjoy delicious, traditional cuisine in this ferme-auberge, whose dining room is housed in its spacious old stables. Access for travellers with special needs.

Les Champs de l'Adour – *5 r. Morancy –* ☎ *05 58 56 92 81 – leschampsdeladour@club-internet.fr –*

closed 24 Dec-6 Jan; Sun to Thu eve. Decorated in a pleasing mix of old (19C stone walls) and new (attractive modern furniture), the focus in this excellent little restaurant near the cathedral is on fresh ingredients and traditional fare.

Le Moulin de Poustagnacq – *40990 St-Paul-lès-Dax – 6km/3.6mi E of Dax via the D 459 –* ☎ *05 58 91 31 03 – closed Nov school hols, Tue noon, Sun eve and Mon.* You'll be enchanted with this old mill on a lake surrounded by peaceful woods. Part of the building has been converted into a restaurant; the striking dining room decor has white stucco arches. Appetising, innovative cuisine.

ENTERTAINMENT

Casino de Dax – *8 r. Eugène-Milliès-Lacroix – On the banls of the Adour in the city centre –* ☎ *05 58 58 77 77 – open Mon-Fri 11am-3am, Sat, Sun and eve of public hols 11am-4am.* This casino has a traditional games room, slot machines, a bar and a restaurant. Tea dances and themed evenings are occasionally held here.

Casino César Palace – *R. du Centre-Aéré-Lac de Christus – 40990 St-Paul-lès-Dax –* ☎ *05 58 91 52 72 – casino.stpaullesdax@ moliflor.com – casino: daily 11am-3am (4am Fri-Sun); bowling: 5pm-2am, Wed-Sat 3pm-2am, Sat 3pm-3am.* This complex comprises a casino, a bowling alley, two restaurants, two bars, a hotel and a popular discotheque *(open weekends only; closed in summer).* Large terrace overlooking the Lac de Christus.

Arènes de Dax – *Parc Théodore-Denis – open for shows.* The bullring was built in 1913 and enlarged in 1932 to its current 8,000-seat capacity. Visit the *patio de caballos,* the *chapelle des matadors* (where bullfighters gather their forces before battle) and the infirmary. Bullfights are organised in Dax each summer around 15 August and in the second half of September.

L'Atrium – *Cours du Mar.-Foch –* ☎ *05 58 90 99 09 – ticket office run by the Régie Municipale des Fêtes et des Spectacles.* The Atrium's auditorium was built in what was left of the 1928 Dax casino, now in ruins. The ceiling, walls and stage offer a spectacular setting for the many concerts, plays and ballets that are performed here.

Régie Municipale des Fêtes – *Pl. de la Fontaine-Chaude* – ☎*05 58 90 99 09* – *www.dax.fr* – *open mid-Jul to end Aug, Mon-Sat 10 am-6.30 pm; Sep to mid-Jul, Mon-Fri 9.30am-noon and 1.30pm-5.30pm.* The Régie is where you'll find tickets for most of the shows and festivities organised throughout the city – bullfights, *courses landaises*, pop concerts and performances at the Atrium.

SPORT AND LEISURE

Parc municipal des Sports – *Bd des Sports* – ☎*05 58 74 12 29* – *open daily 8am-9pm.* This large sports complex includes the US Dax rugby pitch, a Jaï Alaï court, a fronton, football fields, an athletics track and a sports room. Basque pelota matches are held every Wednesday from June to September *(5.30pm at the fronton; 8pm at the Jaï Alaï).*

Calicéo – *355 R. du Centre-Aéré – Lac de Christus – 40990 St-Paul-lès-Dax* – ☎*05 58 90 66 66* – *www.caliceo.com* – *open daily 10am-8.30pm. 11.50€ for 2 hours.* This fitness centre features three mineral water pools, jacuzzis, whirlpools, hydrojets, geysers and a fastwater river. Other features include a gym for cardio-vascular training, hammams and saunas, a bar and a restaurant.

CAFES

Le Salon Valmont – *42 r. des Carmes* – ☎*05 58 90 85 92* – *open 9am-7pm* – *closed for 3 weeks in Mar and Sun.* This 16C-17C building is now home to a pleasant tea room serving a good selection of mixed salads, savoury flans, cakes and pastries. Exposed beams and stonework in the dining room. Attractive patio.

La Tourtière – *12 r. St-Vincent* – ☎*05 58 74 00 75* – *open Mon-Fri 8am-7.30pm, Sat 8am-8pm, Sun 8am-noon. Closed early Feb to early Mar, public hol afternoons, Sun afternoon.* Specialities of this attractive pâtisserie include *tourtière* (a light flaky pastry with apples or prunes, flavoured with Armagnac), *nid d'abeille* (cream cake), *pastis pyrénéen* (an aniseed-flavoured brioche) and peach soufflé.

SHOPPING

A. Cazelle – *6 r. de la Fontaine-Chaude* – ☎ *05 58 74 26 25* – *open Mon-Sat 8.30am-12.15pm and 2pm-7.15pm.* The Cazelle family has been making Dax madeleines since 1906. These small cakes are freshly baked each morning, using only 100% natural ingredients.

Roger Junca – *22 bis pl. de la Fontaine-Chaude* – ☎*05 58 90 01 43* – *www.rogerjunca.com* – *open Mon-Sat 8am-12.30pm and 3-7pm, Sun morning in summer* – *closed 2 wks in Feb and public hols.* An expert in the traditional gastronomy of the Landes region, Roger Junca has been producing *foie gras, confits de canard, patés* and other duck products since 1949. His foie gras won a gold medal in the 2002 Paris concours général agricole (agricultural show).

Additional Sights

Musée de Borda

27 rue Cazade. ◷*Daily except Sun and Mon 2-6pm.* ◷*Closed public hols.* ◷*3€* ☎*05 58 74 12 91.* The museum is housed in a 17C mansion and contains collections of Gallo-Roman and medieval archaeology (statuettes and 1C bronzes discovered in Dax), 18C to 20C paintings, memorabilia belonging to the scholar Jean-Charles de Borda and the Minister of French Colonies, Milliès-Lacroix. One room is devoted to regional folklore, and another to breeds of cattle from the Landes region.

Parc du Sarrat

Rue du Sel Gemme. ♿◷◞◞*Guided tours (1hr 30min) Mar-Nov Tue, Thu and Sat at 3.30pm.* ◷*Closed Dec-Feb, and public hols.* ◷*3.50€.* ☎*05 58 56 86 86.*

The park contains a house designed by the American architect Frank Lloyd Wright. The façade, consisting entirely of plate glass, brings nature right into the house. The park is arranged in a series of theme gardens with a wide variety of vegetation, interspersed with winding canals – a French garden, leading to a pond surrounded by magnolias, a little Japanese garden, a watercress bed, a vegetable plot, etc.

Musée de l'Aviation Légère de l'Armée de Terre (ALAT)

Dax Aerodrome is due S of the town. Take the D 6 in the direction of Peyrehorade, then the D 106 and turn right onto avenue de l'Aerodrome.

& ☉ *Mar-Nov daily except Sun and public hols 2-6pm.* ⊜*5€ (children 1.80€).* ☎ *05 58 35 95 20.*

Created in 1954, ALAT is a descendent of the balloon corps which first appeared in the French Army in 1794 and the captive balloon units used in the First World War. ALAT had a high profile in Algeria during air operations, reconnaissance and rescue missions. In 1977, this air force subdivision was restructured into helicopter combat regiments. The museum houses an historical gallery with collections of documents, memorabilia, uniforms, etc. A hangar contains about 30 aeroplanes and helicopters, including a Hiller UH 12 A which is of particular interest as it was flown to Indo-China by Valérie André, the first woman General in the French Army.

Excursion

Préchacq-les-Bains

16km/10mi NE. Leave Dax by the N 124 heading E and at Pontonx-sur-l'Adour turn right on the D 10, then right again.

Spa The small spa, once used by the writer Montaigne, stands among oak woods on the south bank of the Adour, and like Dax, specialises in the treatment of rheumatism and respiratory complaints. In the gardens beyond the thermal treatment centre, pools of plant and mineral-containing mud can be seen.

ESPELETTE★

POPULATION 1 661
MICHELIN MAP 342: D-2

This village dates from medieval times, and remains a sprawling collection of Basque-style red and white houses lining narrow, winding streets. Espelette specialises in growing a regional variety of red pepper but there is also a brisk local trade in a breed of pony called a **pottock** (a Pottock Fair is held in late January: exhibitions and competitions of pottocks, market with local produce, pelota). The ponies live in herds, in a semi-wild state, on the uninhabited slopes of the mountains along the Spanish border. Once used in the mines because of their docile nature and diminutive stature, these animals are now perfectly suited to pony trekking.

▶ **Orient Yourself**: Espelette lies 6.5km/4mi from Cambo-les-Bains in the foothills of the Pyrenees.
▣ **Parking**: Park at the top of the village and explore on foot.
& **Also see**: CAMBO-LES-BAINS, AINHOA.

A Bit of History

Espelette peppers

In autumn, the façades of the houses in Espelette are draped with garlands of dark red peppers drying in the sun. The peppers were brought to the Basque country from America and Spain in the 17C and very quickly became the favourite local condiment. Baked in the oven and ground into a powder they were

WHERE TO STAY

◎**Hôtel Euzkadi** – *285 Karrika Neagusia –* ☎*05 59 93 91 88 – hotel. euzkadi@wanadoo.fr – closed Tue off-season and Mon – 32 rooms – restaurant* ⊜ ⊜*.* This typical Basque establishment has a striking red façade, comfortable rooms, leisure facilities and restaurant.

initially used in chocolate (Bayonne was the first town to make chocolate in France). They soon replaced ordinary pepper in local dishes such as Poulet Basquaise (chicken with ratatouille), Tripotxa (veal sausage) and Axua (veal cutlets). Today, Espelette peppers are an all-purpose remedy – used as a foot bath, they are said to cure colds and bronchitis! The Espelette Pepper Fair is held on the last weekend in October. Festivities start with the blessing of the red peppers, followed by processions through the streets. At the end of the day, nominations are made for the *Chevaliers du Piment d'Espelette* (Knights of the Espelette Pepper).

Sights

Église
The church contains a gilt-wood reredos; in the nearby cemetery you will find 17C and 18C discoidal headstones unique to the Basque culture (perhaps a remnant of an ancient cult of sun worship).

Ancien Château
♿🕐*Daily except Sun and public hols 8.30am-12.30pm and 2-6pm, Sat 9.30am-12.30pm. No charge. ☎05 59 93 95 02. www.espelette.com*. The town hall, housed in a former 11C castle destroyed and rebuilt several times, holds a permanent exhibition on red pepper.

FONTENAY-LE-COMTE
POPULATION 13 792
MICHELIN MAP 316: L-9

Fontenay was the capital of the Vendée until 1804. This attractive town lies in a sheltered spot on the banks of the River Vendée, bordering the plain, the *bocage* (farmlands criss crossed with hedgerows) and the Poitou marshlands. Its limestone houses, sometimes coated with rough cast, sprawl between two thoroughfares perpendicular to the river. The name of the town is derived from the Quatre-Tias fountain.

- **Information:** Place de la Bascule, 85200 Fontenay-le-Comte. ☎02 51 69 44 99. www.cc-pays-fontenay-le-comte.fr.
- **Orient Yourself**: Fontenay-le-Comte lies 37km/23mi NW of Niort. Place Viète, now the centre of the town, occupies the site of a bastion which was once part of the old curtain wall. The old town lies to the east, beyond rue des Loges in the areas around Église Notre-Dame and Église St-Jean. The modern part of Fontenay extends southwest of the line traced by rue Clemenceau and rue de la République.
- **Parking**: There are car parks in place Viète and near the river in the town centre.
- **Don't Miss**: The bell tower of Église Notre-Dame; Château de Terre-Neuve.
- **Also see**: NIORT, LUÇON.

A Bit of History

In the Middle Ages and during the Renaissance Fontenay, the capital of Lower Poitou, was a fortified town accustomed to violent attacks. In 1372, a local heroine, Jeanne de Clisson, defended it against Bertrand du Guesclin, one of the generals responsible for ousting the English from France. At the end of the 16C, Fontenay was disputed by the Protestants and Catholics. Two centuries later, the Republicans twice fought the Royalists in the Vendée region, beneath its walls.

A Renaissance centre – In the 16C, Fontenay was a centre of Renaissance exuberance. In 1520, the young **Rabelais** knocked at the gates of the Franciscans' headquarters, which stood on the site of the present town hall. He had left the Franciscans of Angers and hoped to study Greek literature under Friar Pierre Amy, a precursor of the Reformation. Amy put him in touch (by letter) with the Hellenist scholar Guillaume

The Town

Budé (1467-1540), a humanist whose
later *Correspondance* with Rabelais and
others became an important document
in the literary history of the period.

In Fontenay Rabelais and his friends
would meet at the home of **André
Tiraqueau** (1480-1558), a learned legal
writer, proud father of 30 children and
author of a treatise on matrimonial laws
for which Rabelais composed an epi-
graph in Greek verse. In 1523, however,
Rabelais was constrained to seek refuge
with the Benedictines in Maillezais after
his Father Superior discovered books in
favour of the Reformation among Rabelais' belongings.

In the second half of the century, other
Fontenay humanists found fame, including Barnabé Brisson, Head of the Paris
Parliament, who was hanged in 1591
during the disputes concerning the
Catholic League, and **François Viète**
(1540-1603), the brilliant mathematician
who invented algebra. The poet and
strict magistrate **Nicolas Rapin** (c1540-
1608) was another major local figure.
During the *Grands Jours* of Poitiers, he
took part in a poetry competition, the
theme of which was to be a flea frolick-
ing on the snow-white bosom of Mademoiselle de Roches, a noted Poitou
bluestocking. Rapin won the prize with
his piece *La Puce* (The Flea), which was
followed by *L'Anti-Puce*. Later, in Paris,
he was one of the chief instigators of *La
Satire Ménippée* (a political pamphlet
directed against the Catholic League
and published in 1594) before retiring
to his country residence, Château de
Terre-Neuve (*see below*).

Église Notre-Dame

The church is marked by a slender, elegant 15C **belfry★** which was remodelled in 1700. The 82m/270ft tower,
crowned by a spire decorated with
crockets, is similar to that of Luçon cathedral. The main doorway is Flamboyant
Gothic, with a large stone filigree opening replacing the tympanum. Wise Virgins with upright lamps and Foolish
Virgins with their lamps upside down
are carved in the coving. A delicate 19C
Madonna adorns the pier niche.

A Louis XVI pulpit is among the features
worth noting inside the church. Others
include the Brisson chapel and the apsidal chapels, dating from the time of
François I, which are now partly concealed
by the outsized 18C altarpiece.

The small 9C **crypt**, (*Reservtions
required for guided tours.* ☎02 51 69 78
08) discovered by chance in the 19C, is
a rare and important example of early
architecture in the Lower Poitou region.
Roman mortar was used for the groin
vaulting. The capitals of the supporting
pillars are in the Byzantine style.

Rue du Pont-aux-Chèvres

A number of interesting old houses can
be seen in this street. The former Benedictine priory at no 3 has a staircase tower.
At no 6, the Villeneuve-Esclapon mansion
is adorned with a monumental Louis XIII
entrance surmounted by a Laocoon (an
antique sculpture group representing
Laocoon, the priest of Apollo, strangled
with his two sons by serpents. The original
is in the Vatican). The figures are flanked
by statues of Hercules and Diana. No 9
boasts a fine balustraded staircase. The
property belonged in the 16C and 17C
to the Bishops of Maillezais. No 14 is a
splendid example of a Renaissance private house. It belonged once to André
Rivaudeau, mayor of Fontenay in the late
16C and author of the tragedy Aman,
which inspired Racine to compose *Esther*.

Place Belliard

The statue in the quiet square represents
General Belliard (1769-1832) who saved

the life of Napoleon Bonaparte at Arcole by shielding him with his own body. The General was born at no 11.

Five interesting houses (three of them with arcades), flanking one side of the square, were built by the architect Jean Morisson during the reign of Henri IV. Morisson himself lived at no 16 – the pediment is crowned by a statue of the architect holding a pair of compasses, the emblem of his profession. His personal motto, *Peu et Paix* (roughly equivalent to "Less is More") is carved above the first-floor bay.

Fontaine des Quatre-Tias

In the local dialect, the word tias means pipes. The fountain, built in 1542 by the architect Lienard de Réau, bears the Latin inscription *Fontanacum Felicium Ingeniorum Fons et Scaturigo* (The Fountain and Source of Fine Minds) – a motto bestowed on the town by François I. The King's coat of arms, complete with emblematic salamander, is engraved on the pediment.

Rue des Loges

In the 18C, this street, flanked by quaintly named lanes and alleys – rue du Lamproie (Lamprey Lane), rue de la Grue (Crane Street), and rue de la Pie (Magpie Alley) – was the town's main street. Today rue des Loges is a pedestrian shopping precinct, still bordered by a number of houses with fine old façades. Among these are the house at no 26 with wrought-iron balconies and carved human faces, no 85, with an impressive late 16C doorway of carved stone, and no 94, a medieval building with projecting upper floors. On the corner of rue St-Nicolas stands a carefully restored early 16C half-timbered house.

Additional Sights

Musée Vendéen

East side of place Viète. 👤🕐 *May–Sep daily except Mon 2-6pm. Oct–Apr daily except Mon and Tue 2.30-6pm.* 🕐*1 Jan, !May and 25 Dec.* 👛 *2.20€ (children no charge).* ☎*02 51 69 31 31.*

M.Thiery/MICHELIN

Place Belliard, a quiet square in a quiet town

The ground and first floors of this regional museum contain collections of archaeology (Gallo-Roman glassware from local tombs), ornithology (stuffed birds) and ethnography (furniture from the south of Vendée).

The second floor is given over to the history of the town and to artists with Vendée connections, including the painters Paul Baudry *(Diana Surprised)*, August Lepère *(The Squall* – a storm at sea – and *Views of the St-Jean-de-Monts Dunes)* and Charles Milcendeau *(View of the Wet Marsh, The Embroideresses, The Spinning-Wheel).* Also on view are sketches by Lepère which served as a basis for engravings.

A small modern art department includes works by Émile Lahner *(The Kitchen, The Egyptian Woman* and highly coloured abstracts dating from 1959 and 1960). A huge sculpture, by the brothers Jan and Jol **Martel**, represents *An Olonne Woman Wearing a Shawl.*

Château de Terre-Neuve

Take rue Rabelais west out of place Viète and turn first left onto rue Barnabé-Brisson to the château.

🕐👄 *May-Sep guided tours (50min) 9am-noon and 2-7pm.* 👛*6.10€ (children 2€).* ☎*02 51 69 17 75 www.chateau-ter-reneuve.com.*

Jean Morisson, who built the houses in place Belliard, was also the architect of this country retreat commissioned by his friend Nicolas Rapin at the end of the 16C. It was here that Rapin wrote his well-known work, *Plaisirs du Gentil-homme Champestre* (The Pleasures of a Country Gentleman). The archaeologist and engraver Octave de Rochebrune restored the château in c 1850, adding to the decoration and collecting a number of works of art which generally lent the property a fine Renaissance air tempered by Classical influences. The building comprises two main blocks at right angles to one another, with turreted bartizans at each corner. The façade is adorned with Italian Renaissance muses in terracotta, and a porch, which was originally part of another château.

The **interior**★ has a number of remarkable features – Louis XIV woodwork from Chambord Château on the Loire, a door from François I's study, fine Louis XV and Louis XVI furniture, 17C and 18C paintings and a handsome chimney piece, designed by Philibert Delorme, with carvings evoking the symbolic system devised by the Renaissance alchemists. Weapons, costumes, mortars, keys and a collection of carved ivory pieces are on display. The Renaissance decoration of the dining hall includes a monumental doorway with a splendid frame, an imposing chimney piece supported by two griffins, and a coffered ceiling of carved stone.

Driving Tour

Forêt de Mervent-Vouvant★

▷ *55km/34mi round tour from Fontenay-le-Comte – allow 4hrs*

This National Forest lies at the junction of the Vendée plain and the mixed woodland, farmland and pasture known as **le bocage**. It covers 5 000ha/20 sq mi of a granite plateau carpeted with clays and sand, and gashed by deep, steep-sided valleys. Three of these have been flooded to form a 130ha/320 acre reservoir enclosed within four separate dams. In the 12C the forest belonged to the

house of Lusignan which owned both the Château de Mervent and the Château de Vouvant. The forest was annexed to the royal domain in 1674 and then assigned to the Comte d'Artois in 1778 on a grace-and-favour basis (it would return to the Crown on the death of the family's last surviving male heir). Following the French Revolution, it became the property of the State.

Numerous well-marked footpaths, cycle tracks and bridle paths cross the area.

▷ *North along the D 938 for la Châtaigneraie; 1.5km/0.9mi beyond Pissotte, take a one-way road on the right.*

Barrage de Mervent★

The approach to Mervent Dam is marked by a stone sculpture representing a Siren, the work of the Martel Brothers (20C). The 130m/426ft long dam plugs the valley of the Vendée and supplies water to the southern half of the département.

▷ *Continue along the one-way road, then turn left onto the D 65ter, and left again, following the signs to Mervent.*

Mervent

The small town is perched on a rocky spur in thick woodland. From the town hall gardens near the church square there is a fine **view**★ down over the reservoir with its beach) on the eastern shore behind Mervent dam.

▷ *Follow D 99; right on the D 99A.*

Grotte du Père Montfort

Louis-Marie Grignion de Montfort, a humble and devout Catholic preacher from Brittany who was later canonised, sought refuge for meditation in the forest around 1715, while on a mission to convert Protestants. The cavern in which he found shelter subsequently became a place of pilgrimage. The footpath leading to it starts behind a wayside shrine on road D99A, where cars may be parked. The grotto opens onto the slope of a valley above the River Mère. From there the path descends to La Maison du Curé, where another priest retired in seclusion.

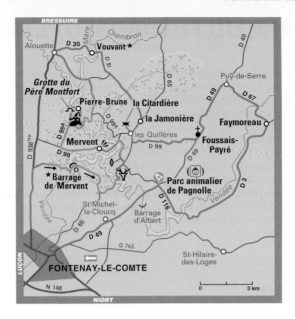

> *Continue along the D 99A, then turn left; 2km/1.2mi farther on, turn left again towards the D 938TER (right). When you reach Alouette, turn right onto the D 30.*

Vouvant★
⌖ *See VOUVANT.*

> *Leave Vouvant along the D 31 to the SE towards Foussais-Payré; 5km/3mi farther on, turn right onto the D 65 towards Mervent.*

La Jamonière Musée des Amis de la Forêt
🕐*Open Apr-Sep 2-6pm. Oct-Mar, daily except Fri and Sat 2-6pm.* 🕐 *Closed 25 Dec–1 Jan.* ✆*3€.* ☎*02 51 00 00 87.* This museum contains leaflets, books, exhibitions, videos etc. on the forest, its flora and fauna, and traditional woodland activities.

> *Continue SW on the D 65 to Quillères.*

Château de la Citardière
The château, partly hidden behind a belt of ancient trees, has a fine 17C façade reflected in a wide moat. A restaurant now occupies the interior.

> *Leave Quillères by the D 99 and continue SE.*

Foussais-Payré
A number of fine Renaissance houses and a 17C covered market distinguish this small town renowned for its annual folklore festivals. Note a fine corner house dated 1552 to the right of the church.
Church – The entrance and west front feature a remarkable collection of religious scenes carved in the 11C by Giraud Audebert, a monk from the Abbey of St-Jean-d'Angély.

> *Drive SW out of Foussais-Payré along the D 49 towards Fontenay-le-Comte.*

PARC DU FUTUROSCOPE★★★

MICHELIN MAP 322: I-4

This modern, original complex was constructed in 1987 on the outskirts of Poitiers, between the River Clan and the A 10 motorway. Sporting a futurist decor, designed by the French architect Denis Laming, Futuroscope offers a range of exciting shows, games and interactive attractions.

- **Information:** Parc du Futuroscope, BP 3030, 86130 Jaunay-Clan.
  ☎05 49 49 30 10. www.futuroscope.fr.
- ▶ **Orient Yourself**: Futuroscope lies 10km/6mi N of Poitiers and is easily accessible either via the A 10 motorway or by TGV high-speed train.
- 🕐 **Organising Your Time**: There's plenty to keep you occupied for a two-day visit here; spending a night will also allow you to watch the spectacular evening show.
- **Kids Especially for Kids**: Le Monde des Enfants.
- 👣 **Also See**: POITIERS.

Le Parc Européen de l'image★★
(European Park of the Moving Image)

🕐From 10am to nightfall or to the end of the late show beginning between 7-10pm according to the season. ☜33€ (children: 24€) for 1 day, 63€ (children 44€ for 2 days. Evening show 16€ (children: 10€). 🕐Closed early-Jan–mid-Feb. For further information on opening times, contact:☎05 49 49 30 80 or www.futuroscope.com.

Kids The 70ha/173-acre park introduces the public to the realities of modern technology and the changes brought about by an image-dominated society. Paths fan out from a shop-lined square to the various attractions scattered throughout the grounds. The visitor is immediately plunged into a modernistic architectural universe of glass and steel. Every building is a work of art, integrated into a thoughtfully landscaped park, providing both force and movement. A play area and an attractive footbridge spanning two man-made lakes contribute to the overall harmony. Most films are renewed every year.

Futuristic architecture

M. Thiery/MICHELIN

Cybernetics

La Cité du Numérique du Futuroscope★(n°3) – This building, erected in 1986 on a hill and combining two volumes – a crystal and a sphere – was the starting point for the park's neo-Futuristic architectural design. Symbolic of major transformations in the world today, it houses interactive challenges and big screen gaming.

Cyber Avenue (n°19) – This underground space covering some 800m²/957sq yd has a great number of video games (charge) which require suppleness and a great deal of anticipation. Spread over two levels, Cyber Avenue is the favourite haunt of young people. always out to test the latest interactive creatio n.

3-D Imagery

Les Ailes du Courage (n°6) Relive the exciting adventures of the Aéropostale airmail service pilot as he battles to clear the Andes Mountains. Wearing special glasses, you have the impression that you are actually part of the film, an effect created by two slightly staggered images.

Adventures in Animation 3D★★★(n°12) Wearing polarising spectacles the audience lives through the creation of the £D animated her and his subsequent adventures in the boxing ring.

Sous les Mers du Monde★★(n°7) Wearing liquid-crystal glasses, spectators see an Omnivax image on a 900m²/ 1 062 sq yd **screen.** The illusion creates a sensation of being suspended in the water surrounded by the fauna of the sea. It is so complete that you want to reach out and touch the fish as they swim past.

For Your Eyes Only

Expédition Nile Bleu★(n°9) In one of the park's original buildings, now its architectural point of reference, experience the trip of a lifetime down the the Blue Nile in a raft. The building, a cluster of giant rock crystals pointing their many facets skywards, reflects the whims of the weather and the changing colours of the seasons. It houses a 600m²/2 000 sq ft **Imax screen**, seven-storeys high and as wide as a tennis court that transports the audience right into the heart of the picture.

L'Etalon Noir★★(n°1) The doors of this transparent half-sunken cube lead into

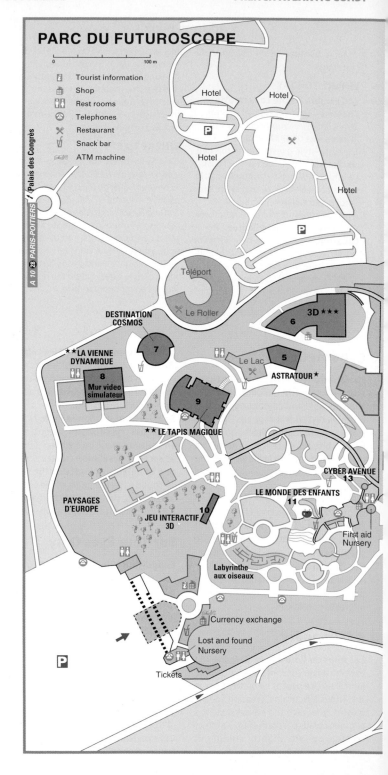

PARC DU FUTUROSCOPE

0   100 m

🛈   Tourist information
🏬   Shop
🚻   Rest rooms
☎   Telephones
✕   Restaurant
▯   Snack bar
🏧   ATM machine

A 10 🛣 PARIS-POITIERS ✓ Palais des Congrès

Hotel

Hotel

Hotel

Hotel

Téléport

Le Roller

DESTINATION COSMOS

3D ★★★

6

7

★★ LA VIENNE DYNAMIQUE

8
Mur video simulateur

Le Lac

5

ASTRATOUR ★

9

★★ LE TAPIS MAGIQUE

CYBER AVENUE
13

LE MONDE DES ENFANTS
11

PAYSAGES D'EUROPE

First aid
Nursery

10

JEU INTERACTIF 3D

Labyrinthe aux oiseaux

Currency exchange

Lost and found
Nursery

Tickets

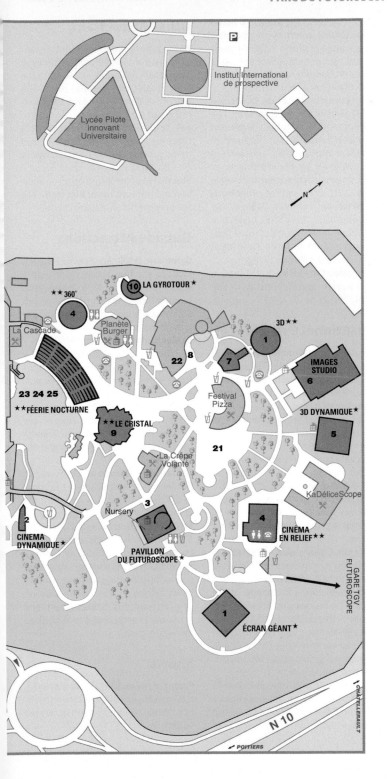

La Gyrotour ★

★★ 360°

4

La Cascade

Planète Burger

3D ★★

1

22 8

7

IMAGES STUDIO
6

23 24 25

★★FÉERIE NOCTURNE

Festival Pizza

3D DYNAMIQUE ★

★★LE CRISTAL
9

La Crêpe Volante

21

5

KaDéliceScope

3

Nursery

4

CINÉMA EN RELIEF ★★

2

CINÉMA DYNAMIQUE ★

PAVILLON DU FUTUROSCOPE ★

GARE TGV FUTUROSCOPE

1

ÉCRAN GÉANT ★

CHÂTELLERAULT

N 10

POITIERS

Lycée Pilote innovant Universitaire

Institut International de prospective

a cinema with a 900m²/3 000 sq ft **hemi-spherical Imax screen** covering the entire human range of vision – 180 degrees. The spectator is bathed in an ocean of images produced by a fish-eye lens in a projection room beneath the seats.

Voyageurs du Ciel et de la Mer★★ (n°14) (Travel by Air and Sea). The building's anthracite tubes sparkle and shimmer in the lake below. The audience is whisked away over sea and land – a feat achieved by the double Imax screens, one **vertical screen,** measuring 672m²/2 210 sq ft**,** and the other **horizontal screen,** measuring 748m²/ 2 460 sq ft**.** The latter, 25m/100ft beneath a glass floor under the spectators' feet, projects a series of fantastic images which create the illusion of flight.

Destination Cosmos★★(n°15) Explore the universe and beyond with the Hubble Telescope .

Sensational Experiences

Le Meilleur du Dynamique★★(n°13) (The Best of Dynamique Cinema) This tiered building houses a moving cinema. The audience, seated on long benches that are move by hydraulic jacks in synchronisation with the images and special effects, are given one final warning before being thrust into a world of virtual reality at the dizzy speed of 60 frames per minute.

Défi d'Atlantis (n°5). This simulator which makes the spectators' seats move in perfect synchronisation with the 3D images brings to life the mystical city of Atlantis.

La Vienne Dynamique + d'Effets★★ (n°16) This pavilion was built in 1994. Water streams down its glass façade into a pool spanned by a footbridge. giving access to the building. Inside each seat is a simulator that produces realistic movement effects that match the on-screen images as you travel through the Vienne department in various modes of transport. real white-knuckle ride.

Péril sur Akryls(n°2) A dynamic cinema where the seats mimic the sensation of speed and movement of a futuristic adventure in 3D.

Other Attractions

Danse avec les Robots★★ (n°4) Seated on the end of a 7m/22ft robotic arm you are whisked through a wild waltz to the beat of salsa, hip hop and disco. The arms move along seven axes and acceleration can reach 3Gs.

Les Yeux Grandes Fermées(n°22) (Journey into the Dark) With a blind guide, journey through a world where eyes do not see.

Star du Futur (n°6) Turn up for an audition and then vist major film studios to see how special effects are created.

Outside Attractions

Gyrotour★ (n°10) A gigantic wheel which looks like a film spool spirals up a 45m/148ft high pylon. It continues to turn at the top, providing the visitor with a panoramic view of the spectacular grounds below.

Le Monde des Enfants (n°18) (Children's World) This playground, surrounded by pools of water, has open-air attractions (giant slides and water games), as well as a games and hands-on room (interactive games, virtual reality, video adaptations, musical house). Tokens are required for most of the games. Children too small for the other rides (under 4ft) enter free.

Les Jardins d'Europe (n°17) (European Gardens) Take a stroll above the water to discover gardens that represent the landscapes of Europe.

Mission Eclabousse★(n°11) New for 2007 this outdoor water attraction will be sure to produce floods of fun. You navigate a boat, armed with water cannon to shoot floating targets and other boats, around an island while avoiding geysers, water jets, hidden snipers and other boats attacking you with their own water guns.

Shows

Forest of Dreams (n°23) Every evening after dark there is a light and pyrotechnic show projected onto water screens.

Fantaisie Aquatique (n°24) This aquatic show of fountains, water jets and water falls synchronised to music is one of the most impressive in Europe.

Illusions Magiques (n°25) A daily live show of magic and other illusions.
Open Air Exhibition of Images (n°21)

HAGETMAU

POPULATION 4 403
MICHELIN MAP 335: H-5

Imposing public buildings (colleges, a covered market) in 1950s style testify to the post-war prosperity of Hagetmau, an agricultural trade centre and a major chair-manufacturing base.

The discovery of numerous prehistoric remains indicate very ancient and very large settlements at various times. In 778, Charlemagne founded the Abbaye de St-Girons, which was destroyed in 1569 by the Protestants.

▶ **Orient Yourself**: Hagetmau is situated 12km/7.5mi S of St-Sever along the D 933.
⊙ **Don't Miss**: The capitals in the crypt at St-Girons.

Sights

Crypte de St-Girons
From the church at Hagetmau, follow signs to Dax until you get to the crossroads at Larrigade; turn right. The crypt is sign-posted on the right.
⊙*Open Jul and Aug daily except Tue 3-6pm; Sep-Jun, contact the town hall.* ⊜ *1.60€.* ☎*05 58 05 77 77.*
This crypt, which was a halt on the pilgrims' road to Compostela (⊙ *see INTRODUCTION, THE WAY OF ST JAMES*), is all that remains of an abbey built to house the relics of St-Girons, the 4C evangelist who preached the Gospel in the Chalosse region. The ceiling of the crypt rests on four central marble columns and eight recessed columns around the walls. The tomb of the saint lay between the marble columns. Scenes carved on the 12C **capitals★** represent his battle against the forces of evil and the dangers surrounding his missionary activities.
Other capitals in the crypt show the deliverance of St Peter and the parable of the rich man.

Excursions

Brassempouy
12km/7mi W. Leave Hagetmau to the south-west via the road to Orthez; after 2.5km/1.5mi turn right onto the D 2. Just before St-Cricq turn left onto the D 21.
This small Chalosse village, the main street of which appears to be straddled by the stone tower of the Romanesque-Gothic church, is among the world's most important prehistoric sites. They include the earliest known representation of a human face, carved c 23 000 years BC – the celebrated 3.6cm/1 inch ivory carving known as the **Vénus de Brassempouy** or Figurine à la Capuche (Lady with the Cowl), now exhibited in the Musée des antiquités Nationales in St-Germain-en-Laye. Though many important discoveries had been made over the preceding hundred years, huge archeological tracts still remained untouched when excavations resumed in 1982.

Maison de la Dame de Brassempouy★
♿ ☞ *Open Jun-Sep 11am-7pm, guided tour available (1hr). Mar-May and Oct daily except Mon 2pm-5.30pm. Nov-Feb Sat-Sun, Tue and public hols 2-5.30pm.*

🕐Closed 1 May. ∽4.50€ (children aged 6-11: 3€); combined ticket with the Jardin de la Dame de Brassempouy 7€ (children aged 6-11: 5€). ☎05 58 89 21 73.

The museum displays some of the prehistoric discoveries made in the Chalosse district (a millstone, polished axe-heads) along with items found at Brassempouy since excavations were resumed (tools, bones and the remains of animals which had been eaten). Period documents recall the original 19C excavations. An exhibition of prehistoric female statuary includes reproductions of the world's most famous statuettes and copies of nine figurines discovered at Brassempouy.

Jardin de la Dame de Brassempouy

☞Open Jul-Aug guided tour (1hr) 10am-12.30pm and 2.30-7.30pm. Apr-Jun and Sep-Oct daily except Mon 2.30-6.30pm. 🕐Closed Nov-Mar. ∽4.10€ (children 6-11: 3.10€); combined ticket with Maison de la Dame de Brassempouy 7€ (children aged 6-11: 5€). ☎05 58 89 25 89.

Return to prehistoric times during a tour in a reconstructed environment (habitat, flora, fauna) with an archaeologist, and experience prehistoric daily life by taking part in workshops (pottery, flint carving).

Château d'Amou

16 km SW of Hagetmau. Take the D 933 then the D 13. In Amou, follow signs to Gaujacq, first road on the right. The carpark is located on the left hand side after the grid. ☞Open Jul-Sep guided tour (45 min) Mon, Tue and Sun 3pm, 4pm and 5pm. ∽4€ (children under 16 no charge). ☎05 58 89 00 08. www.chateauamou.com.

The marquis d'Amou, ancestor of the current landlord, had this château built at the behest of Louis XIV. A fine 18C gate opens onto an alley of plane trees leading to the château built in 1678 according to the plans of Mansart, the architect of Versailles. The vestibule is paved with a remarkable Gallo-Roman mosaic surrounded by a large staircase. Close to it,

a restored 18C sedan chair. In the dining-room, the silver cutlery is set à la française, as it was then the custom. On the first floor, the four bedrooms in a row have kept their original style, with their 17C floor-tiles and their Louis XIV wooden floor. Note that Théophile Gautier used to occupy the "best one" (the smallest, therefore the best heated!) when he stayed at Amou. In the chapel, fitted out in the 19C, a trompe-l'œil painting imitates wood.

The **outbuildings**, gathered around a square yard, represent an interesting example of regional architecture, alternating a dovecot from Béarn and Gascon buildings covered with special tiles. An agricultural estate used to go along with the château, a former wine press is there to remind visitors of the fact that in the past, Chalosse wine used to be exported throughout all Europe.

Samadet

10km/6mi E along the D 2.

The hey-day of this small town was from 1732 to 1811 when its faïences (glazed earthenware) were known throughout the world. The factories here were able to produce both deep and strong tones using the grand feu technique (high-temperature firing) and more delicate colours using the gentler petit feu. The **Musée de la Faïencerie** (♿🕐open Apr–mid-Oct daily except Mon 10am-12.30pm and 2-6.30pm. Mid-Oct–the end of Mar daily except Mon 2-6pm; 🕐closed 1 Jan, 1 May, 1 and 11 Nov and 25 Dec; ∽4€, no charge on the 1st Sun of the month; ☎05 58 79 13 00; www.museesamadet.org), in the old abbot's house, contains rare and beautiful collections of celebrated Samadet wares; there are items decorated with roses, carnations, butterflies, and dishes in green monochrome with grotesques and chinoiseries. An 18C bourgeois interior, 18C costumes, various workshops and reconstructions of the Royal faïencerie are also of interest.

HENDAYE ☼ ☼

POPULATION 12 596

MICHELIN MAP 342: B-2

Hendaye is a border town lying on the east bank of the River Bidassoa, which forms the Franco-Spanish border at that point.

- **Information:** 12 r. des Aubépines, 64700 Hendaye.
  ☎ 05 59 20 00 34. www.hendaye.com.
- ▶ **Orient Yourself**: Hendaye contains three separate districts: Hendaye-Gare, Hendaye-Ville and Hendaye-Plage, corresponding to the area around the railway station, the town proper and the sea-front.
- **Don't Miss**: The 13C crucifix in Église St-Vincent; Château d'Antoine-Abbadie.
- **Also See**: ST-JEAN-DE-LUZ.

Sights

Hendaye-Plage

The resort benefits from uninterrupted views over the open sea and a climate which encourages luxuriant vegetation: magnolias, palm trees, tamarisk, oleanders, eucalyptus and mimosa line the avenues and shade the gardens everywhere. An unusual Moorish-style building houses a bustling shopping arcade with cafés and restaurants; it also marks the beginning of the GR 10 long-distance footpath. From the beach, the coastal view to the northeast is marked by the rock outcrops known as Les Deux Jumeaux (Twins), just off Pointe de Ste-Anne. In the other direction Cabo Higuer (Cape Fig Tree) marks the mouth of the Bidassoa. A cycle track links the beach to the town centre via Chingoudy Bay.

Église St-Vincent

This large Basque-style church has been rearranged inside, enabling the visitor to study fragments of reredos and polychrome statues in detail. On the right is an unusual Romanesque baptismal font installed in a 17C niche with a pediment, embellished by a Basque cross. In the organ loft, the decoration of the beautiful gilded instrument portrays the Annunciation. In the Chapelle du St-Sacrement, note the 13C **crucifix★**.

Pointe Ste-Anne Excursion

Domaine d'Abbadia

Leave Hendaye by D the 912 towards St-Jean-de-Luz (the cliffroad). Turn left and follow the signs "Domaine d'Abbadia".

Les Deux Jumeaux – "Twin Rocks"

B. Kaufmann/MICHELIN

Address Book

For coin ranges, see the Legend on the cover flap.

WHERE TO STAY

Hôtel Valencia – *29 bd de la Plage – ☎05 59 20 01 62 – closed 15 Dec-Jan – P – 22 rooms.* The first-floor breakfast room and four of the simply furnished guest rooms have good views of the sea and Spanish coast.

Serge Blanco – *Bd de la Mer – ☎05 59 51 35 35 – info@thalassoblanco. com – closed 11-26 Dec – 90 rooms.* This sea-water therapy resort is the ideal place for a relaxing break. The functional rooms have balconies and bay windows overlooking the sea or the courtyard.

WHERE TO EAT

Marco Polo – *2 bd de la Mer – Résidence La Croisière – ☎05 59 20 64 82 – polom@ wanadoo.fr – closed 7-27 Jan, evenings Nov-Mar except Sat.* You'll think you're on a cruise ship in this restaurant with its light wood furnishings, handrails and copper objects. Lovely views of the Baie d'Hendaye, the Estuaire de la Bidassoa, the sea and Spain from the large bay windows. The accent here is on fish and seafood.

The protected area of Domaine d'Abbadia on Ste-Anne headland has the geographical features typical of the Basque coastline; its gorse and heather-covered meadows go right up to the grey cliffs overlooking the sea. The path along the cliff edge provides an excellent view of the two famous "Jumeaux" rock formations to the west.
Return to the D 912 and turn left to enter the castle grounds.

Château d'Antoine Abbadie★★

Open Jun-Sep guided tours (1hr, last admission 30min before closing time) daily except Sat-Sun 10-11.30am and 2-6pm; unaccompanied visit Sat-Sun 2-6pm. Feb-May and early Oct to mid-Dec guided tour daily except Sun, Mon 2-5pm. Closed mid-Dec–Jan and public hols. 6.40€. ☎05 59 20 04 51.

The château was built in the 19C by the explorer and astronomer **Antoine d'Abbadie** (1810-1897) on plans by Viollet-le-Duc. Modelled on the medieval fortress, it has crenellated towers and pepper pots which were previously used as an astronomical observatory.
The park contains exotic plants and trees. The decoration and furniture, designed by Viollet-le-Duc, illustrate the life and taste of Antoine Abbadie. The polychrome ornamentation of the chapel, which is repeated throughout the castle, is reminiscent of Basque churches. The French-style ceilings are decorated with Amharic inscriptions (Abbadie studied this language in Ethiopia). The **Grand Salon★**, housed in a round tower, is painted in deep blue as a background for the initials of Antoine and his wife Virginie. In all the rooms there are verse and mottoes in English, in Basque and in Amharic, illustrating Abbadie's personality (his motto was "Better to be than to seem"). From the large library which Abbadie created for the Observatory of the Science Academy, one walks down to the observatory where one can still see the telescope used by priests until 1975 to establish the position of the stars in the sky.

Biriatou

5km/3mi SE. Leave Hendaye via the rue de Béhobie.
Beyond Béhobie the road follows the course of the Bidasoa before twisting up towards this tiny village, where it ends beside a parking area. The small square with its pelota court, adjoining inn and the church at the top of a flight of steps makes a charming ensemble. The view here embraces the wooded mountains, the frontier river below and the first few miles of Spain on the far side.

Donostia/San Sebastián★★ (St-Sebastien)

25km/15.5mi SW of Hendaye. Take the A 8 towards Bilbao, or the N 10 which becomes the N 1 in Spain. San Sebastián is located in the Spanish Basque country.

L'Île des Faisans (Pheasant Island)

This river isle downstream from the Spanish frontier post at the Béhobie bridge is today no more than a wooded strip increasingly threatened by the current; no trace remains of the important historical role it once played. In 1463 Louis XI met Henry IV, the King of Castile, on its banks; in 1526 François I, held prisoner in Spain after the battle of Pavia, was exchanged here for his two sons. Since the island was deemed suitable for occasions in which royal and diplomatic etiquette were involved, it was used again in 1615 as "neutral" ground on which two royal brides-to-be could officially be introduced to their new countries: they were Elizabeth, the sister of Louis XIII, chosen as the wife of the Infante of Spain (the future Philip IV), and Anne of Austria, the Infante's sister, chosen for Louis XIII himself.

The **Treaty of the Pyrenees** was signed on Pheasant Island in 1659. A commemorative stone recalls the event.

In the spring of 1660 the island was the scene of feverish preparations. The painter Velasquez (who died soon afterwards of a chill caught during the work) decorated the pavilion in which the marriage contract, provided for in the Treaty of the Pyrenees, was to be signed by Louis XIV and Maria Theresa, the daughter of Philip IV of Spain. As each delegation wished to remain on its own soil – protocol in fact forbade the King of Spain to leave his own territory – the building on the mid-stream islet was divided inside by an imaginary frontier line.

It is always a pleasure to go beyond the Spanish border to dine on tapas and seafood in the port of the old Spanish city. In the evening, stroll around the **plaza de la Constitución**, once used as an arena for races held in San Sebastián; above the high arcades, you can still make out the section numbers that divided up the seating. The best way to see the site called the Concha, a scallop-shaped **bay**★★★ stretching between Monte Urgull and Monte Igueldo, is to walk along the sea between beaches, gardens and opulent-looking buildings. The city is a thriving bathing resort. If you take the funicular, you will discover the **view**★★★ from **Mount Igueldo**: the islet of Santa Clara and the city surrounded by mountains. The **view**★★ from **Mount Urgull** is also excellent: you can see the fort of Santa Cruz de la Mota. From the top, you can watch both the Concha and the monuments of the old city.

LES HERBIERS

MICHELIN MAP 316: J-6

This little town is the ideal starting point for a drive through windmill country. The manufacture of clothes and shoes remains the traditional economic activity of Les Herbiers.

- **Information:** 10 rue Nationale – 85500 Les Herbiers. ☎02 51 92 92 92.
- ▶ **Orient Yourself**: Les Herbiers stands on a bluff overlooking the River Grande Maine, 19km/12mi NW of Pouzauges.
- **Don't Miss**: The windmill at Mont des Alouettes.
- **Organising Your Time**: Allow a day to explore the region, following the Route des Moulins.
- **Especially for Kids**: Chemin de Fer de la Vendée.
- **Also See**: LA ROCHE-SUR-YON.

Address Book

⚅For coin categories, see the Legend on the cover flap.

WHERE TO STAY

⊜⊜**Chambre d'hôte La Métairie du Bourg** – *5km/3mi NE of Les Herbiers. Take the D 755, D 11 and a side road – ☎02 51 67 23 97 – ⌷ – 3 rms.* This bed and breakfast on a typical Vendée cattle farm has spacious, well-maintained bedrooms. Substantial breakfasts and a warm welcome make this a pleasant place to stay. Good value for money.

WHERE TO EAT

⊜**Auberge du Mont Mercure** – *Rue de l'Orbrie – 85700 St-Michel-Mont-Mercure – ☎02 51 57 20 26 – contact@ aubergemontmercure.com – closed during Feb and Nov school hols, Mon eve Sep-June, Tue eve and Wed .* This family auberge at the top of the village has a warm, friendly ambience. The decor here is rustic with exposed beams, an open fireplace and old farming tools on display. Traditional cuisine at reasonable prices. Children's menu.

A Bit of History

Windmill Country

In the past the Vendée hills offered both strategic and tactical advantages to armies. The Romans built a road linking the crests, and a temple crowned Mont Mercure. For centuries the heights were dotted with countless windmills which turned every time the sea winds blew – sometimes throughout the night – grinding wheat and rye from the fertile plains nearby. During the Revolution, however, local Royalist supporters used their mills as a kind of rural semaphore system, altering the position of sails and vanes to telegraph information concerning the movements of the enemy. As a result, many were burned down by Republican troops. Mechanisation in the 19C put any surviving windmills out of business.

Many mills are again being restored to working order.

A typical example is stone-built, cylindrical in shape, and topped by a movable, conical roof or "cap" covered with shingles (this type is known as a tower mill because of its fixed, tower-like base). Four sails are fixed to the revolving roof to which a *guivre* is frequently attached (a long pole reaching to the ground), to help turn the sails to face the prevailing wind. The wooden sails are either covered with canvas (hemp in earlier times) or made of wooden slats articulated using the Berton System, invented in 1848.

Sights

Church

It has an impressive belfry-porch with a Flamboyant doorway framed by St Peter and St Paul.

Chemin de Fer de la Vendée

&⃝*Open Mid-May to mid-Sep, possible to have a meal in "Orient Express" dining car, leaving from Mortagne-sur-Sèvre (journey time 3hrs); call for dates, departure times and prices.Reservations advised at least 24hrs in advance ☎ 02 51 63 02 01 www.members.lycos.fr/vapeurvendee.*
Kids In season, this quaint train runs on an old line linking Les Herbiers and Mortagne-sur-Sèvre. It is an original way of peacefully exploring 22km/14mi of Vendée farmland, with a stop at Les Épesses station. **Gare des Épesses**, on the Herbiers-Mortagne line, is typical of the architecture of early 20C country stations. **Musée de l'Histoire des Chemins de Fer en Vendée** – In this little station museum, posters, exhibits and documents trace the short but eventful history of the railways.

Route des Moulins Driving Tour★

Round-trip 90km/56mi – allow a full day

▷ *Leave Les Herbiers going west via the N 160 towards La Roche-sur-Yon.*

Forêt des Bois-Verts

This little wood and lake is a popular spot for picnics and walks in fine weather.

▷ *Return via the N 160 for 4km/2mi then go left.*

Abbaye de Notre-Dame-de-la-Grainetière

🕐 *Open 9am-7pm.* 👝*2€.* ☎*02 51 67 21 19.*

The Abbey, devoted to Our Lady of the Corn Chandlers, was build on the edge of Soubise Forest in 1130 by Benedictine monks from the Monastery of Fontdouce, near Saintes. With the help of the local overlords, the monks became sufficiently powerful in the 13C to build the fortifications which enabled them to resist the English when they laid siege to the abbey in 1372. In the 15C, however, the monks' power waned, becoming even weaker during the Wars of Religion. Revolutionary uprisings and the Vendée Wars finally destroyed the abbey at the end of the 18C. Subsequently used for farming and as a quarry, it underwent restoration in 1963. In 1978, a Benedictine priory was established in the abbey.

Only the west end of cloisters remain, with an ambulatory of fine twinned columns. Opposite, the 12C chapter house still has its original vaults resting on granite pillars. Three apsidioles are all that remain of the abbey-church. The southwest tower, or Tour de l'Abbaye with its one arrow slit, is the only part of the fortifications still standing.

▷ *Return to the crossroads and turn right, then right again 500m/547yd farther on.*

Mouchamps

This village, situated above the Petit-Lay Valley, is the birthplace of Commandant Guilbaud who, in 1928, was lost in the arctic aboard his seaplace, *Latham 47*, as he was attempting to rescue the airship *Italia*. Since the 17C, Mouchamps has been a Protestant enclave in a Catholic area: until recently, Catholic houses were singled out by a white cross above the door.

▷ *Leave Mouchamps towards the northwest along the D 13.*

Château du Parc-Soubise

The estate once belonged to the powerful Rohan-Soubise family; the 16C-17C castle was burnt down in 1794 (during the Revolution) and 200 women, children and old people perished; the roof alone has been restored. Situated near a 28ha/69-acre lake surrounded by ancient oak trees, the edifice has retained memories of Henri IV who stayed there in 1589 and tried to seduce his cousin, Anne de Rohan. When he asked her the way to her bedroom, she is said to have replied: "through the chapel, your Majesty!"

▷ *Return to Mouchamps and continue eastwards along the D 13.*

Tombe de Clemenceau

Following the Petit-Lay Valley, the road leads to the 16C manor of **Le Colombier,** which belonged to the Clemenceau family. At the end of the road, walk through the doorway opening onto an alleyway. Below, on the way down to the Petit-Lay, you can see the graves of Clemenceau and his father beside a cedar tree.

▷ *Return to the D 13, for Pouzauges.*

Église du Boupère

This curious 13C church, fortified in the 15C. Its façade is surrounded by buttresses pierced with arrow slits and loopholes and two bartizans linked by a crenellated watchpath. The sides were defended by gatehouses.

▷ *Continue along the D 13 then turn left onto the D 960.*

Pouzauges

👟*See POUZAUGES.*

▷ *Leave Pouzauges north-west via the D 752 in the direction of les Herbiers.*

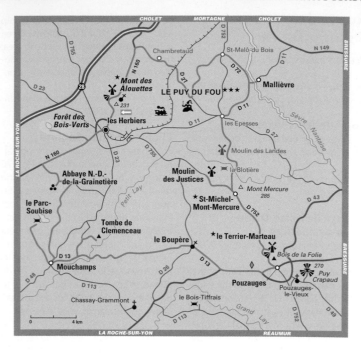

Moulins du Terrier-Marteau★
See POUZAUGES.

▶ *Go back along the D 752 in the direction of les Herbiers.*

The road winds back down into the small valley separating Pouzauges from St-Michel-Mont-Mercure.

St-Michel-Mont-Mercure★

Moulin des Justices
Closed to visitors

This mill, built at the end of the 19C, owes its name to the fact that it is perched on top of a bluff, 275m/900ft above sea level, from which justice was administered in former times. The mill, which still grinds organic flour, has a shingle roof which can be rotated using an inside winch. The width of the sails, made of wooden slats articulated using the Berton System, can be varied.

▶ *Return to St-Michel and follow the D 752 on the left.*

After St-Michel, D 752 winds its way through the valley, past a hill with a windmill

without sails (Moulin des Landes) to Les Épesses with its two churches standing side by side.

Mallièvre
This old weaving centre is built on a granite outcrop overlooking Vallée de la Sèvre Nantaise. The village can be toured on foot by taking the Sentier Génovette, punctuated with water fountains and information points.

▶ *Leave Mallièvre, going back over the River Sèvre Nantaise, then turn right on D 72 towards St-Malo-du-Bois.*

Puy du Fou★★
See Le PUY DU FOU.

▶ *Drive north along the D 27 and take the Cholet road.*

Mont des Alouettes★
This 231m/758ft high hill marks the northwestern limit of the Vendée hills. The name is derived from the bronze skylarks *(alouettes)* which decorated the helmets of Gallic warriors when they enlisted in the Roman legions based in the area. In 1793, the seven mills on

Mont des Alouettes – Windmill and chapel

these moors were among those most frequently used to send signals by the "Whites" or Royalists. Subsequently, all were set afire by the Republicans. After many ups and downs, one of them was started up again in 1989.

The mills are all typical of the region, with their rough-hewn oak *guivres* or tails and shingled conical roofs. One of them is dedicated to the Vendée writer Jean Yole.

Mill – ○*Open Jul-Aug 10am-7pm; Jun and early Sep to mid-Sep daily except Tue 10am-12.30pm and 2-6pm; Apr-May, Sat-Sun and public hols 10am-12.30pm and 2-6pm.* ○*Closed from mid-Sep to end of Mar.* ≋*3€ (children under 14 : 2€).* ☎*02 51 66 80 32 www.villedesherbiers.com.* This

mill, with its canvas-covered sails, still grinds corn. The small granite chapel in the Troubadour neo-Gothic style was started in 1823 in honour of the royalist Catholic Army. The windows and other finishings were only added in 1968.

The wide-reaching **view★★** encompasses Nantes, the Atlantic Ocean and, towards Pouzauges, the chain of hills dominated by the church of St-Michel-Mont-Mercure. It is from here, too, that the impressive, almost mysterious effect of the surrounding farmland, with its intricate mixture of copse and spinney and hedgerow, is most strongly felt.

▷ *Continue on N 160 to Les Herbiers.*

HOSSEGOR

POPULATION 3 390

MICHELIN MAP 335: C-13

Hossegor is a pleasant seaside resort bordered by the Canal du Boudigau, which separates the town from neighbouring Capbreton. Thanks to the efforts of successive generations of local architects, writers and painters since the beginning of the century, this choice natural site wooded with pines, cork-oak and arbutus has been carefully developed into a holiday centre complete with parks, gardens, hotels, a casino and a golf course.

- **Information:** Place des Halles – Hossegor. ☎ 05 58 41 79 00. www.hossegor.fr
- ▷ **Orient Yourself**: 23km/14mi N of Bayonne and 28km/17mi W of Dax.
- **Don't Miss**: The lake and surrounding pine forest.
- **Organising Your Time**: Allow half-a-day to explore the resort and its surrounding area. The lake offers plenty of options for swimming and water-sports.
- **Kids Especially for Kids**: Atlantic Park aquapark *(see Address Book)*.

Geographical Notes

The climate, influenced by the coast, the lake and the forest, is temperate, the humidity ideal, making the town an invigorating place to vacation.

Some way off-shore is the famous Gouf de Capbreton, an undersea canyon 3 000m/9 800ft deep and over 60km/37mi long. The huge groundswell produced by this submarine phenomenon has made Hossegor a playground for surfing enthusiasts and each summer, in the second half of August, the "Hossegor Rip Curl Pro", a World Championship for professional surfers, is held here.

The Resort

Le Lac★

Where once the River Ardour flowed, there is now a long tidal salt-water lake, ringed by the pine forest and villas in the local style . The lake is linked directly to the ocean by Boudigau Canal.

Lac d'Hossegor is ideal for water sports. Its beaches, with their gently lapping waters, are perfect for small children, while Plage du Rey, on the east bank, offers a wide choice of equipment and lessons.

Capbreton ☆☆

Separated from Hossegor by Boudigau canal, the town was an important **port** up until the diversion of the River Adour. Decline soon followed but today, its attractive apartment buildings, large marina and sandy beach, have turned it into a prosperous **seaside resort**. The jetty, known locally as *l'estacade*, is a popular vantage point for contemplating the coast, the Pyrenees and the mouth of the canal.

Capbreton is also known for its **"gouf"** or swallow-hole – a phenomenon of underwater topography which is invisible from the surface, but which was well-known to local fishermen centuries before it was scientifically identified. It is the main geomorphologic trait of the continental shelf in the Bay of Biscay. The swallow-hole is an east-west chasm running for over 60km/37mi from the exit of the harbour.

It is 3-10km/2-6mi wide and up to 3 000m/nearly 10 000ft deep. Various hypotheses have been put forward to explain its existence but none has been conclusively proved – that it is the result of a complex process of underwater fluvial erosion, a fracture linked to buckling of the Pyrenees, or a canyon gouged out by the River Adour during the great glaciations of the Quaternary Age when sea levels lowered.

Écomusée de la Pêche et de la Mer

&⚲Open Jul and Aug 10am-noon and 2-6.30pm; Apr-Jun and Sep 2-6pm; Feb–Mar and Oct–Nov, Sun and public hols 2-6pm. ⚲Closed Dec–Jan. ⚲4.50€ (children: 3€). ☎05 58 72 40 50.

Kids Located above the municipal casino, this museum focuses on marine geology and the history of the fishing industry around Capbreton and the Landes coast. Note the skeleton of an Arctic whale beached near Le Penon in 1988. The terrace provides a **panoramic view** of the surrounding area.

La pinède des Singes

8km south via the D 652, N 10 and D 126. ⚲Open mid-Apr to end of Sep: 10am-noon and 2-6pm. ⚲6.50€ (children: 3€). ☎ 05 59 45 43 66.

Kids This wooded area is home to monkeys from Java, which are allowed to roam here freely.

Driving Tour

Around the Lakes

38km/24mi itinerary from Hossegor to Vieux-Boucau-les-Bains.

▷ *Leave Hossegor N along the D 152.*

The road leads to **Le Penon**, a seaside resort which combines waterfront apartments and villas set among the forest pines.

▷ *Turn right onto the D 89 then left just before Seignosse.*

The road overlooks Étang Noir before running north towards Étang Blanc.

Address Book

☺ *For coin ranges, see the Legend on the cover flap.*

WHERE TO STAY

Chambre d'hôte Le Bosquet – *4 r. du Hazan (rte de St-Vincent-de-Tyrosse) – 40230 Tosse – 10km/6mi E of Hossegor via the D 33 and D 652 – ☎05 58 43 03 40 – ✉ – 3 rooms.* Pine and oak trees surround this low, modern house near Hossegor, with direct access to the garden from the guestrooms. Meals here are taken in the Basque-style dining room in the winter or on the terrace with barbecue in fine weather. Calm, peaceful ambience and friendly, hospitable hosts.

Chambre d'hôte Ty-boni – *1831 rte de Capbreton – 40150 Angresse – 3km/1.8mi E of Hossegor via the D 133 – ☎ 05 58 43 98 75 – www.ty-boni.com – ✉ – 3 rooms.* This quiet bed and breakfast has an attractive large garden with a swimming pool and small lake. The modern house, built in traditional regional style, has pleasant, simply furnished rooms. Fully-equipped kitchen at guests' disposal. Friendly welcome.

Les Hortensias du Lac – *Av. du Tour-du-Lac – ☎05 58 43 99 00 – reception@hortensias-du-lac.com – closed 15 Nov-1 Apr – ⛶ – 11 rooms.* This attractive hotel situated on the lakeshore only 500m/550yd from the sea is the perfect place for a relaxing holiday. Its white facade and round arched windows overlook the peaceful waters of the lake. Comfortable, elegant rooms decorated in white with light wood furnishings. A few duplexes for family holidays.

WHERE TO EAT

Sporting Grill – *119 av. Maurice-Martin – Casino Barrière d'Hosegor – ☎ 05 58 41 99 99 – casinohossegor@lucienbarriere.com.* This typical 1930s restaurant on the banks of the canal is a listed building. Its woodwork and copper evoke the colonial and Art Deco styles. Grilled meat and fish on the menu; tranquil terrace.

SPORT AND LEISURE IN HOSSEGOR

Parc municipal des sports Jaï Alaï – *Av. Maurice-Martin – ☎05 58 74 19 40 – tournaments: Jul-Aug Mon and Thu 8.45pm.* *Pala corta* and *cesta punta* matches are played at this covered Jaï Alaï fronton neighbouring the Sporting Casino. *Grosse pala* and *grand chistera* matches are played at the Casino's fronton outdoors.

Hossegor Surf Club – *22 imp. de la Digue Nord – ☎05 58 43 80 52 – www.hossegorsurfclub.com – contact: Mon-Fri 9am-12.30pm; school hols 9am-12.30pm and 2-5pm; Jul-Aug: daily – closed mid-Dec to end Jan and Sun off-season.* Located next to the Fédération Française de Surf, this club organises surfing and bodyboard courses. Weekly courses for groups and individuals, with accommodation included if required.

Yacht Club Landais – *2987 av. du Touring-Club-de-France, BP 69 – ☎05 58 43 96 48 – yachtclublandaid@wanadoo.fr – Jul-Aug daily 9am-7pm; mid-Mar to mid-Nov: Mon-Sat 10am-noon and 2-5.30pm – closed Jan-Feb.* This yacht club, which organises courses and private lessons, also rents boats, windsurf boards and canoes.

Atlantic Park – ☺ – *Le Penon Plage – 40150 Seignosse – ☎05 58 43 15 30 – mairie-seignosse@seignosse.com – open May-15 Jun and Sep, 11am-6pm, mid-Jun-end Aug, 10.30am-7.30pm – closed 15 Sep-May.* If you want a change from the beach, this aquapark has a host of attractions that will keep the whole family entertained. Facilities include a spa, swimming pool and waterslides, as well as table tennis, volley ball, badminton and a children's play area. Bar, fast food and picnic area on site.

VTT Loisirs – *116 av. des Tisserands – ZA de Pédebert – ☎05 58 41 75 41 – www.vtt.france.com – open daily except Sun 9am-noon and 3-7pm; daily in summer – closed Jan and afternoons of public hols.* Mountain bike rental.

Golf-Hôtel – *Av. du Belvédère – ☎05 58 41 68 30 – golfseignosse@wanadoo.fr – open daily except Thu 8am-7.30pm, winter 9am-5pm – closed 1 Jan-1 Mar.* This

attractive 18-hole golf course is situated in a rolling estate surrounded by pine trees. Clubhouse, hotel and restaurant.
Casino Barrière d'Hossegor – *119 av. Maurice-Martin* – ☎*05 58 41 99 99* – *www.casinos-barriere.com – open Jul-Aug, daily until 5am; rest of the year, Sun-Thu 10am-3am, Fri-Sat until 4am*. Built in 1923, this building is an excellent example of the architecture of the Basque-Landes region. In 1998, the Barrière Group turned it into a games complex with a casino (50 slot machines), tennis courts, mini-golf, swimming pool, fronton, discotheque and restaurant.

SHOPPING

Rip Curl – *407 av. de la Tuilerie* – ☎*05 58 49 99 71 – open Mon-Sat 10am-1pm and 3-7pm*. This is the factory outlet of Rip Curl, manufacturer of surfboards, swimsuits and surfing accessories. The company organises world surfing championships here every year. A second shop can found on Avenue du Touring-Club-de-France.

BARS AND CAFES

Marcot' – *Av. du Touring-Club-de-France* – ☎ *05 58 43 52 15 – summer, daily 8am-1am; rest of the year, Tue-Sun 8am-8pm*. Founded in 1927, this pastry shop-cum-tea room sells a wide selection of home-made cakes, ice creams and chocolates.

SPORT AND LEISURE IN CAPBRETON

Bowling du Port – *Av. Maurice-Martin* – ☎*05 58 72 33 72 – Apr-Sep, 5pm-3am; Oct-Mar, Wed, Sat-Sun 3pm-3am, Tue-Fri 5pm-3am*. This little complex near the marina has eight bowling lanes and a beer and cocktail bar with a lively atmosphere. Terrace overlooking a busy street. Salads and pizzas to eat in or take away.

Capbreton Surf Club – *Bd François-Mitterrand* – ☎*05 58 72 33 80 – www. capbretonsurfclub.com – Mar-Nov, Mon-Sat 10am-noon and 2-5pm*. This club organises surfing and bodyboard courses.
Centre équestre L'Appaloosa, Parc-de-Loisirs-du-Gaillou – *Bd des Cigales* – ☎*05 58 41 80 30 – open daily 9am-noon and 2pm-midnight; covered riding arena open all year*. This little riding school has around 30 horses and organises rides through the woods or on the beach all year round. The centre also holds riding lessons with a certified teacher in a covered riding arena.
Parc des Sports – *R. du Stade* – ☎ *05 58 72 49 93 – open daytime*. The facilities available at the Parc des Sports include football and rugby pitches, a fronton, a gymnasium, tennis courts and a grass-covered athletics track.
Le Jean B – *Av. Georges-Pompidou* – ☎ *06 09 73 83 27 – open late Jun to late Aug, daily 10.30am-noon and 2-6pm*. This fisherman organises ocean fishing and sight-seeing boat trips.

SHOPPING

Marché aux poissons – *Av. Georges-Pompidou – open summer, daily 9am-12.30pm and 3-6pm; rest of the year, 3-6pm*. For authentic local colour, pay a visit to the local fish market, where the catch is sold off the docks, right by the *capitainerie*. The market is also the site of festivities such as the *Tournade* that takes place in the summer. If you happen to be in Capbreton for Christmas, you will see Santa Claus himself arrive from the sea on the St-Nicolas lifeboat.

Étang Blanc

This delightful "white pool" is bordered by fishermen's huts and circled by a narrow road looping through the charming countryside and along the inviting shore.

▷ *Continue north along the D 189 which veers east after Gaillou-de-Pountaout and passes between Étang Blanc and Étang Hardy. Turn left onto the D 652 towards Soustons.*

Étang de Soustons★

The figure-8 shape of this 730ha/1 800-acre lake, fringed by reeds and surrounded by dense pine woods, makes it impossible to see the whole of it at once. All parts of the lake, however, are easily accessible through the woods.

🚶*30min round-trip on foot*. To reach it from Soustons, follow allée des Soupirs (left of the church) and then avenue du Lac as far as the landing stage, banked with flowers. Take the GR 8 signposted rambling path, to Pointe des Vergnes, to enjoy the view. Continue along the south bank, which goes round the urban development zone *"ZAC des Pêcheurs"*. A pine forest leads to a picnic area on the water's edge.

▷ *Leave Soustons west along D 652 and turn right onto a minor road just beyond the bridge spanning the Vieux-Boucau channel; Tropica Parc is 5km/3mi farther on.*

▷ *Return to the D 652 and turn right to Vieux-Boucau-les-Bains.*

Vieux-Boucau-les-Bains

The town was renamed Vieux-Boucau (Old Estuary in the local dialect) and almost abandoned in 1578, when the course of the River Adour was deviated. Today, Vieux-Boucau-les-Bains has been revived by the construction of Port d'Albret, a large tourist resort built on a 50ha/120 acre lagoon among the sand and pines. The waters of the lake are renewed each day by a dam with tide-activated locks. An **esplanade** joins Vieux-Boucau to Port-Albret, a charming spot for an evening stroll, when lights on the water sparkle and flow.

GROTTES D'ISTURITZ ET OXOCELHAYA★★

MICHELIN MAP 342: E-2

This rich archaeological site consists of two prehistoric caves hollowed out deep in the Colline de Gaztelu. The caves contain spectacular examples of colourful stalactites and stalagmites, as well as cave drawings dating back to the Palaeolithic Era.

▷ **Orient Yourself**: The caves are located between St-Palais and Hasparren; they can be reached from the village of St-Martin-d'Aberoue *(turn left down Rampe des Grottes)*.

🅿 **Parking**: Park near the entrance to the caves; there is also a picnic site here.

Ⓒ **Also see**: CAMBO-LES-BAINS, ESPELETTE.

The Caves

👐*Visit by guided tours (45min) every 20min, Jul and Aug 10am-noon and 1-6pm; Jun-Sep at 11am, noon and 2-5pm; mid-Mar to end of May and Oct to mid-Nov 2-5pm, extra tour Sun, school hols and public hols at 11am.*⊕*6.60€ (children 7-14: 3.30€).* ☎*05 59 29 64 72. www.grottes-isturitz.com.*

One above the other, the caves correspond to two different levels, each abandoned long ago, of the subterranean course of the River Aberoue. A single visit encompasses both. They witness the presence of human occupation during the Palaeolithic age, between 80 000 and 15 000 BC.

Grotte d'Isturitz

It is through this upper cave that visitors enter the lime-stone stronghold of the

mountain. It is mainly of scientific interest; you will see a **pillar** on which three reindeers have been carved one above the other, following the relief of the stone, as well as a horse. Traces of occupation by Palaeolithic Man from the

Grotte d'Oxocelhaya

B. Kaufmann/MICHELIN

Mousterian period to the Magdalenian have been discovered, showing an exceptional continuity. Excavations have revealed semi-rounded staffs incised with curvilinear ornamentation, and a number of carvings, examples of which are on display in the local museum.

Grotte d'Oxocelhaya

The second stage of the tour, in the lower cave, 15 metres below, reveals a fascinating series of chambers richly decorated with natural rock **concretions**: stalactites, stalagmites, columns, discs, translucent draperies and a glittering petrified cascade.

Moreover, two reproductions illustrate the 30 **drawings** (outlines drawn with charcoal, scraped or drawn with fingers on clay) discovered on the walls, but which you will not be able to see because of the need for preservation.

JARNAC

POPULATION 4 659

MICHELIN MAP 324: I-5

The town of Jarnac is now linked with the name of **François Mitterrand** (1916-1996) former President of France who chose to be buried in his home town in Grands' Maisons cemetery to the west of the town. The local economy is based on the distillation and shipping of brandies.

▶ **Orient Yourself**: Jarnac stands on the north bank of the River Charente in a pleasant wooded site on the edge of the "Grande Champagne" district, 14km/9mi E of Cognac.

- **Don't Miss**: Donation François-Mitterrand; Maisons Courvoisier and Louis Royer.
- **Also See**: COGNAC, ANGOULÊME.

Sights

Donation François-Mitterrand

&. ◑Open Jul and Aug daily 10am-noon and 2-6pm (last admission 30 min before closing time); Sep-Oct and Feb-Jun, daily except Mon and Tue 2-6pm. ◑Closed Nov, Dec and 1 May. ⊚5€. ☎05 45 81 38 88.
The museum, known as the Orangerie Cultural Centre, is housed in an former brandy store on the banks of Charente River. The library contains the complete collection of speeches given by François Mitterrand during his fourteen years as French president.

The vast glass building contains some of the many works of art (ceramics, engravings, paintings, sculptures, etc.) presented to François Mitterrand during his presidency by people from all over the world.

Maison Courvoisier

Place du Château. Entrance near the bridge. &.⬚Visit by guided tour (45 min), Jun -Aug 10am-6pm; May and Sep daily except Sat 10am-6pm. ◑Closed 1 May. ⊚4€ (children under 18 no charge). ☎05 45 35 56 16.
A small **museum** traces the history of spirit distillation and the different stages in the production and refinement of Cognac. The silhouette of Napoleon I on the bottles of the Courvoisier brand recalls that Emmanuel Courvoisier, the founder of the company, supplied the Emperor himself, and that in 1869 the

---

WHERE TO EAT

◔◔◔**La Ribaudière** – Port-Bourg – 16200 Bourg-Charente – 6km/3.5mi W of Jarnac. Take the N 141 and a secondary road – 05 45 81 30 54 – closed Feb school hols, 15 Oct-1 Nov, Tue lunch, Sun eve and Mon. Beyond the spruce façade of this establishment, awaits modern decor and some innovative cooking. Try the cepe and foie gras de canard soup in the winter or the thin tomato and cray-fish tart in the summer. Then let yourself be tempted by their fine Cognac.

Jarnac Thrust

In 1547 Gui Chabot, Baron de Jarnac, having been insulted by La Chataigneraie (a close friend of Henri II and one of the finest swordsmen in Europe), challenged him to a duel. The encounter, organised as a "single combat" affair subject to the will of God, took place on 10 July at St-Germain-en-Laye near Paris, in the presence of the King, the Queen, Diane de Poitiers and the entire Court. Jarnac, on the point of losing, vanquished his opponent with a thrust that was within the rules but entirely unexpected, severing La Chataigneraie's hamstring. The term **coup de Jarnac** (Jarnac thrust) has been used to describe this type of attack ever since – but with an added sense of treacherousness which may seem unfair, in the circumstances, to the memory of the battling Chabot.

firm was appointed purveyor to the Court of Napoleon III by Royal decree. A visit to one of the brandy *chais* (storehouses) includes a slide show projected onto a sphere.

Maison Louis Royer

Quai de la Charmille. &○*Open Jul-Aug daily except Mon and Tue 11am-1pm and 3-7pm, Sat 11am-1pm and 3-8pm, Sun 2-6pm.* ⊗*No charge.* ☎*05 45 81 02 72 www.louis-royer.com.*
An entrance hall with beautiful inlaid work leads into the *Espace Voyage,* an original exhibit on the various stages in the production of cognac, from the vineyard to exportation throughout the world. After this imaginative introduction, the tour continues through the *chais de vieillissement*, redolent with the aroma of ageing brandy. A temporary exhibit and reconstructed workrooms bring to life the various trades associated with the production of brandy.

Excursion

Abbaye de Bassac
7km/4.3mi E.
Bassac Abbey, founded soon after the year 1000 by Benedictine monks, was abandoned at the time of the Revolution and returned to religious life in 1947 by the Missionary Brothers of St Theresa of the Infant Jesus. A number of important relics were preserved here, including the Holy Bonds said to have been used to tie up Christ during the ritual Flagellation.
Abbey Church★ – In the 15C, the interesting façade in the Saintonge Romanesque style was given special defences,

including a gable pierced with arrow slits and flanked by watch towers. During the Revolution, an anonymous patriot inscribed the words of Robespierre on the wall: *The people of France recognise the Supreme Being and the immortality of the soul.*
Inside, the single nave with its convex vaulting and flattened east end, testifies to the far-reaching influence of the Angevin Gothic style.
On the southern side, there is a 17C painted panel representing the Entombment. The enormous monks' chancel was remodelled in the early 18C. The 40 delicately carved stalls, the monumental eagle lectern, the high-altar reredos and two small altarpieces backing the choir screen are all the work of Benedictine fathers helped by local craftsmen. This sober and elegant decoration perfectly

Bassac Abbey

complements the medieval architecture of the sanctuary.

Monastery buildings &⁀Visit by guided tour (45min) Jul–Aug daily except Mon 3-7pm. ⌨2.50€ (no charge Aug 15). ☎05 45 81 94 22. These were rebuilt in the 17C and 18C. A majestic doorway framed by Ionic columns leads to the old cloisters. The cloister galleries were demolished in 1820 (marks where the charges were rammed in are still visible) but the monastic buildings still exist. The ground floor contains the kitchens, the calefactory, a balustraded staircase in the south wing, and the old chapter-house, nowadays used as a chapel (fine 17C vaulting and modern – 1954 – stained-glass windows). There is a small garden and terrace in front of the façade overlooking the River Charente.

LACANAU-OCÉAN
POPULATION 3 142
MICHELIN MAP 335: D-4

Built along the ocean front, where huge rollers come crashing on the shore, Lacanau is a picturesque resort lying at the foot of a large expanse of sand dunes, carpeted with sea pines; these have long been exploited for timber and resin. The geometrically arranged plantations, rising and falling over sandy valleys, offer a pleasant contrast to the wide sandy beaches extending over a distance of 20km/12.4mi. It is the ideal place for cycling and surfing enthusiasts.

- **Tourist Office**: Pl. de l'Europe, 33680 Lacanau-Océan. ☎05 56 03 21 01. www.lacanau.com.
- **Orient Yourself**: Lacanau lies 55km/34mi NW of Bordeaux along the D 6. Take care driving along the roads between Bordeaux and the Atlantic Coast, which are narrow and busy with locals.
- **Don't Miss**: The nature reserves of the Étang de Cousseau and the Lac d'Hourtin.
- **Also See**: BASSIN D'ARCACHON, THE HAUT-MÉDOC (see VIGNOBLE DE BORDEAUX).

Excursions

Streams prevented from reaching the sea by a long line of dunes eventually formed a string of lakes linked by canals.

&For coin ranges, see the Legend on the cover flap.

WHERE TO STAY

⊜⊜**Hôtel Domaine Aplus** – Rte de Baganais – ☎05 56 03 91 00 – info@vitalparc.com – closed Dec and Jan – P – 57 rooms – restaurant ⊜⊜⊜. This modern hotel resort situated in the middle of a pine forest is also a riding school. Rooms, apartments and stabling for horses are all available here. The rooms are quiet, with balconies. The complex also has Indoor and outdoor swimming pools and a fitness room.

Lac de Lacanau★

This lake, a popular spot for family holidays, covers an area of 2 000ha/5 000 acres. Its 8km/5mi length teems with freshwater fish, including eels, pike and perch. It offers every imaginable water sport – swimming, sailing, windsurfing, water-skiing, canoeing and kayaking (⌐boats available for hire). The lake can also be toured on foot or by bicycle.

Étang de Cousseau

⚡⌐Guided tours: ☎05 56 91 33 65. Allow half a day; bring drinking water and mosquito repellent. Access to the lake, a natural reserve, is via a footpath through Lacanau Forest or along paved bicycle paths (leave your bike in the areas indicated at the entrance to the park as they are not allowed in the park itself).

sand. Dunes, sometimes up to 60m/197ft high, line the west bank.

Lac d'Hourtin-Carcans★

This vast, secluded and unspoiled lake, 19km/12mi long and about 3.5km/2mi wide, covers an area of more than 6 000ha/ 14 800 acres. It is like an inland sea set in a landscape of moors and forests, fringed by marshes in the north and in some parts of the east, most of which is covered in

Hourtin ≙

The village, a popular departure point for travels through the network of lakes, lagoons and canals in the south-west suitable for canoeing, is also a base for pleasure boats, following the development of a lakeside marina.

PARC NATUREL RÉGIONAL DES LANDES DE GASCOGNE★

MICHELIN MAPS 335: E-6 TO H-10

The area was once a marine depression, subsequently filled with distinctive fine sands during the Quaternary Era. The vast tract is poorly drained and below the surface is a hard impermeable layer, further reducing its fertility.

▶ **Orient Yourself:** The regional park comprises 40 municipalities of the Landes and Gironde *départements* and covers 301 500ha/745 037 acres in the heart of the mountain forests of Gascony. It stretches from the far east of the Arcachon basin to the Val de l'Eyre, including the valleys of the Grande and Petite Leyre rivers in the south and the wooded areas of the Grande-Leyre.

🐾 **Don't Miss:** Walking or cycling through the park; the Écomusée de la Grande Lande.

🕐 **Organising Your Time:** You can drive through the park in a day, but if you want to spend time walking, swimming and visiting the area, there is plenty to keep you occupied for two to three days.

Kids **Especially for Kids:** Marquèze; leisure activities such as swimming, cycling and horse-drawn carriage rides through the park.

👣 **Also See:** BASSIN D'ARCACHON, ARCACHON, BORDEAUX, BISCAROSSE, CHÂTEAU DE LA BRÈDE, MIMIZAN, MONT-DE-MARSAN.

A Bit of History

Development of the region since the Second Empire has concentrated on the extension of the forest, with pine and deciduous forests planted thickly between the Gironde Landes and the River Adour. Part of this territory has now been given special protection as the Parc naturel régional des Landes de Gascogne (Landes of Gascony Regional Nature Park). The park was designed for the protection of wildlife and its environment: permission was given for the restoration of several churches along the route of Santiago de Compostela, the creation of the **Écomu-** sée de la Grande Lande★ (an open-air museum including the sites of Marquèze, Luxey, Moustey), the **Parc Ornithologique du Teich** (👣 *see BASSIN D'ARCACHON*), as well as reserves, study centres, etc.

Heart of the Park Tour

127km/79mi – allow all day

This route goes through the great Landes Forest, crossed by the Grande and Petite Leyre rivers, with its areas of regeneration, its glades, its hunting grounds and

Address Book

⏱ For coin ranges, see the Legend on the cover flap.

WHERE TO STAY

⊜**Chambre d'hôte Mme Boschetti** – *46 rte de Badet – 33770 Salles – 8km/5mi NW of Belin-Béliet dir. Arcachon –* ☎*05 56 88 47 24 – ⊭ – 4 rooms.* Built in 1905, this reasonably-priced bed and breakfast situated on the edge of the Landes forest has light, spacious rooms furnished in 1950s style. Bourgeois-style breakfast room. Calm, peaceful environment.

⊜**Chambre d'hôte Les Arbousiers** – *Le Gaille – 40630 Sabres – 7.5km/4.5mi W of Sabres via the D 44 –* ☎*05 58 07 52 52 – ⊭ – reserv. required – 6 rooms – meals ⊜⊜*. This typical Landaise house with its handsome wooden frame is simple and elegant. Set in a clearing of the pine forest, it has plain, cosy rooms and a friendly owner with a passion for birds.

⊜⊜**Chambre d'hôte Chez M. et Mme Clément** – *1 r. du Stade – 33830 Belin-Béliet –* ☎*05 56 88 13 17 – maison.clem@ wanadoo.fr – ⊭ – 5 rooms.* A handsome 19C bourgeois house in a park graced by venerable old trees. The refined decor features oak woodwork, waxed parquet floors and marble fireplaces; the rooms are bright and most have direct access to the garden. One self-catering cottage.

WHERE TO EAT

⊜⊜**Le Haut-Landais** – *Pl. du Bourg-40410 Moustey –* ☎*05 58 07 77 85 – info@lehautlandais.com – closed mid-Oct-Feb and Mon.* On the village square, this auberge has been welcoming travellers since the 17C. Dutch-born but Landais by adoption, the restaurant owner serves specialities from both places: duck, roast pigeon and the 'Port d'Amsterdam' platter. The restaurant also has two self-catering cottages.

⊜⊜**Café de Pissos** – *Au bourg – 40410 Pissos –* ☎*05 58 08 90 16 – closed 20-27 Jan, 12 Nov-6 Dec, Sun eve, Tue eve and Wed except Jul-Aug.* Century-old plane trees shelter the terrace of this family auberge in the middle of town which also serves as the villagers' local watering hole. Simple regional cuisine. A few modest rooms.

⊜⊜**Ferme-auberge du Jardin de Violette** – *Manoir des Jourets – 40120 Lencouacq –* ☎*05 58 93 03 90 – closed Sun eve, Mon-Tue – ⊭ – reserv. required.* Home-grown produce has pride of place in this restaurant, which is housed in attractively renovated old stables in the heart of the Landais forest. Unusual varieties such as Chinese artichokes and golden purslane accompany poultry raised on the farm. Home-made Armagnac and aperitif. One self-catering cottage available.

---

typical low houses. The **Écomusée de la Grande Lande★**, comprising three separate sites near the villages of Sabres, Luxey and Moustey in the heart of the Parc naturel régional des Landes de Gascogne evokes the daily life and traditional activities of the region in the 18C and 19C. The whole region is ideally suited to outdoor tourism and can be explored on horseback, by foot or by bicycle: a bicycle path goes from Hostens to Mios.

Belin-Béliet

Eleanor of Aquitaine was born in this village in 1123. A bas-relief in her memory stands on the site of the castle built by the dukes of Aquitaine *(access via rue Ste-Quitterie; follow signpost to Hôtel Aliénor)*.

To the north of town is the **Centre d'Animation du Graoux**, which offers courses about the environment and outdoor sports activities.

▶ *Leave Belin-Béliat eastwards via the D 110. At Joué, turn right along the D 110ES to Moustey via Peyrin and Biganon.*

Moustey

Two churches made of ferrous rock known locally as **garluche** stand side by side on the town's main square. A walled-up doorway in the south wall was originally used by *cagots* (outcasts). Église Notre-Dame, to the south, houses the **Musée du Patrimoine Religieux et des Croy-**

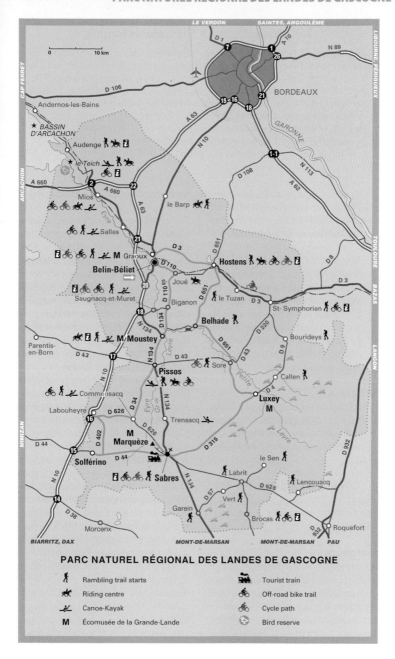

PARC NATUREL RÉGIONAL DES LANDES DE GASCOGNE

Symbol	Description	Symbol	Description
🚶	Rambling trail starts	🚂	Tourist train
🐎	Riding centre	🚵	Off-road bike trail
🛶	Canoe-Kayak	🚲	Cycle path
M	Écomusée de la Grande-Lande	🐦	Bird reserve

ances **Populaires** devoted to local religious heritage and popular beliefs. ⏱*Open Jul–Aug 10am-noon and 2-7pm.* 🎟*4€ (children: 2.50€).* ☎*05 58 08 31 31.*

▸ *Take the N 134 S to Pissos.*

Pissos

The church, just outside the village, has a belfry with a shingle roof. Route de Sore, which runs through an old Landes inn, leads to the **Airial artisanal** in which contemporary art, regional gourmet specialities and crafts are exhibited (cera-

Houses and Huts of the Landes Region

An integral part of the landscape are the whitewash roughcast houses typical of the Landes region. They are usually built in glades, inherited from the former *airial*, or forest clearing. They are built on one level and only have an attic with a skylight in the tiled roof. A wide canopy, supported by wooden pillars, the *estantade*, protects the front of the house. Small huts once used by resin tappers to store their tools can still be seen along the forest roads. These low, rectangular, rather basic huts are made of Landes pine (planks assembled horizontally) and covered with a gently sloping tiled roof. Two huts are often joined together.

mics, wood and copper crafts, fabrics and jewellery). Opposite the centre an old shepherd's fold has been transformed into a **glass-blowers' workshop.**

▶ *Take the D 34 S. At Commensacq, the D 626 right leads to Labouheyre. As you enter the town there is a former stopping place on the pilgrimage route to Santiago de Compostela. A road to the left, by the church (follow the signs for the gendarmerie), leads to Solferino. It crosses the Parc de Peyre (forest cabins and a riding centre).*

Solferino

In 1857, Napoleon III bought some 7 000ha/ 16 800 acres of marshland. After draining it, he set up an experimental area with model farms. A village was created in 1863.

▶ *Take the D44 E to Sabres*

The train for Marquèze leaves from **Sabres** station.

Marquèze★★

Access only by train from Sabres. ♿ ⓒ *Tourist steam train from Sabres every 40min from early Jun–mid-Sep 10am-noon and 2-5.20pm; Apr-May and mid-Sep–end of Oct 2-4.40pm, Sun and public hols 10am-noon and 2-4.40pm.* ⊛*9.50€.* ☎*05 58 08 31 31 www.parc-landes-de-gascogne.fr.* 🄺🄸🄳🅂This sector of the Écomusée covers almost 70ha/173 acres in the protected region of the Vallées de l'Eyre and comprises a delightful collection of traditional buildings – some original, others reconstructions on their former site – from the 30 or so structures which stood

here when the clearing was occupied by three families.

The **airial**, for centuries an oasis in the bleak moorland and subsequently a glade in the pines which replaced the moorland, is a sort of huge esplanade, mainly planted with oak trees, where the houses and farm buildings were grouped. It is here that the master's house *(marquèze)*, dating from 1824, stands. It combines stout beams, cob walls and a three-pitched roof, and, like the other buildings, has no foundations, relying on sound timber construction for its stability.

Nearby, the more modest house with less massive beams was where the servants **(brassiers)** were lodged. Beyond is the tenant farmer's house with its barns, pigsties, beehives and chicken runs.

A path beneath the trees leads to the miller's house (1834) and the **mill** itself, with its two separate millstones for grinding the smaller and the larger varieties of grain. The woodland walk ends at the **charbonnières** (charcoal burners), where old trees were burnt very slowly to produce charcoal, before returning to the airial where an information centre presents a selection of documents, maps, models and an illustrated commentary *(in French)* on the museum and the agricultural and pastoral life of the region. A nearby sheepfold contains a flock of grazing sheep; they were once used to clear the moorland for agricultural use and enrich it with their droppings.

On the other side of the railway, between an aviary and an ancient well, there is a second big house, known as Le Mineur, which was transferred from another *airial*, and an exhibition explaining the old pastoral farming system. In the

Back in Time in Marquèze

The Écomusée de la Grande Lande organises several events aiming at reviving 19C traditions from the Landes region.

La Maillade, which takes place on 1 May, is the festival of spring: Maypoles, decorated with flowers are planted in order to honour a young lady or a friend.

Mid-May is the time for **shearing sheep**. Their wool will then be carded, spun and knitted.

Haymaking takes place during the first half of June: hay is cut in the fields and saved to feed cattle in winter.

The biggest **laundry** of the year; known as the *bugade*, takes place in the middle of June. Ash replaces washing powder. The washing is rinsed in the river.

The 24 June is the **feast of St John** and midsummer's night. Large wooden crosses are burnt in the hope of securing good crops.

Finally, throughout the fine season (from the end of March to October), it is possible to watch craftsmen at work: tapping of pine trees, kneading and cooking bread, grinding rye, ploughing with oxen etc.

Information – ☎*05 58 08 31 31 www.parc-landes-de-gascogne.fr.*

model orchard over 1 600 species of fruit trees native to the Grande Lande are tended; they include varieties of apple, plum, cherry, medlar and quince.

▶ *Return to Sabres or go left via the D 315 in the direction of Luxey.*

Luxey

The **Jacques and Louis Vidal Resinous Products Workshop** illustrates the traditional local industry based on resin products which dates from the beginning of the Industrial Revolution; the workshop operated commercially from 1859 to 1954. Visitors may follow every stage from the arrival of the tapped pine-tree sap to the final storage of refined turpentine. ⏱*Open early Jun–mid-Sep daily 10am-noon and 2-7pm; end of Mar–end of May and mid-Sep –early-Oct 2-6pm, Sun and public hols 2-7pm.* ☜*4€ (children: 2.50€).* ☎*05 58 08 31 31; www.parc-landes-de-gascogne.fr*

▶ *The D 651 leads to Belhade via Sore and Argelouse.*

Belhade

In the Gascon dialect, this town's name means beautiful fairy. It has a church with a belfry-wall and a doorway with attractive sculpted columns. To the west, on the left, there is a view of the Château de Belhade with round crenellated towers.

Hostens

Between 1933 and 1963, lignite was excavated out of open quarries. The quarries were then flooded by the rising water table, forming the lakes of Lamothe and Bousquey. The **Domaine départemental d'Hostens**, a leisure park covering 500ha/1 200 acres, has been developed on the site. A nature trail guides visitors through the park.

▶ *Return to Belin-Bélietvia via the D 3 and the N 10.*

ABBAYE DE LIGUGÉ

MICHELIN MAP 322: H-5

Ligugé claims the title of the Oldest Monastery in the West. After more than three centuries of interruption, monastic life here was resumed in 1853 by Benedictine monks from Solesmes.

▶ **Orient Yourself**: 8km/5mi S of Poitiers on the west bank of the River Clain.

A Bit of History

Under the sign of St Martin

In the year AD 361 a soldier, born in what is now Hungary, established a monkish cell here in the ruins of a Gallo-Roman villa in the Clain Valley; he later became St Martin, the patron saint of France. Martin was a young officer in the Roman army when he encountered a beggar numb with the cold one day at the gates of Amiens; he at once took off his cloak, sliced it in two with his sword and gave half to the shivering pauper. Subsequently in a dream, he saw Christ wrapped in the shared cape, he had himself baptised.

Martin became a disciple of Hilaire (Hilary), the Bishop of Poitiers, and spent almost 10 years here at Ligugé. His burning faith and profound sense of charity were soon spoken of throughout the region, and in the year 370 the inhabitants of Tours entreated him to become their bishop. Not far from Tours, he founded the monastery of Marmoutier.

St Martin died at Candes, on the banks of the Loire, in 397. The monks of Ligugé and those of Marmoutier disagreed over who was to have charge of the body, but the men of Tours had their way by placing the corpse in a boat and rowing silently away after nightfall while their rivals slept. It was then that the miracle occurred: although it was November, as the vessel neared the town leaves appeared on the trees, flowers blossomed and birds sang. The warm autumn days of Indian summer are known in France as l'été de la St Martin.

Abbey Sights

Excavations

The digs here, which were started in 1953 in front of and beneath the nave of the present St Martin's Church, have revealed an exceptional series of pre-Romanesque structures which incorporate the remains of a Gallo-Roman villa, an early basilica (discovered in 1956) dating from before the year AD 370, a 4C martyrium (votive chapel), a 6C church and a 7C basilica. Some noteworthy features include:

♦ On the left, the wall of one room of the Gallo-Roman villa, with a floor made of a kind of concrete. On the right is an arcade of the martyrium, which succeeded this room.

♦ The south transept of the 7C basilica, which forms the foundation of the present belfry; a vault dating from AD 1000; a 4C Ionic capital (reused); a model and plans of the original buildings.

♦ Beneath the present nave, the crypt of the 7C basilica. Behind this is the apse of the primitive basilica built by Martin in the 4C.

♦ The southern apsidal chapel of this same 7C basilica. The ornamental tiling, enamelled segments in geometric patterns, is the oldest of its kind in France.

Église St-Martin

Today this is the parish church of Ligugé. It was rebuilt in the early 16C by Geoffroy d'Estissac, at that time Prior of Ligugé. The **west front** and its belfry, both in the Flamboyant Gothic style, are extremely elegant. On one leaf of the carved Renaissance doors St Martin is depicted dividing his cloak.

Monastery

A number of ancient features are included within the monastery as a whole. A round tower in the outer wall is known as the Rabelais Tower because the celebrated story-teller spent a lot of time here between 1524 and 1527, when he was working as secretary to Geoffroy d'Estissac.

A community of 40 Benedictine monks inhabits the monastery today. The site so impressed the writer **J-K Huysmans** (1848-1907) that he stayed here as an oblate – a lay person attached to a religious community in order to benefit from its spiritual support – in 1901. The painters Rouault and Forain and the poet Louis Le Cardonnel were received at the same time. The poet Paul Claudel, brother of the sculptress Camille Claudel, was also a postulant here.

In the **galerie d'émaux** there is an exhibition of the enamelwork that has made this monastery famous throughout the world. *Open daily 10-11.15am and 2.30-5.45pm, Sun and public hols 11.15am-noon, 3-4.15pm and 5.15-6pm.* 05 49 55 21 12 www.abbaye-liguge.com.

The visit ends with a tour of the small **museum** (*As for the Galerie d'Émaux*) in which the monastic history and geography of the area is illustrated.

LUÇON

POPULATION 9 311

MICHELIN MAP 316: I-9 – LOCAL MAP SEE MARAIS POITEVIN

This charming episcopal town, on the borders of the Poitou marshlands and plain, was once a seaport. Today, it is an important trading and agricultural centre.

- **Tourist Information**: Sq. Édouard-Herriot, 85400 Luçon. 02 51 56 36 52. www.ville-lucon.fr.
- **Orient Yourself**: Luçon lies W of Fontenay-le-Comte and SE of La Roche-sur-Yon, some 21km/13mi inland from the coast.
- **Don't Miss**: Cathédrale Notre-Dame; Jardin Dumaine.
- **Also See**: FONTENAY-LE-COMTE, LES SABLES-D'OLONNE, LE MARAIS POITEVIN.

A Bit of History

Richelieu

On 21 December 1608, in the cathedral here, a pale-faced young man accepted the homage of a handful of canons: Armand du Plessis de Richelieu, aged only 23, was taking over "the ugliest bishopric in France, a mud-caked backwater" – as he himself described it to a friend soon after his arrival.

He was hardly exaggerating: the town had been ruined by the Wars of Religion and by illness and fever brought on by the damp of the surrounding marshes. Such fevers forced the young bishop to retire from time to time to his 16C country château, for the Bishop's residence, which had been deserted for 30 years, had not a single fireplace in working order.

Richelieu refused to be discouraged, however, and persevered with his mission, restructuring the See and its clergy, restoring the cathedral and residence, and founding a seminary. He was also responsible for the creation of a town bearing his name south-west of Tours, near the River Loire.

At the same time, the man who was later to play an important role as State Adviser to Louis XIII was enhancing his prospects by intensive study of history and theology; by cultivating friendships with diplomats and such influential figures as Father Joseph (who subsequently became Richelieu's mentor on matters of foreign policy), Cardinal de Bérulle (a major force during the Catholic renais-

WHERE TO EAT

L'Oranger – 2km/1.2mi N of Luçon on the La Roche-sur-Yon road – 02 51 56 11 32 – contact@oranger.fr – closed mid-Sep-early Oct, Sun eve and Mon. Dine either on the veranda or in the contemporary-style dining room in this charming restaurant just outside Luçon. L'Oranger also has a few simple guestrooms on the premises.

M. Thiery/MICHELIN

The cathedral in Luçon

sance in the 17C) and the Abbot of St-Cyran (whom he was to have imprisoned, many years later, at Vincennes).

Sights

Cathédrale Notre-Dame

This former abbey church became a cathedral in 1317. As well as Richelieu, the See counts at least one other celebrated bishop on its roll: Nicolas Colbert, the brother of the Minister, who governed the bishopric from 1661 to 1671. The church, built of fine honey-coloured limestone, is largely in the Gothic style, although the northern arm of the transept dates back to Romanesque times. The west front was entirely remodelled in the late 17C under the supervision of the architect François Leduc. The overall balance and strictly Classical layout of this façade (superimposed antique orders, scrolled decoration etc) contrast vividly with the slender, tapered Gothic spire which was rebuilt in 1828 and rises to a height of 85m/279ft. The façade as a whole serves today as a belfry-porch. The well-proportioned nave and chancel date from the Gothic period; the latter is adorned with ornamental woodwork and a rich 18C canopy. Richelieu himself is said to have preached from a pulpit, delicately painted with fruit and flowers, in the north aisle. In the south transept is a 16C *Deposition (restored)* from the Florentine School. The 19C organ in the gallery is by Cavaillé-Coll.

Évêché (Episcopal Palace)

South of the cathedral is the 16C façade of the old bishops' residence. Entrance – via the **cloisters** – is through a doorway surmounted by a Gothic arch framing the armorial bearings of Louis, Cardinal de Bourbon, who was Bishop of Luçon from 1524 to 1527. Galleries juxtaposing both Gothic and Renaissance elements were added in the 16C. The western side is pierced by Renaissance windows.

LUSIGNAN

POPULATION 2 677
MICHELIN MAP 322: G-6

This small Poitou town lies along the crest of a promontory overlooking on one side the valley of the River Vonne, on the other a vale in which a business district has been built flanking the main road to Poitiers.

- **Tourist Information**: Pl. du Bail – BP 10, 86600 Lusignan. ☎05 49 43 61 21.
- **Orient Yourself**: Between the N 10 and A 10 motorway SW of Poitiers.
- **Also See**: POITIERS, TUMULUS DE BOUGON.

A Bit of History

Mélusine the Fairy

A long time ago, according to legend, Raimondin, the young Comte du Poitou, accidentally killed his uncle with a hunting spear while the two men were grappling with an enraged wild boar. Wandering distraught in Coulombiers Forest, not far from Lusignan, Raimondin saw a spring suddenly well up at the foot of a bluff on top of which appeared the filmy white silhouettes of three enchanting female figures. One of them was the fairy Mélusine, whom the young noble determined to make his bride.

Despite her mortal marriage, Mélusine retained her magic powers; with a wave of her wand, she conjured up dream palaces. In this way she created not only Lusignan Castle, on the spot where she met Raimondin, but also the fortresses of Pouzauges, Tiffauges, Mervent, Vouvant, Parthenay and Châteaumur. Yet the fairy bride hid a shameful secret from her past. Having murdered her own father, she was condemned to be transformed, every Saturday night, into a creature with the head and torso of a woman, while below her navel she was an odious serpent.

One fine Saturday, however, consumed by jealousy at Mélusine's repeated absences, Raimondin burst through the door of the room where she bathed. Stupefied, he discovered his wife's changed and writhing body as she combed her long golden tresses. Mélusine at once dived out of the window, assumed the form of a giant snake, and slithered sinuously three times around the town and the castle before hurtling down onto the gatehouse tower of the château, and vanishing into thin air.

Sights

Castle ruins

The fortress, built at the extremity of the promontory overlooking the steep-sided Vonne Valley, belonged originally to the Lusignan family, whose members, at one time, ruled over Jerusalem and Cyprus. All that remains of the castle today is a group of buildings occupied by a museum, along with subterranean chambers and the foundations of several towers which were once part of the surrounding fortifications. In the 18C the castle grounds were transformed into the Promenade de Blossac, named after the steward. An avenue of lime trees surrounded by flower gardens now leads to a terrace from which there is an attractive **view** of the Vonne Valley, spanned by a 432m/475yd viaduct.

Church

This fine example of Poitou Romanesque architecture with particularly impressive proportions was built by the Lusignan family in the 11C. The recumbent statue in the south aisle is Gothic. The high altar stands above a crypt with triple barrel vaulting. Outside, a porch added to the southern elevation in the 15C faces an interesting house with half-timbered, projecting upper storeys which dates from the same period.

MAILLEZAIS★

POPULATION 934

MICHELIN MAP 316: L-9 – LOCAL MAP SEE MARAIS POITEVIN

A little way outside this Poitou village, on the edge of the flat marshlands which make up the Marais Poitevin, stand the imposing ruins of Maillezais Abbey.

▶ **Orient Yourself**: The abbey is situated 12km/7.5mi SE of Fontenay-le-Comte.
◉ **Also See**: FONTENAY-LE-COMTE, NIORT, LE MARAIS POITEVIN.

A Bit of History

Foundations

The abbey was founded by Guillaume Fier-à-Bras, Comte de Poitou, at the end of the 10C. At that time the limestone rise on which it is built was washed by the Atlantic surf – part of the enormous Gulf of Poitou, since silted up and sealed in to become the Marais Poitevin wetlands. The abbey, dedicated to St Peter, was first inhabited by monks of the Benedictine order, who honoured the arms of St Rigomer here. In the 13C it was sacked by Geoffroi la Grand-Dent, a member of the Lusignan family who claimed to be the son of Mélusine, and who was subsequently used by Rabelais as a model for the boisterous and brave giant Pantagruel in his novel of the same name. In 1317 the French pope John XXII elevated Maillezais to the status of a bishopric but allowed the monks to remain in the abbey. During the Wars of Religion most of the buildings were destroyed and the Bishop of Luçon, Richelieu, ordered the episcopal seat to be transferred to La Rochelle.

Geoffroy d'Estissac

Between 1518 and 1542 the Bishop of Maillezais was Geoffroy d'Estissac, a Périgord man who seemed to collect livings as a hobby: he was Abbot of Celles-sur-Belle, of St-Liguaire near Niort, of Cadouin in Périgord, Prior of Ligugé and Hermanault, near Fontenay-le-Comte, and Dean of St-Hilaire de Poitiers.

Geoffroy was a great builder, constantly altering and improving the establishments for which he was responsible; it was he who started the construction of the castle at Coulonges-sur-l'Autize, decorative elements of which were subsequently transferred to the Château de Terre-Neuve at Fontenay-le-Comte.

The erudite and liberal bishop welcomed Rabelais to Maillezais when the young monk was expelled from Fontenay in 1523, and for three years employed him as secretary. Rabelais followed him to

several other ecclesiastical residences in the Poitou region. Later, from Rome, he sent d'Estissac the first seeds of the green vegetable which became known as *Salade Romaine* (Cos Lettuce).

Agrippa d'Aubigné

The writer Agrippa d'Aubigné (1552-1630) was born in the Saintonge region and later became a close friend of Henri IV; he was the grandfather of Mme de Maintenon *(for her biographical sketch, see NIORT)*. An ardent Protestant, he was condemned to death four different times for his religious views. A scholar as much as a poet, he wrote among many other works a Huguenot *chanson de geste* entitled *Les Tragiques* (Tragedies). From 1584 to 1619 Aubigné spent much of his time either in his fort at Doignon, near Maillé south of Maillezais, or within the abbey itself, where he was host to Protestant troops fortifying the outer walls.

Abbaye de Maillezais★

Allow 45min. ⊙*Open Jun-Sep 10am-7pm; Oct-May 9.30am-12.30pm and 1.30-6pm.* ⊙*Closed the last 3 weeks of Jan.* ⊛*5€.* ☎*02 51 87 22 80.*

Much of the fortified wall built around the monastery on Aubigné's orders is still standing. The work transformed the abbey into a true fortress: on the left of the entrance a bastion shaped like the

Abbaye ruins

B. Kaufmann/MICHELIN

prow of a ship faces the Marais wetlands. It was surmounted by a bartizan watchtower, and because the prow pointed due south, it also served as a giant sundial.

Abbey church

Building of the church began in the early 11C, though only the narthex and the wall of the north aisle remain from this period. The narthex was flanked by two square towers, following a pattern established in Normandy where abbey churches were distinguished by tower strong points on either side of the west front. The façade of the church here was later incorporated into the fortified wall built by Aubigné.

The three tall, crowned openings piercing the existing aisle wall reveal that the nave was altered in the 13C. The aisles were originally topped by galleries – again as in Norman abbeys.

The transept, of which only part of the northern arm remains, was a 14C Gothic addition. It is possible to climb to the top of one of the truncated turrets flanking its gable, from which there is a good general view of the ruins, the village and the marshes. The outlines of the huge chancel, which was rebuilt in the 16C by Geoffroy d'Estissac, can still be made out.

Monastery

Most of the monastic buildings date from the 14C. The foundations of the old cloisters have been uncovered, along with sections of the paving, a 12C storeroom, a *lavabo* where the monks washed their hands before entering the refectory, a well and a number of abbots' or bishops' tombstones.

One wing of the monastery still stands and includes the ancient salt cellar (basement); the octagonal kitchen, now housing an exhibition of items discovered during the excavations – scrolled modillions, capitals etc – and the refectories (ground floor); the guests' dorter (dormitory) and infirmary with its large central fireplace (first floor).

Boat trip

Pedestrian access from the parking area of the abbey. ⛵ *Embarcadère de l'Abbaye,* ☎*02 51 87 21 87; Aria-Loisirs,* ☎*02 51 87 14 00; or Le Petit Port Sauvage,* ☎*02 51 00 71 77.*

A ride in a typical flat-bottomed boat propelled by a long pole along the canals of **Green Venice**, as this part of the Marais Poitevin is known locally, is an excellent complement to the tour of the abbey (interesting views of the abbey).

Nieul-sur-l'Autise

8km/5mi NE.

This village grew around an old **abbey** (♿🕐*open Jun-Sep 10am-7pm, Oct-May 9.30am-12.30pm and 1.30-6pm;* 🕐*closed the last 3 weeks of Jan;* ⛵*5€, children under 18 no charge);* ☎*02 51 50 43 00)* founded in 1068. In the 13C monks began to drain the neighbouring marshes. The abbey was secularised in 1715 and soon abandoned. The Romanesque abbey church in Poitou style was restored in the 19C and features a richly carved west front. The square **cloisters**⋆ are original and have Romanesque galleries offering good views.

Maison de la Meunerie

🕐*Open Jun-Sep 10.30am-12.30pm and 2-7pm; Easter and Nov school hols 2.30-6pm; May, Sat-Sun 3-6pm.* ⛵*3.50€.* ☎*02 51 52 47 43.*

This restored old watermill now houses a museum: the mill workings and domestic rooms of the miller and his family are on view.

LE MARAIS BRETON-VENDÉEN★

MICHELIN MAP 316: E-6 TO F-7

This coastal marshland stretches from Bourgneuf to St-Gilles-Croix-de-Vie. The entire area covers more than 20 000ha/49 500 acres.

▸ **Orient Yourself**: North of the Beauvoir hills, the Machecoul wetlands are separated from the former island of Bouin by the Dain saltwater canal. To the south, wetlands known as Monts and Challans are divided by the Perrier Canal.
🞈 **Don't Miss**: The Passage du Gois.
🞈 **Also See:** LOGIS DE LA CHABOTTERIE, ÎLE DE NOIRMOUTIER.

A Bit of Geography

In times past, the coastline was dotted with islands (Bouin, Beauvoir, Monts, and Riez) which acted as dams, slowly silting up the gulf. Like the Marais Poitevin, these salt-marshes have been drained over the centuries as canals and saltwater channels were dug out first by 17C monks, then by Dutch engineers.

Today, the open expanse seen from above is a patchwork of green fields, preferred grazing ground for local species of horses, cows and sheep. The old salt flats have mostly been transformed into pastureland or dammed and flooded for commercial fishing purposes (raising eel and mullet). On higher ground (hillocks known as *mottes*), there are still a few remaining *bourrines,* the traditional marshlander's dwelling; a low house made of straw and mud, thatched with reeds. The region's trademark windmills are found on the highest points, in the company of little villages; many of these sites were once islands. On the canals, boatmen pole their flat-bottomed *yoles* among the waterfowl.

Driving Tours

1 From Grand Étier to Étier du Dain★

Round-trip from Challans – 105km/63mi – allow 6hrs

Challans

This farm town is the region's main economic centre. Renowned for the ducks raised here, in demand by the greatest

chefs, Challans has diversified production by increasing black chicken stock as well.

In season, during the **Four Thursdays Fair,** the whole town dons an air of the early 1900s, and by-gone traditions are brought back to life: the duck market, a schoolroom, folk dancing, games, cycle races, and more.

▸ *Leave Challans to the NW on the D 948 towards Beauvoir-sur-Mer.*

Sallertaine

In the 11C, this town was still an island, when monks from Marmoutier (near Tours) founded a priory here, building a Romanesque church with a cupola.

The novelist René Bazin (1853-1932) chose Sallertaine for the setting of *La terre qui meurt,* proclaiming his attachment to the land and ancestral values. In summer, the Île aux Artisans (a crafts centre) is the starting point for a canoe trip through the marsh.

▸ *Leave Sallertaine NW for St-Urbain.*

Moulin de Rairé

🞈 *Visit by guided tour (45min) Jul and Aug 10am-noon and 2-6.30pm; Apr-Jun and Sep 2-6pm. Rest of the year by appointment.* 🞈 *3.50€ (children: 1.60€).* ☎ *02 51 35 51 82 www.moulin-a-vent-de-raire.com.*

Standing tall above the marshland, this tower windmill has been catching the breeze since its construction in the 16C. The rotating cap can be adjusted from inside the mill, and the white canvas sails use the Berton system. Along the road, you soon cross over the Grand Étier

Le Marais breton-vendéen – Saltwater canal

– *étier* means "tide channel or marsh creek".

La Bourrine à Rosalie

🕐*Open Jul and Aug 10.30am-12.30pm and 2.30-7pm; mid-Jun–end Jun and Sep 2.30-6.30pm; Easter hols and early-May–mid-Jun, Sat-Sun and public hols, 2.30-6.30pm. 1.60€ 02 51 49 43 60.*
This typical marshlander's house has a reed roof, a common room with a raised bed (in case of flooding), and a "reception room" for entertaining special guests.

▶ *Carry on along the D 199, then turn right onto the D 82.*

Salle panoramique

♿🕐*Open Jul-Aug 10am-7pm, Sun and public hols 3-7pm (last admission 1hr before closing time); May-Jun and Sep daily except Mon, Sun and public hols 10am-noon and 2-6pm; Feb-Apr, Oct and Nov school hols, daily except Mon 2-6pm. 3.40€ (children aged 7-16: 2.60€). 02 51 58 86 09.*
A lift installed in a **water tower** makes it possible to reach a vast terrace at 70m/230ft above sea level, where a lovely **view★** opens all round: to the east, the wetlands bordered by the hedgerows around Challans; to the north, the Bourgneuf Bay and the bridge to Noirmoutier Island; to the west and south, the forest of Côte des Monts.

▶ *Continue along the D 82.*

Notre-Dame-de-Monts⌂

This seaside resort is a regional landsailing centre. A bike trail leads to La Barre-de-Monts through a sweet-smelling pine forest.

Pont d'Yeu – On the south side of town, a wooden staircase has been built in the dunes to provide access to the beach at Pont d'Yeu. When the tidal reach is strongest, the sea withdraws to reveal 3km/1.8mi of rocky strand, quickly invaded by alert fishermen *(as soon as the tide turns, return to the beach without delay)*. This tidal flat may be all that remains of an isthmus which once connected Île d'Yeu to the continent, during the Ices Ages of the Quaternary Era.

▶ *Leave Notre-Dame-de-Monts to the N by a little road running parallel to the D 38.*

The picturesque **Route de la Rive** traces the border between the **Pays des Monts Forest** and the first glimmerings of the marsh. Many paths lead from the forest to the ocean, through the sea oats waving atop the dunes.

Pey de la Blet

At 41m/135ft, this is the highest point of the former island of Monts. The site has been attractively planted in pine and green oak, making it a pleasant walk to the **scenic overlook**.

Fromentine

This modest seaside resort is nestled between the ocean and the forest. Gateway to the islands, it is the point of departure for boats to Île d'Yeu (regular departures from the jetty) and for Île de Noirmoutier (by the bridge).

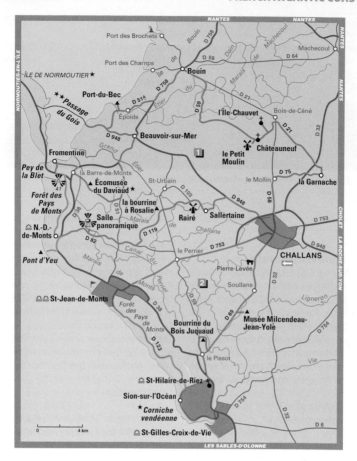

▶ *Go to the centre of Barre-de-Monts and take the road in front of the church.*

Écomusée du Marais Breton-Vendéen – de Daviaud★

&. ⓘ*Open early May–mid-Sep 10am-7pm, Sun and public hols 2-7pm; Feb-Apr, mid-Sep–early Dec daily except Mon 2-6pm. ⓘClosed Dec and Jan. ⊘4€. ☎02 51 93 84 84; www.ecomusee-ledaviaud. com.*

Housed in a late-19C sharehold farm, the **centre de découverte du Marais breton-vendéen** is a living museum of local architecture, providing visitors with a picture of the traditional lifestyle of marshland inhabitants in bygone days. In a typical *bourrine* sod house, an animated model describes the different construction methods and the way the old farms were organised; the salt store, located next to the marsh where salt

was collected, displays an exhibit on that process. The Écomusée is in a white-washed building made of clay and straw, with a reed roof, once used as a barn and stable and now featuring presentations on the local environment and wildlife (geomorphology, fauna, flora, migratory birds). A bit farther on, a reconstitution of the inside of an ordinary dwelling at the turn of the 20C gives a good idea of the austere lives led there.

You can try your own hand at some of the marshlanders' special skills, by manoeuvring a *yole* down the canal, or vaulting over a stream with a long pole.

▶ *Continue until you reach the D 51, then turn left.*

Beauvoir-sur-Mer

This village used to be on the shore, and the site of an 11C castle which was laid to siege by Henri IV in 1588, then destroyed one year later. The church, **St-Philibert**, also dates from the 11C; the bulky bell-tower rises in contrast to the elegant doorway.

▶ *Take the D 948 W out of Beauvoir-sur-Mer.*

Passage du Gois★★
See ÎLE DE NOIRMOUTIER.

▶ *Head back towards Beauvoir-sur-Mer, and turn left after 2km/1mi.*

Époids
The oyster beds of **Port-du-Bec**, situated in the bay of Bourgneuf, have been contributing to the local economy since the 1950s. South of the Bouin polders, related activities have developed, including fish hatcheries, shellfish breeding and algae farms. When the tide is low and the channel known as the Étier du Dain empties out, a veritable forest of wooden piles and foot bridges is revealed, an unusual landscape which gave the wharf the nickname of **port chinois.**

▶ *At Époids, take the D 51A, then turn left onto the D 758.*

Bouin
Once an island encircled by the ocean and the Dain tidal channel, this town suffered repeated flooding up until 1940, when a sturdy dike, 14km/8.4mi-long, was built to protect the charming streets and oyster beds of Bouin.

▶ *Leave Bouin SE on the D 21, after 2km/ 1mi, turn right on D 59.*

Châteauneuf
The bell in the church tower was made in 1487.

Le Petit Moulin – *Visit by guided tour Jul–Aug 10am-noon and 2-7pm; Feb–Jun and Sep–11 Nov, 2-7pm.* 3.50€ (children: 1.75€). 02 51 49 31 07. www.chez. com/petitmoulin. Since 1703, when it was erected to replace a wooden mill, this restored tower mill has been grinding grain. The cap can be turned from inside to face the sails to the wind, and the Berton system of adjustable vanes increases efficiency.

▶ *Leave Châteauneuf on the D 28 NE.*

Abbaye de l'Île-Chauvet
Open Jul–Sep, daily except on the last week 2-6pm. 4.50€ (children under 15: no charge). 02 51 68 13 19.
The abbey was founded around 1130 by Benedictine monks beckoned by the lord of La Garnache. The site was then a deserted island. The building was damaged during the Hundred Years War, and abandoned by the monks in 1588, in the heat of the religious wars ravaging France. In 1680, the abbey came back to life when members of the Camaldolite order moved in; they lived there until 1778. The French Revolution finally closed the book on the abbey's history.
Among the vestiges, admire the pointed arch of the doorway, its covings and decorative interlaced patterns.

S. Sauvignier/MICHELIN

Port du Bec

Address Book

☕ *For coin ranges, see the Legend on the cover flap.*

WHERE TO STAY

🛏 **Chambre d'hôte Le Pas de l'Île** – *Le Pas-de-l'Île – 85230 St-Gervais – 4 km/2.4mi SE of Beauvoir. Take the D 948, D 59 and a secondary road –* ☎02 51 68 78 51 *– closed 15 Nov-15 Mar – ⊅ – 3 rms.* This pretty little house has a strong regional flavour: arranged around a square courtyard, its ground-floor rooms have their own private entrance and are decorated with antiques. Take a stroll through the wetlands just behind the house or enjoy foie gras made from ducks reared on the property.

🛏🛏 **Antiquité** – *14 r. Gallieni – 85300 Challans –* ☎02 51 68 02 84 *– antiquitehotel@aol.com – closed 20-27 Dec – 16 rms.* A modern house built in the local style. The second-hand furniture from antique shops gives each room its own individual style. All rooms overlook the courtyard; those in the annexe are particularly attractive. Swimming-pool.

WHERE TO EAT

🍽🍽 **La Pitchounette** – *48 r. Bonne-Brise – 85230 St-Gervais – 3 km/1.8mi SE of Beauvoir on the D 938 –* ☎02 51 68 68 88 *– closed for a week in Jan, a week in Jun, 2 weeks in Sep, Mon and Tue except Jul-Aug.* This charming little white house with blue shutters is situated on the road in to St. Gervais. Thought has been given to the lighting and decor, resulting in a cosy atmosphere in the dining room. The baroque decor is original and attractive; unfortunately the terrace is rather noisy.

🍽🍽🍽 **Gite du Tourne-Pierre** – *85300 Challans – 3 km/1.8mi – take the D69 SW of Challans –* ☎02 51 68 14 78 *– closed 7-29 Mar, 5-23 Oct, Fri off-season, Sat lunch and Sun eve – reservations required.* A bit off the beaten track, this typical Vendée-style restaurant serves contemporary, home-made cuisine. The dining room opens onto an attractive garden, complete with terrace and swimming-pool. The owner, also the cook, makes everything herself, from the hors d'oeuvres to the cherries preserved in liqueur.

Nothing is left of the Camaldolite buildings. In the Benedictine wing, the dormitory and its impressive 13C roof beams are open to visitors. The pilgrims' hostel stands next to it.

▸ *Before arriving in Bois-de-Céné, take the D 21 straight ahead.*

La Garnache

Once a fortified medieval refuge in the hands of powerful feudal lords who possessed much of the surrounding land, La Garanche stands at the north-eastern border of the Marais.

Château – ⏲*Open Jul-Aug daily except Mon 2-7pm.* 👛*6€.* ☎02 51 93 11 08. The once-proud edifice was long left to sleep beneath a thick cover of vines. First erected in the 12C, it was renovated in the 13C and 15C, before Louis XIII ordered it razed in 1622; the Vendée Wars finished the task. Time has left the ramparts and two hollow towers erect, and the base of the square keep still marks the ground.

Musée Passé et Traditions – ⏲*Open Jul-Aug daily 2-7pm; mid-Jun–late Jun and early Sep–mid-Sep Sat-Sun 2-7pm.* 👛*3€ (children under 14: no charge); guided tours 4.50€.* ☎ 02 51 35 00 66 or 02 51 35 23 00. This museum offers a reconstruction of a peasant dwelling, with its common and reception rooms. There is also a collection of headdresses and clothing, farm tools, and a dairy.

▸ *Leave Garnache on the D 75 W.*

The road is bordered by pine groves.

▸ *At Mollin, the D 58 leads back to Challans.*

② **From the Shore Inland**

Round-trip from Challans – 60km/36mi – allow 3hrs

Challans
👛*See above.*

▷ *Leave Challans on the D 753 W.*

St-Jean-de-Monts ⌂⌂

A popular seaside resort (casino, golf, high-rise buildings along the promenade), the big sand beach at St-Jean is part of the long stretch reaching from Fromentine to Sion, 26km/15.6mi interrupted only by the rocky Pont d'Yeu tidal flat.

The town centre is sheltered by wooded dunes; the church was reconstructed in 1935, with due respect for its 14C charms, and the shingled belfry is 17C.

▷ *Take the coast road S (D 123).*

Corniche Vendéenne★

South of Sion, the coast road overlooks rocks sculpted by the sea into shapes reminiscent of ancient ruins; a set of five clustered together are known as **les Cinq Pineaux**. The rocky cliff face is pierced by tidal inlets and creeks. At the far end of a promontory, a plaintive wail made be heard rising from the **Trou du Diable** (Devil's Hole). When the incoming tide is strong, the sea booms into this cove and the spray seems to explode from the rocky ground of the cliff top.

The corniche ends at Grosse Terre Point; take the steps near the lighthouse to reach the bottom of the cliff.

▷ *The road continues along the Corniche de Boisvinet, lined with Belle Epoque villas. From the scenic overlook, take in the view of Pointe de la Garenne and the entrance to the port.*

St-Gilles-Croix-de-Vie ⌂

🕭 *see ST-GILLES-CROIX-DE-VIE.*

▷ *Leave St-Gilles-Croix-de-Vie via the D 38B N towards Perrier.*

To the right, the marshlands stretch all the way to the horizon.

St-Hilaire-de-Riez ⌂

This village looks out over the Vie Valley; the **church** was rebuilt in the 19C (three 17C polychrome altarpieces). ⏲*Open Jul–Aug (guided tours available) Tue 11am-noon.* ☎*02 51 54 33 89.*

▷ *Go back to the D 38B. At Pissot, go straight on via the D 59 towards Perrier.*

Ecomusée de la Bourrine du Bois Juquaud

♿⏲*Open Jul-Aug 10am-12.30pm and 2-7pm, Sun and public hols 3-7pm; May-Jun and Sep 10am-noon and 2-6pm; Sun and public hols 3-7pm; Feb-Apr, Oct, Nov and Christmas school hols daily except Mon 2-6pm.* ⏲*Closed 1 Jan, All Saints and 25 Dec.* ☜*2.20€ (children under 10 no charge).* ☎*02 51 49 27 37.*

Tucked away in a grove, this typical marsh-lander's property has been faithfully restored part and parcel.

In the farmyard, or *tcheraïe*, are several small buildings: the *bourrine* with early-20C furnishings and adjacent bread oven; the barn; shelters for keeping the wheelbarrow and the firewood dry; the chicken coop; the dairy. The vegetable garden is in the farmyard too.

▷ *Continue along the country lane, then turn left onto the D 69 towards Soullans.*

Musée Milcendeau-Jean-Yole★

♿⏲*Open Jul-Aug 10am-7pm, Sun and public hols 3-7pm; May-Jun and Sep, daily except Mon 10am-noon and 2-6pm; Feb-Mar and Nov school hols, daily except Mon 2-6pm, Sun and public hols 3-6pm.* ⏲*Closed Jan, 25 Dec.* ☜*3.80€ (children under 16 2.80€).* ☎*02 51 35 03 84.*

The museum is devoted to two artists with roots in the Marais Breton-Vendéen, the painter Charles Milcendeau (1872-1919) and the author Jean Yole. The house, in a pleasant shady grove, was purchased by Milcendeau in 1905. A student of Gustave Moreau, the young artist used sketching and pastel techniques. Influenced by Spanish styles, as the decoration of his studio illustrates, he was inspired by the daily lives of marshlanders. Indeed, the portraits and domestic scenes he painted are like an ethnological record. An audio-visual presentation provides further information.

▷ *From Soullans, the D 69 towards Challans runs along a wooded area; a menhir (Pierre Levée) testifies to prehistoric inhabitants.*

LE MARAIS POITEVIN★★

MICHELIN MAP 316: H-6 TO L9

Since 1975 the Poitou Marshlands have been a conservation area extending over three *départements*. Under clear, luminous skies, meadows are bordered by poplar and willow trees; the black boats of the marshlanders glide along innumerable watercourses.

▶ **Orient Yourself**: The Marais Poitevin is divided into the Dry Marsh, near the sea, where the Atlantic winds blow, and the Wet Marsh, farther inland, bounded on the north by the limestone plain of the Vendée and southwards by the hills of Aunis.

🧒 **Especially for Kids**: Miniature Train at Coulon; Boat Trips.

👣 **Also See**: NIORT, FONTENAY LE COMTE, ÎLE DE RÉ.

Topographical Notes

The Marshland Epic

Aiguillon Bay, an Atlantic inlet which is gradually silting up, is all that remains of the vast gulf which stretched in ancient times from the limestone plain in the north to the hills of the Aunis. The gulf, which penetrated inland as far as Niort, was scattered with rocky islets (now towns such as Maillezais, Marans and St-Michel-en-l'Herm). The former shoreline is apparent in the remains of cliffs, laid out along Moricq, Luçon, Velluire, Fontaines and Benet to the north, and Mauzé-sur-le-Mignon, Nuaillé-d'Aunis and Esnandes to the south.

Little by little the rivers Lay, Vendée, Autise and Sèvre Niortaise discharged their alluvium into the gulf, while at the same time sea currents were piling up a clay-like silt known locally as *bri*, and as a consequence the marine inlet was transformed into a huge salt-marsh.

Drainage work began in the 13C when monks from the neighbouring abbeys dredged out the Canal des Cinq-Abbés (Five Abbots' Canal) which drained the northern part of the swamp.

The work, interrupted by wars, was resumed under Henri IV by an engineer from Bergen-op-Zoom in Holland, leading to the progressive colonisation of the marshlands. Around Aiguillon Bay itself Dutch-style polders protected by dikes were reclaimed from the sea between the 16C and the 19C.

The Marais Today

The marshes, extending on either side of the River Sèvre Niortaise, cover an area of 80 000ha/198 000 acres.

The general configuration of the Marais includes a network of embankments or

---

Eels

Abundant in both the Marais Poitevin and the Marais Breton-Vendéen, the European eel *(Anguilla anguilla)* remains for some 10 years in fresh water, where it acquires its characteristic silver colour, before swimming down estuaries and across the Atlantic Ocean, a journey of about 6 000km/3 728mi, in order to breed at great depths in the Sargasso Sea (near Bermuda).

The larvae then migrate back across the Atlantic and reach the coasts of Europe between seven and nine months later. Upon their arrival, the transparent young eels swim up estuaries and rivers between November and March. While they are growing, they are called yellow eels.

Eels are caught with wicker hoop nets or with a *vermée*, a piece of rope on which worms have been tied and which is hung from a long rod. As eels do not like light, fishing is usually done at night.

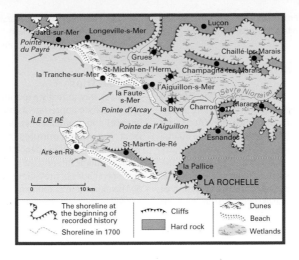

dikes, known locally as *bots*, along the top of which run roads and tracks and below which are the principal channels *(contrebots)*. When the rivers draining into the marshes are in spate, excess water surges into subsidiary channels *(achenaux)*, which divert the flow again into *rigoles* and finally *conches*, marked by lines of small trees. Between these waterways the land, which is extremely fertile, is used both for crops and for grazing.

Fauna

The marshes attract a multitude of birds, some of them migratory, looking for food, for a place to rest or somewhere to nest.

Various species can be observed, depending on the season: gulls and terns, wild ducks, geese, large waders such as herons, egrets, spoonbills and storks, and small wading birds such as sandpipers, plovers, redshanks, oystercatchers, stilts, avocets and lapwings.

The furry snout of the **nutria** *(Myocastor coypus)*, a large, reddish-brown rodent which proliferates in the Wet Marsh, can often be seen skimming along the water. The discreet **common or Eurasian otter** *(lutra lutra)* with its sleek brown coat is more difficult to spot, as it rarely comes out of its burrow in the day time. You can see where it has been on the banks, however, by its droppings, with their pungent odour of fish. Due to pollution and the sometimes sudden changes in its

habitat, the otter now has difficulty in finding food (mainly fish).

Traditions

The marshlanders lived in low, white-washed houses grouped in villages either on limestone islets or on the dikes, where there was no risk of flooding. Each householder owned some kind of cabin in an isolated spot. Most houses were flanked by a *cale* – a miniature creek in which boats could be moored. Boats were the normal means of transport, manoeuvred either with a *pigouille* (a hooked pole or gaff) or a short oar called a *pelle*. There were two types of boat: the slim, lightweight *yoles* used for going to church, to market or to school and the larger, more heavily built *plates* taking the place of vans or trucks, delivering farm produce or ferrying horses and cows.

The marshlanders delivered their milk to local cooperatives, which produced much-praised butter, returning the whey for the fattening of pigs. Fishing brought in mullet, perch, carp, crayfish and eels. Hunting for waterfowl and other game birds (duck, plover, snipe) was restricted to the winter months.

Ecological threat

The increase in cereal growing during the last few years is gradually causing the marsh to dry up and the use of fertilisers and pesticides is threatening the entire ecosystem. Plans have been forwarded to return to traditional agriculture.

Marais Mouillé★★

The Wet Marsh, sometimes called **Venise Verte** (Green Venice), is the more picturesque, particularly east of the Autise, on either side of the Sèvre; it covers 15 000ha/ 37 000 acres. A profusion of alders, lofty ash trees, willows and poplars of the species known as Poitou Whites lines the banks, and overhangs the labyrinth of narrow channels parcelling the rich fields in which herds of Friesians, Normans and locally-bred cattle graze. The plots under cultivation produce an abundant harvest of artichokes, onions, garlic, melons, courgettes, broad beans and the delicious haricots, usually white, known as *mojettes*. In summer, the relatively cool Wet Marsh offers charming pastoral landscapes. During the February and March floods however, visitors can appreciate how difficult the marshlanders' life was in the

past. At that time, the Wet Marsh often floods its meadows and roads.

Proceed with care; some roads can be impassable.

Kids Boat trips

The best way to really experience the Wet Marsh, to appreciate its poetry, its silences and its uniqueness, is to go by boat. The vessels, mirrored in the still water, glide in summer beneath a dense vault of foliage filtering the bright light through shades of grey-green to jade.

The expansion of tourism in the area has led to the creation of many landing-stages. For your first exploration of this maze of waterways, it would be better to rent a flat-bottomed boat (the traditional wooden one has unfortunately been replaced by a plastic one), steered by a guide. Prices (indicated per person) vary according to the starting point: the most tourist-oriented spots do not necessarily offer the most interesting trips. The following trips take in a few small harbours at the heart of the marsh.

Eastern Venise Verte Driving Tour

30km round-trip – about 2hr 30min

Coulon★

This small town is the capital of the Wet Marsh and the main departure point for **boat trips** through this attractive canal country, locally known as Green Venice.

⚓With or without a guide. Contact Embarcadère Prada ☎05 49 35 97 63; Auberge-embarcadère La Pigouille ☎05 49 35 80 99; DLMS Tourisme ☎05 49 35 02 29; Embarcadère Cardinaud ☎05 49 35 90 47.

The marshlands can also be explored by **Kids miniature train** (Le Pibalou) which leaves from Coulon. ⏱Easter–early-Nov tours (20km/12mi, 1hr 15 min) of the Marais Poitevin. Contact DLMS Tourisme, 6 r. de l'Église. ☎05 49 35 02 29.

Below the bridge across the River Sèvre Niortaise, the river flows peacefully between quays lined with boatmen's houses. Going back along the jetties on the right bank, **place de la Coutume** recalls the customs duties on transported goods which boatmen had to pay to go up the Sèvre Niortaise.

Église – This initially Romanesque church later remodelled in the Gothic style (west and south doors), is one of very few in France to have a preacher's pulpit outside; this one is shaped like a small canopied tower.

Maison des Marais Mouillés – ⏱Open Jul–Aug 10am-8pm; May, Jun and Sep: 10am-noon and 2-7pm, Sat-Sun, 10am-1pm and 2-7pm; Feb-Apr and Oct-Dec, daily except Mon 10am-noon and 2-7pm. ⚓5€ (children: 2.50€). ☎ 05 49 35 81 04. www.parc-marais-poitevin.fr. The museum, housed in the old customs house, has various exhibits on life in the marshes over the centuries. The main room on the ground floor is reserved for temporary exhibitions on the Poitou marshes. The first floor includes a reconstruction of the interior of a typical 19C marshlander's house and the **Maraiscope**, a simulated

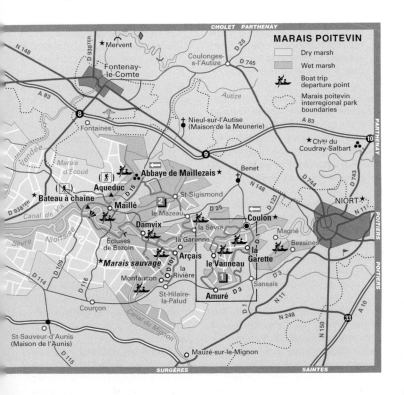

model based on audio-visual aids, of the main stages in the formation of the Wet Marsh. A nature room illustrates the environment (fauna and flora) and the traditional activities of the marshlanders, such as eel fishing and dike building. The visit ends with a presentation of local boat building *(balai)* and objects from the Bronze Age found during excavations of various sites around Coulon.

▶ *On leaving Coulon, drive W along the D 123. At the end of the village, take rue du Port-de-Brouillac (dairy) towards Grand Coin. At the end of the road, turn left and cross the canal. Immediately after the bridge, turn left again.*

The Grand Coin dam offers a good example of **boat transfer** technique. The road skirts the canal lined with poplars and weeping willows providing shade for anglers. After crossing a small bridge, one discovers a sturdy Poitou farmhouse with remarkable stone bond.

▶ *At the end of the canal, turn right onto the D 123 towards Irleau.*

Ash trees mark the beginning of the Wet Marsh; planted to consolidate the banks, they owe their unusual aspect to the way they are trimmed every five or seven years.
The right bank of the Sèvre Niortaise offers striking views of charming cabins (some of them are only accessible by boat). The course of the river is punctuated by conches and rigoles and its gradient suddenly drops at the **Sotterie lock** from 30cm per km (1ft per 0.6mi) to less than 5cm (2in); the

flow of water, considerably slowed down floods the marsh.

▶ *Beyond the Pont d'Irleau, follow the first road on the left. Turn right at the end of the road. At the crossroads, continue straight on then turn left onto the D 102.*

Le Vanneau
This boatmen's village has a well-equipped **harbour**★: the remarkable view embraces a pastoral setting (landing-stage, characteristic footpath, line of willows). The main conche penetrates into the Wet Marsh beyond a screen of poplars.

▶ *Rue de Gémond (right) then rue des Vergers (left) lead to the D 102: turn left towards Sansais; 200m/219yd farther on, take a small road on the right (bike tour no 1 markings).*

There has been a change of scenery: cereal crops enclosed by hedges have replaced the woods.

▶ *At the end of the road, turn left (unsurfaced road), then right (surfaced road): 200m/219yd farther on, turn left.*

Surrounded by greenery once more, visitors can cross a bridge to appreciate the beauty and charm of the site.

▶ *Turn right at the next intersection and, a little way farther on, cross a small bridge. Turn right at the crossroads.*

Trees suddenly give way to cultivated fields: on the left, a blue silo adds a touch of colour to the austere landscape.

▶ *At the crossroads, drive straight ahead and join the D 115. Turn left as you leave St-Georges-de-Rex, then, at the Chausse intersection, turn left again onto the D 3 towards Sansais. 400m/437yd farther on, take the V 8 on the left.*

Amuré
The old cemetery (15C Hosanna cross and graves raised on piles) is 300m/328yd away from the new cemetery where two megaliths are said to have healing powers.

Continue eastwards along the D 3 to Sansais; after 1.7km/1mi, turn left onto a minor unsurfaced road (Bike tour no 3 markings); 900m/0.5mi farther on, turn left onto the surfaced road.

At a place called Vollette, look for a fine example of a traditional Poitou farmhouse, turned into a *gîte rural*.

▷ *At the crossroads, follow the D 102 on the right and turn left 400m/437yd farther on; at the next intersection (700m/765yd), turn left and stop following the bike tour markings.*

From Pont de la Chaume du Château, one re-enters the Wet Marsh. This section of road may be closed during flooding or when wild ducks cross the area *(morning and evening)*.

▷ *Follow the surfaced road. After 2.2km/1.3mi, the road is closed by a wooden gate; turn right, cross a small bridge and turn left 600m/0.5mi farther on.*

La Garette

This former boatmen's hamlet is characteristic of the area with its rows of houses built without foundation, which open onto a conche on one side and onto the road on the other. The high street *(closed to traffic)*, lined with small landing-stages, extends as far as the Vieille Sèvre.

▷ *From the car park follow the street to the D 1; turn left at the crossroads.*

The road goes through the eastern part of La Garette and crosses the Vieille Sèvre: from the bridge, there is a fine view of the river and its banks. The D 1, which takes you back to Coulon, marks the border between the wet area *(on the left)* and the dry area *(on the right)*.

2 Sèvre Niortaise to Autize Driving Tour

50km/31mi round-trip – allow 3hrs

Maillezais★

🔗 *See MAILLEZAIS.*

▷ *Drive S out of Maillezais along the D 15. In Croix-de-Maillé, turn right onto the D 25 and continue to the bridge N of Maillé. Leave the car and follow the towpath on the right.*

Aqueduc de Maillé

1km/0.6mi there and back.

🚶 Set in pastoral surroundings, this hydraulic complex enables the Canal de Vix (Dry Marsh) to cross that of La Jeune Autise (Wet Marsh).

Maillé

This old village is at the centre of many legends as testify the characters (acrobats, athletes carrying lions) which decorate the recessed arches of the **Romanesque doorway** of the Église Notre-Dame. Conveniently situated along the shaded banks of the Canal du Bourneau, the landing-stage nestles under a group of willow

This chain boat is the traditional method used for crossing the marshland canals

trees. Beyond the lock-bridge, it is possible to take a trip to the Île de la Chatte.

▶ *Take the road signposted Dognon, Millé opposite the church.*

Agrippa d'Aubigné's keep (where *Les Tragiques* was printed in 1616, *see MAILLEZAIS*) used to stand in **Fort Dognon.** The

road crosses a small bridge offering extended view of the marsh. Stran white-plastic rafts can be seen along th conches: they are meant to trap the proliferating nutrias.

▶ *1.3km/0.8mi beyond the Millé farm, a footpath starts in a bend (the path*

Address Book

For coin ranges, see the Legend on the cover flap.

WHERE TO STAY

Chambre d'hôte M. and Mme. Ardouin – *Basse-Brenée – 85580 St-Michel-en-l'Herm* – ☎02 51 30 24 09 – *www.visite-vendee.com* – 🍴 – *3 rooms.* This 1766 farm in the heart of the marshlands couldn't be more isolated. Its no-nonsense rooms all open onto the countryside, where birds of all feathers abound. The ground level room with kitchenette and terrace is particularly pleasant.

Chambre d'hôte Le Logis d'Elpénor – *5 r. de la Rivière – 85770 Le Gué-de-Velluire – 10 km/6mi SE of Chaillé-les-Marais on the D 25* – ☎02 51 52 59 10 – *www.lelogisdelpenor.fr – closed Dec–mid-Feb – 5 rooms – meals* . This is our kind of address! On the bank of the river, this enchanting 18C house in a private garden is a delightful place to stay. Its large rooms are nicely furnished with period pieces. Don't miss the home-baked brioche for breakfast – it's heavenly!

Chambre d'hôte La Closeraie – *21 r. de la Paix – 85450 Champagné-les-Marais* – ☎02 51 56 54 54– *www.closeraie.fr – closed 30 Dec-15 Jan – 5 rooms – meals* . This charming 19C building, with all guest rooms on the ground floor, is furnished with antiques. The rooms are arranged around a lovely walled garden. Regional breakfast with home-made preserves and Vendée brioche. Special weekends organised around themes; an independent cottage is also available (4-5 people). Before leaving, stop in the small shop to purchase local specialities.

Hôtel Au Marais – *quai Louis-Tardy – 79510 Coulon – 11km/7mi W of Niort via the D 9 and D 1* – ☎05 49 35 90 43 – *information@hotel-aumarais.com – closed*

15 Dec-1 Feb – 18 rooms. Right next to the quay, these two august houses are the perfect starting point for discovering the Poitevin marshlands – just a few steps down and you're at the edge of the Sevre river. Sunny bedrooms, modern and well cared for.

WHERE TO EAT

Theddy-Moules – *72 r. du 14-Juillet – 17230 Charron – 10 km/6mi W of Marans on the D 105* – ☎05 46 01 51 29 – *closed Oct-Apr – reservations recommended.* You'll have your meal under a wooden lean-to built against the house of this native shellfish farmer. A very popular address among the locals who gather here to savour the famous *moules* (mussels) *à la Theddy*, cooked in cream and Pineau. Fresh produce for sale.

Le Central – *pl. de l'Église – 79510 Coulon – 11 km/6.5mi W of Niort. Take the D 9 and D 1* – ☎05 49 35 90 20 – *le-central-coulon@wanadoo.fr – closed 16 Feb-10 Mar, 27 Sep-10 Oct, Sun eve and Mon.* Would you prefer your meal under the patio parasols or in the pretty dining room? It's up to you. A friendly welcome in this old auberge by the church where you can savour tasty cuisine chosen from several set-price menus.

Les Mangeux de Lumas – *access on foot in summer – 79270 La Garette – 12 km/8mi W of Niort via the D 9 and D 1* – ☎05 49 35 93 42 – *closed 3-23 Jan, 2-28 Nov, Mon and Wed eve (except 12 Jul-31 Aug) and Mar.* In a pretty little village, this ancient farm opens its petite terrace on the waterway at the stroke of dawn. In the winter, you'll be nice and warm in its country-style dining room. Accent on regional cuisine. Grilled food in the summer.

is closed off by means of a chain: no vehicles allowed).

Sentier du bateau à chaîne★

▷ Take the street in front of the church, then follow "Dognon, Millé." The path is 1.5km/0.9mi away on your left, after the farm of Millé. 600m/656yd there and back. Follow the marked itinerary Entre Sèvre et Autizes.

🚶 This unusual itinerary offers the discovery of the hidden side of the marsh (fauna and flora). The narrow path runs alongside a *conche* through thick vegetation which can slow one down considerably. It leads to one of the last **bateaux à chaîne** (flat-bottomed boats propelled by pulling on a chain) in the area, which can be used (with care) to cross a conche.

▷ Continue along the same road. At the crossroads, turn left onto the D 25B. Cross the River Sèvre then turn left as you come off the Pont du Sablon.

The itinerary follows the left bank of the Sèvre Niortaise and offers fine views of the Île de la Chatte and its fishermen's cabins.

☺ A picnic area is available near the lock of the Rabatière Canal.

▷ At the intersection of the Croix-des-Mary bridge, carry straight on towards Damvix. At the next crossroads, turn left and cross over the lock.

Several bridges in succession make it possible to reach the right bank of the Sèvre Niortaise across the Bazoin locks, an important intersection of waterways.

Damvix

This small marshland village in a pleasant location on the Sèvre Niortaise contains a number of low cottages linked by footbridges which span the narrow canals.

▷ Cross the Sèvre Niortaise and follow the D 104 towards Arçais; 200m farther on, turn right onto a minor road (Camping des Conches) which runs across a bridge. Beware: the itinerary

leading to the village of la Rivière through the Marais Sauvage follows an unsurfaced road only suitable in dry weather; in rainy weather, go to Arçais by the direct route.

Le Marais Sauvage★

A few planks of wood across a *conche* followed by (take the left-hand road) the dam of La Garette (fine view) give access to the Marais Sauvage (turn right at the fork). This conservation area covering 1 600ha/3 954 acres is crisscrossed by 100km/62mi of waterways forming a real maze.

The village of **la Rivière**, with its fine traditional houses, stands on the edge of the marsh. To the north, the road which joins the D 101 offers a striking contrast between the wooded marsh (on the left) and the vast expanse of rolling fields (on the right); **Monfaucon** to the south has a fine landing-stage.

Arçais

Set up in the bend of a reach, the **Grand-Port★★** consists of a large paved dock; the landing-stage faces a typical wooden cabin. At each end of the harbour, two wooden cranes have been left as a reminder of the time when trunks of poplars travelling along the waterways were hoisted onto the quayside. There are remarkable farmhouses along the Minet reach in the northern district of **la Garenne.**

▷ From the Grand-Port, follow the D 102 towards Damvix. At Les Bourdettes, cross the dam then the lock and take the Chemin de la Foulée on the right.

The itinerary follows the right bank of the Sèvre Niortaise to the Village de la Sèvre. When you reach a typical footbridge, take the road on the left leading to Mazeau harbour (landing-stage after the bridge).

▷ Drive NW out of Le Mazeau along the D 68 towards Maillezais; 1km/0.6mi beyond St-Sigismond, at La Ragée, turn left towards Anchais. At the end of the road, turn left onto the path leading to Port d'Anchais.

Port d'Arçaise

L'Espace Marais

A vast barn houses reconstructions illustrating former marshland crafts. In addition, there is a maze, an aquarium (regional fish) and the devil's garden (containing poisonous plants).

▸ *Return to the Quatre Chemins crossroads and drive N; beyond Moulin de Bouteline, the D 68 takes you back to Maillezais.*

Marais Desséché★

The **Dry Marsh** presents a very different aspect. A territory of wide open spaces crossed by canals and dikes, it produces wheat, barley and various types of bean despite the fact that the black earth of the bri needs constant fertilising. The pastureland has been given over to the rearing of salt-pasture sheep and cattle. Around Aiguillon Bay, which is slowly silting up, there are mussel beds *(bouchots)* particularly near Esnandes and Charron.

③ Marais du Petit Poitou Driving Tour

60km/37mi round tour – allow 3hrs

Marans

This is the market town of the Dry Marsh, and noted for its grain storage (silos). The small port, linked to the ocean by a canal, harbours a boatyard. Lock gates maintain the level of the tidal basin, where a number of coasters and pleas-

ure craft are moored. It is possible to have a panoramic view of the marsh from the tower of Notre-Dame Church.

▸ *Drive N out of Marans along the N 137 towards Luçon. In Sableau, turn right onto the D 25A then left in Vouillé onto the D 25.*

Shortly after La Groie *(2km/1.2mi farther on)*, note on the left a dike, known as a *bot*, on the edge of the marsh. The road then skirts the striking cliffs of the Village de l'An VII (a former limestone island) once pounded by the waves.

Chaillé-les-Marais

Built on what is now just a limestone bluff, the town commands the plain which was once under water. It is the centre of the Dry Marsh sector known as Petit Poitou, the first in the province to be drained and dried. From the viewpoint (place de l'Église), there is a fine view of the marsh and of the former islands of Aisne and Sableau to the left.

▸ *Return to the N 137 and turn right (rue de l'An VII) towards Luçon, then left 900m/0.5mi beyond the tourist office.*

Maison du Petit Poitou

🕐*Open Jul-Aug 10am-1pm and 2-7pm; Sun 2-7pm; Jun 2-7pm; Apr and Sep 2-6pm. ⊕3.90€ (children 6-16 2.20€). ☎ 02 51 56 77 30.*

Kids The former house of the dike master offers comprehensive information on the drying out of marshes, their flora and

...una, and the activities of its inhabitants. Outside, animals whose traditional
habitat is the Marais – local donkeys,
goats, cows and Marans chickens – roam
about.

▶ *Continue along the N 137 towards Luçon;*
   700m/0.4mi farther on, cross Pont de la
   Coube and turn immediately left onto
   the D 10.

The road skirts the picturesque **Canal
du Clain** offering an interesting view of
the Chaillé cliffs. The canal is lined with
sparse farmhouses, damp meadows on
the left and cereal crops on the right.

▶ *Turn right onto the D 25 at Ste-Rade-*
   gonde-des-Noyers crossroads. As you
   leave Champagné-les-Marais, turn
   left before the bridge onto the chemin
   Sud du canal.

The **Canal de Champagné,** one of the
favourite haunts of anglers, crosses cultivated fields. The typical fauna (herons)
and flora (thistles, reeds) of the Dry Marsh
can be seen on either side of the road.

▶ *Turn left at the end of the long straight*
   section of road, then continue straight
   ahead at the next crossroads (3km/
   1.9mi).

The road skirts round the Marais Fou. A
belfry and a water tower emerges from
a vast expanse of fields on the right.
Farther on, the view embraces the small
Port de l'Épine where a few fishing
boats are moored and, beyond, a farmhouse surrounded by umbrella pines
(rare in this area).

▶ *Follow the D 10A on the right then,*
   1.1km/0.7mi farther on, turn left onto
   a minor road which crosses the Canal
   de Vienne; continue for another 100m/
   110yd and turn right.

At the crossroads, stop in front of the warehouse to look at the *bac à râteau*, once
used to dredge the silted-up canals. This
cleaning-up process was undertaken
every seven or eight years in wintertime
and festivities were organised for the
occasion.

The road crosses several locks including
the picturesque Grands Greniers lock.
To the south, the Sèvre Niortaise supplies
five canals (Vienne, Clain, Cinq Abbés,
Mouillepied, Vix), thus forming an important network of waterways.

▶ *Turn right at the end of the long straight*
   road skirting the Mouillepied Canal,
   then left at Hutte de la Briand.
▶ *At the lock-bridge, turn right onto the*
   N 137 to return to Marans.

④ Le Marais Maritime Driving Tour

70km/44mi round tour – allow 3hrs

St-Michel-en-l'Herm

Benedictine abbey ⌂⌂ *Visit by guided
tour (45min) Jul–end of Aug on Tue, Thur
and Fri at 10am, 10.40am, 11.20am, 3pm,
3.40pm and 4.20pm.* ⊘*Closed public hols.*
⊜*2.80€.* ☎ *02 51 30 21 89.*
here dedicated to archangel St Michael.
Notice the elevated placement of statues of this saint in local churches and
sanctuaries; this is a reflection of his
reputation for appearing from on high.
The abbey, founded in the 7C by Ansoald,
Bishop of Poitiers, prospered until the
9C when it was devastated by the Normans. Wars with the English during the
14C and 15C, the Wars of Religion in the
16C and the Revolution brought only
more destruction. It was rebuilt each
time, though only partly the last time,
in the late 17C, when François Leduc was
involved. Of particular note are the Gothic
chapter-house and calefactory, with a
refectory and the monks' building by
Leduc.

Musée André Deluol – ♿⊘*Open mid-
Jun–end Sep daily except Tue, 3-7pm; Oct
to mid-Jun, Sat-Sun, Mon and public hols
3-5pm.* ⊜*3€.* ☎*02 51 30 25 15.* Paintings,
drawings, pastels and sculptures by a
local artist.

▶ *Leave St-Michel S along the D 60.*

La Dive mound comes into view on the
right, past a silo. Shortly afterwards, the
D 60 *(straight ahead at the crossroads)*
crosses several dikes and polders
(reclaimed from the sea). The road ends

at the foot of the **Digue du Maroc** (1912), bristling with strange perches intended for birds of prey (falcons, owls).

▶ *Return to the crossroads and turn left.*

La Dive

This was still an island in the 17C. From the entrance of a former quarry, the road rises and runs along the mound, above the marsh, over a distance of 700m/0.4mi. The view extends from Pointe d'Arçay to the Aiguillon creek, encompassing Île de Ré and its viaduct-bridge. Back at sea level, one can see the cliffside indented by the sea, now partly covered over with ivy.

▶ *Continue towards the sea then turn left at the crossroads.*

Digue de l'Aiguillon

The famous dike, conceived and built by Dutch engineers, is a slender 6km/3.6mi tongue of land protected by a breakwater. To the left are former salt-marshes turned into oyster beds; from Les Sablons, there is a succession of beaches bordered by sand dunes.

▶ *Go to the end of the dike.*

Pointe de l'Aiguillon★

The south-east extremity of the dike where there is a wildfowl hunting reserve (Réserve de Chasse Maritime), projects into the grey waters of the silting-up bay. The wide **view** extends from the narrow estuary of the River Lay and Pointe d'Arcay (north-west) to the Île de Ré (south-west) and

the port of La Pallice (south). The famou mussel beds are visible only at low tide.

▶ *Follow the dike in the other direction.*

L'Aiguillon-sur-Mer

The low-built houses overlooking the estuary of the Lay face a denuded countryside, bleak beneath an immense sky. The local economy is based on nursery gardening, coastal fishing and the cultivation of oysters and mussels.

▶ *Cross the Lay.*

La Faute-sur-Mer

Although it boasts a casino, La Faute remains basically a small family seaside resort, with a long beach of fine sand. The string of dunes stretches southwards to **Pointe d'Arçcay** (national hunting reserve).

La Tranche-sur-Mer⌂

This seaside resort, with a wide beach of fine sand, stretches for 13km/8mi. Behind, pine woods extend over an area of 600ha/1 483 acres. Maupas Lake offers facilities for learning various water sports, including windsurfing, boogie-boarding, and sailing. A flower festival takes place in spring (⌂ *see CALENDAR OF EVENTS*).

▶ *Drive N out of La Tranche-sur-Mer along the D 747.*

Angles

One of the gables on the old abbey church here is adorned with the repre-

Baie de l'Aiguillon

J. Damase/MICHELIN

entation of a large bear which, according to legend, was changed into stone by a hermit named Martin. Inside the church, the chancel and transept are Romanesque whereas the nave is in the Plantagenet style.

▶ *Return to the crossroads and continue straight ahead.*

Tour de Moricq

This large 15C square tower standing isolated in the middle of a field once guarded a small harbour on the River Lay.

▶ *Follow the D 25 towards Grues. Continue for 2km/1.2mi beyond St-Denis-du-Payré.*

Réserve Naturelle de St-Denis-du-Payré

🕐*Open Jul–Aug 9.30am-12.30pm and 3-7pm (specialised tour guides available); early-Nov public hols and Christmas school hols, 9.30am-12.30pm and 2-5pm (other school hols, 6pm).* 🕐*Closed 1 Jan,* *1 May, and 24, 25 and 31 Dec.* ⊕*5.35€ (children 3.80€).* ☎*02 51 27 23 92.*

The nature reserve (2km/1mi east) encompasses 207ha/512 acres of marshland frequented by large numbers of birds, both nesting and migratory. A diorama with slides which can be viewed at the **Maison de la Réserve,** situated at the heart of the village, illustrates the various species which can be identified through telescopes from the nearby **observatory**.

▶ *Continue along the D 25. In Triaize, turn right onto the D 746.*

Just before crossing the Chenal Vieux, note the former limestone islet on the right, at La Dune; 500m/547yd farther on, a farmhouse stands on a mound made up of oyster shells, said to be going back a very long time; this curious pile of shells, once crushed to powder to feed poultry, can be seen from the roadside.

▶ *Continue along the D 746 to return to St-Michel-en-l'Herm.*

MARENNES

POPULATION 4 685
MICHELIN MAP 324: D-5

More than half the oysters eaten in France come from the Marennes-Oléron basin. "Marennes-Oléron" is the name given to the renowned, greenish oyster fattened in the *claires* (special beds) of the basin which lies between the mouth of the River Seudre, the coast north of Marennes and the eastern coast of the Isle of Oléron. Oysters grow to maturity in *parcs à huîtres*, but it is only in the *claires* of this region that the adult mollusc is fattened, refined and subjected to the effects of microscopic algae known here as Navicules Bleues which give the seafood its delicate perfume and subtle hue.

🔲 **Information:** Pl. Chasseloup-Loubat, 17320 Marennes. ☎05 46 85 04 36.
▶ **Orient Yourself**: Marennes, once an island in the Gulf of Saintonge, is situated on the right bank of the Seudre estuary, 22km/14mi SW of Rochefort.
😊 **Don't Miss**: The view from the tower of Église St-Pierre-de-Sales.
👁 **Also See**: ROCHEFORT, SAINTES, ÎLE D'OLÉRON.

Sights

Église St-Pierre-de-Sales

This 15C church is built in a style known, in France, as English, with a tall square tower, buttressed at the corners, crowned by a spire decorated with crockets. The spire, rising to a height of 85m/279ft, is a landmark visible from miles away and used as a navigation mark by sailors.

The interior is noteworthy for its wide nave flanked by chapels beneath balustraded galleries. Eight-branched rib vaulting arches above the bays.

For coin ranges, see the Legend on the cover flap.

TOURIST INFORMATION

Tourist office – *Pl. Chasseloup-Loubat, 17320 Marennes –* ☎ *05 46 85 04 36.*

WHERE TO STAY

☺☺ **Grand Chalet** – *2 av. La Cèpe – 17390 Ronce-les-Bains – 9km/5.4mi SW of Marennes via the D 728E –* ☎ *05 46 36 06 41 – frederic.moinardeau@wanadoo.fr – closed 11 Nov-8 Feb. – 26 rooms – restaurant* ☺☺*.* Facing the Île d'Oléron, this 1850s hotel with an unusual chalet-style façade has an enviable location right on the water's edge, its garden extending down to the sea. The guestrooms either overlook the garden or offer attractive sea views.

Terrasse de la Tour

🕐*Open Jul-Aug 10am-12.30pm and 2-7pm; Sep-Jun, Mon-Fri 2-6pm, Sat-Sun and public hols by prior arrangement.* ☜*2€ (children 1€).* ☎*05 46 85 03 86.*
Accessible up 291 steps, this tower platform offers an impressive **panorama**★ – 55m/180ft high – over the oyster farms, the islands, the Avert peninsula and a stretch of the marshes.

Cité de l'huître★

Access is from the car park by free shuttle. 🕐*Open Jun–Aug 10am-8pm; Apr–May, Sep and school hols daily 10am–7pm; Oct daily except Mon noon–7pm; Nov–Dec daily except Mon and Tue noon–7pm.* ☜*Jun–Sep 9€ (children 6€); Oct–May*

Oystermen near Fort Louvois

S. Sauvignier/MICHELIN

7€ (children 4€) ☎*05 46 36 78 98 www. lacitedhuitre.com*
This brand new interpretation centre in a series of five old cabins built on stilts over the **Chenal de la Cayenne** houses an exciting and interactive exhibition on the oyster. In one hut the life cycle of the oyster and the secrets of the breeders are revealed. Details of the ecosystem and how it affects the oyster are detailed in another hut while in another hut the history of the oyster is retraced using the latest in multimedia techniques. One cabin is devotes o the life of several generations of oyster farmers. In addition there is a restaurant and activities for children.

Château de la Gataudière

1.5km/1mi N. ☜*Visit by guided tour (30 min) Jun-Sep 10am-noon and 2-6pm; Mar-May and Oct-Nov, daily except Mon 10am-noon and 2-6pm.* ☜*6€ (children aged 5-12: 4.50€).* ☎ *05 46 85 01 07. www. gataudiere.com.*
The château was built c 1749, in the Louis XIV style, by François Fresneau (1703-70), an engineer who studied the production of rubber from the hevea tree in French Guyana and returned to France to lay the base for its industrial use. The château stands on the site of a medieval house in the heart of an old marsh village known as Les Gataudières. On the garden front, a terrace with a wrought-iron balustrade runs the length of the façade. A Classical pediment embellished with a Triumph of Flora (the goddess of flowers) surmounts a central block decorated with trophies symbolising the resources of the region (oyster farming, salt-marsh agriculture, winemaking etc).
Inside, the main reception floor is notable for the Grand Salon with its stone walls set with fluted Corinthian pilasters representing the arts, the sciences and the four seasons. Fine Louis XV furniture can be seen in the dining hall and the Blue Salon. A building in the courtyard houses an exhibition of horse-drawn vehicles.

Excursions

Brouage★
6.5km/4mi NE. ☜*See BROUAGE.*

rt Louvois★

km/4mi N. ⏱ *Open Jul-Aug, 10.30am-*
.30pm; Mid-Sep–end Sep and mid-Jun–
end Jun at low tide (contact the tourist
office for further information). ⚭*5€ (chil-*
dren 2€). No charge for boat trip at high
tide. ☏*05 46 85 07 00.*
Access to the fort (also known as Fort
Chapus) is by foot at low tide, and by boat
when the tide is in.

MAULÉON

POPULATION 7 327

MICHELIN MAP 322: B-3

From May to October 1793, Mauléon, (then called Châtillon-sur-Sèvre), was the
capital of the military resistance in Vendée, a stronghold of Royalist support
during the Revolution. Royal vouchers, corresponding to the promissory notes
issued by the French Revolutionary government, were even printed.

▶ **Orient Yourself**: Located north-west of Deux-Sèvres, and straddling the neighbouring *départements* of Vendée and Maine-et-Loire, Mauléon looks down from
a rocky outcrop over the Ouin Valley.

👓 **Also See**: BRESSUIRE, POUZAUGES.

Sight

Musée du BRHAM

⏱*Open 10am-noon and 2-6pm, Sat-Sun*
and public hols 2.30-6pm. ⚭*2€.* ☏*05 49*
81 86 23.

The local Historical and Archaeological
Research Society (French acronym BRHAM)
is housed in the beautiful granite Abbaye
de la Trinité, remodelled in the 19C in the
Louis XIV style.

One of the rooms in the abbey contains
eight **engraved rocks★** from Les Vaux.
In the 19C, more than 200 of these slabs,
carved with various motifs, such as crosses,
stars, circles and stylised figures, the date
and meaning of which remain an
enigma, were discovered in the
surrounding area. The other
rooms contain exhibits on the
Vendée Wars and folk traditions
(religious art, Poitou headdresses,
local cabinetry).

Excursions

St-Aubin-de-Baubigné

5km/3mi E via the D 759. A statue
by Falguière was erected in 1895
in honour of **Henri de La Rochejaquelein**, who was buried in the
funerary chapel of the church near

his cousin, the Marquis de Lescure, head
of the Vendée armed forces.

Château de la Durbelière

2km/1mi N of St-Aubin-de-Baubigné via
the D 153.

The old 15C-17C château, now in ruins,
formed part of a vast rural development.
The seigniorial lodgings, surrounded by
a water-filled moat, were flanked by massive square pavilions. In one of these, in
1772, **Henri de la Rochejaquelein** was
born.

It was in the courtyard of this château that
Monsieur Henri, at the age of 21, rallied
2 000 peasants, calling upon them to

La Rochejaquelein

M. Thiery/MICHELIN

follow him to the Vendée Wars under the Royalist flag with the memorable words:

> *"If I advance, follow me;*
> *If I retreat, kill me;*
> *If I die, avenge me!"*

In October 1793 the very young and ha some La Rochejaquelein was appoint General of the Royalist-Catholic arm, After the army moved into Brittany, he was killed by a Republican at Nuaillé, near Cholet, in 1794.

MAULÉON-LICHARRE

POPULATION 3 533

MICHELIN MAP 342: G-3

Mauléon is an old stronghold and the smallest capital in the seven Basque provinces. It rises on the right bank of the River Saison, at the foot of a hill where the ruins of the old castle stand. Mauléon is also the capital city of espadrille sandals. 70% of the French production is manufactured there.

▶ **Orient Yourself**: Mauléon-Licharre lies 30km/19mi W of Oloron-Ste-Marie and 40km/25mi E of St-Jean-Pied-de-Port in the foothills of the Pyrenees. The district of Licharre sits on the west bank of the River Saison and is home to the Renaissance Château d'Andurain.

😊 **Don't Miss**: Exploring the Soule region to the S of the town.

🕐 **Organising Your Time**: Allow half a day to explore the Basse Soule region and a full day for the Haute Soule.

Kids **Especially for Kids**: The Aventure Parc Aramits in the Basse Soule region (&see Address Book).

& **Also See**: OLORON-STE-MARIE, ST-JEAN-PIED-DE-PORT, THE BÉARN.

Sights

Château

Visit by guided tour (1hr, last admission 30min before closing time) Jul to mid-Sep daily except Thu 11am-noon and 3-6pm, Sun 3-6pm. 4.50€. 05 59 28 04 18.

This Renaissance château was built towards the beginning of the 17C by Arnaud I de Maytie, the bishop of Oloron. Of particular interest are the carved fireplaces and the 17C-18C furniture inside the château.

Château fort de Mauleon

Steep ascent to the castle. Access for cars. 🕐*Open mid-Jun to end Sep and Easter school hols, 11am-1.30pm and 3-7pm; early May to mid-Jun, Sat-Sun and public hols 11am-1.30pm and 3-7pm. 2.50€ (children under 7 no charge).*

Built in the 12C on a hill overlooking the valley of the River Saison, this castle was demolished in the 17C on the orders of the king. The castle well is still visible in the courtyard. Note the three cannons dating from 1685 on the path around the battlements.

Excursion

Château de Mongaston

12km/7.4mi N. *Visit by guided tour (1hr 30min) May-Oct, daily except Tue 2.30-6.30pm. 4.60€ (children under 10: 2.30€). 05 59 38 65 92.*

This fortified 13C keep was used to watch the Vallée de la Soule and to communicate with Mauléon by the sound of a bell or luminous signals. A turret was added in the 14C, and the castle underwent other modifications in the 16C. In 1929, it was destroyed by a fire and deserted. The present landlady, whose ancestors had sold the castle in 1896, has started its rebuilding.

On the ground floor, 19C family belongings and furniture. On the first floor, the library houses a tearoom, and a **musée historique de la Figurine** (historical

Address Book

⟨ For coin ranges, see the Legend on the cover flap.

WHERE TO STAY

⊜⊜**Chambre d'hôte Maison Elichondoa** – *64120 Pagolle – 13km/8mi W of Mauléon-Licharre via the D 918 and D 302 – ☎05 59 65 65 34 – ⊠ – 4 rooms – meals ⊜⊜.* In a small mountain village, this well-restored 17C farm is the perfect place for a relaxing break. Surrounded by a landscape of countryside and hills, the farmhouse interior is an attractive mix of old beams, exposed stone and colourful decor.

WHERE TO EAT

⊜**Auberge du Lausset** – *64130 L'Hôpital-St-Blaise – 13km/8mi E of Mauléon-Licharre. Take the D 24 and D 25 – ☎05 59 66 53 03 – closed 10-24 Jan, 4-25 Oct, Sun eve and Mon off-season.* This quiet, family-run inn opposite a delightful 12C Romanesque church serves traditional cuisine in a large, contemporary-style dining room. Eat out on the shaded terrace in summer. The

auberge also has a few reasonably priced rooms.

⊜⊜**Le Chalet Pedro** – *In the Iraty forest (near the D 18) – 64220 Mendive – ☎05 59 28 55 98 – ⟨ open Easter to 11 Nov, school hols and Sat-Sun in winter – closed Tue in Apr-May – ⊠.* A stone's throw from the Spanish border, this charming chalet is nestled in a small valley in the middle of the forest. Simple bistro-style decor with oak tables. River trout in season. Apartments to let in the house across the way.

SPORT AND LEISURE

Aventure Parc Aramits – [Kids] – *Espace Forêt-Loisirs – 64570 Aramits – ☎05 59 34 64 79 – www.aventure-parc-aramits – open 10am-6pm – closed Nov-Apr.* This exciting adventure park offers a range of climbing activities through the tree tops (children must be at least 1.5m/4.9ft tall with arms raised), as well as bungee jumping, hiking, canyoning and pot-holing. The park has a dedicated area for younger children (aged 3-8), a bar-restaurant and a picnic-area.

---

museum of figurines) is on the second floor.

La Soule★

The province, which shares many cultural influences with Béarn – including, for instance, the types of houses – has retained the dances and folk traditions most characteristic of the region.

1 Lower Soule and the Barétous Driving Tour

78km/49mi – allow 3hrs

This area is rich in souvenirs of the famous musketeers who inspired Alexandre Dumas to write his classic story of d'Artagnan and his three friends.
Stop at Gotein-Libarrenx in order to admire its characteristic steeple with three spires.

▶ *Continue along the D 918.*

Gotein

This Pyrenean village has a church and belfry-calvary typical of the region.

Trois-Villes

The name of the village recalls the military career and the personality of Mr de

Gotein – Belfry-calvary

B. Kaufmann/MICHELIN

Tréville, Captain of the King's Musketeers under Louis XIII. The château was built by François Mansart (1598-1666), the great classicist architect.

The **Barétous**, a transitional region between Béarn and the Basque provinces, offers the visitor a checkerboard of maize fields and magnificent meadows punctuated by thickets of oak trees, with the limestone summits of the mountains in the background.

Lanne

The pretty church, with its double porch, was originally the chapel attached to the château owned by Isaac de Porthau (Porthos in Dumas' *The Three Musketeers*).

Aramits

This village was once the capital of the Barétous. Aramis, another of d'Artagnan's musketeers, was a lay brother at an abbey here which has now disappeared (Athos, the third musketeer, was named after a village of that name near Sauveterre).

Arette

The small town was rebuilt after an earthquake on 13 August 1967. A mountain road leads to **Arette-Pierre-St-Martin**✵, a small winter sports resort.

After a pleasant, twisting climb above the Arette basin, the road traverses a slope of the Aspe Valley.

▷ *At Asasp, cross the Aspe torrent.*

St-Christau
 See LE BÉARN, GAVE D'ASPE.

The road runs down to Oloron along the east bank of the river.

Oloron-Ste-Marie
 See OLORON-STE-MARIE.

▷ *Take the D 936, NW, for 12km/7mi then turn left onto the D 25.*

L'Hôpital-St-Blaise

A tiny village on the Basque-Béarn border. The **church**★ – a rare example of Hispano-Moorish art on the northern side of the Pyrenees – is in the form of a Greek cross, the four arms radiating from a central tower. *Audio-guided tours 10am-7pm.* ☎ *05 59 66 11 12.*

▷ *Return to Mauléon-Licharre.*

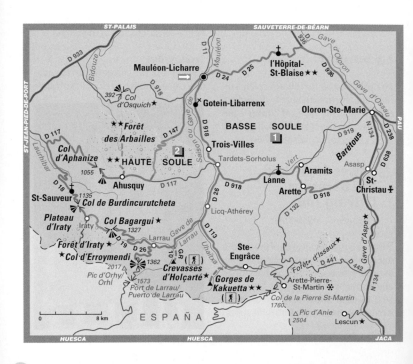

② **Upper Soule★★ Driving Tour**

130km/80mi – allow one day

Upper Soule is a magnificent region of forests and pastures, separated from the St-Jean-Pied-de-Port depression by the massifs of Iraty and Arbailles – a difficult barrier because of the rough terrain and the density of the woodland covering it. This is a region particularly suitable for forest rambles, fishing and, in winter, cross-country skiing.

▶ *Leave Mauléon S along the D 147.*

Forêt des Arbailles★★

This is an upland forest carpeting the higher reaches of a limestone bastion standing clear of the gullies carved by the Saison, the Laurhibar and the Bidouze torrents. The forest rises to a height of 1 265m/4 150ft at Pic de Behorléguy. The beech groves, hiding slopes strewn with boulders, riddled with hollows, give way in the south to a pastoral zone ending in a sheer drop facing the Spanish frontier.

▶ *Turn right onto the D 117.*

Ahusquy

There is a *(restored)* mountain inn standing on this **panoramic site★★**, once a gathering place for Basque shepherds, whose piercing cries echoed off the surrounding hills. Farther uphill, clearly visible at the top of a footpath, is a drinking trough filled with Ahusquy spring water. The water was at one time popular as a kidney and bladder ailment cure.

Col d'Aphanize

Wild horses can be seen grazing on the slopes around the pass. The pastureland here is the summer home of many flocks of sheep. East of the pass the **view★★** opens out wide: from Pic des Escaliers, immediately south, to Pic de Ger on the south-eastern horizon, by way of Pic d'Orthy, Pic d'Anie and the Massif de Sesques between Aspe and Ossau. Ossau-Iraty is a refined local cheese made from ewe's milk; gourmets like to eat it with black cherry jam.

▶ *In Mendive, turn left onto the D 18.*

Chapelle St-Sauveur

From a distance this chapel looks like a sheepfold. It was once a hostel-chapel on a pilgrimage route followed by the Knights of the Order of Malta on Corpus Christi day. A line of small columns outside marks the Stations of the Cross. A number of naïve statuettes are housed inside.

Col de Burdincurutcheta

Alt 1 135m/3 724ft. *Park 1km/0.6mi below the north side of the pass, where the road approaches a rocky crest.* Walk to the edge. The view extends over the jagged foothills, extensively lacerated, of the frontier massif, gashed by bleak, deserted valleys; in the distance the basin of St-Jean-Pied-de-Port, centre of the Cize region, opens out.

Plateau d'Iraty

Horses and cattle roam here in summer along with the sheep; locally made sheep's cheese is a fresh delight.

Forêt d'Iraty★

This forest of beech groves straddling the frontier supplied wood for masts for the French and Spanish navies from the 18C onwards; it is one of the largest wooded areas in Europe (in France alone 2 310ha/5 710 acres).
Ski area – The small resort village of Chalets d'Iraty was built in the 60s in the heart of Iraty Forest. At an altitude of 1 200m/4 000ft to 1 500m/5 000ft, the 109km/68mi of cross-country ski runs and numerous hiking paths offer a unique view of the mountain.

Col Bagargui★

There is a **view★** to the east of the Upper Soule mountains and the High Pyrenees in the Aspe and Ossau regions. In the foreground, on the right, is the heavy mass of Pic d'Orthy; farther away rise the elegant limestone summits of the Pic d'Anie chain, and behind them the silhouette of Pic du Midi d'Ossau. Scattered among the forest trees below are the buildings of the picturesque village of Iraty.

▶ Continue towards Larrau then along the
road to Port-de-Larrau (usually blocked
by snow from November to June).

Col d'Erroymendi★

Alt 1 362m/4 469ft. 7.5km/4mi from Larrau, by the Port de Larrau road (generally
blocked by snow from November to June).
From here there is a vast mountain **pano-
rama★** which highlights the pastoral and
woodland activities in the Upper Soule
region. A few yards east of the pass there
is a different view: the fan of the Upper
Saison valleys and, on the horizon, the
rocky mass of Pic d'Anie.

Crevasses d'Holçarté★

🚶1hr 30min round-trip on foot, via the
footpath marked GR 10, which is visible
soon after the café and the Laugibar Bridge.

▶ At Pont de la Mouline, leave the GR 10
on the left and take the right-hand
alternative.

After a steep, stiff climb, the entrance to
the crevasses is reached: these are in fact
very narrow gorges sliced from the limestone to a depth of 200m/656ft. The
path rises to the top of the Olhadubi
tributary gorge, which is crossed by a
dizzily impressive footbridge slung
171m/561ft above the torrent in 1920.

Gorges de Kakuetta★★

Access via the D 113, which leads to Ste
Engrâce. 🚶Take the footbridge across the
Uhaïtxa, climb up the opposite bank and
go down into the gorge. ⊙This excursion
is a demanding one, best undertaken
when the water level is low (early Jun to
late Oct). Stout footwear is essential as the
ground can be slippery. ⊙Open mid-Mar
to mid-Nov, 8am to dusk (last admission
6pm). ⊜4€. ☎05 59 28 70 56 (Bar La Cascade) or ☎05 59 28 60 83 (town hall).

These limestone gorges are beautiful as
well as impressive, with the beginning
of the Grand Étroit (the Great Narrows),
the most grandiose of all.

This splendid canyon, more than
200m/656ft deep, is no more than
3m/11ft to 10m/33ft wide at the top of
its sheer sides. The torrent roars through
the long fissure with its dense clumps
of vegetation. The path, frequently difficult, eventually arrives at the water's
edge, crossing the stream by a number
of footbridges here and there. It ends
within sight of a 20m/65ft-high water-
fall sustained by a resurgent spring,
where a cave, replete with giant stalactites and stalagmites, marks the end of
the walk.

Ste-Engrâce

This is a shepherds' village, surrounded
by wooded mountains fissured by steep
valleys. The Romanesque church, a former
11C abbey church, stands with its asymmetric roof and its heavy masonry on a
pastoral **site★** in the upper coomb of
the Uhaotxa, marking one of the ancient
routes to Santiago de Compostela.

Gorges de Kakuetta

B. Kaufmann/MICHELIN

The chancel, closed off by a robust 14C grille, has richly ornamented capitals. These include (left) scenes involving buffoons and jesters; hunting scenes and a Resurrection in the centre; and (right) **Solomon and the Queen of Sheba**, the royal visitor's elephant bearing on its back a palanquin in the Indian manner.

▶ *Return to Mauléon along the D 113, D 26 and D 918.*

MELLE★
POPULATION 3 851
MICHELIN MAP 322: F-7

Melle owes its existence to the silver-bearing veins of lead in the hills of St-Hilaire, on the west bank of the Béronne: they were used in medieval times for the production of coins in a local mint. Melle is unusual for its three Romanesque churches. Two of them, originally attached to Benedictine monasteries, accommodated pilgrims on the road to Compostela. The town was won over at the time of the Reformation and enjoyed a certain prosperity after the foundation of its college in 1623. Melle was once famed for raising the local breed of donkey, the Poitou Baudet (*see DAMPIERRE-SUR-BOUTONNE*).

▶ **Orient Yourself**: Melle is tucked into the angle where the narrow, heavily wooded Béronne gorge meets a smaller valley. The best view of the town is from the D 950, driving north-east from St-Jean-d'Angély.

Don't Miss: The Église St-Hilaire.

Especially for Kids: The Mines d'Argent des Rois Francs.

Also see: NIORT, LUSIGNAN.

Sights

Église St-Hilaire★

St Hilary's Church, built in the Poitou Romanesque style at its purest, was part of St-Jean-d'Angély Abbey. The sober east end and the west front with its coned pinnacles are particularly attractive. Above the north doorway stands a carving of a **horseman** *(le cavalier de Melle)* which is famous in the history of religious art for the controversy the figure has provoked: the crowned rider has been identified at various times as Charlemagne, as Jesus Christ suppressing the Ancient Law, or even as the Emperor Constantine triumphing over paganism. The east end includes three apsidal chapels with buttress-columns and carved modillions radiating from an ambulatory joined to the transept. Two more chapels lead off the transept itself; above the crossing rises a belfry-tower.

Interior – The scale of the nave, aisles and ambulatory indicates that the church was designed as a place of pilgrimage. The barrel-vaulting is supported by pillars, quadrilobed in section, with interesting carved capitals; the third on the right, entering from the west front, depicts a wild boar hunt. A doorway leading into the south aisle is – most unusually – decorated on its inner side: on the archivolt, Jesus and the Saints accompanying Him overcome fantasy animals

For coin ranges, see the Legend on the cover flap.

WHERE TO EAT

Les Glycines – *5 pl. René-Boussard – ☎05 49 27 01 11 – contact@hotellesglycines.com – closed 26 Jan-1 Feb, Sun eve off-season and Mon from Oct to Mar.* In the past, this lively restaurant, attractively decorated, was the village café. Now popular with locals and visitors alike, it specialises in traditional, regional cuisine. The restaurant also has guest rooms on the premises.

Le Cavalier de Melle

representing the forces of evil. At the far end of this aisle a sound system diffuses a continuous programme of sacred or ritual music from all over the world.

Église St-Pierre

This church dedicated to St Peter once belonged to a priory attached to St-Maixent Abbey. It was built, like St Hilary's, in the Poitou Romanesque style, and stands on a hill overlooking the Béronne. The east end and the side entrance are remarkable for their carved ornamentation: a cornice above the south doorway is supported by historiated modillions (symbols of the Evangelists) between which are carved Signs of the Zodiac, and Christ in Glory occupies a niche above this cornice. The east end is noteworthy for the decoration of the bays, the charming modillions of the axial chapel, and – crowning one of the buttress-columns – a capital featuring two peacocks, the symbols of immortality.

Mines d'Argent des Rois Francs (Kings' Silver Mines)

Visit by guided tour (1hr 30min) Jun–Sep 10am-noon and 2.30-7.30pm; Mar–May and early Oct–mid-Nov Mon-Fri at 3pm, Sat-Sun and public hols 2.30-6.30pm; 6.70€ *(children: 4€).* 05 49 29 19 54; www.mellecom.fr/mines.

Kids The porous limestone on which Melle stands harbours a quantity of geodes – pockets or cavities containing crystallised minerals, in this case lead ore with a small proportion (3%) of silver. The mine from which the ore was extracted, which had been worked since the 5C, became, under Charlemagne, the supplier of silver to a local mint designed to strike the royal coinage. In the 10C the mint was moved elsewhere and the disused mine was forgotten until the 19C.

Since then, the build-up of rubble has been cleared from the ancient galleries to render them accessible to visitors. During the underground tour, primitive ventilation chimneys can be seen, along with a number of concretions, a small lake and traces of the oxidisation caused by the firing which broke up the rock. Sound effects within the galleries evoke an atmosphere of mining.

Chemin de la Découverte
Arboretum

This pedestrian-only trail, which follows stretches of disused railway line, encircles nearly the whole of the old town within its 5km/3mi circuit. Vegetation native to the region alternates with zones in which 650 different species of foreign and exotic trees and shrubs have been planted, all of them labelled for identification purposes. Of particular interest is the **Bosquet d'Écorces** (Bark Grove) north of St Hilary's Church.

MIMIZAN

POPULATION 6 864
MICHELIN MAP 335: D-9

Ségosa-la-Mimizan, which dates back to Gallo-Roman times, was buried by sand in the 6C. The township of Mimizan was built at the end of the 10C, at the foot of a Benedictine abbey. Buried again by the remorseless advance of the sand hills in the 18C *(on the road to Mimizan-Plage)*, the ruins were saved by a local man called Teixores, who was the first to use couch-grass and rushes to consolidate the shifting dunes. The belfry of the **old abbey church**, built in the 13C, is still standing. Richly sculpted, it is surmounted by a Christ in Glory surrounded by statues of the saints, including St John, which is the oldest of its kind in the region of Aquitaine.

- **Information**:38 av. Maurice-Martin, 40200 Mimizan-Plage.
  ☏05 58 09 11 20; www.mimizan-tourism.com.
- **Orient Yourself:** Mimizan is located 33km/19.8mi SW of Biscarosse. The town comprises two different resorts: Mimizan-Ville and Mimizan-Plage, which lie about 6km/3.7mi away from each other.
- **Organising Your Time:** It's worth spending a whole afternoon at the Étang de Léon. Explore the area either on foot or by a boat trip along the Courant d'Huchet.
- **Especially for Kids:** The beach; the farm at St-Paul-en-Born
  (**see Address Book**).
- **Also See:** BISCARROSSE, PARC NATUREL RÉGIONAL DES LANDES DE GASCOGNE

The Resort

Mimizan-Plage

At the end of the street, on the left, a short flight of steps leads to a monument commemorating the landing of the aviators Lefèvre, Assolant and Lotti on 16 June 1929, after their epic North Atlantic flight. The view in all directions from the top of the dunes is superb.

Mimizan-Plage has four beaches along the ocean with supervised bathing and one along the Mimizan channel. Cycle tracks link the ocean and Lac d'Aureilhan as well as Mimizan-Plage and Contis. A footpath runs along the Mimizan channel.

Mimizan has obtained the "Station Kid" label, awarded to resorts which are especially adapted to children: activities, sports, games, adventure playgrounds have been organised for them.

Lac d'Aureilhan-Mimizan

There are pleasant perspectives on this lake from the roadway.

Driving Tour

From Mimizan to Courant d'Huchet

50km/31mi itinerary – allow 2hrs

- ▶ *Follow the D 652 S and turn right just before St-Julien-en-Born.*

Courant de Contis

The Contis channel takes the waters of several local streams down to the ocean through areas of vegetation as dense as they are varied. It winds slowly through the marshes and on through the dunes, beneath a cool canopy of leaves or between high natural hedges of bracken, reeds and alder bushes, intermingled with wild vines.

- ▶ *At St-Julien-en-Born take the D 41 to Lesperon.*

Lévignacq

This charming village, typical of the Landes, boasts an ancient church and low, timber-framed houses with tiled roofs. The church, fortified in the 14C, is unusual with its

Address Book

For coin ranges, see the Legend on the cover flap.

WHERE TO STAY

Hôtel Atlantique – *38 av. de la Côte-d'Argent (Mimizan-plage) – 05 58 09 09 42– www.hotelatlantique-landes.com – P – 38 rooms – restaurant.* This Landaise house from the early 20C is near the beach yet far from the bustle of tourist crowds. There are two room categories here; the more expensive rooms have a balcony. Attractive decor of wooden beams and exposed red brick in the dining room.

Hôtel Airial – *6 r. de la Papeterie – 05 58 09 46 54 – pascal.basset5@wanadoo.fr – closed Nov-Apr – P – 16 rooms.* A small family hotel built in the 1970s in a quiet residential neighbourhood. Friendly reception, simple, well-kept rooms and reasonable prices. Pleasant garden.

WHERE TO EAT

L'Auberge de St-Paul – *Quartier Villenave – 40200 St-Paul-en-Born – 7km/4.5mi E of Mimizan via the D 626 – 05 58 07 48 02 – ste.s@wanadoo.fr – closed Oct-Mar and Mon except Jul-Aug.* An ideal place for a family meal, this auberge amid the pines has something for everyone -excellent food with an emphasis on regional specialities, farm animals, extensive grounds and a children's play area.

LEISURE ACTIVITIES

La Ferme du Born – *Kids – Lavignasse – 40200 St-Paul-en-Born – 05 58 04 80 14 – www.lafermeduborn.fr – open Jul-Aug, daily except Sat 10am-7pm; Apr-Jun, Sep, Oct: Wed, Sun, school and public hols 2.30-6.30pm; 5€ (children under 12 3.50€).* This animal park offers the perfect introduction to farm animals such as sheep, goats and ducks. Children can take part in organised activities, including feeding the animals. Children's play area, picnic tables and shop selling local produce.

SHOPPING

Market – *Place Félix-Poussade – Fri morning.* A wide range of produce from all over south-west France can be bought in this lively market – fruit from the Lot-et-Garonne; hams and cheeses from the Pyrénées-Atlantiques; and foie gras and oysters from the Landes. Popular with locals and tourists.

---

porch and doorway in the Louis XIII style and its belfry-tower. The **wooden vaulting★** inside was decorated in the 18C with paintings. In the chancel is an altarpiece surrounded by cabled columns, whereas in front of the altar itself there is a gilt wood representation of Jesus in the Garden of Olives.

▶ *Return via the D 105 to the D 652, turning left at Miquéou. At Vielle a little road leads to the Étang de Léon.*

Étang de Léon

The cool, clear water in a peaceful countryside setting attracts tourists and water sports enthusiasts.

▶ *Return to Vielle and follow the D 328 to Moliets-et-Maa.*

The road circling the lake goes through rough terrain, alternating between pine forests and marshes, and revealing typical Landes houses with their diagonal brick facing.

Just before the hamlet of Pichelèbe, a bridge crosses the River Huchet. A small path provides a delightful walk through peaceful surroundings (30min there and back).

Courant d'Huchet★

This capricious coastal river, popular with eel fishermen, runs through lush, exotic-looking vegetation and makes for lively **boat trips**, especially enjoyable on hot summer mornings. *Departures Apr-Sep, in the morning for Île aux Chênes (2hrs, 11.50€); in the afternoon for Pichelèbe Bridge (3hrs, 14.50€) and Plage d'Huchet (4hrs, 18.50€). Reservations required (3 days in advance). 05 58 48 75 39.*

MONT-DE-MARSAN

POPULATION 29 489

MICHELIN MAP 335: H-11

This is the capital of the Marsan region in the south-east of the Landes. The town lies at the confluence of the River Douze and River Midou, which join to form the River Midouze. It enjoys a climate that is hot in summer and mild in winter. Palm trees, magnolias and oleanders flourish in the open air, spiced with the tang of pines. Mont-de-Marsan is an important administrative centre, with a curious collection of public buildings in the style known as Empire-Restauration. Some sculptures, formerly in the Despiau-Wlérick museum, can now be seen in the streets.

- **Information:** 2pl. du Général-Leclerc - BP 305 - 40011 Mont-de-Marsan. ☎05 58 05 87 37.
- ▶ **Orient Yourself**: Mont-de-Marsan is situated 130km/81mi S of Bordeaux via the A 63 and the N 134, and 60km/37mi E of Dax along the N 124.
- P **Parking**: There is a free car park at the Préfecture, on boulevard Lattre-de-Tassigny.
- **Don't Miss**: Musée Despiau-Wlérick.
- ⏱ **Organising Your Time**: Allow half a day for a leisurely stroll through the town and a visit to the Musée Despiau-Wlérick, and a full day for exploring the surrounding area. Don't miss the St-Roch market (⏱ see ACTIVITIES).
- **Especially for Kids**: Théâtre Municipal (see Address Book).
- **Also See**: PARC NATUREL RÉGIONAL DES LANDES DE GASCOGNE, SAINT-SEVER.

Town Activities

The market held at place St-Roch every Tuesday and Saturday morning is one of the most picturesque in France.

To the north of the town there is a huge racecourse, with local stabling for 300 horses. The 12 meetings a year here include flat racing, steeplechases and trotting events.

The bullfights and contests pitting men against combative cows (the animals are not put to death in these events), a popular tradition in this region, are held in the town arena.

Sights

Musée Despiau-Wlérick★

⏱ Open daily except Tue and public hols 10am-noon and 2-6pm (last admission 30min before closing). ≈3.40€, no charge Mon. ☎05 58 75 00 45.

The two sections of this museum in the heart of the old town are housed in a pair of beautifully restored 14C buildings (a Romanesque house, a chapel and a keep (donjon Lacataye), linked by a gallery where temporary exhibits are held. The monumental sculptures in the garden are by Charles Despiau (1874-1946), a native of Mont-de-Marsan who was among the artists promoting the revival of interest in sculpture at the beginning of the 20C.

The **Musée Despiau-Wlérik**, located in the old keep, is devoted to modern figurative sculpture. Over 700 works by 100 different artists are on display, most of them dating from the 1930s.

The sculptors include Orloff (Pregnant woman), Bourdelle, Bouchard, Zadkine (Seated Melancholy), Manolo and Gargallo (Urano). The upper floors are reserved for local artists. The stairway linking them is adorned with fine examples of glazed earthenware from Samadet.

Works by **Charles Despiau** occupy one whole floor: they include several female busts, among them Paulette, a marble which was admired by Rodin, and a strikingly naturalistic Liseuse (Woman reading). On another floor The Child in Clogs is an early work by **Robert Wlérik** (1882-1944), the Mont-de-Marsan sculptor responsible

Address Book

For coin ranges, see the Legend on the cover flap.

TOURIST INFORMATION

Tourist office – 2 pl. du Général-Leclerc – BP 305 – 40011 Mont-de-Marsan – ☎ 05 58 05 87 37.

WHERE TO STAY

Le Domaine de Paguy – 40240 Betbezer-d'Armagnac – 5km/3mi NE of Labastide d'Armagnac via the D 11 and D 35 – ☎ 05 58 44 81 57 – albert.darzacq@wanadoo.fr – meals: open daily except Wed 1 Jul-15 Sep – reserv. required – 4 rooms – meals. This 16C manor house stands in the centre of a vast wine-growing estate overlooking the Douze valley. Spacious, attractive rooms, partly renovated, open onto the landscaped park and the vineyards, where hens and ducks roam free. Fine local Landes cuisine takes pride of place in the kitchen of this handsome property.

WHERE TO EAT

Richelieu – 3 rue Wlérick -Mont-de-Marsan – ☎ 05 58 06 10 20 – le.richelieu@wanadoo.fr – closed 1-12 Jan, Sun eve and Sat. Conveniently situated near the Musée Despiau-Wlérick in a quiet street in the town centre, this hotel-restaurant makes an ideal base for exploring Mont-de-Marsan. Reasonably priced regional cuisine is served in the contemporary-style dining room.

BARS

La Cidrerie – 7 r. du 4-Septembre – ☎ 05 58 46 07 08 – Mon-Sat 6pm-2am, Tue 10am-2am. Housed in an old stable, this auberge carries on the Basque cider tradition. The large wooden tables make for a friendly atmosphere.

ENTERTAINMENT

Arènes de Plumaçon – Pl. des Arènes – ☎ 05 58 75 39 08/05 58 75 06 09 – Mon-Fri 8.30am-noon and 2-6pm. Mont-de-Marsan bullring hosts a range of shows, including bullfights, *vaches landaises* competitions, concerts and the Fête de la Madeleine in mid-July. Guided tours daily.

Comité des Fêtes – 39 pl. Joseph-Pancaut – ☎ 05 58 75 39 08 – Jun-Aug, Mon-Sat 9am-noon and 2.30-7pm; Aug-Mar, Mon-Fri 8am-noon; Apr-May, Mon-Fri 8.30am-noon and 2-5.30pm. Tickets for the town's bullfights can be purchased from this organisation.

Espace François Mitterrand – 480 r. de la Ferme du Conte – ☎ 05 58 46 62 40 – ticket office run by the Service Culturel Municipal. This cultural centre with a 3,500-seat capacity holds major concerts, operas and ballets, as well as sports events.

Théâtre Municipal – 9 pl. Charles-de-Gaulle – ☎ 05 58 75 30 71 – performance evenings: ticket office run by the Comité des Fêtes. Plays, dance, song shows and children's entertainment figure on this theatre's programme.

---

for the equestrian statue of Marshal Foch in place du Trocadéro, Paris.

Viewpoint

From the bridge just downstream from where the two rivers meet there is a pleasant view, upstream, of the old houses beside the river banks.

Excursions

Villeneuve-de-Marsan

17km/11mi E via the D 1.
Villeneuve-de-Marsan, a former 13C bastide, still has its original church and ancient tower. The imposing brick church of **St-Hyppolite** is flanked by buttresses and surmounted by a beautiful square fortified tower. Inside, a 1529 fresco recounts the life and martyrdom of St Catherine of Alexandria. The top of the ancient crenellated tower (beautiful brick decoration) looks out over the vineyards which produce Grand Bas Armagnac (brandy).

▶ *Drive SE along the D 1 towards Eauze for 2km/1.2mi then turn right to Perquié.*

Château de Ravignan

Visit by guided tour (1hr) Jul-Aug 4pm and 5.30pm, Sat-Sun and public hols 3-6pm;

May-Jun and Sep-Oct, Sat-Sun and public hols 3-6pm. ₰5€. ☎05 58 45 28 39.
This castle, built on a classical plan, is surrounded by a French garden. The interior is richly furnished and decorated with family portraits and engravings of Henri IV and a particularly beautiful collection of costumes from the court of Louis XVI.

Saint-Justin
A map is available at the tourist office, located under the arches of the place.
This is the oldest *bastide* in the Landes (1280). In its heyday, such notables as Gaston Fébus and Henri IV stayed here. Contemporary visitors will find the hamlet's charm intact.

Court dress from the period of Louis XVI

Roquefort
22km/14mi NE via the D 933.
The home of the Vicomtes de Marsan in the 10C, Roquefort with its 12C and 14C ramparts and towers was once a fortified town. Founded by the Benedictines of St-Sever in the 11C, the **church** later housed an order of Antonites, a hospitaller order who cared for people suffering from St Anthony's Fire (that is, poisoning). The building is mainly Gothic, with fortifications such as arrow slits in the apse and a square tower used as a keep. On the south side, a Flamboyant Gothic portal leading into the church is decorated with the Roquefort arms (three rocks and three stars). Nearby stands the former priory with its Flamboyant Gothic doors and windows.

Église St-Pierre-du-Mas
The large Gothic door to this church is adorned with carvings relating to the Last Judgement. Inside the church, note the **sarcophagus of Sainte Quitterie**★ in the crypt.

Labastide d'Armagnac★
29km/18mi NE.
This picturesque *bastide*, with its old half-timbered houses built around the main square, was founded in 1291. There is an impressive bell tower.

Barbotan-les-Thermes
43km/26mi via Labastide d'Armagnac.
🅂🅟🅐 This spa resort nestles in a peaceful wooded valley.

MOUILLERON-EN-PAREDS
POPULATION 1 177
MICHELIN MAP 316: K-7

Two of the most outstanding men in the recent history of France, **Georges Clemenceau** and **Jean-Marie de Lattre de Tassigny**, were born in this small village typical of the Vendée *bocage*. It was also the birthplace of the celebrated 19C astronomer **Charles-Louis Largeteau** (1791-1857).

▶ **Orient Yourself**: The village is situated on the D 949bis 9km/6mi W of La Châtaignerie.
ⓒ **Also See**: LUÇON, FONTENAY-LE-COMTE.

Musée Jean-de-Lattre-de-Tassigny

A Bit of History

Jean-Marie de Lattre de Tassigny (1889-1952) – The life of Jean de Lattre is interwoven with the history of the first half of the 20C. Scion of an aristocratic Vendée family, he was admitted to the elite St-Cyr military academy; he became a dragoon and then an infantry officer during the First World War. In 1920 he was posted to Morocco, where he distinguished himself in the Rif War. A brilliant tactician, he was promoted to Colonel, and then General in 1939. After the fall of France in the Second World War, he was arrested by the Germans in 1942 but escaped a year later and made his way to London to join the Free French, and from there went to Algiers. In 1944 he led the French 1st Army during the invasion of Provence, subsequently liberating Alsace, crossing the Rhine and advancing as far as the Danube. He was among the Allied leaders who signed the German Act of Capitulation on 8 May 1945. In 1950 he was appointed High Commissioner of Indo-China. De Lattre died in Paris in January 1952; four days later he was posthumously elevated to the rank of Marshal of France.

National Museums

◔Open mid-Apr–mid-Oct 9.30am–noon and 2-6pm; mid-Oct–mid-Apr 10am–noon and 2-5pm. ◔Closed 1 Jan and 25 Dec. ◕3€, (children under 18 no charge). No First Sun of the month no charge. ☎02 51 00 31 49 www.musee-deuxvictoires.fr.

The town hall, which stands not far from the **church** with its 12C belfry (the 13-bell carillon rings daily on the hour), houses the **Musée des Deux Victoires**. As much a memorial as a museum, this establishment reviews in parallel the destiny and the career of two extraordinary men, Clemenceau and De Lattre, caught in the maelstrom of two world wars. Among the documents, souvenirs, trophies and other items on display are a walking stick presented to Tiger Clemenceau by his *poilus* (soldiers; the handle is carved in the shape of a tiger's head), as well as the eagle's head surmounting the pediment of the Reichstag, which was presented to De Lattre in 1945 by the Soviet Marshal Zukov.

In the village, commemorative plaques identify the birthplaces of Clemenceau and De Lattre, who was called *Le Roi Jean* (King John) by his troops. The birthplace of the latter is now the **Musée Jean-de-Lattre-de-Tassigny**. The De Lattre family's lifestyle, characteristic of that enjoyed by a generation of Vendée notables, has been carefully recreated. The house retains its original furniture and there are a number of display cases evoking the life and the career of the Marshal. Opposite the house is the cemetery where the body of De Lattre lies beside his son, who was killed in Indo-China. Two sites are devoted to the memory of De Lattre: the **Mémorial** at La Boinière and the **Oratoire** (memorial chapel) housed in an old windmill situated on **Colline des Moulins** *(2km/1mi E)*. From this quiet hillside there is a fine view of the *bocage*.

NIORT ★

POPULATION 56 663
MICHELIN MAP 322: D-7

Niort rises beside the green waters of the Sèvre Niortaise, distilling a charming air of placid bourgeois prosperity, especially in season when the many flowers around the town come into bloom. Local gastronomic specialities include eels and *petit-gris* (snails) from the nearby marshes, *tourteau fromager*, a cake made with fresh goat's cheese, and **angelica** treats made from *angelica archangelica*, an aromatic plant whose stalks are crystallised (confectionery), cooked (jam) or distilled (angelica liqueur).

- **Information:** 16 r. du Petit-St-Jean, place Martin-Bastard, 79000 NIORT. ☎05 49 24 18 79; www.niortourisme.com. The tourist office organises guided tours of the town (1hr 30min) all year (except Sun). Reservation required. 5€.
- **Orient Yourself**: Niort lies just off the A 10 motorway SW of Poitiers, some 60km/37mi from the coastal town of La Rochelle. It makes a good base for excursions into the Poitou marshlands (&see MARAIS POITEVIN).
- **Parking**: There are several car parks in the town centre, as well as a large car park at the bus station in place de la Brèche (&see MAP).
- **Don't Miss**: The Donjon; the Pilori.
- **Especially for Kids**: Zoorama Européen in the Forêt de Chizé S of Niort.
- **Also See**: TUMULUS DE BOUGON, MARAIS POITEVIN.

A Bit of History

Madame de Maintenon
Françoise d'Aubigné, the granddaughter of the poet Agrippa d'Aubigné, was born in Niort in 1635, in a house on rue du Pont that stood in the shadow of the castle where her father was locked up for non-payment of debts. Sent in disgrace to an Ursuline convent at the age of 14, she escaped and eventually married the poet Scarron, 25 years her senior. After his death the young widow became part of the Court, as governess to the children born to Louis XIV by his mistress Madame de Montespan, and soon caught the king's eye herself; he subsequently created her Marquise de Maintenon. Françoise and the king were secretly and morganatically – that is, her rank remained unchanged – married in

---

Address Book

&For coin ranges, see the Legend on the cover flap.

WHERE TO STAY
Hôtel Le Moulin – *27 r. Espingole – ☎05 49 09 07 07 –* P *– 34 rms.* Built in 1988, this modern hotel was designed by its architect owner. Somewhat removed from the old city centre, not far from the Sèvre, the hotel's rooms are spacious and simply furnished; those to the back of the buidling are quieter.

WHERE TO EAT
La Table des Saveurs – *9 r. Thiers – ☎05 49 77 44 35 – tablesaveurniort@* wanadoo.fr – closed Sun except hols. This old fabric shop near the market hall is now an attractive restaurant decorated in warm, cheerful colours. Excellent daily specials and wonderful chocolate desserts!

La Belle Étoile – *115 quai M.-Métayer – 2.5km/1.5mi W of Niort (near the West ring road) – ☎05 49 73 31 29 – info@la-belle-etoile.fr – closed 2-23 Aug, Sun eve and Mon.* This pretty house on the banks of the River Sèvre is the perfect place for a quiet meal. Dine on the terrace or in one of the elegant dining rooms and enjoy regional cuisine with a contemporary flavour.

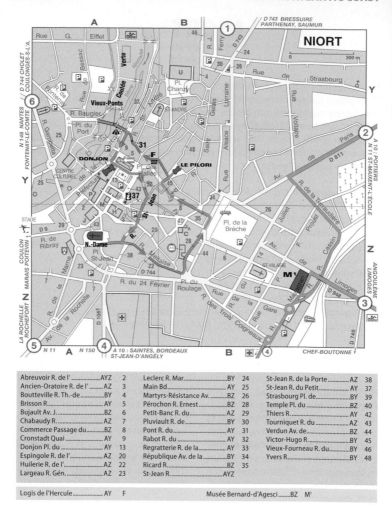

Abreuvoir R. de l'	AYZ	2	Leclerc R. Mar.	BY	24	St-Jean R. de la Porte	AZ	38

Abreuvoir R. de l' .... AYZ 2
Ancien-Oratoire R. de l' .... AZ 3
Boutteville R. Th.-de .... BY 4
Brisson R. .... AY 5
Bujault Av. J. .... BZ 6
Chabaudy R. .... AZ 7
Commerce Passage du .... BZ 8
Cronstadt Quai .... AY 9
Donjon Pl. du .... AY 13
Espingole R. de l' .... AZ 20
Huilerie R. de l' .... AZ 22
Largeau R. Gén. .... AZ 23

Leclerc R. Mar. .... BY 24
Main Bd .... AY 25
Martyrs-Résistance Av. .... BZ 26
Pérochon R. Ernest .... BZ 28
Petit-Banc R. du .... AZ 29
Pluviault R. de .... BY 30
Pont R. du .... AY 31
Rabot R. du .... AY 32
Regratterie R. de la .... AY 33
République Av. de la .... BY 34
Ricard R. .... BZ 35
St-Jean R. .... AYZ

St-Jean R. du Petit .... AY 37
Strasbourg Pl. de .... BY 39
Temple Pl. du .... BZ 40
Thiers R. .... AY 42
Tourniquet R. du .... AZ 43
Verdun Av. de .... BZ 44
Victor-Hugo R. .... BY 45
Vieux-Fourneau R. du .... BY 46
Yvers R. .... BY 48

Logis de l'Hercule .... AY   F   Musée Bernard-d'Agesci .... BZ   M¹

1683, the year Madame de Montespan fell from favour.

When the Sun King died in 1715, Madame de Maintenon retired to the establishment she had founded in St-Cyr in 1685: an institution for the education of impoverished daughters of the nobility. After a remarkable ascension from barnyard to palace, she died there in 1719.

Local Activities

Today, while still a centre of glove-making and *chamoiserie* (tanning and oiling skins to make them supple), Niort is home to more modern activities including insurance. A number of French *mutuelles* (mutual insurance companies) have established their headquarters in

the town, and the industry has made Niort one of its French capitals.

Walking Tour

The town is built on the slopes of two facing hillsides: on one stands the castle keep and the Church of Our Lady; on the other the former town hall and the St-André district. The heart of the town, rue Victor-Hugo, crosses the site of the old medieval market in the lowest part of the valley. At the eastern extremity of place de la Brèche, a huge square bordered with trees, the main roads leading to the town centre converge. Here ancient houses roofed with round tiles line the narrow, twisting streets climbing the slope, many of which have retained their original names: rue de l'Huilerie (oil mill street), rue du Tourniquet (turnpike lane), rue du Rabot (wood plane street) etc. Rue du Pont and rue St-Jean were once shopping streets bustling with market stalls.

▷ *Leave the car in the car park on place des Halles where the walk starts.*

Donjon★

☞ *Currently closed for restoration. For further information, call ☎05 49 28 14 28.*

This **keep** was the most important element in a fortress begun by Henry II Plantagenet in the 12C and completed by his son Richard the Lion Heart. It was surrounded by a defensive perimeter 700m/770yd in circumference. The ensemble formed a small town within the town, which included houses, gardens and a parade ground flanked by the collegiate church of St-Gaudens, destroyed during the Wars of Religion. Under the Bourbons the keep was used as a state prison.

Today its unusual silhouette still towers over the Sèvre. The plan and elevation are original; two tall, massive bastions, square in shape and linked by a 15C building which replaced the primitive curtain walls, are bordered by turrets which also act as buttresses.

Inside the keep, at the entrance level, the **Hall of Glove-making and Chamoiserie**★ focuses on Niort's traditional trades. The lower rooms, vaulted in the 18C, house the town's **archaeology collection.** This includes stone tools, an early Bronze Age gold necklace, ceramics discovered during excavations at Bougon, a 9C BC chariot wheel, Merovingian sarcophagi, coins from the Carolingian era found at Melle, a late Gauloise stele, and a 14C knife-handle of carved ivory representing a shepherd playing the bagpipes. The ethnology department on the upper floor has a reconstructed Poitou interior (c 1830) complete with costumes, furniture, domestic utensils etc.

From the platform at the top of the keep there is a view of the town and the river.

▷ *From place des Halles, take the rue du Rabot and turn left onto rue St-Jean.*

Rue St-Jean

The oldest and most interesting houses in Niort stand in rue St-Jean and adjacent streets. Among them are the 15C Governor's residence (no 30) and, at no 3 rue du Petit-St-Jean, the Hôtel Estissac, an elegant Renaissance mansion.

▷ *Turn right onto rue Notre-Dame which leads to the church.*

Église Notre-Dame

The elegance of this church's 15C belfry is due in part to a lightening of the square tower by the addition of serrated pinnacles to the buttresses; four of the niches hollowed from these still contain statues. The difference in size between the tower and the spire is further emphasised by the placing of dormers and more pinnacles at the base of the latter. Finally the steeple itself, rising to a height of 76m/250ft, is reinforced by superimposed relief arches forming a chevron design.

The north façade, on rue Bion, has a fine doorway in Flamboyant Gothic style.

Inside the church – the layout was reversed in the 18C – the first chapel off the north aisle contains some curious tombs dating from 1684: Charles de Baudéan-Parabère, Governor of Niort, his wife and his son, also Governor in his day, are all represented climbing out of their graves on Resurrection Day. In the third chapel hangs *St Bernard Trampling the Decree of Pope Anaclet*, an 18C painting by Lattainville. The early-16C font was used for the baptism of Françoise d'Aubigné. A Way of The Cross and the carved wood pulpit in the Gothic style date from 1877.

▷ *Follow rue Mellaise, then rue Pérochon which leads to the tourist office. From there, walk to the vast place de la Brèche then turn left towards the Pilori.*

Le Pilori★

This odd structure is the old town hall, built on the site of a medieval pillory. The building, on a ground plan that is practically triangular, was modified in the 16C by the architect Mathurin Bertomé, who bordered it with semicircular towers, crowned it with machicolate parapets and pierced it with mullioned windows. The upper part of the belfry dates from the 17C and the pinnacle from the 19C. Le Pilori is now used for displaying temporary exhibitions.

Logis de l'Hercule
⚬⚮ *Closed to the public.*
It was in this hostelry, which at one time traded under the sign of Hercules, that the first case of the plague epidemic that was to decimate the population of Niort over seven months was reported in May 1603.

Rue du Pont
Old houses with projecting upper storeys line this street and at no 5, out of sight in a courtyard, is the house where Françoise d'Aubigné was born.

▸ *It is possible to continue this stroll through the gardens on the opposite bank of the Sèvre Niortaise, or to return to place des Halles.*

Coulée Verte
This promenade comprises the renovated Cronstadt, La Regratterie and La Préfecture quays and is a pleasant place for a quiet riverside stroll. From the **old bridges** (Vieux Ponts) linking the two halves of the town there is a splendid view of the castle keep.

Museum

Musée Bernard d'Agesci
🕐 *Open May–15 Sep daily except Mon 10am-6pm; 16 Sep–Apr daily except Mon 10am-5pm.* 🎟3.60€ *(children no charge)* ☏*05 49 78 72 00.* Set up in the former Lycée Jean Macé (secondary school), the museum contains all the exhibits from the town's various museums. Named after the local painter and sculpter Bernard d'Agesci, the museum also houses some of his work and there is another room dedicated to the contemporary local sculptor, Pierre-Marie Poisson. Both the **Musée de Beaux Arts** (Fine Arts Museum) and the **Musée Histoire Naturelle** (Natural History Museum) are located in the building.

Forêt de Chizé

20km/12mi S via N150 and the D1.
The Forêt de Chizé south-east of Niort, once part of the vast Argenson Forest which covered the whole region in the Middle Ages, contains more than 5 000ha/13 500 acres of oak and beech which grow in a chalky soil ideal for the cultivation of meridional species. This picturesque forest, crossed diagonally by D1, offers numerous starting points for forest walks; the road is also lined with attractive picnic areas.

Zoodyssée★
🕐 *Open May-Aug daily 9am-7pm; Apr 10am-7pm; Feb-Mar and Sep-Nov daily except Tue 1-6pm.* 🎟9€ *(children: 5€).* ☏*05 49 77 17 17; www.zoodyssee.org.*
Kids The zoo, in the heart of the forest, occupies a former military base sealed off by the Americans during the last world war.
The aim of the zoo is to facilitate the observation and study of European fauna including nearly 600 animals in a 25ha/62-acre forest setting. The first part of the park is devoted to predatory mammals (wild cats, marten, civet, wolves, otter, lynx, brown bears and red fox), birds (diurnal and nocturnal predators, web-footed species and waders), reptiles and amphibians (vivarium), all of whom live in conditions resembling their original habitat as closely as possible.
The rest of the zoo is inhabited by larger mammals free to roam in huge wooded enclosures – graceful spotted deer, skia, roe-deer, agile ibex, chamois and moufflons (wild mountain sheep from Corsica) and an imposing herd of rare European bison and wild boar. The park also has a number of auroch (wild bulls) and tarpan (wild horses), two almost extinct species which have been re-established. A distinctly local animal is the delightful Poitou donkey, which has successfully escaped threatened extinction here.

Moulin de Rimbault
Built in 1682 on the north-east edge of Forêt de Chizé, the windmill, overlooking the Niort plain, was abandoned 1928. It is being restored, complete with a revolving cap on a greased wooden rail, a guivre

(long pole used to turn the sails to the wind), part of the internal machinery and sails with adjustable wooden slats using the Berton system.

Les Ruralies

9km/6mi SE along the A 10 (both ways) or the D 948 (a minor road branches off the D 174 S of Vouillé.

This enormous complex, conceived mainly as a rest area for motorway users, groups together not only the usual restaurants, shops selling regional specialities, and petrol and service stations but also a hotel, an exhibition centre, the local agricultural Chamber of Commerce and a couple of museums.

Musée agricole

&⚪*Open daily10am-6pm.* ⚪*Closed 1 Jan and 25 Dec.* ⚲ *5€ (children aged 8-16 2€; children under 8 no charge).*

The museum illustrates the development of farming techniques through the tools, implements and machinery involved: ploughs and harrows, olive oil presses, stills, harvesters, tractors etc. In the section devoted to apiculture, a hive in full production buzzes behind a transparent panel. Video films are shown.

Châteaux

Château du Coudray-Salbart★

11km/7mi N by the D 743. The path up to the ruins starts near the bridge over the river. 👣*Visit by guided tour (1hr 30min)*

Forêt de Chizé

S. Sauvignier/MICHELIN

Jun–early Sep 10am, 3.30pm and 5pm; Feb-May and mid-Sep to mid-Nov Wed, Sat and Sun 10am and 4pm. ⚲*5€ (children 2.50€).* ☎*05 49 25 71 07.*

The castle, which rises on an escarpment overlooking the Sèvre Niortaise, is an unusual and fascinating example of 13C military architecture. Its construction (1202-25) is linked to the final phase of the battle between the Capetians (Philippe Auguste, Louis VIII) and the Plantagenets (King John, Henry III) for possession of the Guyenne region.

Château de Cherveux

15km/9mi NE along the D 8. 👣*Visit by guided tour Apr-Oct Thu-Sun 10am-noon 3-7pm.* ⚲*5€(children 3€).* ☎*05 49 75 06 55; www.chateau-de-cherveux.com.*

This castle is a fascinating example of 15C military architecture with its keep and machicolated towers.

ÎLE DE NOIRMOUTIER★

MICHELIN MAP 316: C 5-6

The low-lying island, blessed with a mild climate, luminous skies and numerous beauty spots, is a delightful and popular holiday retreat. Auguste Renoir, having stayed here with paintbrush and palette, wrote to a friend: "It is an admirable place, lovely as the South, but the sea is beautiful in a different way."

▶ **Orient Yourself**: The long thin island of Noirmoutier frames the western margin of a gulf south of the Loire estuary, separated from the mainland only by a narrow channel that recedes at low tide.

👁 **Don't Miss**: Passage du Gois.

Kids **Especially for Kids**: Aquarium-Sealand.

A Bit of History

This haven of peace was not spared by the Vendée War, since it was of strategic importance for both sides. The island changed hands several times, which led to the inevitable massacres.

Since Roman times, successive subsidence has been reducing the area of Noirmoutier so that although the island is still 20km/12mi long, it is now scarcely 1km/0.6mi wide at La Guérinière – where, in 1882, heavy seas almost cut the place in two.

The islanders live in low-built houses with red-tiled roofs and whitewashed walls. Since 1959 an undersea pipeline has supplied them with fresh water from the mainland.

A 700m/2 300ft-long prestressed concrete bridge on 9 twin piers has spanned the Fromentine Channel since 1971.

Geographical Notes

Noirmoutier comprises three sectors. To the south, the Barbtre dunes stretch towards the Vendée coast, from which they are separated by the **Fosse de Fromentine**, a gap only 800m/880yd across but scoured by violent currents. The centre of the isle is similar to the Dutch landscape, with **polders** (stretches of land reclaimed from the sea) and saltmarshes below sea level, protected by dikes. The area is crisscrossed by canals, the most important of which, the Étier de l'Arceau, crosses the island from one side to the other.

To the north, a series of creeks indent a rocky coast carpeted with oak, pine and acacia – the flowers, commonly sold as mimosa, are exported each year by the tonne. Here again there are dunes, planted this time with maritime pines, on which several windmills stand.

Resources - The **salt marshes** (see below) glittering beneath the sun yield several hundred tonnes of salt per year. This production is largely due to the unusually high proportion of sunshine, to the generous tidal range and, paradoxically, to bad weather. Of the 700ha/1 730 acres of salt-marsh on the island,

only 100ha/247 acres are exploited, by 40 *paludiers* – proprietors grouped into syndicates or co-operatives which manage the upkeep of the channels and oversee the extraction and sale of the salt.

The island's resources are mainly agricultural. The soil, enriched with seaweed and other marine vegetation washed ashore, favours the production of new potatoes and forced fruit and vegetables which are highly prized. Dry-stone walls, embankments, tamarisk hedges or rows of cypress trees protect the crops from the sea winds.

The riches of the ocean itself, however, are not neglected: oysters are farmed in the Baie de Bourgneuf; fishermen from the port at L'Herbaudière are famed for their catches of sea bass as well as crab, lobster and other crustaceans. The harbour at Noirmoutier-en-l'Île serves mainly as a haven for wintering craft.

Salt Marshes

Jul–Aug (late afternoon). Michel Gallois, 02 51 39 52 72; Véronique Gendron, 02 51 39 58 67; Cathy Guérin, 06 18 01 06 08; Christine and Normand Hallais, 02 51 35 90 14; Martine Ruffio, 06 63 64 79 76; Valérie Simon, 02 51 35 97 22.

Several of the island's salt producers open their salt marshes to visitors (tours last 1hr.

Noirmoutier-en-l'Île

Noirmoutier is the island capital, a white town with sun-bleached buildings extending parallel to a canal-port drained of water at low tide. The 1km/0.6mi-long Grande-Rue (main street) ends at a former parade ground opening onto the port.

Place d'Armes

The royalist **General d'Elbée** was executed by a Republican firing squad on this parade ground in 1794. A little way back from the esplanade, the castle and the church stand side by side on a slight rise. Two fine 18C buildings are nearby: on the right, facing the castle, the Lebreton des Grapillières mansion (now a hotel); on the left the Jacobsen house, named

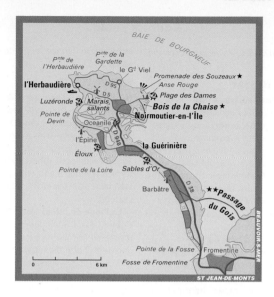

after a Dutch family who worked on the draining of the island during the 18C.

Château

🕐Open mid-Jun–mid-Sep 10am-7pm; early Feb–mid-Jun and mid-Sep–early Nov daily except Tue 10am-12.30pm and 2.30-6pm. ⚫3.80€. ☎02 51 39 10 42.
The 15C defensive perimeter, bare and austere, forms a rectangle interrupted only by two corner towers with bartizan turrets. Picturesque views of the town, the salt-marshes and the sea can be seen from the covered way running around the castle's circumference. Inside the enclosure are the old Governor's residence and a square 11C keep which houses a **museum**.

Ground floor – This floor is devoted to local history: archaeology and the Vendée Wars. The armchair in which General d'Elbée was shot is on display; incapable of moving because he had not recovered from wounds suffered in the battle of Cholet, the General was transported in this chair to place d'Armes, where the executioners waited. A 19C painting by Julien Le Blant illustrates the drama.

First floor – This section contains a diverse assortment of items connected with the ocean: ships' figureheads, model boats, a pirate's axe and sabre, an early-19C cross made from seashells.

Second and third floors – These floors, devoted to the fine arts, contain works by artists attracted by the beauty of the island (A Baudry, F Palvadeau, O de Rochebrune); temporary exhibitions are held during the high season.

Logis du gouverneur – This floor houses a splendid collection of English **Staffordshire pottery**★ (18C and 19C), some of it known as **Jersey pottery** because it was there that the pieces were stored. The variety of shapes, the decorative motifs and the colours used lend this collection a particular brilliance.

From La Vigie turret there is a **panorama** of Noirmoutier and the coast: the view extends as far as La Baule on the mainland to the north and Île d'Yeu to the south.

Église St-Philbert

This former Benedictine abbey church combines the Romanesque (chancel) and Gothic (nave) styles. Beneath the chancel, flanked by sumptuous Baroque altars, a fine 11C **crypt** occupies the site of the original Merovingian chapel. The crypt houses the cenotaph of St Philbert – an empty tomb installed in the 11C, the original sarcophagus having been transferred at the time of the Norman invasions.

Aquarium-Sealand

🕐Open Jul-Aug 10am-8pm; early Feb–Jun and Sep–mid-Nov 10am-12.30pm and

Address Book

For coin ranges, see the Legend on the cover flap.

WHERE TO STAY

Camping Le Caravan'Île – *R. de la Tresson – 85680 La Guérinière – ☎02 51 39 50 29 – contact@caravanile.com – open Mar-15 Nov – reserv. recommended – 385 pitches.* After having pitched your tent behind the dunes, dive right into the pleasures of swimming in the sea or the large heated pool. Direct access to a gigantic beach of fine sand, children's playground, mini-golf, games room and mobile home rentals.

Chambre d'hôte Baranger – *8 r. de la Mougendrie – 85330 Noirmoutier-en-l'île – ☎02 51 39 12 59 – yvan.baranger@wanadoo.fr – 5 rooms.* In a peaceful side street of downtown Noirmoutier, two steps from the château, this house offers guests simple rooms that open onto a small enclosed garden. One studio with kitchen and terrace, perfect for independent-minded travellers.

Château du Pélavé – *9 allée de Chaillot – Bois de la Chaize – 85330 Noirmoutier-en-l'île – ☎02 51 39 01 94 – château-du-pelave@wanadoo.fr – 18 rooms – restaurant.* At the heart of the Bois de la Chaize, this sizable late-19C granite villa is surrounded by a pretty park landscaped with trees and flowers. Its sunny rooms, four of which have big private terraces, are decorated with modern furniture. Lower rates off-season.

Hôtel Fleur de Sel – *85330 Noirmoutier-en-l'île – ☎02 51 39 09 07 – contact@fleurdesel.fr – closed 2 Nov-1 Apr – 35 rooms – restaurant.* Right near the Sableux beach, this low house with white walls and round tiles is quite charming. The rooms are posh, decorated with yew or waxed pine furniture and matching draperies, creating an island-type

WHERE TO EAT

L'Île d'Her – *2 quai Jean-Bart – 85330 Noirmoutier-en-l'Île – ☎02 51 39 11 93 – liledher@wanadoo.fr – closed Sun eve and Mon; open daily Apr-Sep – reserv. recommended in high season.* A popular address with locals, especially the large terrace. A varied menu, with an understandable slant towards fish and seafood.

La Plage de Jules – *At the Plage des Dames – 85330 Noirmoutier-en-l'Île – on the approach to Noirmoutier en l'Île, towards Bois de la Chaize, then Plage des Dames – ☎02 51 39 06 87 – laplagedejules@wanadoo.fr – closed Oct to early-Apr – reserv. recommended.* A delightful setting surrounded by rocks, sand and the green oaks of the Bois de la Chaise. Fish and seafood a speciality, accompanied by the island's famous potatoes.

Marine – *5 r. Marie-Lemonnier – 85330 L'Herbaudière – ☎02 51 39 23 09 – closed 1-24 Oct, Sun eve, Tue eve and Wed except Jul-Aug.* Across from the fishing docks, this white house with blue shutters is run by a young couple. Under its exposed frame ceiling, amid old brass and wood fishing contraptions, you can savour fresh cuisine that's a blend of land and sea. Small garden-terrace in the summer.

Le Grand Four – *1 r. de la Cure – behind the château – 85330 Noirmoutier-en-l'île – ☎02 51 39 61 97 – info@legrandfour.com – closed Dec, Jan, Sun eve and Mon out of season.* Don't miss this little restaurant behind the château. In a vine-covered house, it's as quaint as can be with its comfortable armchairs, fresco-painted ceiling, knick-knacks and omnipresent flowers. The cookery, based on seasonal produce, marries regional flavours with the sea.

---

atmosphere. Terrace service in summer and pool.

2-7pm. 9€ (children 3-12: 7€). ☎02 51 39 08 11.

Local and tropical sea creatures are on show here in a setting featuring underwater caverns and the hulks of sunken ships. A huge pool is reserved for sea-lions.

Musée de la Construction Navale

Open Jul–Aug 10am-7pm; Apr–Jun and Sep daily except Mon, 10am-12.30pm and 2.30-6pm. 3.20€ (children: 1.60€). ☎02 51 39 24 00.

This museum, housed in a former *salorge* (salt loft) once used as a yard by local artisan boat-builders, illustrates the traditional techniques of boat-building. Plans, blueprints, templates, sails and rigging, and demonstrations of wood-sawing and the construction of hulls faithfully reproduce the atmosphere of the old marine workshop.

Excursions

Bois de la Chaize★
2km/1.2mi NE via the D 948 (follow the signs towards Plage des Dames).
This fragrant, harboured wood overlooking the sea could be a corner of the French Riviera: clumps of umbrella pines, ilex trees and flowering mimosa thickets, scenting the air during the mild February weather, combine to give the place its deservedly exotic reputation.
Plage des Dames owes its name to the fact that Gallic Druidesses practised their rites here in ancient times. The sheltered beach, an elegant curve of fine sand, is the starting point of the **Promenade des Souzeaux★**, a charming walk *(45min round trip)* past the rocky, wooded creeks of the island's north-eastern coast.

Leave the beach via the footpath under the ilex trees on the left of the small landing-stage, then follow the first track climbing upwards, again on the left.

After the lighthouse, pines are again interspersed with the ilex. The rocky cliffs here overlook a sea studded with reefs and there are views of the Côte de Jade (Jade Coast), west of Pornic on the mainland. The clifftop path passes above the pretty Anse Rouge (Red Cove), dominated by Plantier Tower, before leading to Souzeaux beach.

L'Herbaudière
5km/3mi NE along the D 5.
A busy traffic of brightly coloured boats animates this small fishing port where the catch (lobsters, crawfish and various white fish) is sold daily at quayside auctions. The multicoloured pennants which serve to mark the position of lobster-pots out at sea give a festive air to the vessels which carry them. A forest

M. Thiery/MICHELIN

The salt marshes, the church and château in the distance

of masts rises above the pleasure craft moored in a neighbouring basin.
From the jetty separating this marina from the fishing port there is a view of l'Île du Pilier, a small island crowned by a lighthouse, which was once linked to Noirmoutier by a causeway.

La Guérinière
4km/2.5mi S along the D 948.
The Port du Bonhomme with its oyster-breeders' cabins shelters on the north coast of the village, whereas the south coast is lined with sand beaches overlooked by the Bois des Éloux and a row of windmills.

Musée des Arts et Traditions Populaire
Open Jul-Aug daily 10am-7pm; Apr-Jun and early Sep–mid-Oct 2.30-5.30pm. Closed 1 May. 3.50€. 02 51 39 41 39.
This museum presents a survey of local activities and folk art in the late 19C and early 20C: agriculture, fishing, crafts and life around the salt-marshes are among the subjects treated. The museum also houses reconstructed local interiors, collections of costumes and head-dresses, and such local folk art as sea-scapes painted on fragments of sail canvas by *cap-horniers* (Cape-Horners) – sailors who had worked aboard the

full-rigged clippers navigating the dangerous seas around Cape Horn in the cargo races of the 19C.

Passage du Gois★★
12km/7.5mi SE via the D 948.
This 4.5km/3mi submersible causeway was the only way for vehicles to reach the island until 1971, when the toll bridge was opened. Shoals formed the Gois causeway; the name is derived from a local term, *goiser*, meaning to wade, which is what you will have to do if you don't read the tide tables correctly. Floats are provided at regular intervals along the way so that people caught by the rapidly rising waters can hoist themselves to safety until the waves subside. It is a busy spot for fishermen, oyster and mussel farmers.

ABBAYE DE NOUAILLÉ-MAUPERTUIS★

MICHELIN MAP 322: I-5

The remains of this ancient Benedictine abbey, half hidden from the road in a small wooded valley, convey the charm and austerity of great Romanesque buildings.

▸ **Orient Yourself**: The abbey is situated 10.5km/6.5mi southeast of Poitiers.
◔ **Also See**: POITIERS; FUTUROSCOPE.

A Bit of History

Battle of Poitiers (1356) – It was not far from the abbey, on the north bank of the River Miosson, west of the minor road to Les Bordes, that one of the bloodiest battles of the Hundred Years War took place. Known to historians as the Battle of Poitiers, this was the encounter in which the French King **Jean II le Bon** (1319-64) was defeated and taken prisoner by the **Black Prince**, son of Edward III of England. The King, surrounded by a few companions, had advanced onto a knoll known as Alexander's Field when he was attacked by the Anglo-Gascon army. Jean, wearing the royal armour garnished with gold fleurs-de-lis, resisted long and bravely, helped by his youngest son Philippe, still only a child, who called out to him warning him of oncoming blows. Eventually, however, totally exhausted and wounded in the face, the King was obliged to give in. To regain his freedom he had to abandon to the English the western half of his kingdom, pay an enormous ransom and allow two of his other sons to be taken as hostages to London. When one of them escaped, Jean himself went to the English capital to replace him, and died there soon afterwards.

Sights

The D 12 from Poitiers offers an attractive view down over the abbey; the old defensive perimeter has been cleared and renovated. Aside from these defensive walls and towers – some have been partly levelled – the abbey was protected by moats fed from offshoots of the River Miosson.
A small, charming drawbridge leads to the vaulted north gate and through to the abbey courtyard beyond. The 15C abbot's residence attached to the entrance is served by an attractive staircase turret.

Abbey church
On the right, the 12C belfry-porch is lightened by a large bay pierced in the 15C. The lateral wall in the centre has a curious elevation: two levels of arching, superimposed, are themselves surmounted by arches and bays; both sets of features are Romanesque but the lower date from the 11C and the upper from the late 12C. The upper parts of the transept and chancel were altered in the 17C: it was then that the semicircular apse was replaced by a flat east end. The impressive dome on squinches, reinforced by ribs, rises above the first bay of the nave, which is

framed by very narrow aisles and has 12C barrel vaulting. Note, near the north entrance, the Romanesque column of blue-grey marble, it was relocated here when the church was remodelled.

A fine ensemble of 17C woodwork (rood screen, choir stalls, lectern eagle) adorns the middle of the church. At the far end of the chancel, behind the 17C high altar, stands an enormous mass of carved and painted stone: the 9C **tomb★** known as the Shrine of St Junien. Staircases on each side of the chancel (restored in the 17C) lead down to the crypt (⊶ *not open to the public*) in which the relics of the saint were venerated.

The abbey behind its walls

Monastic buildings

There remains, south of the church, one wing crowned with a strange Romanesque chimney (said by some to have been a former *Lanterne des Morts*) and, beyond, a 17C building facing the Miosson.

OIRON★★

POPULATION 945

MICHELIN MAP 322: F-3

The small village of Oiron is the home of two splendid but little-known architectural monuments: the château of the Gouffier family and a delightful Renaissance collegiate church.

▶ **Orient Yourself**: The village is located midway between the towns of Thouars and Loudun.

⊙ **Don't Miss**: The château and collegiate church.

A Bit of History

The Gouffier family

Artus Gouffier, chamberlain to François I, accompanied his sovereign to Italy and was so overwhelmed by Italian art that on his return, in the early 16C, he began building a church in the Renaissance style. At the same time he organised the construction of a tower and one wing of the château. Both church and château were completed under the direction of his eldest child, Claude, who also began collecting the works of art to be displayed in the residence. Master of the King's Horse and extremely wealthy, Claude Gouffier held the title of Comte de Caravas: in legend he became the Marquis de Carabas (the fictitious title given to his impoverished master by *Puss in Boots*, the hero of Charles Perrault's fairy tale of 1697).

In 1705 Mme de Montespan acquired the château; she stayed here often until her death in 1707.

Part of a project combining **contemporary art** and historical monuments, the château now houses a collection of specially commissioned works. The contemporary artists drew inspiration from the 16C fashion of cabinets of curiosities – or miscellanea, assembled by scientifically minded people – and the theme of the five senses and four elements, as well as the château itself.

M. Thiery/MICHELIN

Château★★

Open Apr–Sep 10.30am-5.30pm (last admission 1hr before closing); Oct–May, 10.30am-4.30pm. Closed 1 Jan, 1 May, 1 and 11 Nov and 25 Dec. 6.10€ (children no charge). 05 49 96 51 25 www.oiron.fr.

Beyond two small pavilions stands the main body of the château, a central block flanked by two square pavilions crowned by balustrades, and two wings – one 16C with an upper floor, the other 17C with a terrace – framing the central courtyard. On the left, the first floor wing, begun by Artus Gouffier in 1515, was completed by his son, Claude. Of Gothic inspiration, the **galerie des Chevaux** with its basket-handle arcades is surmounted by marble medallions depicting Roman emperors in profile. On the walls of the gallery, the Master of the King's Horses commissioned paintings of Henri II's best mounts. Over the years, the paintings slowly decomposed, leaving behind only a yellowish colour where they hung on the wall, and the brands of the stud farms (still visible) where the horses were bred. In 1992, these ochre panels framed by the arcades were painted in pure, dancing lines by Georg Ettl; the elegant horses they depict trot gaily down the length of the gallery.

A beautiful staircase, its ramp formed by the spiral moulding of the central newel, leads to the next floor forming a majestic **gallery★★**. Here, 14 paintings of remarkable composition and draughtsmanship, their colours now faded, line the walls with subjects taken from the history of Troy and the Aeneid. The Louis XIII ceil-ing was commissioned by Louis Gouffier. Its 1,670 caisson panels depicting various subjects – mammals, birds, weapons etc – are like an overhead encyclopaedia. The gallery leads to the Pavillion des Trophées and the former chapel of Claude Gouffier. The **central pavilion**, begun by Louis Gouffier and completed by La Feuillade, still contains its original 16C works. The admirable Renaissance staircase, with its hollow central newel and straight flight of stairs, was inspired by that of Azay-le-Rideau. The **Salle du Roi** (also known as the *Salle des Armes*), has a remarkable polychrome ceiling, dizzying in its mul-titude of images. Rather than the usual hunting trophies, the walls here are hung with surprising works by Daniel Spoerri, 12 *Corps en Morceaux* (1993), composi-tions of objects reflecting the diversity of nature, chaos controlled.

The **Pavillon du Roi** houses two rooms with the decorative exuberance charac-teristic of the Louis XIII style. The King's Chamber has an extraordinary ceiling overloaded with heavy gilt motifs fram-ing painted caissons.

The *Salon des Ondes* houses the highly original *Étuis d'Or* by Hubert Duprat (1993), gold and pearl cases, which appear to be insects in metamorphosis.

Reflecting the Renaissance passion for the study of nature, the tower's *Cabinet des Monstres* includes imaginary animals (such as a bird's head on a fish's body) created by Thomas Grünfeld in 1992.

Sol Lewitt's *Wall Drawings Room* on the second floor is worth a detour and so are the ground-floor rooms.

Surprising works of contemporary art await inside the Renaissance château

D. Mar/ MICHELIN

In the **Tour de Madame de Montespan** *(south wing)*, from the **Salles des Ouvrières de la Reine** wafts a penetrating fragrance, emanating from a wall of beeswax erected by Wolfgang Laib. Under the domed tower, one of the most marvellous pieces in the château is the *Decentre Acentre* (1992), by Tom Shannon. The smooth aluminium forms fit perfectly into the luminous, round room: a disk is suspended from the ceiling, it slices a sphere in two (the upper half is floating on a magnetic field), creating an image reminiscent of planets and galaxies.

Collegiate Church★

The Renaissance façade includes twinned doors and a large arch surmounted by a pediment bearing the arms of the Gouffier family.

In the transept lie the family tombs, executed by sculptors from Tuscany named Juste, who had settled in Tours. The two largest date from 1537; the smaller pair, from the studio of Jean II Juste, from 1559. In the northern arm of the transept is the tomb of Philippine de Montmorency, second wife of Guillaume Gouffier, who died in 1516. Her recumbent effigy is represented clothed in the garments of a widow. Nearby is the mausoleum of her son, the Amiral de Bonnivet, killed in 1525 while fighting with François I during the French defeat after the siege of Pavia.

The tomb of Artus Gouffier, founder of the church and brother of the admiral, is in the south transept, beside that of his son Claude; the figure of Artus is clothed in armour. A 16C painting after Raphael represents John the Baptist.

The seigneurial chapels, on either side of the chancel, are magnificently decorated in the Renaissance style. The south chapel contains a 16C portrait of St Jerome; the painting of the *Holy Family* in the north chapel dates from the 18C. The keystones in each chapel are very elaborately worked. Also noteworthy are the picturesque 16C statues of the Apostles on the high-altar reredos, the portrait of Claude Gouffier on the north wall of the chancel, and a fine Resurrection, painted in the Flemish mannerist style of the 16C, on the south wall.

ÎLE D'OLÉRON★

MICHELIN MAP 324: B-3 – C-5

The Isle of Oléron is just off the coast between Royan and La Rochelle. The island is a popular holiday resort with families in search of sun, sea, fresh air, the scent of pines and, of course, Oléron's famous oysters.

Since 1966, Oléron has been linked to the mainland by an elegantly curving road bridge, the longest in France at 3 027m/almost 2mi. The viaduct is built of pre-stressed concrete in simple, modern lines and rests on 45 rectangular piles; the central spans, 79m/259ft wide, rise 23m/75ft above the highest of high tides. A 7m/23ft carriageway, two cycle lanes and two walkways for pedestrians are incorporated in the viaduct's total width of 10.6m/35ft. From the mainland, the best view of the bridge is from the old ferry landing-stage at Le Chapus.

🕐 **Organising Your Time**: Allow a full day to explore the island.
Kids **Especially for Kids**: Le Marais aux Oiseaux, Parc Ornithologique de Maisonneuve.
♿ **Also See**: MARENNES, ROCHEFORT, LA ROCHELLE.

Geographical Notes

Oléron, a prolongation seawards of the old province of Saintonge, is except for Corsica, the biggest of all the French islands (30km/18mi long and 6km/3.6mi wide). The Pertuis (Straits) of Antioche and those of Maumusson, ravaged by dangerous currents, separate it from the Charente coast.

The limestone foundation of the low-lying isle is streaked with areas of sand forming long strings of dunes, wooded in the north (Saumonards Dune) and west (on the Côte Sauvage). The white houses of Oléron are surrounded by mimosa, oleander, tamarisk, fig trees and the grey-green spines of agave. Windmills sprout up unexpectedly on the hill tops.

Natural resources – To the east, the coastline and the lowlands between Boyardville and St-Trojan are exclusively reserved for oyster farming – the island's principal economic asset, along with early fruit and vegetables and the cultivation of vines. The vineyards, mainly grouped around St-Pierre and St-Georges, produce white or rosé wines with an agreeable, slightly iodized flavour characteristic of the region. The salt-marshes, once numerous near Ors, St-Pierre and La Brée, have largely been transformed into oyster *claires*.

A more recent development on the island is the establishment of several fish farms raising eels, trout and clams.

The most important fishing port on Oléron is La Cotinière on the west coast but an unusual form of coastal fishing also survives around the Chassiron headland at the isle's northernmost extremity. Here, visitors may see the local catch caught in specialised **fish locks** – walled enclosures fitted with grilled apertures at the seaward end, through which the water filters as the tide goes out. At low tide the fishermen wade out in the shallow water which remains and capture their prey with the aid of *fouënes* (a kind of harpoon) or *espiottes* (a type of sabre).

On the Côte Sauvage (Wild Coast), locals go spear fishing – especially in June and September – for bar and meagrest.

A Bit of History

The Rules of Oléron

In 1199, the 76-year old **Eleanor of Aquitaine**, now a penitent following her turbulent life and scandalous youth, returned to her island possession and stayed in the château here before retiring to Fontevraud Abbey where she died in 1204.

Aged but not resigned, she set about restoring law and order to the island she ruled. The dangerous Côte Sauvage, for instance, had long been at the mercy of wreckers who looted and pillaged ships driven ashore and robbed any survivors from their crews – a practice euphemistically known as *le droit d'aubaine* (windfall rights). Eleanor decreed that henceforth such brigands must be punished:

> *"They must be put in the sea and plunged under water repeatedly until they are half dead, and then taken out and stoned to death as one would dispose of wolves or mad dogs".*

Subsequently the dowager drew up a set of rules "concerning the seas, the vessels sailing upon them, their masters, crew companions and also merchants". This maritime code, known as *Les Rôles d'Oléron*, served as a base for all subsequent charters regulating conduct on the high seas. After the reign of Eleanor (a statue of her stands in the museum in St-Pierre) Oléron was coveted both by the French and the English. In 1372 the English abandoned the isle, taking away with them all the official documents.

The Oléron Pocket

The island was occupied by the Germans in 1940 and liberated on 30 April and 1 May 1945, though not without difficulty: overcoming the stubborn resistance of the 15 000-strong occupiers' garrison and forcing a German capitulation required a large-scale combined operation, which was code-named Jupiter and involved Allied land, sea and air forces.

St-Pierre d'Oléron

St-Pierre is situated in the centre of the island, on the edge of the marshes, and is both the commercial and the administrative capital of the island. In the summer months the town, with its attractive pedestrian precincts, becomes extremely busy.

Church

A pale, octagonal belfry dating from the 18C serves as a landmark for sailors at sea. On each side of the chancel, a chapel is preceded by clover-leaf arching supported by black marble pillars.

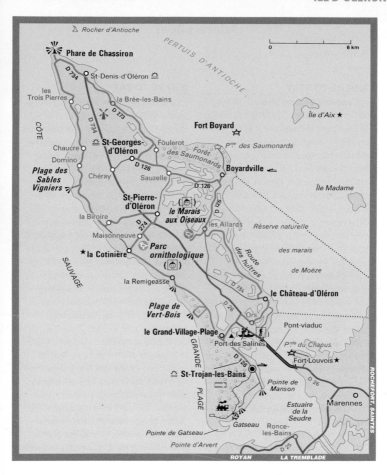

From the platform at the top of the tower (32m/105ft high), the whole of the island is visible in the foreground of a **panorama★** embracing the Île d'Aix, the Île de Ré and the estuary of the River Charente.

Lanterne des Morts

This Lantern of the Dead, rising to a height of 30m/98ft, stands in place Camille-Memain on the site of a former cemetery. The monument was built at the time of the English occupation in the 13C and its slender, sober lines are typical of the early Gothic style. It is crowned by an 18C pyramid roof.

Inside, a staircase still leads to the beacon at the top where the priest used to light the flame symbolising the immortality of the soul. An altar stands against one of the walls.

Maison des Aïeules

It was in this ancestors' house, home of his maternal grandparents at no 13 in the street now bearing his name, that the novelist Pierre Loti, member of the French Academy, spent many of his school holidays. In 1923 Loti was buried – like his Huguenot ancestors – in the family garden, here "beneath the ivy and the oleanders". His childhood bucket and spade were placed near his body, following his wishes. In front of the town hall a bust of Loti, who was born in Rochefort, commemorates the writer's link with St-Pierre.

Address Book

For coin ranges, see the Legend on the cover flap.

WHERE TO STAY

Camping Le Verébleu – *17190 St-Georges-d'Oléron – 1.7km/1mi SE of St-Georges-d'Oléron. Take the D 273, then the road towards Sauzelle* – ☎05 46 76 57 70 – *verebleu@wanadoo.fr – open 26 May-11 Sep – reserv. recommended – 360 pitches – restaurant.* They've got it all! A big aquatic theme park based on Fort-Boyard, a mini-golf, a children's playground, a tennis court, archery, bike rentals…and if you've forgotten your tent, mobile homes, chalets and cottages are also available.

Chambre d'hôte Les Trémières – *5 rte de St-Pierre – 17310 La Cotinière –* ☎05 46 47 44 25 – ✄ *– 4 rooms: 49/51€.* 200m for the la Cotinière port and its shops, this early 20C house is charming indeed. The pocket garden, hidden behind the blond stone wall façade with its blue shutters, is the perfect place for a delicious summertime breakfast under the horse-chestnut. Bedrooms and suites.

Chambre d'hôte Micheline Denieau – *20 r. de la Legère – La Menounière – 17310 St-Pierre-d'Oléron – 3km/1.8mi W of St-Pierre-d'Oléron –* ☎05 46 47 14 34 – *denieau-jean-pierre@wanadoo.fr –* ✄ *– 5 rooms.* Simple, well-cared-for bedrooms have been built in the outbuildings of this typical regional-style house. There's a common room with an additional kitchen. Your hosts, who make wine and pineau for a living, will invite you into their own dining room for breakfast.

Hôtel L'Albatros – *11 bd du Dr-Pineau – 17370 St-Trojan-les-Bains –* ☎ 05 46 76 00 08 – *closed 5 Nov-13 Feb –* 🅿 *– 13 rooms – restaurant* ◷◷◷. This old oyster breeder's house on the edge of the public forest has its toes in the water. The dining-room has a marine style, and theI double-decker terrace opens onto the deep – the ideal place to savour a seafood meal.

WHERE TO EAT

La Belle Cordière – *17370 St-Trojan-les-Bains –* ☎05 46 76 12 87 – *closed 11-31 Jan, Mon and Tue except Jul-Aug.* This family-run and simply furnished restaurant occupies a traditional house in a street close to the church and town hall. Depending on the time of year, dine in the dining room-veranda or on the terrace. The emphasis here is on fish and seafood.

Les Alizés – *4 r. Dubois-Aubry – 17310 St-Pierre-d'Oléron –* ☎05 46 47 20 20 *– closed mid-Nov to mid-Dec, mid-Jan to early Mar, Tue and Wed (except Jul-Aug) and public hols.* The two brightly coloured dining rooms provide an interesting contrast to the white exterior. Local dishes to the fore, including *chaudrée charentaise*, sole, eel etc.

Le Bout au Vent – *Le Port – 17370 St-Trojan-les-Bains –* ☎05 46 76 05 43 *– open 15 Jun-15 Sep –* ✄. If you follow the right bank of the port, you will happen upon this amusing fisherman's house on piles. You can't beat the view of the Oléron bridge from its covered terrace. Leave your hurries behind, the owner works alone. Eglade de moules (mussels cooked with pine needles) on demand and home-made bread.

Les Bains – *on the harbour – 17190 Boyardville –* ☎05 46 47 01 02 – *hotel.des.bains@net-up.com – closed 20 Sep-19 May, Wed from 26 May-7 Jul, Wed lunchtime and 14 Jul-15 Sep.* You can enjoy the liveliness of the Boyardville yachting harbour from the terrace of this modest restaurant as soon as the weather obliges. Rustic dining rooms and appetizing menu. Spic-and-span bedrooms from another era.

Le Relais des Salines – *on the Salines harbour, Petit Village – 17370 Grand-Village-Plage –* ☎05 46 75 82 42 – *closed 3 Nov-15 Mar.* On the harbour, this wooden oyster-breeder's cabin is a pleasant stopping place. Colourful walls and tablecloths and bistro chairs for a lovely view of the salt marshes, their grasses billowing in the wind. Simple à la carte seafood menu.

t-Trojan-les-Bains ⚓

St-Trojan is a pretty seaside resort with Mediterranean-like vegetation. Warm water from the Gulf Stream laps its four sandy bathing beaches; the attractive villas scattered among the trees on the edge of a magnificent pine forest are fragrant with the scent of mimosa flower from January to March.

A thalassotherapy centre (salt-water and sea-air cures) treats rheumatism and other complaints.

Forêt de St-Trojan

This huge stretch of woodland, thickly carpeted with parasol pines relieved here and there by an undergrowth of ilex or clumps of broom, covers an area of 2 000ha/almost 5 000 acres. Much of the forest, commercially harvested, grows on dunes, cresting as high as 36m/118ft.

Grande Plage

3km/1.8mi W of St-Trojan via the D 126E1. This splendid fine sand beach rising to a line of dunes, exposed to the west wind and the Atlantic rollers of the Côte Sauvage, stretches as far as the eye can see in every direction.

Pointe de Manson

2.5km/1mi SE of St-Trojan. The road to the Point ends by an *estacade* (dike). From the top of this there are **views** of the viaduct, the headlands of Ors and Le Chapus, the Seudre estuary and La Tremblade peninsula – which frame what is in effect a small inland sea.

Plage de Gatseau

4km/2mi S of St-Trojan. The road leads to a delightful beach of fine sand, very popular with bathers. On the way there are fine **views** of the Arvert headland, Ronce-les-Bains and the landmark tower of the church at Marennes on the mainland.

Pointe de Gatseau

This isolated promontory at the southern extremity of Grande Plage, separating it from the more sheltered beach at Gatseau, is one of the most evocative spots on the Côte Sauvage (Wild Coast). Access is by a small **tourist train** (⏱open Easter–end of Oct; A special "dusk" service operates in Jul and Aug; ☜10€ (children 7€); ☎05 46 76 01 26) which runs between St-Trojan and the Côte Sauvage.

Island Driving Tour

Round-trip from St-Trojan-les-Bains

85km/53mi – allow 1 day

St-Trojan-les-Bains ⚓
♨See ST-TROJAN-LES-BAINS.

Le Grand-Village-Plage

This seaside resort combines leisure, sport and cultural activities.
La Maison Paysanne de la Coiffe et du Costume – ♿⏱Open Jul-Aug daily except Sun 10am-noon and 3-6pm. ☜4.50€ (children 3.50€). ☎05 46 47 43 44. This local costume museum has preserved the island's folk history by recreating the atmosphere of country life in the past. The farmhouse with its single room and window is fully furnished in the local style. The outbuildings – wine stores, stables and barns – contain exhibits of traditional activities relating to the sea and vine-growing.

The neighbouring **Maison de la Coiffe et du Costume Oléronais**★ includes an attractive display of traditional costumes

M. Thiery/MICHELIN

Oysterman's cottage

(both everyday and festive wear) worn on the island during the last century.

Port des Salines – ○*Open Jun–Sep 9.30am-1pm and 2.30-7pm, Sun and public hols 9.30am-12.30pm and 3-7pm (guided tour daily, except Sat-Sun at 11am and 5pm); Apr–May 9.30am-12.30pm and 2.30-6.30pm, Sun and Mon, 2.30-6.30pm.* *Ecomusée 4€, guided tour 3.50€.* ℡*05 46 75 82 28.* Set in an enclave formed by the road to the viaduct, oyster beds and a forest, this port is a revival of the old salt-marshes.

Two well-marked trails allow visitors to discover the site. At the entrance, brightly coloured **oyster huts** contain exhibits retracing the island's recent history: salt production in Saintonge, fish locks and oyster farming.

Visitors can learn how salt is collected in a salt-works developed around a **cabane à Sau** designed to store up to 200t of salt (the island's last salt maker retired in 1990).

Fine examples of trawlers and oyster boats are anchored in the waters of a small port which provides access to a channel encircling the tidal reservoir. **Boat trips** provide the opportunity to discover the flora and fauna of the salt-marshes. Quai des Hôtes offers visitors a selection of regional food products.

▶ *Return to the road bridge. In Ors, follow the D 275.*

Le Château-d'Oléron

The remains of a 17C fortress, a citadel originally built on Richelieu's orders, stand here. In 1666 the construction of the port at Rochefort led Louis XIV to order the establishment of a *ceinture de feu* (girdle of fire) to protect the Charente estuary leading to this new port. Fouras and the Île d'Aix were therefore heavily fortified and the Oléron citadel redesigned and reinforced. Numerous deportees, both lay and religious, were imprisoned here during the Revolution.

The town is arranged geometrically around a huge central square containing a pretty Renaissance fountain with four cabled columns. The port penetrates the built-up area: a picturesque local sight is the arrival and departure of boats bound for the oyster farms.

The small coast road heading north toward Les Allards is known locally as the **Route des Huîtres** (the oyster road). This narrow roadway permits the servicing of the many canals, sheds and ports strung out opposite the east-coast oyster farms – and gives visitors a fascinating insight, especially at low tide, into the island's ostreicultural activity.

Le Marais aux Oiseaux

&.○*Open Jul–Aug 10am-7pm; Apr-Jun and Sep, 10am-1pm and 2-6pm (Sat-Sun, 2-6pm); Oct–Mar, during school hols, daily except Sat 2-6pm.* ○*Closed 1 Jan and 25 Dec.* *4.20€ (children aged 6-14 2.60€).* ℡*05 46 75 37 54 www.sauvegarde-oleron.com.*

Kids This area of former salt-marshes surrounded by oak trees is now a **bird sanctuary** and nature reserve, providing a winter retreat for some species of migratory birds and a nesting site for others. Herons, egrets, pelicans and wild geese are among the numerous species enjoying the swamp conditions of their natural habitat.

▶ *Return to Les Allards and continue along the D 126.*

Boyardville

The name of the resort derives from a hutted camp established here for the army of workmen building **Fort Boyard.** Boyardville, once a training centre for the crews of torpedo boats, is today enlivened with a small marina. The 8km/5mi beach is in fact the seaward side of the Dune des Saumonards, an undulating 450ha/1 100-acre sand mass covered with plantations of pine trees – an ideal site for ramblers. A forest track leads to the old Saumonards Fort (military territory).

Fort Boyard

○═*Closed to the public.*

This is a curious stone structure rising, offshore, from the shallow sea in the middle of the Straits of Antioche, between the Île d'Oléron and the Île d'Aix. The fort, another project designed to protect the mouth of the Charente, was started in 1804 and completed in 1859 under Napoleon III; progress in the science of artillery, however, which was developing much more rapidly than

Fort Boyard

B. Kaufmann/MICHELIN

...k on the fort, made it militarily out of date before it was even finished. In 1871 it was used as a prison: a large number of Communards (members of a Parisian workers' rebellion who were savagely crushed after the Franco-German War of 1870-71) were incarcerated there before their trial and deportation to New Caledonia.

At the beginning of the 1990s, astute television producers turned the abandoned fort into the striking setting of a televised game which brought international fame. In high season, boats take visitors to within a short distance of the fort.

▶ *Continue along the D 126.*

St-Georges-d'Oléron ⌂

The façade of the 11C-12C Romanesque church in this small town is attractively decorated with geometric motifs. The crowned arch of the central doorway was rebuilt in the 13C and the Gothic vaulting over the nave dates from the same period. The church as a whole was restored in 1618 and again in 1968. There is a fine covered market in the town square.

▶ *Drive NE to join the coast road and turn left towards St-Denis-d'Oléron.*

Phare de Chassiron

🕐 *Open Jul-Aug 10am-8pm; Apr-Jun and Sep 10am-12.15pm and 2-7pm; Oct-Mar 10am-12.15pm and 2-5pm.* ✆ *2€ (children: 1€).* ☎ *05 46 75 18 62.*

This black and white lighthouse built in 1836 is 50m/164ft high. The 224-step climb to the top is worthwhile for the huge **panorama**★ it reveals: apart from the Île d'Oléron itself, the view takes in the Île d'Aix, the Île de Ré, the port of La Rochelle, La Pallice and, offshore, the Rocher d'Antioche with its warning beacon, which looks like a town swallowed up by the sea. Below the lighthouse, at low tide, the fish locks around the cape are visible.

▶ *Follow the coast road S towards Chaucre via Les Trois-Pierres.*

The road, running above low cliffs which mark the beginning of the **Côte Sauvage,** is flanked inland by a plain scattered with market gardens.

Plage des Sables Vigniers

The beach, between two rock spurs at the foot of wooded dunes, offers views of the Côte Sauvage and over a sea that is frequently stormy.

▶ *Continue along the coast road and turn left in La Biroire.*

St-Pierre-d'Oléron

👁 *See ST-PIERRE D'OLÉRON, ABOVE.*

▶ *Leave St-Pierre-d'Oléron S along the D 274.*

Parc d'Oiseaux

♿🕐 *Open Easter–Sep 10am-7pm; Oct–Nov 2-7pm.* ✆ *6.70€ (children 5€).* ☎ *05 46 47 10 32.*

Kids Over 200 species of birds can be seen in this sanctuary, including, among the brightly coloured exotics, the crowned yellowcrest crane, the toucan, the macaw and the blackheaded lory of New Guinea.

La Cotinière★

This is a busy, picturesque port half way down the Côte Sauvage. Thirty small trawlers are based in the harbour, fishing mainly (in summer) for shrimps, prawns, lobster, crab and sole. Once landed the catch is sold immediately at **La Criée** the local term for a fish auction in the covered market. 🕐 *Daily except Sun at 6am and 4pm.* 🕐 *Closed on public hols.* ☎ *05 46 76 42 42.*

A Sailors' Chapel (1967) stands on the dune overlooking the port.

The route crosses the Côte Sauvage dunes, passes **La Remigeasse** and then penetrates an area of woodland (pines and holm oaks) offering tantalising glimpses of the ocean.

Plage de Vert-Bois

The road follows a one-way system to loop through another patch of tree-covered

dune-land fringed with reeds before ... ing at this beach; from here is an impr ... sive **view**⋆ of the ocean, with long lin ... of breakers rolling shorewards every time the wind rises.

▸ *Continue along the same road via Grand-Village-Plage and follow the D 126 back to St-Trojan-les-Bains.*

OLORON-STE-MARIE

POPULATION 11 067

MICHELIN MAP 342: I-3 – LOCAL MAPS SEE LE BÉARN

In the past Oloron and Ste-Marie were an important stage on the pilgrim's route to Santiago de Compostela, one of the last before the climb to Col de Somport, the pass on the Spanish border. In memory of this tradition, contemporary sculptures by artists including Guy de Rougemont, Carlos Cruz-Dies and Michael Warren have been placed at strategic points of historic interest around the town. This unusual urban initiative is part of an overall project to mark out the ancient pilgrims' road, to be continued along Vallée d'Aspe and from there into Galicia via Hecho (Spain). Other sculptures can now be seen in Agnos, Gurmençon, Sarrance and on the Sebers Bridge.

🚩 **Information:** Allée du Comte-de-Tréville.
☎ 05 59 39 98 00. www.ot-oloron-ste-marie.fr
▸ **Orient Yourself**: The town is situated 32km/20mi southwest of Pau.
☺ **Don't Miss**: The doorway of the Église Ste-Marie.
⏱ **Also See**: PAU, VALLÉE D'OSSAU, VALLÉE D'APSE.

A Bit of History

Oloron was once two separate towns, joined together in 1858. It is believed to have been originally an Iberian outpost and subsequently a late Roman citadel surrounded by ramparts on the present-day hillside quarter of Ste-Croix. Rebuilt into a military stronghold at the end of the 11C by the viscounts of Béarn, it served as a staging post along the route of the Reconquista – the wars against the Saracens in northern Spain. It is located at the junction of the Aspe and Ossau which join to form the River Oloron. The river's name derives from *Iluro*, an Iberian place name and a local mountain deity.

Ste-Marie, which was both a rural and episcopal town, developed around the middle of the 11C on the terrace overlooking the west bank of the Aspe. Originally a Roman town, it became a bishopric the beginning of the 6C before it was

destroyed during the Basque incursions in the late 7C.

Église Ste-Marie

This former cathedral dates from the 12C and 13C. The belfry-porch shelters a magnificent Romanesque **doorway**⋆⋆, one of the rare examples of its period which, miraculously, has suffered no serious damage in spite of local invasions and religious wars. The exceptional hardness of the Pyrenees marble used in its construction is responsible for the well-preserved condition: over the centuries the stone has become as smooth as polished ivory.

Among the doorway's most **impressive features** are:

◆ Two atlantes in chains (thought by 19C archaeologists to be Saracens – an allusion to the Moors Gaston found installed in France on his return from the Holy Land, and whom he subsequently drove out); *A Deposition; Daniel in the Lion's Den (left)* and the *Ascension of Alexander (right)*, both of which were reconstructed in the 19C.

* Coving representing Heaven: The 24 elders of the Apocalypse, carrying long-necked jars of perfume, are playing violas or rebecs – three-stringed violins used by minstrels – as they worship the divine Lamb, which carries the Cross. Evil is represented by a dragon's head. This is a literal translation into sculpture of the *Vision of St John in the Apocalypse*.

* Coving representing Earth: the craftsmen used local models to re-create the entire peasant life of the place and the period: boar hunting, salmon fishing and filleting (from 1 000 to 1 500 salmon were caught then each day at Oloron), cheese-making, preparation of hams, barrel-making, goose-plucking etc;

* An equestrian statue of the Emperor Constantine trampling on paganism; and a monster devouring a man.

Interior
There are two light switches, one behind the third pillar of the nave on the left and one at the entrance to the chancel on the left. A lepers' stoup is inset into the first pillar supporting the organ loft on the north side (capital originally from the cloisters). At the entrance to the chancel, note the 18C gilded oak sanctuary lamp and 16C lectern carved from the trunk of a single tree.

Other features of note include the 16C pulpit, the fine organ loft (1650), a 17C crib with carved wood figures (north aisle).

Villa Bourdeu

⊙*Open Jul-Aug daily except Sun 9am-7pm, Sun and public hols 10am-1pm; rest of the year, daily except Sun 9am-12.30pm and 2-6.30pm.* ☎05 59 39 98 00.
This late-19C manor houses the tourist office which is a good starting point to discover the surroundings: a giant map helps visitors appreciate the extent of the territory. A wide walkway is lined with

Elders of the Apocalypse

B. Kaufmann/MICHELIN

a kaleidoscope of photographs of the region (each one showing the distance from Oloron). An old-fashioned train has been turned into a cinema showing short films that create the illusion that you are riding through the landscapes.

Quartier Ste-Croix

The Holy Cross district, the old town surrounding the château of the Vicomtes (destroyed in 1644), is built on a projecting spur between the two torrents.

Église Ste-Croix
Inside, there is an unusual Spanish-Moorish dome, added in the 13C, above the 11C transept crossing. Inspired by the mosque at Cordoba, Spain, the architects of this dome mounted it above star vaulting supported by columns with historiated capitals.

Old houses
Near the church are two fine Renaissance houses; lower down in rue Dalmais is the stately **Grède tower** (14C) with its twinned bays. Beside it is a 17C building which houses the **Maison du Patrimoine** departments of archaeology, ethnography and mineralogy relating to the town and the Upper Béarn region occupy two floors of this museum, together with paintings and souvenirs of the wartime internment camp at Gurs. ⊙*Open Jul-Sep daily except Mon 10am-noon and 3-6pm; Apr-Jun and Oct-Nov, Tues, Thu and Sat (for precise opening times, please enquire).* ◎3€ ☎05 59 39 98 00.

Promenade Bellevue

West of the church, by the terrace overlooking the Aspe torrent and the Ste-Marie district. Follow, on the right, the route along the top of the old ramparts. From here the is a striking **view** up the Vallée d'Aspe t the mountain chain beyond it, which extends westward as far as the Basque country.

ORTHEZ

POPULATION 10 121

MICHELIN MAP 342: H-2

Orthez was the capital of Béarn before Pau; today it is a busy and picturesque town and its most interesting architectural feature is an ancient fortified bridge.

▶ **Orient Yourself**: The town is situated 47km/29mi northwest of Pau and 74km/46mi east of Bayonne.

☺ **Don't Miss**: The Pont Vieux.

☌ **Also See**: DAX, HAGETMAU, MONT-DE-MARSAN, PAU.

A Bit of History

Gaston VII Moncade, Vicomte of Béarn, was behind the town's development in the 13C. After the union of Foix and Béarn, Gaston Fébus held court here. The writer and court poet Jean Froissart (c 1337-c 1400) described in his Chroniques the brilliance of the château receptions after he had been a guest there in 1388 and 1389. Francis Jammes (1868-1938) was another poet of note associated with Orthez. He lived in the town from 1897 to 1907; the wooden-balconied house that was his home can be seen on the way out of town, on the route to Pau.

Old Town

In the days of Gaston VII and Gaston Fébus the ground plan of Orthez did not lie parallel to the river, as it does now: the main axis of the town then was at right angles, clustered on each side of a line drawn from the fortified bridge to Château Moncade. Reminders of this period remain in the dignified old houses, some with decorated porches, which line rue Bourg-Vieux, rue de l'Horloge and rue Moncade.

Pont Vieux★

The 13C bridge, guarded by a tower pierced with an arched gateway, guarded the entrance to the town. The tower was still 'n use as a defence feature in 1814, at the time of the struggle against Wellington. From the bridge there is an attractive view of the Pau torrent, tumbling past the huge blocks of limestone half-blocking the river bed. Another way of having a good view of the bridge is to go under it by canoe!

Château Moncade

◔*Open Jun-Aug daily 10am-12.30pm and 3-7pm; May and Sep 10am-12.30pm and 2.30-6.30pm.* ◉*2€.* ☎*05 59 69 37 50.* The tower is all that remains of the grandiose fortress built by Gaston VII in the late 13C and early 14C. Inside, a model fortress enables visitors to imagine the building as it used to be. Exhibition on the life of Gaston Fébus and his **Livre de chasse** (reproductions). From the terrace (33m/36yd high), view on the roofs of Orthez.

Église Saint-Pierre

Once connected to the town's ramparts, this 13C church was a defensive post, as in the arrow slits in the north wall. Inside the original double nave is devoid of side aisles; along with the chancel with its ribbed vaulting (four very fine carved keystones), this is all that remains of the 13C building.

Musée Jeanne-d'Albret

On the corner of rue Roarie and rue Bourg-Vieux. The elegant 16C mansion once belonged to Jeanne d'Albret, the mother of Henry IV. The building has an octagonal

The Lacq Gas Field

In December 1951, during exploratory drilling by La Société Nationale des Pétroles d'Aquitaine, the Lacq 3 borer hit one of the largest known gas fields at that time, at a depth of 3 500m/11 500ft.

tower which adds to the charm of the main entrance, leading to a paved inner courtyard. The steeply sloping tiled roof is typical of the region. The carefully restored façades reveal the warm tones of the stonework. It now houses the tourist office. On the first floor, an interesting museum retraces the **history of Protestantism in Béarn,** from the Reformation to the 20C (it is not a religious museum), with the help of written documents, objects, medals and small-scale models. This clear exhibition on a complex subject is worth the visit. *Open daily except Sun and Mon 10am-noon and 2-6pm. Closed Jan. 4.50€. (children aged 3-15 2€). 05 59 69 14 03.*

Monument du Général Foy

3.5km/2mi N, on the road to Dax.
The monument is a memorial recalling the Battle of Orthez (1814) in which Marshal Soult's 30 000 men were defeated by Wellington's army of 45 000. The monument sits in a pleasant location surrounded by fine Béarnaise farms crowned by tall sloping roofs, with views of the distant Pyrenees.

Keystone in Saint-Pierre

A. Thuillier/MICHELIN

Maison Chrestia

Open Jul-Aug daily 0am-noon and 3-6pm; rest of the year 8.45am-12.45pm. Closed on public hols. 05 59 69 11 24. www.francis-jammes.com.
The writer Francis Jammes lived in this typical 18C house from Béarn, before he moved to another house, in front of the school, after his wedding. The Francis Jammes Association has been installed there since 1982. They have been gathering documents and books about the author.

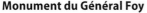

Address Book

For coin ranges, see the Legend on the cover flap.

WHERE TO STAY AND TO EAT

Ferme-Auberge Baron-Maisonnave – *40700 Castaignos-Souslens – 10km/6mi S of Hagetmau on the D 933 towards Orthez – 05 58 89 08 10 – claude.maisonnave@ libertysurf.fr – closed 1 week during Feb school hols –.* Drive slowly on the way to this B&B otherwise you might disturb the fowl wandering freely around the farm! The former barns and stables are now equipped with a rustic dining room. House specialities include dusk, chicken and veal. The owners also sell preserves to carry home with you.

Chambre d'hôte Costedoat – *64370 Hagetaubin – 15km/9mi NE of Orthez on the D 933. Head towards Hagetmau then turn right onto the D 945 – 05 59 67 51 18 – – 4 rooms.* Tempted by life on the farm? This is the spot for you. You can choose to help the owner with his daily chores, unless you prefer a game of billiards, tennis or a dip in the pool. The rooms are spacious and you are sure to fall for the delicious home-made jams served at breakfast.

SHOPPING

Market – Traditional duck and goose product market *(marché au gras),* Tue 7.30-10am from Nov-Mar.

LE HAUT OSSAU★★

MICHELIN MAP 342: J 5-6

Upstream from the village of Eaux-Chaudes, the Vallée d'Ossau separates into three different branches – the Bious, Soussouéou and Brousset – which together are known as the Haut Ossau (the Upper Ossau region). High above this towers the imposing silhouette of the Pic du Midi d'Ossau. The greater part of the Upper Ossau region lies within the Parc national des Pyrénées.

- **Parc National des Pyrénées:** 59 rte de Pau, 65000 Tarbes.
  ☎05 62 44 36 60. www. parc-pyrenees.com
- ▶ **Orient Yourself**: The tours described below start in Gabas, situated 53km/33mi S of Pau via the D 934.
- **Don't Miss**: Lacs d'Ayous; Pic de la Sagette; Lac d'Artouste; Col du Portalet.
- **Especially for Kids**: The train that runs from La Sagette to the Lac d'Artouste.
- **Also See**: Pau.

Driving Tours

1 Vallée du Gave de Bious★

15km/9mi, then 45min on foot.

Gabas

This is a mountain village lying in the hollow where the torrents rushing down from Pic du Midi d'Ossau meet. The 12C village chapel, with vaulting supported by semi-cylindrical pillars and thick, crossed joints, has been redecorated in a modern style. Sheep's cheese prepared (pressed) in a special way is a local delicacy. From Chêne de l'Ours *(2km/1.2mi beyond Gabas)* there is a fine view of the Pic du Midi.

▶ *Drive 5km/3mi N along the D 934. A wide forest track starts on the left, just before the bridge spanning the Bitet.*

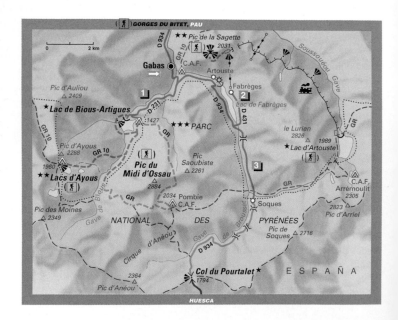

Lac d'Ayous

Gorges du Bitet
🚶 *1hr round trip on the forest track.* A climb through this shady gorge takes the visitor past a series of fascinating cascades, rapids and pools. A hydroelectric pipeline marks the walk's end.

▸ *Turn back, drive through Gabas then turn right onto the D 231.*

The road climbs very steeply, leading to the dam which has effectively drowned the Bious amphitheatre.

Lac de Bious-Artigues★
Looking south from the west bank of the lake, not far from the dam, there are superb **views★** of Pic du Midi d'Ossau: at sunset the andesite rock-faces fade through every shade of red to deep violet. To the south-west is the impressive bulk of Pic d'Ayous.

Pic du Midi d'Ossau
Alt 2 884m/9 462ft.
This mountain peak, recognisable from as far away as Pau, is in the form of a fang – a silhouette which contrasts with the normal Pyrenean crestline, and which is striking less for its boldness than for its delicacy.
A tour of the peak starting at Artigues *(signposted as an alternative to GR10)* is a walk which should be attempted only by fit and experienced climbers. It can be broken by an overnight stop at the

Pombie CAF Refuge. Hundreds of chamois live on the slopes of the peak's eastern foothills.

Lacs d'Ayous★★
🚶 *Climb (on foot): 2hr 30min; descent: 1hr 30min; difference in altitude: 560m/ 1 837ft.* Follow the Parc National signs and the red-and-white markers of the GR10 trail. From the refuge west of these three mountain lakes there are grandiose **views★★★** of Pic du Midi reflected in the waters.

② Vallée du Soussouéou

Allow 4hrs
This excursion combines a ride in a gondola to La Sagette, leaving from the eastern side of the Fabrèges reservoir (Lac de Fabrèges), and a trip on the Lac d'Artouste mountain railway.

Cable-car to La Sagette
🚠 *Jul-Aug, 8.30am-6pm (15min every 30min); Jun-Sep, 9.30am-5.30pm.* ⊜*6€ (children: 4.20€). Combined ticket with the tourist train.* ☎*05 59 05 36 99.*
From the upper station (alt 1 950m /6 398ft) a marvellous **view★★** of the glaciated valley of the Brousset far below – partly drowned now by the reservoir – forms part of the same mountain panorama dominated by the silhouette of Pic du Midi d'Ossau. A look at the **Pic de la Sagette★★** viewing table is worth

Address Book

USEFUL ADDRESSES

Maisons du Parc – The Maisons du Parc National give information on the park's flora and fauna, as well as walks through the park. They also display various permanent or temporary exhibitions, as well as multimedia films or documents:
Maison du Parc (vallée d'Aure) – *65170 St-Lary-Soulan,* ☎ *05 62 39 40 91;*
Maison du Parc et de la Vallée (vallée de Luz-Gavarnie) – *65120 Luz-St-Sauveur,* ☎ *05 62 92 38 38;*
Maison du Parc (vallée de Luz-Gavarnie) – *65120 Gavarnie,* ☎ *05 62 92 42 48;*
Maison du Parc (vallée de Cauterets) – *65100 Cauterets,* ☎ *05 62 92 52 56;*
Maison du Parc et de la Vallée (vallée d'Azun) *65400 Arrens-Marsous,* ☎ *05 62 97 43 13;*
Maison du Parc (vallée d'Ossau) – *65440 Laruns,* ☎ *05 59 05 41 59;*
Maison du Parc (vallée d'Aspe) – *64880 Etsaut,* ☎ *05 59 34 88 30.*

WHERE TO STAY

Refuges du parc – Camping is forbidden. There are two types of mountain refuges: those managed by an on-site caretaker *(open mid-Jun to mid-Sep)* and those that are not. The former get very crowded in summer and you are advised to reserve your place ahead of time. Those that do not belong to the Parc national des Pyrénées are generally managed by the Fédération des Clubs alpins français.

SPORTS AND ACTIVITIES

Hiking – More than 350/217mi of marked paths make the national park a paradise for hikers. Hunting, picking flowers, campfires and dogs are forbidden in the park. Fishing in rivers and lakes (salmon) is, however, allowed with a permit.
Skiing in Artouste-Fabrèges – Altitude: 1400/2100m/4593-6890ft. 10 lifts and 15 pistes for downhill skiing and snowboarding, others for cross-country skiing. (♻ *See PLANNING YOUR TRIP).*

---

the climb (🚶1hr on foot round trip). 🚠 In winter, there is a cable-car service to the slopes of the small family style ski resort of Artouste.

Train from From La Sagette to Lac d'Artouste

🕐 *Jul–Aug 9am-5pm (every 30min); Jun and Sep 10am-3pm (every 1hr).* ☎ *17€ cable-car and train round-trip (children aged 4-12: 13€).* ☎ *05 59 05 36 99; www. trainartouste.com.*
The little train winds and twists its way among the mountain slopes at 1 950m/6 398ft. The 10km/6.2mi **journey**★★ offers striking views of the Vallée du Soussouéou, 500m/1 640ft below.
🚶 From the terminus *(stop limited to 1hr 30min)* a footpath leads to **Lac d'Artouste**★ *(30min round trip).* A dam has now raised the surface level of the lake, which laps the granite slopes of an amphitheatre surrounded by peaks which rise to 3 000m/ 9 850ft.

③ **Vallée du Gave de Brousse**

15km/9mi starting from Gabas via the D 934.

The road skirts the Fabrèges and Artouste hydroelectric power stations then climbs to the level of the Fabrèges reservoir. Ahead, on the Spanish frontier, are the slopes of Pic de Soques – a mountain with a particularly contorted geological structure. Still climbing, the road runs through a narrow channel and leads finally to the Anéou cirque.

Col du Pourtalet★

Alt 1 794m/5 886ft. This border pass is normally blocked by snow from November to June. Looking back towards the north there is a fine **view**★ of the immense pastoral Anéou cirque – dotted in summer with countless sheep – and, farther north still, of Pic du Midi d'Ossau.

ZOO DE LA PALMYRE★★★

This attractive 14ha/33-acre zoo is one of the most visited in France. Shaded by maritime pines and oaks, visitors can admire the scenery from one of the many benches along the path winding through the zoo. Every year 250t of hay, 180t of fruit and vegetables, 70t of straw, 50t of meat, 20t of fish and 7 000l of milk are used. The zoo breeds species threatened with extinction (such as elephants and cheetahs); the lion cub nursery brings pleasure to young and old alike.

▸ **Orient Yourself**: The zoo is situated in the middle of the Forêt de La Palmyre, at the eastern end of the seaside resort of La Palmyre, 15km/9mi NW of Royan.

🕐 **Also See**: ROYAN, ÎLE D'OLÉRON.

The Zoo

&🕐*Open Apr -Sep 9am-7pm; Oct-Mar 9am-6pm.*👝*14€ (children aged 3-8 10€).* ☎*05 46 22 46 06 or 08 92 68 18 48; www. zoo-palmyre.fr.*

Kids Pink flamingos at the foot of a water-fall welcome visitors to La Palmyre. In order to avoid missing something, it is advisable to follow the marked 4km/2.5mi trail; all along the way, panels explain the habits and characteristics of the various species.

More than 1 600 animals from every corner of the globe are scattered throughout the pine forest with its numerous lakes and hills, in areas similar to their natural habitat.

Carnivorous species – The most dangerous predators (cheetahs, lions, wolves, Siberian tigers) live next to smaller mammals (small pandas, suricates).

Birds – A great variety of species are represented here including exotic birds with magnificent plumage like the parrots, cockatoos and midnight blue macaws who use their beak as a third foot!

Hoofed animals – The large species (elephant, hippopotamus, rhinoceros) offer a striking contrast with the more agile species (blesbok, impala and zebra).

Polar bears – Otters and sea-lions are often seen showing off in their pool, but to see polar bears swimming and playing about is certainly unusual. The polar-bear enclosure is a huge pool (1 000m³/1 308cu yd) set up as an ice floe. Below, a wide glass panel enables visitors to see the agility and ease with which these 450kg/992lb giants swim.

Reptiles – A vivarium houses crocodiles from the Nile, royal pythons from Africa and tortoises from the Seychelles Islands.

Monkeys – There is a wide variety of shrewd little monkeys such as the silky golden lion marmoset from Brazil with

Polar bear

S. Sauvignier/MICHELIN

its bright orange fur or the male emperor marmoset with its magnificent white moustache. Only a sheet of plate glass separates visitors from families of African gorillas, the most imposing of all the apes, with their highly amusing antics.

Shows – Additional attractions are the lions' feeding time, a sea-lion show, during which these delightfully playful animals demonstrate their amazing agility, and performing parrots and cockatoos, riding bicycles, driving cars and roller skating.

PARTHENAY★

POPULATION 10 466

MICHELIN MAP 322: E-5

Parthenay is the capital of the Gâtine region, an agricultural area renowned for its sheep farming, dairy products, apple orchards and above all cattle-breeding. The **cattle market**, held every Wednesday in the Bellevue district (behind the railway station), is the second largest in France for animals destined for slaughter. The town is also home to a number of aeronautical, mechanical and electronics industries, and its importance is reflected in the number of trade fairs held each year in the Parthenay Palais des Congrès (conference hall and exhibition centre). From Pont-Neuf there is a fine **view**★ of the oldest part of Parthenay, in particular of the picturesque architectural group formed by Pont-St-Jacques and the ancient fortified gateway beside it.

- **Information:** 8 r. de la Vau-St-Jacques, 79200 Parthenay, ☎05 49 64 24 24. For information on guided tours, contact the Association Atemporelle, ☎05 49 63 13 86; www.cc-parthenay.fr
- ▶ **Orient Yourself**: Parthenay is picturesquely sited on a rocky spur circled by the River Thouet, 43km/27mi NE of Niort.
- **Parking**: There are two car parks in the old town, one near the Porte de la Citadelle and the other near the château *(see map)*.
- **Don't Miss**: The view from the Pont Neuf; Pont et Porte St-Jacques; Rue de la Vau-St-Jacques; Église St-Pierre.
- **Especially for Kids**: The cattle market held every Wednesday morning in the Bellevue quarter.
- **Also See**: NIORT, FONTENAY-LE-COMTE, BRESSUIRE.

A Bit of History

Mélusine

The legendary **Mélusine**, the maid with a serpent's tail, is said to have created the castle at Parthenay in the wink of an eye, – as she is supposed to have done with many fortified towns in the region. Parthenay is, nevertheless, different; the seigniors here were directly de-scended from Mélusine until the Middle Ages, being members of the Larchevêque family, a branch of the Lusignans.

Pilgrims' Way

In medieval times Parthenay was one of the important stops on the pilgrims'

route to Santiago de Compostela. Arriving from Thouars, the ex-hausted travellers would go first to the church (a chapel still exists on the road to Thouars). Having left there those who had fallen ill on the journey, the pilgrims would cross the bridge, go through the fortified gateway and enter the town. Once they had found accommodation in the inns and taverns of rue de la Vaux-St-Jacques they would then pay ritual visits to the local sanctuaries (there were 16), churches such as Notre-Dame-de-la-Couldre and Ste-Croix. Once these devotions were completed, the pilgrims were free to disperse among the taverns in the town or to admire the charms of

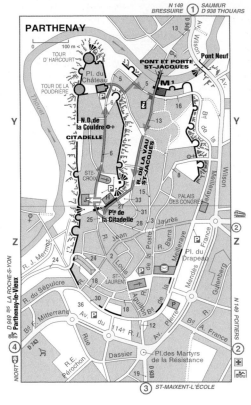

the graceful women of Parthenay, so renowned for their looks that they were celebrated in a popular folk song of the day.

Medieval Town Walking Tour

1hr. The walk starts from the town hall.

Citadel

Perched high up at the extremity of the promontory, the citadel protected the castle keep, the seigneurial residence and two churches behind its massive ramparts (12C). Down below, the fortifications were strengthened by the natural barriers of the river and the Vaux-St-Jacques Valley. In the Middle Ages Parthenay had the reputation of being impregnable.

Porte de la Citadelle (or Porte de l'Horloge) – a powerful Gothic fortification framed by pointed towers – leads into the fortress. In the 15C the gateway

served also as a belfry; a huge bell dating from 1454 still hangs here. Farther on along rue de la Citadelle, on your right are the collegiate church of Ste-Croix (12C) then **Église Notre-Dame-de-la-Couldre,** which has retained a fine Romanesque doorway characteristic of the Poitou region. The street leads to the vast esplanade where the castle used to stand (only two towers remain) and which offers bird's-eye views of the River Thouet meandering below and the Vau-St-Jacques district.

▷ *Take the steps down and follow the narrow rue du Château.*

Pont and Porte St-Jacques★

The narrow 13C bridge across the River Thouet was, and is, the entrance to the town from the north. A drawbridge unites it with the St-Jacques gateway, dating from the same period, which retains its tall, twin towers and its machicolated watch-path.

Address Book

WHERE TO STAY

⊝⊝⊜**Chambre d'hôte Château de Tennessus** – *79350 Amailloux – 9km/ 5.4mi NW of Parthenay. Take the N 149 towards Nantes, then the D 127 towards Lageon – ☎05 49 95 50 60 – closed 24-31 Dec – ⊟ – 3 rms.* A magnificent fortified 14C castle complete with moats, a draw-bridge and spiral staircases. Sleep in a four-poster bed in one of the enormous, medieval guestrooms. One self-catering cottage with a garden and swimming pool.

WHERE TO EAT

⊝**La Truffade** – *14 pl. du 11-Novembre – ☎05 49 64 02 26 – closed 3 weeks in spring, 3 weeks in autumn, Tue and Wed.* Copious portions of hearty Auvergne specialities such as *truffade*, *tripous* and Auvergne ham are served in this traditional restaurant. The decor evokes the Massif Central, with photos of volcanoes on the wall, a display case of Laguiole knives and a collection of cow bells hanging from the rafters.

Rue de la Vau-St-Jacques★

This was once Parthenay's main shopping street and links the two town gateways, Porte St-Jacques and Porte de la Citadelle. The street's medieval aspect still recalls the days of the pilgrims. Some of the ancient half-timbered houses with projecting upper storeys have wide bays at street level, marking the location of former shops and stalls.

The road continues up through place du Vau-Vert (Green Vale Square), skirting the walled citadel – although the towers were long-since levelled, their remains are still visible.

▶ *A footpath running below the ramparts leads back to Porte de la Citadelle.*

Sights

Musée Municipal Georges-Turpin

&⊙*Open Jun–Sep 10am-noon and 2-6pm, Sat-Sun 2.30-6.30pm; May daily except Sat 10am-noon and 2-6pm; Oct-Apr Wed-Fri 10am-noon and 2-6pm.* ⊙ *Closed Tue, Sat and public hols.* ⊜*2€ (children under 15 no charge).* ☎05 49 64 53 73.

Housed in the **Maison des Cultures de Pays**, a contemporary building, the museum has two entrances, one from Porte St-Jacques and the other from the north bank of the Thouet *(car park)*.
Animated models retrace the history and development of Parthenay. Numerous display cases (including archaeology,

The old town by night

D. Mar/MICHELIN

coin collections and furniture), as well as temporary exhibits, offer the visitor a broad picture of the past in Gâtine. One of the rooms is entirely devoted to **Parthenay earthenware** represented by pieces (1882-1916) made by the Jouneau-Amirault duo, who revived this popular art.

Cattle market

🕐 *Open Wed 7.30-10.30am. Enquire at Parthenay market.* ☎ *05 49 94 03 44.*

Kids The cattle market taking place on Wednesday mornings (behind the railway station) is the second most important beef market in France. Sheep and local produce are also sold here.

PAU★★

POPULATION 78 732

MICHELIN MAP 342: J-3 OR LOCAL MAPS SEE LE BÉARN

Pau is the most elegant and pleasantly situated of all the towns on the fringe of the Pyrenees. Pau was highly prized as a tranquil winter resort by the British in the 19C, but its consistently soft and healing climate is still appreciated today. Pau's main tourist attractions are its historical links with Henry of Navarre (Henri IV of France), its particularly fine mountain views and excellent recreation and sports facilities including golf, horse racing, fox hunting and other pastimes introduced by the British in the 19C. Regular events include the **Grand Prix de Pau**, a tough challenge for drivers and their vehicles competing on the 3km/1.8mi circuit through the main streets of the city, and the **Festival de Pau**, which attracts high quality performers every summer.

- **Information:** Pl. Royale, 64000 Pau. ☎05 59 27 27 08. www.ville-pau.fr.
- ▶ **Orient Yourself**: Pau lies just off the A 64, which runs between Biarritz and Toulouse. It is also on the high-speed TGV line from Bordeaux to Tarbes.
- **Parking**: The main car parks can be found in place Clemenceau in the city centre, place Recaborde in the Hédas quarter (near the château) and in cours Bosquet (near the Musée des Beaux-Arts – 👉 *see MAP*). It is very difficult to find a parking place in the old town.
- **Don't Miss**: The view from the Boulevard des Pyrénées; the Château; the doorway of the Romanesque church in Morlaàs; the historiated capitals of Cathédrale Notre-Dame in Lescar.
- 🕐 **Organising Your Time**: It is worth spending at least a couple of days in Pau to explore the town.
- Kids **Especially for Kids**: The Haras National de Gelos; the Cité des Abeilles in St-Faust.
- 👉 **Also See**: OLORON-SAINTE-MARIE, VALLÉE D'OSSAU, SITES DE BÉTHARRAM.

A Bit of History

Gaston Fébus

In the 14C he built a wall around Pau and laid the foundations of the present castle. His successors continued his work and, in 1450, the town followed Lescar, Morlas and Orthez as the provincial capital of Béarn. It was, however, modest as capitals go: each time the States (provincial assembly) met, there were always some deputies who had to sleep under the stars owing to the shortage of lodgings.

An English Town

The English, drawn to the warm climate, settled in Pau from 1840, building sumptuous villas around the town centre. Eclectic architectural styles were adopted, similar to numerous 19C public and private buildings. Each villa has its own grounds and outbuildings: greenhouses and stables, both essential parts of the British lifestyle. Villas, usually private, can still be seen today in the area around Lawrence Park, north of the town centre and the Trespoey district due east.

Address Book

For coin ranges, see the Legend on the cover flap.

WHERE TO STAY

Hôtel Central – 15 r. L.-Daran – ☎05 59 27 72 75 – contact@hotelcentralpau.com – closed 20-26 Dec – 28 rooms. Guests receive a friendly welcome in this modest hotel right in the centre of Pau. The rooms, of varying comfort and sizes, are very clean and well-soundproofed. Lounge with billiards table.

Hostellerie de l'Horizon – 64290 Gan – 9km/5.5mi S of Pau via the N 134 – ☎05 59 21 58 93 – pierreeyt@free.fr – closed 23 Dec-2 Feb, Sun eve, Tue lunchtime and Mon. This pleasant building with a blue and ochre facade overlooks a pretty park with many trees. The structured rooms are furnished in the style of the 1930s-40s, and the dining room has a Japanese flavour. Lovely view of the neighbouring hills from the terrace.

WHERE TO EAT

Au Fin Gourmet – 24 av. G.-Lacoste – ☎05 59 27 47 71 – au.fin.gourmet@wanadoo.fr – closed Feb school hols, 26 Jul-9 Aug, Sun eve, Wed lunch and Mon. Across from the train station and at the foot of the funicular, this restaurant with a big, glass-walled dining room is reminiscent of a bandstand. Brick tiles on the floor and pleasant hues make for a genteel ambience. Contemporary cuisine.

BARS

Le Boucanier – La Flibuste – 64 r. Émile-Garet, Quartier du Triangle – ☎05 59 98 89 12 – open Sep-Jun, Mon-Sat 6pm-2am; Jul-Aug, Mon-Sat 9pm-3am – closed Sun and public hols. One of Pau's most attractive bars, fitted out like a ship's hold. Good choice of beer (130 different varieties) and cocktails.

ENTERTAINMENT

Zénith – Bd du Cami-Salié – ☎05 59 80 77 66 – www.zenith-pau.fr – ticket office: Mon-Fri 9am-noon, 2pm-6pm. This enormous, up-to-the-minute performance hall can seat as many as 6,500 spectators. Operas, classical and pop music concerts, cabarets, circuses, ice shows – they've got it all.

Casino Municipal de Pau – Allée Alfred-de-Musset – parc Beaumont – ☎05 59 27 06 92 – www.groupetranchant.com – open Sun-Thu 10am-3am, Fri-Sat and pre-holiday evenings until 4am. This casino boasts a hundred slot machines in addition to a traditional games room, a restaurant and a bar. Live music on Fridays.

SHOPPING

Au Parapluie des Pyrénées – 1 r. de Laussat – ☎05 59 27 53 66 – open Mon-Fri 8am-noon and 2-7pm, Sat 9am-noon and 2-6pm. Since 1890, the enormous parapluies des Pyrénées, or Pyrenees umbrellas, which provide shelter from the region's heavy outbursts of rain, have been made here. It is the last remaining enterprise of its kind in France.

Confiseur-chocolatier Verdier – 6 r. des Druides – leaving the motorway, take the rocade towards Bordeaux then the N 134 towards Pau city centre – ☎05 59 72 70 30 – open Mon-Fri 9am-noon and 2-6pm, Sat 9am-noon – closed 2 weeks in Aug. Monsieur Verdier wanted to be a musician, but he bowed to his father's wishes and became a pastry and confectionery chef instead, specialising in chocolate making. Today, his many mouth-watering delicacies include raisins au jurançon, cailloux au chocolat and dents d'ours.

Francis Miot – Uzos roundabout – D 37 – ☎05 59 35 05 56 – www.feerie-gourmande.com – open Mon-Sat 10am-noon and 2-6pm – closed Sun and public hols. Francis Miot has been making jam since 1985 and has collected a host of prestigious awards: in 2000 he was awarded the Best Bonbon of France prize for his coucougnettes. A visit to his workshop includes demonstrations, tastings and a special "tasting school" for children.

Josuat – 2 r. du Mar.-Joffre – ☎05 59 27 65 67 – open Tue-Sat 9am-noon and 2.30-7.15pm – closed Sun and public hols except Easter and Christmas. Founded in 1880, this confectioners makes homemade pastries, chocolates and other sweets.

Henri Burgué – Chemin des Bois – Bas de Saint-Faust, 64110 St-Faust – 11 km/6.6 mi SW of Pau via the D2 and D 502 – ☎05 59 83 05 91 or 06 85 20 53 23 – open daily

9am-8pm. This producer makes sweet and dry Jurançon wine, which is aged in oak barrels for a period of three years. The wine is tasted directly from the barrel using glass pipettes.

SPORTS AND LEISURE

Hippodrome du Pont Long – *462 bd de Cami-Salié* – ☎*05 59 13 07 07 – open racing and training days.* This is one of the largest horse-racing tracks in France. 28 events are held here every year. This is also where the Centre d'Entraînement de Sers, with its 600 horses, is located.

Le Plantier de Pau – *5 allée du Grand-Tour* – ☎*05 59 62 37 96 – open Mon-Fri 2-7pm.* Played in the Landes, the Pyrénées-Atlantiques and the Hautes-Pyrénées by 650 card-carrying members, the *quilles de neuf* (nine pin) game is bowling's ancestor. It is played with a 6.2kg ball and nine 96cm-high pins. The players, most of them retired, gather here for a game every afternoon.

Palais des Sports de Pau – *R. Suzanne-Bacarisse* – ☎*05 59 02 54 69 – open Mon-Fri 9am-noon and 2-7pm.* This is the head-quarters of the Elan Béarnais basketball team, five-time champion of France and once champion of Europe. The ultra-modern building, capable of seating 8,000 spectators, is considered to be one of the finest sports arenas in Europe.

Stade Nautique – *Av. Nitot* – ☎*05 59 11 20 10 – schedule varies according to school calendar – open Jun-Aug, Mon-Sun and public hols 10am-7pm – closed mid-Sep to mid-Jun.* This outdoor swimming pool has two sections – one Olympic-style pool for swimming and a deeper pool for diving.

Marguerite of Marguerites

In 1527 Henri d'Albret, King of Navarre, sovereign lord of Béarn and Comte of Foix and Bigorre, married Marguerite of Angoulême, the sister of the French king François I. The celebrated Marguerite of Marguerites transformed the castle in accordance with Renaissance taste, surrounded it with luxuriant gardens and used them as background for pageants and plays which she composed herself, and turned the castle into the foremost intellectual centre of the time.

Birth of Henri IV

Henri and Marguerite's daughter **Jeanne d'Albret** married a de-scendant of St Louis, and her son, Henry of Navarre, later became Henri IV of France as a consequence (©see BÉARN).

Jeanne returned from campaigning in Picardy to Pau for the birth of her son. She arrived on 3 December 1553 and was confined 10 days later. As Jeanne's father had advised, she sang songs in the Béarnaise tongue during labour so that the child "might neither cross nor tearful be". According to custom, directly Henri was born Grandfather d'Albret rubbed his lips with a clove of garlic and then moistened them with the local Jurançon wine, before laying the baby in the turtle-shell that was to be his cradle.

An English Discovery

As early as the July Monarchy of 1830 there were English residents in Pau, and they gradually grew in numbers to form a colony. Some of these expatriates were retired officers who had fought with Louis XVIII on his victorious return from Britain in 1814. It was however a Scot, Doctor Alexander Taylor (1802-79), who brought the town fame and fortune: in 1842 he published his theory – which was rapidly translated into most European languages – that Pau could serve as a winter resort providing cures for various ills, and many visitors came to test his claim; many did indeed find a stay here beneficial.

The local enthusiasm for sports dates from the same period the colony introduced the steeplechase in 1841 (the racetrack at Pont-Long is, along with the Grand National course at Aintree in England, one of the most important in Europe). Fox-hunting followed a year later and, in 1856, the first golf links on the continent were inaugurated. The year 1889, when Queen Victoria instead chose Biarritz for a one-month visit, saw the start of Pau's decline as an international winter resort.

A Green City

Half of the city is covered with parks (750ha/1853acres). Many of them have exotic species, which adds something to the charm of the city. Just to name a few of them: the parks and the gardens of the château, the contemporary gardens in the lower city and the Johanto gardens close to the boulevard des Pyrénées.

Sights

Boulevard des Pyrénées★★★

At the initiative of Napoleon I, place Royale was extended to form a splendid terrace overlooking the valley and the fast-flowing waters of the Gave de Pau, which was aptly named boulevard des Pyrénées.

At the end of the boulevard, the municipal casino stands in the middle of **Parc Beaumont,** with its many varieties of trees and ornamental lake. The boulevard overlooks terraced gardens and a funicular connecting place Royale to the railway station below and offers a spectacular view of the Pyrenees described with great lyricism by many writers.

Panorama★★★ – Beyond the vine-covered slopes of the Gelos and Jurançon foothills, the sweeping view stretches from Pic du Midi de Bigorre to Pic d'Anie, with Pic du Midi d'Ossau standing out clearly in the background. In fine weather, particularly in the early morning and evening and notably in winter, the view can be quite spectacular. Plaques indicating the altitude of each peak are fixed to the railing exactly opposite each summit.

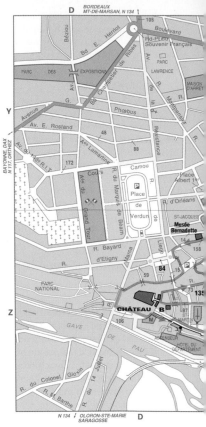

Old quarter

East of the castle, a network of picturesque streets lined with antique shops and restaurants offers a pleasant stroll. Maison Sully, built in the 17C, stands

Boulevard des Pyrénées

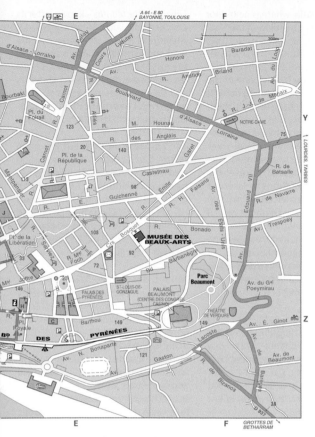

opposite the castle, whereas next door stands the former building of the Navarre parliament, restored in the 18C. Close to Place des États, a crossroads for transhumance until the Renaissance, you can see rue du Moulin, one of the oldest in the city. The adjoining tower is the old belfry of Église St-Martin, built in the 15C. The arcaded place Reine-Marguerite was once the market place where the gallows and wheel were erected for capital punishment. Rue René Fournets, on the left, crosses the quartier des Hédas, formerly reserved to craftspeople. Turn left and join rue du Tran leading to place Gramont, which represents a renovated 19C architectural unit. Behind the fountain, the passage under the porch followed by a staircase leads to the ramparts and to the Tour de la Monnaie and to a canal (15C), which was used for the flour-mill of the château.

Château★★

Visit by guided tour (1hr 15min) mid-Jun–mid-Sep daily 9.30am-12.15pm and 1.30-5.15pm. Rest of the year daily 9.30-11.45am and 2-5pm. Closed 1 Jan, 1 May, 25 Dec. 4.50€, free on the 1st Sun of the month. 05 59 82 38 07; www. musee-chateau-pau.fr.

The castle, built by Gaston Fébus in the 14C on a spur overlooking the river, has lost its military aspect despite the square, brick keep – in typical Sicard de Lordat style – which still towers over it. Transformed into a Renaissance palace by Marguerite d'Angoulême, the building was completely restored in the 19C in the time of Louis-Philippe and Napoleon III.

Royal Apartments – This fine suite of rooms sumptuously redecorated in the 19C includes a superb collection of **tapestries★★★** removed from the royal storehouse during the reign of Louis-Philippe (numerous Gobelins tapestries). The tour starts in the elegant 16C kitchen, where a scale-model of the whole castle is on display.

The **hundred-place dining hall** – with a table large enough to accommodate that number of revellers – has a ceiling with exposed joists. Splendid Gobelins tapestries from the early 18C representing *The Hunts of Maximilian*, and part of the series of 17C tapestries showing the

Labours of the Months – known, after its creator, as the Lucas Months Tapestries – hang on the walls. Elsewhere, note the large and lavish first-floor reception hall, the rest of the Lucas tapestries, Sèvres porcelain vases, neo-Gothic chandeliers and 18C Japanese-style vases.

In the **royal bedroom** stands an unusual, monumental bed fashioned in the Louis XIII style.

The **Empress' Apartment** has been restored to its second Empire style; a washstand complete with toiletries can be seen in the boudoir. Also displayed is the turtle shell from the Galapagos Islands, which is said to have been Henri IV's cradle. The historical rooms contain portraits of Henri IV (16C-17C) and stories relating to his life.

Musée des Beaux-Arts★

Rue Mathieu-Lalanne. Open daily except Tue 10am-noon and 2-6pm. Closed 1 Jan, 1 May, 14 Jul, 1 Nov, 25 Dec. 3€. 05 59 27 33 02.

In the Fine Arts Museum old masters are exhibited next to local little-known artists in tasteful thematic displays of old and contemporary works. For instance, El Greco's *St Francis in Ecstasy* (1590), a feverish expression of mystical fervour, hangs next to an abstract work dating from 1993, *Metaphysical Reflections*.

Paintings from the French, Italian, Dutch, Flemish, Spanish and English schools from the 15C to the 20C include the works of Jordaens, Rubens, José de Ribera, Zurbaran, Nattier, Van Loo and others. In 1878, the Fine Arts School of Pau purchased Degas' *Cotton Exchange in New Orléans*, marking the entry of Impressionism into the museum. The modern era is also represented, with paintings by Berthe Morisot, Armand Guillaumin and André Lhote.

The museum also displays numerous examples of the various trends in contemporary art. Sculpture is particularly worthy of mention, with works by Jean Arp, Gillioli, Lasserre among others.

A regional tone is given by the romantic paintings of Eugène Devéria (1805-65) – mountain landscapes, *Birth of Henri IV* – and visions of fast-flowing mountain streams with the sublime ring of the Pyrenees on the horizon by his pupil

Victor Galos (Pau 1828-79), an exceptionally talented painter from Béarn.

Musée Bernadotte

8 rue Tran. ⓘ*Open daily except Mon 10am-noon and 2-6pm.* ⓘ*Closed 1 Jan, 1 May, 14 Jul, 1 Nov, 25 Dec.* ⚫*3€.* ☎*05 59 27 48 42.*

The museum is in the birthplace of Charles Bernadotte (1763-1844), the Marshal of France who succeeded to the Swedish throne in 1818 under the name of Charles XIV. The salons on the first floor are devoted to the display of family magnificence; on the second floor is an old Béarnaise kitchen and the room where the future monarch was born. The Bernadotte family rented the second floor of this house, built in a traditional style, of beaten cob.

Excursions

Haras National de Gelos

Leave Pau S on the road to Oloron then follow the road to Nay.
1 rue Maréchal-Leclerc in Gelos. ☞ *Visit by guided tour (1hr 30min) 9 Jan–23 Dec daily 10am, 2.30pm, 4.30pm; Sat-Sun 2.30pm, 4.30pm. Public hols on request.* ⓘ*Closed 1-15 Jan, 1 May, 24 and 25 Dec.* ⚫*5€.* ☎*05 59 35 06 52.*

Kids The Haras de Gelos is an equestrian breeding and rearing centre, founded in a former 18C château by Napoleon in 1807. There are breeds ranging from pure-blood Arabs and Anglo-Arabs, breeds from Brittany, the Ardennes and Franche-Comté, Pottok ponies and ponies from the Landes.

La Cité des Abeilles (City of Bees)

11km/7mi W. Leave Pau by the D 2 to Mourenx. At Laroin, take the D 502 hairpin road towards St-Faust-de-Bas and continue for 2km/1mi. ⓘ*Open Jul–Aug, 2-7pm (last admission 1hr before closing time); Apr–Jun, early Sep–mid-Oct daily except Mon 2-7pm; mid-Oct to end Mar: Sat-Sun and public hols 2-6pm.* ⓘ*Closed mid-Dec to mid-Jan.* ⚫*5.50€ (children 3.75€).* ☎*05 59 83 10 31; www.citedesabeilles.com.*

Kids This fascinating, open-air museum, which is undergoing continuous development, is devoted to the bee and its

existence. Visitors follow a footpath climbing a slope planted with sweet-smelling, nectar-bearing flowers to discover the world of apiculture, ancient and modern: traditional old beehives from different regions of France; a covered apiary from a monastery; a glass-walled observation hive in which the workers can be studied tending their allotted honeycombs.

Arzacq

32km/19.8mi NW of Pau. Take the D 943 then the D 39 as you leave Morlaas, then take the D 944 towards Hagetmau.
Maison du jambon de Bayonne – ⓘ *Open Jul-Aug daily 10am-1pm and 2.30-6.30pm;. Rest of the year daily except Mon 10am-1pm and 2.30-6.30pm.* ⓘ*Closed Sun 5 Feb-26 Mar, 1 Jan, 1 Nov, 25 Dec.* ⚫*6€ (children 2.30€).* ☎*05 59 04 49 35 or 05 59 04 49 93 www.jambon-de-bayonne.com* This museum, dedicated to Bayonne ham, has ham-tasting sessions.

Former Capitals

Morlaas

After Lescar was destroyed in the 9C, and until Orthez replaced it, Morlaas became the capital city of Béarn in the 9C. Nowadays, only its **Romanesque church** indicates former glory.

Morlanne

The small brick castle used to be one of the fortresses raised by Gaston Fébus at the end of the 14C.

▹ *Take the D 269 and join the D 945 towards Lescar.*

Lescar

After the Normans had destroyed Beneharnum (about 850), a major Roman city which had given its name to Béarn and had become its capital city, a new town was constructed on the hill.

▹ *Climb up the slope and enter the old city through a fortified door.*

The **cathédrale Notre-Dame** (Notre-Dame cathedral) was built from 1120 on, starting with the choir. The Romanesque **capitals**★ are particularly remarkable.

PEYREHORADE

POPULATION 3 056

MICHELIN MAP 335: E-13

Peyrehorade is the main town in Pays d'Orthe in the Landes département. A particularly interesting example of architectural development in southern France, the town marks the beginning of river navigation on the converging mountain streams of Pau and Oloron known as the Gaves Réunis, which flow into the Adour. Along the quays, yachts are gradually replacing the sailing barges of the past. It is best to visit the town on Wednesdays when the long central market place is busy with stalls and vendors. Peyrehorade is one of only four fish-auction centres dealing with *pibales* (tiny elvers), a great delicacy particularly appreciated by Spanish gourmets.

- **Information**: 147 av. des Évadés. ☎05 58 73 00 52
- **Orient Yourself**: Peyrehorade is situated 35km/22mi E of Bayonne and 30km/19mi W of Orthez on the N 117.
- **Parking**: Quai du Sablot (along the bank of the Gaves Réunis). On Wednesdays (market day), the town centre is closed to traffic.
- **Don't Miss**: The Benedictine monastery at Sorde-l'Abbaye; the Abbaye d'Arthous.
- **Organising Your Time**: Allow half a day to visit Peyrehorade. Note that the Benedictine monastery at Sorde-l'Abbaye and the Abbaye d'Arthous are closed on Monday and only open in the afternoon in low season. A picturesque medieval market takes place in Peyrehorade on the last Wednesday in July.
- **Especially for Kids**: The museum at the Abbaye d'Arthous; the Aire d'Hastingues.
- **Also See**: SAUVETERRE-DE-BÉARN, DAX, HOSSEGOR.

Sights

The **Château d'Orthe** with its four corner towers (16C-18C) stands on the riverbank. Nearby, on the main square is the tourist office where a leaflet describing the walk to the Aspremont castle ruins (11C) is available.

Driving Tour

Banks of the Gaves and Adour

66km/41mi – allow half a day.

- *Take the D 29 East of Peyrehorade.*

Sorde-l'Abbaye

This former *bastide* owes its development to Benedictine monks who used to possess a vast agricultural domain along with a salmon farm and a mill. The interest of the village lies in the vestiges of its abbey, listed as a UNESCO World Heritage site in 1998, and located on the banks of one of the finest stretches of smooth water.

Benedictine monastery

Visit by guided tour (30 min) Apr–Oct daily except Mon 10.30am-noon and 2.30-7pm (last admission 30 min before closing time); Nov–Mar daily except Sat-Sun 9-noon and 1.30-530pm. Closed last week in Dec and first week in Jan, 1 May. 2€. ☎05 58 73 09 62.

In the chapter house are gathered Celtic discoidal steles from the graveyard of Peyrehorade. The only remaining element from the cloister is a pillar and from the main building façades made of stone from Bidache (the marble frames of the parlour have been plundered). From the terrace, there is a nice view on the gave d'Oloron. In the basement, the landing stage remains, as well as the **crypt-portico** which counts fourteen cellars. Note that the steeple of the monastery has been restored with briquettes.

Address Book

For coin ranges, see the Legend on the cover flap.

WHERE TO STAY

Maison Bel Air – 40300 Bélus – ☏05 58 73 24 17 – www.maison-belair.com – ☕ – 4 rooms – meals ☕ ☕.
Surrounded by a garden, this pretty 18C house, typical of the region, has been tastefully restored. Stone walls, exposed beams and old furniture make the lounge and bedrooms (non-smoking) quite cosy. The rooms are large and comfortable, with parquet floors. Gîte also available.

Chambre d'hôte Maison Basta – 335 chemin de Basta, quartier Nord – 40300 Orthevielle – 8km/5mi N of Peyrehorade on the D 33 rte de St-Vincent-de-Tyrosse – ☏05 58 73 15 01 – www.gite-basta.com – closed 2 weeks at Christmas – ☕ –

4 rooms – meals ☕ ☕.
The welcoming landlords of Maison Basta have filled their home with souvenirs from their exotic travels. The lovely 18C house is decorated with attractive furniture and pleasant colour schemes. Swimming pool.

WHERE TO EAT

Ferme-Auberge "Cout de Ninon"– [Kids] – 40300 Sorde l'Abbaye – ☏05 58 73 06 66 – closed Tue noon in Jul-Aug; Mon, Fri and Sun eve – ☕ – reservations required. Chickens, ducks, donkeys, calves, cows and other farm animals give this working farm a charm no child can resist. The dining room is decorated very simply, enabling you to focus on the delicious food made with farm-fresh ingredients.

▶ *Return to Peyrehorade, then leave the town via the bridge over the river and the D 19. Just before the rise, turn right.*

Abbaye d'Arthous

Open Apr-Oct daily except Mon 10.30am-1pm and 2-6.30pm; Nov-Mar, daily except Mon 2-5pm. Closed 20 Dec-1 Feb, 1 May, 1 and 11 Nov. 3€; 1st Sun ech month no charge. ☏05 58 73 03 89.
The abbey, converted into farm buildings in the 19C, was founded in the second half of the 12C and served as a staging post for pilgrims on the route to Santiago de Compostela. The abbey buildings were restored in the 16C and 17C recreating the charm of the traditional half-timbered houses of the Landes region.
The church is especially noteworthy for its completely restored east end. Note the decoration in the apse and two apsidal chapels; billet-moulding is supported by modillions: figures often in pairs, geometrical designs reminiscent of a bed of reeds or a pan-pipe and interwoven patterns. The modillions in the south apsidal chapel depict the seven capital sins. The chancel still has a few patterned capitals with interlaced designs. The south-west pillar in the crossing is surmounted by a carved capital depicting a centaur with an elephant's body (late 12C).

Under the half-timbered gallery of the monastic buildings are two beautiful 4C mosaics from a Gallo-Roman villa in Sarbazan.

▶ *Turn back along the D 19 which becomes the D 10 and goes through Vallée de la Bidouze at the foot of the ruins of Château de Gramont in Bidache. Then turn right onto the D 936 towards Bayonne.*

The road climbs into the open countryside of the Basque foothills. When Bardos comes into sight, pull over onto the left for a **view★★** of the Basque Pyrenees with Pic d'Anie in the background, the first summit (alt 2 504m/8 238ft) in this high chain of border mountains.

▶ *After Bardos, continue along the D 936 to Séquillon. Turn right onto the D 123, and after about 3km/1.8mi, go left to Urcuit.*

Urcuit

Like the neighbouring town of Urt, this little town has a very strong Basque character, featuring a fine Basque-style **church** with an outer gallery. Typical discoid Basque headstones can be seen in the adjoining cemetery.

The church in Urcuit

▶ *Return to Urt on D 257; then take D 261.*

The road follows the River Adour alongside orchards of kiwi trees grown on trellises.

▶ *After 6km/3.6mi, turn right towards Guiche.*

Guiche

Above the entrance to the cemetery is an amusing house on stilts known as Maison du Fauconnier (Falconer's House) which was once the town hall. A little farther along, in Guiche-Bourgade, are the ruins of a castle with a square keep.

▶ *Go down to the old port on the Bidouze and take the D 253 to Aire Hastingues.*

Aire d'Hastingues

▶ *On the A 64 motorway in the Pau-Bayonne direction. Access to the rest area is possible from Bayonne and the neighbouring villages.*

Its geometric layout, which includes the service station, symbolises the nearby intersection of the French roads leading to Santiago de Compostela. Pathways lined with box hedges and panels illustrating well-known sites, lead to a circular building given over to the history of the famous pilgrimage. Inside, information panels, reproductions of art works, slide shows and interactive terminals recount the history of St James the Apostle and the daily lives of the pilgrims as they faced the many trials and tribulations of their journey. An exhibit entitled *La Fin des Terres* (World's End), featuring the *Tree of Jesse* which decorates the pillar of the structure dedicated to the *Glory of Saint Jacques*, recounts the end of the pilgrimage.

▶ *Take the D 3 on the right; the road follows the river.*

Hastingues

This tiny *bastide* is named after the King of England's seneschal, John Hastings, who founded the town in 1289 under the orders of Edouard I Plantagenet, Duc d'Aquitaine. All that remains of the upper town, perched on a headland overlooking the meadowland of Arthous below, is a single fortified gateway to the south-west and several 15C and 16C houses. Take time to admire the charming place de l'Église, shaded by cypresses from the old cemetery.

▶ *Return to Peyrehorade via the D 23. Take the D48 towards Came and then the D 936 towards Bidache.*

Bidache

This picturesque village with its single street and attractive old houses is typical of the Navarre region. From the 14C, the lords of Gramont controlled this area which lies on the borders between Navarre, Béarn and France.

▶ *Return to Urt on D 257; then D 261.*

The road follows the River Adour alongside orchards of kiwi trees grown on trellises.

▶ *After 6km/3.6mi, turn right towards Guiche.*

Guiche

Above the entrance to the cemetery is an amusing house on stilts known as Maison du Fauconnier (Falconer's House) which was once the town hall. A little farther along, in Guiche-Bourgade, are the ruins of a castle with a square keep.

▶ *Go to the old port on the Bidouze; take D 253 to Aire Hastingues.*

POITIERS★★

The most impressive view of Poitiers is from the Plâteau des Dunes in the St-Saturnin suburb east of the town, below the cliff on the east bank of the River Clain. The medieval districts in the heart of the city have much of general interest to sight-seers; a busy student life centring on the nearby university gives the town a lively atmosphere, especially around the square in front of the town hall.

- **Information:** 45 pl. Charles-de-Gaulle – 86009 Poitiers. ☎05 49 41 21 24. www.ot-poitiers.fr.
- ▶ **Orient Yourself**: The old town of Poitiers is built on a promontory surrounded almost entirely by the River Boivre and River Clain. The city lies 102km/64mi S of Tours and 113km/70mi N of Angoulême.
- 🅿 **Parking**: There are three large car parks (fee payable) signposted in the town centre: Charles-de-Gaulle (at Notre-Dame-la-Grande), Carnot (at the town hall), and Rivaud (near the Parc de Blossac). There are also free car parks at boulevard Bajon, Pont Joubert, rue du Jardin-des-Plantes and boulevard du Maréchal -de-Lattre-de-Tassigny *(see map)*.
- **Don't Miss**: Église Notre-Dame-la-Grande; Église St-Hilaire-le-Grand; Cathédrale St-Pierre; Musée Ste-Croix.
- 🕐 **Organising Your Time**: Allow a day or two to explore the old town and visit its churches and museums; an additional couple of days will also give you time to visit Futuroscope 12km/7mi outside Poitiers.
- **Also See**: FUTUROSCOPE.

A Bit of History

Dawn of Christianity

The earliest Christians in the region gathered together in the centre of the Roman city here in the 3C and 4C: St John's Baptistery was one of their sanctuaries. Their first important bishop, the gentle **St Hilaire** (St Hilary, died AD 368), was an outspoken champion of orthodoxy; he also taught St Martin, who was his favourite disciple. Arriving uninvited at the Council of Séleucée, Hilaire found that the monks refused to make room for him – "when suddenly, miraculously, the earth itself rose up and assumed the form of a splendid chair, higher than the others, and all those present were lost in wonderment," according to the chronicler of La Légende Dorée (The Golden Legend).

Another renowned name in the history of the Church in Poitou was **St Radegund,** the wife of Clotaire I, who fled to Poitiers in 559 and founded Holy Cross Monastery – where her confidant, St Fortunat, would recite poems he had written in Latin.

A Momentous Date

Of the three conflicts known as the **Battle of Poitiers**, that in which Charles Martel vanquished the army of the invading Arabs in AD 732 and saved Christianity is by far the most famous – and the most important.

The Arabs – Moors, Saracens – having conquered Spain flooded into Gaul from the south. Checked for the first time by Eudes, Duke of Aquitaine, they decimated his forces near Bordeaux and continued towards the centre of the country, sacking and pillaging everything on their way. Eudes asked for help from the Merovingian leader Charles Martel; the Arabs, who had just burnt down Église St-Hilaire in Poitiers, found themselves confronted by the Frankish troops a few miles north of the town.

Martel's cavalry cut the Moslem army to ribbons, and little by little the invaders began to retreat from Aquitaine. The year 732 remains as an important symbol of Western Christianity's first true victory over the Moslems.

Address Book

For coin ranges, see the Legend on the cover flap.

WHERE TO STAY

Hôtel Gibautel – *rte de Nouaillé* – ☎05 49 46 16 16 – *hotel.gibautel@wanadoo.fr* – 📂 – *36 rooms*. This modern hotel situated opposite a clinic on the outskirts of Poitiers has small, modern and well-equipped rooms.

Chambre d'hôte Château de Vaumoret – *r. du Breuil Mingot – 10km/6mi NE of Poitiers. Take the D3 towards La Roche-Posay, then the D 18 to Sèvres-Anxaumont* – ☎05 49 61 32 11 – 🍽 – *5 rooms*. Although only a few kilometres from Poitiers, this B&B is surrounded by peaceful countryside. Housed in a delightful 17C château in grounds of 15ha/37 acres, the guestrooms here are attractively furnished in traditional style. The perfect place to unwind.

Hôtel Château de Périgny – *Périgny – 86190 Vouillé – 17km/12mi NW of Poitiers via the N 149 and a secondary road* – ☎05 49 51 80 43 – *info@château-perigny.cim* – 📂 – *39 rooms – restaurant*. Right in the middle of a park, this 15C château is a haven of peace and tranquillity. The rooms are furnished in period or modern style; those in the annexe are a little more basic.

WHERE TO EAT

Les Bons Enfants – *11 bis r. Cloche-Perse* – ☎05 49 41 49 82 – *closed 20-29 Feb, Sun eve and Mon*. Amid the many schools of this neighbourhood, this little restaurant with a green façade boasts a large painting of a group of late-19C schoolchildren. The restaurant specialises in regional cuisine. Friendly ambience.

L'Orée des Bois – *86280 St-Benoît* –☎05 49 57 11 44 – *Closed Sat noon, Sun eve and Mon*. This building covered in Virginia creeper is a restful place for a meal away from the bustle of the city centre. There are two country-style dining rooms, one with a fireplace. Traditional local fare.

Poitevin – *76 r. Carnot* – ☎05 49 88 35 04 – *closed 19 Apr-2 May, 11 Jul-3 Aug, 23 Dec-3 Jan and Sun*. The accent is on traditional regional cuisine in this busy restaurant which is popular with locals.

Sample specialities such as *mouclade charentaise* or *farci poitevin* in one of four comfortable contemporary-style dining rooms.

Le Chalet de Venise – *in the village – 86280 St-Benoît – 4km/2.4mi S of Poitiers via the D 88* – ☎ *05 49 88 45 07 – closed 1-10 Mar, 23 Aug-2 Sep, Sun eve and Mon*. This charming restaurant is situated just outside Poitiers in the village of St-Benoît. The outdoor terrace overlooking a peaceful garden with a stream is the perfect spot for a meal in summer, while the comfortable dining room has a cosy ambience in winter. Pleasant rooms.

CAFES

Jasmin Citronnelle – *32 r. Gambetta* – ☎05 49 41 37 26. This delightful tea-room situated opposite a flower-filled courtyard serves a wide variety of teas, pastries and ice cream, as well as quiches and salads at lunchtime. Attractive terrace in summer. Exhibitions of paintings.

Chez Cul de Paille – *3 r. Théophraste-Renaudot – city centre* – ☎05 49 41 07 35 – *Mon-Sat 9am-11pm – closed 2nd week of school hols in Feb, in May, for a week in Aug, and Sun*. A charming auberge with flagstones on the floor, straw stools and old varnished tables. The graffiti on the ochre walls includes some famous signatures, including those of Arletty, Brel and Coluche.

SHOPPING

Market – *Mon-Sat*. The main food market takes place in the market hall near Église Notre-Dame-la-Grande. There is an excellent choice of fruit and vegetables, fish, meat, cheese and bread.

Bajard – *8 r. Carnot* – ☎ *05 49 41 22 49*. This elegant pâtisserie specialises in home-made cakes and pastries. Specialities include Le Ventou, a macaroon biscuit topped with nougat and raspberry coulis, and the Ambré, a mixture of caramel cream and pear mousse.

Rannou-Métivier – *30 r. des Cordeliers – open Mon afternoon to Sat, 9am-7pm* – ☎ *05 49 30 30 10*. For five generations, the Rannou-Métivier family has perfected its skills in the art of almond confectionery. The award-winning house speciality is the delicious Montmorillon macaroon.

Jean de Berry's Court

The city of Poitiers, having twice fallen under English domination – in the 12C by Henry Plantagenet and Eleanor of Aquitaine, in the 14C after the second Battle of Poitiers in 1356 – was finally restored to the French crown after General Bertrand du Guesclin (c 1320-80) had chased the English from the region. The royal representative was the brother of Charles: Jean, Comte de Poitou and holder of the Berry and Auvergne dukedoms.

De Berry's rule, which extended from 1369 to 1416, brought fame and prosperity to Poitiers. Jean de Berry was ostentatious and sophisticated, a generous patron of the arts, and never travelled anywhere without his menagerie and a retinue of talented artists.

Poitiers During the Renaissance

The intellectual reputation of the renowned 4 000-student university drew many thinkers and writers to Poitiers.

Following his patron and protector Geoffroy d'Estissac, **Rabelais** stayed here several times between 1524 and 1527; Calvin was also a visitor. This city of monks and priests (there were 67 churches then) – "A big town and confident, teeming with scholars" as it was described at the time – became for a while France's third most important cultural centre after Paris and Lyon. Certain members of the humanist philosophical and poetic group known as Les Pléiades came to rub shoulders with the learned at the university. They included the mathematician Jacques Pelletier, Ronsard, the leading light of the group, the poet Jean-Antoine de Baïf and Joachim du Bellay, another poet who modelled his style on the Hellenistic lyricism of antiquity.

Four-Hundred Years of Sleep

Poitiers was not spared by the Wars of Religion. Destruction, misery, famine were visited upon the town, which in addition twice suffered the rigours of a siege. From then on life in Poitiers went into decline; even the university, despite the fame of some of its students – Descartes for instance – shared the same fate.

Despite the strenuous efforts of the Intendant **Comte de Blossac,** this slumber persisted until after the Second World War. Since then the influence of a younger generation has injected a new dynamism into the town and has enabled it to reclaim its position as capital of the Poitou-Charentes region.

Église Notre-Dame-La-Grande★★

The name of this former collegiate church stems from S. Maria Maggiore Church in Rome. The building, with its perfect lines and the aesthetic balance of its architectural features, stands as a supreme example of Romanesque art in France. The west front, which has blackened over the centuries, is one of the most famous in the country.

The dimensions of the church are: length 57m/187ft, width 13m/43ft, height 16.6m/54ft.

West front★★★ – The elegant west front, magnificently restored in recent years, dates from the 12C and typifies the Poitou Romanesque style – even if the architects were influenced by the art of the Saintonge area. It is densely carved and the lively figures are further accentuated, according to the time of day, by the play of light and shade. In the centre, at ground level, is an arched doorway with four receding lines of coving, flanked by arcades framing twinned arches within. Above these three arched elements are

The west front of Notre-Dame-la-Grande

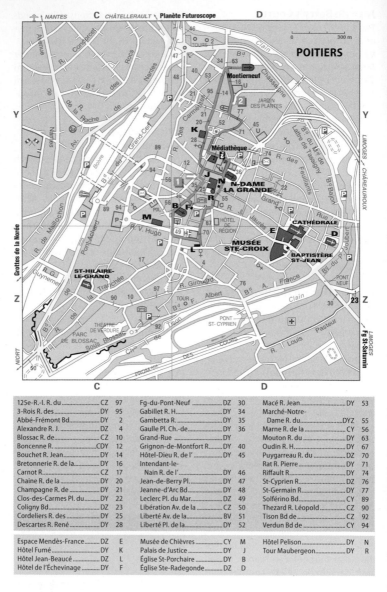

POITIERS

bas-relief sculptures of (read from left to right and from the lower level to upper) *Adam and Eve; Nebuchadnezzar on his Throne; the Four Prophets Moses, Jeremiah, Isaiah and Daniel;* the *Annunciation; the Tree of Jesse;* the *Visitation;* the *Nativity;* the *Bathing of the Infant Christ;* the *Meditation of St Joseph.*

The central doorway is surmounted by a large, very tall arched window bay, itself flanked by a double row of blind arcades housing the Apostles and (at the extremities of the upper row) two figures said to be St Hilary and St Martin. The coving of the arcades is decorated with fine carvings representing plants and fantastic creatures.

Christ in Majesty gazes down from an oval-shaped frame in the great gable above. The figure is surrounded by the symbols of the Evangelists and crowned by a stylised sun and moon, metaphors for eternity in the Romanesque period.

At each side of the west front a cluster of columns supports a pierced lantern with straight or arched cornices and a roof in the shape of a pine-cone, covered with scales.

North Wall – The chapels flanking this side of the church were added in the 15C *(against the chancel)* and the 16C *(along the aisle)*. Note the unusual silhouette of the square-sectioned 12C belfry with a pierced turret, again topped by a pine-cone roof.

Interior – The interior of the church, which is in the Poitou style but without a transept, was unfortunately repainted in 1851. On each side of the barrel-vaulted nave are very high rib-vaulted aisles.

A 17C copper goblin can be seen in the chancel. Behind the high altar stands a 16C statue of Notre-Dame-des-Clefs (Our Lady of the Keys), installed to replace the original which was destroyed in 1562: the statue recalls a miracle said to have occurred in 1202, when the keys of the town were spirited away from the traitor who was going to hand them over to the besieging English. The oven vault above the chancel – painted in the 12C with a fresco depicting the *Virgin in Majesty* and *Christ in Glory* – is supported by six heavy, round columns arranged in a semicircle. The original apsidal chapel, on the south side of the ambulatory, was replaced in 1475 by another, now dedicated to St Anne. This was founded by Yvon du Fou, the Seneschal (Steward) of the city, whose armorial bearings can be seen above the fine Flamboyant funerary niche where his tomb was lodged. In its place now is an Italian version of the *Entombment*, in polychrome stone, which dates from the 16C. The work was once in Trinity Abbey in Poitiers.

Town Walks

The town hall has laid out three coloured itineraries drawn on the ground, starting from Église Notre-Dame-la-Grande, which enable visitors to explore the town without getting lost. Below you will find two short walks and some additional sights which cover the town's main centres of interest.

1 City Centre

▸ *Starting from Église Notre-Dame-la-Grande (place Charles-de-Gaulle), follow rue de la Regratterie then turn left onto rue du Palais.*

Palais de Justice

🕐 *Open daily except Sat-Sun 8.45am-noon and 1.45pm-5.30pm.* 🚫*Closed public hols.* 💰*No charge.* ☎05 49 50 22 00.
The Restoration façade of the law courts masks the Great Hall and the original keep of the ancient ducal palace, rare examples of urban civic architecture dating from the Middle Ages.
The **Great Hall★** (47m/154ft long and 17m/55ft wide) was reserved for important trials, solemn audiences and sessions of the Provincial Estates. In 1418, four years before he was proclaimed king, the fleeing Charles VII set up his court and parliament here. In March 1429 Joan of Arc was subjected to a gruelling interrogation by an ecclesiastical commission, to emerge after three weeks with an enhanced sense of her sacred mission – and official recognition that the mission was religiously inspired.
Although construction of the vast hall was started under the Plantagenets, it was De Berry who commissioned the architect Dammartin to build the great gable wall with its three monumental chimneys, its balcony and Flamboyant windows. Up above, four fine statues represent (left to right) Jean de Berry, his nephew Charles VI, Isabeau of Bavaria, and Jean's wife Jeanne de Boulogne.
The early-12C keep, known as **Tour Maubergeon**, which was transformed into a residence for Jean de Berry in the 14C, are visible from rue des Cordeliers. Remains of the original Gallo-Roman defensive wall can be seen in the adjacent square.

▸ *Walk from the Palais de Justice along rue Gambetta then turn left onto rue Paul-Guillon.*

Hôtel de l'Échevinage

This 15C building with its contemporary chapel was once the town hall. It originally housed first the university's Grandes Écoles (seats of higher learning) and then the local magistrate *(échevinage)*.

▶ *Return to rue Gambetta.*

Église St-Porchaire

All that remains of the original 11C church built on this site is the belfry-porch with its four-sided pyramid roof.

Three tiers of arcades and bays stand above the great Roman arch, decorated with Romanesque capitals, which serves as an entrance to the two-aisle church restored in the 16C.

Up in the belfry hangs the great bell of the university, which was cast in 1451. At one time it was used to announce the start of student classes.

Musée de Chièvres

◉*Open Jun-Sep Mon-Fri 10am-noon and 1.15-6pm (9pm Thu), Sat-Sun and public hols 10am-noon and 2-6pm; Oct-May Mon-Fri 10am-noon and 1.15-5pm, Sat-Sun and public hols 2-6pm.* ◉*Closed Mon morning, 1 Jan, Easter, Whitsun, All Saints, 25 Dec.* ◈*3.60€, no charge Tue and 1st Sun in the month (children no charge).* ☎*05 49 41 42 21.*

Fine 16C-18C furniture, also tapestries, ceramics, and enamels from Limoges.

Hôtel Pélisson

Its finely decorated façade is a good example of architecture from the Renaissance period (mid-16C).

▶ *Go up to rue du Marché-Notre-Dame until you reach place Charles-de-Gaulle.*

②Trois Quartiers

Walking through this pleasant but steep district requires a certain amount of energy!

▶ *Starting from place Charles-de-Gaulle, follow rue de l'Université and walk past the multimedia library.*

Médiathèque

♿◉*Open Jun-Sep daily except Sun and Mon 11am-6pm, Sat 11am-5pm, Tue 11am-8pm; Oct-May Tue and Thu 11am-10pm, Wed and Fri 11am-6pm, Sat 11am-5pm.* ◉*Closed public hols.* ◈*No charge.* ☎*05 49 52 31 51.*

The multimedia library is one of the most attractive modern buildings in Poitiers.

Inaugurated in 1996, it contains a fine medieval collection and works in close association with the Bibliothèque Nationale de France in Paris.

▶ *Walk down rue Cloche-Perse on the right until you reach place de la Liberté then follow rue Pierre-Rat.*

Église de Montierneuf

This church belonged to an abbey of the Cluniac order. The sanctuary dating from the 11C was completely remodelled during the Gothic and Classical periods. The west front was rebuilt in the 17C.

▶ *Walk along the north side of the church to the garden situated behind the east end.*

In the lower Romanesque part of the edifice, note the east-facing transept chapels and the radiating chapels of the apse. The Gothic upper part is flanked by graceful flying buttresses.

▶ *Walk up rue Jean-Bouchet and rue de la Chaine which leads onto rue René-Descartes.*

Hôtel Fumé

Note the Flamboyant dormer windows adorning the restored façade of no 8, a 16C building belonging to the university. There is an attractive courtyard with stair turret, **gallery** and corbelled balcony.

▶ *Return to place Charles-de-Gaulle via place Charles-VII and rue de la Regratterie.*

Quartier Épiscopal

Cathédrale St-Pierre★

St Peter's Cathedral was begun at the end of the 12C and almost completed by the end of the 14C – the date of its consecration; it is striking for its huge dimensions.

Exterior – The wide west front, with its rose window and three 13C doorways, is flanked by two asymmetric towers. That on the left *(northern)* side, supported by a series of engaged colonnettes, retains an octagonal storey topped by a balustrade.

The tympana of the doorways are carved with fascinating sculptures, among them the *Crowning of the Virgin (left)*; the dead hurrying from their graves and the heavenly elect separated from the damned delivered to Leviathan *(centre)*; the teaching of St Thomas, patron of stone-carvers – the miraculous building of a mystical palace for the King of India *(right)*.

▶ *Walk around the northern flank of the cathedral as far as rue Arthur-de-la-Mauvinière.*

Note on the way around the massive strength of the buttresses and the absence of flying buttresses. At the far end of the building the dizzy height (49m/161ft) of the flat **east end** can be appreciated – especially as this is emphasised by a falling away of the land.

Interior – On entering, visitors are struck by the sheer power of the architecture: the wide shell of the cathedral is divided into three aisles of almost equal height, and the impression of a perspective soaring away towards the east is accentuated by a progressive narrowing of the aisles and a lowering of the central vault from the chancel onwards.

Twenty-four domed rib vaults – a Plantagenet influence – crown the eight spans of each of the three aisles. Despite its flat exterior, the east end is hollowed out enough to form three apsidal chapels. A cornice embellished with historiated modillions supports a narrow gallery running around the walls above a series of blind arcades.

Among the stained-glass windows at the far east end is a late-12C representation of the *Crucifixion* showing a radiant Christ flanked by the Virgin and St John. Above and below this are: the Apostles, with their faces raised towards a Christ in Glory, set in a mandorla; the crucifixion of St Peter and the beheading of St Paul.

The **choir stalls★**, dating from the 13C, are said to be the oldest in France. The carved corner-pieces represent the Virgin and Child, angels carrying crowns and the architect at work.

The 18C organ, built by François-Henri Clicquot (1732-90), member of a cele-

brated dynasty of organ-makers working in Reims and Paris in the 17C and 18C, is located on the inner side of the west front, within a beautiful shell-shaped loft with basket-handled arching.

▶ *Walk along rue Ste-Radegonde which starts behind the cathedral then continue along rue Arthur-de-la-Mauvinière.*

Église Ste-Radegonde★

This former collegiate church was founded around AD 552 by Radegund with the idea that it would eventually become the last resting-place of her nuns from Holy Cross Abbey. The church is characterised by a Romanesque apse and a belfry-porch which stand at opposite ends of a nave in the style known as Angevin Gothic. The belfry-porch, majestic and massive in its proportions, square in plan and then octagonal, was enhanced in the 15C with a Flamboyant portal in the niches of which today stand modern statues of the patron saints of Poitiers. At the base of the tower there remains a chamber, lined with stone benches, where ecclesiastical justice used to be dispensed.

A small garden east of the church offers an agreeable view of the **east end** and the pleasing lines of the church as a whole.

Baptistère St-Jean★

🕓*Open Jul and Aug daily 10am-12.30pm and 2.30-6pm; Apr-Jun and Sep daily except Tue 10.30am-12.30pm and 3-6pm; Oct-Mar daily except Tue 2.30-4.30pm.* 🕓*Closed 1 Jan and 25 Dec.* ⬬*0.80€.* ☎*05 49 41 21 24.*

St John's Baptistery, dating from the middle of the 4C, is the oldest example of Christian architecture in France.

Originally the baptistery comprised two rectangular chambers: the baptismal hall and a narthex, preceded by an entrance corridor framed by two changing-rooms. The rectangular baptismal hall still exists, together with a 6C-7C quadrangular apse and two apsidal chapels, originally square but changed to a semicircular shape in the middle of the 19C. The former narthex, however, which was restored in the 10C, is now polygonal. Panels of Romanesque brickwork brace the window embrasures, which are partly blocked up and pierced

Frescoes projected on the walls of St-Jean

with oculi. Beneath the gables are strange pilasters with capitals carved in bas-relief.

Interior – Inside, the baptistery is notable for the intricately carved capitals of its marble columns, covered with beading, strapwork and foliage in the antique manner; for the colonnettes supporting the arcades; for the three tall arcades, pierced in the wall set back from the entrance doorway, which link the narthex and the baptismal chamber. The apse and its two chapels are surmounted by oven vaults. In the centre of the baptismal chamber is the **octagonal pool** which was used for baptism by total immersion: the novice convert, whose clothes would have been removed in one of the changing rooms, was first lowered into the water to receive the ritual unction from the bishop, then dressed in a white tunic and solemnly received in the cathedral. In the 7C use of the pool was superseded by baptism by affusion (holy water poured over the head) following the installation of a cistern supplying the font; until the 12C this was the only place in Poitiers where baptisms could be consecrated. The building now houses an interesting lapidary museum.

Romanesque frescoes – partly overpainted in the 13C and 14C – adorn the baptistery walls: an *Ascension* above the apse; *Christ in Majesty* decorating its oven vault; four horsemen, including the Emperor Constantine, on one of the walls in the rectangular chamber; peacocks, the symbol of immortality, on the left-hand wall. Between 10pm and midnight in summer, the frescoes are projected onto the outer wall of the edifice *(the show lasts approximately 30min)*.

Musée Ste-Croix★★

🕐*Open Jun-Sep Mon-Fri 10am-noon and 1.15-6pm (Tue 8pm), Sat-Sun and public hols 10am-noon and 2-6pm; Oct-May Mon-Fri 10am-noon and 1.15-5pm, Sat-Sun and public hols 2-6pm.* 🕐*Closed Mon morning, 1 Jan, Easter, Whitsun, All Saints, 25 Dec.* 🎟3.60€, *no charge 1st Sun in the month and Tue (combined ticket with the Musée des Chièvres).* ☎05 49 41 07 53. www.musees-poitiers.org.

The museum is housed in a modern building standing on the site of the former Holy Cross Abbey (Abbaye Ste-Croix).

Archaeology – *Basement: access down a staircase at the far end of the first hall.* The collections here concentrate on the Poitou of prehistory to medieval times. The chronology of the Palaeolithic Era is set out, with displays of flint implements, tools and other items discovered during digs (fragments of a bronze roasting spit from the 7C BC, an ingot of pure copper, objects buried c 700 BC). A number of Gallo-Roman finds are presented against a backdrop of the remains of antique walls: inscriptions, fragments of columns, bas-relief sculptures and statues, among them the head of a man and a famous **Minerva** in white marble (1C AD) unearthed in Poitiers. Fine funerary stones from Civaux, including Man as a Child, are also on show.

The rest of the collections are displayed in a number of rooms on several different levels linked by stairways or steps.

Painting – The staircase at the end of the archaeology gallery leads to a fine series of paintings from Abbaye Ste-Croix by the Dutch painter Nicolas Van der Maes depicting the 17C **Mysteries of the life of Christ.**

Other paintings include works from the **late 18C:** the local artist, J-A Pajou *(Oedipus cursing Polynices)*, Géricault's circle *(Masculine Anatomy)*. The **19C** is represented by Alfred de Curzon, a local painter *(The Convent Garden)*, Octave Penguilly-l'Haridan *(The Parade of Pierrot)*, Charles Brun *(Portrait of Germaine Pichot)*, and Léopold Burthe *(Ophelia)*. A number of works by **Orientalists** are grouped together, they include: *Jewish Fête in Tangier* by Alfred Dehodencq, *Fantasia* by Eugène Fromentin and *A Street in Constantinople* by André Brouillet.

Sculpture – The collections include a medieval bas-relief, the *Stone-cutter*, found near St-Hilaire-le-Grand, a Renaissance medallion embossed with the features of Christ, a marble bust of Louis XIII from the Château de Richelieu as well as 19C exhibits: an Auguste Ottin marble, a Carrier-Belleuse terracotta, a recumbent plaster effigy of Mademoiselle de Montpensier by James Pradier and a marble by Jean Escoula symbolising Sleep. There is also a reconstruction of the studio of sculptor Jean-René Carrière (1888-1982).

Bronzes include small works by Rodin *(The Man with the Broken Nose* and *The Despairing Adolescent)*, Maillol *(Prairie Nymphs)* and Camille Claudel. A room recently refurbished and devoted to Camille Claudel displays *Desertion* (1888), *The Waltz* (1893), *Deep Thought* (1900) and *Fortune* (1900-04).

Ethnological Collections – The first floor houses an exhibit on trades in the urban areas, such as cobbler, wood turner or textile worker, and a curious carousel made by a local postman, Mr Bonnet.

Espace Mendès-France

♿🕑*Open Jul and Aug Tue-Fri 9.30am-6.30pm, Sat and Mon 2-6.30pm; Sep-Jun Tue-Fri 9.30am-6.30pm, Sat-Sun and Mon 2-6.30pm.* 🕑*Closed public hols.* ∾*5€ (children 2.50€).* ☎*05 49 50 33 08; www.maison-des-sciences.org*

This modern building houses scientific, technological and industrial exhibitions. The **planetarium** offers a multimedia show about the town. (♿🕑 *Open school hols (zone B), daily except Sat at 5pm; otherwise, Sun at 5pm.* 🕑*Closed public hols.* ∾ *6€ (children under 18: 3€).* ☎ *05 49 50 33 08; www.maison-des-sciences.org)*

Faubourg St-Saturnin

This district lies to the east of the city centre on the opposite bank of the River Clain. Climb boulevard Coligny to the top of the plateau des Dunes, where the **statue of Notre-Dame-des-Dunes** overlooks Poitiers. There is a splendid **view★** of the city from here *(viewing table)*.

St-Hilaire-le-Grand★★

Archaeological enthusiasts consider this ancient church dedicated to St Hilary to be the most interesting in Poitiers. Before going inside, it is worth walking around the church to admire the group of chapels grafted onto the transept and ambulatory. Each chapel is surrounded by columns with intricately worked capitals, and boasts a cornice decorated with modillions carved with horses' heads, small monsters and foliage.

Interior – The church of St-Hilary-the-Great, which was completed in 1049, was always an important sanctuary as well as being a large one; the three aisles, covered with timber ceilings, frequently sheltered members of the earliest pilgrimages to Santiago de Compostela. Unfortunately in the 12C the church was ravaged by fire and the gutted timbers were replaced by stone vaults; however, as the distance it was possible to span in stone was naturally less than it was with wooden beams, the architects charged with the restoration were obliged to narrow the aisles. They solved the problem by dividing each of the original side aisles longitudinally in two, adding central columns to support the ribbed vaulting above; at the same time two rows of columns were added to the nave, linked ingeniously to the original walls and bearing a whole series of small domes. The final arrangement – the church as it is today – has a central nave bordered by three aisles on either side – the only seven-aisle church in Europe.

Columns were added to St-Hilaire-le-Grand in the 12C to support the vaulting

Two of the northern aisles incorporate the 11C belfry, the base of which forms an impressive room with massive columns and remarkable archaic capitals. The vaulting is reinforced with huge string courses. It is from the transept that the vision and originality of the architecture can best be appreciated. Both transept and **chancel** are raised some way above the level of the aisles. The floor at the front of the chancel is covered with a fine mosaic. The pillars framing it have interesting capitals, notably, on the north side, that representing the burial of St Hilary himself. The ancient frescoes on the four pillars preceding the transept represent bishops of Poitiers. In the chapels, more frescoes illustrate episodes in the lives of St Quentin and St Martin.

The chancel is separated from the ambulatory by a semicircle of eight columns, linked at the base by fine 12C wrought-iron grilles. In the ambulatory, on the main axis of the church, is an unusual statuary group of the *Holy Trinity*: God the Father presenting his Son on the Cross, above which stands the dove of the Holy Spirit.

In the **crypt** is a casket (19C) containing the relics of St Hilary.

PONS

POPULATION 4 427

MICHELIN MAP 324: G-6

The attractive little town of Pons (pronounced Pon) is built on a hillside, its keep and ramparts overlooking the languid waters of the Seugne, a tributary of the Charente, as it branches out into a myriad of streams flowing through meadows, poplars and willows.

A staging post on the road to Santiago de Compostela in the Middle Ages, Pons became a stronghold of military radicalism and anticlericalism at the turn of the 20C, in the person of its mayor, Émile Combes (1835-1921).

- **Information:** Donjon – Pl. de la République – 17800 Pons – ☎05 46 96 13 31.
- **Orient Yourself**: Pons lies 20km/12mi S of Saintes and 23km/14mi SW of Cognac.
- **Don't Miss**: The Donjon (keep) of the old château; the wood pannelling at the Château d'Usson outside Pons.
- **Also See**: COGNAC, SAINTES.

WHERE TO STAY

⎈**Auberge Pontoise** – *23 r. Gambetta – ☎05 46 94 00 99- auberge-pontoise@ wanadoo.fr – closed Sun eve from 15 Sep-15 May.* Set right in the village, this cosy auberge, a former biscuit factory, has a busy restaurant which is popular with locals. Traditional cuisine, with an emphasis on local produce, is served in the comfortable dining room. The auberge also has some simple rooms.

⎈⎈**Hôtel Bordeaux** – *1 av. Gambetta – ☎ 05 46 91 31 12 – hotel-de-bx@hotel-de-bordeaux.com – closed Sun eve from Oct to Easter – 15 rms – restaurant ⎈⎈.* Housed in an old building, the interior decor of this hotel is fairly modern. Its small rooms are simple and functional. Don't miss the restaurant – the innovative cuisine is excellent and the prices reasonable. Terrace in the summer and a great choice of Cognacs.

Castle

The castle once covered the area now occupied by the square and public gardens. Its owners, the lords of Pons, answered to no one but the King of France; they commanded more than 60 towns and villages and more than 600 parishes and domains, giving rise to the motto, "What the King of France cannot be, the lord of Pons will."

Donjon★

⏰*Open Jul-Aug 9.30am-12.30pm and 2-6pm; May-Jun daily except Sat-Sun 9.30am-noon and 1.30-5pm, Sat-Sun 10-11.30am and 3-5.30pm; Sep-Journées du Patrimoine, 9.30am-12.30pm and 2-5.30pm; rest of the year, Mon-Fri 9.30am-12.30pm and 1.30-5pm.* ⏰*Closed 1 May, 14 Jul, 15 Aug, 1 Nov.* ⎈*2.50€ (children aged 6-12 1€).* ☎*05 46 96 13 31.*

The 12C **keep**★ is 30m/100ft high; it was reached by ladders which could be withdrawn if there was a threat. Although the roof ridge, renovated in 1904, is rather fanciful, the rest of the building, supported by narrow buttresses, gives a powerful impression. From the top, there is a **panorama** of the town and valley.

At the foot of the slope, the old seigneurial abode includes a main 17C building flanked by an older staircase turret. It now houses the town hall.

Farther on, the charming public gardens forming a terrace along the ramparts offer attractive views overlooking the streams branching out from the Seugne.

Château des Énigmes (Usson)

1km/0.6mi S on the D 249. ⏰ *Easter to early Nov, 10am-7pm (ticket office closes at 5pm).* ⎈ *10€ (children aged 4-18: 8€).* ☎ *05 46 91 09 19.*

A fine example of Renaissance architecture, the château was built by the Rabaine family near Lonzac, two leagues east of Pons. Threatened with destruction at the end of 20C, it was transported and rebuilt, stone by stone, on its present site. The courtyard is interesting for the variety of its ornamentation: at the back, the gallery with its basket-handle arches is remarkable for its medallions (the 12 Caesars), statues of marmosets and engraved maxims. At the end of one of the wings, a tower with its original roof is carved with coats of arms and emblems (shells and crescents from the Rabaine arms) and, just under the edge of the roof, a frieze divided into panels by short, hollow columns.

Inside, note the drawing room decorated with fine Regency **wood panelling**★, white with gold borders, from the château in Choisy-le-Roi and, in the main hall, the door of the former chapel, sculpted by Nicolas Bachelier, a pupil of Michelangelo.

PORNIC

POPULATION 11 903
MICHELIN MAP 316: D-5

Pornic is a popular seaside resort with a narrow inlet sheltering a small fishing port, historical quarters clustered on a hillside, stately homes with gardens full of parasol pines, a golf course, sheltered sandy beaches, a large marina and a thalassotherapy centre. The town boasts a long list of famous visitors from the 19C onwards, including George Sand, Gustave Flaubert, Auguste Renoir, Lenin, Marc Elder and Max Ernst.

- **Information**: La Gare – BP 1119, 44210 Pornic. ☎02 40 82 04 40. www.ot-pornic.fr.
- ▶ **Orient Yourself**: Situated 25km/15mi SE of St-Nazaire, Pornic is linked to Nantes by the D 751.
- **Don't Miss**: The Corniche de la Noéveillard.
- **Especially for Kids**: The Maison du Pêcheur at Passay; Planète Sauvage near Port St-Père.
- **Also See**: ÎLE DE NOIRMOUTIER, MARAIS BRETON-VENDÉEN.

Sights

Old town

Once a fortified town, it was naturally protected to the south by the port and to the west by the valley known today as the Jardin de Retz. The castle and ramparts, are now replaced by promenade de la Terrasse and Rue de la Douve.

The fishing port - From the end of the port which mainly shelters fishing boats and an occasional coastal vessel, see the buildings of town cluster on the hillside, and directly opposite, the cove and the silhouette of the castle at its entrance.

Castle

Hidden deep in the greenery, Pornic Castle, of granite construction, overlooks Plage du Château below. Once surrounded by water, access was via a drawbridge later replaced by a fixed bridge over rue des Sables.

Built in the 13C-14C, it belonged to the famous Gilles de Rais or Bluebeard (*see TIFFAUGES*); it was renovated in the 19C.

Promenade de la Terrasse - Built on the site of the old ramparts, the view from the walkway is lovely: the castle and the Jardin de Retz, with its many plant nurseries.

Pornic – View of the old town from Gourmalon

M. Thiery/MICHELIN

Address Book

ⓒ *For coin ranges, see the Legend on the cover flap.*

WHERE TO STAY

⊜⊜ **Chambre d'hôte Cupidon** – *Plage du Portmain – 44210 Ste-Marie-sur-Mer – 6km/3.5mi W of Pornic on the coast road – ☎02 51 74 19 61 – gagnot-catu@ clubinternet.fr – closed mid-Jan to mid-Feb – �🛏 – 4 rms.* 50m/55yd from Portmain beach, this B&B built in beach-chalet style has a cosy feel. The beach is directly across the street, but if it's too crowded you can always take a dip in the pool or borrow a bicycle!

WHERE TO EAT

⊜**L'Estaminet** – *8 r. du Mar.-Foch – ☎02 40 82 35 99 – closed Sun evening and Mon ist fornight in Oct, 25 Dec–1 Jan.* The restaurant near the port serves traditional specialities such as veal with cream sauce with pineau de Charentes

Corniche de la Noéveillard★

30min round trip on foot. Take the path along the coast from Plage du Château. It joins another path jutting out over the sea; as you walk along, the view over Pornic cove, the rocks and ocean changes. Eventually, the path overlooks the facilities of the large marina, before winding its way to the fine sandy beach of Plage de la Noéveillard.

Corniche de Gourmalon

The road runs along the edge of the corniche, above Anse aux Lapins Beach, then on to Pointe de Gourmalon headland. Views of Pornic, the castle, Corniche de la Noéveillard.

Dolmen des Mousseaux

Signposted from Plage du Château. This double walkway, covered by stones arranged in tiers, apparently doubled as a tomb and a prestigious monument for Neolithic farmers in about 3500 BC. The two chambers have a characteristic commonly found near the Loire Estuary: a corridor joins the side chambers, somewhat like the transept of a church.

Driving Tours

①Côte De Jade

14 km/8.4mi via the D 751 – 45min

From Pornic to St-Brévin-les Bains, popular seaside resorts adorn the coastline of the Pays de Retz, known as the **Jade Coast,** in honour of the deep green colour of the water there. Between Pornic and St-Gildas, the line of schist cliffs is broken by creeks and sandy alcoves, making the landscape especially appealing.

Ste-Marie

Near Mombeau Beach, a cliff top path provides a pretty **view** of the rocky coastline speckled with sandy beaches. Fishing nets hang from poles upright in the water.

▶ *Follow the signs Le Porteau par la Côte.*

From Sablons beach to Porteau, the road goes along the sea above the ragged coastline.
From Porteau to Préfailles, the road leaves the coast; ramblers can continue on the Tour de Pays de Retz trail high above the ocean.

Pointe de St-Gildas★

ⓒ*Leave the car in the car park near the marina.*
The point of land is covered with short grass, growing fitfully over the vestiges of the Atlantic wall; shell cliffs extend out to meet the breakers. It was off Pointe St-Gildas that the steamship *St-Philibert* sunk in June of 1931, drowning 500 day trippers returning from Île de Noirmoutier.
From the far end of the point, the view opens up to the coast of Brittany, between St-Nazaire and Le Croisic and all the way to Noirmoutier, sitting low on the horizon.

②Pays De Retz

130km/80 mi – allow one day

▶ *Drive SE out of Pornic.*

The road runs along the coast to Moutiers-en-Retz which offers fine views of Bourgneuf Bay and Noirmoutier Island.

Bourgneuf en Retz

Important crossroads on the way to the beaches of Bourgneuf Bay (north) and the oyster beds of the Vendée region (south).

Musée du Pays de Retz

6 rue des Moines ⚓ ◐Open Jul–Aug daily 10.30am-1pm and 2-6.30pm; Apr-Jun and Sep-Oct daily except Mon 10am-noon and 2-6pm (open Mon public hols). ⚋ 4€ (children: 2€). ☎02 40 21 40 83; www. museepaysderetz.com

This musem is housed in the 17C buildings of an old monastery. It includes sections on archaeology, collections of local headdresses and costumes and reconstructions of traditional workshops.

▶ *Leave Bourgneuf E along the D 13.*

Machecoul

The historic capital of Pays de Retz stages shows illustrating the history of the region.

▶ *Drive NE on the D 64, turn right onto the D 71 2km/1.2mi beyond St-Mêmele-Tenu and right again onto the D 61 in St-Lumine-de-Coutais.*

St-Philbert-de-Grand-Lieu

Abbatiale St-Philbert

Acces via the tourist office. ◐Open Apr-Sep 10am-12.30pm and 2.30-6.30pm; Oct-Mar, 10am-noon and 2-5.30pm, Sun and public hols 2-5.30pm. ⚋2.50€ (combined ticket with the Maison du Lac). ☎02 40 78 73 88.

Erected in the 9C, the abbey church was altered during the Revolution and again in 1870 but was later partly restored to its original aspect. Inside, note the austere nave with its massive pillars (it was built of brick and stone, a technique in-herited from the Romans) and some of the stones date from the Roman period. The crypt has openings designed to enable the congregation to see the 7C marble sarcophagus which, until 858, contained the remains of St Philbert.

Maison du Lac

Acces via the tourist office. ◐Open Apr-Sep, 10am-12.30pm and 2.30-6.30pm; Oct-Mar, 10am-noon and 2-5.30pm; ◐Closed 1 Jan, 25 Dec. ⚋2.50€ (combined ticket with the abbey); children aged 6-12 1.50€. ☎02 40 78 73 88.

This ornithological museum is devoted to the 225 species of sedentary and migratory birds living close to Lac de Grand-Lieu. There is an audio-visual presentation of the local fauna and flora.

▶ *Drive N out of St-Philbert on the D 65.*

Lac de Grand-Lieu

This was once a true lake but over the past 100 years, an insidious invasion of vegetation has gradually converted it into a forbidding swamp-like marsh.
The shores are thick with rushes, reeds and clumps of furze making it an exceptional ornithological site.
The lake, which is linked to the Loire estuary by the Achenau (*cheneau* is a local word for canal), was officially declared a nature reserve in 1980. It covers 4 000ha/ 10 000 acres in summer and 8 000ha/ 20 000 acres in winter. The rocky bottom, at depths ranging from 1m/3ft- to 2m/ 6ft depending on the season, is sometimes covered with a thick bed of silt. It is said that the ancient town of Herbauge, cursed for its dissolute morals, is buried beneath this shroud. According to legend, the muffled tolling of its church bell can be heard in the middle of the swamp at midnight on Christmas Eve.
The lake lies directly below one of the regular Atlantic migration routes and is the temporary home of more than 200 species of birds, including ducks, geese, teal, snipe, corncrake, rail and grebe. It is also an important nesting site for grey heron and the rare spoonbill.

Passay

This typical inland fishing hamlet is the only place from which it is possible to approach the mysterious Lac de Grand-Lieu.

Maison du Pêcheur – ⊙Open Jun-Aug, daily except Mon 2.30-7.30pm; mid-Apr–May and Sep–11 Nov Wed and Fri-Sun 2.30-6.30pm. ⊙Closed 1 Jan and 25 Dec. ⊚2.50€ (children aged 6-17 1.50€). ☎02 40 31 36 46.

Kids This small museum, housed in an **observation tower** overlooking the marsh and its surroundings, reveals the secrets of an unusually rich ecosystem. The fauna and flora of the area, as well as associated activities – especially local fishing techniques – are clearly and simply presented and explained. Indigenous species (perch, pike, carp and eel) can be viewed in the museum's aquariums.

▸ *Continue NE along the D 65 and, in Pont-St-Martin, turn W onto the D 11. In Bouaye, take the road to the S, which leads to St-Mars-de-Coutais.*

Planète sauvage★★

♿⊙Open Jul-Aug, 10am-5.30pm; Apr-Jun and Sep-Oct 10am-5pm; Mar and Nov Sat-Sun 10am-4pm. ⊚16.50€ (children aged 3-12 10.50€). ☎02 40 04 82 82. www.planetesauvage.com.

Kids More than 2 000 animals roam freely through the sparsely wooded hills and plains, interspersed with lakes and ponds. The park consists of two tours: one by car and the other on foot.

Safari track – After passing through the disinfecting basin, the driver must proceed very slowly along the 10km/6mi of tracks winding through bushland and savannah. There are 13 enclosures, where visitors can discover different animals at close quarters: hippopotami and elephants playing water games, a herd of galloping bison, agile impalas and springboks, majestic stags in full-antler combat, bears napping on the rocks, tigers wrestling, lions regally sprawling in the sun, painted hyenas snarling, giraffes placidly nibbling greenery, and more. While car windows must be closed at all times, it is still quite exciting to see wild animals at such close range, in natural habitats.

Safari Village – The village has various leisure facilities including a playground, a picnic area, restaurants, shops, cultural facilities (a very attractive thematic exhibition room), and walking paths through a replica of a bush village.

The tour can begin with the **Arche des Reptiles** (a vivarium containing snakes and crocodiles in a dimly lit environment) and a miniature animal farm (20 species), followed by the **Sea Lion show** and **Île des Siamangs** where screeching monkeys mingle with flocks of pink flamingos, marabou and pelicans along the banks of the lake. An exotic garden leads to the **Forêt de Singes** (keep to the marked footpaths), inhabited by rhesus monkeys.

▸ *Drive to Port-St-Père and continue N on the D 103.*

Le Pellerin

Here you can catch a ferry across the River Loire.

▸ *Drive westwards along the D 58 via Rouans to the D 266 and turn left. The road runs through Princé Forest. Turn right to Chauvé and pick up the D 6 which leads back to Pornic.*

POUZAUGES

POPULATION 5 473
MICHELIN MAP 316: L-7

Pouzauges stands on the slope of a hill crowned by the Bois de la Folie, overlooking an attractive rural landscape of fields and hedgerows.

▸ **Orient Yourself**: Pouzauges is located in the heart of the Vendée hills, 19km/11mi SE of Les Herbiers.

🏷 **Don't Miss**: The windmills at Le Terrier-Marteau.

🕭 **Also See**: LE PUY DE FOU, BRESSUIRE.

Sights

Château

This medieval fortress comprises walls incorporating 10 ruined towers, and a square keep, flanked by turrets, which protected the entrance. A cross recalls the 32 Vendée Royalists who were shot here during the Revolution.

Église St-Jacques

St James' Church was built of granite in the Vendée style with a square tower over the crossing; it has a short nave and a 12C transept which is in a transitional Romanesque-Gothic style. The large, Flamboyant Gothic chancel with three bays is 15C.

Excursions

Moulins du Terrier-Marteau★★

1km/0.6mi along the D 752 and a minor road on the right.
Guided visit on prior request to Henri Marquis – 21 r. Catherine-de-Thouars – 85700 Pouzauges – 5€.
On the right-hand side are the quaint white windmills of the region with their shingle roofs. It is pleasant just to watch the canvas sails go round. These two windmills, built in the 19C, have been restored and still have their mobile roof, so that the sails can be turned to catch the wind, using a *guivre* (long pole). Attractive **view**★ of the farmland criss-crossed with trees and hedges to the west.

Bois de la Folie

Near Le Terrier-Marteau.
This was probably a *luccus*, or sacred wood, in Roman times, after being a meeting place for the Druids who gathered mistletoe and performed ritual sacrifices.
The wood, situated on a mound of granite, has oak, pine and beech trees. This thick, isolated clump of trees, visible from afar, was known to the locals as *Pouzauges Bouquet*, or the Vendée Lighthouse. It affords a **view**★ of the typical farmland to the north-east.

Driving Tour

Between Sèvre Nantaise and Grand Lay

Round trip 75km/145mi – 6hrs

▷ *Leave Pouzauges SW along the D 43 and turn right onto the D 113.*

Château du Bois-Tiffrais

The château houses a museum which traces the trials and tribulations of Protestantism in western France, especially in the region of Poitou.

Musée de la France protestante de l'Ouest

Open mid-Jun–mid-Sep daily except Mon 2-7pm. 2.50€. 02 51 66 41 03.
Well-documented explanatory panels illustrate the major events – Calvin's sermon in Poitou (1534), the Edict of Nantes (1598), revocation of the Edict of Nantes (1685), which led to Protestant emigration and the practice of secret worship during the period known as The Desert, and finally, the Edict of Tolerance (1787). Various exhibits, including Bibles and copies of *méreaux* (medals which enabled the pastor to identify the clandestine faithful) and a collapsible pulpit (for assemblies held in secret), recall the days of oppression.

▷ *Continue along the D 113 then follow the Chantonnay road, turning right after 2km/1.2mi.*

Prieuré de Chassay-Grammont

Open mid-Jun–end Sep 10am-7pm. 3€ (children no charge). 02 51 66 47 18 (in season) or 02 51 50 43 16.
This monastery founded by Richard the Lionheart in c 1196, has been massively restored. It is a good example of the architecture of the Order of Grammont, a community of hermits who lived in secluded spots and attached great importance to poverty. Their monasteries were sober and without ornamentation.
At Chassay, all of the monastic buildings as well as the church, are built around a cloistered courtyard. The church has a

Sails to the wind

single nave stripped of all embellishments. The only light came from three windows in the apsidal chapel. On the ground floor, the chapter-house with its Romanesque vaulting and the large refectory, whose 13C Anjou-Gothic vaulting has been restored, have a certain elegance. The monks' dormitory is on the first floor.

▷ *Return and cut across the D 960bis. Turn left in Sigournais then right in Chavagnes onto the D 89.*

Mouilleron-en-Pareds

⌕ *See MOUILLERON-EN-PAREDS.*

▷ *Leave Mouilleron NE along the D 8.*

Église de Pouzauges-le-Vieux

The granite **church** dates from the Romanesque period, apart from the chancel which was remodelled in the 14C, and stands in an attractive landscape dotted with cypresses. The pure lines of its architecture – its strong, simple doorway, extended transept and short, square tower over the crossing – became a model for many other churches in the region.

▷ *Take the D 49 in the direction of Montournais.*

Puy Crapaud

At an altitude of 270m/885ft, it is one of the highest points on the Vendée hills. It is crowned with the remains of a windmill, converted into a restaurant. *For access to the viewing table (steep staircase), ask at the local bar.* From the top of the windmill, there is a vast **panorama★★** of the whole of the Vendée region as far as the sea. The view of the hills stretching out between Pouzauges and St-Michel-Mont-Mercure is particularly attractive.

▷ *Continue on the D 49; at Montournais, take the D 8 N to St-Mesmin.*

About 1km/0.6mi beyond St-Mesmin, on the road to Cerisay, are the medieval ruins of the picturesquely located **Château de St-Mesmin** – the machicolations of the keep are still intact.

▷ *At the crossroads, turn left on the small road which joins the D 27.*

La Pommeraie-sur-Sèvre

In the Gothic **church**, with its elegant Plantagenet vaulting in the nave, 15C frescoes depict the seven capital sins, symbolised by figures on animals. There is a Roman bridge across the Sèvre.

▷ *Leave La Pommeraie-sur-Sèvre and take the D 43 W to return to Pouzauges.*

LE PUY DU FOU★★★

MICHELIN MAP 316: K-6

On summer evenings the château sparkles under the lights of its famous Son et Lumière show in which a cast of hundreds stages an open-air historical pageant. By day, the museum evokes the past of the Vendée region while various attractions lure visitors into the 12ha/30 acres of grounds. The name Puy du Fou is derived from the Latin: *puy* (from *podium*) means a knoll; *fou* (from *fagus*) designates a beech tree. Thus, a 'hill where a beech tree grows', or more lyrically, Beechmount.

▶ **Orient Yourself**: Puy de Fou is located SW of Cholet and NE of La-Roche-sur-Yon.
⊚ **Don't Miss**: The Cinéscénie Sound and Light Show.
Kids **Kids**: The park has many shows and attractions that children will love.
⚑ **Also See**: POUZAUGES; BRESSUIRE.

Sights

Cinéscénie★★★

⊘*Closed to the public during the day. 13 500 seats.* ♿⊘*Show (1hr 45min) Jun-Jul Fri and Sat 10.30pm (last entrance 10pm); early Aug-early Sep Fri-Sat 10pm (last entrance 1hr before show).* ⊚*23€ (children 13€). Reservations required. Dress warmly.* ☏*02 51 64 11 11; www.puydufou. com*

Kids The terrace below the rear façade of the château, together with the ornamental lake below it, makes an agreeable background for the Cinéscénie spectacular, in which the story of Jacques Maupillier, peasant of the Vendée, and the history of the Vendée region come to life with the help of 800 actors and 50 horsemen in a dazzling show, including an impressive array of special effects, fountains, fireworks, laser and other lighting displays.

Château

It is likely that the original castle, built in the 15C and 16C, was never completed; it was in any case partly destroyed by fire during the Vendée Wars. A fine late Renaissance pavilion remains at the far end of the courtyard, preceded by a peristyle with recessed Ionic columns. This now serves as the entrance to the museum. The left wing of the château is built over a long gallery.

Grand Parc★★

&🕒Open Jul-Aug daily 10am-7pm; Jundail except Mon and Wed 10am-7pm; Late Apr–May and Sep enquire about times and dates. ✆25€ (children aged 5-13 15€). ✆02 51 64 11 11. www.puydefou.com.

The entire Puy du Fou estate extends over 35ha/86 acres. Numerous paths surrounding the château, skirting lakes or crossing dense woods of chestnut trees offer pleasant walks with a choice of interesting diversions.

Fauna

On the way up to the castle, explanatory panels line the path linking several **aviaries★★** containing birds of prey. **Farm animals★**, among them the famous *baudets*, graze inside large enclosures and

a peasant can be seen guiding his team of oxen in and out of the old stables. Reconstructed **underground galleries** show the liv es of rabbits and foxes. In the **wolves' lair**, you can hear the story of the last wolf who roamed the area in 1908.

Flora

A pleasant trail through the **Arboretum de France★** provides useful information about a great variety of plants.
There is also a **heather trail** and a **Renaissance rose garden★** containing 100 different species.
Another trail, known as the **Vallée fleurie★★**, lined with various plants and trees, winds round ponds and waterfalls.

Remembering the Vendée Wars

⟨🔞⟩This historic trail can upset young children and sensitive persons.
The underground trail is lined with dramatic scenes of massacres perpetrated during the Vendée Wars.

Music

Every 15min, a **peal** of 21 bells plays ancient melodies and regional characters come alive every 30min. Costumed musicians forming a **brass quintet★** play Baroque music. It is possible for visitors to control the play of fountains from a distance.

Shows

Bataille du Donjon – *30min show; 3 500 seats.* Reconstruction of the battle which

The legend of Saint Philibert

S. Sauvignier/MICHELIN

led to the first Puy du Fou castle being taken by the English in 1429. Stunts and special effects.

La bal des oiseaux fantômes★★ – *30min show; 1 700 seats*. The ruins of a 13C **castle** provide the background for a display of falconry – free-flying trained birds – with running commentary by a falconer in period costume.

Les Viking★★★ – *30min show; 3 000 seats*. Spectacular special effects (a long-ship emerging from the water), caval-cades and fighting illustrate the story of this monk who died in Noirmoutier in 685.

Le magicien-ménestrel★ – *20min show; 800 seats*. Jugglers vie for the applause of bystanders with feats of skill and virtuosity beneath the ramparts of the medieval city.

Gladiateurs★★ – in a reconstruction of a **Gallo-Roman amphitheatre★** watch a Roman circus of gladiators in hand-to-hand combat, chariot racing and fighting wild animals.

Mousquetaire de Richelieu★ – In the **Grand Carousel★** with its 2 800sq m stage, the atmosphere of theatres from 17C has been recreated. Here there is a show of combat, fencing, acrobatics, dancing and horsemanship from mus-keteers.

Théâtre d'eau★★ – *20min show; 600 seats*. A fairy-like display of 1 500 computer-controlled fountains enhanced by spec-tacular light effect.

Théâtre pour enfants – *15min show; 400 seats*. Puppet show for children.

Villages

Three villages of different periods have been reconstructed north of the site. Inside the **Fort de l'an Mil★★**, craftsmen can be seen at work in their thatched stone houses.

A drawbridge leads to the **Cité médié-vale★★★** protected by its ramparts. Inside, craftsmen and minstrels walk about their business along the narrow lanes. In the **18C village★★**, the work of crafts-men in period costume can be admired while musicians perform a serenade and jugglers demonstrate their virtuosity.

ÎLE DE RÉ ★
OFF THE COAST NEAR LA ROCHELLE
MICHELIN MAP 324: C-3

The surface of this unspoilt island is broken only by vineyards and an occasional pinewood. It has become a favourite retreat for summer holiday-makers in search of sunshine, sea air and wide open spaces. Although a bridge now links it to the mainland it retains most of its insular character and its famous salt-marshes. Numerous marked and peaceful cycle-tracks crisscross the island.

▷ **Orient Yourself**: The Île de Ré is situated just off the port of La Rochelle, cutting in two the gulf between the Île d'Oléron and the Vendée coast. The island is bordered to the north by the Breton Straits (Pertuis Breton) and to the south by the Straits of Antioche.

☺ **Don't Miss**: St-Martin-de-Ré, Phare des Baleines.

Kids **Especially for Kids**: Réserve Naturelle de Lilleau des Niges, l'Arche de Noé.

ఉ **Also See**: LA ROCHELLE.

A Bit of History

Anglo-French rivalry

From the Hundred Years War to the fall of Napoleon, the Île de Ré was closely involved in the conflict between the English and the French, during which the "red-coats" (the English) made many attempts to storm its shores: it would have been an invaluable base so close to mainland France. Nor was the isle spared during the Wars of Religion, which brought misery and deprivation to the inhabitants.

In 1625 the brave Marquis de **Toiras** (1585-1636), a deeply spiritual and fiercely warlike man, was governor of the island, which he had wrested from the Protestants and then reinforced by building the St-Martin citadel and the fort of La Prée. At that time, the whole island was under arms. An English fleet commanded by the Duke of Buckingham anchored off Les Sablanceaux and columns of infantry poured ashore to lay siege to the town of St-Martin, defended by 1 400 French, and the fort of La Prée. In no time there was an acute shortage of provisions. There were rations for less than a single day left when the miracle occurred: a squadron of 30 ships from the French fleet appeared in the Breton Straits and, with a favourable wind, managed to penetrate the harbour at St-Martin.

The siege, nevertheless, continued. On 6 November 1625, 6 000 Englishmen, encouraged by a mass singing of psalms, hurled themselves at the town walls. After a bloody hand-to-hand battle they were however repulsed.

It was then that Louis XIII, arriving at La Rochelle, despatched a contingent of reinforcements to the island, under the leadership of Marshal de Schomberg. The English, caught between two fires, were attacked at Pont de Feneau, near Loix, and massacred, leaving 2 000 dead on the field together with 6 cannon and 46 flags. Toiras was created Marshal of France in 1630.

Geographical Notes

L'Île de Ré, sometimes known as "L'Île Blanche", extends in a northwesterly direction for almost 30km/18mi. It largely comprises a series of Jurassic limestone outliers forming islets – principally Loix, Ars and Ré proper – which have become linked together.

In the north the deeply indented bay of Fier d'Ars, and the marshes surrounding it, constitute the Kids **Réserve Naturelle de Lilleau des Niges**, the home of thousands of different species of birds including grey curlews, widgeon, teal, silver plovers and geese. In the south a line of sand dunes has formed on a rocky plateau which stretches far away beneath the sea; the jagged cliffs eaten away by the encroaching tides have given rise to the name of this area: La Côte Sauvage (The Wild Coast).

The southeastern part of the Île de Ré, the widest and most fertile, is broken up into tiny smallholdings producing early fruit and vegetables, asparagus and above all vines (the wine, red, white and rosé, is full-favoured, with a hint of algae in the after-taste). The fortified apéritif-wine made here on the island is as good as the better-known Pineau des Charentes.

To the north and west the vines share the land with pines, as far as La Couarde. Beyond that, Ars-en-Ré is salt-marsh country – although the marshes are fast disappearing.

The people of Ré – the Rétais – are landlubbers rather than seafaring folk. Of the riches of the ocean they deal only in *sart* (seaweed and other wrack), harvested with huge rakes, shellfish and the prawns which teem on the rocky *platin* exposed at low tide. In addition, oyster farming has been introduced to the Fosse de Loix and Fier d'Ars inlets.

S. Sauvignier/MICHELIN

Dunes on pointe du Fier

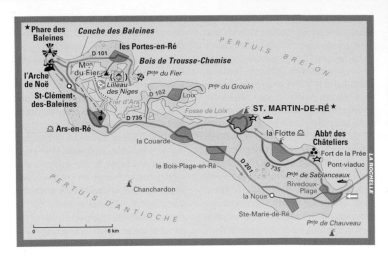

In the past the women of the island wore a long, narrow headdress to protect them against the fierceness of the sun; its name, the **quichenotte**, is said to derive from "kiss not", as its function was also, allegedly, to discourage the advances of amorous invading Englishmen. Today this tradition, like many others, has all but vanished – the island donkeys, for instance, which have disappeared entirely, were bedecked with straw hats and picturesque striped or plaid "trousers" to keep away flies and mosquitoes in the salt-marshes. Such things can now be seen only on postcards in the village shops. The villages are scattered all over the island, their single-storey houses, dazzling white, with typically green shutters, are brightened with hollyhocks, delphiniums and scarlet salvia, or a wisteria on a trellis.

Quichenotte headdress

St-Martin-de-Ré★

The island capital, formerly an active port and a military stronghold, has turned gracefully into a charming tourist centre. The narrow streets, quiet, spotlessly clean, still bumpy with cobblestones, have largely managed to retain the atmosphere of the Grand Siècle (the 17C in France).

Fortifications★

These date back to the early 17C but were entirely refashioned by Vauban after the siege of 1625 (℗ *see above*). Vauban came to inspect the Île de Ré in 1674 with the aim of strengthening the defences of the naval installations created by Colbert at Rochefort in 1666; the fortifications he designed for St-Martin were completed in 1692.

The **citadel**, built in 1681, was used as a prison under the Ancien Régime (19C) and later became a religious penitentiary. The citadel is not open to the public but a walk around the bastions on the seaward side reveals pleasing **views** of the Breton Straits and the mainland; note also the interesting watch-turrets and the cannon embrasures.

Parc de la Barbette

This park, sheltered by the fortifications, is a pleasant place for a shady stroll, looking down on the sea and the distant southern coast of the Vendée. Holm oaks, acacias,

Address Book

🪙 *For coin ranges, see the Legend on the cover flap.*

WHERE TO STAY

⌾**Hôtel L'Hippocampe** – *r. du Château des Mauléons – 17630 La Flotte – ☎05 46 09 60 68 – 12 rooms.* This 1927 house profits from the calm of a peaceful street in the village. Albeit modest, the interior design is slowly evolving. Breakfast served outside in the summer.

⌾⌾**Sénéchal** – *6 r. Gambetta – 17590 Ars-en-Ré – ☎05 46 29 40 42 – hotel.le.senechal@wanadoo.fr – closed 3 Jan-14 Feb and 13 Nov-19 Dec – 18 rooms.* This old island hotel has just received a facelift. White stones, blond wood and colourful textiles in the renovated rooms. Pleasant patio.

⌾⌾**Chambres d'hôte Le Clos Bel Ébat** – *17 r. de la Grainetière – 17630 La Flotte – ☎05 46 09 61 49 – closed Jan-Mar – ⊟ – 3 rooms.* The pretty little rooms (two-night minimum in season) of this ancient spirit storehouse are perfect for a romantic sojourn as well as for large families because they have communicating doors. A nice touch: the breakfast basket set in front of your bedroom door each morning.

⌾⌾⌾**Chambre d'hôte Domaine de la Baronnie** – *21 r. Baron de Chantal – 17410 St-Martin-de-Ré – ☎05 46 09 21 29 – infodomainedelabaronnie.com – closed 4 Nov-28 Mar – 6 rooms.* A unique address on the island! This superb registered mansion, tastefully restored, offers calm rooms of refined comfort. One of them, a duplex in the tower, has a splendid view of the garden and roofs of St. Martin. Breakfast served in a charming room.

WHERE TO EAT

⌾⌾**Les Embruns** – *6 r. Chay-Morin – Îlot – 17410 St-Martin-de-Ré – ☎05 46 09 63 23 – helene.berenguer@wanadoo.fr – closed Sun eve and Wed off-season.* Behind its green shutters, this little restaurant serves food fresh from the marketplace with a spotlight on fish. The menu is seasonal and blends perfectly with the fishing paraphernalia decor on the obligatory white and blue background.

⌾⌾**La Bouvette** – *Le Morinand – 17580 Le Bois-Plage-en-Ré – 2km/1.2mi SE of St-Martin-de-Ré via the D 201E2 – ☎05 46 09 29 87 – closed 20 Nov-20 Dec.* Next to the Morinand mill, this former wine storehouse is now a restaurant. Step inside and try just-caught fish grilled on a wood fire or a meat dish. The slate menu changes with the seasons. Very relaxed atmosphere.

⌾⌾**Le Bistrot de Bernard** – *1 quai de la Criée – 17590 Ars-en-Ré – ☎05 46 29 40 26 – bistrot.de.bernard@wanadoo.fr – closed 6 Jan-15 Feb, 11 Nov-20 Dec, Mon and Tue from Oct to Mar.* On the wharf, this old, typical house has charm to spare. With its terrace in front in the summer and its pretty dining room looking out on a courtyard garden, this is a very pleasant place to dine. Marine decor in keeping with the fish on the menu.

⌾⌾**Le Chat Botté** – *r. de la Mairie – 17590 St-Clément-des-Baleines – ☎05 46 29 42 09 – closed 1 Dec-1 Feb and Mon from 15 Sep-15 Jun.* You go through the bar to enter this regional-style house near the church. It has been owned by the same family since its building in 1920. Its large, recently renovated dining room gives onto a terrace and garden. Decor in shades of wood and modern furniture for traditional cuisine, proposed in fixed-price menus.

---

parasol pines and locust trees lend the park an almost Mediterranean air.

Hôtel de Clerjotte

Tall slate roofs crown this fine building constructed in a style midway between Flamboyant Gothic and Renaissance. It was originally the headquarters of an organisation owing allegiance to the local ruler, the Officiers des Seigneurs de Ré, and was at one time used as the town arsenal.

Today the building houses a museum and the tourist information centre. In the courtyard, bordered with Renaissance galleries, stands a staircase-tower at the foot of which is an elegant Flamboyant doorway.

Musée Ernest-Cognacq – *Until completion of renovations in 2009 only the area for temporary exhibitions is open ◷Open Jul-Sep daily except Tue 10am-7pm; rest of the year daily except Tue 10am-noon and*

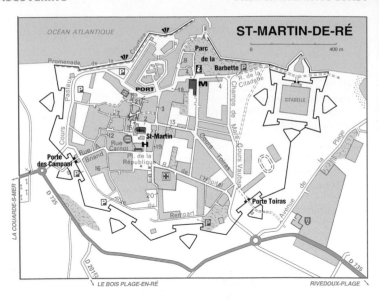

Bailli-des-Écotais Cours	2	Cothonneau R. Suzanne	12	Job-Foran Quai	18
Baron-de-Chantal R.	3	Dechézeaux Cours	13	Lapasset R. du Général	19
Bouthillier Av. Victor	4	France Pl. A.	15	Père-Ignace R.	20
Citeaux R. de	7	France R. Gaspard	16	Poithevinière Quai de la	21
Clemenceau Quai Georges	8	Gabarets R. des	17	Sully R. de	22

Ancien hôtel des Cadets de la marine (Hôtel de ville)	H	Hôtel de Clerjotte (ancien arsenal) Musée Ernest-Cognacq	M

2-6pm. ◔*Closed 1 Jan and 25 Dec.*
*4.20€. *05 46 09 21 22.

The maritime history of St-Martin and the island as a whole is presented through models, ships' figureheads, ancient weapons and tableaux (combat scenes, portraits of mariners and Napoleon's return from the Isle of Elba aboard the brig Inconstant). These seafaring displays are supplemented with a collection of pottery from Delft and porcelain from China, a reminder of the island's former maritime trade with the rest of the world.

The Port

Trade with Canada and the West Indies brought the port of St-Martin great prosperity during the 17C. Pleasure craft and a few fishing boats have now, however, replaced the tall ships sailing from the north in search of salt or wine, and the schooners from the Caribbean laden with spices. Port and harbour between them girdle the old sailors' district, now busy with shops, forming a picturesque islet which is popular with visitors. The quays

are paved with the ballast of long-gone merchant ships.

Église St-Martin

◔*Open Jul-Aug 9.30am-11.30pm; Sep–Jun 10am-nightfall.* *1.60€.* *05 46 09 58 25.*

The church dates from the 15C and was nicknamed "the big fort" because of the fortifications (still visible from the transept) which protected it. Ruined by the Anglo-Dutch naval bombardment of 1696, it was restored in the early 18C. A chapel dedicated to sailors contains 18C and 19C votive offerings.

Ancien Hôtel des Cadets de la Marine

This building houses both the town hall and the post office. It was built in the 18C to be used as barracks for a company of naval cadets. At the beginning of the 20C Ernest Cognacq, a merchant who founded the famous La Samaritaine department store in Paris, made a gift of it to his native town.

Port de St-Martin-de-Ré

Driving Tour

Round-trip from Pointe de Sablanceaux

75km/47mi – allow one day
The road, the D 735, follows the coast as far as Fort de La Prée, built as part of the ring of defences around La Rochelle.

▶ Take the first road to the right.

Ancienne Abbaye des Châteliers

The ruins of this Cistercian abbey founded in the 12C and destroyed in 1623 stand, with the wind whistling through them, on the bleak moorland carpeting Les Barres promontory. The remains of the abbey church include the west front and walls tracing the outline of a nave and a flattened east end in the style of Cîteaux Abbey. The chancel was lit via an elegant window. On the left of the church a series of pillars crowned with the beginnings of ribs indicate that cloisters once stood here. Excavations have unearthed capitals, coins, even skeletons.

▶ *Continue along this minor road through the seaside resort of La Flotte.*

St-Martin-de-Ré★
See ABOVE.

▶ *Leave St-Martin and drive west along the D 735.*

Ars-en-Ré

This small port with a network of lanes and alleys so narrow that the corners of houses had to be shaved off to allow carriages to turn into them was once frequented by Dutch and Scandinavian vessels loading cargoes of salt.

In the main square, once a cemetery but now covered over and planted with elms, stands **Église St-Étienne** (St Stephen's Church), its needle-sharp belfry spire, painted black and white as a landmark to sailors. A fine Romanesque entrance, partly below the new ground level, leads to a nave of the same period reinforced with thick ribs. The Gothic chancel, longer than the nave, is flanked by wide side aisles. The domed vaulting here is in the Angevin style.

Just south of the church is the Seneschal's (Steward's) House, dating from the Renaissance period and embellished with two corner turrets.

Réserve Naturelle de Lilleau des Niges

Guided tours by appointment at the Maison du Fier. Unaccompanied tours of the reserve's peripheral areas. 5.50€ (children 3€). 05 46 29 50 74. www.lilleau. niges.reserves-naturelles.org.

This nature reserve is inhabited by thousands of birds, including: curlews, grey plovers, teals and barnacle geese, which you can observe from the cycle

369

Staircase, Phare des Baleines

M. Thiery/MICHELIN

track which skirts the southern part of the reserve.

▶ *Bear right towards the D 101.*

Les Portes-en-Ré

This former salt-marsh workers' village is known locally as the "tip end of the island". Note the Chapelle de la Redoute, which is in fact a former powder magazine.

Bois de Trousse-Chemise

This pleasant pine wood surrounds the vast beach of **Pointe du Fier**.

Conche des Baleines

A forest track leads to this wide bay backed by dunes which describes a graceful curve indenting the coast. The use of the word *baleine* (whale) in names in this area derives from the fact that, in Roman times, hundreds of whales were washed up on these shores.

Phare des Baleines★

🕐 *Open Jul-Aug 9.30am-7.30pm; Apr-Jun 10am-7pm; rest of the year 5.30pm.* 🎫 *2.50€ (children 1.30€).* ☎ *05 46 29 18 23.*
The lighthouse, rising 55m/180ft above the headland, was built in 1854 to replace a 17C beacon-tower which had a light that did not carry very far. The tower can be reached by a pathway.
A spiral staircase of 257 steps leads to the gallery of the lighthouse. From here there is a splendid **panorama★** over the Breton Straits, the Vendée coast and

Pointe de l'Aiguillon to the north and east, over the Île de Ré to the southeast and the Île d'Oléron to the south. At low tide it is possible to see the **fish-locks** around the cape.

L'Arche de Noé

♿🕐 *Open Jun-Aug 10.30am-8pm; Sep–mid-Oct 2-6pm; Mid-Oct–May Sun and school hols 2-6pm.* 🎫 *10€ (children aged 3-10 7€).* ☎ *05 46 29 23 23. www.parc-archedenoe.com*
Kids This "Noah's Ark" amusement and culture park not far from Phare des Baleines offers visitors a trip through a magical world which presents the history of navigation at sea through models and dioramas, a collection of crustaceans and corals ("Océanorama"), displays of stuffed birds native to Île de Ré, a maze and exotic animals. The **Naturama★** houses a remarkable collection of stuffed animals from all over the world, grouped according to their habitat; decoratively-presented exotic butterflies and insects; a number of aquariums, and a turtle weighing 537kg/1 175lbs which was washed up on one of the island's beaches in 1978.

St-Clément-des-Baleines

The village is known for its beaches.

▶ *Continue along the D 735 then, at La Couarde, bear right onto the D 201 and return to Pointe de Sablanceaux via Le Bois-Plage-en-Ré and Ste-Marie-en-Ré.*

CHÂTEAU DE ROCHE COURBON★

MICHELIN MAPS 324: F-4

This château overlooks a graceful series of balustraded terraces and formal gardens in the French manner. The building stands isolated at the heart of the oakwoods that novelist **Pierre Loti** loved so much.

▸ **Orient Yourself**: The castle is located 15km/9.5mi northwest of Saintes and 19km/11mi southeast of Rochefort.
- **Don't Miss**: The gardens.
- **Also See**: ROCHEFORT, SAINTES.

A Bit of History

"Sleeping Beauty's Castle"

This was the title of an article written by Loti in 1908, which appeared in Le Figaro newspaper, to stimulate interest in his campaign to save the woods around the old château, itself long abandoned. Loti recalled the memories of his youth, when his holidays were spent with a friend – later to be his brother-in-law – who became the tax-collector in nearby St-Porchaire. Often as an adolescent, he wrote years later, he would stray "into the density of these oaken groves" sliced by a ravine buried beneath the foliage and pitted with small grottoes where "the greenish half-light filtered through leafy branches".

The campaign – harnessed to another run by fellow writer André Hallays – was a success: not only was the forest saved from the woodsman's axe; from 1920 onwards the château was restored and its gardens brought back to life.

Visit

The estate is entered via Porte des Lions (Lions' Gate), a monumental 17C structure with three arches, adorned with caryatids on the inside. Having crossed a moat, which was bordered with balustrades in the 17C, visitors pass below the "keep", an ancient machicolated tower.

M. Thiery/MICHELIN

Does a princess sleep within?

Château

&.♿🚻 Castle: by guided tour (45min) Apr-Oct 10am-noon and 2-6pm; Nov–Mar 10am-noon and 2-5pm. Gardens: unaccompanied visit 9am-7pm; Nov to Mar 9am-5.30pm. ⊘Closed Thu from mid-Sep to mid-May, Sun am in winter, 1 Jan and 25 Dec. ⊸Castle and gardens 8€ (children aged 7-14 4.50€), gardens 5.50€ (children aged 7-14 4.50€). ☎05 46 95 60 10.

The château, like the keep, dates from the 15C but was substantially altered by Jean-Louis de Courbon in the 17C when windows, dormers and skylights were refashioned and arcades added at the foot of the garden façade to support a balcony. This façade is remarkable for the balance of its elements and its balustraded stairway.

Inside, the tour of the château starts with a library-cum-study furnished in Louis XIII style which serves as a gallery for the paintings, most of them from the old chapel: they include biblical episodes, allegories, landscapes and a series of painted panels illustrating The Labours of Hercules which date from the time of Louis XIV.

The 18C Grand Salon, with panelling and furniture from the same period, contains a bust of Hubert Robert after Pajou, and a painting by the Dutch artist Hackaert which shows the château as it was in the 17C. Visitors then pass through a Louis XVI vestibule hung with rare, early 19C, illustrated panoramic wallpaper, and landscapes painted by Casanova, the brother of the notorious libertine. The tour finishes with two 17C rooms with Louis XIII ceilings: in the first of these is an enormous stone fireplace bearing the Latin inscription: Fide, Fidelitate, Fortitudine

(By Faith, Fidelity and Courage); the second room is a kitchen-banqueting hall with regional furniture and faience and a curious, very old roasting jack.

Gardens★

Beyond the château formal parterres and basins, separated by clipped yew hedges and graced with statues, form a magnificent and colourful perspective focusing on a double stairway flanking an ornamental waterway. Partially laid over marshland, these gardens were preserved from flooding by having their supporting piles regularly rebuilt (works lasting 17 years). Skirting these waters and the nymph at their far end, visitors reach a terrace offering a stunning **view★★** of the château, reflected in the smooth surface of the pool below it. The wide tree-lined walk leads to a column surmounted by a sphere; from here, by turning suddenly around, it is possible to experience that same sense of magic and surprise that so stimulated Pierre Loti.

Salle des Fêtes

Within this "festival hall" there is a superb late 16C stone stairway with balustrades.

Grottoes

30min round trip on foot.

🚶he woodland walk ends in an avenue of holm oaks which leads to the narrow valley carved out by the Bruant, a tributary of the River Charente. It is this stream which feeds the pools and waterways in the castle gardens.

The caves in the steep wall of the ravine which intrigued the young Loti were inhabited by prehistoric man.

ROCHEFORT★★

POPULATION 25 797
MICHELIN MAP 324: E-4

Rochefort, known as the "town of Pierre Loti," is on the border of the Aunis and Saintonge regions, between the right bank of River Charente and the marshes, not far from the Atlantic coast. The town takes great pride in its illustrious maritime history. There is still something exotic in the air around the arsenal, in which the great expeditions of the time were masterminded. Despite its air of severity, due to the grid pattern of Its rectilinear roads set at right-angles to each other (some of which still have their original blue Quebec cobblestones), Rochefort, created by Colbert in the 17C, is famous for the dignity and harmony of its architecture: one and two-storey buildings, private mansions (highly decorated façades, wrought-iron balconies) and Royal Rope Factory, built of fine pale-coloured dressed stone. Its excellent museums, such as La Maison de Pierre Loti, Le Centre International de la Mer, which is laid out in the Rope Factory, Le Musée de la Marine and many others, add interest to the town. Rochefort's thermal springs were reopened in 1953

- **Information:** Av. Sadi-Carnot, 17300 Rochefort.
  ☎05 46 99 08 60. www.tourisme.fr/rochefort.
- ▶ **Orient Yourself**: Rochefort is situated 38km/24mi southeast of La Rochelle and 44km/27.5mi northwest of Saintes.
- **P** **Parking**: A number of car parks are dotted around the centre (&see town plan).
- **Don't Miss**: Corderie Royale, Arsenal district, Maison de Pierre Loti, Musée d'Art et d'Histoire.
- **Also See**: ÎLE D'OLÉRON, CHÂTEAU DE LA ROCHE COURBON, LA ROCHELLE, SAINTES.

A Bit of History

The Days of Sailing Ships

In the middle of the 17C Jean-Baptiste Colbert (1619-83), Louis XIV's minister in charge of the Navy, was looking for a base from which the Atlantic coast could be defended against the incursions of the English. Brouage was silting up and the roadstead of La Rochelle was not sufficiently sheltered. Rochefort, 15km/9mi upriver from the mouth of the Charente, seemed the ideal choice. It was protected off-shore, moreover, not only by the Île de Ré, Île d'Aix and Île d'Oléron, but also by the Fouras and Le Chapus

Pierre Loti (1850-1923)

The author Pierre Loti, whose real name was Julien Viaud, was born in Rochefort at No 141 of the street that now bears his nom-de-plume. He was the son of a municipal official. Loti, a much-travelled naval officer, accomplished sportsman and something of a dandy with a distinguished bearing, was also a novelist of great sensitivity and an exceptional story-teller. Inspired by his voyages to exotic destinations, he wrote *Pêcheur d'Islande* (Iceland Fisherman), *Aziyadé, Ramuntcho* and *Madame Chrysanthème*, books that were instrumental in his acceptance as a member of the élite Académie Française at the unusually young age of 41.

Maison de Pierre Loti, Rochefort

Address Book

For coin ranges, see the Legend on the cover flap.

WHERE TO STAY

Hôtel La Belle Poule – *3km/1.8mi S of Rochefort on the Royan road – ☎ 05 46 99 71 87 – closed 8-29 Nov, Sun eve and Fri off-season – 🅿 – 20 rooms – restaurant*. Just next to the Martrou bridge, this house in a flower-filled garden is an enjoyable stop. A cable's length from the islands, the centre of Rochefort and therefore of Pierre Loti's house, it offers big rooms and a pleasant dining room with a fireplace.

Hôtel Corderie Royale – *r. Audebert – near the Corderie Royale – ☎ 05 46 99 35 35 – info@corderieroyale-hotel.com – closed 1 Feb-6 Mar, Sun eve and Mon from Nov-Easter – 🅿 – 45 rooms*

– restaurant. This hotel accross from the port has been constructed out of the magnificent 17C buildings of the Royal Artillery. An excellent halt in the very centre of the Arsenal quarter, even if the 1980s decor doesn't suit everyone's fancy. Superb view of the Charente river from the restaurant. Pool.

WHERE TO EAT

Ferme Aquacole de l'Île Madame – *17730 Port-des-Barques – ☎ 05 46 84 12 67 – closed Feb, Nov school hols, evenings in Nov and Wed – reservation recommended*. This farm on an island is only accessible at low tide. Surrounded by pools and salt marshes, you can savour seafood and congers raised here. Occasionally, the sea covers the passage to terra firma at lunchtime, but don't fret, it doesn't last!

---

promontories – all of them easy to fortify.

It was decided therefore, starting from scratch, to turn Rochefort into a military port with an arsenal as powerful as the one in Toulon, and from 1666 onwards work started on the docks and fortifications. By 1671 Rochefort could boast a population of 20 000, and 13 men-of-war, a galley and several brigantines had been launched.

The town, originally constructed of wood, was rebuilt in stone in 1688 on the orders of the naval governor Michel Bégon – the man who gave his name to the begonia family: these exotic plants discovered in the West Indies by a priest, Father Plumier, were brought back to France at the governor's request.

Arsenal

Colbert's arsenal was, by 1690, "the biggest, the most complete and the most magnificent in the kingdom": 47 warships had been armed and provisioned there with ammunition, among them several three-deckers such as the famous *Louis-le-Grand*. Between 1690 and 1800 three hundred new vessels sailed into the waters of the Charente from Rochefort's naval yards.

The *Sphinx*, the French navy's first steam-powered warship, was built in the first half of the 19C, followed by the *Mogador*, the most powerful paddle-wheel frigate ever to be built in France. The arsenal was closed in 1926.

Between 5 000 and 10 000 workmen were employed in the arsenal. Every morning and evening the flagship fired a cannon shot to signal the opening or closing of the gates.

It was from Rochefort, on 21 March 1780, that General La Fayette set sail for the second time to reinforce the "Insurgent" troops in America onboard a brand new frigate, *L'Hermione*, built at the arsenal. In 1816 the frigate *La Méduse* sailed from Rochefort for Senegal in West Africa, only to be wrecked off the coast of what is now Mauritania. The loss of the ship inspired Géricault to paint his celebrated dramatic work *The Raft of the Medusa*.

The Hulks of Rochefort

In the autumn of 1792 the Republican "cleansing" of the clergy began. Hundreds and hundreds of priests who had refused to swear that they accepted the "civil" status of the Church under the new Constitution were sent to Rochefort, where they were destined to embark on ships taking them to the

Guyana penal colony in South America. Anchored in the Charente were two decrepit ships (known as *pontons* or hulks) awaiting them. In the event the prisoners were transferred to two even more dilapidated slave traders. The "villains" were crammed between decks in batches of 400, lying on filthy straw, with nothing but sea-water to wash in. A communal tub of broth with a few broad beans floating in it was all they had for food, the *sans-culottes* (revolutionaries) having already sold part of the rations destined for the prisoners.

One day, after a short voyage, the hulks weighed anchor. Instead of deportation to Guyana, the priests found they were kept aboard ship off the Île d'Aix. On deck shots were fired and cries of "Long live the Republic! Long live Robespierre!" rang out over the water. By now the deportees, lacking everything, had only one aim: to survive. In January 1794, however, typhus made its grim appearance. Twelve or thirteen priests died every day; at each death there was a noisy celebration by the crew. The corpses, at first thrown into the sea, were later transported to Aix or Île Madame – a tiny offshore islet linked to the mainland at low tide: fatigue parties drawn from the surviving priests were forced to carry out this gruesome task; many of them died doing it.

Transferred at last to Île Madame, all of those still living were freed in 1795.

Arsenal District★

The arsenal was built on the banks of the River Charente in two sectors which still exist, interspersed with launching slipways and entrances to dry docks. From 1830 the entrance was via the famous Porte du Soleil. The arsenal contained 11 shipbuilding yards and four refitting basins, including **La Vieille Forme**, the oldest masonry dry dock (1669) in the world. The complex also housed a foundry that specialised in copper-plated nails, a boilermaking shop, forges, sawmills, rope-makers and a cooperage works that produced barrels for gunpowder as well as enormous warehouses for quartermasters' stores. Huge mast pits could contain up to 50 000m³/65 400yd³ of wood rendered rot-proof by the briny water. A workshop of "Naval sculptors" carved figureheads and embellished poops and prows.

Porte du Soleil

This entrance to the arsenal, dating from 1830, is in the form of a triumphal arch.

Chantier de Reconstruction de l'Hermione

🕐 *Open Apr-Oct 9am-7pm; Nov-Mar 10am-6pm.* 🔧 *Guided tours (1hr 30min) available Fri-Sun 2.30-16.30pm.* 🕐 *Closed 1-15 Jan and 25 Dec.* 💶 *4.60€ (children 2€, under 8 no charge); guided tours 6€ and 3€.* ☎ *05 46 87 01 90. www.hermione. com.*

Rebuilding the Hermione

M. Thiery/MICHELIN

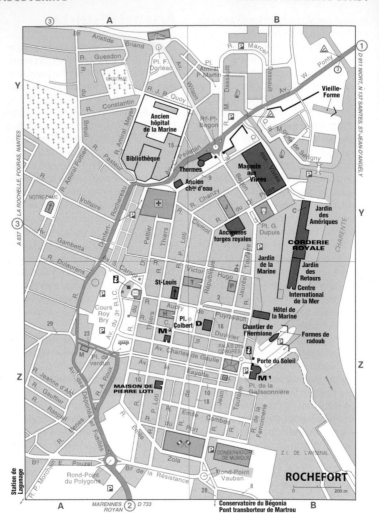

The double dock (1728) was specially restored and equipped for the construction of a replica of the *Hermione*, the frigate (fitted with guns using 12lb cannonballs) in which La Fayette sailed to America *(see above)*. Work began on 4 July 1997 using the same techniques as in 1779, when the *Hermione* was first built.

Hôtel de Cheusses

A magnificent gateway leads to the courtyard of this 17C mansion which was once the local Admiralty headquarters. Today the building is a naval museum.

Musée de la Marine

Open Apr to mid-Sep 10am-6.30pm; mid-Sep to Mar daily except Mon 10am-

noon and 2-6pm. *Guided tours available.* **Closed mid-Dec–late-Jan and 1 May.** *5€ (children under 18 no charge), combined ticket with the Ancienne École de Médecine Navale.* ☎05 46 99 86 57. www.musee-marine.fr.

Model ships, ships' figureheads, navigational equipment, paintings, charts, weapons and flags evoke the history of the French Navy from the 17C to the 20C. Maps, documents and explanatory models illustrate the story of Rochefort's old naval dockyard. Particularly impressive are the very large ship models (and those of windmills) in the outer hall.

Of particular note is the enormous capstan from the privateer commanded by René Duguay-Trouin (1673-1736), whose great exploit was the capture of Rio de Janeiro in 1711 with "a feeble fleet".

Hôtel de la Marine

Napoleon Bonaparte once stayed here, and the oldest part of the building dates back to the time of Louis XIV. In front of it is a monumental 18C gateway. A tall, square-sectioned tower at one side was formerly used for the exchange of visual signals with ships.

Jardin de la Marine

The tree-lined riverside walks and terraced lime trees of this quiet, sheltered garden date back to the 18C. A handsome staircase terminating in a doorway with three arches leads down to the former royal rope factory.

Corderie Royale★★

This rope factory below the garden and overlooking the Charente was founded by Colbert in 1666 and completed four years later; it stands on a kind of "raft", a grid of heavy oak beams, because of the nature of the soil. The factory supplied all the rigging for the entire French fleet from the time the factory was opened until the Revolution; once steam took over from sail, however, its activity declined and it was closed at the same time as the arsenal.

The Corderie Royale was severely damaged during World War II but has been the subject of an extensive restoration programme which has replaced the original lengthy and very harmonious façade

(374m/1 227ft long). This is surmounted by a blue slate mansard roof with pediment dormers. The rear façade is reinforced by elegant scrolled buttresses. The building as a whole is a classic – and rare – example of 17C industrial architecture.

The **Centre International de la Mer** (**Open Apr-Oct 9am-7pm; Nov-Mar 10am-5.30pm (last admission 1hr before closing).** *Guided tours possible.* **Closed 1-14 Jan and 25 Dec.** *5€ (children 2€); guided tours 7€ and 3€.* ☎05 46 87 81 40. www.corderie-royale.com) houses a permanent exhibit on ropes and rigging: once the hemp had arrived from the Auvergne it was spun, assembled in strands and then twisted into its final form before being tarred – the length of the building both limiting and conditioning that of the rigging. Among the exhibits is an imposing 19C machine corder (twisting machine) which runs on rails. Temporary exhibits on maritime themes are also held here.

Surrounding the Corderie is the **Jardin des Retours**. Its rare and exotic species make it easy to imagine great expeditions returning to the port, laden with unknown plants such as begonias and magnolias. The riverside **Jardin des Amériques** includes the **Aire des Gréements** (Rigging Zone), evoking the vessels of the past; while the **Labyrinthe des Batailles Navales** is a maze of clipped yew hedges.

Magasin aux Vivres

This late 17C naval storehouse, next to the provisioning dock and facing the marina, was the site of a bakery able to produce 20 000kg/ 44 100lbs of bread each day.

Ancienne École de Médecine Navale

Visit by guided tour Jul-Aug at 11am, 2.30pm and 4pm. Jun and Sep, at 2.30pm and 4pm; Feb-May and Oct–mid-Dec Wed and Sat-Sun at 3pm. **Closed mid-Dec to end Jan and 1 May.** *5€, combined ticket with Hôtel des Cheusses.* ☎05 46 99 59 57. www.musee-marine.fr.

This 18C building stands at the heart of a park. The chapel, crowned with a pinnacle, lies behind a façade with a carved pediment. The École de médecine navale et tropicale was established in 1722.

The library and various collections of anatomy, surgery and natural history can be visited.

Thermal springs

Nearby is a small centre for thermal cures: the springs were first tapped after Napoleon I's visit in 1808 and rehabilitated once again in 1953, when the virtues of thermal treatment regained their popularity. The naturally hot waters (42°C/108°F) gush forth from the depths of the marshes. **La Source de l'Empereur** (Emperor's Spring) is especially effective in the treatment of rheumatism, osteoarthritis and dermatitis.

Opposite stands the old **water tower**, a fine quadrangular structure in stone, dating from 1900, which at one time supplied the whole town.

Additional Sights

Église St-Louis

The church, built on the site of a chapel belonging to an old Capuchin monastery (1672), is imbued with the majesty of the Classical style.

Place Colbert

This fine square, huge and rectangular in shape and bordered by elegant façades, is the true city centre. On the western side, the town hall is installed in the Hôtel d'Amblimont. The 18C monumental fountain on the other side of the square represents the Ocean and the River Charente mingling their waters.

Pierre Loti's house, Rochefort

Maison de Pierre Loti, Rochefort

Many of the scenes in the 1967 Jacques Demy musical film, *Les Demoiselles de Rochefort*, were shot in this square. (👆 See *PLANNING YOUR TRIP*)

Musée d'Art et d'Histoire★

Enquire for opening times and tarifs. ☎05 46 82 67 80

The museum is housed in the former Hôtel Hèbre-de-Saint-Clément. A large picture gallery and an adjoining exhibit room contain a sketch by Rubens (*Lycaon Changed into a Wolf by Jupiter*), a number of 17C flower paintings, portraits from the 16C Italian School, and others by Roques (Ingres' teacher) and a series of landscapes, portraits and sentimental scenes from the Empire and Romantic epochs. These include Gauffier's *Return of the Prodigal Son* and work by Belloc, Rouget (*Portrait of Lola Montès*) and Michallon. More recent paintings hang nearby.

Fine collections of ethnographic interest from Africa and the South Pacific, including superb Polynesian masks, may be found in the Lesson Gallery.

In the following room hang seascapes and a copy of Géricault's dramatic work inspired by the Medusa tragedy. The Local History department has an extraordinary plan of Rochefort, in relief, from 1835, and Vernet's painting, *The Port of Rochefort*. The Camille Mériot Room is reserved for collections of shells.

Maison de Pierre Loti★

👆*Visit by guided tour (50 min, departure every 30 min); reservation required, daily except Tue at 10.30am, 11.30am, 2pm, 3pm and 4pm.* ⏱*Closed Jan, 1 and 11 Nov and 25 Dec.* ⬤*7.80€ (children under 8 no charge).* ☎*05 46 99 16 88.*

Loti's house is in fact two intercommunicating buildings – his birthplace and the house next door, which he acquired as soon as he was able – concealing a remarkable interior behind a relatively plain façade. The rooms are sumptuously furnished and decorated, and full of souvenirs from his many voyages.

There are two salons on the ground floor. Loti's piano stands in the first, which is hung with family paintings, some by his sister; the second houses Louis XVI furniture and a number of mementoes and objets d'art. The **"Renaissance" Dining**

Room – furnished in the Spanish style and hung with five 17C Flemish tapestries – includes a huge chimney piece and a dais for musicians. On the mezzanine floor, the former studio used by the author's painter sister, transformed into a "15C salon", was the site of a famous "Louis XI dinner" in April 1888.

The spartan furnishings of the first-floor master bedroom are in striking contrast to the three apartments around it: the **Mosque**, with décor largely from a mosque in Damascus (collection of prayer mats, candelabra, weapons, a painted cedarwood ceiling); the **Turkish Salon** with its sofas, cushions, exotic wall hangings and a stucco ceiling inspired by the Alhambra in Granada; the **Arab Room**, glittering with enamel-work and adorned with a *moucharabieh* (a carved wood screen placed in front of a window).

Musée des Commerces d'autrefois

Open Jul-Aug 10am-8pm; Apr-Jun and Sep-Oct 10am-noon and 2-7pm, Sun and public hols 2-7pm; Nov-Mar 10am-noon and 2-6pm, Sun and public hols 2-6pm.
Closed Jan and 25 Dec. 5.80€ *(children under 10 no charge). 05 46 83 91 50.*

Here a series of workshops and stores dating from 1900 to 1940 have been re-created in meticulous detail within an old warehouse dating from the turn of the century. The picturesque evocation of life in days gone by includes a Rochefort bar with its Belle Epoque façade, a pharmacy, a hatter's, a grocery store, a forge and a dyer's workshop.

Conservatoire du Bégonia

Visit by guided tours (1hr) May–Sep daily except Sun and Mon, at 2.30pm, 3.30pm and 4.30pm (Sat, at 2.30pm and 3.30pm); Feb-Apr and Oct-Nov daily except Mon at 3.30pm and 4.30pm.
Closed on public hols. 4€. *05 46 99 08 26.*

Plumier was the botanist priest who first brought begonias back from the West Indies in the 17C. The plant was not, however, commercially available in France until the end of the 18C. Here, in a huge hothouse, over 850 species, natural and hybrid, are grown, cared for and brought to perfection.

Pont Transbordeur de Martrou

2.5km/1.5mi S, in rue Jacques-Demy which becomes avenue du 11-Novembre.
Open Jun-Aug, 10am-noon and 2-8pm, Mon, 2-8pm; May and Sep, 10am-noon and 2-7pm, Mon, 2-7pm; Apr, 10am-noon and 2-6pm, Mon, 2-6pm, Oct, 10am-noon and 2-5pm, Mon, 2-5pm; Nov-Jan, Sat-Sun, 10am-noon and 2-5pm; Feb-Mar, 2-7pm, Mon, 10am-noon. 1.80€ *(return). 05 46 99 08 60.*

This iron transporter bridge, a splendid example of industrial art dating from 1900, is 176m/577ft long and stands more than 50m/164ft above the surface of the Charente. Five of these bridges were built in France by the engineer Ferdinand Arnodin: in Marseille, Rouen, Brest, Nantes and Rochefort. Transporter bridges enabled both pedestrians and vehicles to cross from one side of the river to the other, without sea-going ships being hindered by the structures of a fixed bridge. Martrou is the only one to have been re-instated (1994). It can be used by cyclists and pedestrians. A new toll-bridge for vehicles was opened in 1991.

Pont-l'Abbé-d'Arnoult

This formerly fortified city on the canalized Arnoult river, with its whitewashed houses, developed around a Benedictine priory built in the 11C, on the behest of Geoffroy Martel, comte d'Anjou. The explorer René Caillé, born in Mauzé-sur-le-Mignon 11km/7mi North-East of Surgères) in 1799, was buried in the graveyard of Pont-l'Abbé in 1838. He was the first explorer who came back alive from Timbuktoo.

The lower part of the façade of the church is adorned with Romanesque sculptures. The centre of the first arch of the doorway, depicts the mystical Lamb honoured by the angels. The second and the fourth arches represent Virtues and Vices, wise Virgins and mad Virgins, and the third one is dedicated to the saints.

The tympanums of the lateral arcades represent, on the left a hardly visible scene, Saint Peter leaving jail, and on the right Saint Peter crucified.

A porch nearby gives access to the yard of the priory (15-16C). Its façade is adorned with an elegant turret.

LA ROCHEFOUCAULD
POPULATION 3 228
MICHELIN MAP 324: M-5

La Rochefoucauld is a small town with picturesque half-timbered houses, set on the banks of the River Tardoire. Near the old fairground (Champ de Foire) is a 17C **bridge,** slightly humpbacked, with two half-moon ravelins, face to face, built so that pedestrians could get out of the way of carts and carriages. From here there are pleasant views of the river and the old château rising grandly above it. The prosperity of La Rochefoucauld depends on several small industries, among them the production of charentaises – a comfortable form of slipper. It was in the time of Louis XIV that this began as a cottage industry; the slippers were partly made from fabric left over from the manufacture of sailors' reefer jackets while the soles were cut from felt used to dry paper pulp in the paper factories of Angoulême. The slippers were so successful that they even found their way into the Court.

Information: 1 R. des Tanneurs, 16110 La Rochefoucauld. ☎05 45 63 07 45.

Sights

Château★★★
🕐 Apr–Dec 10am-7pm; Jan–Mar: from 2pm (by appointment). ✺8€ (children 3€). ☎05 45 62 07 42.
The Château de La Rochefoucauld was the home of an illustrious line whose chief has traditionally always had the Christian name of François; the best known is probably **François VI de La Rochefoucauld** (1613-80), the pessimistic author of the famous *Maxims*. The château, still the property of the same family, is constructed of soft white stone. The remains of a square Romanesque keep are still visible, but the place as a whole, with its elegant Renaissance façade and beautiful **main courtyard**★★, recalls the châteaux of the Loire more than any military stronghold. Note in particular the **spiral staircase**★ (108 steps) and it elegant vaulting, as well as Marguerite d'Angoulême's **boudoir**★, decorated with 17C painted panels depicting the French properties of the La Rochefoucauld family.

Château de La Rochefoucauld

The river front is framed by a medieval tower and the castle chapel. Noteworthy here are the pedimented dormers with their candelabra and their tabernacle motifs stamped with a shell.

Ancien Couvent des Carmes

Rue des Halles. A restored chapter-house and huge cloisters with groined vaulting and trefoil arching supported by delicate small columns comprise the main points of interest in this former Carmelite monastery. Part of the building has been turned into a laboratory of paleontology.

Église Notre-Dame-de-l'Assomption-et-St-Cybard

The church is built in a style rarely found in the Angoulême region: 13C Gothic.

Ancienne Pharmacie de l'Hôpital

Place du Champ-de-Foire. Visit by guided tour (30min) by prior appointment (48hr) at the Tourist office. No charge. ☎05 45 63 07 45.

The old pharmacy of the hospital, which dates back to the 17C, houses an interesting collection of chemist's pots, flasks, mortars (16C and 17C) and a complete surgeon's instrument case from the Empire period; its original owner was attached to the army of Napoleon. Also on display, a fine 17C Christ fashioned from ivory.

Excursions

Chasseneuil-sur-Bonnieure, Memorial de la Résistance and Cimetière National

11km/6.6mi NE along N 141. Unaccompanied visit to the memorial. Guided tour of crypt (45min), Apr-Sep: daily except Sat-Sun 9-11.45am and 2-5.45pm; Oct-May daily except Sat-Sun 9-11.45am and 2-4.45pm. No charge. ☎06 83 53 68 98.

This monument to the French Resistance occupies the centre of a cemetery laid out in terraces on the hillside – 2 026 soldiers and members of the Resistance, killed between 1940 and 1945, rest in peace beneath the rose-bush covered lawns.

WHERE TO STAY

⊜⊜**Château L'Âge Baston Bed and Breakfast**– *l'Âge Baston – 16110 St-Projet-St-Constant – 3km/1.8mi S of La Rochefoucauld dir. Angoulême, then Pranzac on the D 33 –* ☎*05 45 63 53 07 – lagebaston@aol.com –* ⊟*– 4 rms.* On the heights overlooking La Rochefoucauld, this solid 16 and 17C edifice has preserved its authenticity with its old parquets and asymmetrical walls. The spacious rooms are old-fashioned; the reception and ambience are casual.

Église de Ste-Colombe

12km/7.5mi NW along D 6 and D 91. The church in this typical little Charente village has an interesting Romanesque façade adorned with statue-columns (St Colombe, St Peter) and bas-reliefs with symbols from the gospels.

Forêt de la Braconne

The Braconne massif (around 4 000ha/ 9 884 acres) is a limestone plateau extensively carved by underground waters which have produced dolines or sink-holes caused by subsidence of the surface. The best-known – and the most spectacular – is **La Grande Fosse** (*the big pit*), a huge funnel-shaped depression 55m/180ft deep and 250m/820ft in diameter. Although it is smaller, **La Fosse Limousine** (*south-east of the Grande Combe roundabout*), hidden by tall beech trees, is also attractive. As for **La Fosse Mobile** (*not open to the public*), legend has it that a wicked son who had murdered his father tried in vain to dump the body in this sink-hole – but the nearer he approached the edge of the depression, the more it moved away from him. In fact the depths of this abyss, which lies in an isolated spot in the silence of the woods, are used for training local cavers.

▶ *Return to La Rochefoucauld via D 88.*

LA ROCHELLE★★★

POPULATION 76 584

MICHELIN MAP 324: D-3

La Rochelle is the capital of the Aunis, a region founded by the Romans and fought over in the attrition between the English and the French in the Middle Ages. The town is popular with painters, seduced by the bustling atmosphere of its daily life. The old fortified port, the hidden streets lined with arcades, the ancient wooden houses and stately mansions, whether under the brilliance of summer skies or the most romantic of drizzles, all combine to make La Rochelle the most attractive town on the coast from Nantes to Bordeaux.

- ▤ **Information**: Quartier du Gabut, pl. de la Petite-Sirène, 17000 La Rochelle. ☎05 46 41 14 68.
- ▶ **Orient Yourself**: The town is situated 23km/14mi northwest of Rochefort.
- ▣ **Parking**: A number of car parks are dotted around the centre (*see town plan*).
- ⌾ **Don't Miss**: Old town, Vieux Port, Tour St-Nicolas, Tour de la Lanterne, Maison Henri-II, Hôtel de Ville, Musée d'Histoire Naturelle, Neptunéa.
- 🄺🄸🄳 **Especially for Kids**: Aquarium, Musée des Automates, Musée des Modèles Réduits.

A Bit of History

The English connection

Henry II of England, who was Eleanor of Aquitaine's second husband, granted La Rochelle its charter in 1199, thus liberating the city of its feudal and ecclesiastical ties. Ramparts were erected as early as the 13C and La Rochelle entered into commercial agreements with England and Flanders, importing canvas and wool, exporting wine and salt. The town became an international trading centre, with banks and merchants from Spain, England and Flanders. From the 15C onwards, La Rochelle prospered through the fur trade with Canada and the slave trade with the West Indies.

A Protestant stronghold

La Rochelle was sometimes known as "the French Geneva" as it was, like its Swiss counterpart, a haven for numerous disciples of Calvin before 1540; in the early days of the Reformation his teachings were even preached in the city churches. Between 1562 and 1598 the Wars of Religion brought a bloodbath to the region. In 1565 priests were hurled into the sea from the top of the tall Lantern Tower. Three years later a National Synod was held here under the presidency of Calvin's follower, the writer and theologian Théodore de Bèze. The staunchly Calvinist queen Jeanne d'Albret, her son Henri de Navarre (the future Henri IV) and the Prince de Condé took part in the debates.

In 1573 the royal army, led by the Duc d'Anjou, laid siege to the city. But La Rochelle held out. The inhabitants made use of a machine, derisively known as *L'Encensoir* (the censer), which drenched the assailants with boiling water and melted pitch. After six months of continued attacks the city still had not fallen, and the royalists had lost 20 000 men, when the siege was lifted.

The siege of La Rochelle (1627-28)

55 years later a second royalist army stood at the gates of La Rochelle – though this time the town was allied with the English, who had invaded Île de Ré.

Two equally determined figures were pitted against each other on this occasion: outside was **Cardinal Richelieu**, determined to impose a unity on France, whatever the cost; inside was **Jean Guiton** (1585-1654), a small, abrupt man, un-cultivated yet fanatic in temperament, who had been an admiral in the navy and was now Mayor of La Rochelle.

Unfortunately for Guiton the blockade was organised by a masterly hand, both on land and at sea, from where help for the besieged from the English was expected: Richelieu himself took charge of the siege. What was in effect a gigantic dike was erected across the bay to block the entrance to the harbour. Both infantry and artillery were posted on top of the dike with the result that the English fleet was unable to sail through and relieve the beleaguered garrison.

At first the people of La Rochelle were not overly concerned at the building of the dike: storms, they were convinced, would sweep it away. In fact it held, though it took the besiegers 15 months to starve the town into submission. Richelieu made his victorious entry on 30 October 1628, followed two days later by Louis XIII.

From Rabelais to Fromentin

La Rochelle has always been a popular town with writers. **Rabelais**, one of the first, broke his journey here and described the light from the Lantern Tower in Pantagruel. **Choderlos de Laclos**, the author of *Les Liaisons Dangereuses*, was garrisoned here c1786 as an engineer officer overseeing the construction of the arsenal. He lived in a house linked, via a concealed stairway and an underground passage, with the mansion owned by Admiral Duperré. It can only be guessed at whether de Laclos' marriage to Solange, the Admiral's sister, was in any way connected to this ease of access.

The writer associated more than anyone with La Rochelle is **Eugène Fromentin** (1820-76), who was a painter and an art critic as well as a novelist. He was influenced by the artists Corot and Delacroix, and his painter's eye is obvious everywhere in his beautiful romance, *Dominique*, published in 1862 and dedicated to George Sand. In this novel he describes with the precision of a naturalist the life in 19C La Rochelle; the landscapes, the skies and the light of the Aunis are suggested with an incomparable lightness of touch.

Fromentin was a native Rochelais but many other eminent men from other parts of France were also associated with the town. They include Voltaire and Laclos, Corot, the Impressionist painters Signac and Marquet, Joseph Vernet who painted the port, and distinguished naturalists and scientists like Lafaille, d'Orbigny and Bonpland. Jean-Paul Sartre was at school in La Rochelle; Georges Simenon lived here for a while: his novel *Le Voyageur de la Toussaint* (The All Saints Day Traveller) is set in the town. An annual convention, held since 1732, brought together some of these eminent figures in sailing.

The port of La Rochelle is regularly on the route of several sailing races (Open UAP, Le Figaro, Hong Kong Challenge and others). The port's main asset is the presence of shipyards, renowned sail-makers and specialists in outfitting of ships' superstructure. It is therefore not surprising that several famous sailers should have chosen La Rochelle as their base including Philippe Poupon and Isabelle Autissier.

Siege of La Rochelle, by H. Motte

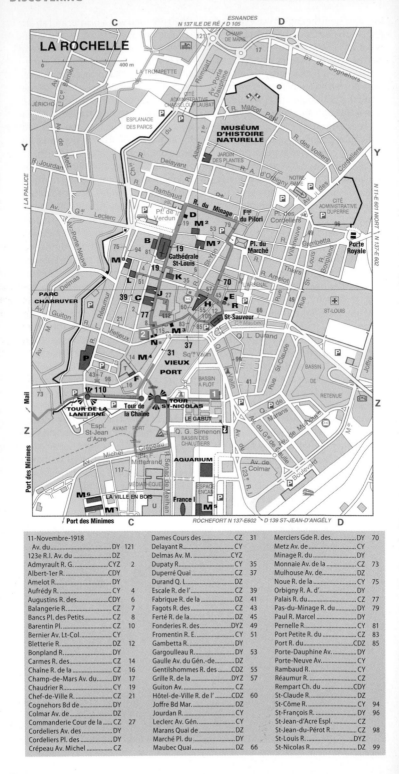

LA ROCHELLE

Walking Tours

① Old Port★★

Starts at the tourist office. 1hr 30min.

The old harbour (the modern harbour has been transferred to La Palice) is located deep inside a narrow bay. You can see the forward harbour, the old harbour, the small dock used by yachts, the outside dock used by trawlers and the reservoir supplied by a canal with water from the River Sèvre.

Gabut district

A picturesque residential and shopping development has been built on the site (east of Tour St-Nicolas) of an old bastion which was once part of the town's ring of fortifications (demolished in 1858). The façades with their wood cladding

recall the fish-lofts and sheds of old-time sailors, while vivid colours and wide windows lend the place a Nordic air.

Tour St-Nicolas★
&See SIGHTS.

▶ *Turn south, cross a small bridge and turn right onto the alleyway running alongside avenue Marillac.*

Walk along the quayside past the multimedia library inaugurated in 1998 and admire the view of the towers and Vieux Port. Take the small boat which ferries passengers to the foot of Tour de la Chaîne.

Cour des Dames

Once the haunt of sardine mongers and fishermen repairing their nets, this esplanade, which is one of the most animated parts of the old port, now features a cin-

M.Thiery/MICHELIN

The old harbor

Address Book

For coin ranges, see the Legend on the cover flap.

WHERE TO STAY

Chambre d'hôte Margorie – *17139 Dompierre-sur-Mer – 8km/5mi NE of La Rochelle on the N 11, then take the road to Mouillepied –* ☎*05 46 35 33 41 – 4 rooms.* A relaxing stop in the local countryside, this isolated old farm is surrounded by stone walls and its inviting garden is full of flowers and trees. In the outbuildings, the rooms are arranged around a second courtyard; some come with a mezzanine.

Hôtel de la Plage – *bd de la Mer – 17340 Châtelaillon-Plage –* ☎*05 46 56 26 02 – hotelaplage-chatel@wanadoo.fr – P – 10 rooms – restaurant.* This tiny hotel facing the beach is nothing fancy, but it is impeccably managed and nicely situated. The small rooms are appealing and soundproofed, and their very reasonable prices should win over the wariest wayfarer. A sure bet.

Hôtel France-Angleterre et Champlain – *20 r. Rambaud –* ☎*05 46 41 23 99 – hotel@france-champlain.com – 36 rooms.* A spot of the country in the city. On a busy street near the historic district, this old 16C convent features a discrete, pleasant garden – a marvellous place to unwind after a busy day in town. In this genteel setting, the rooms, some quite spacious, are decorated with period pieces.

Hôtel Les Brises – *Chemin digue Richelieu, (av. P.-Vincent) –* ☎*05 46 43 89 37 – P – 46 rooms.* How delightful to open one's windows in the morning, contemplate the ocean and breathe the sea air! This 1960s hotel is well situated between earth and water. Lovely view from the panoramic terrace and most of the rooms.

Hôtel de la Monnaie – *3 r. de la Monnaie –* ☎*05 46 50 65 65 – info@hotel-monnaie.com – 31 rooms.* Right behind the Tour de la Lanterne, this splendid 17C mansion where coins used to be made is an agreeable address. You'll appreciate the serenity of the rooms between courtyard and garden, as well as their modern furnishings and spaciousness.

WHERE TO EAT

Le Café de la Mer – *Port du Plomb – Lauzières – 17137 Nieul-sur-Mer – Take the D 106E1 4km/2.5mi W of Nieul-sur-Mer –* ☎*05 46 37 39 37 – closed Oct-Mar.* Mouclades (mussels in a spicy cream sauce), oysters and crepes in the summer, hearty simmering dishes in the winter. This little restaurant opens its bay windows onto a view of the Île de Ré bridge. Enthusiastic appetites will be more than satisfied with the generous portions.

Le Boute-en-Train – *7 r. des Bonnes-Femmes –* ☎*05 46 41 73 74 – closed 26 Aug-9 Sep, Sun and Mon.* Near the markets, this charming restaurant serves a variety of quiches and food fresh from the marketplace. Children's drawings adorn the walls of the bistro dining room; grab a crayon and add to their collection. More mature customers may prefer to visit the vaulted cellar to choose their bottle of wine.

Le Mistral – *10 pl. Coureauleurs, in the Le Gabut district –* ☎*05 46 41 24 42 – restaurant.lemistral@wanadoo.fr – closed 23 Feb-8 Mar, 23 Oct-4 Nov and Sun to Thu eve except Jul-Aug.* This wood-clad house is located at the heart of the Le Gabut district, a stone's throw from the tourist office. The maritime-style dining room is on the first floor; the terrace, on the same level, overlooks the old fishing port.

À Côté de chez Fred – *32-34 r. St-Nicolas –* ☎*05 46 41 65 76 – barregilles@wanadoo.fr – closed Sun from Oct-Mar – reser. recommended.* Here the fish couldn't be fresher! And no wonder – this little restaurant gets its provisions from its neighbour and sister–the fishmonger. Result: a slate menu that changes as the fishing boats come to moor and an authentic atmosphere just behind the docks.

Le Petit Rochelais – *25 r. St-Jean-du-Pérot –* ☎*05 46 41 28 43 – closed Sun except public hols.* A friendly and competent team has taken over this ex-pizzeria cum bistro. The menu chalked on slate and the inviting atmosphere complement food prepared with brio, cooked fresh each day and served with enjoyable wines.

André – *pl. de la Chaîne –* ☎*05 46 41 28 24 – barandre@wanadoo.fr.* A visit to La Rochelle is not complete without a meal at André! On the old docks, facing the Tour de la Chaîne, this enormous restaurant is comprised of a dozen bistro-style dining rooms where customers sit elbow to elbow to feast on seafood. Nautical ambience, marine paintings and objects de rigeur.

BARS AND CAFÉS

Cave de la Guignette – *8 r. St-Nicolas –* ☎*05 46 41 05 75 – open Thu-Sat, 3pm-8pm – closed hols except Ascension Thursday and 8 May*. This charming and colourful wine bar used to be the watering hole of the local fishermen (who have since changed towns). Try the house speciality, la Guinguette, an aperitif made of wine and fruit.

Café de la Paix – *54 r. Chaudrier –* ☎*05 46 41 39 79 – open 7am-10pm – closed Sun, 25 Dec and 1 Jan.* Behind its carved wood facade, this big café covered with mirrors and mouldings has a long history. A hospital in 1709, a theatre during the Revolution, since 1900 it has been a café popular with visiting artists such as Colette, Jean Gabin and Lino Ventura.

LEISURE ACTIVITIES

Casino de la Rochelle – *Allée du Mail –* ☎ *05 46 34 12 75 – www.lucienbarriere.com – casino: open daily, 10am-3am; le Cosy: Wed-Sat, 10:30pm-5am; traditional games: 9pm-5am; restaurant: daily for lunch and dinner.* Le Casino Barrière de la Rochelle awaits you with its 140 slot machines. From 9pm on you can also try your hand at traditional gambling games: blackjack, roulette or boule. After 10pm you can catch your breath at the Cosy with a cocktail while planning your next bet. This chic bar merits its name – note the tartan carpet, marble counter, leather armchairs and terrace overlooking the ocean.

Cours des Dames – This is the place to go if you want to discover the Charantais archipelago by boat. In this part of the port, several ventures offer cruises to Fort Boyard, l'île de Ré, l'île d'Oléron or l'île d'Aix. You can also charter a boat for an excursion along the River Charente.

---

ema, a museum (Grévin) and terrace restaurants.

La Coursive

Now a theatre, formerly the Ancienne Chapelle des Carmes (chapel), has an imposing 17C doorway surmounted with a scallop shell. Inside, there is a fine arcaded courtyard.

Tour de la Chaîne

See SIGHTS.

Rue Sur-les-Murs

The tower is linked with Tour de la Lanterne by this narrow street which follows the top of the old medieval rampart – the only section not demolished by Richelieu, who hoped to use it as a defence against the English (at that time the foot of the wall was at the water's edge).

Tour de la Lanterne★

See SIGHTS.

▶ *Continue along the sea front then through the gardens.*

Parc Charruyer★

This park, built on the mounds and ditches of the old fortifications, encircles the town (2km/1mi long and 200m/658ft wide); alongside, runs a river – home for swans and herons – and winding avenues. To the west, the park becomes the **mail** – a favourite with strollers – finishing up at the monument to the dead, one of Joachim Costa's major works. Between this majestic avenue of elms and the sea, stretch the gardens and terrace of the casino and Parc d'Orbigny, followed by Parc Delmas.

Préfecture

The *préfecture* (administrative headquarters of the *département*), housed in the former Hôtel Poupet, built in the period of Louis XVI presents architecture typical of local private buildings; the magnificent doorway crowned with balustrades faces onto the square.

▶ *From the Préfecture, walk to Porte de la Grosse-Horloge; here you have the choice of starting on the second walk or returning to the Gabut district via quai Duperré.*

Quai Duperré

The cafés lining this quay offer a fine view of the waterfront activity. Beyond the masts and the rigging, the embarkation and disembarkation and the manoeuvring of small boats, the perspective is closed by the two towers guarding the harbour mouth – Tour St-Nicolas on the left, Tour de la Chaîne on the right. On the extreme right, the conical roof of the Lantern Tower is visible.

The picturesque Rue du Port and Petite-Rue du Port, inhabited mainly by fishermen and sailors, lead to the quay. On the western side, facing the big clock, stands a statue of **Admiral Duperré**, who was born in La Rochelle in 1775 and commanded the French fleet at the time of the taking of Algiers in 1830.

2 Old Town★★

The oldest district of La Rochelle, which was built to a regular plan and protected, until 1913, by Vauban's fine ramparts, still exudes an atmosphere part mercantile and part military. The busy, lively **shopping centre** is based around the town hall, its principal axes Grande-Rue des Merciers and Rue du Palais. Narrow streets still paved with ancient stone slabs, secret passages, some of them vaulted, arcades and darkened "porches" where passers-by can stroll sheltered from bad weather – all these give the area plenty of character. Many of the houses are designed on a plan particular to La Rochelle. Almost all of them have two entrances, one on the main street, the other on a lane parallel to it. At ground-floor level, these buildings have one huge room – often converted into a shop – an interior courtyard with a staircase leading to a balconied gallery, and a rear courtyard surrounded by outhouses. On the upper floor, above the shop, is a room looking out on the street, a kitchen overlooking the courtyard, and a "dark room" with no direct light from outside. **Half-timbering** on the oldest houses is over-hung with slates to protect the wood from the rain.

The **beaux quartiers** – the fashionable areas – are west of Rue du Palais. The most stately are Rue Réaumur and Rue de l'Escale. Here, behind high walls pierced with imposing gateways and sometimes (Rue Réaumur) topped with balustrades, the old families live in their solemn 18C mansions midway between courtyard and garden.

▷ *Follow the itinerary marked in green on the town plan.*

Porte de la Grosse-Horloge★

This gateway with its outsize clock was the entrance to the town, coming from the port. The original Gothic tower was modified in the 18C by the addition of a belfry surmounted by a dome and lantern. The turrets on either side are decorated with nautical emblems.

On the far side of the gateway is Place des Petits-Bancs, a small square with a statue of Fromentin in the middle. On the corner of Rue du Temple stands a charming house (1654) with a Renaissance façade.

Rue du Palais★

This is one of the most important streets in La Rochelle, linking the shopping centre with the residential district.

On the right, lines of shops extend beneath a succession of galleries varying in style according to the period in which they were built. Public buildings alternate with galleries on the left-hand side, and there are some fine old houses – the fourth one

Porte de la Grosse Horloge

B. Kaufmann/MICHELIN

along, for example, has windows adorned with miniature arches and carved masks. **Hôtel de la Bourse★** – This 18C Stock Exchange building, the seat of the local Chamber of Commerce since its founding, is an example of the early Louis XVI style. The attractive courtyard has an unusual layout which includes a portal and peripheral galleries. The inner façade is adorned with the sterns of ships and other maritime emblems. In a corner on the left is a fine wrought-iron staircase. A passageway across the road from the Stock Exchange (by no 29 Rue du Palais) leads via Cour de la Commanderie to Cour du Temple (old half-timbered houses). **Palais de Justice** – The law-courts façade, majestic with its fluted Corinthian columns and frieze of carved foliage, was completed in 1789. The inscription on the pediment reads "Temple of Justice"; it is flanked by the two traditional symbols of justice, the sword and the scales. At the intersection of Rue Chaudrier and Rue E.-Fromentin stands a fine 17C house with a corner turret and staircase on carved corbels. Opposite, at the entrance to Rue Dupaty, is an old half-timbered house protected by slates.

▷ *Turn left onto rue E.-Fromentin.*

Maison Venette

The picturesque **Rue de l'Escale★** is paved with pebbles which were once used as ballast by ships from Canada, and is bordered partly by arcades and partly by the projecting porches behind which the homes of 18C nobles were concealed. Maison Venette was built in the 17C for a doctor of that name. The façade of the house is sculpted with motifs representing celebrated doctors from antiquity to medieval times including: Hippocrates, Galen and Avicenna, among others.

▷ *Return to Rue du Palais.*

Rue Chaudrier★

At No 6 stands an old half-timbered house with slate cladding. A plaque in front of the building bears an inscription glorifying Chaudrier, a famous and heroic defender of La Rochelle.

▷ *Turn right into Rue des Augustins and continue to No 11 bis.*

Maison Henri II

ⓒ *See SIGHTS.*

▷ *Return to Rue Chaudrier.*

Cathédrale St-Louis

The cathedral, sober and severe in aspect, was constructed in part on the site of a church dedicated to St Bartholomew. The plans were drawn up by the architects Gabriel, father and son. The west

Francofolies: When Music Takes the Town by Storm

Every year, around 14 July, a musical storm hits La Rochelle. For 6 days, the old port resonates with music and applause. The idea of the festival originated in Quebec where Jean-Louis Foulquier, a radio broadcaster, was captivated by the lively success of a "Francofête" of French songs. In 1985, he chose his home town to host the Francofolies, hanging a bright banner between the towers of the old port. The first year, 25 000 people attended the outdoor celebration. Over the years, a wide variety of entertainers, including Jacques Higelin, Charles Aznavour, Francis Cabrel, Johnny Halliday, Larra, MC Solar, Rita Mitsouko, Samson, Sapho and Alain Souchon, have enchanted the eclectic audience.

The festival is open to every style of music from hard rock to jazz and rap. At the foot of Lanterne tower, on Esplanade Jean-d'Acre, a huge stage welcomes big names in the entertainment business (decibels and lighting effects guaranteed). A few yards away, La Coursive, Le Grand Théâtre and La Salle Bleue are better suited to more intimate performances and new talent. Le Carré Amelot (regional venue), l'Encan (the hip-hop spot) and Magic Mirrors (improvisation and jam sessions until the wee hours) complete the official Francofolies. Unofficially, the beat on the street goes on and on. An autograph session is held in Cours des Dames every afternoon, so be sure to take your camera!

front is surmounted by a scrolled pediment in the Louis XVI manner.

In the third chapel of the north aisle simple votive paintings by sailors contrast with the "literary" and academic compositions by A D Bouguereau (1825-1905), a native of La Rochelle, which cover the dome above the axial chapel. The **treasury** contains 18C and 19C liturgical items. ○*Open Jul-Aug daily except Sun and public hols 2-5pm.* ☞*No charge.*

Café de la Paix

This is the sole remaining example in La Rochelle of those opulent, flamboyant cafés of the last century, gleaming with gilt and glass, where the local burghers read their newspapers or played billiards. Glass panels in the form of arcades, decorated with designs in frosted glass, adorn the façade. The resplendent interior is decked out with carved wood and gilded designs, and huge arched mirrors beneath chandeliers and ceiling medallions painted in trompe-l'œil (1895).

Rue du Minage

Old **arcades★** on each side of the street are irregular in shape – which brings an eccentric element into the perspective down the street. Some of the very old houses are adorned with friezes and sculptures, others with windows beneath a triangular pediment (nos 43, 22, 4 and 2). At the end of the street stands the **Fontaine du Pilori**, which dates from the 16C but was rebuilt in the 18C.

▷ *Continue, via rue Pas-du-Minage, towards the market.*

Place du Marché

At the entrance to the Tout-y-Faut cul-de-sac two well-preserved old houses face one another. The half-timbered one, with mullion windows and a high-up dormer, dates from the 15C; the other (16C) is stone-built with narrow, pedimented window bays.

Grande-Rue des Merciers★

This shopping street is one of the most characteristic arteries of La Rochelle, bordered by numerous galleries and houses built in the 16C and 17C. The medieval buildings, half-timbered under the familiar slate covering, alternate with Renaissance homes built of stone and distinguished by fantastic gargoyles. The wood-and-slate house on the corner of Rue du Beurre, and those at nos 33, 31, 29 and, at the far end, no 17, are all 17C buildings with pedimented windows. No 8 is late 16C, with very narrow windows and heavy pediments; no 5 is early 17C with strange carved figures. No 3 dates from 1628. Mayor Jean Guiton lived in the last two.

▷ *Take rue de la Grille on the right, then turn left onto rue de l'Hôtel-de-Ville.*

Hôtel de Ville

○*See SIGHTS.*

▷ *Follow rue de la Ferté on the left. The Protestant church is on your left, on the corner of rue St-Michel.*

Protestant Church

This church has a charming façade, with sculpted palm leaves and drapery. It is the former Récollets chapel, constructed in 1708. It houses the Musée Protestant (○*see SIGHTS*).

Cloître des Dames Blanches

These cloisters, located next to the Protestant Temple, are part of the former Récollets' Convent. It has now become a cultural centre, and beneath the 32 arches exhibits and concerts are held (in season).

Église St-Sauveur

This 17C and 18C church is crowned by a lofty 15C bell tower.

▷ *Take rue St-Sauveur then rue du Temple back to Porte de la Grosse-Horloge.*

Additional Sights

Old Port★★

Tour St-Nicolas★

○*Open Jul-Aug 10am-7pm; mid-May–Jun and first two weeks in Sep 10am-12.30pm and 2-6.30pm; mid-Sep to mid-May, daily except Mon 10am-12.30pm and 2-5.30pm.* ○*Closed 1 Jan, 1 May and 25 Dec.* ☞*4.60€ (children under 17 no charge); combined ticket for the three towers 10€. ☎05 46 34 11 81.*

This slightly leaning tower, 42m/138ft high, and dedicated to the patron saint of sailors, is a fortress in itself. It was built in the 14C on a pentagonal plan, its five corners reinforced by three engaged circular turrets, a rectangular turret and a higher square tower forming a keep. An outside staircase forming a buttress leads to the main room, octagonal beneath elegant ribbed vaulting. From here, other staircases built in the thickness of the walls lead to a second chamber, which branches off into several rooms including a chapel, and out onto the lower parapet, surrounded by merlons. Scale models, dioramas and water-colour maps from the Musée Maritime (*see below*) trace the development of the port from the 12C to the present day. The upper parapet, surrounded by high machicolated walls with arrow-slits, affords views of the entrance to the harbour, the bay and Île d'Aix.

Tour de la Chaîne

Same opening times and charges as the Tour St-Nicolas. ☎05 46 34 11 81.

The tower owes its name to a huge and heavy chain which used to be stretched across the harbour mouth between this tower and Tour St-Nicolas at night, closing the port to ships. According to Rabelais the chain – still visible at the foot of the tower – was used to keep the giant Pantagruel in his cradle.

Tour de la Chaîne, built in the 14C, was for a long time used as a powder magazine. Originally there was a turret attached to it but this was demolished in the 17C to widen the narrow channel. Inside, a superb vaulted chamber houses an exhibition devoted to the siege of La Rochelle.

Tour de la Lanterne★

Same opening times and charges as the Tour St-Nicolas. ☎05 46 41 56 04.

The Lantern Tower is not as old as the other two (it dates from the 15C), and was built with strictly functional concerns in mind, eschewing aesthetic considerations in favour of military imperatives. The great mass of the building, its walls 6m/20ft thick at the base, contrasts starkly with the elegant octagonal spire and the fine lantern – originally used as a beacon

Tour St-Nicolas

– which surmount it. At ground level is the old guard-room in which the history of La Rochelle is now recounted through illustrated panels.

Within the spire are four rooms one above the other, the walls of which bear **graffiti★** scrawled by soldiers as well as prisoners, mostly dating from the 17C and 18C. The best are glass-protected. At the second level of the spire, a projecting balcony affords a **panorama★★** that embracing the old town, the port, the ocean and the off-shore islands. At low tide it is possible to make out the foundations of Richelieu's dike, level with Fort-Louis, beyond the promenade.

Old Town

Maison Henri-II★

This grand house, built in 1555 for Hugues de Pontard, the Seigneur de Champdeniers, rises at the far end of a garden. The façade, with its twin pavilions, gallery and loggia, is in the Henri II style. It includes a frieze sectioned by triglyphs (tablets with vertical grooves), medallions and bucranes (carved oxen masks). At ground-floor level two buttresses supporting the left-hand pavilion are decorated with *(right)* a satyr playing a guitar and *(left)* a winged woman grappling with a serpent.

Hôtel de Ville★

Visit by guided tour (45min) Jul-Aug at 3pm and 4pm; Jun, Sep and school

hols at 3pm; Oct–May, Sat–Sun and public hols at 3pm. ○*Closed 25 Dec and 1 Jan.* ⊗*4€ (children over 10 1.5€).* ☎*05 46 41 14 68. www.larochelle-tourisme.com.*

The town hall, a late 15C–early 16C composite building, is notable for its rich decoration. The rectangular central courtyard is protected by a walled Gothic enclosure surmounted by a machicolated watch-path reinforced by a belfry-tower. The **main façade★**, built in the reign of Henri IV in the Italian style, overlooks the courtyard. Behind its fluted columns the ground-floor gallery of the façade hides a fine coffered ceiling. The decoration includes trophies, medallions and monograms entwining the initials of Henri IV and Mary de' Medici.

Finer still is the upper level, reached via a balustraded stairway. Here there are pillars and niches in the Tuscan manner, the niches housing effigies representing the four cardinal virtues: (left to right) Prudence, Justice, Fortitude and Temperance.

The **interior** contains Jean Guiton's study, complete with his armchair in Cordoba leather and the desk he struck forcefully with his dagger to emphasise his famous pronouncement before the siege; the walls are hung with Aubusson tapestries.

Henri Motte's 19C painting of the siege can be found in another room, along with a Jacques Callot engraving and a 1628 canvas by Van der Kabel depicting the same tragic event in the town's history.

The rear **façade** looks out over rue des Gentilshommes and also dates from the time of Henri IV; it includes a door studded with bosses which is known as the "Porte des Gentilshommes" because it was through here that the city aldermen filed on the day that the mandate granting them each "the style and title of Gentleman" expired.

Musée Protestant

○*Open Jul–mid-Sep daily except Sun, 2.30-6pm; mid-Sep–Jun by prior arrangement.* ⊗*2€.* ☎ *05 46 34 17 09.*

The museum relates the history of Protestantism, particularly around La Rochelle. Among documents and objects on display: copy of the Confession of Faith of La Rochelle (1571) with ministers' signatures; a bible from 1606 printed in La

Rochelle; A collapsible altar and pulpit and a collection of *méreaux* (medals worn by Protestants for mutual recognition), reminders of the period of clandestine meetings, known as the *désert*.

Musée d'Histoire Naturelle★★

⊶*Closed for renovation until the beginning of 2008.* ☎*05 56 41 18 25.*

The museum stands by the entrance to a park, the Jardin des Plantes, and is housed in two facing buildings:

Musée du Nouveau Monde★

○*Open Apr-Sep daily except Tue 10am-12.30pm and 2-6pm, Sun 2.30-6pm; Oct-Mar daily except Tue 9.30am-12.30pm and 1.30-5pm, Sat-Sun 2.30-6pm.* ○ *Closed 1 Jan, 1 May, 14 Jul, 1 and 11 Nov, and 25 Dec.* ⊗*3.50€ (under 18s no charge).* ☎*05 46 41 46 50. http://perso.wanadoo. fr/musees-la-rochelle.*

The Hôtel Fleuriau, acquired by a shipowner of that name in 1772, houses within panelled Louis XV and Louis XVI salons a number of collections tracing the relationship between La Rochelle and the Americas since the Renaissance. Ship owners and merchants grew rich trading with Canada, Louisiana and especially the West Indies, where they possessed huge plantations producing spices, sugar, coffee, cocoa and vanilla. They prospered enormously too in the "black gold" trade, known more politely as "triangular commerce": sale of cloth and purchase of slaves on the African coast; sale of these slaves and purchase of colonial products in America; sale of the latter in Europe.

Among the displays, ancient maps, coloured engravings, allegories of America, wallpapers (*The Incas* by Dufour and Leroy) and everyday objects used by the Indians are of particular interest. Note also the section on slavery, the fall of Quebec, West Indian engraving and relevant literary themes, including Chateaubriand's novel *Atala*, about the impossible love between an Indian and a Christian girl.

Musée des Beaux-Arts★

○*Open Apr-Sep daily except Tue 2-6pm, Sun, 2.30-6pm; Oct-Mar, daily except Tue 1.30-5pm, Sat-Sun 2.30-6pm.* ○*Closed 1*

Jan, 1 May, 14 Jul, 1 and 11 Nov, and 25 Dec.
3.50€ (under 18s no charge). 05 46
41 64 65. http://perso.wanadoo.fr/musees-
la-rochelle

The Fine-Arts Museum occupies the second floor of the old bishop's palace, which was built during the reign of Louis XVI; following local custom the courtyard is separated from the gardens by a high balustraded wall. A wrought-iron staircase with ovoli leads to the alcoved gallery and rooms in which the paintings hang. The most interesting work among the older paintings is an *Adoration of the Magi*, the last known painting by Eustache Le Sueur (17C French School). Portraits by local artists dating from the 18C include works by Brossard de Beaulieu and Duvivier. The 19C is represented by Bouguereau, Corot, Chassériau and Eugène Fromentin – including several evocative studies of Algeria.

A separate department is devoted to 20C work (glass by Maurice Marinot, Georges Rouault's **Miserere**), some of which is displayed in rotation.

Musée d'Orbigny-Bernon★

Open Apr-Sep daily except Tue 10am-12.30pm and 2-6pm, Sun 2-6pm; Oct-Mar daily except Tue 9.30am-12.30pm and 1.30-5pm, Sat-Sun 2-6pm. Closed 1 Jan, 1 May, 14 Jul, 1 and 11 Nov, and 25 Dec.
3.50€. 05 46 41 18 83. http://perso.
wanadoo.fr/musees-la-rochelle.

This museum specialises in local history and ceramics from Europe and the Far East. Mementoes of the siege of La Rochelle include liturgical items used by Cardinal Richelieu when he celebrated the first Mass after the fall of the town. A number of documents relate to the economic prosperity and intellectual life in the Aunis capital during the 18C.

On the first floor an exceptional collection of ceramics centres on the faïence (glazed earthenware) of La Rochelle but there are fine pieces also from Marseille, Nevers, Strasbourg and Moustiers. An interesting series of pharmacy flasks and bowls is displayed in a number of 18C medicine cabinets.

The second floor is devoted to the Far East (precious Chinese porcelain from the Sung to the Ch'ing dynasties and musical instruments), while the basement

houses an archaeology section including a celebrated 12C tomb, attributed to Laleu but probably work of a monk.

La Ville-en-Bois

The "wooden town" lies to the west of the larger tidal basin; it is an area of low wooden houses mainly used in the past as workshops for ships' repairs or chandlers and spare-part shops. Reorganised after a fire, this district has added cultural activities (university, museums) to its handicraft tradition.

Aquarium★★

Allow a minimum of 1hr 30min.
Open Jul-Aug 9am-11pm; Apr-Jun and Sep 9am-8pm; Oct-Mar 10am-8pm.
12.50€ (children aged 3-17 9.50€).
05 46 34 00 00. www.aquarium-larochelle.com.

This very large, ultra-modern aquarium founded by René Coutant presents a vast panorama of underwater fauna and flora from around the world in 65 tanks. Several rooms are devoted either to a particular ocean or to a specific marine area (such as the Atlantic, the Mediterranean and various tropical seas), their species displayed in superbly arranged tanks. A tunnel with transparent walls allows visitors to wander freely through a tropical marine environment, while an immense basin containing 2 500hl/ 55 000 gallons of water accommodates turtles and sharks. There is a large tropical house, a shop and a café with a terrace.

Neptunéa: Maritime Museum★

Open Jul and Aug 10am-7pm; Apr-Jun and Sep, 10am-6.30pm. 7.60€. 05 46 28 03 00. www.museemaritimelarochelle.fr.
Spreading along the eastern quays of the Chalutiers docks, the entrance to this complex is distinguished by a slipway. Two separate museums tell the tale of maritime history in La Rochelle.

Musée à Flot – A small armada of boats of all shapes and sizes are anchored along the quays (rowing boats, trawlers, open-sea tugs and yachts), including **Joshua**, the elegant red ketch manned by Bernard Moitesier in the Golden Globe Challenge, the first round-the-world solo race (1967-68). Formerly a meteorological frigate, the 76m/249ft long **France 1** is the fleet's most impressive ship; visitors are free to wander up and down its five decks and take a closer look at interesting exhibits on life onboard and meteorology.

Musée des Automates

&. ⊙Open Jul-Aug 9.30am-7pm; rest of the year 10am-noon and 2-6pm. ⊚7.50€ (children 5€). ☎05 46 41 68 08. www. museeslarochelle.com.

Kids Three hundred figures move to the sound of music against a sumptuous backdrop, ingeniously vying with each other for the attention of visitors. The astonishingly life-like figures are animated by a cam system, demonstrated on a Harlequin figure cut in cross-section. Note, in particular, some more recent works, one of which evokes the inventor de Vaucanson and his famous duck, as well as animated shop windows, exhibits for children and historical reconstructions. An imitation Paris metro entrance leads to **"Place de Montmartre"**★★ where the cosmopolitan atmosphere is faithfully recreated. Children will marvel at the mechanical billboards decorating the shops while adults can stroll in the cobbled, lamplit streets and be taken by surprise as an overhead metro rattles by.

Musée des Modèles Réduits

&.⊙Open Jul and Aug 9.30am-7pm; rest of the year, 10am-noon and 2-6pm. ⊙Closed first 3 weeks of Jan. ⊚ 7.50€

(children:5€). ☎05 46 41 68 08. www. museeslarochelle.com.

Kids A miniature train takes children through the museum. The tour starts with a collection of superb model cars and lorries, some remote-controlled. The inside of a galleon tells the story of the great sea-going expeditions while a fabulous water setting provides the backdrop for a **naval battle**. An underwater world plunges the visitor into the ocean depths while train-spotters can admire model trains circuits, one of which includes a model of La Rochelle railway station, and gleaming locomotives of every shape and size, some of which are steam-operated.

Port des Minimes

Three thousand two hundred craft of all types can be accommodated at Minimes marina, on the southern side of the bay sheltering La Rochelle, which makes it the largest pleasure port in Europe on the Atlantic side. Three deep-water tidal basins – Bout-Blanc, Marillac and Lazaret – have been developed. Around the port is a zone of artisans: ship-fitters, sail-makers, painters and experts in repair work provide every service needed by the owners of yachts and cruisers. A sailing school of repute is based here, and there is also a residential area with apartment blocks and holiday homes.

☞A regular waterbus service operates between Les Minimes and Vieux Port.

LA ROCHE-SUR-YON

POPULATION 49 262
MICHELIN MAP 316: H 7-8

This unusual town is striking for its straight streets crossing each other at right angles, its large central esplanade and an impressive equestrian statue of Napoleon. Further exploration will reveal an attractive modern building housing the offices of the département and a renowned stud farm that raises pure-bred horses. Spend some time in the town in July or August and you'll enjoy free musical concerts in the evening as part of the "Cafés de l'été" festival.

🛈 **Information**: R. Clemenceau, 85000 La Roche-Sur-Yon.
   ☎02 51 36 00 85. www.ot-roche-sur-yon.fr.

▶ **Orient Yourself**: La Roche-sur-Yon is situated on a plateau overlooking the River Yon and a landscape of fields and hedgerows. Its geometric, grid-like street plan is typical of the architectural town planning of the mid 19C.

🅿 **Parking**: Main car parks are in the place de Vendée and place Napoléon.

A Bit of History

La Roche-sur-Yon was born out of an imperial wish to install – if necessary by force of arms – a strategic military stronghold designed to prevent further uprisings in the Vendée. In 1804 Napoleon transferred the provincial capital from Fontenay to La Roche-sur-Yon, a modest small town which was subsequently renamed "Napoléon-Vendée". Plans for a military transformation were drawn up by the engineer Duvivier but the lack of stone in the region constrained him to build in cob; as a consequence, when Napoleon passed through in 1808 to have a look at the new fortifications, Duvivier was sacked, being reproached for having created "a mud-walled town".

It was in fact during the Restoration that La Roche found its definitive shape: a geometric, straight-line plan with a grid of streets crossing each other at right-angles, the wide main arteries converging on a huge esplanade which served as a parade ground or barrack square. This town took the form of an irregular pentagon from which six main routes permitted a rapid rectilinear deployment of troops. This innovation in urban planning reflected precisely the politico-architectural thinking in France in the middle of the 19C. The name of the town was nevertheless changed several more times: it became Bourbon-Vendée under the Restoration and the July Monarchy, Napoléon-Vendée at the time of the Second Empire and returned to La Roche-sur-Yon in 1870.

Sights

Place Napoléon
The great esplanade, designed to accommodate 20 000 soldiers, is surrounded by neo-Classical buildings. In the centre of the square stands an equestrian statue (1854) of Napoleon I.

Hôtel du Département
This comprises an old Napoleonic hospital in which exhibitions are held and, just behind it, a modern building (1990) by Roland Castro and Jean-Luc Pellerin. The latter, with its immense glass façade scarcely hiding a large pink tower, cuts vividly across the austerity and rigour of the 19C town-planning.

Museum
&.◯*Open daily except Sun and Mon, 1-6pm. No charge. Museum currently under restoration: open only for temporary exhibitions. ☎02 51 47 48 35.*

As well as archaeological collections from the prehistoric, Gallo-Roman and medieval periods, the museum offers a panorama of 19C Parisian academic painting and a series of canvases by local artists of the same period – Milcendeau, for instance, who recorded the life around the marshes (a museum is devoted to his work in Soullans), and Baudry, who created the decor in the Paris Opera House.

The museum has a collection of works by contemporary artists (Beuys, Boltanski, and others) based on photographic material and holds temporary exhibits highlighting works by living painters.

Haras (Stud Farm)
&.◯*Open Jul-Aug 10am-7pm; Apr–Jun and Sep Wed, Sat and Sun 10am-7pm. Reservation required for visit by guided tour (1hr). 4.50€ (children: 2€). ☎02 51 46 14 47.*

This is one of the most important stud-farms in France. A number of thoroughbred stallions and French trotting horses are stabled here.

ROYAN ☼ ☼ ☼

POPULATION 17 102
MICHELIN MAP 324: D-6

The town of Royan, capital of the Côte de Beauté (Coast of Beauty), was rebuilt after the bombardments that flattened it in 1945. Today in the guide of a modern town it has once more found the popularity and prosperity that characterised it at the end of the 19C. In the holiday season there is a substantial increase in the population. Royan is ideally located on a headland at the entrance to the Gironde. The town is flanked by choice holiday resorts: the stately Pontaillac, **Meschers-sur-Gironde★** and the more family-oriented St-Palais and **St-Georges-de-Didonne**. Beaches of fine sand curve enticingly at the inner end of the town's four **conches** (coves or bays indenting the coastline). The largest cove harbours a strand 2km/ 1mi long; the smaller ones, warm and sheltered from the wind, are separated by cliffs or dunes carpeted with a forest of holm oaks and parasol pines that give off a pleasant summer fragrance. Apart from the natural beauty of the area and a particularly mild climate, Royan also benefits from a seaweed-cure centre and numerous other attractions, hence its popularity.

- 🛈 **Tourist Office**: Palais des Congrès -17200 Royan.
  ☎05 46 23 00 00; www.royan-tourisme.com.
- ▶ **Orient Yourself**: Royan is located on the Atlantic Coast, 35km/22mi SW of Saintes.
- 🅿 **Parking**: There are a number of car parks along the seafront, as well as in the town centre *(see map)*.
- ⊚ **Don't Miss**: The seafront; Église Notre-Dame.
- 🄺🄸🄳🅂 **Especially for Kids**: Les Jardins du Monde.
- ☼ **Also See**: SAINTES, ÎLE D'OLÉRON, LA PALMYRE.

A Bit of History

The Royan Pocket

At the time of the Liberation of France, in the autumn of 1944, Nazi troops stationed in the southwest withdrew to a number of coastal enclaves – St-Nazaire, Verdon, Royan – and dug themselves in with the intention of holding out as long as possible. Royan was besieged by the French forces of General de Larminat when, on 5 January and 14-15 April 1945, two violent aerial bombardments almost totally destroyed the town. The Germans surrendered on 17 April, only three weeks before the armistice on 8 May.

Royan today

Anyone who knew Royan before World War II will remember, not without a certain nostalgia, its ornate villas and chalets half-hidden among the palms, its great Victorian hotels with their heavily decorated façades, the casinos like Baroque temples or palaces from the Renaissance. All that has gone: only the Pontaillac area today can evoke such memories; Royan town centre has been rebuilt following the norms of late 20C town planning. Huge perspectives have been opened up, bordered by apartment blocks with wide balconies and red-tiled roofs in the Charentais manner.

Sights

Église Notre-Dame★

The church was built between 1955 and 1958 to plans by the architects Guillaume Gillet and Hébrard. It is a structure of reinforced concrete coated with resin to protect it from wind erosion.

From Place Notre-Dame, at a slightly lower level, the ascending perspective of the east end, forming a kind of prow, is accentuated by the belfry which soars to a height of 65m/213ft.

On the left, detached from the nave, is a pyramidal baptistery.

Inside the church, visitors are at once struck by the weightless quality of the

Address Book

⚭ For coin ranges, see the Legend on the cover flap.

TOURIST INFORMATION

Tourist office – *Palais des Congrès -17200 Royan* – ☎ *05 46 23 00 00; www.royan-tourisme.com*

TRANSPORT

Buses – Several bus companies run services in Royan and from Royan to nearby towns, including Meschers, St-Palais, St-Georges-de-Didonne, Vaux-sur-Mer, La Tremblade, Ronce-les-Bains, Médis, Saujon and Saintes. For further information, contact the tourist office or SEMAAAS (Aunis-Saintonge) at ☎ 05 46 97 52 06.

WHERE TO STAY

⊖ **Hôtel Pasteur** – *40 r. Pasteur* – ☎ *05 46 05 14 34 – hotel-le-pasteur.sarl@ wanadoo.fr – closed Oct-Mar except school hols – 15 rms.* In a calm Royan neighbourhood, this big, renovated post-war house has reasonable prices for the area. The rooms are tidy and sensibly furnished, even if the style is a bit out-moded. Family boarding-house ambience.

⊖⊖ **Belle-Vue** – *122 av. Pontaillac* – ☎ *05 46 39 06 75 – belle-vueroyan@ wanadoo.fr – closed 1 Nov-31 Mar – 18 rms.* This modernised 1950s villa is situated on a wide avenue. The well-soundproofed rooms on the ground floor overlook a small garden. Mini-golf nearby.

⊖⊖⊖ **Hôtel Primavera** – *12 r. Brick, via av. de la Grande Côte – 17420 St-Palais-sur-Mer* – ☎ *05 46 23 20 35 – contact@ hotelprimavera.com – closed 15 Nov-15 Dec and Feb school hols –* 🅿 *– 45 rms – restaurant* ⊖⊖. Built in the late 19C, this elegant seaside villa is enhanced by a peaceful park. Whether in the old building or the new wing, the decor is bourgeois and most of the rooms have a view of the sea. Two simpler annexes, a covered swimming pool and a tennis court. Traditional cuisine with an emphasis on seafood.

WHERE TO EAT

⊖ **La Siesta** – *140 r. Gambetta* – ☎ *05 46 38 36 53 – closed mid-Dec to mid-Jan and Wed.* This restaurant, rebuilt on the exact site of the Brasserie des Bains where Pablo Picasso once stayed, faces a sailing harbour. Try the bruschetta, a slice of good Italian toast with a choice of toppings, before moving on to fish, Italian pasta or a Tex-Mex dish.

⊖ **Le Relais de la Mairie** – *1 r. du Chay* – ☎ *05 46 39 03 15 – Alain.gedoux@ wanadoo.fr – closed 15-31 Mar, 15 Nov-7 Dec, Thu eve, Sun eve and Mon off-season.* Appearances can be deceiving! Behind the rather gloomy exterior, this retaurant's narrow dining room is colourful and pleasant. Interesting fixed-price menu offered daily. A la carte menu a bit pricey.

⊖⊖ **Le Petit Poucet** – *La Grande Côte – 17420 St-Palais-sur-Mer* – ☎ *05 46 23 20 48 – closed Jan, 12 Nov-20 Dec and Wed from Oct to late Mar.* A magnificent view of the sea, especially from the terrace! This is the best feature of this unusual 1950s edifice built overlooking the beach. Cosy atmosphere in the dining room and simple cuisine at affordable prices.

⊖⊖ **La Jabotière** – *espl. de Pontaillac* – ☎ *05 46 39 91 29 – closed 2 Jan-2 Feb, Christmas school hols, Sun eve and Mon off-season.* White and blue parasols, a wooden terrace and big bay windows overlooking the Conche de Pontaillac – this shoreside restaurant a stone's throw from the casino is a very enjoyable place for a meal. Less expensive fixed-price menu at lunchtime.

BARS AND CAFÉS

La Maison Blanche – *Prom. de la plage de Nauzan – 17640 Vaux-sur-Mer* – ☎ *05 46 38 01 06 – www.maisonblanche.fr – daily 9am-2am – closed Nov-Feb.* An unbeatable view of the sea, a big swimming pool surrounded by palm trees, a labyrinth of benches scattered throughout a huge 'casbah' decorated with African cloths and masks. This establishment with three bars is jam-packed until closing.

L'Astoria – *42 av. du maréchal-Leclerc – ☎ 05 46 05 85 75 – summer: daily 8am-2am; rest of the year: 4pm-2am.* This is a popular meeting place for locals in Royan. Although it may not be as large or impressive as some of the other bars in town, this café-cum-exhibition centre has a pleasant, intimate, bistro-style atmosphere.

LEISURE ACTIVITIES

The seaside resort of Royan offers a wide range of leisure facilities, including the new **Espace nautique** (☎ 05 46 05 44 13), the town **casino**, run by the Lucien Barrière group, (☎ 05 46 39 03 31), and its **Thalassotherapy Institute** (*Thalazur Royan*, ☎ 05 46 39 96 96).

Royan Croisières – Enjoy a boat trip along the Gironde estuary (2hrs 15min; 16€, children under 13: 11€); visit the impressive Cordouan lighthouse (Phare de Cordouan, 4hrs – you will get your feet wet on arrival as you disembark in the water). This company runs several boat trips in summer. Reservation recommended (Apr-Oct). On certain dates, the lighthouse trip does not run because of crab fishing. 28€ (children under 13: 19€). ☎ 05 46 06 42 36.

SHOPPING

Market – The market takes place daily (except Mon from mid-Sep to mid-Jun) in and around the central market hall. Closes 2pm.

Regional specialities – Look out for the chocolate sardines, oysters and snails made by confectioners and pastry chefs in the town, which recall the town's once active fishing industry.

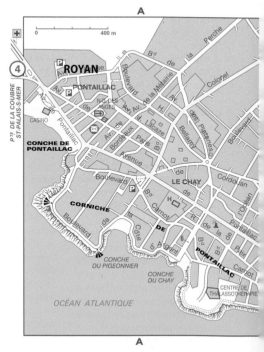

single nave, flying away, spacious and light. The great organ, the work of the Poitou master Robert Boisseau, has a case of hammered pewter and is renowned for the quality of its tone.

Two contrasting statues face one another beneath the northern gallery: a 14C carved wood St Joseph with a recumbent Christ, and a modern, copper figure of Joan of Arc.

Front de Mer★

Royan's seafront curves around the northern end of the **Grande Conche** – an imposing crescent of buildings, commercial as well as residential, its line emphasised by a columned peristyle in the shelter of which people can shop or admire the view of the Gironde estuary. Off to the right the distinctive silhouette of Cordouan lighthouse can be recognised.

At the western end of the seafront is the port. This comprises a dock for trawlers and the sardine boats which fish for the famous royan, a marina for yachts and cruisers, and a tidal basin with the jetty from which the ferry to Pointe de Grave leaves.

Boat trips are organised in summer, especially out to Cordouan lighthouse.

Corniche de Pontaillac

This walk should be taken at high tide for the best views. Follow Boulevard Carnot and Boulevard de la Côte-d'Argent.

Having skirted the tennis courts and the old Fort du Chay, the route runs above a number of small coves (Conche du Chay, Conche du Pigeonnier) from which there are fine views of the Gironde and the Côte de Beauté, from Pointe de Suzac (south east) to Pointe de la Coubre (northwest). The walk ends at the **Conche de Pontaillac★**, a sheltered inlet surrounded with smart villas scattered among the sub-tropical foliage. This small beach fringed with a perfect curve of fine sand is the most popular in Royan.

Église Réformée, Marché Central – Market with original fine-concrete

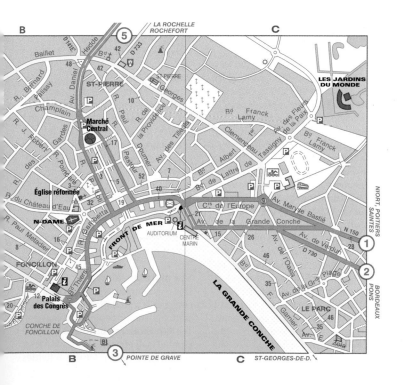

The sea spray at La Grande Côte

dome, **Palais des Congrès** – Glass-walled building.

Les Jardins du Monde★

5 r. des Fleurs-de-la-Paix. &. *Open Jul-Aug 10am-8pm; Sep-Jun 10am-6pm. Closed Jan.* 8.50€ *(children 4-12 5.50€).* 05 46 38 00 99; www.jardins-du-monde.com

On the banks of the marais de Pousseau (Pousseau marsh), in an area which has been drained after the war, this 7.5ha/18.5acres floral garden, open since 2002, is enshrined within a high metallic structure and three large steel sails. The vast semi-circular entrance is followed by a large tropical greenhouse which shelters a very beautiful **collection of orchids★**. The atmosphere changes completely as you reach the bonsai pavillion where you can admire rare specimens, which are sometimes more than centuries old. Then, in the open air, the gardens offer various styles: the Japanese zen garden, the Louisiana forest, the marsh house, the labyrinth of mist (bamboo forest):

The park can partly be visited by electrical boat: a 20 min tour will enable you to cross the marsh canals and give you access to the swamp and the bamboo forest. You will also find a shop, a restaurant and activities for children.

Driving Tour

Pointe and Forêt de la Coubre★

31km/19mi NW – allow 3hrs.

▶ *Drive north-west out of Royan along the D 25.*

Vaux-sur-Mer

On one side of the valley stands a charming Romanesque church rising from an old cemetery planted with elms and cypress trees. Inside, note the capitals at the transept crossing, especially the figure of the bear trainer on the southern side.

▶ *Continue south to Nauzan.*

Nauzan

A cove with a beach of fine sand, sheltered from the wind by cliffs on either side.

St-Palais-sur-Mer

This small, popular resort with its stylish elegance is surrounded by smart villas scattered among the pines and ilex trees. The **Parc du Marais du Rhâ** (behind the covered market), laid out around a lake, is well equipped for leisure activities (miniature golf, cycle-track, tennis, boating, fishing etc.). From the cove there is a view of the Cordouan light.

At the far end of the beach (on the right, looking at the cove), take rue de l'Océan and then **Sentier de la Corniche**★ *(signposted, 45min round trip on foot).*

🚶The path, also known as the Sentier des Perrières (path of the slate quarries), twists through the woods and then crosses a gash in the cliff into which, at high tide, the ocean rollers hurl themselves with a thunderous noise. The path ends at a promontory where the jagged rocks have been smashed into bizarre shapes: Monk's Rock, the Devil's Bridge, the Quarrymen.

La Grande Côte★★

▷ *Park in the car park, on the left, where the D 25 turns away from the coast and plunges into the woods. Walk to the rock platform. Telescope available.*

From this viewpoint, when the weather is bad – or even unsettled – sightseers can enjoy the grandiose spectacle of huge waves breaking violently on the rocks, sending bursts of spray jetting high in the air. From left to right, the **view** embraces the Gironde, Pointe de Grave, the Cordouan light, and the promontory and light-house of La Coubre.

A few yards away, on the right, there is a view sideways down onto the beaches and dunes of La Grande Côte, where long lines of breakers roll shorewards and bathing is very dangerous. Rod and reel fishing with cast weights is practised along the almost-deserted strand, especially for bass.

Zoo de la Palmyre★★★

👶 *See ZOO DE LA PALMYRE.*

The route emerges from the forest to pass the resort of **La Palmyre** then skirts **La Bonne Anse** – a lagoon refuge for small boats during bad weather, where coastal currents have turned the extremity of Pointe de La Courbe back on itself to form a spit shaped like a shepherd's crook.

Phare de La Coubre★

La Coubre Lighthouse has had to be rebuilt several times because the dune on which it stands is "mobile". The present version dates from 1905 and rises to a height of 60m/199ft. Its slender, soaring, two-tone tower overlooks the Point from a position near the semaphore station. This is one of the most powerful lighthouses in France, with a beam that carries 53km/33mi, signalling the approaches to the Gironde. From the top – 300 steps and then a metal ladder – there is an extensive **panorama**★ over La Coubre Forest and the Isle of Oléron *(north and east)*; the extremity of the point and its coastal spit, La Bonne Anse, and Cordouan lighthouse standing alone on the horizon *(south)*. In the distance Pointe de Grave and the Côte de Beauté as far as the cliffs of Meschers-sur-Gironde are visible.

Forêt de la Coubre★

Most of this 8 000ha/19 768 acre forest is composed of maritime pines and ilex trees; there are still a few deer to be seen. Extensive reforestation has all but eradicated the traces of the devastating fire which ravaged the area in 1976.

The forest serves to stabilise the dunes along the Arvert coast, better known as the **Côte Sauvage** (Wild Coast), which was studded during World War II with bunkers built by prisoners of war under the German Todt Organisation. Bike paths wind through the woodlands and lead to the beaches.

Half a mile north of La Coubre lighthouse *(car park)* a sandy track twists through the dunes to the strand, from which there is an impressive view of Atlantic rollers crashing on the shore.

About 8km/5mi farther north, beyond the metallic Gardour tower, there is a wooded knoll on the right of route D 25. Crowning this rise, at the end of a forest road known as Chemin des Fontaines, is a panoramic tower made of wood: this is the **Tour des Quatre Fontaines**. From it there are wide-ranging views over the forest and the ocean beyond.

LES SABLES-D'OLONNE ☼ ☼ ☼

POPULATION 15 532
MICHELIN MAP 316: F 8-9

Les Sables-d'Olonne is an important seaside resort on the Côte de la Lumière (Coast of Light), built on the sands of what was once an off-shore bar. Port Olona is the starting point for the round-the-world yacht race held every four years known as the "Vendée Globe" – a tough challenge for single-handed sailing boats with no ports of call allowed and no help on the way.

> ☺ *During the summer season's folklore festivals: visitors will see the traditional, ancestral costume of short skirts with pleated petticoats, black stockings, sabots with heels, and tall headdresses with quivering "wings."*

- **🛈 Tourist Office**: 1 prom. Jaffre – 85104 Les Sables-d'Olonne Cedex. ☎02 51 96 85 85. www.ot.lessablesdolonne.fr
- ▸ **Orient Yourself**: Les Sables-d'Olonne stretches between a small port and an immense beach of fine sand running for more than 3km/1.8mi at the foot of the Remblai (an embankment-promenade).
- **🅿 Parking**: There are a number of car parks along the seafront, as well as in the town centre (☝*see MAP*).
- ☺ **Don't Miss**: The Remblai promenade.
- **Kids Especially for Kids**: The town's long sandy beach; the Parc Zoologique de Tranchet.
- ☝ **Also See**: LA ROCHE-SUR-YON.

A Bit of History

Origins

In the Middle Ages the site here was no more than an outer port for Olonne, a small town on the Vertonne estuary now a little way inland. Then, little by little, the inlet silted up, finally turning into a swamp and then a salt-marsh; Les Sables-d'Olonne (the sands of Olonne) was created.

Under the patronage of Louis XI, who visited the area with the chronicler Commynes, the Seneschal (Steward) of Poitou, the port was dredged out and shipyards were built. Some of the vessels launched here took part in the great voyages of discovery. In the 17C a local sailor, **Nau the Olonnais**, distinguished himself in the West Indies during the bloody guerrilla warfare waged against the Spaniards by the buccaneers of Turtle Island and the privateer-pirate gang

La Grande Plage

B. Kaufmann/MICHELIN

Address Book

For coin ranges, see the Legend on the cover flap.

WHERE TO STAY

Hôtel Antoine – *60 r. Napoléon – ☎02 51 95 08 36 – antoinehotel@club-internet.fr – closed mid-Oct–mid-Mar – 20 rms.* Between the harbour and the beach in the old fishermen's quarters, this elegant hotel doubles as a family boarding house where regulars come for an annual visit. Spick-and-span rooms of varying sizes, friendly reception. Half-board available in season.

Atlantic Hôtel – *5 prom. Godet – ☎02 51 95 37 71 – info@atlantichotel.fr – 30 rms.* This 1970s hotel is on the promenade, directly across from the Sables d'Olonne bay. Its pleasant rooms are spacious. Ask for a seaside room – you'll get a balcony as well as a view. The hotel's Le Sloop restaurant specialises in seafood. Partially covered swimming pool.

Chambre d'hôte Château de la Millière – *85150 St-Mathurin – 9km/5.4mi NE of Les Sables via the N 160 – ☎02 51 22 73 29 or 02 51 23 85 75 – chateaudelamilliere@club-internet.fr - closed Oct–Apr – ⊄ – 5 rms.* This elegant 19C residence is nestled in a 25ha park. Its large rooms, decorated with period furniture, open onto trees. The pool is set in a pretty garden with pavilions. French billiards for fans. Two self-catering cottages available year round.

WHERE TO EAT

L'Affiche – *21 quai Guinée – ☎02 51 95 34 74 – closed 2-15 Jan, Wed from 15 Jun-15 Sep, Sun and Thu eve and Mon all day from 15 Sep-15 Jun.* You can't miss this little eatery on the fishing docks – its sunshine yellow exterior catches the eye! Pleasant, simple decor and a varied menu, with an accent on seafood.

Auberge Robinson – *51 r. du Puits-d'Enfer – La Pironière – 85100 Château-d'Olonne – 4km/2.4mi SE of Les Sables; take the coast road – ☎02 51 23 92 65 – closed 15 Feb–8 Mar, 19–27 Oct, Sun eve, Tue eve from Jun to Sep, Tue in Jul-Aug.* Follow the coast road out of Les Sables d'Olonne to this charming auberge with its charming little garden and attractive awnings. Barbecued meat on the terrace in the summer and delicious cuisine in the candy-pink dining room full of trinkets and curios in the winter.

Cayola – *76 prom. de Cayola – Anse de Cayola – 85100 Château-d'Olonne – 7km/4.2mi SE of Les Sables on the coast road – ☎02 51 22 01 01 – closed 1-25 Jan, Sun eve and Mon.* Perched high upon a cliff, this handsome contemporary villa has a majestic view of the ocean. Its large modern dining room with French windows opens onto a teak terrace, overlooking the swimming pool and the sea in the distance…Vertigo guaranteed! Tasty, well-prepared contemporary cuisine.

BARS AND CAFES

Casino des Pins – *Av. Rhin-et-Danube – Casino des Pins bus (line 6) – ☎02 51 21 69 00 – www.casinodespins.fr – daily 10am-4am.* In addition to its 105 slot machines and traditional games, this casino has a classy and comfortable pub with a big shady flower-filled terrace around an ornamental pool. One concert per week in the summer.

Hot Blues Café – *24 prom. Clemenceau – ☎02 51 95 91 01 – hot-blues-cafe@wanadoo.fr – winter: Mon-Fri 11.30pm-1am, Sat-Sun 11.30pm-2am; summer: daily 11pm-2am – closed Mon and Tue in winter.* The walls of this little basement hideout are painted with a large fresco of a blues concert. Situated at the end of the Remblai promenade, the café has an outdoor terrace which is covered and heated in winter. Choose from a range of snacks, cocktails and different varieties of rum.

SPORTS AND LEISURE

Les Circaètes – *Base de mer (petite jetée) – Les Circaètes are located near the harbour master's office (Capitainerie) – ☎06 09 80 28 70 – www.chez.com/les circaètes – daily 9am-9pm – open from mid-Jun to mid-Sep.* A wooden garden shack is the office for this friendly couple of diploma-holding sports devotees. Water-skiing and para-boating for the daring – at 80 metres above the sea, it's a real high!

Le Ranch – *Centre équestre de Sauveterre – 56 r. des Rochers – 85340 Olonne-sur-Mer – ☎02 51 90 76 96 – summer: daily 7.30am-noon and 2-9pm; rest of the year: 9am-noon and 2-5pm.* Come winter or summer, this ranch offers rides through the forest, in the wetlands and along the shore for riders of all levels. In summer, two 2-hour rides are organised on the beach, at 7.30am and 7.30pm.

Le Kifanlo – *Organisme de Culture, d'Étude et d'Action Maritimes – 48 r. Parisse – ☎02 51 95 53 11 – www.multimania.com/ocean – sign up at the l'Office du tourisme (02 51 96 85 85); schedule varies depending on the tides.* Learn all about the perils and excitement of life as a deep-sea fisherman on board a superb trawler (a listed historical vessel). The boat carries up to 12 people.

Base Canoë – Les Salines – *120 rte de l'Aubraie – ☎02 51 90 87 74 – lessalines@wanadoo.fr – Jun-Aug 9am-7pm; Sep, Oct*

and May, by prior arrangement – closed Nov-Apr. Explore over 1 400 ha/3 460 acres of wild marshland by canoe. Les Salines offers a number of different routes of varying lengths along the salt river.

SHOPPING

La Poissonnerie Pilote – *Quai Franqueville – Jul-Aug, Mon-Sat 7.30am-12.30pm and 2-7.30pm; Sun, 7.30am-12.30pm; Sep-Jun, Mon-Sat 7.30am-12.30pm and 2-7pm.* Fish lovers will be in their element at this fish market, where the daily catch is displayed on stalls alongside the port. A wide choice of fresh fish and seafood.

---

known as the "Brothers of the Coast". The seafarer met a gruesome fate, devoured by hostile natives.

Economic life – The harbour comprises a dock for fishing boats, a wet dock (Bassin flot) for cargo ships, and a marina known as **Port Olona** with 1 100 berths for yachts and cruisers which lies farther upriver, just south of the long, straight by-pass road linking Les Sables with the ancient fishermen's district of La Chaume west of the town.

Trawlers with their modern gear are engaged in both coastal and deep-sea fishing, generally in the southern part of the Bay of Biscay, although vessels sometimes travel as far north as St George's Channel, between Great Britain and Ireland. Because of the tonnage landed the town ranks 12th among France's fishing ports.

The **salt-marshes** north of the town are no longer exploited: plans have been approved to transform them into a zone of aquaculture. Market gardens in La Chaume, on the other hand, well-fertilised with marine compost, continue to produce high-quality early strawberries, artichokes etc.

Sights

Le Remblai★

This embankment was built in the 18C to protect the town from the incursions of the sea. Today the fine promenade

along its top is bordered by shops, hotels, cafés and luxury apartment blocks with splendid views of the beach and the bay. At the western extremity of Le Remblai is the municipal swimming pool and one of the casinos (Casino de la Plage, which includes a 700-seat theatre and a conference hall which can accommodate 1 000). Behind the modern blocks, the narrow streets of the old town beckon.

La Corniche

This southerly prolongation of Le Remblai leads to the new residential district of La Rudelière. After 3km/1.8mi the cliff-top route arrives at **Le Puits d'Enfer** (Hell's Well) – a narrow and impressive cleft in the rock, where the sea foams and thrashes.

Quartier de la Rudelière

This district is near the **Lac de Tanchet**, with its lakeside sailing school. In the same area are the town's second casino, Casino des Sports, a sea-water cure centre (Centre de Thalassothérapie), sports grounds and a zoo.

Parc Zoologique de Tranchet – ㅤ ㅤ*Open Easter–Sep 9.30am-7pm; mid-Feb–Easter 2-6.30pm; Oct to early Nov 2-6pm.* *11€ (children aged 3-10 6€).* ☎02 51 95 14 10 www.zoodessables.fr ㅤIn this pleasantly laid out "green belt" environment, visitors can observe a vari-

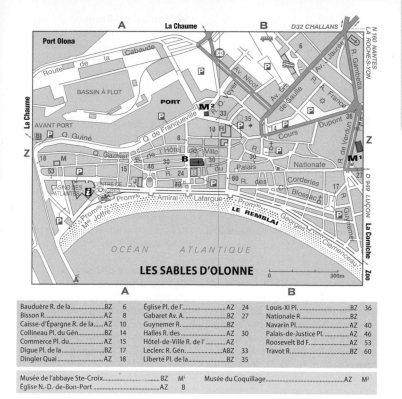

LES SABLES D'OLONNE

ety of wildlife including camels, llamas, kangaroos, monkeys and rare birds.

Église Notre-Dame-de-Bon-Port

The church was built in 1646 by Richelieu. In the nave, which is an excellent example of late Gothic architecture, the Gothic vaults are perfectly complemented by the pilasters of the Corinthian order supporting them.

Musée de l'Abbaye Ste-Croix

🕐 Open mid-Jun–Sep daily except Mon 10am-noon and 2.30-6.30pm; early Oct to mid-Jun daily except Mon 2.30-5.30pm. 🕐 Closed public hols. ☞4.60€ (children aged 12-18 2.30€); no charge 1st Sun in the month. ☎02 51 32 01 16.

The old Holy Cross Abbey, founded in the 17C by Benedictine monks, is now a cultural centre. The ground floor of the museum is devoted to the last works of Victor Brauner: Mythologies et Fêtes des Mères (1965)

On the first floor are works by Gaston Chaissac (one of the leaders of the Art

Brut movement, 1910-64). A second room is devoted to temporary exhibitions.

The second floor houses works by contemporary painters: Baselitz, Beckmann, Cahn, Magnelli, Marquet etc. The 17C attics contain collections of **popular art and traditions** including a marshland domestic hut interior, traditional costumes from Les Sables and the surrounding marshlands, seascapes by the local painter Paul-Emil Pajot, and a number of model boats.

Olonne Country Driving Tour

40km/25mi round tour – allow half a day.

▶ *Drive west out of Les Sables-d'Olonne.*

La Chaume

The redeveloped, former fishermen's district has retained its small houses with tiled roofs which contrast starkly with the planned modernism of the resort. A

Lighthouse on the jetty

shuttle service links La Chaume to Les Sables (departure from quai Guiné).

Tour d'Arundel – This tower, once the keep of a fort built in the 12C for Lord Arundel, is used today as a lighthouse. There is a fine view of the bay from the top.

Prieuré St-Nicolas – The 11C priory chapel, transformed into a fort in 1779, stands on a pleasant site commanding the entrance to the port and offering a splendid view of the bay. A garden has been laid out around the building, with a mosaic memorial (1971) to sailors lost at sea. Fine view of the bay.

▶ *D 87 north from La Chaume.*

On your right lies the abandoned **salt-marsh zone**.

Forêt d'Olonne

This stretch of woodland standing alone between the ocean and the Vertonne marshes shimmering beneath the sun extends for 15km/9mi north of Les Sables. Oak thickets beneath clusters of tall pines carpet over 1 000ha/2 470 acres of dunes crisscrossed by footpaths; the quick eye may catch sight of one of the herds of deer wandering freely.

▶ *At Champclou turn left onto the D 80.*

St-Nicolas-de-Brem

The church here is curious. It was built in the 11C and partially reconstructed in the 17C. There is a statue of St Nicolas above the entrance. Nearby is a tumulus, an ancient medieval mound probably thrown up to protect the port.

▶ *Drive south-east out of St-Nicolas-de-Brem along the D 38. At L'Île-d'Olonne, turn right onto the D 87.*

The road crosses the Olonne marsh, the eastern part of which has been transformed into a bird sanctuary. The marsh was originally formed because of the gradual silting up, in prehistoric times, of what was the Bay of Olonne.

Observatoire d'Oiseaux de l'Île-d'Olonne

○*Open Jul and Aug, 9.30am-6pm; Easter weekend, last weekends in Apr, mid to end of Jun and beginning to mid-Sep 10am-5pm.* ∞*2.50€ (children aged 7-18:1.30€).* ☎*02 51 33 12 97. www.adev-asso.org.*
Well-placed on a rise overlooking the marsh, the observatory allows visitors, with the help of telescopes, to study the birds in the Chanteloup Hunting Reserve. Every summer the 38ha/94 acre reserve accommodates, among many other species, an important colony of avocets.

▶ *Return to L'Île-d'Olonne and continue along the D 38.*

Olonne-sur-Mer

This one-time coastal port now stands a little way inland, the effect of the silting up of the Bay.

▶ *Leave Olonne-sur-Mer east via the D 80.*

Château de Pierre-Levée

This charming 18C folly in the Louis XVI style was built by Luc Pezot, a tax collector for Les Sables district.

▶ *The N 160 leads back to Les Sables-d'Olonne.*

ST-ÉMILION★★

POPULATION 2 345

MICHELIN MAP 335: K-5 – LOCAL MAP SEE VIGNOBLE DE BORDEAUX

The renowned wine centre of St-Émilion is a delightful town surrounded by vineyards. Ancient ramparts, monuments, a maze of narrow streets and stone stairways linking picturesque small squares, combine to form an overall picture that never fails to impress visitors. In fine weather the sun accentuates the golden tones of the old stone walls, while the ever-changing contrasts of light and shade enliven a stroll through the medieval quarters. The town is known not only for its fine wines but also for the local macaroons (small crushed almond cakes).

- **Information**: pl. des Creneaux.
  ☎05 57 55 28 28. www.saint-emilion-tourisme.com.
- **Orient Yourself**: St-Émilion lies 10km/6mi E of Libourne on the slopes of a limestone plateau overlooking the Dordogne Valley.
- **Parking**: Car parks (admission fee payable) are located outside the old ramparts, at the top and at the bottom of the city.
- **Don't Miss**: The Église Monolithe; the Cloître des Cordeliers.
- **Also See**: BORDEAUX, VIGNOBLE DE BORDEAUX.

A Bit of History

Centuries after the Latin poet Ausonius settled in the locality – he had property on the hillside, and his name today remains allied to one of the prestigious wine "houses" – it was a hermit named **Émilion** who found here the peace and tranquillity necessary for meditation. Émilion, originally from Brittany, was a baker by trade before embracing the monastic life at Saujon, near Royan. Withdrawing subsequently to the limestone slopes of the Dordogne Valley, he discovered a grotto watered by a natural spring in the rocky centre of what is now the town bearing his name, and lived there until his death towards the end of the 8C.

Ten centuries later it was a fugitive who sought sanctuary in St-Émilion: **Élie Guadet**, a native of the town and a prominent member of the Girondin Party at the beginning of the Convention. Suspected of "Moderantism" – what today would be termed deviation from the party line – Gaudet became a victim of the Revo-

Jurats and the Jurade

In the Middle Ages the famous red wines of St-Émilion (see VIGNOBLE DE BORDEAUX) were qualified as "honorific" because it was the custom to offer them to royalty and persons of note. From then on it was decided that, in order to maintain the excellence and reputation of wines permitted to bear that name, they should be subject each year to evaluation by a committee of professionals. The body appointed by the town council to carry out this task was called the Jurade and its members the Jurats. The Jurade was reformed in 1948 and still operates today.

In the spring of each year, a procession of Jurats wearing scarlet, ermine-trimmed robes and silken hoods attends a solemn mass and then proceeds towards the cloisters of the collegiate church for ceremonial events. At the end of the afternoon, the Jurade pronounces its judgement on the new wine from the top of the King's Tower.

In the autumn these same Jurats assemble at the top of the King's Tower to proclaim the official start of the grape harvest. Such solemn rites are accompanied by ritual banquets – suitably washed down with local wines – held in the Dominican Room of the local wine-growers' association.

Address Book

For coin ranges, see the Legend on the cover flap.

GETTING AROUND

Le petit train touristique, which has been operating since 1992, is a good alternative for those who want to tour the town but can't do it on foot. The 35-min trip *(Easter to mid-Oct)* carries vistors past some presitigioius wine-growing châteaux and the main monuments of the town. Departures every 45min from in front of the Collégiale church (upper town) from 10.30am-6.30pm (5€; children 4€).

WHERE TO STAY

Château Meylet – *La Gomerie – 1.5km/1mi W of St-Émilion, rte de Libourne via the D 243 – ☎05 57 24 68 85 – http://chateau.meylet.free.fr – ⌷ – 4 rooms.* Built in 1789, this Girondin residence is situated among 2ha of grapevines. The charming, rustic rooms are furnished with fine period pieces. Breakfast is served on the veranda in the winter, and under the garden bower in the summer.

Château Monlot Capet – *1 r. Conte – 33330 St-Hippolyte – 3km/1.8mi E of St-Émilion dir. Castillon via the D 245 –* ☎05 57 74 49 47 – www.belair-monlot.com – *5 rooms.* The foundations of this château with its chalky facade and handsome tiled roof were laid when the Capetians ruled the land. Old photographs hang in the rooms, each of which is named after a different vintage. The breakfast room is decorated in a grapevine theme. Visits to the wine storehouses and tastings available.

WHERE TO EAT

Le Bouchon – *1 pl. du Marché – ☎05 57 24 62 81 – franck.herman@tiscali.fr – closed Nov-Feb.* One of the best addresses on the marketplace. The recently repainted dining room has aerial photos and Botero prints on the green and blue walls. Traditional cuisine prepared with care and an excellent choice of wines.

L'Envers du Decor – *11 r. du Clocher – ☎05 57 74 48 31 – enversdu-decors@nerim.fr – closed 22 Dec-9 Jan.* With its back against the collegiate church, this attractive wine bar has a lovely, peaceful terrace with a fig tree and flowers. The dining room is simply decorated with wood, metal and old stonework. The cuisine here focuses on fresh ingredients. Wine on sale.

lutionary leader Robespierre's hatred for the Girondins, and was obliged to flee Paris disguised as an upholsterer. He took refuge first in Normandy and later rejoined a couple of Girondin colleagues in St-Émilion. It was here, one day in 1794, that he was discovered, arrested, and taken to Bordeaux, where he died on the scaffold.

Walking Tour

The Town★★

St-Émilion faces due south, nestling within a horse-shoe between two hillsides. At the junction of the two slopes, a tall belfry rises above a rocky spur honeycombed with caves, catacombs, a hermitage, a chapel and an extraordinary underground church. At the foot of this promontory, below the church, lies Place du Marché, the main square at the heart of this busy small town. The square acts as a link between the districts sprawled over the two hills, one the site of the royal castle, the other the site of a deanery (clerical residence), reflecting the age-old rivalry between civil and religious powers.

Saint-Emilion is a pedestrian city. Make sure you wear comfortable shoes, as the streets are paved and steep. The picturesque network of narrow streets is ideal for a leisurely stroll.

Place du Marché

St-Émilion's main square and market place, in a picturesque setting at the foot of the spur, offers a fine view of the troglodyte church and its great belfry soaring heavenwards (fine view from the top).

▶ *A ramp leads to Porte de la Cadène.*

Porte et logis de la Cadène

This gateway stands at the end of a street off the main square, with a 15C timber-framed house beside it. The name of the arch derives from the Latin word *catena* ("chain"), and is a reminder of nights past, when access to the town centre was blocked by a chain across this gateway. The span frames the church belfry.

▶ *Turn right onto rue de la Porte-Brunet.*

Of the old **Logis de la Commanderie** (the abbot's lodgings), nothing remains but a covered watch-path and a corner bartizan.

Cloître des Cordeliers

For information, call ☎05 57 74 49 31.
The Cordeliers – Franciscans of a strict order distinguished by a knotted cord worn around the waist – built this sanctuary in the 14C. The handsome ruins of their square **cloisters**★ include slender twinned columns supporting Romanesque arches. At the far end, on the right, a 15C Gothic archway precedes the stairway which led to the monks' cells.

On the left, the belfry of the old church (15C) is supported by two unusual super-imposed arches. Inside, the nave is sepa-rated from the apse by a triumphal arch in the Flamboyant Gothic style, which gives access down to a series of caves quarried out 20m/66ft deep in the bed-rock where sparkling white and rosé wines are left to age.

There is an interesting view of St-Émilion from the Esplanade nearby (place du Cap-du-Pont).

▶ *Continue along rue de la Porte-Brunet to the ramparts.*

Porte Brunet

It is one of the six gates which allowed access through the ramparts erected in the 13C and reinforced later by a machico-lated watch-path. It was through this gate, one night in January 1794, that the out-lawed Girondins escaped from Robes-pierre's men after the arrest of their companion Guadet

From Porte Brunet, there are impressive views of the vineyards. The Tour du Roi (the king's tower) and the spire of the church tower can be seen rising above the narrow winding streets .

▶ *Turn back and take rue de la Liberté on the left. Take the stairs on the left (after number 3), continue on the left, then turn right in rue de la Tourelle.*

Château du Roi

🕐*Open Jun-Sep 10.30am-8.30pm; Low season enqire at the Town Hall. Entrance at the top of the Tour du Roi. ⌘1€. ☎05 57 24 61 07.*
The King's Castle, founded according to some by Louis VIII and to others by Henri III Plantagenet in the 13C, was used as the town hall until 1720. From the top of the King's Tower (a rectangular keep with latrines on its outer face, standing on an isolated spur of rock) there is a fine viewa over the huddled rooftops of the town and across to the valleys of the Dordogne and the Isle rivers.

Follow rue de la Grande-Fontaine then the steep ruelle du Tertre-des-Vaillants which wends its way between houses dug out of the rock.

Collégiale

Place Pioceau.
This huge church (Collégiale is used to refer to churches which are endowed for a chapter of canons, but do not host the bishop's see) has a Romanesque nave with a Gothic chancel. The entrance is on the north side of the chancel, via a superb 14C porch built at a time when Gaillard de Lamothe, the nephew of Pope Clement V, was Dean of the resident canons. The carved tympanum repre-sents The Last Judgement. Below, only the lower parts of the statues of the Apos-tles remain in their niches, the figures having been mutilated during the Wars of Religion and during the Revolution. The 15C choir stalls in the chancel are carved with an entertaining variety of characters.

Inside the nave, two 12C mural paintings – *The Virgin* and *The Legend of St Catherine* – adorn the far end of the right-hand wall.

Logis de Malet de Roquefort

Opposite the *église collégiale*, a 15C man-sion is incorporated into the ramparts; the old covered watch path of the forti-

St-Émillion vineyards

B. Kaufmann/MICHELIN

fied town with its corbelled crenellations passes beneath the roof of the house.

▶ *Head to place des Créneaux.*

Cloître de la collégiale

&. ⓒ*Open same as for the Monolithic church bell-tower (see below).* ⊘*No charge. Enter via the tourist information centre.*
The cloisters, which lie to the south of the church, date from the 14C and are still in very good condition; they have much in common with the Cordeliers' Cloisters, particularly in the design of their twinned columns, which are extremely elegant. Arches reinforce the corners separating the galleries – one of which houses an impressive series of covered niches formerly used as tombs.
The deanery – comprising the old refectory and the monks' dormitory – has been restored and is occupied today by the tourist information centre.

Clocher de l'église monolithe

ⓒ*Open Jul-Aug 9.30am-8pm; mid-Jun–late Jun and early Sep–mid-Sep 9.30am-7pm; mid-Sep–late Oct and early Apr–mid-Jun 9.30am-12.30pm and 1.45-6.30pm; Nov-Mar 9.30am-12.30pm and 1.45-6pm.* ⊘*1€.* ☎*05 57 55 28 28.*
You will not have climbed the 187 steps in vain: you will have a full view on the village, its monuments and the vineyards, the whole picture being listed as a UNESCO world heritage site.

▶ *Return to place du Marché.*

Place du Marché

Combined tours of the four sights below with a tour guide (45 min). Buy your ticket at the tourist office.

Ermitage St-Émilion

Enlarged to form of a Latin cross, this grotto contains "St Émilion's Bed", his armchair carved from the limestone, and a spring, now guarded by a 17C balustrade; right at the end is an altar surmounted by a statue of the saint.

Catacombes

Near the chapel, the cliff face opens out into catacombs – rock galleries once used as an ancient burial ground, with tombs gouged from the rock. Later, the main part of this subterranean maze was used to store corpses. At the top of a central dome is an opening through which bones from a cemetery on top of the cliff were disposed of. At the base of the dome is a primitive representation depicting the resurrection of the dead: three carved figures emerging hand in hand from their sarcophagi.

Chapelle de la Trinité

Holy Trinity Chapel, a miniature sanctuary built by Benedictine monks in the 13C, includes a harmonious – and, in the southwest, rare – example of a timber-framed Gothic apse (frescoes). Inside, elegant High Gothic ribbed vaulting converges on a keystone embossed with the symbolic Lamb.

Église Monolithe★

Inelegant reinforcing pillars make the site, currently being restored, less aesthetically pleasing. The church, the largest monolithic sanctuary in Europe to be carved from a single solid block of rock, is a great rarity. It was fashioned between the 8C and the 12C by enlarging natural grottoes and caverns which already existed in the porous strata. The main entrance was through a tall 14C Gothic porch decorated on the tympanum with a Last Judgement and a Resurrection of the Dead. The interior of the church is impressive as much for the size of those three aisles carved from the rock as for the perfect symmetry of its vaulting and squared pillars – only two of which support the belfry (concrete supporting posts have been added temporarily, during restoration work). At the back of the central nave, beneath the arcade of the bay, there is a bas-relief of two four-winged angels or cherubims.

The majestic belfry (198 steps) offers a fine view of the town, its monuments and the neighbouring vineyards.

Driving Tour

St-Émilion Vineyards

Round trip of 52km/32mi. ℭ *See VIGNOBLE DE BORDEAUX.*

ST-GILLES-CROIX-DE-VIE ⚓

POPULATION 6 797
MICHELIN MAP 316: E-7

The Vie estuary is a geographical curiosity. Approaching the sea, the stream first runs up against a line of sand dunes, the Pointe de la Garenne, and then against the rocky headland known as the Corniche Vendéenne, looping itself as a result into a number of meanders: it finally emerges into the Atlantic between the beaches of Croix-de-Vie (Plage de Boisvinet) and St-Gilles (Grand-Plage) via a bottleneck at the harbour mouth. In the summer boat trips are organised around the coast, leaving from the port. The fishing boats here supply wholesale fish merchants and factories with lobsters, crabs, tuna fish and sardines for canning or freezing. A sheltered marina can accommodate up to 600 craft.

▸ **Orient Yourself**: The lively fishing port of Croix-de-Vie and the town of St-Gilles-sur-Vie, on the south bank of the Vie estuary, north-west of Les Sables-d'Olonne, combine to make the single commune of St-Gilles-Croix-de-Vie. When St-Hilaire-de-Riez *(northeast)* is included, the combined area is also known as Havre-de-Vie.

ℭ **Also See**: ROCHE-SUR-YON, SABLES-D'OLONNE, MARAIS BRETON-VENDÉEN.

St-Gilles-Croix-de-Vie

B. Kaufmann/MICHELIN

Coëx
14km/8mi E via the D 6.

Jardin des Olfacties★
&♿ ◷*Open Mid-Jun–Aug 10.30am-7pm; mid-Apr–mid-Jun and early to mid-Sep, daily 2-7pm.* ✆*6.70€ (children under 12 no charge).* ☎*02 51 55 53 41.*
The Gué-Gorand stream runs through this pleasantly undulating floral garden. A path takes visitors through a series of "fragrant chambers" combining different plants and scents. Colourful flower beds giving off various fragrances (artemisia, varieties of mint, sage, sweet-smelling

🍽**La Crêperie** – *4 r. Gautté* – ☎*02 51 55 02 77 – closed 7-21 Mar and 3-16 Oct; Mon off-season except school hols.* This pretty 17C house has exposed stonework, period floor-tiles, wooden tables, cast iron chairs, fishing nets and ropes and modern art. The batter is hand-beaten in the kitchen and the pancakes cooked before your eyes. Covered terrace in the back.

geraniums, roses, etc.) encircle an attractive pond surrounded by sculptures, cultural exhibitions and leisure facilities.

ST-JEAN-DE-LUZ★★
POPULATION 13 247
MICHELIN MAP 342: C-2

As a smart summer and winter seaside resort, St-Jean-de-Luz only dates back to 1843; however as a fishing port, the town is ancient. Today only one house survives from before the great fire of 1558, when the place was sacked by the Spanish. The sea-front is determinedly modern. Ste-Barbe headland, which can be reached on foot via Promenade de la Plage and Boulevard Thiers, offers a fine view southwards across the bay to Socoa fort on its rocky promontory. St-Jean-de-Luz, the most Basque of the towns lying north of the Spanish border, offers all the attractions and amenities of a beach resort together with the picturesque and briny delights of a busy fishing port.

- **Tourist Office**: Pl. du Maréchal Foch – 64500 St-Jean-de-Luz – ☎05 59 26 03 16; www.saint-jean-de-luz.com.
- **Orient Yourself**: St-Jean-de-Luz is located on the Atlantic Coast, S of Biarritz and just 13km/8mi from the Spanish border.
- **Parking**: Park in place du Maréchal Foch near place Louis-XIV and the port.
- **Don't Miss**: The port; Église St-Jean-Baptiste; Maison Louis-XIV; the Corniche Basque.
- **Especially for Kids**: The cog-railway from Col de St-Ignace to La Rhune.
- **Also See**: BIARRITZ, BAYONNE, ESPELETTE.

A Bit of History

The Marriage of Louis XIV
The outstanding historical event connected with St-Jean-de-Luz is the marriage of Louis XIV and Maria Theresa. The wedding between the King of France and the Infanta of Spain, provided for in the Treaty of the Pyrenees, was delayed be-cause of the monarch's passion for Marie Mancini, the niece of Cardinal Mazarin. The situation was resolved when the Cardinal – successor to Richelieu and Louis XIV's chief minister – eventually

sent the young girl into exile and the King yielded for "reasons of State". Louis arrived in St-Jean-de-Luz on 8 May 1660 and was lodged, together with the royal retinue, in an imposing mansion which had been built for the shipowner Lohobiague; Maria Theresa stayed in an elegant brick and stone house nearby. On the morning of 9 June the King presented himself at the Infanta's house to claim his bride. The procession moved off towards the church between the Swiss Guards lining the route, and was led by two companies of Gentlemen-at-Arms followed by Cardinal Mazarin dressed in sumptuous robes. Behind him came Louis XIV, in black with lace trimmings, and then the Infanta who wore a dress of spun silver and a cloak of heavy purple velvet, with a gold crown on her head. The King's brother, known in royal circles simply as "Monsieur", was a few paces behind with their mother, the imposing Anne of Austria. They were followed by the rest of the court.

The marriage was solemnised by the Bishop of Bayonne and the service lasted until halfway through the afternoon. The door through which the royal couple left the church was walled up after the ceremony.

The cortège returned to the Infanta's house. From the balcony there the King himself and Mazarin threw commemorative medals to the crowd below. Later the newlyweds dined with the court in Lohobiague's mansion.

Following a strict etiquette they were then led to the nuptial couch, and given the traditional blessing by the Queen Mother as she drew its curtains.

Louis XIV found in Maria Theresa a gentle and worthy wife, and when she died the King remarked: "This is the first and only time she has ever made me unhappy."

Wedding Gifts

The young Queen was showered with gifts worthy of the Thousand and One Nights. From her husband she received six dazzling sets of jewellery encrusted with diamonds and other precious stones; from Monsieur, twelve jewelled dress ornaments. The present from Mazarin, who was phenomenally wealthy, outshone them all: 1 200 000 livres-worth of diamonds and pearls, a great dinner service in solid gold, and two state coaches, one drawn by six Russian horses, the other by six Indian horses, each with trappings and livery to match the colours of the carriages.

Sights

Port★

With whaling a thing of the past, local fishermen nowadays rely on hauls of sardines, anchovies and especially tuna fish for their livelihood.

The port is at the inner end of the only anchorage to break the long straight line of the Atlantic coast between Arcachon and the Bidasoa River. The estuary, nestling between the Socoa and Ste-Barbe headlands, is further protected from westerly gales by massive dikes and the Artha breakwaters.

From the quays there are picturesque views across the busy harbour of the old town and inland, in the distance, the great pyramid bulk of La Rhune.

The imposing **Maison de l'Infante** seems to be guarding the boats. This elegant building in the Louis XIII style, constructed of brick and stone with Italian-style galleries overlooking the port, belonged to the rich Haraneder family. The Infanta stayed here with her future mother-in-law, Anne of Austria. In the

La Maison de l'Infante

B. Kaufmann/MICHELIN

Address Book

For coin ranges, see the Legend on the cover flap.

WHERE TO STAY

Chambre d'hôte Arrayoa – *at the village edge – 64310 Ascain – ☎05 59 54 06 18 – closed 1-7 Oct – ⊠ – 4 rooms.* This peaceful sheep and duck farm is located outside the village. The charming reception, big common room with a corner kitchen and bookshelves, country-style bedrooms, private fronton and reasonable prices make this a popular place to stay. Homemade duck confit and foie gras for sale.

Hôtel Bolivar – *18 r. Sopite – ☎05 59 26 02 00 – closed Oct-Apr – 16 rooms.* If you've come to the region to spend most of your time by the sea, this family hotel 50m from the beach is for you. The rooms, though smallish, are simple and clean, and the bathrooms well equipped.

Hôtel Le Petit Trianon – *56 bd Victor-Hugo – ☎05 59 26 11 90 – lepetittrianon@wanadoo.fr – closed Jan – 26 rooms.* A simple, well-maintained hotel. The rooms, rather cramped, come with 1960s-style bathrooms. In season, you can have breakfast in the inner courtyard decorated with an immense Basque fresco.

Chambre d'hôte Villa Argi-Eder – *Av. Napoléon III, – Plage Lafitenia – 5km/3mi NE of St-Jean-de-Luz. Take the N 10 towards Biarritz, then a secondary road – ☎05 59 54 81 65 – villa-argi-eder@wanadoo.fr – ⊠ – 4 rooms.* This attractive Basque house has a pretty, quiet garden and a surfers' beach just 100m away – an ideal spot for a holiday. The large, simple rooms open onto private terraces overlooking the garden.

Chambre d'hôte Olhabidea – *64310 Sare – 13km/8mi SE of St-Jean-de-Luz via the D 918 and D 4 – ☎05 59 54 21 85 – closed Dec-Feb – ⊠ – 4 rooms.* This typical 17-18C house was restored by local craftsmen. The rooms, with their pretty Basque colours and waxed furniture, are smart and comfortable. Make sure that you book in advance in season – this is a popular B&B with a growing reputation.

Chambre d'hôte Château d'Urtubie – *r. Bernard-de-Coral – 64122 Urrugne – 2km/1.2mi S of St-Jean-de-Luz via the N 10 (dir. Hendaye) – ☎05 59 54 31 15 – chateaudurtubie@wanadoo.fr – closed 16 Nov-14 Mar – P – 10 rooms.* Enjoy a taste of château life in the charming, traditional bedrooms of this historic monument that has belonged to the same family since 1341. Don't be put off by the nearby road – the air-conditioned rooms are well sound-proofed. Park and museum.

WHERE TO EAT

Salon de thé L'Acanthe – *31 r. Garat – ☎ 05 59 26 85 59 – www.lacanthe.com – off-season 9am-7pm, Jul-Aug daily 9am-10pm – closed 15-30 Jan and Mon off-season.* Has swimming in the sea given you an appetite? This pleasant tea room is conveniently situated just 50m from the beach. Breakfast is served from 9am-noon; at other times of the day snacks include salads, quiches and simple meals.

Venta Insola – *Col d'Ibardin – 64500 Vera de Bidasoa – after the Venta Gloria, take the first left after 3km/1.8mi – ☎00 349 48 63 12 28 – closed weekdays in winter and Mon in summer – ⊠.* Who could resist this authentic venta nestled in the bottom of the valley? The dining room has retained its traditional flavour with a large wooden counter and liqueurs, cigarettes and foodstuffs on display on the shelves. Terrace by a stream.

Muscade – *20 r. Garat – ☎05 59 26 96 73 – closed beg. Nov to end March.* Quiches, pies and tarts of all varieties are enticingly displayed in the window of this little restaurant, which has an attractive dining room decorated in pastel hues. Reasonable prices.

Chez Théo – *25 r. de l'Abbé-Onaindia – ☎05 59 26 81 30 – closed mid-Nov to end Dec, 2 weeks in Mar, Sun eve and Mon except school hols.* A family auberge in the Spanish Basque country where you'll find azulejos, posters of ferias, cob walls, solid wood furniture as well as a wide choice of tapas and more substantial fare served in a convivial ambience.

Restaurant Ibaïa – *39 r. Tourasse – ☎05 59 51 12 21 – closed Jan, Sun eve off-season and Mon.* A handful of tables are set on the pavement in front of this old house a few steps from the beach. The decor is typical of the region, with an open fireplace, exposed beams and hot pepper garlands hanging in the windows. Local cuisine.

⊜⊜**Au Chipiron** – *4 r. Etchegaray – ☎05 59 26 03 41 – closed mid-Nov to mid-Dec, Oct to 15 Mar except school hols, open Fri eve to Mon noon.* This restaurant describes itself as a "house of fish and regional specialities", the most celebrated of which is their *chipirons à l'encre* (squid in ink). The dining rooms, decorated in Basque country colours, are cosy and attractive. Games corner for children.

⊜⊜**Petit Grill Basque** *"Chez Maya" – 4 r. St-Jacques – ☎05 59 26 80 76 – closed 27 May-3 Jun, 20 Dec-20 Jan, Thu lunch and Wed.* This small, hospitable neighbourhood restaurant has been run by the same family for three generations. The Basque interior is traditional in style, with old plates, copperware and wall frescos. Plentiful regional cuisine.

SPORTS AND LEISURE

Association Sportive de la Nivelle – *Pl. William-Sharp – 64500 Ciboure – ☎ 05 59 47 18 99 – golf.nivelle@etxe.fr – summer: daily except Thu 7am-8.30pm; off-season: daily except Thu 8am-7pm or 7.30am-7.30pm.* While the general French enthusiasm for golf is a recent phenomenon, it has always been one of the most popular sports in the Basque country. In addition to the 18-hole golf course, this association has 3 tennis and 2 squash courts.

Fronton Municipal – *1 av. André-Ithurralde – ☎05 59 26 13 93 – luzean2@wanadoo.fr – Jul-Sep: Mon, Thu 8.30-11pm.* From July to September, you can watch chistera matches played on Mondays and grand chistera matches on Thursdays (9:15pm), often accompanied by traditional singing and dancing. Open to the public except during competitions, the fronton is often used by local groups which run courses for adults and children alike.

Jaï Alaï – *Av. André-Ithurralde – ☎05 59 51 65 30 – www.saint-jean-de-luz.com – Mon-Fri 9am-12.30pm and 2-7pm.* Cesta punta is one version of the emblematic sport of the Basque country, pelota. Like jai alai in Latin America, it is played against a three-wall fronton. From June to September, professional cesta punta matches take place here on Tuesdays and Fridays.

Le Spot – *16 r. Gambetta – ☎05 59 26 07 93 – lespot64@aol.com – Mon-Sat 10am-12.30pm and 2.30-7.30pm; Jul-Aug: Mon-Sat 9.30am-8pm – closed Mon morning.* This sports shop organises surf and bodyboard lessons. Two other shops in the same street, Bakea (n° 37) and H2O (n° 72) offer similar courses.

Sports Mer – *7 bd Thiers – Digue aux Chevaux – ☎ 05 59 26 96 94 or 06 80 64 39 11 – sportsmer.com – Jul-Aug: daily 10am-8pm; office open year round – closed public hols except summer.* Exciting activities such as para-boating (solo or tandem) and jet-skiing run by qualified instructors are organised by this company.

Trinquet Maïtena – *42 r. du Midi – ☎05 59 26 05 13 – daily 9am-10pm.* The Basques practice many sports, like squash, tennis and golf, but their heart belongs to pala, played in a trinquet (small covered court). After a game, they come here to relax and sing together.

École de Voile Internationale – *Parking de Socoa – 64500 Ciboure – 4 km/2.4 mi W of St-Jean-de-Luz via the N10. ☎ 05 59 47 06 32 or 06 80 13 79 22 – guyonnetT@wanadoo.com – May-Sep: daily 9am-noon and 2-7pm.* This school offers sailing and water-skiing courses and rents boats and windsurf boards.

BARS AND CAFES

Le Brouillarta – *48 prom. Jacques-Thibaud – ☎05 59 51 29 51 – summer: daily 9am-3am; off-season: Tue-Sat 9am-2am, Sun 9am-6pm – closed Jan, Sun eve and Mon.* An unbeatable view of the ocean and the hundred-year-old Artha dyke make this the perfect observation point for watching the dark and fearsome *brouillarta,* the storm that comes suddenly from the sea, make its way towards the shore. Simple, classic decor.

Le Duke – *Pl. Maurice-Ravel – ☎05 59 51 12 96 – summer: daily until 3am; off-season: 8am-2am.* This contemporary bar is run by Michel Chardié, a former surfing champion who named it after his idol, The Duke, a Hawaiian surfing star who rode the waves in the 1950s. Trendy music and clientele.

Maison Adam – *6 r. de la République – ☎05 59 26 03 54 – www.macarons-adam.com – Tue-Sun 7.45am-12.30pm and 2-7.30pm; from mid-Jun to end-Sep: daily – closed early Jan to mid-Feb.* Since

1660, La Maison Adam has continued to make the same macarons that were a favourite delicacy of Louis XIV. Indeed, it was in 1660 that the Sun King and his wife Marie-Thérèse d'Autriche visited St-Jean-de-Luz and stayed in a house across the way from the boutique. **Maison Pariès** – *9 r. Gambetta – ☎05 59 26 01 46 – www.paries.fr – mid-Feb to mid-Jan: daily 8.30am-1pm and 2.30-7.30pm; summer: until 11pm – closed mid-Jan to mid-Feb.* Founded in 1910 by Robert Pariès, a master chocloate-maker, this shop is one of the most popular confectioneries in the town. Among the specialities, make sure you try the *mouchou basque* (macaroon

made of almonds, sugar and egg whites), the soft caramel Kanougas and the chocolates made in the Bayonne tradition.

SHOPPING

Maison Thurin – *32 r. Gambetta – ☎05 59 26 05 07 – maisonthurin@wanadoo.fr – open Tue-Sat 8.30am-12.30pm and 3.30-7pm; in season, Mon-Sun lunchtime 8.30am-12.30pm and 3.30-7pm.* This shop stocks an excellent choice of local specialities, such as Bayonne ham, sheep's cheese, bright red Espelette chilli peppers, local foie gras and poultry. There is also a selection of

---

large 17C room, note the immense sculpted and painted fireplace and the beams decorated with paintings from the school of Fontainebleau.

Rue Mazarin

17C shipowners used to live on the strip of land separating the roadstead from the harbour. The area has retained a few elegant houses; note in particular Maison St-Martin at no 13 rue Mazarin.

Town centre

Modernised now with many pedestrian precincts (rue de la République, rue Gambetta) – the town centre has a special charm of its own. The famous "oldest house", its solid dressed-stone construction contrasting with the red-roofed, white-walled Basque buildings nearby, is at 17 rue de la République, near the harbour.

Maison Louis-XIV★

Visit by guided tours (30min) Jul-Aug 10.30am-12.30pm and 3-6.30pm, Sun and public hols 3-6.30pm; Jun and Sep 10.30am-noon and 3-5.30pm, Sun and public hols 3-5.30pm. Call ahead for price information. ☎05 59 26 01 56.

The house now named after the monarch who stayed here was built by the shipowner Lohobiague in 1643. It is an imposing building beside the port, with the façade facing the town distinguished by corbelled turrets at the corners. Inside, the "Old Basque" character of the

house is evident in the sturdy, straight-flight staircase which was built by ship's carpenters: like the original floorboards in all the rooms, the treads are kept in place by large, visible, heavy-headed nails which make sanding or planing impossible. From the second-floor landing a passage leads to the apartments where Lohobiague's widow received Louis XIV in 1660; a south-facing, arcaded gallery here offers a splendid view of the Basque Pyrenees.

The huge kitchen boasts an impressive fireplace. The green-panelled dining-room contains a marble Directoire table and – a gift from the royal guest to his hostess – a three-piece service in silver-gilt with inlaid enamel work.

Église St-Jean-Baptiste★★

This is the largest and most famous of all the Basque churches in France; it was founded in the 15C and was being enlarged at the time of Louis XIV's wedding. The bricked-up doorway through which the royal couple left can be seen just inside the main entrance, on the south side.

Externally the architecture is sober, even severe, with high walls and small windows. A vaulted passageway tunnels beneath the massive tower. A fine wrought-iron stairway leads to the galleries.

Interior – The sumptuous, largely 17C interior presents a striking contrast to the church's exterior. Three tiers of oak galleries (five on the end wall) surround the broad, single nave; these, traditionally, are reserved for men. The vaulted roof above the nave is lined with remarkable painted panels. The chancel, raised high as in all Basque churches, is separated from the nave by a handsome wrought-iron screen. The dazzling gold **altarpiece**★ dates from c 1670 (restored 1987). Between the columns and entablatures that divide it into three levels, shallow niches hold statues of the Apostles, angels and local saints.

Among other items of interest are the 17C pulpit supported by sphinxes and – in the embrasure of the walled-up doorway – a statue of **Notre-Dame-des-Douleurs** (Our Lady of Sorrows). Beside this is a small Virgin of the Rosary in ceremonial dress.

Driving Tours

1 **La Corniche Basque**★★
(The Basque Coast Road)

30km/19mi round-trip – allow 1hr.

▶ *Leave St-Jean-de-Luz west via the D 912.*

The route approaches the cliffs of Socoa, offering superb sea **views**★★. Before snaking down to Hendaye, it passes near **Domaine d'Abbadia**, the Second Empire home of Antoine Abbadie (1810-97) which the scholar left to the French Academy of Sciences (🕭 see HENDAYE, Pointe Ste-Anne).

Socoa
3km/1.8mi W via the D 912.

▶ *Park at the port and continue (45min round-trip on foot) towards the jetty.*

⬛The beginning of the dike offers a good view of the harbour and the town. Entrance to the anchorage at St-Jean-de-Luz was formerly defended by Socoa fort, which was built under Henri IV and improved by the celebrated military architect Vauban. Turn right, leaving the port, and climb to the lighthouse along Rue du Phare, then follow Rue du Sémaphore to the

coastal signal station: to the southwest there is a superb **view**★★ of the Basque coastline from Cape Higuer (Cabo Higuer) in Spain all the way to Biarritz. Below, in the foreground, the foliated strata of the cliffs drop steeply down to the crashing waves of the Atlantic.

Hendaye ⌂⌂
🕭 See HENDAYE.

▶ *Leave Hendaye by the N 10 east towards Béhobie and St-Jean-de-Luz.*

Urrugne
The church at the centre of the town presents an almost military aspect, with high walls and few windows. The face of the adjoining belfry-porch bears a sundial.

▶ *From the main square in Urrugne, take the hill leading up to Notre-Dame-de-Socorri.*

Notre-Dame-de-Socorri
This pilgrimage chapel dedicated to the Virgin lies in a lovely **setting**★: the shady clearing on the site of the former cemetery offers views of the undulating countryside dominated by the great spur of La Rhune and, on the horizon, the heights of Jaozkibel and Les Trois Couronnes.

▶ *Beyond Urrugne, turn left below the N 10.*

Socoa

B. Kaufmann/MICHELIN

Château d'Urtubie★

🕐Visit by guided tour (1hr) Mid-March–early Nov 2-6pm; unaccompanied visit at 11am. ☞5.50€. ☎05 59 54 31 15.

This castle was built in the 14C with the authorisation of King Edward III of England; it has undergone many changes since and has become an elegant classical manor house. Its two towers which, in the 19C, used to stand on each side of the draw bridge, have now rooves à l'impériale. In the central tower, note a remarkable suspended cork screw staircase from the 16C. In the chapel built in the 17C, the gilding of the choir was restored in the 19C. A bathroom was fitted out behind the sacristy in 1830.

The walls of the château are decorated with large 16C tapestries from Brussels. The château, surrounded with moats until the 18C, is now enshrined within lovely English gardens. The orangery houses an exhibition about cider.

▸ Return to St-Jean-de-Luz by the N 10.

2 Le Labourd★

116km/72mi round tour – allow 1 day
The Labourd coastline offers a picturesque alternation of rugged cliffs and sandy coves; away from the ocean rollers the landscape is one of gentle hills and wide moors known as touyas. Mountains stand out against the clear skies but they are not high: La Rhune, the culminating peak in the range, rises to no more than 900m/ 2 953ft above sea level. This excursion will lead you through the traditional villages and rolling hills of this picturesque region.

▸ Leave St-Jean-de-Luz via the N 10, drive to Urrugne; left on the D 4 to Ascain.

Ascain★

The pretty village square, with its church, pelota court, traditional houses and welcoming hotels, has a great deal of character. The Basque church with its three-tiered galleries is preceded by a massive belfry-porch; on the right of the cemetery behind it is an interesting disk-shaped stele dating from 1657. In one of the Ascain restaurants there is a trinquet – a rectangular indoor court marked out

for a variant of pelota, reminiscent of the English game of fives.

▸ Continuing south, the road (D 4) rises beside an attractive valley to reach Col de St Ignace (St Ignatius Pass), at an altitude of 169m/555ft.

La Rhune★★

From Col de St Ignace – 1hr round-trip by rack railway. 🕐Mid-Mar to early-Nov departures 10am and 3pm, supplementary departures according to weather conditions and numbers. Summer generally every 30min from 9am. ☞11€ return (children aged 4-10 6.50€ return). ☎05 59 54 20 26.

Kids The journey aboard the wooden train dating from 1924 is well worth it. It is possible to come back on foot (👟wear suitable walking shoes). Enquire before leaving about the visibility on the summit. La Rhune (in Basque larrun means good pastureland) is regarded as the symbol of the French Basque country. From the summit (alt 900m/2 952ft; television transmitter) of the frontier-mountain, there is a superb **panorama★★★** over the ocean (Bay of Biscay), the Forest of the Landes, the Basque Pyrenees and, southwards, the Bidassoa Valley.

Maison Ortillopitz

▸ 1km from Col de St-Ignace. Take the route communale in front of the station de la Rhune.

A ship-owner had this fine and large farm built (600m²/717.6sq yards on three floors), hence the comfort of the place. A visit will enable you to discover the daily life of a Basque family. The most remarkable features of the house are the straight wooden stairways looking like a ship, the kitchen with its bread oven, the elegant framework of the attic (built with 600 trees!); the cider press and the washtub. 18ha/44.4 acres of land also belong to the estate of Ortillopitz: a vegetable garden, an orchard, vineyards, hemp and pepper cultivation.

Sare★

This charming village was described, under the name of Etchezar, by the author Pierre

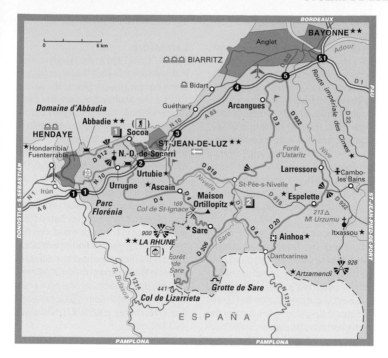

Loti in his novel *Ramuntcho* (1897). The high fronton wall of the pelota court, the shaded streets, and the fine church with its galleries, raised chancel and Baroque altarpieces are all typical of the Basque country.

Sare is also known as "wood pigeons' hell" due to the local method of snaring the migratory birds as they fly south in the autumn. The upper Sare valley, a pastoral landscape of sheep, dairy cattle and Pottok ponies between scattered hamlets with some fine dovecotes is particularly appealing.

▶ *Take the D 306 south.*

Grotte de Sare

Visit by guided tour (1hr) Jul Aug 10am-7pm; Apr-Jun and Sep 10am-6pm; Oct 10am-5pm; Nov-Dec and Feb-Mar, 2-5pm. ⊘*Closed 1 Jan, 7 Jan-6 Feb and*

Petit train de la Rhune

B. Kaufmann/MICHELIN

25 Dec. ⊚ *6.50€ (children under 13 3.5€).*
☏*05 59 54 21 88. www.sare.fr.*

The grotto or *lezea* (a Basque word meaning cave) is part of a vast series of galleries gouged from the limestone at the beginning of the Quaternary era by waters hurtling down from Pic d'Atchouria. Corrosion, abrasion and dissolution of some of the rock's mineral constituents have produced over the millennia every kind of karstic cavity. The discovery here of flint tools and the remnants of bones shows that many of these caves were at one time occupied by humans, particularly during the Upper Perigordian period (20 000 BC).

The enormous entrance, which opens to the northeast, leads into a subterranean labyrinth illuminated by blue lights. The natural marvels to be seen on the tour (900m – about half a mile) are explained in an audiovisual presentation (in French). 🚶*2 hours there and back.* The **sentier des contrebandiers** (smugglers' path) leads to the caves of Zugarramurdi (Navarre).

▷ *Return to D306 and turn left.*

The road continues beside attractive undergrowth flourishing on the banks of a stream, then rises into the oak-filled Forêt de Sare.

Col de Lizarrieta

Alt 441m/1 447ft. The pass, with its hides and snare centres all along the crests, is a hive of activity during the pigeon-shooting season.

▷ *Return to the D 4 and continue eastwards.*

Aïnhoa★
⚲*See AÏNHOA.*

▷ *Head northeast along D 20.*

Espelette★
See ESPELETTE.
Before the road plunges down into the valley of the Nive, the view opens out again onto the Basque Pyrenees, La Rhune and the Artzamendi (behind), and the heights of Cambo-les-Bains and the gentle green slopes of Mont Ursuya (ahead).

▷ *Turn left (D 20) to Larressore.*

Larressore
From 1733 to 1906 a seminary founded in this village by Abbot Daguerre trained many Basque priests. Beside the pelota court is the **Atelier Ainciart-Bergara**; this workshop was established before the French Revolution by a craftsman of that name and is still family-operated today. Using their own time-honoured methods, the workshop produces the traditional Basque staff or *makhila*, from the wood of the medlar tree. The canes are seasoned and decorated with a pattern of dried sap which has oozed from incisions cut in the fresh wood. Besides the workshop, you will find an exhibition and a documentary about the different stages in the making of makhilas *(30 min)*. ⊙*Open daily except Sun and public hols 8am-noon and 2-6pm.* ⊘*Closed early Sep.* ⊚*No charge.* ☏*05 59 93 03 05. www.makhila.com.*

▷ *Follow the D 932 towards Bayonne and turn left onto the D 3 just before reaching the motorway.*

Arcangues
This picturesque village is particularly attractive around the church, the inn and the pelota court. Inside the church, with its carved galleries, there is a large Empire-style chandelier and a bas-relief representing the beheading of John the Baptist, patron saint of the parish. The landscaped cemetery with its characteristic Basque tombstones (a stone disc on a plinth) offers a panoramic **view**★ of the Basque Pyrenees.

▷ *Continue along the D 3.*

The winding road snakes through Ustaritz Forest. Beyond, the descent towards St-Pée offers distant glimpses of La Rhune, the Irun depression, the promontory of Jaizkibel and the sea. To the east, the minor Artzamendi range closes off the upper Nivelle basin.

▷ *In St-Pée-de-Nivelle, turn right (west) onto the D 918 to St-Jean-de-Luz.*

ST-JEAN-PIED-DE-PORT★

POPULATION 1 417

MICHELIN MAP 342: E-4

The old town of St-Jean-Pied-de-Port on the north bank of the Nive is encircled by 15C ramparts dating from the time of Navarrese domination. The citadel and fortifications on the south bank, built to defend the road to Spain after the Treaty of the Pyrenees, are part of the 17C military complex designed by Vauban.

▶ **Orient Yourself**: The town, once the capital of Lower Navarre, lies in a mild, picturesque basin watered by the Nive and Petite Nive rivers, its red sandstone houses grouped around a spur crowned by the old citadel. It is situated in the foothills of the Pyrenees, not far from the Spanish border.

🅿 **Parking**: Park near the Porte de France and follow the ramparts to the stairs that lead up to the Porte St-Jacques.

👁 **Also See**: GROTTES D'ISTURITZ ET OXOCELHAYA, AINHOA, IXTASSOU.

A Bit of History

Pilgrims' Way

In the Middle Ages St-Jean was a great rallying centre for *Jacquets*, the pilgrims en route for Santiago de Compostela, who journeyed from all over Europe. They wore a heavy grey cloak, a broad-brimmed felt hat turned up at the front and marked with three or four scallop shells (the emblems of the pilgrimage), and carried a bread bag and an eight-foot stave with a water flask attached. Whenever a devout procession of the pious was announced, the town became a hive of activity: church bells pealed, priests intoned prayers, children ran out to escort the pilgrims, and the inhabitants, standing on their doorsteps, offered provisions. Then the pilgrims would move on, chanting the responses; those too tired to continue could stop in rue de la Citadelle, where the monks from Roncesvalles had organised a refuge for them. The name St-Jean-Pied-de-Port is a reminder that the town lies at the foot of a port or pass: for travellers heading for Spain it was the last stop before the climb to Puerto Ibaêeta, or Port de Roncevaux as it is known on the French side (alt 1 058m/3 468ft), 25km/16mi away on Spanish territory. Beyond the crest, the monastery of Roncesvalles (Roncevaux to the French) has maintained a tradition of Christian hospitality since the 12C – and preserved the memory of the brave hero Roland, who fell in the year 778 when the rear guard of Charlemagne's army

Houses along the River Nive

B. Kaufmann/MICHELIN

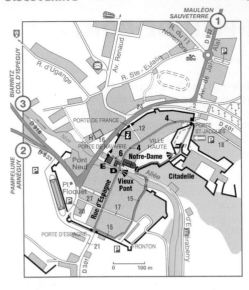

was overwhelmed by Basque mountain people on the way back from a campaign against the Saracens in Spain. According to the tale, Roland, though urged to do so by his councillors, was too proud to blow his horn to sound the retreat in time to save his men. In the ancient epic of *The Song of Roland* the mountain people themselves are transformed into Saracens. In one version of the legend, the cleft in the rock formed when Roland tried to break his magic sword is near the Cirque de Gavarnie; in another it is here at Roncesvalles.

Walking Tour
Allow 1hr 30 min

Rue de la Citadelle
The street, sloping down towards the river, is bordered by charming 16C and 17C houses with rounded doorways and carved lintels. At number 41, the "**prison des évêques**" (bishops' jail) houses an exhibition which evokes the paths to Santiago de Compostella in the Middle-Ages. On the way, you will find a city map and posters in front of the Tourist Information Centre (at each door, rue d'Espagne and at the citadel).

Église Notre-Dame
The Gothic church, dedicated to the Virgin, has handsome sandstone pillars.

Rue de l'Église
This street leads from the church to Porte de Navarre, passing the former hospital which now houses a library and the **house of the Jassu family**, paternal ancestors of St François-Xavier (1506-52).

▶ *Return to the church, pass through the vaulted passage beneath the belfry and cross the river.*

Vieux Pont
From the Old Bridge there is a picturesque view of the church, which is incorporated into the ramparts, and the old riverside houses.

Rue d'Espagne
The street, which climbs uphill to Porte d'Espagne through which the pilgrims left the town, has always been one of the main shopping areas.

▶ *Follow avenue du Fronton to the left, cross the river again, walk to the back of the church and take the steps.*

Citadelle
From the bastion facing the entrance to the citadel, the view stretches over the St-Jean basin and the neat little villages within it (viewpoint indicator).

▶ *Return to Porte St-Jacques.*

ST-SAVIN★★

MICHELIN MAP 322: L-5

St-Savin is famous for its Romanesque abbey church, which is decorated with the finest and most complete series of mural paintings in France. The site is now on UNESCO's World Heritage List.

▶ **Orient Yourself**: The Abbaye de St-Savin is situated on the west bank of the River Gartempe, 42km/26mi E of Poitiers.

Also See: ANGLES-SUR-L'ANGLIN, POITIERS.

A Bit of History

Part of the Legend

Towards the middle of the 5C in Macedonia, two brothers, Savin and Cyprien, were summoned to appear in front of the proconsul Ladicius for having refused to worship certain idols. The brothers were condemned to death, and all pleas for mercy were in vain. They were imprisoned but managed to escape and left for the Gauls, though their executioners caught up with them on the banks of the Gartempe: the brothers were decapitated on the spot. Savin's body was buried by priests on a height known at the time as Three Cypresses Mount, not far from where the town of St-Savin stands today.

The Building Stages

The first abbey church was erected in the 9C, near the sacred burial site, and placed under the patronage of the martyr Savin. Louis the Debonair installed twenty Benedictine monks in the abbey under the tutelage, it is said, of Benoît d'Aniane.

In 878 the abbey was pillaged by the Normans, despite it being protected by a line of fortifications. Reconstruction did not begin until the 11C but was finished in a relatively short space of time. The painted decoration, which completely covered the interior of the church, was added as the building work progressed.

Decline and Rebirth

The Hundred Years War brought to an end the period of relative prosperity enjoyed by the monks up to that time; the abbey was caught up in violent battles between soldiers loyal to the King of France and those fighting for the Black Prince. In the 16C the Wars of Religion saw the Catholics and the Huguenots in furious conflict over possession of the abbey: it was devastated in 1562 and 1568 by the Huguenots, who burnt the choir stalls, the organ and the timber roof, and pillaged six years later by the Royal army. Most of the buildings were later demolished as their upkeep was too expensive.

From 1611 to 1635 an adventurer who liked to call himself the Baron of the Francs installed himself in the church as though it were a stronghold. The arrival, in 1640, of monks from Saint-Maur finally brought an end to the profanities to which the abbey had been subjected for three centuries. However, though the monks saved the buildings from total ruin, the wall paintings suffered from various efforts to restore them.

In 1836 Prosper Mérimée, the writer and Inspector of Historic Monuments, had the church listed as a historic monument and organised important restoration works which continued for almost a century.

An unrelated historical anecdote: it was an engineer from St-Savin, Léon Edoux, who in 1867 invented the hydraulic elevator and perfected it in trials within the bishop's lodgings; he gave it the name *ascenseur*.

Visit

🕐 *Church open all day; visitors are requested to be quiet and discreet during services.* *Guided tour of the church and abbey buildings (1hr 15min + 30min film); the tour schedule varies with the season, call ahead for information.* **⊘***Closed Jan, 11 Nov, 25 and 31 Dec.* ⊚ *6€ (children aged 12-18 4.50€).* ☏*05 49 84 30 00.*

Wall Paintings★★★

Some paintings were destroyed during the devastation visited on the abbey, others were damaged by whitewash which the monks applied, still others suffered as a result of the first phases of restoration.

Unlike most frescoes painted from a preliminary sketch, the paintings here were drawn directly onto the wall, using a process halfway between the fresco technique and distemper-painting: the colours were applied to old plaster, thereby penetrating only the top level of this coating and forming a very thin layer. The few colours used include yellow-ochre, red-ochre and green, mixed with black and white.

The overall effect is one of gentle tones but avoids being insipid through the use of contrast: the different characters are portrayed with great liveliness, their feet suggesting movement, their forms revealed by the moulding of their clothes, their hands often disproportionately long, accentuating the expressive qualities. This dancing, rhythmic allure is also found in Romanesque sculpture. Faces have large, simple, bold features, with red and white marks describing cheeks, nostrils and chins.

In the **narthex** the various painted scenes recount episodes from the Apocalypse: Christ in Majesty in Celestial Jerusalem, Combat between the Archangel and the Beast, the New Jerusalem, the Plague of Grasshoppers. The predominantly pale tones (green, yellow-ochre, red-ochre) allow the scenes to be clearly read despite the darkness inside the porch.

The **nave**, however, is the setting for the true masterpiece which is highlighted by the purity of the architecture. The stories told in the carefully-restored paintings on the vaulting unfold at a height of over 16m/52ft and cover an area of 412m^2/1 351sq ft. The most strik-

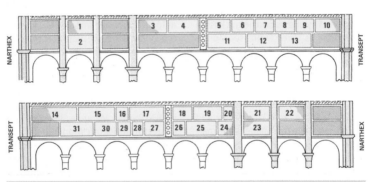

1. Creation of the stars (God adds the Sun and the Moon to the firmament).
2. Creation of Woman – God presents Eve to Adam – Eve and the serpent.
3. Eve, seated, spins.
4. The offerings of Cain and Abel (Abel, God's chosen one, is the only one haloed).
5. Abel's murder – Cain's curse.
6. Enoch, his arms raised to heaven, invokes God – God tells Noah of the forthcoming flood and invites him to build the ark.
7. Noah's ark during the flood.
8. God blesses Noah's family leaving the ark (showing the famous "Beau Dieu" representation of God).
9. Noah sacrifices a pair of birds and a lamb in thanksgiving.
10. Noah's vineyard. Before continuing with the story of Noah on the right-hand section, note the scenes on the lower register which tell the end of Exodus and include the life of Moses.
11. Passage through the Red Sea: the waters swallow up the Egyptian cavalry and Pharaoh's chariot.
12. The Angel of God and the column of fire separate the Egyptians and the Hebrews and protect the latter who march in rows, led by Moses.
13. Moses receives the Tables of Law from God.
14. Noah drinks and dances, a goblet in hand.
15. Drunken Noah lies asleep, his robes in disarray; Ham mocks his father, while his brothers Shem and Japhet cover him with a blanket.
16. Noah curses Canaan in front of Shem and Japhet.
17. Construction of the tower of Babel.
18. The call of Abraham (♿ see illustration).
19. Abraham and Lot's separation.
20. Announcement of the combat of the kings and call for help from Lot of Abraham.
21. The combat of the Kings *(removed)*.
22. Meeting between Abraham and Melchizedeck, King of Salem and priest of Most High, who brings him bread and wine *(removed)*.
23. Death of Abraham.
24. Isaac blesses his son Jacob.
25. Joseph sold by his brothers.
26. Joseph bought by Potiphar, one of Pharaoh's officers.
27. Joseph, Potiphar and his wife (the temptation of Joseph).
28. Joseph in prison.
29. Joseph explains Pharaoh's dream.
30. Pharaoh puts his ring on Joseph's finger and makes him his administrator.
31. Joseph's triumph.

The nave

ing thing initially is the soft tones – beige and pink – of the columns supporting the vaulting. The vaulting itself is covered with famous scenes from the Book of Genesis and the Book of Exodus, ranged in two rows along either side of the centre ridge, which forms a decorative band. A painting behind the main door shows the Triumph of the Virgin.

Two sections are distinguishable in the nave. The first three bays, which make up the first part of the nave, are separated by transverse ribs, while the rest of the vaulting is a continuous barrel which made painting that section of the ceiling easier; the painter nevertheless added a false rib between the 5th and 6th bays.

Stand in the south aisle to see the frescoes on the left-hand side of the nave (illustration p423). Then cross the transept crossing and stand at the beginning of the left-hand aisle to view the paintings on the right-hand side of the ceiling (illustration above).

The scenes listed in the illustrations are recognisable.

Abbey buildings★

These were rebuilt in the 17C in the extension of the church's transept arm; they have since been restored.

The old **refectory**, to the right of the entrance, houses exhibits of contempo-

rary mural art organised by CIAM, the International Centre for Mural Art, which is based within the abbey.

To the left, in the **chapter house**, photographs reveal the appearance of the church crypt (*closed for conservation reasons*).

From the garden, which the river runs through, there is an attractive view over the elegant rear face of the abbey buildings, from the bishop's lodgings (on the left), which are of medieval origin, although remodelled in the 17C and 19C, across to the east end of the church with its apse, apsidal chapels and belfry.

Abbey Church★★

The church, a handsome combination of harmony and sobriety, is also striking for its sheer size: 76m/250ft long with a transept 31m/101ft across and a spire rising to 77m/252ft.

Inside the church, in the nave, there are fine **capitals** deeply-carved with foliage and animals; those by the chancel are decorated with acanthus leaves and lions. The best **view★** of the church is from the far side of the river. On the left extend the abbey buildings and the elegant belfry-porch – overshadowing the apse, the apsidal chapels and the squat belfry; it is crowned by a crocketed spire surrounded by turrets. On the right stands **Vieux Pont** (the Old Bridge), which dates from the 13C and 14C.

SAINT-SEVER

POPULATION 4 455

MICHELIN MAP 335: H-12

St-Sever offers good views of the River Adour and the enormous sea of pines that covers the neighbouring Landes. The one-time "city of scholars" is a useful base for excursions through the Chalosse region and the departure point of a corniche (D 32) winding above local meadows bordering the course of the Adour.

▶ **Orient Yourself**: St-Sever is situated 12km/7mi S of Mont-de-Marsan.
▣ **Parking**: Follow signs to the "centre historique" and park near the church.
◔ **Also See**: HAGETMAU, MONT-DE-MARSAN.

Sights

Église

The Romanesque abbey church (partly restored in the 17C and 19C) features a chancel with 6 apsidal chapels of decreasing depth, and transept arms which end in galleries resting on a single column which develops, above, into a purely decorative arcade. The marble columns of the chancel and transept were taken from the old palace of the Roman governors of Morlanne; their remarkable **capitals★** include water-leaf (11C) and lion designs, historiated capitals (inside the west front) showing Herod's banquet and the beheading of John the Baptist, and a mixture of figures symbolising the predominance of the New Testament over the Old. The **sacristy** leads to the cloisters, only two sides of which remain. Outside, the **east end** of the church is crowned with a dome and a lantern, and surrounded by the Romanesque apsidal chapels which have amusing modillions.

A historiated capital

A. Thuillier/MICHELIN

Rue du Général-Lamarque

This street is lined with a few 18C mansions (nos 6, 18, 20 and 26); others dating from the 19C include General Lamarque's former residence at nos 8 and 11; note the neo-Classical doorway of the edifice and the two pavilions flanking it. 16C mansion at no 21.

The former **Jacobin convent**, which has been turned into a cultural centre, has late-17C brick-built cloisters. ◷Open Jul-Sep daily 2.30-6pm. Rest of the year on request 1 week in advance at the tourist office. ☎05 58 76 34 64

Promenade de Morlanne

Access by car. From the viewpoint, the panorama encompasses the River Adour below and the vast "sea of pine trees" offering a striking contrast with the rolling hills of the Chalosse.

Driving Tours

① Le Tursan★

63km/38mi – about 4hrs.

▶ *Leave St-Sever southeast on the D 944; left on D65 in Aubagnan.*

Vielle-Tursan

From the terrace of the town hall, there is a nice view over the rolling landscape of the Tursan region. Wines from the area were exported in the 17C and have recently experienced a renewed popularity. *Courses landaises*, the regional sport involving deftly avoiding cows with very sharp horns, are held in local arenas.

Address Book

For coin ranges, see the Legend on the cover flap.

WHERE TO STAY

Hôtel Alios – 40500 Bas-Mauco – 4.5km/0.54 mi NE of St-Sever via rte de Mont-de-Marsan – 05 58 76 44 00 – hotel.alios@club-internet.fr – closed 2-22 Aug – 10 rooms – restaurant. A practical address for an affordable overnight stay. The rooms are simple and functional. Traditional cuisine is served in a bright dining room with a veranda.

WHERE TO EAT

Auberge du Moulin – Rte de Dax – 40330 Amou – 11km/6.6mi S of Gaujacq.

Take the D 158 then the D 15 (dir. Dax) – 05 58 89 30 09 – closed Nov-May – . Canard gras (fattened duck) is the speciality of this country inn. The pretty, rather old-fashioned dining room features coloured tiles and Basque tablecloths. Peace and quiet guaranteed on the terrace.

Le Relais du Pavillon – 2km/1.2mi N of St-Sever at the crossroads of the D 933 and D 924 – 05 58 76 20 22 – relaispavillon@club-internet.fr – closed 3-17 Jan, Sat eve, Sun eve and Mon. This restaurant housed in a building dating from the sixties stands near a busy crossroads outside the city. The attractive dining room, terrace and guestrooms all overlook the garden and pool.

▶ *Continue along the D 65. The twisting road crosses the rise that separates the parallel valleys carved out by affluents of the River Adour.*

Eugénie-les-Bains   Spa

The town, created in 1861, is named for the Empress Eugénie, considered the "godmother" of the town. Two springs, L'Impératrice and Christine-Marie, provide relief to visitors suffering from rheumatism; obesity, urological and intestinal problems. The spa also offers short stays for quick weight loss.

▶ *Take the D 11 south to Geaune, and enjoy the views of the mountains.*

Geaune

This former English *bastide* is now home to the coopérative des vignerons du Tursan, the local winegrowers' coöp. There is a lovely square with arcades along three sides.

▶ *Take the D 2 west to Samadet.*

Samadet

See HAGETMAU.

▶ *Continue along the D 2. Hagetmau is in the Chalosse region. Return to St-Sever on the D 933.*

2 Chalosse★

71km/44mi round trip from St-Sever. Allow half a day.

▶ *Drive south-west out of St-Sever along the D 21.*

Chalosse, a hilly region nestling within the great curve of the River Adour, has yet to be discovered by the crowds. Fertile patches of "wild" sand – visible in cuts and ditches – stud the region. Despite the modest aspect of the smallholdings and villages, which are in the Landes style, the agriculture is productive and well-balanced. Chalosse has a long history: it is in this region that Palaeolithic man fashioned such primal masterpieces as the celebrated Lady of Brassempouy; later, pilgrims passed through on their way to Santiago de Compostela.

Audignon

The village has an interesting church enclosed within a seemingly fortified cemetery. Note, in the chancel, the remarkable stone altarpiece with its coloured frescoes. The Romanesque east end contrasts with the belfry-porch and its octagonal Gothic spire. In the 14C, the medieval keep became the church tower.

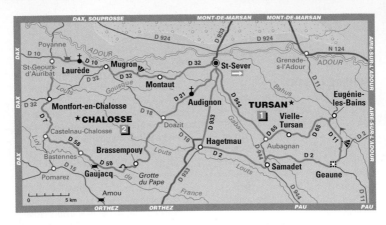

> *Continue along the narrow D 21 which winds through the wooded hills.*

Brassempouy
See HAGETMAU.
Between Brassempouy and Bastennes, the D 58 runs through rolling hills.

Château de Gaujac
Visit by guided tours (1hr) Jul-Aug 11am, 2pm, 3pm, 4pm, 5pm, 6pm; Jun, daily except Wed 3pm, 4pm, 5pm, 6pm; mid-Feb–end May and early Sep–mid-Nov daily except Wed 3pm, 4pm, 5pm. 5€ (children 2€). 05 58 89 01 01.
The elegant château (17C) is visible behind a screen of magnolias, with the Pyrenees in the distance. The courtyard forms a cloister with a garden and a gallery. Several rooms are open to the public. They are furnished, decorated with wooden panelling. In the guard's dining room, in which the table is set, note the cupboard with several pieces of earthenware and a marble fountain. Don't miss the chest-of-drawers from the school of Boule in the green sitting room. The room called "chambre du Cardinal", in memory of François de Sourdis, archbishop of Bordeaux, who gave their nuptial benediction to Louis XIII and Anne of Austria in 1615, contains a remarkable *bargegno* (cabinet) from the 15C.
Plantarium *Open Jul-Aug and Feb-Mar 2.30-6.30pm; rest of the year, daily except Wed 2.30-6.30pm. Closed mid-Dec to mid-Jan. 5€ (children: 2€). 05 58 89 24 22.* This is located at the back of the castle (entrance on the right) and is

divided into eight colourful and fragrant flower beds and surrounded with a pergola.

> *In Castelnau-Chalosse, turn north onto the D 7 to Montfort.*

Montfort-en-Chalosse
The nucleus of this small town is a hillock criss-crossed by narrow lanes and steep, stepped streets. **Musée de la Chalosse** and the nearby Médiathèque are both devoted to country life and the economy of this pleasant rural region. *Open Nov-Mar daily except Mon, Sat and Sun 2-5.30pm; Apr-Oct daily except Mon 10am-noon and 2-6.30pm, Sat-Sun 2-6.30pm. 4.80€. 05 58 98 69 27.*

> *Continue along the D 7 then the D 10, passing the 17C Poyanne Château to Laurède.*

Laurède
The village **church** boasts a striking Baroque interior. Of particular note are the monumental high altar surmounted by a baldaquin, the pulpit and lectern, and the woodwork in the sacristy. *Guided tours available (1hr) Fri at 3pm by appointment at the tourist office of Mugron. 05 58 97 99 40.*

> *Continue on D10*

Mugron
This small town is the "county town" of the region and is heavily involved in the development of agriculture in the Cha-

losse (wine co-operative, grain silos). At the time of the Intendants, the small port on the Adour nearby used to export the local wine as far as Holland. From the public gardens around the town hall, once the hillside home of a rich bourgeois family, there are fine **views★** of the valley.

▶ *Take D32 E*

Between Mugron and Montaut there are frequent views of the rear of the plateau, the promontories dropping down in succession towards the Adour and the pignada (a local term for the forest of maritime pines).

Montaut

The main street of this old fortified village runs along the crest crowning the last fold of the Chalosse plateau; its charming houses look out over the plain of the Adour and the forests of the Landes. The church tower, which is also the gateway to the town, was rebuilt after the ravages perpetrated by the bands under Montgomery. The two altarpieces inside the church reveal interesting stylistic differences: that on the right-hand (south) side features a strict rhythm of perpendiculars, in contrast with the sinuous, flowing lines of the Baroque reredos on the left. The former dates from the early 17C, the latter from the 18C.

▶ *The D 32 leads back to St-Sever.*

ST-VINCENT-SUR-JARD

POPULATION 871
MICHELIN MAP 316: G-9

St-Vincent, a seaside village on the Vendée coast, evokes the fighting spirit of the French political leader Georges Clemenceau (1841-1929) who spent the last years of his tumultuous life here.

- 🛈 **Tourist Office**: Rte du Jard – 85520 St-Vincent-sur-Jard.
  ☎02 51 33 62 06. www.ot.saintvincentsurjard.com
- ▶ **Orient Yourself**: St-Vincent-sur-Jard is situated on the Atlantic Coast, S of La Roche-sur-Yon and N of the Île de Ré.
- 🕭 **Also See**: MARAIS POITEVIN, SABLES-D'OLONNE, ROCHE-SUR-YON, ÎLE DE RÉ.

A Bit of History

Clemenceau, the son of a bourgeois family in the Vendée, launched himself into politics in 1869 after studying medicine and visiting the United States. He was Mayor of Montmartre by 1870 and a member of the National Assembly (Parliament) a year later. Representing the extreme Left of the time, he earned a reputation as a fighter of duels and a destroyer of ministers (he earned the nickname "the Tiger" because of the ferocity of his parliamentary attacks).

In 1906 Clemenceau became a minister (for Home Affairs) and also President of the Conseil (Cabinet), and instituted a vigorous policy of reform. Ousted by the Radicals in 1909 after he had harshly repressed a series of strikes in the South,

he founded a newspaper which bitterly attacked every government until 1917, when he was recalled to the Presidency of the Conseil. It was then that he began to mobilise the enthusiasm of the French, visiting the Western Front, encouraging the troops, sustaining the morale of the civilians: the Tiger had become the Father of Victory. He presided over the 1919 peace conference, resigned his chairmanship in 1920 and retired to his house in St-Vincent after over half a century of politics.

Visit

Maison de Georges Clemenceau

🕭♿*Visit by guided tour (30min, last admission 1hr before closing time) mid-May–mid-Sep 9.30am-12.30pm and 2-*

M. Thiery/MICHELIN

Clemenceau's house

6.30pm; mid-Sep–mid-May daily except
Mon 10am-12.30pm and 2-5.30pm.
🕐Closed 1 Jan, 1 May, 1 Nov, 25 Dec.
🎟4.60€, no charge the first Sun of the
month. ☎02 51 33 40 32.
The house is a short distance from the
village, at the end of route D 19A.
The site, facing the ocean and the Île de
Ré, has a hint of grandeur about it, and
is a suitable resting-place for the wild
and restless spirit of the old warrior.
The low building, typical of the Vendée,
has been preserved exactly as it was when
Clemenceau died. The tour includes the
salon, Clemenceau's bedroom-study, a
kitchen-dining room containing a hammered copper watering-can which is
believed to have belonged to Marie-
Antoinette, and the thatched summer-
house, all of which are filled with souvenirs recalling his political life.
In the garden, which flowers with the
roses Clemenceau always loved, there
is a bust of the grand old man.

Le Talmondais
Driving Tour

Round-trip of 55km/34mi – 3hrs.

▶ *Leave St-Vincent-sur-Jard by the west.*

Abbaye Notre-Dame-
de-Lieu-Dieu

The imposing mass of this ancient abbey,
founded in 1190 by Richard the Lionheart,

lies between the marshes of Talmont and
the coastal pine woods of Jard. Sacked
and pillaged during the Hundred Years
War, ruined by the Protestants in the 16C,
the abbey was rebuilt by Premonstratensian monks in the 17C, when the storey with octagonal corner bartizans was
added. By the end of that century, however, the abbey was again abandoned.
Today the fine Plantagenet vaulting can
still be admired in the chapter-house,
which opens onto a garden laid out on
the site of the old cloisters.

▶ *Follow the road to a car park in front
of a farm called St-Nicolas.*

Pointe du Payré★

🚶The best way to explore this nature
reserve is on foot *(2hrs 30min round trip)*.
A path leads through a forest of evergreen oaks, holly and ivy, among dunes
and marshes. Closer to the shorelines,
the sea winds and salt spray have twisted
the evergreen oaks into fantastic shapes.
The view from the water's edge takes in
the charming sandy Plage des Mines on
the right and the cove of St-Nicolas framed
by cliffs overlooking the rocky foreshore
on the left. On the way back through the
undergrowth along the shoreline, it is
important to keep to the footpath in
order to protect the ecosystem. The view
can be admired from the rocky outcrops
along the way. The path sometimes passes
beneath curious canopies formed by the
criss crossed branches of the evergreen
oaks on either side. Pointe de Payré affords
a fine view of Le Veillon cliffs.

▶ *Return via Jard-sur-Mer then take
the D 21 northwards. After 2km/1mi,
turn left.*

La Boulière marshes run along the side
of the road to the left.

▶ *Turn left along the D 180.*

The road leads to the **port** which marks
the beginning of a zone of oyster farms
at the junction of the Île Bernard and
Payré channels.

▶ *Rejoin the D 108 and continue
northwards.*

Talmont-St-Hilaire

The town is in the marshy alluvial zone of the Payré Estuary, east of the Sables-d'Olonne. The **château** in ruins (11C) rises up above the former port; the view from the top of the keep extends as far as the sea. ◷ *Open mid-Jun–mid-Sep, daily 10.30am-7pm; early Mar–mid-Jun, 10.30am-12.30pm and 2-6.30pm; end Sep–early Nov, 2-6pm.* ✆ *telephone for tarifs* ☎*02 51 90 27 43.*

Tourists can also admire the nearly 140 vehicles in the **Musée Automobile de Vendée**★, 2.5km/1.5mi northwest of town. The vintage automobiles on display, made between 1885 and 1970, are restored and in working condition. Among the many models built before the First World War are a Léon Bollé (with an odd resemblance to a railway car), a 1906 Renault, 1908 Monobloc and a Peugeot Lion from 1910. ⛭◷*Open Jun-Aug, 9.30am-7pm (last admission 1hr before closing time); Apr-May and Sep, 9.30am-noon and 2 6.30pm;* ◷*Closed 1 Jan, 25 Dec.* ✆*8.10€ (children 4.40€).* ☎*02 51 22 05 81; www.musee-auto-vendee.com*

▸ *Leave Talmont east along the D 949 for 4km/2mi. At Poteau, turn right.*

St-Hilaire-la-Forêt

This little village is the gateway to the Talmondais megalithic region with its astonishing number of dolmens and menhirs. Together with Île d'Yeu *(⛭see ÎLE D'YEU)* this area has the richest collection of Neolithic upright stones in Vendée.

Centre Archéologique d'Initiation et de Recherche sur le Néolithique – ⛭◷*Open Jul–Aug 11am-7pm; Apr–Jun and Sep, daily except Sat 2-6pm.* ✆*5.80€ (children aged 7-11 2.50€.* ☎*02 51 33 38 38.*

This archaeological research centre focuses on the Neolithic period. Explanatory panels convey information on this ancient civilisation and there is a fine display of photographs illustrating the principal sites in western France. A visit to the centre is completed by a diorama presentation on the Neolithic megaliths of the Talmont *(illuminated map)* and a video-recording. Outside, in season, there are **demonstrations of prehistoric techniques**★: the

---

Address Book

⛭*For coin ranges, see the Legend on the cover flap.*

WHERE TO STAY

◿**Camping Les Écureuils** – *rte des Goffineaux – 85520 Jard-sur-Mer – 3km/ 1.8mi W of St-Vincent on a secondary road –* ☎*02 51 33 42 74 – camping-ecureuils@wanadoo.fr – open 15 May-15 Sep – reservation recommended – 261 pitches – restaurant.* In a holm oak and pine forest 300m from the ocean, this campsite has friendly staff, a well-designed layout and attractive surroundings that make up for the slight lack of space. Swimming pool and kids' club.

◿◿**Hôtel de l'Océan** – *1km/0.6mi S of St-Vincent –* ☎*02 51 33 40 45 – hotel. locean@wanadoo.fr – closed 15 Nov-27 Feb and Wed from Apr to Sep –* ▱ *– 37 rms – restaurant*◿◿. Right next to Georges Clemenceau's house and 50m from the beach, this family hotel is appreciated by a clientele of regulars who come back year after year to enjoy a holiday by the seaside. Traditional decor, friendly atmosphere and peace and quiet guaranteed.

WHERE TO EAT

◿**Le Chalet St-Hubert** – *rte de Jard –* ☎*02 51 33 40 33.* You will be welcomed at the bar before entering a light, modern dining-room with large French-windows. Traditional food served at reasonable prices. If you choose to stay at the hotel, ask for one of the ground-level rooms – they're bigger and open onto the garden.

◿◿**Le Menhir** – *Av. du Gén.-de-Gaulle – 85440 Avrillé –* ☎*02 51 22 32 18 – closed 15 Jan-28 Feb, Sun eve from Sep to Jun and Mon.* A convivial auberge siuated in a village famous for its menhir, the tallest of Vendée. Country-style decor with an inviting fireplace; traditional, simple cuisine.

building of a dolmen, stone polishing techniques, etc. A number of plants known to have flourished in Neolithic times have been sown.

Bicycles may be hired for exploring the megalithic sites in the area *(the trail is indicated by arrows)*.

▶ *Leave St-Hilaire north-east via the D 19.*

Avrillé

In the municipal park behind the town hall stands the **Caesar's Camp Menhir**. This, the tallest menhir in Vendée and one of the biggest in France (rising 7m/ 23ft above ground), is the sole survivor of what was once a group of stones.

▶ *Leave Avrillé west via the D 949.*

Château de la Guignardière

Open mid-Jun–Aug 10am-7pm; early Apr to mid-Jun and Sep, 11am-6pm. 9.50€ (children: 7€). 02 51 22 33 06. The château was founded in c 1555 by Géhan Girard, the Panetier (officer charged with the safeguard and distribution of bread) of Henri II, but was never finished because Girard was murdered.

The original garden façade is in the Renaissance style with granite courses and tall, double-mullioned windows. The high chimney stacks are built of brick. A number of alterations – in the same style – were made in the 18C.

Of particular note inside are the monumental chimney pieces in granite; a fine stairway, also in granite, which is halfway between a spiral staircase and one with half-landings; the attics with their magnificent three-stage rafter-work in oak; the vaulted cellars.

A trail through the grounds leads to a series of ponds fringed by bald cypress, with unique structures called "knees" (conical outgrowths of lateral roots) projecting upwards, and – hidden in Fourgon Wood – to three groups of menhirs which were once part of an ancient alignment. The tallest of these megaliths measures about 6m/20ft.

▶ *Return to Avrillé and take the D 105 south-east, then turn left along the D 91A. At Bernard, turn left along the D 91, then left again at the calvary.*

The three **Savatole dolmens** can be seen on the right-hand side of the road (explanatory panel).

Dolmen de la Frébouchère

This impressive granite monument, of the so-called Angevin type, consists of a stone portico leading to a rectangular chamber. The single slab of rock (now cracked) covering the chamber weighs about 80 tonnes.

Frébouchère dolmen

B. Kaufmann/MICHELIN

▶ *Continue south along the D 91. At Longeville-sur-Mer, take the D 105 for 1km/0.6mi towards La Tranche-sur-Mer, then turn right.*

The road along the north side of the Longeville forest leads back to St-Vincent-sur-Jard.

SAINTES★★

POPULATION 25 595

MICHELIN MAP 324: G-5

With its plane trees, white houses and red-tiled rooftops, Saintes has a distinctly Mediterranean feel. This prosperous, regional capital on the banks of the River Charente has a rich cultural and historical heritage, with monuments dating from every period since the Romans. The town has given its name to the Saintonge, an old province in the western Charentes.

🗊 **Information:** Villa Musso – 62 cours National – 17100 Saintes.
☎05 46 74 23 82. www.ot.saintes.fr

▶ **Orient Yourself**: Saintes is located just off the A 10 motorway between Cognac and Royan. The town is crossed by avenue Gambetta, cours National and cours Lemercier, busy shopping streets which are shaded by plane trees.

🅿 **Parking**: There are a number of car parks in the town centre *(see map)*.

◉ **Don't Miss**: Abbaye aux Dames; the old town; Arc de Germanicus; Musée des Beaux-Arts; the Arènes.

◔ **Also See**: COGNAC, ROCHEFORT, ÎLE D'OLÉRON, ÉGLISE ST-PIERRE D'AULNAY.

A Bit of History

Origins

"Mediolanum Santonum", capital of the Santons during the Roman domination of the Vendée, was built on the hillside sloping up from the west bank of the Charente; the river was spanned by a bridge on which the Arch of Germanicus was erected. The Latin poet Ausonius died in this town, in his Villa Pagus Noverus, at the time St Eutrope was beginning to preach the Gospel.

In the Middle Ages, when Saintes was under Plantagenet rule, religious buildings sprang up all over the town; pilgrims on the way to Santiago de Compostela *(see Introduction, The Way of St James)* filed continuously across the bridge. They were welcomed and sent on their way to two suburbs which had developed around religious establishments: St-Eutrope and, on the east bank of the Charente, the Abbaye aux Dames.

Until the Revolution – under which Saintes became the county seat of Lower Charente but was deprived of its bishopric – so many luxurious mansions were built by local nobles and lawyers that the town could serve as a lesson in the evolution of Classical architecture.

Town planning had its place in 18C Saintes, laying out the thoroughfares on the perimeter of the old town along the site of the ancient ramparts. In the 19C Cours National (the principal axis of the modern town) was bordered with neo-Classical public buildings; among them, on opposite sides of the avenue, are the law courts and the theatre.

A Determined Man

In c1539 a man called **Bernard Palissy** (1510-90) was working in Saintes as a surveyor. He decided, however, to renounce this profession and devote his time to the art of ceramics, and set up a studio-workshop near the ramparts. Here, in a state of complete privation, he struggled day and night to survive until he discovered the secret of enamelling. "Maistre Bernard, the worker in earth", as he was known, became celebrated for his enamelled terracotta work.

A philanthropist

Against his will perhaps, **Joseph Ignace Guillotin** (1738-1814), a doctor living in

Saintes, lent his name to France's notorious machine for judicial executions. Until then, decapitation had been reserved for those of noble birth. The doctor believed that all men should be equal at death – and he was anxious to spare the condemned unnecessary suffering. He therefore proposed to the National Assembly in 1789 "a rapid-action beheading machine". Guillotin, himself a deputy, was gratified when the invention was approved; he was less pleased when the death machine was not unnaturally christened, in 1792 when it was first used, La Guillotine.

Walking Tour

Old Town★
Walking Tour

▶ *Park the car on the market square where the walking tour begins.*

The Old Town district around the cathedral on the west bank of the river is characteristic of Saintes, proud of its distinctive image.

Cathédrale St-Pierre

St Peter's Cathedral was built on the site of a Romanesque church; all that remains of the early building is a dome above the south transept. Its construction, under the direction of three successive Bishops of

Saintes, all members of the Rochechouart family, dates in the main from the 15C. It was severely damaged by the Calvinists in 1568. The massive bell tower, made heavier still by enormous buttresses with projecting features, was never completed: a dome with lead panels replaced the spire proposed in the original plans. Angels, saints and prophets adorn the Flamboyant doorway within the porch at the foot of the tower.

Unity and simplicity characterise the architecture of the interior. Stripped of ornamentation, the large round columns of the nave, like the Gothic pillars in the chancel, support a bare upper wall roofed with visible timbers. Only the side aisles are vaulted in stone.

Both nave and aisles date almost in their entirety from the 16C, the great organ from the 16C and 17C. A door in the south transept opens onto the former canons' cloisters (13C), of which two galleries and the ruins of the chapter house remain.

The axial chapel, with its niches surmounted by elaborately carved canopies, exemplifies the final effervescence of the Flamboyant Gothic style; the credences were already Renaissance. The **treasury**, in an annex chapel, displays a collection of sacred vessels and vestments.

▶ *Leave place du Marché, which is beside the cathedral, and follow the whole length of rue St-Michel then turn left onto rue Victor-Hugo.*

The old town along the Charente

M. Thiery/MICHELIN

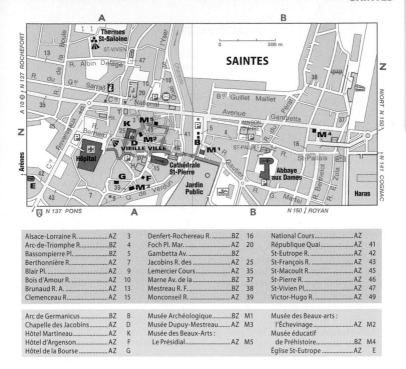

A succession of pretty stone houses in the characteristic Saintonge style, can be seen in Rue Victor-Hugo, once known as Grande-Rue, which follows the course of the old road which led via the Germanicus arch to the bridge across the river.

Présidial★ (Musée des Beaux-Arts)
2 rue Victor-Hugo. Open Jun-Sep daily except Mon 1.30am-6pm; Oct–May daily except Mon 1.30-5pm. Closed 1 Jan, 1 May. 1.60€ (children under 18 no charge), no charge Sun and Wed. 05 46 93 52 39. www.ville-saintes.fr.
Set back at the far end of the garden, the mansion, a former presidential residence (President Le Berthon, 1605), today houses a **fine arts museum** mainly devoted to paintings from the 15-18C (Flemish, Dutch and French schools). Architecturally its façade, with wide bays and dormers topped by triangular pediments, marks the beginning of the Classical period.

▶ *Continue along rue Victor-Hugo as far as rue d'Alsace-Lorraine. Turn left here and continue to place de l'Échevinage.*

Ancien Échevinage
Beyond the Classical gateway, an 18C façade is attached to a turret dating from the 16C. The spiral staircase of this former belfry leads to the **Musée des Beaux Arts de l'Échevinage**, a fine arts museum housing 19C and 20C paintings as well as a splendid collection of Sèvres porcelain from 1890 to 1910. *Open Jun-Sep daily except Mon 1.30am-6pm; Oct–May daily except Mon 1.30-5pm. Closed 1 Jan, 1 May. 1.60€ (children under 18 no charge), no charge Sun and Wed. 05 46 93 52 39. www.ville-saintes.fr.*

▶ *Return to place de l'Échevinage and take rue du Dr-Mauny. Pass through the triple-arcade porch to the Hôtel Martineau courtyard.*

Hôtel Martineau
This mansion is now the home of the municipal library.

Chapelle des Jacobins
This chapel has an elegantly designed bay in the Flamboyant style.

Address Book

⏱*For coin ranges, see the Legend on the cover flap.*

WHERE TO STAY

⊜**Hôtel Avenue** – *114 av. Gambetta – ☎05 46 74 05 91 – contact@hoteldelavenue. com – closed 24 Dec-3 Jan –* 🅿 *– 15 rms.* The rooms of this 1970s hotel in the centre of town are relatively calm because they all face away from the street. Attractive breakfast room.

⊜**Chambre d'hôte Anne et Dominique Trouvé** – *5 r. de l'Église – 17810 St-Georges-des-Coteaux – 9km/5.4mi NW of Saintes. Take the N 137 dir. Rochefort then the D 127 – ☎05 46 92 96 66 – adtrouve@yahoo.fr – closed 15 Nov-28 Mar –* ⊠ *– 4 rms.* Bookworms will love this old farmhouse where the bedrooms are named after authors and contain their works. Enjoy a good read among the old furniture or venture outside to see the 'bujour', the former washing-place.

⊜⊜**Messageries** – *r. des Messageries – ☎05 46 93 64 99 – info@hotel-des-messageries.com – closed 19 Dec-7 Jan –* *33 rms.* Near the historic district, this old stagecoach inn built around a courtyard dates from 1792.

WHERE TO EAT

⊜⊜**Auberge des Glycines** – *4 quai des Gabarriers – 17350 Taillebourg – 16km/10mi N of Saintes. Take the D 114 dir. St-Savinien – ☎05 46 91 81 40 – auberge-des-glycines@wanadoo.fr – closed Feb and Nov.* This bourgeois house is in a charming village on the banks of the Charente. Enjoy the view from the windows of its cosy dining room or have your meal in the secret garden behind the house in the summer. A tranquil restaurant in which to sample excellent regional cuisine.

⊜⊜**Le Bistrot Galant** – *28 r. St-Michel – ☎05 46 93 08 51 – bistrot.galant@ club-internet.fr – closed Sun except noon on public hols and Mon.* This little restaurant in a calm pedestrian street in the centre of Saintes is highly recommended. Interest-ing fixed-price menus, contemporary cuisine and two small, colourful dining rooms.

▸ *Rue des Jacobins. The route passes the rear façade of Hôtel Martineau. Turn left to reach the steps leading up to the hospital.*

Hôpital

This 16C building stands in the middle of attractive flower-filled gardens over-looking the old town.

▸ *Go back down the steps and walk past the cathedral to quai de Verdun.*

Quai de Verdun is lined with the terraced gardens of some 17C and 18C mansions adorned with wrought ironwork and balusters.

▸ *Take the footbridge across the River Charente.*

Jardin public

These public gardens, laid over the town's former parade ground, are decorated with Roman ruins. One end is closed off by a façade built in 18C style and an orangery.

Arc de Germanicus★

This fine Roman arch with its twin arcades stood until 1843 on the bridge that carried the main thoroughfare in Saintes across the River Charente. Threatened with de-struction when the bridge, itself Roman, was about to be demolished, the arch was saved by the intervention of the writer Prosper Merimée, who held the post of Inspector of Historic Monuments. It was dismantled and rebuilt on the east bank of the river.

The structure, built of local limestone and erected in the year AD19, was a votive – not a triumphal – arch. Inscriptions still visible dedicate it to Germanicus, to the Emperor Tiberius, and to his son Drusus. The name of the donor, Caius Julius Rufus, also appears. In the centre of the arch the groins of the three pillars supporting the double arcade are emphasised by fluted columns with Corinthian capitals.

Musée Archéologique

🕐*Open Jun-Sep 10am-6pm, Sun 1.30-6pm; Oct-May 10am-5pm, Sun 1.30-5pm.*

🚫*Closed 1 Jan, 1 May, 25 Dec.* 🎫*1.60€, no charge Sun and Wed.* ☎*05 46 74 20 97. www.ville-saintes.fr.*

The museum houses an interesting lapidary collection, deriving mainly from discoveries made when the wall of the ancient Gallo-Roman *castrum* (fort) was demolished. It includes columns, capitals, architraves and remarkable bas-reliefs. Further traces of Roman remains can be seen in the neighbourhood of the museum.

▶ *From here it is possible to make a detour to Abbaye aux Dames and to come back to the market square via the footbridge.*

Abbaye Aux Dames

🕐*Apr-Sep, 10am-12.30pm and 2-7pm; Oct-Mar daily except Mon 1-6pm.* 🚫*Closed between Christmas and New Year's Day.* 🎫*3€ (children under 16 no charge). 05 46 97 48 48.*

This "Ladies' Abbey", which stands on the east bank of the Charente, was consecrated in 1047. The abbey was dedicated to St Mary, and owed its prosperity to Agnès de Bourgogne, whose second husband was Geoffroy Martel, Comte d'Anjou and seigneur of the Saintonge. The Abbey, placed in the hands of Benedictine nuns, was directed by an Abbess – customarily chosen from among the most illustrious families in France – who then bore the title "Madame de Saintes". Charged with the education of young daughters of the nobility, the convent counted among its boarders at one time Athenaos de Rochechouart, the future Marquise de Montespan and mistress to Louis XIV. After the Revolution and during the Empire period the Abbey fell into decline. It was transformed into a barracks, freed after World War I, but required a great deal of restoration before it could be returned to the Church for religious use.

Abbey Church★

The Abbey Church is in the local Saintonge Romanesque style; it is reached via an 18C porch leading to the Abbey's first courtyard, where it is surrounded by the usual convent buildings. The most remarkable features of the church are the façade and the bell tower. The **façade** presents a richly-ornamented **doorway** at the centre, flanked by blind arcades. The carved coving in the doorway shows, from bottom to top: six angels adoring the Hand of God; the symbols of the Evangelists around the Lamb; the suffering of the martyrs, menaced by a whip, an axe or the Sword of Justice; 54 old men wearing crowns, facing each other two by two as they play music. The coving of the right arcade portrays the Last Supper; that on the left, the presence of a divine Christ facing five other figures suffused with light whose significance is uncertain. Note also the historiated capitals (a knight, monsters) and, on the gable, the arms of Françoise I de La Rochefoucauld, Abbess from 1559 to 1605.

The lower level of the **bell tower**, situated above the transept crossing, is square in section and pierced with three arcades on each face. Above this is a shallow octagonal level flanked by pinnacles which is in turn surmounted by a dome pierced by 12 twinned bays separated by small columns. The whole tower is topped by a scaled conical roof, the slopes of which are slightly convex.

Interior – In the first half of the 12C the interior was the subject of alterations, generally thought to have been made by the architect Béranger (an inscription carved into the outside of the north wall dates the work as pre-1150). The quadripartite vaulting in the transept arms – and the Gothic chapel in the northern arm – are later (15C) additions. The two-bay nave, lined with six heavy 12C pillars erected in front of the 11C walls, is covered with a timber ceiling which replaced the two original domes on pendentives, destroyed by fire in 1648. On the southern side of the transept entrance, a console supports a 12C head of Christ.

At the intersection of the nave and the transept, before the transept crossing and the belfry above it, four more heavy pillars support a dome on squinches. Half-barrel vaulting over the Romanesque chancel is prolonged by a slightly recessed, terminal oven vault.

Convent buildings

The façade of the long 17C central block has been restored to its original purity of line: two storeys pierced by narrow windows and surmounted by an upper level punctuated by dormers with pediments.

On the left, adjoining three renovated bays of the old 14C cloisters, is a fine 17C doorway, the pilasters of which are adorned with exuberant sculptures that contrast strikingly with the severity of the façade.

Arènes★

West of the town centre. ⏰*Open Jun-Sep, 10am-8pm; Oct-May, Mon-Sat 10am-5pm, Sun 1.30-5pm.* ≈*1€.* ☎*05 46 97 73 85.*

A short distance from the centre, the Roman arena – in reality an amphitheatre – owes part of its sylvan attraction and evocative atmosphere to the fact that grass covers a large proportion of the stepped terracing. This is one of the oldest amphitheatres of the Roman world – it was built in the 1C AD – but is relatively small. Overall dimensions of the ellipse are 125m long x 102m wide (413ft x 335ft), while the actual arena, where performances took place, measures 64m x 39m (210ft x 128ft). The terraces could accommodate 20 000 spectators.

Halfway up the terraced slope, on the southern side, there is a gap in which a small fountain plays. This is dedicated to St Eustelle, a young female disciple of St Eutrope who was beheaded here.

Driving Tours

① **Romanesque Churches in the Saintonge★**

Round-trip of 75km/47mi – 4hrs

▸ *Leave Saintes heading west (N 150 then the D 728).*

Église de Corme-Royal

The church, a dependency of Abbaye aux Dames in Saintes, is noted for its two-storey west front decorated with a profusion of delicate carvings. The interior, which has regained its original vaulting, is lit by modern stained-glass windows.

▸ *Return via the D 728. At Nancras go left along the D 117.*

Abbaye de Sablonceaux

⏰*Open year round;* ↩*Guided tours Jul-Aug daily except Tue 3-6pm; rest of the year, guided tour 1st Sun of the month and by advance reservation 3-6pm. Mid-Jul–mid-Aug, son et lumière Wed, Thu, Fri, Sat nights.* ☎*05 46 94 41 62.*

This abbey was founded in 1136 by Guillaume X, the father of Eleanor of Aquitaine. Partially destroyed five times since the 14C, the abbey church with its Romanesque nave and tall Gothic tower has been restored to something like its original splendour. The convent buildings are being restored.

The Roman Amphitheatre

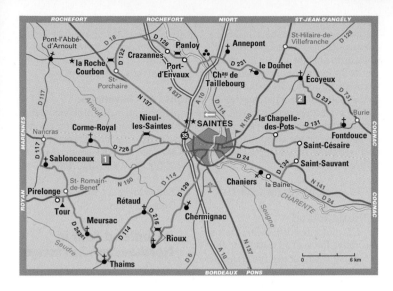

▶ *Take the D 243E1 to St-Romain-de-Benet.*

Hameau de Pirelonge

The hamlet, which has a number of historical houses renovated using traditional methods, boasts a series of small museums which together preserve the local heritage.

Musée des Alambics – Housed in a distillery, this museum displays a collection of alembics (stills) from the Charente region, of the type still in use for the refinement of cognac. The museum also shows a series of "mobile" stills used by home distillers to make alcohol from wine or fruit. A collection of alcoholmeters is interesting.

Musée Charentais de l'Imprimerie – *Same admission times and charges as the Musée des Alambics.* An immense workshop containing about 30 machines (linotype machines and old printing presses) are used to demonstrate the printing methods of the past. Young visitors will discover the amazing history of the printing industry before the age of the computer, when lead still reigned supreme. Some of the houses have displays of **church vestments** (albs, copes and chasubles), paper money (from promissory notes issued during the French Revolution to modern bills) and reconstructions of

craftsman's workshops (blacksmith's, weaver's, barrel-maker's, etc.).

In the autumn, the **Alembic and Harvest Fairs** held in the hamlet revive local traditions.

About 200m/218yd from the hamlet *(behind the railway line)* the **Tour de Pirelonge**, a Roman tower, is still partially roofed with carved stones. Between vineyards and woods, the tower stands on the edge of an old Roman road but its function remains a mystery – boundary marker or religious monument?

▶ *Return via the N 150 towards Saintes. After 500m/550yd turn right onto the D 243E1.*

Église de Meursac

The Gothic church, shored up by powerful buttresses, ends in a Romanesque chancel with half-barrel vaulting. Romanesque capitals in the chancel depict birds pecking lions and a human figure strangling two lions. The altarpiece and tabernacle are of carved and gilded wood. A 5C crypt was discovered beneath the church in 1972; the large chamber was hollowed from the bedrock and has a domed roof (access via a narrow spiral staircase near the chancel).

▶ *Follow the D 243E1 south-east.*

Église de Thaims

The modest church was built on the site of a Gallo-Roman villa (remains of the villa walls, up to a height of 2.5m/8ft, can be seen at the foot of the octagonal church tower, on the north side). In the garden on the southern side of the church are a number of Merovingian sarcophagi. The cornices of the transept crossing inside are Merovingian too, although scenes engraved there, including the Flight of St Peter, are later (Carolingian).

▷ *Leave Thaims north-east via the D 114.*

Église de Rétaud

The 12C church is worth seeing for the decorative frieze of its west front, the octagonal belfry above the transept crossing, and especially for the richly carved, faceted walls of the apse. The consoles, fashioned into grotesques, are interesting. Noteworthy features inside include the two capitals at the entrance to the apse, the small columns framing its bays, and part of a funerary litre (a black band on the church wall decorated with the armorial bearings of the dead).

▷ *Leave Retaud heading south via the D 216.*

Église de Rioux

This simple rural church with a low nave and belfry-porch, is known to art enthusiasts for its brilliant sculptured décor; the **east end★** is particularly noteworthy.

▷ *Leave Rioux north-east via the D 129.*

East end of the church in Rioux

On the way to Chermignac the road passes within view of the Château de Rioux, which belonged in the Middle Ages to the family of the Seigneurs of Didonne, vassals of the Comtes de Poitou.

Église de Chermignac

Frightening animals and different types of human characters adorn the covings above the church entrance. Near the church is a fine example of a **hosanna cross** (*see INTRODUCTION, ARCHITECTURE*).

▷ *Return to the D 129 which leads back to Saintes.*

② **Woodland Tour in Northeastern Saintonge**

Round-trip 39km/24mi – allow 4hrs. Leave Saintes heading east along the N 150.

Château du Douhet

The 17C château, with its sober lines, is thought to have been built from plans drawn up by Jules Hardouin-Mansart (1646-1708), the brilliant classicist architect responsible for the Grand Trianon at Versailles and Place Vendôme in Paris. The château and its dependencies, together with the gardens, park and pools, extend over an area of 20ha/49 acres.

Don't miss the tour of the grounds (1hr on foot), from the Renaissance dovecote to the two mirrored pools of the southern esplanade. These elegant, square, balustraded basins are still fed by the 1C Gallo-Roman aqueduct which once serviced the thermal baths at Saintes. Stop to admire and breathe in the fragrance of the centenary **boxwood★**. Beyond the trees, from the terrace which overlooks the pools, there is a beautiful view across the water to the majestic south face of the château. Inside the château *(access via the steps below the south front)* – where the period furniture and fittings have only partly been preserved – interest centres mainly on the curious salon named The Lantern, with its 17C woodwork. In the right wing a museum of local traditions has been installed, with the reconstruction of an early 19C bourgeois interior in the Saintonge style, and collections of regional prehistoric, Gallo-Roman and mineralogical items.

▶ *Drive east along the D 231 which soon crosses the N 150.*

Écoyeux

The church here is an imposing 12C building, fortified in the 15C – witness the two turreted watchtowers framing the west front.

▶ *Leave Écoyeux south-east via the D 231.*

Abbaye de Fontdouce

🕐 *Open Jul-Aug daily 10.30am-7.30pm. May-Jun and Sep-Oct daily 2.30-6.30pm; Apr, Sun and public hols 10.30am-6.30pm. Guided tour (1hr) available Apr-May and Sep-Oct every Sun 4pm. ☞6€. ☎05 46 74 77 08. www.fontdouce.com.*

This prosperous Benedictine abbey, half hidden in a steep, wooded valley, was sacked by the Huguenots. All that remains today is a small collection of monastic dependencies: a 12C cellar, a heating house with a 15C campanile, the main block dating from the 12C and 13C, and a Charente-style residential hall added to it in the 19C. Visitors can tour the parlour, the two Romanesque chapels one above the other, and especially the magnificent **chapter house★**, with its twelve bays in which the ribbed vaulting rests on a forest of pillars. Notable here are the finely carved keystones, among them a curious three-faced head with four eyes, probably symbolising the Holy Trinity. The abbey church is now only a few ruined columns and a huge pillar base which would have been at the transept crossing.

▶ *Take the D 131 towards Saintes.*

La Chapelle-des-Pots

Locally fashioned ceramics, in a tradition dating back to the 13C, are still made in this village today.

▶ *The D 131 joins the N 141 which leads back to Saintes.*

SAUVETERRE-DE-BÉARN★

POPULATION 1 304
MICHELIN MAP 342: G-2

The small town lies on a picturesque site★ above an escarpment overlooking the Oloron Torrent.

🛈 **Tourist Office**: Pl. Royale – Sauveterre.
☎05 59 38 58 65. www.tourisme-bearn-gaves.com.
▶ **Orient Yourself**: Sauveterre-de-Béarn lies S of the A 64 motorway between Pau and the Atlantic Coast.
👁 **Don't Miss**: The view from the old bridge.
👣 **Also See**: GROTTES D'ISTURITZ ET OXOCELHAYA, ORTHEZ, BAYONNE, PAU.

A Bit of History

The Judgement of God

In the year 1170 Sancie, the widow of Gaston V of Béarn was accused of having killed a child born after her husband's death and was submitted to a trial known as the Judgement of God. On the orders of her own brother, the King of Navarre, she was bound hand and foot and thrown into the river from the top of the town's fortified bridge (👣 *see below*). However, the strong current cast her up on the bank, safe and sound, further downstream – so Sancie was pronounced innocent and had her rights restored.

Sights

Terraces by the Church and the Town Hall

From here there is a wonderful view: the old bridge, the torrent, a tree-covered island, a ruined tower, the Romanesque belfry of the church, the outline of the distant Pyrenees – a most romantic landscape.

Vieux pont

One arch of the ancient bridge remains, surmounted by the town's 12C fortified gateway. The legend of Sancie is explained *(in French)* on a panel. From here again there is a magnificent **view**★★ of the river, the fortifications, the church and the splendid Montréal Tower.

Église St-André

⊙*Open daily 9am-noon and 3-6pm.* ☎*05 59 38 58 65.*

The tympanum above the entrance to St Andrew's Church depicts Christ in Glory surrounded by the four Evangelists. The ribbed vaulting harmonises perfectly with the Romanesque design of the interior. A pillar on the north side of the chancel is topped by a historiated capital representing Scandal-Mongering and Gluttony. The east end, flanked by two apsidal chapels, is surmounted by a quadrangular bell tower pierced by twinned windows.

Excursion

Chapelle de Sunarthe

1.5km/0.9mi E, follow the signs. ☜*Visit by guided tour (1hr) Jul-Aug Tue, Thu, Sat at 3pm and 4pm, Wed and Fri at 3pm; mid-Apr–Jun and Sep Wed and Sat 3pm and 4pm.* ⊛*5€ (children 2.50€).* ☎*05 59 38 58 65 or 06 70 36 79 05.*

There's a *son et lumière* display on the small-scale model of the medieval city of Sauveterre-de-Béarn.

Château de Laàs

9km/5mi SE via the D 27. ☜*Visit by guided tour (1hr, last visit 1hr 30min before closing time) Jul-Aug 10am-7pm; Apr–May and Sep-Oct daily except Tue 2-7pm; Jun daily except Tue 10am-7pm.* ⊛*4€ (ticket provides access to the whole site).* ☎*05 59 38 91 53.*

This is an extraordinary château-museum: by collecting together **furniture**★, objets d'art and family paintings from three different homes, Monsieur and Madame Serbat, the last owners of this 17C manor house, created a decorative arts museum which also serves to illustrate the art of living in the Hainaut region (in the north of France) during the 18C.

LouisXVI panelling adorns the bedchambers and salons. Mme Serbat's room is decorated with illustrations of the *Fables* of La Fontaine. Tapestries and hand-

Sauveterre-de-Béarn

A. Thuillier/MICHELIN

painted fabrics (music room) set off the fine Northern School paintings (Watteau de Lille). Nor is historical anecdote forgotten: a first-floor bedroom recalls the aftermath of Waterloo, for here is the bed Napoleon slept in at Maubert-Fontaine on 19 June 1815. In the library, a curious collection of eleven 17C fans which have not been sewn together.

The 12ha/29.6 acre **park** has both a French and an English garden. On the terrace, above the gave d'Oloron, you can see a rose garden and, below, a bamboo garden *(picnic area)*.

SOULAC-SUR-MER ☀

POPULATION 2 720
MICHELIN MAP 335: E-1

This seaside resort is sheltered by pine-covered dunes on one side, and from the surging surf on the other, by a high sand bank, once the site of the ancient city of Noviomagus, which was swallowed up by the sea in the 6C. Until the 16C, Soulac had a large natural harbour giving on to the Gironde estuary, where pilgrims would come ashore on their way to Santiago de Compostela. It was overrun by marshes in the 17C. From the waterfront there is a fine view of the Phare de Cordouan. Bathing is supervised along the resort's four beaches and there are numerous possibilities for water sports, hikes and cycle tours.

▶ **Orient Yourself**: Soulac-sur-Mer lies on the Atlantic Coast near the Gironde estuary.
Kids **Especially for Kids**: Children will love the resort's long, sandy beaches.
◔ **Also See**: PHARE DE CORDOUAN, VIGNOBLE DE BORDEAUX.

Sights

Basilique Notre-Dame-de-la-Fin-des-Terres

At the end of the 18C, this Benedictine abbey church was almost entirely covered by sand. It was uncovered and restored in the 19C.

The church includes elements of 12C Romanesque architecture and has a 14C belfry which replaced the original one which stood over the transept crossing. The Poitou style of building is apparent in the windowless nave, and dimly lit by tall bays in the side aisles which are almost as high as the nave itself. Some of the historiated capitals remain.

Three capitals show the tomb and shrine of St Veronica (left pier before the chancel) who evangelised the Médoc region and died in Soulac; one portrays St Peter in prison (at the entrance to the chancel, left), and another depicts Daniel in the lions' den (inside the chancel). A polychrome wood statue of Our Lady of Land's End, to whom the church is dedicated, stands in the south transept.

Musée d'Art et Archéologie

🕓 *Open Jul-Aug 3-7pm; Apr-Jun and early Sep–mid-Sep daily except Wed 3-6pm.* 🕓 *Closed 20 Sep-31 Mar.* ✆*2.15€.* ☎*05 56 09 83 99.*

The town boasts an **archaeological museum** displaying flint axes, chisels, decorated pottery, arrow heads from the Neolithic and Bronze Ages, and military ensigns, money, ceramics and glassware from the Gallo-Roman period.

The museum also houses the **Fondation Soulac-Médoc**. On view, inside, are paintings and sculptures by contemporary local artists.

Excursions

Montalivet-les-Bains

18km/11mi S.

This small seaside resort is best known as a centre of naturism, due to the presence of a large resort nearby, and for its lively daily market in the summer.

There are 12km/7mi of beach, 2 hiking trails in the marshes and cycle paths in the forest.

443

WHERE TO STAY

⌂ **Camping Les Lacs** – *126 rte des Lacs – 33780 Soulac-sur-Mer – 3km/1.8mi S of Soulac via the D 101 – ☎ 05 56 09 76 63 – info@camping-les-lacs.com – open 29 Mar-2 Nov – reserv. recommended – 187 pitches.* The facilities at this friendly campsite include two pools (one covered and one outdoors), a games room, a bar, a pizzeria and a shop. As well as pitches for tents and caravans, the site has mobile homes to let.

Pointe de Grave

10km/6.2mi N.

Park the car by the monument. Pointe de Grave is the tip of a headland at the northernmost limit of the Landes, which curves across to narrow the mouth of the Gironde. It lies directly across the water from the beach resort of Royan.

The present monument replaces a 75m/246ft pyramid erected to commemorate the landing of American troops in 1917 and demolished by the Germans in 1942. The Point was a strategic coastal defensive position. German forces occupying western France held on to it after the Allied landings in 1944; and it was not recaptured until April 1945, only weeks before the armistice.

The old blockhouse on top of the dune offers a vast panoramic viewa of the Cordouan lighthouse 9km/5mi out to sea, the peninsula and lighthouse of La Coubre, the Gironde and the harbour at Le Verdon, the coves around Royan and the splendid expanse of the Atlantic Ocean.

Another lighthouse, on the Point itself, houses the **Musée du phare de Cordouan** (*120 steps* ◷*Open Jul-Aug, 10am-noon and 2.30-6.30pm, May-Jun Sun and public hols 3-6pm;* ⌕*2.50€ (children under 12 1.50€);* ☎*05 56 09 61 78; www.littoral33.com/Le_Verdon.htm;* **Phare de Cordouan★**⌕*See Phare de CORDOUAN).*

This museum highlights the exceptional architecture of the off-shore Cordouan lighthouse and gives some idea of the daily life of the keepers. Children's drawings on the theme of lighthouses, and an aquarium with exotic marine species complete the exhibition; from the gallery, admire the view of the estuary.

As well as providing access to the lighthouse, Pointe de Grave is the departure point for various boat trips. There is also a scenic railway.

Le Verdon-sur-Mer

Le Verdon is a large container terminal in an advantageous location at the mouth of the estuary, protected from the ocean by Pointe de Grave. It has a deep-water port unrestricted by locks or tides, and offers direct access up the Gironde. Its disposition, combined with the excellent facilities (fast cargo handling, ample warehouse space), makes it particularly suitable for the huge container ships and oil tankers which dock here before sailing for Central America, South America, West Africa and the Indian Ocean.

Moulin de Vensac

From Soulac take the D 101E6 left and follow the orange signposting to the mill. ⌕*Visit by guided tour (30min) Jul-Aug 10am-12.30pm and 2.30pm-6.30pm; Jun and Sep, Sat-Sun and public hols 10am-12.30pm and 2.30-6.30pm; Apr-May and Oct, Sun 10am-12.30pm and 2.30-6.30pm; public hols 2.30-6.30pm.* ◷*Closed Nov–Mar.* ⌕*3€.* ☎*05 56 09 45 00.*

This traditional 18C windmill, consisting of a stone tower with a conical roof, was moved to its present location in 1858. Visitors can follow the different stages of flour-making from the grinding of corn to the final sifting. Some of the machinery, fashioned from oak, is as old as the mill itself.

TALMONT-SUR-GIRONDE★

POPULATION 83
MICHELIN MAP 324: E-6

The charming "walled town" of Talmont, modelled on the bastides of Aquitaine, was built in 1234 on a peninsula by Edward I of England. Talmont is famous for its Romanesque church dedicated to St Radegund; walk along the ramparts and through streets lined with hollyhocks.

▶ **Orient Yourself**: Talmont-sur-Gironde lies 16km/10mi SE of Royan.
▣ **Parking**: It's best to leave your car in the car park situated at the entrance to the village.
◔ **Also See**: ROYAN, SAINTES.

Sights

Église Ste-Radegonde★

St Radegund's church, a fine example of the Saintonge Romanesque style, stands on an impressive **site**★ at the tip of the promontory, on the edge of a sheer cliff dropping into the Gironde. It is continually threatened by the tides which unceasingly attack the horizontal strata of the sedimentary beds it rests upon. The cliff face has more than once been consolidated and the church restored to its original 12C appearance. This stone sentinel standing apart from the village and its tiny port is surrounded by a small cemetery from which there is a fine **view** of the estuary and, off to the right, the white chalk cliffs of Meschers.

The building is squat and compact, with a traditional apse and apsidal chapels.

A square tower with a shallow pyramid roof surmounts the transept crossing. One bay of the nave was lost to the sea in the 15C.

From the mud flats and seaweed-covered rocks exposed at the foot of the cliff when the tide is out, the spectacular site of the church can be admired to the full, along with the particular elegance of its east end. Rhythmically punctuated by buttress-columns, this is enlivened by a ring of tall, blind arcades which frame windows at first-floor level; a neat row of smaller blind arcades with small columns decorates the second storey.

The fine doorway in the northern arm of the transept has coving adorned with angels adoring the Lamb, acrobats, and men pulling a rope tethering two lions. Note the dome on pendentives, and the capitals around the half-domed apse.

Address Book

◔ *For coin ranges, see the Legend on the cover flap.*

WHERE TO EAT

◌◌ **L'Auberge des Monards** – *16 Le Port des Monards – 17120 Barzan – 4.5km/ 3mi SE of Talmont via the D 145 – ☏ 05 46 90 44 44 – closed Mon eve, Tue eve, Wed eve and Thu off season.* Located in one of the small ports typical of the estuary, this restaurant is popular with locals. Fish and meat are grilled all year round in the big fireplace on the veranda. Simple decor and evenings based on culinary themes, such as *piballes* or spare rib of beef.

◌◌ **L'Estuaire** – *Au Caillaud – 1 av. de l'Estuaire – ☏ 05 46 90 43 85 – closed Oct-Mar, Mon, Tue and Wed.* This attractive restaurant enjoys a stunning location with magnificent views of the Gironde estuary. The rustic-style dining room is decorated in cheerful pastel shades and the home-made regional cuisine is excellent. The restaurant also has a few well-maintained rooms to let in season.

Musée d'Histoire locale
🕑 *Open Jun-Aug 10.30am-12.30pm and 2-7pm; Apr–May and Sep 2-6pm.* 🎟*2€ (children under 16 no charge).* ☎*05 46 90 43 87.*

Near the seamen's cemetery, the old school houses a museum designed to provide visitors with detailed information of the town and the traditional fishing activities practised in the lower estuary of the Gironde.

THOUARS★

POPULATION 10 656
MICHELIN MAP 322: E-3

The best view of the site★ of this old town is from the southern approach (D 39), across the bridge over the River Thouet. From Pont Neuf (New Bridge) there is a fine view of the rocky promontory, cradled by the river on the Poitou-Anjou border, and of the roofs – a mixture of Romanesque tiles and Angevin slates – of the houses clustered below the castle walls. Celebrations in traditional and medieval costume bring the town to life in the summer.

▸ **Orient Yourself**: Situated on a rocky promontory encircled by the River Thouet, Thouars is located N of Parthenay and NW of Poitiers.

🅿 **Parking**: There are several car parks on the outskirts of the old town, as well as near place St-Médard in the town centre.

🔎 **Don't Miss**: The façade of Église St-Médard; the houses in the old town.

🕐 **Also See**: OIRON, BRESSUIRE, LE PUY DU FOU.

A Bit of History

Origins
For many years Thouars remained faithful to the Plantagenets but the town eventually fell to **Bertrand du Guesclin** (1320-80), one of the generals who chased the English from the region, after a memorable siege in 1372. Having purchased Thouars from the Amboise family, Louis XI stayed here several times, and his wife, Margaret of Scotland, expressed a wish to be buried here. Charles VIII gave the town to the House of La Trémoille, and the family remained seigneurs of Thouars until the Revolution. The Protestant faith had been embraced by the inhabitants; after the Revocation of the Edict of Nantes Thouars lost fifty per cent of its population.

Thouars was the birthplace of the medieval general Louis de La Trémoille. In 1619 his heir Henri de La Trémoille married Marie de la Tour d'Auvergne, sister of Turenne. She razed the old gothic château-fort to build the present château.

Walking Tour

Old Town

Allow 1hr.

▸ *The walk starts from place St-Médard, where you can park the car.*

Église St-Médard★
The church, standing adjacent to a 15C square tower with overhanging corner turrets, is a Romanesque building despite the Gothic rose-window adorning its fine Poitevin **west front**★★.

The extensively-decorated entrance is surmounted by a Christ in Glory worshipped by angels. The archivolts – the last one breaks the ranks with a resurrected Christ Rising from the Tomb – spring from historiated capitals depicting the Punishment of the Vices. Splendid effigies of St Peter, St Paul, the Prophets and the Sibyls stand above the lateral arcades. The Romanesque doorway with festooned arches on the north

View of Thouars

M. Thiery/MICHELIN

side of the church is of Moorish inspiration. Inside, the three original Romanesque naves were replaced in the 15C by a single nave with lowered vaulting.

▷ *Follow rue du Château which prolongs rue St-Médard.*

The two streets once formed the town's high street and led to the old bridge.

Old houses★

Rue du Château boasts two brick-and-timber houses including the Hostellerie St-Médard, flanked by a vaulted passageway, and several corbelled façades beneath sharp, steep gables – notably that of the 15C Hôtel des Trois-Rois (Three Kings Mansion) at no 11. It was here that the future Louis XI slept when he was still *dauphin* (heir to the throne). A moulded corbel on the façade supports a bartizan where guards could mount to keep watch over the street.

Opening onto the esplanade, that was once the seigneurial courtyard, are the Chapelle Notre-Dame and the Château.

Chapelle Notre-Dame

This chapel was built above a series of crypts, one of which is still the family tomb of the La Trémoilles. The superb Flamboyant Gothic façade is surmounted by a Renaissance gallery with shell decorations.

Château (Collège Marie-de-La-Tour-d'Auvergne)

Visit by guided tour (2hrs) Jul-Aug Wed, Sat and Sun 3.30pm, also some dates from Oct-Apr. For further information, contact the tourist office. ◉5€ (children under 12 no charge). ☎05 49 66 17 65.
A domed pavilion housing a monumental staircase projects from the central block and there are two other pavilions at the extremities.

▷ *Walk up avenue de La-Trémoille to Abbaye St-Laon.*

Ancienne Abbaye St-Laon

This former abbey first staffed by Benedictine monks and then, after 1117, by Augustinians includes a 12C-15C church with a fine, square Romanesque belfry. Margaret of Scotland is buried here. The present town hall is installed in the old (17C) monastic buildings.

▷ *Follow rue Régnier-Desmarais, rue St-Médard and turn right towards Chapelle Jeanne-d'Arc.*

Chapelle Jeanne-d'Arc

Built in 1892, the chapel now houses regular exhibitions of contemporary art.

▷ *Walk along rue Du-Guesclin to Porte au Prévôt.*

Address Book

For coin ranges, see the Legend on the cover flap.

WHERE TO STAY

Hôtellerie St-Jean – *Rte de Parthenay* – ☎05 49 96 12 60 – hotellerie-st-jean@wanadoo.fr – P – *closed 7-20 Feb, 8-21 Aug and Sun evening*. Enjoy this wonderful retreat but with a view over the old town of Thouars. Rooms are decorated to and impeccable standard. Dining-room is immaculate and welcoming; classique cuisine.

WHERE TO EAT

Le Logis de Pompois – *(Centre d'Aide par le Travail), Pompois – BP 86 – 79102 Ste-Verge – 5km/3mi NW of Thouars. Take dir. Doué-la-Fontaine and Pompois* – ☎ 05 49 96 27 84 – *closed Sun eve, Mon and Tue*. Enjoy outdoor dining in summer at this old winery dating from the 18C and 19C. In the winter, guests eat in the elegant dining room, which is an attractive blend of modern and traditional styles. 'Jazz' dinners two Saturdays a month. Fine cuisine.

Porte au Prévôt

This is the gateway forced by Du Guesclin when he penetrated the town in 1372 to end the siege. It is framed by two projecting ravelin towers on octagonal bases.

▶ *Follow rue du Président-Tyndo.*

Tour du Prince-de-Galles

🕐 *School hols in spring and summer, daily except Mon and public hols 10.30am-12.30pm and 2.30-6.30pm; other periods from Apr-Sep, Sat-Sun 2-6.30pm.* ⊗ *No charge.* ☎ *05 49 66 66 52.*

The Prince of Wales Tower, also known as the Granary Tower because it was used as a grain store when it formed part of the town's defensive perimeter, is round and massive and capped with small bartizans. It has also gone under the name of Faux-Sauniers, in reference to unscrupulous salt dealers who were locked up here by members of the "salt police". Before its abolition in 1709, the highly unpopular and iniquitous salt tax spurred vast smuggling operations; bandits ended up in narrow cages visible on the second floor of the tower.

▶ *Rue Prince-de-Galles and rue Saugé lead back to place St-Médard.*

VILLENEUVE-SUR-LOT

POPULATION 22 782
MICHELIN MAP 336: G-3

Villeneuve was founded in 1253 on the borders between Périgord and Guyenne by Alphonse de Poitiers. It was built to serve as a "support centre" for the strongholds scattered throughout the upper Agenais region; In its day, Villeneuve was one of the largest and most powerful bastides in the southwest. Numerous alleys and ancient houses have been preserved from the Middle Ages, especially around Place La Fayette, a typical old square.

The town is today largely spread around the banks of the River Lot. The river's fertile alluvial valley produces plentiful crops of fruit and vegetables: it has turned Villeneuve into a busy trading centre and, like Agen, a regional market for plums.

- **Tourist Office:** 3 place de la Libération, 47300 Villeneuve-sur-Lot. ☎05 53 36 17 30. www.villeneuve-sur-lot.fr.
- ▶ **Orient Yourself**: Villeneuve-sur-Lot is situated 33km/20mi N of Agen.
- P **Parking**: Park in place La Fayette near Église Ste-Cathérine and explore the town centre on foot.
- **Especially for Kids**: The museums in Clairac in the Lot valley.
- **Also See**: AGEN, CHÂTEAU DE BONAGUIL.

Sights

Town gates

The two town gates – **Porte de Paris** north-east of the old town and **Porte de Pujols** south-west – are the only traces of the old ramparts. The gates are both built of brick and stone, are both crowned with crenellations and machicolations, and both covered by a roof of brown tiles. Porte du Pujols is three storeys high with mullioned windows; Porte de Paris was instrumental in the fierce resistance to Mazarin's troops during the siege of 1653.

Église Ste-Catherine

Open 9am-6pm.
This brick-built church, in Romanesque-Byzantine style, resting on a granite plinth, was consecrated in 1937. It is both stately and and somewhat austere. Its north-south orientation is extremely unusual. The interior is decorated, apart from the chancel, with a series of restored stained-glass windows; those dating from the 14C and 15C – which came from the old church – have been attributed to the school of **Arnaud de Moles**, the master-enameller and painter who worked on the cathedral in Auch. Beautiful 17C and 18C gilt wood statues (of Our Lady of the Rosary, St Joseph, Mary Magdalene and St Jerome) adorn the four pillars of the nave above the doorway into the baptistery. The marble font stands bathed in blue-tinged shafts of light. The paintings in the nave by Maurice Réalier-Dumas (see MUSEUM OF GAJAC) show a procession moving towards the chancel.

Bell tower, St Catherine's

Address Book

🪙 *For coin ranges, see the Legend on the cover flap.*

WHERE TO STAY

🛏 **Hôtel La Résidence** – *17 av. L.-Carnot – ☎ 05 53 40 17 03 – hotel.laresidence@wanadoo.fr – closed 18 Dec-3 Jan – 18 rooms.* A small family hotel with reasonably priced accommodation. The rooms in the main house are very basic; those in the building just behind are quieter and more comfortable.

🛏🛏 **Chambre d'hôte Château de Seiglal** – *47380 Monclar-d'Agenais – 6km/3.6mi N of Fongrave. Take the D 238 then the D 667, kilometre post n° 25 – ☎ 05 53 41 81 30 – decourty-chambres-hotes@wordline.fr – ✍ – 5 rooms – meals 🍴🍴.* This attractive 19C bed and breakfast surrounded by century-old trees is the perfect place for a relaxing stay. The comfortable guestrooms, named after the owner's five sisters, have fine views of the park and fields. Convivial table d'hôte meals served in the dining room with sculpted furniture and fireplace.

SHOPPING

Place Lafayette – Place Lafayette, also known as Place des Cornières, is the hub of Villeneuve-sur-Lot. The busy streets leading from the square are full of shops, bars and cafés.

La Boutique des Pruneaux – *Pl. de la Libération – ☎ 05 53 70 02 75 or 06 07 44 52 31 – www.boutique-des-pruneaux.fr – Mon-Sat 9am-12.30 pm and 2-7.45pm, Sun 9am-12.30pm.* Many of the famous pruneaux d'Agen are grown and processed in Villeneuve-sur-Lot and its surrounding area. This boutique, at the foot of the Porte de Paris, specialises in prunes and other regional delicacies, including chocolates and vintage Armagnacs (40 to 50 years old).

SPORT AND LEISURE

Aviron Villeneuvois – *Quai d'Alsace – ☎ 05 53 49 18 27 – office hours: Mon-Fri 9am-noon and 2-5pm.* This rowing club, situated in the heart of the city, organises boat trips up the Lot river during summer months.

Centre de Plein Air de Rogé – 👶 – *D 661 – SE of Agen via the D 661 towards Penne-d'Agenais – ☎ 05 53 70 48 13 – Jul-Aug, daily 10am-6pm.* Surrounded by greenery and bordered by a loop of the River Lot, this children's outdoor centre is blessed with an idyllic setting. Kayak, rowing, water-skiing, horseback riding, archery, trampoline and mountain biking courses are held here.

Pont des Cieutats (or Pont-Vieux)

This old bridge with uneven arches, which was built by the English in the 13C, offers a picturesque view over the banks of the river and over the 16C **chapelle N.-D du-Bout-du-Pont**, chapel at the end of the bridge, with its east end jutting over the water. According to a legend, a sailor dived there in order to unfasten his boat, which was mysteriously blocked, and he discovered a small statue of the Virgin Mary.

Musée de Gajac

2 rue des Jardins. ♿🕐21 Jun–1 Oct Mon-Fri 10am-noon and 2-6pm, Sat-Sun, 2-6pm; 2 Oct–17 Jun, Mon and Wed-Fri 10am-noon and 2-6pm, Sat-Sun, 2-6pm. 🕐 Closed public hols. 👝1€. ☎05 53 40 48 00.

The new municipal museum of Villeneuve, housed in an old windmill overlooking the Lot, mainly contains collections of paintings from the 18C (Lebrun school), the 19C (Maurice Réalier-Dumas, Hyppolyte Flandrin, Eva Gonzalès and André Crochepierre) and the 20C (Henri Martin, Brayer). Some temporary exhibitions.

Penne d'Agenais ★

10km/6mi E via the D 661.

This stronghold was once the fief of the kings of England, and so suffered during the wars of religion that it was nothing but ruins by the mid-20C. Greatly restored, it is now a lively summer tourist attraction.

Place Gambetta

This shady terrace is an excellent starting point for a tour of Penne. The "gateway to the town" opens onto two fine 16C houses, one of which served as a local prison for many years.

Notre-Dame-de-Peyragude

This modern sanctuary (in Romanesque-Byzantine style) is built on the top of a hill offering a scenic view of the valley. Very popular pilgrimages in honour of the Virgin are held here.

Viewpoint★

The orientation table overlooks the valley of the Lot, from Villeneuve to Fume: the view extends as far as the Upper Quercy in the distance.

Porte de Ferracap

The gallows used to be near this gate.

Rue de Ferracap

This, and the adjacent streets, are lined with very fine renovated houses (some with half-timbering and corbelling).

Place Paul-Froment

A remarkable brick house preceded by a house with Gothic arches contains a café and exhibit rooms.

Porte et Fontaine de Ricard

This old fortified gate and the fountain below are named after Richard the Lionheart who was responsible for building the town's first fortifications.

Driving Tour

1 Lower Lot Valley

65km/41mi round trip – allow all day

▶ *Leave Villeneuve north-west via the D242 towards Casseneuil.*

Casseneuil

45 allée des Promenades, 47440 Casseneuil,
☎05 53 41 13 33.
The pretty brown-tiled roofs of Casseneuil, built in a bend at the junction of the Lède and the Lot, are clustered around the church which houses beau-

tiful frescoes (13-15C). After living off the river trade for many years, the town has now turned to preserved foods as its chief source of revenue. Many fine old houses, their loggias (15-16C) leaning towards the Lède and surrounded by terrace gardens, are arranged throughout the village and on the roads to St-Pastour and Hauterive.

▶ *Go south-west via the D 217 to Ste-Livrade and turn left along the D 667. After 1km/0.6mi, turn left to Fongrave.*

Fongrave

Fongrave priory was founded in 1130 and placed under the rule of Fontevraud, only accepting nuns of noble birth. The **church** has a monumental 17C carved oak **altar piece**★ with snake-infested vines writhing around its cabled columns; an Adoration of the Magi occupies the centre.

▶ *Go west to Castelmoron-sur-Lot. Take the D 249 then the D 263 to Laparade.*

Laparade

The ramparts of this bastide overlooking the Lot Valley offer a sweeping **view**★ from Villeneuve-sur-Lot, on the left to the junction of the Lot and Garonne, on the right (viewpoint indicator). The river meanders companionably through a checkerboard of crops and orchards.

▶ *From Laparade, take the D 202 west, then the D 911.*

Clairac

Picturesque half-timbered houses with brick facings are witness to Clairac's rich past. The seat of a Benedictine abbey, it was destroyed and rebuilt many times during the Wars of Religion. The Crusaders won the town back from the Cathari (also known as Albigenses, a heretic sect seeking to achieve purity through complete ascetic renunciation), in 1224; it became a Protestant stronghold in 1560. Today, it is home to three museums which will delight children in particular.

Kids The **Musée du Train** presents miniature trains chugging through animated scenes. &. ⊙*Open Jul-Aug, 10am-7pm; Apr-Jun and Sep, 10am-6pm; Feb-Mar and*

Nov-Dec, Wed, Sat-Sun, school hols and public hols 10am-6pm. ⊜8€ (children 6€), 10€ combined ticket with the Abbaye des automates and Musée du train. ☎05 53 79 34 81.

Kids The **Forêt Magique**, also based on animated figures, plunges the visitor into a world of elves and forest animals. ♿ ◷Open Jul-Aug 10am-7pm; Apr-Jun and Sep 10am-6pm; Feb-Mar and Nov-Dec Wed, Sat-Sun, school hols and public hols 10am-6pm. ⊜4.50€ (children 4€), 10€ combined ticket with the Abbaye des automates and Musée du train. ☎05 53 79 34 81.

Kids **L'abbaye des Automates** – Audio-guided tour ◷Open Jul-Aug 10am-7pm; Apr-Jun and Sep 10am-6pm; Feb-Mar and Oct-Dec Wed, Sat-Sun, school hols and public hols 10am-6pm. ⊜8€ (children 5€); 10€ combined ticket with Musée du train and Forêt Magique. ☎05 53 79 34 81. This astonishing museum of automated figures explains the daily life of the abbey monks (it is said that the Clairac monks introduced prunes to the region and brought in tobacco from Brazil in 1555) and retraces the history of the town, which boasts such illustrious figures as the poet Théophile de Viau (born in Clairac in 1590) and Montesquieu, whose wife came from Clairac. Interesting: French historical monuments made of matches and small-scale models of prestigious ships.

Plum delicious

J. Malburet/MICHELIN

▶ Take the D 911 east and follow the signs to "Le Musée du Pruneau," just before Granges-sur-Lot.

Granges-sur-Lot

The **Musée du Pruneau★**, in the Gra-bach estate, surrounded by plum trees whose fruit is used for prunes, shows the various tools used up until very recently to pick and prepare the dried fruit. A film explains the age-old production process and, at the end of the tour, the visitor is invited to taste the estate's home-made specialities, all derived from plums and prunes, of course. ♿ ◷Open mid-Mar–mid-Oct 9am-noon and 2-7pm, Sun and public hols 3-7pm; mid-Oct–mid-Mar 9am-noon and 2-6.30pm, Sun and public hols 3-6.30pm. ◷Closed 1 Jan, last 2 weeks in Jan, 25 Dec. ⊜3.50€. ☎05 53 84 00 69.

▶ Return to Villeneuve via the D 911.

Le Temple-sur-Lot

The jardin des Nénuphars (water lily garden) is located among the botanical gardens of **Latour-Marliac** (founded in 1875), the oldest and most prestigious aquatic tree-nursery in the world. You will see the rarest white water lilies in the ponds and on the lake. This is a nicely landscaped garden which offers a panoramic view on the site, with a pergola, an exotic greenhouse, a fountain, a Japanese bridge, and a bamboo garden. Some species of water lilies here inspired Claude Monet for his *Nymphéas*. He used to buy them here for his garden in Giverny: his signature can be seen on the order register.

② Les Serres du Bas Quercy

49km/31mi round trip – allow all day

▶ Leave Villeneuve SW via the D 118.

The region of Lower Quercy consists of peaceful countryside with low elongated plateaus, cut across by chains of hills *(les Serres)* stretching between the fertile valleys.

Pujols

This very old village is perched on a hill providing an attractive **view**★ of Villeneuve-sur-Lot and the broad valley of the Lot, dotted with market gardens and fruit trees.

A passageway under the St-Nicolas bell tower leads to the old village which is still surrounded by the remains of its 13C ramparts. The main street is lined with timber-framed houses with canopy roofs. The nave of the church of St-Nicolas has rib vaulting, while that of Ste-Foy-la-Jeune, currently used as an exhibit hall, is decorated with 15C frescoes *(in poor condition)*. An old well, vestiges of fortifications, and Renaissance houses add to the pleasure of the tour.

▷ *Left onto D 118, then onto the D 220.*

Grottes de Lastournelles

⏱*Visit by guided tour (45min) Jul-Aug, 10am-noon and 2-6pm; Sun and public hols 2-6pm; rest of the year by prior request.* ✎*5€ (children 3.50€).* ☎*05 53 40 08 09.*

Bones found in the caves are displayed in glass cases at the entrance. Galleries have been hollowed out by the seepage of underground water. Small stalactites are forming on the roof. Seven chambers are open to visitors; Les Colonnes is named for the massive pillars within.

▷ *Join the D 212, then turn left, then left again towards St-Antoine-de-Ficalba.*

Grottes de Fontirou

⏱*Visit by guided tour (40min) Jul-Aug 10am-12.30pm and 2-6pm; mid-Jun–end Jun and early Sep–mid-Sep 2-5.30pm; Easter school hols and early May–mid-Jun, Sat-Sun 2-5.30pm.* ✎*5.80€.* ☎*05 53 41 73 97. www.grottes-fontirou.com.*

The galleries and rooms hollowed out in the grey limestone of the Agenais region are decorated with reddish ochre concretions (due to the clay content), contrasting with a number of lovely white stalagmites. Animal bones from the Tertiary era are displayed in one of the rooms.

▷ *Go back to the N 21, turn right, then left onto the D 110.*

The road goes through the Serres, limestone hills rising above the wide valleys, and through.

a small village which has retained a number of historical houses *(on its southern side)* and an old covered market.

▷ *Take the D 10, then the D 656 to the left, take the third road on the left, towards Frespech.*

Frespech

Surrounded by 11C walls (reinforced during the Hundred Years War), this charming little village's Romanesque church dates from the 11C, as do a few of the stone houses.

Souleille farm (3.5km/2.2mi from Frespech) houses an attractive **Musée du Foie Gras**. ⏱*Open Jul-Aug 10am-7pm; Rest of the year 10am-7pm, Sun and public hols 3-7pm.* ⏱*Closed 1 Jan, 10-31 Jan and 25 Dec.* ✎*4€.* ☎*05 53 41 23 24 www.souleilles-foiegras.com.*

▷ *Turn right, following the signs to Hautefage-la-Tour.*

Hautefage-la-Tour

Near the Gothic-style Notre-Dame-de-Hautefage, whose Flamboyant porch is surmounted by a canopy, there is a beautiful hexagonal tower used as a belfry. A round turret topped by a pinnacle turret is part of the tower, pierced with mullion windows on some of its sides. The upper section is decorated with an open-work balustrade, gargoyles and pinnacles. On the square below, planted with beautiful plane trees, is an old wash-house. Against the church, also below, is a pilgrims' fountain.

▷ *Take the D 103, turn left onto the D 223, then right onto the N 21 to return to Villeneuve-sur-Lot.*

VOUVANT★

POPULATION 867

MICHELIN MAP 316: L-8

Hedgerows, dense woodland and the tranquil waters of the nearby River Mère combined, give Vouvant a peaceful, old-world atmosphere. According to local legend, the Fairy Mélusine is said to have built Vouvant Château in a single night.

▶ **Orient Yourself**: Vouvant lies perched on a bluff near the River Mère, 11km/7mi N of Fontenay-le-Comte.

👍 **Also See**: FONTENAY-LE-COMTE, PARTHENAY.

Sights

Church★

The church was founded by the monks of Maillezais Abbey. The 11C nave was very badly damaged by partisans of the Reformation in 1568 and only the walls of the first three bays remain. The original three apses were rebuilt in the 12C (restored in 1882) along with the crypt below (also restored in the 19C) and the great doorway of the northern transept, which is in the Romanesque style; this doorway, the main **façade★**, flanked by clustered columns and topped by a sharp gable, form a rich and readable page of sculpture.

Main Doorway – The doorway consists of arched doors twinned beneath a common archivolt, surmounted on the tympanum by two interesting stone carvings in relief. On the right, partly damaged by weather, is the figure of Samson overcoming the lion; on the left is Delilah shearing Samson's hair. The covings above the two doors are decorated with floral motifs and the capitals with animals and fantastic figures.

The first coving of the **archivolt** features a line of supporting atlantes, the second a finely carved succession of characters, biblical and mythological. On the left above the arch is a Virgin and Child, balanced on the right by an effigy of John the Baptist. Higher still are two **friezes** on modillions: the Last Supper (below); the Apostles witnessing the Ascension (above).

Château

The old fortress, home of the Lusignans in medieval times, bars the neck of the promontory girdled by a loop of the river. Its defensive walls demarcate Place du Bail, a grassy esplanade planted with chestnut trees now used as a site for country fairs. From the edge there are attractive views over the lazy curve of the River Mere, which widens here upstream from the Pierre-Brune dam.

Capitals on the church doorway

M. Thiery/MICHELIN

Tour Mélusine★

🕐 *Information and tickets at the tourist office or the Café du Centre* 👁️*1.50€ (children: 0.70€).* ☎*02 51 00 80 21.*

Once a keep, the tower was built in 1242. The walls, up to 3m/10ft thick, enclose two chambers, one above the other, with curious pyramid vaulting. The top of the tower can be reached by a stairway of 120 steps. From here, 36m/118ft above the ground, there is a vast **panorama**★ to be admired – from the picturesque site of the village itself to the sombre mass of the forest-covered plateau in the south and the chessboard of bocage farmland in the north.

ÎLE D'YEU★★

POPULATION 4 788

MICHELIN MAP 316: B-7 TO C-7

The Isle of Yeu off the Atlantic Coast has a typical island feel with its unspoiled nature, mild temperature, sunny climate and limited motor traffic. The scenery of the island's often grandiose coastline is very varied. The unspoilt "Côte Sauvage" faces the open sea, its crystalline schist rock formations making the island look much like Belle-Île. However, the eastern and southern coasts look more like the Vendée, with pine trees, evergreen oaks, dunes and long, wide beaches of fine sand.

- 🏠 **Tourist office:** Pl. du Marché, 85350 Île d'Yeu. ☎02 51 58 32 58.
- ▶ **Orient Yourself**: The island's geographic location and geology have earned it many affectionate nicknames such as the **Corsica of the Atlantic** and the **Grain of Granite**. Standing watch over the mainland, the 10km/6mi long and 4km/2mi wide island is one of the furthest from the west coast of France (10 nautical miles).
- 👁️ **Don't Miss**: The Côte Sauvage; Port-de-la-Meule; the views of the coast from the Vieux Château.
- 👣 **Also See**: St-Gilles-Croix-de-Vie; Île de Noirmoutier; Le Marais Breton Vendéen.

A Bit of History

History and activities of the islanders

The island has been inhabited since prehistoric times (there are a large number of dolmens and menhirs) and it is not impossible that this was the island where, according to the Greek geographer Strabo, a religious "college" of Druidesses was established.

A monastery was founded on Yeu in the 6C. The future St Amand, the "Apostle of Flanders", was drawn here at the beginning of the following century. In the 8C the island was given the enigmatic name of *Insula* (isle) *Oya*. In the 16C the entire population of a village in Cornouaille, south-west Brittany, led by its priest, disembarked on Yeu with the idea of settling here. The prefix *ker-*, attached to certain villages is a distortion of the Lower Poitou dialect word *querry*, meaning a village.

Île d'Yeu was ruled by various seigneurs, including Olivier de Clisson, the brilliant warrior who became Commander-in-Chief of the French army, before it was sold to the Crown in 1785.

Aside from tourism, the islanders' main resource is fishing. Specialising in high quality fish, the island's fishermen hold the national record for white tuna (101 tonnes). With a fishing fleet of 81 boats equipped with special trawling nets, the port of Île d'Yeu supports nearly 260 fishermen. Often forced to travel far from their home port to fish using their traditional methods, a number of islanders have been in the news as a result of clashes with other fishermen in southern Europe.

A Marshal detained

On 16 November 1945 a naval escort vessel landed an old man of 90 on the island. He was to be in-carcerated in the

Address Book

◔ For coin ranges, see the Legend on the cover flap.

WHERE TO STAY

⊜**Hôtel l'Escale** – *La Croix de port – 85350 Port-Joinville – ☎02 51 58 50 28 – yeu.escale@voilà.fr – closed 18 Nov-15 Dec – 28 rms.* This hotel is a good base for exploring the island, situated away from the busy port area. The decor is bright and cheerful, with white walls and yellow shutters outside and teak furniture and marine-inspired decor in the breakfast room. Simple, well-maintained rooms.

⊜**Chambre d'hôte M. and Mme Cadou** – *10 r. Ker-Guérin – 85350 St-Sauveur – ☎02 51 58 55 13 – closed Oct – ⊠ – 3 rms.* This house is one of the few places to stay in the picturesque village of Saint-Sauveur. All blue and white, the decor of the spacious rooms is inspired by that of a ship's cabin – hardly surprising when you realise that Monsieur Cadou is a naval carpenter. In fine weather, breakfast is served in the garden.

⊜⊜**Atlantic Hôtel** – *Quai Carnot – 85350 Port-Joinville – ☎02 51 58 38 80 – atlantic-hotel-yeu@club-internet.fr – closed 2-24 Jan – 15 rms.* On the fishing docks above a fishmonger's, this hotel is one of the island's better addresses. Access by a narrow stairway next to the shop. Its small modern rooms are simple but functional and well-kept. Friendly reception.

⊜⊜⊜**Chambre d'hôte Villa Monaco** – *Villa Monaco – 85350 Pointe-des-Corbeaux – ☎02 51 58 76 56 – www.villamonaco.info – 5 rms – meals ⊜⊜.* Situated on the eastern tip of the island, this blue-shuttered Vendée house has an unbeatable location – the view of both coasts from the garden is splendid. Simple rooms tastefully decorated, let by the week in the summer. Self-catering cottage available only in the winter.

WHERE TO EAT

⊜⊜**Le Père Raballand** – *6 pl. de la Norvège – 85350 Port-Joinville – ☎ 02 51 26 02 77 – www.lepereraballand.com – closed early Dec-Feb – reservation recommended summer and weekends.* A very popular address in the port. The large outdoor terrace is perfect for watching the boats and activity in the busy harbour. Off season, meals are served in an attractive dining room decorated with marine paraphernalia. Simple cuisine.

---

citadel at Pierre-Levée. The old man was the "ex-Marshal" Pétain, head of Vichy (collaborationist) France from 1940 to 1944, whose death sentence had been commuted to life imprisonment. In 1951 he was struck by a double pulmonary congestion and removed to hospital. He died on 23 July. Men who had fought under him at Verdun, in the First World War, carried the coffin to the cemetery at Port-Joinville, where he lies.

Sights

Allow 1 day to explore the island

Cliff paths around the coast offer visitors a succession of splendid views – especially in the south and west – as well as the opportunity to explore the attractive coves and beaches below.

Port-Joinville★

This, the largest town on the island, was originally called Port-Breton; the present name derives from Admiral de Joinville, the third son of Louis-Philippe I, who brought Napoleon's body back to France in 1840. It is one of the most important tuna fishing ports in France. Tourists arriving from Fromentine or Noirmoutier can enjoy a picturesque view of the tiny port crammed with fishing boats and small trawlers, their multicoloured pennants, dressed above a series of buoys, fluttering in the breeze. Behind the masts and rigging is a quay bordered by white houses. With the exception of the outer harbour, the port is left dry at low tide. Beyond the waterfront there is one shopping street and a network of lanes close-packed with fishermen's cottages.

The house where Mme Pétain lived while her husband was imprisoned is now **Le**

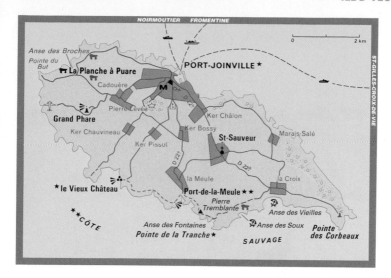

Musée-Historial. One room is reserved for the exhibit of Pétain mementoes: in the remainder of the small museum the history of the island is illustrated. ⏱ *Visits by prior request: contact M. Nolleau, 5 rue du Marché, Port Joinville, 85350 Île d'Yeu. ⏱ 3.50€. ☎ 02 51 58 31 55.*

The Marshal's tomb, a simple white stone slab in a grove of yews and cypress trees, faces the mainland from the local cemetery.

Grand Phare

⊶ *Not open to the public.*

The upper platform (201 steps) of the lighthouse is 41m/135ft above the ground (and 56m/184ft above sea level). There is a splendid **view★** looking out over the island to the ocean and, in clear weather, to the coast from Noirmoutier to St-Gilles-Croix-de-Vie.

Dolmen de La Planche à Puare

This megalith stands on a stretch of moor-land near the **Anse des Broches** cove, at the northwestern tip of the island. It is constructed of schistose granite blocks and is unusual in that it has a central passage with lateral chambers (two each side of the passage in this case). Ancient bones have been found.

Côte Sauvage★★

The rocky coast, extending in a northwest-southeast line from Pointe de But to Pointe des Corbeaux, is indented in an irregular

Île d'Yeu – Port-Joinville

Île d'Yeu – Le Vieux Château

fashion. The ocean views are magnificent. Two of the best are from a cliff path linking the old castle with Port-de-la-Meule. Perched above sheer rock-faces plunging into the sea, the path leads walkers eventually to a picturesque **view**★★ looking down over the creek.

Le Vieux Château★

This old castle occupies an imposing site at the seaward end of a moor. Its ghostly silhouette, almost indistinguishable from the rock on which it is built, is both romantic and spectacular. Its walls rise from a granite spur gashed by a narrow crevasse 17m/56ft deep; down below, the ocean waves boom and echo like thunder.

It was built in feudal times (possibly the 11C) and remodelled in the 16C, and this wild pirates' lair now forms a rough trapezoid flanked by defensive bastion towers. A foot-bridge, replacing the old drawbridge, leads inside the walls. From the top of the keep (*beware: there is no parapet*) there are marvellous **views**★★ of the Côte Sauvage and the sea.

Port-de-la-Meule★★

A long, narrow inlet penetrating the coast. At the inner end is the slipway of the crabbers and lobster boats which sink their pots along the rocky depths of Côte Sauvage. From the moorland heights above, the small white Chapel of Notre-Dame-de-Bonne-Nouvelle watches over the tiny port. The local sailors take part in an annual pilgrimage here.

The cliff path continues beyond the chapel as far as **la Pierre Tremblante**, an enormous boulder perched above the sea which can be made to rock gently by pressing on a certain spot.

Pointe de la Tranche★

A number of rocky creeks surround this headland; Anse des Fontaines, named after its freshwater spring; and another two particularly calm, sheltered and suitable for bathing - the Anse des Soux, where there is a marine grotto, and the **Anse des Vieilles**, the island's prettiest beach.

Pointe des Corbeaux

This is the south-eastern extremity of Île d'Yeu, forming the dividing line from which the astonishing contrast between the island's two different landscapes can best be appreciated – the rocky, storm-tossed, Breton-style coast on the west; a calm, sandy, pine-clad shoreline on the east.

St-Sauveur

This is commonly referred to simply as "the Town" as it was once the island capital and residence of the Governor. There is a Romanesque church with a square tower above the transept crossing.

For the best little places,
follow the leader.

France

reat Britain
& Ireland

Looking for the latest news on today's best hotels and restaurants?
Pick up the Michelin Guide and look for the Bib Gourmand and Bib
Hotel symbols. With 45,000 addresses in Europe, in every category and
price range, the perfect place to dine or stay is never far away.

MICHELIN
A better way forward

INDEX

INDEX

INDEX

INDEX

INDEX

WHERE TO EAT

INDEX

WHERE TO STAY

INDEX

LIST OF MAPS AND PLANS

MAPS AND PLANS

COMPANION PUBLICATIONS

MICHELIN MAPS

Michelin products are complementary: for each of the sites listed in The Green Guide, map references are indicated which help you find your location on our range of maps.

To travel the roads in this region, you may use any of the following:

♦ the Regional maps at a scale of 1:200 000 nos 518, 519, 521, 525 and 526, which cover the main roads and secondary roads, and include useful indications for finding tourist attractions. These are good maps to choose for travelling in a wide area. In a quick glance, you can locate and identify the main sights to see. In addition to identifying the nature of the road ways, the maps show castles, churches and other religious edifices, scenic view points, megalithic monuments, swimming beaches on lakes and rivers, swimming pools, golf courses, race tracks, air fields, and more.

♦ the Local maps that cover all of France are illustrated on the map below.

And remember to travel with the latest edition of the map of France no 721, which gives an overall view of the region, and the main access roads which connect it to the rest of France. The entire country is mapped at a 1:1 000 000 scale and clearly shows the main road network. Convenient Atlas formats (spiral, hard cover and "mini") are also available. Michelin is pleased to offer a route-planning service on the Internet: www.Via-Michelin.com. Choose the shortest route, a route without tolls, or the Michelin recommended route to your destination; you can also access information about hotels and restaurants from the red cover **Michelin Guide**, and tourists sites from **The Green Guide**.

Bon voyage!

Special symbols

◆ Water park

🏖 Beach

🚣 Boat trips
departure

⬚⬚⬚ Fortified town (bastide): in
southwest France, a new town
built in the 13-14C and typified
by a geometrical layout.

Sports and recreation

🏇 Racecourse

⛸ Skating rink

🏊 🏊 Outdoor, indoor swimming pool

🎥 Multiplex Cinema

⛵ Marina, sailing centre

⛺ Trail refuge hut

▫▪▪▪▫ Cable cars, gondolas

▫+++++▫ Funicular, rack railway

🚂 Tourist train

◆ Recreation area, park

🎭 Theme, amusement park

🦌 Wildlife park, zoo

❀ Gardens, park, arboretum

🐦 Bird sanctuary, aviary

🚶 Walking tour, footpath

🙂 Of special interest
to children

Abbreviations

A   Agricultural office
        (Chambre d'agriculture)

C   Chamber of Commerce
        (Chambre de commerce)

H   Town hall (Hôtel de ville)

J   Law courts (Palais de justice)

M   Museum (Musée)

P   Local authority offices
        (Préfecture, sous-préfecture)

POL.   Police station (Police)

🛡   Police station (Gendarmerie)

T   Theatre (Théâtre)

U   University (Université)

MAPS AND PLANS

COMPANION PUBLICATIONS

MICHELIN MAPS

Michelin products are complementary: for each of the sites listed in The Green Guide, map references are indicated which help you find your location on our range of maps.

To travel the roads in this region, you may use any of the following:

◆ the Regional maps at a scale of 1:200 000 nos 518, 519, 521, 525 and 526, which cover the main roads and secondary roads, and include useful indications for finding tourist attractions. These are good maps to choose for travelling in a wide area. In a quick glance, you can locate and identify the main sights to see. In addition to identifying the nature of the road ways, the maps show castles, churches and other religious edifices, scenic view points, megalithic monuments, swimming beaches on lakes and rivers, swimming pools, golf courses, race tracks, air fields, and more.

◆ the Local maps that cover all of France are illustrated on the map below.

And remember to travel with the latest edition of the map of France no 721, which gives an overall view of the region, and the main access roads which connect it to the rest of France. The entire country is mapped at a 1:1 000 000 scale and clearly shows the main road network. Convenient Atlas formats (spiral, hard cover and "mini") are also available. Michelin is pleased to offer a route-planning service on the Internet: www.ViaMichelin.com. Choose the shortest route, a route without tolls, or the Michelin recommended route to your destination; you can also access information about hotels and restaurants from the red cover **Michelin Guide**, and tourists sites from **The Green Guide**.

Bon voyage!

Special symbols

◆ Water park

🏖 Beach

🛶 Boat trips
departure

⠿ Fortified town (bastide): in
southwest France, a new town
built in the 13-14C and typified
by a geometrical layout.

Sports and recreation

🐎 Racecourse

⛸ Skating rink

♒ ♒ Outdoor, indoor swimming pool

🎥 Multiplex Cinema

⛵ Marina, sailing centre

⛺ Trail refuge hut

□─■─■─■─□ Cable cars, gondolas

□─┼┼┼┼┼─□ Funicular, rack railway

🚂 Tourist train

◆ Recreation area, park

🎢 Theme, amusement park

🦌 Wildlife park, zoo

❀ Gardens, park, arboretum

🐦 Bird sanctuary, aviary

🚶 Walking tour, footpath

👶 Of special interest
to children

Abbreviations

A   Agricultural office
(Chambre d'agriculture)

C   Chamber of Commerce
(Chambre de commerce)

H   Town hall (Hôtel de ville)

J   Law courts (Palais de justice)

M   Museum (Musée)

P   Local authority offices
(Préfecture, sous-préfecture)

POL.   Police station (Police)

🛡   Police station (Gendarmerie)

T   Theatre (Théâtre)

U   University (Université)

MAPS AND PLANS

COMPANION PUBLICATIONS

MICHELIN MAPS

Michelin products are complementary: for each of the sites listed in The Green Guide, map references are indicated which help you find your location on our range of maps.

To travel the roads in this region, you may use any of the following:

♦ the Regional maps at a scale of 1:200 000 nos 518, 519, 521, 525 and 526, which cover the main roads and secondary roads, and include useful indications for finding tourist attractions. These are good maps to choose for travelling in a wide area. In a quick glance, you can locate and identify the main sights to see. In addition to identifying the nature of the road ways, the maps show castles, churches and other religious edifices, scenic view points, megalithic monuments, swimming beaches on lakes and rivers, swimming pools, golf courses, race tracks, air fields, and more.

♦ the Local maps that cover all of France are illustrated on the map below.

And remember to travel with the latest edition of the map of France no 721, which gives an overall view of the region, and the main access roads which connect it to the rest of France. The entire country is mapped at a 1:1 000 000 scale and clearly shows the main road network. Convenient Atlas formats (spiral, hard cover and "mini") are also available. Michelin is pleased to offer a route-planning service on the Internet: www.Via-Michelin.com. Choose the shortest route, a route without tolls, or the Michelin recommended route to your destination; you can also access information about hotels and restaurants from the red cover **Michelin Guide**, and tourists sites from **The Green Guide**.

Bon voyage!

Special symbols

◆ Water park

𝒜 Beach

🛶 Boat trips departure

▦ Fortified town (bastide): in southwest France, a new town built in the 13-14C and typified by a geometrical layout.

Sports and recreation

🏇 Racecourse

⛸ Skating rink

≋ 🏊 Outdoor, indoor swimming pool

🎥 Multiplex Cinema

⚓ Marina, sailing centre

🏠 Trail refuge hut

□—■—■—□ Cable cars, gondolas

□—+—+—+—□ Funicular, rack railway

🚂 Tourist train

◆ Recreation area, park

🎭 Theme, amusement park

🦌 Wildlife park, zoo

❀ Gardens, park, arboretum

🐦 Bird sanctuary, aviary

🚶 Walking tour, footpath

👶 Of special interest to children

Abbreviations

A Agricultural office (Chambre d'agriculture)

C Chamber of Commerce (Chambre de commerce)

H Town hall (Hôtel de ville)

J Law courts (Palais de justice)

M Museum (Musée)

P Local authority offices (Préfecture, sous-préfecture)

POL. Police station (Police)

🛡 Police station (Gendarmerie)

T Theatre (Théâtre)

U University (Université)